# THE HOME SCHOOL SOURCE BOOK

THIRD EDITION

JEAN and DONN REED

BROOK FARM BOOKS

BRIDGEWATER, MAINE, USA and GLASSVILLE, NEW BRUNSWICK, CANADA

This book incorporates material previously published in somewhat different form in *The First Home-School Catalogue* (1982, 1986); *"efficient instruction elsewhere"* (1984); *The Home-School Challenge* (1985); *The Home School Source Book* (first edition, 1991; second edition, rev., 1994); *The Homeschooling Book of Answers*, by Linda Dobson; *Homeschooling: An Open House*, by Nancy Lande; and *Home Education Magazine*, *Harrowsmith*, *Nurturing*, *The New Nativity*, and other periodicals.

Portraits and cartoons by Chuck Trapkus, Rock Island, Illinois: Jean and Donn, page 8; Donn and Gus, pages 130, 133, 134, 135; cartoon with skunk, page 136; Gus, page 150; Jean and Donn, page 182; Jean and Donn, page 454; Jean with guitar, page 456. Clip art is from Dover Publications and Frank Shaffer. We truly thank all the publishers that contributed artwork of their book covers, including Aristoplay, Audio Forum, August House, Barker Creek, Boyd Mills Press, Career Press, Cobblestone Publishing, Crabtree, CS Educational Solutions, Dawn Publications, Free Spirit, Fulcrum, Gazelle, Gryphon House, Hammond, Illumination Arts, Independent Publishers Group, January Productions, Kids Can Press, Penton Overseas, Replogle Globes, Ten Speed Press, Troll, and Workman Publishing, and very special thanks to EDC Publishing.

Published simultaneously in Canada and the United States by Brook Farm Books, Box 246, Bridgewater, ME 04735, and Brook Farm Books, Box 101, Glassville, NB E7L 4T4, Canada.

Printed and bound in the United States of America.

Library of Congress Catalog Card Number: 97-97171

National Library of Canada Cataloguing in Publication Data

Reed, Jean, 1943-
The home school source book

3rd ed.
Includes index.
ISBN 0-919761-28-3

1. Domestic education-Canada. 2. Domestic education-United States.
3. Instructional materials industry-Canada-Directories. 4. Instructional materials industry-United States-Directories. 5. Children-Books and reading-Bibliography.

I. Reed, Donn II. Title.

LC37.R46 2001 371.04'2 C97-901238-4

*DEDICATION — 1994*

For Jean —

Whose constant inspiration, support, patience, hard work, and companionship have made this and all things possible; this book, like so many other parts of our lives, is hers as much as mine;

And for Cathy, Karen, Susan, and Derek —
Who have taught us far more than we have taught them; whose curiosity, interests, hopes and fears, increasing awareness, perceptions, and interpretations have all added to our knowledge of ourselves as parents and as people;

All five of whom have given me a life of warmth and meaning far beyond my reasonable expectations. I look back over our lives together, and am very glad we chose to do it all our way.

And our adventure continues ...

June 2000

For Donn, June 13, 1938 - December 21, 1995

Whose courage and vision have given us a living legacy of insight, liberally sprinkled with humor and filled with love. Who has been, and still is, the center of my life.

Who inspires me and supports me, now as much as ever, in all my endeavors. Donn, you were so much more than I ever dreamed of or expected in a husband and father, lover and friend, teacher and mentor, critic and playmate — my spiritual companion. You filled my life with inspiration, love, and companionship that has not been broken — even by death's summons. Although I can no longer hold your hand, I hold you in my heart. You are as much a part of me and this book as you always have been. I too look back over the years, and am very glad we chose to do it our way.

And for Cathy, Karen, Susan, and Derek —

Who held me through the dark days; whose love and support have kept me secure and encouraged me to continue doing what I hold most dear. Each of you, although far away, continues to teach me. I value your thoughts, opinions, and friendship more than you can imagine. Each of you continues to enrich my life beyond my expectations.

And yes, Donn, the adventure continues ...

This book is dedicated to Donn and the kids, but it would not have been possible without the help and support of many others. To name them all would take a separate book.

Special thanks to Dr. J.T. Dancey, B.Sc., M.D.C.M.; Helen Creelman, R.N.; the oncology staff at the DECH; Lynn Drost, R.N.; and the team of Extra Mural nurses, all of whom helped us in our fight against cancer, and to have five more good years together. They gave us the best of conventional medicine, while we proceeded with our own non-traditional regimen. Many thanks also to Dr. Colin Lockhart, Wanda MacFarlane, and all the staff at the Bath Medical Clinic and Northern Carleton Hospital, who made themselves available above the call of duty and offered support whenever it was needed.

A special salute to you, Dad, and Madge — you never wavered in supporting my efforts, even through your own life-and-death struggles. Thanks to Mom and Richard for starting me with a computer.

Thank you, Tim and Lillian Haas, for your much appreciated technical and editing expertise (keeping the egg off my face) and your generosity of spirit, all of which have made this book the best it can be. You've ensured that my education is still continuing. And last but not least, you've kept me sane while I tackled the QuarkXPress publishing program. You are terrific!

Enduring thanks to my cousin Dr. Alfred Alschuler and my friend Judy Tompkins, who have, with incredible patience, inspired me and helped with initial editing of my work, keeping it organized and to the point. Many thanks to Barb Merz for help with the Freebies chapter. And of course, thanks to Lillian Jones for her help, support, suggestions, and encouragement.

Many thanks also go to all my friends and neighbors who have kept me in contact with the world at large while I retreated to my cave and worked. Thanks, Carolyn, for the baking and doing my laundry, for conversation and coffee breaks, for all the great walks, and for help with myriad odd chores. You are a true friend.

*And last, but certainly not least*, to each and every one of you who took the time to write, sharing my sorrow, offering your prayers and your thoughts about Donn and his work, I offer my sincere thanks. You have encouraged me to continue when I've felt overwhelmed. I owe you more than I can possibly express in mere words. I wish it were possible to list all your names, but you and I know who you are. I have saved each and every letter and card. This book is also dedicated to you and your families.

## ORDERING FROM BROOK FARM BOOKS

The Catalog and Directory section of this Source Book offers you a comprehensive guide to more than 4,000 individual items, sources of material and/or information, support groups, and other materials especially useful to children and adults learning independently at home. More than half of these items can be ordered directly from Brook Farm Books, which gives you the convenience of consolidated ordering of materials from scores of publishers, manufacturers, and other suppliers.

**Our criteria for items we sell are the same as for items we used ourselves: They must be fun, challenging, constructive, informative, and relevant to steady mental, physical, and moral growth.**

We don't have a large company. Your orders are processed personally, from opening the mail to sending out the orders. We may not be as efficient as computers, but we're friendlier.

About the age guidelines in this book: If the youngest age given is eight, you could probably use the book with a younger child who is well versed in the subject or a reluctant older student. If our note says "8 and up" it means that's about the right age and that older students new to the subject will find it informative and useful. For those of you with kids of widespread ages, we found we could use one book and make it suitable for all four of our kids by assigning work and research appropriate to each age.

**Instructions for ordering from Brook Farm Books can be found at the end of the book.**

**TO ORDER MORE COPIES OF THIS BOOK**: Additional copies of *The Home School Source Book*, 3rd edition, may be ordered from Brook Farm Books, P.O. Box 246, Bridgewater, ME 04735, or Brook Farm Books, Box 101, Glassville, NB E7L 4T4, for $29.95 plus $3 postage. All orders must be paid in U.S. funds. Checks or money orders are fine. Visa/MasterCard or American Express orders are accepted through our toll-free order number: 877-375-4680. You may also purchase copies from your local bookstore. If they don't have it, they can order it through Baker and Taylor Books, Ingram Distributors, or Bookseller's Edge.

**QUANTITY DISCOUNTS** are available for 10 or more copies. Write for our discount schedule.

**ITEMS NOT SOLD BY BROOK FARM BOOKS**: Ordering instructions are usually given with the listing. If any necessary information (such as price) is missing, write to the publisher or supplier. If it's a small company, send a #10 SASE with your request for information. Using a letterhead, order form, or at least a rubber stamp will often get you better service, and sometimes a substantial discount.

### "UNKNOWN" — "FORWARDING ORDER EXPIRED" — "RETURN TO SENDER"

For every inquiry that is returned to you with the above words, or an equivalent, I sincerely apologize. I've tried to ascertain the accuracy of all listings, but companies, like people, sometimes move and then seem to disappear. Usually, the best one can do in such a case is to look for similar services or materials from other companies.

### ***** "REGISTER" YOUR *HOME SCHOOL SOURCE BOOK* *****

If you didn't buy your *Home School Source Book* from Brook Farm Books, please send us your name and address, telling us when and where you bought it, so we can add your name to our files for future mailings (such as notice of the next edition). We do not sell, rent, or trade our mailing list; your personal information stays with us.

# TABLE OF CONTENTS

## Essays and Commentary



## Catalog and Directory

# BEFORE YOU GET CONFUSED, READ THIS INTRODUCTION!

This edition has a new format. There are now two of us writing for you, and I was stymied for a time figuring out how to make it clear to you who was speaking to you. When Donn wrote the last edition he used the first-person singular and plural, I and we, to indicate that he was speaking for himself, and for the two of us. When I began writing I soon realized that I, too, wanted to speak for myself, and use, I, meaning me, Jean. I didn't want to fill the book with "he says" and "I say" or labels in the margins saying "Jean" or "Donn." I was stumped.

I should have remembered one of the major lessons we learned homeschooling the kids: *Never* under-estimate your kids. When I finally posed this problem to the kids, Susan quickly pointed out the obvious solution. "Mom," she said, "you have a computer. Why not use two different type fonts?"

"Well, why not?" I thought. I'd never seen it done, but that's never been an inhibiting factor for either Donn or me. I tried it and it worked well, but if you were to skip this introduction and start reading through the rest of the book first, I think you would be confused.

**You will find my writing and book reviews all written in the typeface used for the majority of this page (Comic Sans). New listings will be easy to recognize.**

Whenever you see a different typeface, you will know Donn is speaking to you. His essays and book reviews are in Century Schoolbook — all I've done is update the prices. E.g.: **"When we began our 'experiment' in home-schooling in the early 1970s, part of our purpose was to determine what things and conditions are most useful, if not essential, in learning. What are the 'necessaries' of teaching at home — not just the physical materials, such as books and pencils, but the methods, the attitudes, and the objectives? What knowledge is really useful or essential in life, and what are the best ways of obtaining or imparting it?"**

This edition has been a long time in coming. I'm sorry about the delay and wish it could have been done sooner. Many of you have come with us through the years as readers, customers, and longtime friends through correspondence and understand the delay. Some of you deserve a medal for patience. Some of you are about to meet us for the first time. The reason for the delay and the need for me to write using separate fonts is because Donn can no longer do it.

For those of you who don't know, after a ten-year battle with cancer, Donn died in December 1995. He loved writing. He loved finding new and exciting resources and making them available to everyone. *The Home School Source Book* was his baby, and because he loved his work he did almost all of it. I was the coffee server, errand runner, chore doer, and everything else while he worked. I made doughnuts, gardened, did barn chores, hauled wood, played my guitar, and read. I eagerly awaited the next chapter, listened, gave comments, and helped only with packaging books and other minor chores. It was the way we worked together. It wasn't until he was very sick that we started my education into how to run the business. My first lesson was that most of the information I needed was in Donn's head. The transfer of information never was completed.

Over the past five years I've had a massive midlife education in business, writing, publishing, and order fulfillment — the ultimate in adult homeschooling. By continuing Donn's work I feel that we are still working together; it's a continuation of our lives together in a new dimension.

What's Mom going to do now that Dad's not here?

When Donn died I knew I wanted to continue Brook Farm Books and create a new edition of *The Home School Source Book*. I had no idea how much work would be involved. I just knew I had to do it.

# You're going to rewrite Dad's book!!! 

I've had two very good offers from well-known publishers to do this book. Both would have made fundamental changes that I felt would destroy its integrity and its unique qualities. I have continued on my own. I hope you will find enjoyment and useful information within these pages and bear with me as I continue to learn.

**Computer users:** Though not every listing in the book has a Web address (I've underlined them for easy reference), most businesses and organizations do have them nowadays. Try a search engine such as www.google.com for links. Please note that Web and e-mail addresses sometimes break across lines in listings (as google just did). In most cases the break has been made after a period or a slash in Web names and after a period or the "@" in e-mail addresses. If there was no way to avoid having the (dumb) computer hyphenate a word in the middle of a Web address, I have removed the underlining from the hyphen so you'll know not to type it into your browser. Of course, every once in a while Web names do have hyphens that you need to type; in such cases, the underline remains. Another quirk: Some Web addresses include underscores ( _ ), which disappear when the whole address is underlined. If you see what looks like a space in a Web address, type an underscore.

**Any resemblance to my kids in these drawings is intentional but purely accidental.**

# OUR BEGINNINGS

When Henry David Thoreau began his famous experiment in living at Walden Pond, his purpose, he wrote later, was to determine what things and conditions are essential to life. In most parts of the world, he said, only four things are essential for physical survival: food, clothing, shelter, and heat.

"At present day," Thoreau went on to say (mid-1800s), "and in this country, as I find by my own experience, a few implements, a knife, an axe, a spade, a wheelbarrow, etc., and for the studious, lamplight, stationery, and access to a few good books, rank next to necessaries, and can all be obtained at a trifling cost."

When we began our "experiment" in home-schooling in the early 1970s, part of our purpose was to determine what things and conditions are most useful, if not essential, in learning. What are the "necessaries" of teaching at home — not just the physical materials, such as books and pencils, but the methods, the attitudes, and the objectives? What knowledge is really useful or essential in life, and what are the best ways of obtaining or imparting it?

There were no books or magazines about home-schooling then, no directories or catalogs of materials, and we didn't know any other home-schoolers. We found and chose learning materials by hit or miss: browsing in book stores, buying discarded library books (still a good source), searching through garage sales and used-book stores, buying activity books in toy stores, borrowing from public libraries and, when we could, from schools.

When a school principal loaned us a school supplies catalog, we discovered wonderful possibilities we hadn't even suspected — books, charts, posters, toys, games, science kits, film strips, models, and much more. The rustic, rural lifestyle we prefer seldom generates much money (although we have no objection to money, in itself), but that period of discovery was one of the fortunate exceptions during which I was earning a good wage. We promptly spent several hundred dollars on our first order.

When the packages arrived, it was like a childhood Christmas morning for all of us. In the weeks following, we remained very happy with most of the purchases. Some items, however, proved to be very disappointing, and we began to learn that an item isn't necessarily good, or even worth the postage, just because it's offered for sale to "professional educators."

Once we discovered the scores of suppliers and hundreds of educational book publishers, our problem was no longer finding materials, but deciding what would be most useful. How we wished for a comprehensive guide to the materials available! It would have saved us hundreds of dollars, as well as hundreds of hours wasted in trying to use worthless materials.

We continued our search, gradually sifting the excellent from the moderately good and the worthless. Experience was certainly our best teacher.

As public schools continued to get worse, home-schooling became more common, and parents began coming to us for advice about teaching at home. In offering ideas and suggestions, we often discussed the need for a comprehensive directory of materials. One evening, after a couple had left with an armload of borrowed books and many pages of notes, Jean said to me, "No one else is doing it. Why don't you?"

I laughed, but she was serious, and the idea grew on me.

Even after teaching at home for more than ten years, we knew of relatively few families teaching at home. For years we knew nothing about the growing number of home-school newsletters and support groups. Guessing that the finished book would be about a hundred pages, and would take a month or two to finish, I began making notes. I wrote to publishers, government agencies, and the few home-school organizations I knew about. My notes grew. After eight months of researching, evaluating, and selecting, I had compiled nearly 240 pages of sources, resources, organizations, and publications. This was another period of very low income for us, so we decided to finance the publication by selling some of the listed items ourselves. After considering scores of titles, I finally called my book *The First Home-School Catalogue* — because that's what it was, the very first of its kind. I typed it on an ancient Royal and put illustrations in with Glue-Stick. I made fifty copies of the book on a photocopier and had covers printed. Jean and I collated the pages on our kitchen table, bound them, glued on the covers, and had the books trimmed at a print shop. In the spring of 1982, I mailed a few review copies, ran two small ads, and waited.

The response more than paid me for all my time and work. *The First Home-School Catalogue* seemed to be a welcome addition to the home-school movement. It was a very crude book, with no professional expertise whatsoever, but no one mentioned that, nor the many faults and serious omissions of which I was very aware. Orders for *The First Home-School Catalogue* came from all the Canadian provinces, from nearly all of the United States, and even from Spain, Greece, Puerto Rico, Japan, Indonesia, and many other countries, and were quickly followed by enthusiastic letters of appreciation — "Thanks for the information," "Great," "Loved it."

"I like it very much," wrote John Holt. "A wonderful venture." *Mother Earth News* said its "listings, honest reviews, and advice ... should be invaluable to any home-schooling parent."

I was very happy with the positive response, but felt the high praise had been earned more by my intention than by an actual accomplishment. Almost immediately, I began planning extensive additions, revisions, and improvements. I published the second edition in 1986.

I had planned to call the next edition *The Second Home-School Catalogue*, but by then two other resource guides had been published (one in 1985, the other in 1986), each claiming to be the first; so, in weak self-defense, I kept my original title. It's true that imitation can be flattering, but an omission of polite acknowledgment reduces its sincerity.

The changing needs of our four children, the many new products available, and questions and suggestions from readers have all kept me searching and evaluating. Most home-school services and organizations freely exchange ideas and information, but, as in many growing movements, a few have become very competitive. Many new organizations have begun, most of them providing real and needed services, but a few apparently are trying to displace others. A few reviewers of books and other materials for home-schoolers, relying for a large part of their income on advertisers, praise and recommend everything sent to them, even when the products are contradictory in philosophy or purpose, sometimes without fully examining the material being reviewed. "He who praises everybody," wrote James Boswell, "praises nobody."

**Jean and I believe learning materials should be fun, challenging, constructive, informative, and relevant to steady mental growth. We depend on orders from customers to continue the publication of this source book, but we absolutely will not sell or recommend any item that does not meet our criteria.** This book lists a few items with which we don't agree, and you can't buy them from us, but we don't mind telling you where you can buy them if you want them. We also recommend many items we don't sell, sometimes because they are available only from other suppliers, sometimes because we can't give you as low a price as other suppliers can.

As you'll see, we have strong opinions. Whether you agree or disagree with us, you'll always know where we stand, and will not be misled by indiscriminate praise and false "objectivity." We want to make a living, but we want to make it honestly.

Most people who are not home-schooling, whether or not they approve of it, assume that its goals are similar to those of public schooling — to prepare young people for jobs or careers or further education, to make a living, and to be relatively good citizens of the society in which they live. Many home-schoolers agree with those goals, but believe that education at home will provide a better foundation than the public schools can.

We are among the many others who want to reach further, to aim higher. Money-earning skills are certainly useful and perhaps even necessary, but there are other skills of far greater importance. This is, and will continue to be, a period of rapid and radical change — in society, in government, and in the ecology of our planet. We have the duty, as parents and educators, to help our children prepare to meet those changes and challenges creatively and responsibly, and to help them develop skills and attitudes with which they can make positive contributions to the world. The ability to evaluate, to make responsible judgments, to resolve conflicts peacefully, and to create and maintain strong families will be of much more worth to our children and to the world than degrees in business management, welding, or engineering.

Of equal importance, we want our children to be happy now, as children. Childhood is important in and of itself; it shouldn't be spent only in preparation for adulthood.

In selecting learning tools and materials — to recommend, to sell, or to use ourselves — we always try to keep these objectives in mind — to find kits, books, models, and other learning materials that help us define and develop more fully the values and skills we believe are needed for happy, purposeful, creative lives, as children and as adults.

We hope you find this book useful. We welcome personal correspondence with all our readers. If you have any questions, comments, or suggestions, please write.

Donn and Jean Reed
Brook Farm, 1991

Are you feeling uncertain about your ability to homeschool? Does the idea of teaching your child to read make your stomach feel queasy? Do your poor high school algebra grades haunt you? Relax! Uncertainty in beginning a new challenge is normal. It's all right for you to learn right along with your children. As you read through our book you'll see how we resolved various problems, and you'll find other books that will help you find the best way for your family to meet the challenges and adventures encountered when you and your children learn at home. Oh, yes, you'll learn too!

We too, began with many doubts and fears, great expectations, and many more questions than answers. We had no models to follow. Neither our parents nor our own education had given us role models or patterns to follow, though both had given us examples we had no wish to emulate. Our goal was to instill in our children a lifelong love of learning, as well as the confidence in their own abilities to work and live in whatever manner they might desire, and to be people capable of making constructive contributions to the world around them.

Homeschooling can work for you. It worked for us. After twenty-four years of homeschooling, our last child took wing and left home. Do we wish we had done some things differently? Certainly, we were not perfect parents. We learned through the years by our mistakes as well as our successes. Was our homeschooling experience a success? Yes. All four kids have been off on their own for a number of years, some to college, some to work, some following lifelong dreams and others pursuing new interests.

Would we do it again?

Absolutely!

Jean Reed
Brook Farm, 2000

# WHY WE TEACH AT HOME

When Jean and I were expecting our first baby, in 1966, there was very little literature about natural birth. We had read enough to know that we wanted an undrugged birth, but we took for granted the "necessity" of birth in a hospital. All we asked was permission for me to be present during the delivery.

"Oh, no," the doctor said, "we have enough problems without having fainting husbands all over the floor."

So Jean and I decided, tentatively, to have the baby at home. (For the complete story see "Our Way" in "Birthing, Babies, and Parenting.") We studied everything we could find on the subject. Consequently, all four children were born at home. Cathy was born in a little log cabin in northern Vermont, forty miles from the nearest hospital. Karen was born in 1968, in our home, with six feet of snow drifted outside the windows. Susan was born in 1970 and Derek in 1972, both in a log cabin in the mountainous Central Interior of British Columbia, also forty miles from the nearest hospital.

Active fatherhood — that is, participating as a full partner in parenting — has many rewards, but one of the greatest is hearing that first little cry of "Hello" and cradling the new son or daughter even before he or she is fully born.

Jean nursed each of the babies for at least a year. For the first six weeks or more, we never put the babies down or left them alone; we always held them, carried them, and cuddled them. They never woke up crying, wondering where they — or we — were.

"It's good for them to cry," several neighbors and relatives told us. "It develops their lungs." Others told us, "You give them too much attention. It isn't good for them. They'll become too dependent on you."

We thought about these comments, but not in the way others may have wished. Babies are born dependent on their parents. They coo and gurgle when they are happy. They cry for attention when something is not right from *their* perspective. We always felt our babies cried for a reason, and although we may not have understood why, their unhappiness was sufficient reason to do what we could to remedy the situation. Our convenience was not an issue.

The babies slept with us, despite the many warnings (from people who had never tried it) that "You'll roll on the baby in your sleep!" It never happened, of course.

When Cathy became hungry during the night, Jean had only to turn over, still half-asleep, help the baby find the nipple, and doze off again. No fumbling for the light switch, no grumbling at being awakened, no crying, no frustration.

There was only one instance when it didn't quite work — that is, not right away. I woke up enough to hear Cathy's murmur of hunger change to a cry of indignation, and I turned on the bedside light to see why Jean wasn't feeding her. Jean, still asleep, was trying with great determination to put her nipple into Cathy's ear. (A reader of *Nurturing Magazine*, in which part of this story appeared, wrote me, "Ah, the old nipple-in-the-ear trick — I've done it myself many times!")

The objections and fears many people have about home-birth are not greatly different from their feelings about home-school: "Something will go wrong," "You need the experts," "You're sheltering them too much," and so on.

Our main reason for having home-birth was that we loved our children (yes, even before they were born), and we wanted them to have the best start in life. We began teaching them at home for the same reason.

In education, as with birth, it was the narrow-mindedness and insensitivity of the "experts" and "trained professionals" that led us to realize we could probably do much better without their help.

We are confirmed do-it-yourselfers in many areas of life — childbirth, house-building, food production, etc. — and so we thought about teaching our children at home, but didn't have any definite reason for doing so, and assumed that contact with other children would be enjoyable and beneficial.

We had read some of John Holt's books (*How Children Fail*, *How Children Learn*, etc.) and various other books about education, but we thought that small rural schools might somehow have escaped the negative attitudes and academic failings most of the books described.

We were wrong. In nearly every instance, our children returned from school much poorer than they had been when they left home. The girls had learned to read and to enjoy books at least a year before entering school. They soon learned, in the public schools, that reading is a very serious chore; they not only lost interest in reading, but actually lost a great deal of reading ability. They became ill-mannered and bigoted. Far from being "broadened" by social contacts, they were coerced into becoming very narrow and intolerant.

Cathy had always enjoyed books, from the time she was old enough to look at them. Before she was two, she spent hours with her favorites, studying minute details in the pictures and asking us about the letters. By the time she was six, she was entirely familiar with the alphabet, basic phonics, shapes, and colors, and seemed to have an intuitive grasp of elementary psychology (but without knowing any of its jargon). She enjoyed working with us in the garden, the barn, and the kitchen. We talked about school, and decided to give it a try.

Each morning, we drove to the corner, where Cathy boarded the school bus and rode to the two-room schoolhouse twenty miles away. In the afternoon, we met her at the corner to bring her home.

Cathy liked school, she told us. She had many friends and she liked the teacher. Each day, she was eager to meet the bus, and came home with excited stories of new games and new friends.

She began sucking and chewing her lower lip, until it was always red and swollen. She stopped reading, and had no interest in books. She became bossy and whiny. The redness of her lower lip spread down toward her chin.

Cathy's teacher told us she hadn't noticed any problems. Cathy insisted there was nothing wrong; she got along with the other children, she still liked her teacher, and the work was very easy, even if a little boring. She continued to chew her lower lip, and often screamed at us and gave us belligerent orders. The other children no longer looked forward to the time she came home from school.

During the two-week Christmas vacation, she stopped chewing her lip, and the redness almost disappeared from her lip and chin. Toward the end of her vacation, she looked into a few of her favorite books. She became more pleasant to live with, more friendly and agreeable and cooperative — as she had always been before she started school.

When she returned from the first day back at school after vacation, her lower lip was red and swollen. She refused to pick her coat up from the floor, and she was snappy and bossy.

We never returned her to that school. For the rest of that winter and through the following summer, she occasionally looked through her books, but had no interest in reading. We left her alone, and didn't try to give her any "school" work.

We moved, and in the fall Cathy entered a different school in the second grade. Despite having "missed" half of the first grade, she had no difficulties with second-grade work. Her teacher was pleasant, competent, and understanding. Cathy finished the school year with high marks and still had a pleasant personality. We concluded that the first year must have been an unfortunate exception.

Karen, like Cathy, had learned basic reading and math skills long before she entered formal schooling. Her first-grade teacher was one of the most loving and dedicated teachers our children ever encountered. Karen's first-grade experience was nearly everything we thought public education should be — a continuation of skills already learned and the introduction of new subjects and new concepts, both academically and socially. We could see Karen growing, rapidly and happily.

Cathy's third-grade teacher was often hoarse from yelling at her students. One of her favorite punishments for any misbehaving boy was to have him sit on her lap, making him the unhappy object of his classmates' coarse jokes and teasing.

What happens in the mind of a child for whom a customary act of affection becomes a dreaded punishment and humiliation?

I have vivid memories of visiting Cathy's class the day the school held Halloween parties. I went to Karen's class to deliver treats for their party and saw happy, costumed children having a good time. I knew Cathy's class would be different, but I was still unprepared for what I encountered. Her class was the only one in the whole school not having a party or wearing costumes. This teacher did not celebrate Halloween due to her religious beliefs, and therefore she would not permit her class to join in the festivities. I had no quarrel with this teacher's religion, or with her right to choose what to celebrate, but I felt that as a public employee, she had no right to force her personal decision on thirty children of varying beliefs. When I knocked on the classroom door, I could see through the window that the teacher was yelling. She beckoned to me to come in and pointed to a desk in the back of the room, all with hardly a pause in her ranting at one of the boys. I was dumbfounded.

The sound of the teacher's voice made me, even as an adult, cringe and want to disappear. I felt myself tumble emotionally back through time to my school days, gradually getting smaller and smaller. I sat at a child's desk stunned and intimidated. What was she doing to the minds of the children who spent five days a week with her?

As it happened, Cathy was a good student, academically and socially. She disliked the teacher's screaming and bullying, but was relieved (as we were) that she was never the object of the teacher's tirades. We felt it was a very unhealthy environment, whether or not Cathy was learning anything positive or useful. And she wasn't.

Given a writing assignment, Cathy wrote:

> One day I was sweeping the floor. I swept the edge of the counter, and I swept a spray can out. It said Spray broom. I sprayed the broom. The broom said Hi who are you? I'm Cathy I said will you come to the zoo with me? Of course I will I am your friend. So we went to the zoo. We saw a lion and it was loose. We told someone at the zoo. The end.

Not too bad, really. I know many adults who couldn't do as well. But it was much less than we thought should have been achieved in thirty hours a week, four weeks a month, nine months a year, for over two years.

Even worse, Cathy was bored.

"What did you do in school today, Cathy?"

"Oh, nothing. Just more second-grade work. I did it all last year. When will I start learning something new?"

From asking that question to becoming an eight-year-old dropout, with full parental approval and encouragement, was a very short step.

A dropout. No education? How would she get anywhere in life?

Cathy began "going to school" at home. Not yet free of our own educational conditioning, we eased ourselves into the formal teaching business by subscribing to a correspondence course from Calvert School. Each weekday, from nine in the morning until noon, Jean was Cathy's teacher. In those three hours, they easily covered more than two daily lessons, including arithmetic, geography, Greek mythology, art, literature, spelling, history, science, and composition.

At the same time, Jean was raising and teaching Susan and Derek. Karen was doing well in first grade in the public school. (I was taking life easy as an edgerman in a sawmill.)

As a hobby, Cathy studied dinosaurs and fossils, and this was only one of many areas in which we found Cathy was often the teacher and we were the pupils.

Ten weeks after leaving the public school, Cathy wrote:

A JOURNEY TO THE PAST

> I found a time machine. I am going back to 120 million years ago. Dinosaurs roamed the earth and volcanoes erupted a lot. They liked it warm and wet and it never snowed. I saw a Stegosaurus, like a duck; it ate plants. It didn't frighten me but it was about 11 feet tall and four feet wide. I rode on a Triceratops, a three-horned dinosaur. I saw a Tyrannosaurus. I ran back to the time machine and I went to another part of the jungle. I saw a Teranodon, a bird without teeth. I had a ride on it. It took me to an Ankylosaurus and I took the Ankylosaurus home with me.

Did you notice she missed the "p" in "pteranodon"? You wouldn't miss it, of course; and I just looked in my dictionary for the spelling. (If you missed it, don't feel bad. MS Word spell-check did too.) But how much can you expect of an eight-year-old kid, only halfway through third grade?

In spite of a few good experiences with the public schools, we were finally beginning to learn our own lesson. For the next three years we taught all four of our children at home. Then Cathy wanted to try public school again, to be able to spend more time with others her age. After much discussion, we reluctantly agreed to let her try. Her teacher proved to be the second of the best teachers our children ever had in public school, and we never regretted Cathy's year with her.

The next year was quite different. Cathy's English and history teacher, with a master's degree in education, couldn't spell, punctuate, or construct a proper sentence. He taught his students to use colons and semicolons interchangeably. He taught them a punctuation device he called "dot-dot-dot," and met my objection with the explanation that the word "ellipsis" would be too difficult for eighth-graders to remember. He taught that capitalization of the first letter in a sentence is a matter of personal preference.

I haunted him, two or three times a week, after school hours and occasionally at class time, but wasn't surprised that it did no good. He wasn't overly anxious to discuss his methods, although he tried to assure me that his own training had been quite thorough, and that he certainly knew more about English and teaching than anyone without formal training in those subjects.

Cathy and her class were told to find Rio Blanco on a map of Brazil. She spent over an hour searching through her school atlas, our own atlas (which is better), and the Encyclopedia Britannica. Failing to find Rio Blanco anywhere, Cathy was finally convinced that the teacher had made another spelling mistake, and he later admitted it (with a shrug, and not seeming embarrassed). Cathy had learned a lesson, but not the one her teacher had intended. That wasn't the only hour of her life wasted by a teacher's careless spelling or sloppy handwriting.

I made a list of words the teacher consistently misspelled on assignment sheets and showed the list to the principal.

"What grade level," I asked, "should have complete mastery of the spelling of these words?"

He looked the list over and said, "Third grade. A fourth-grader who didn't know these words would be considered slow."

I said it seemed to be a great waste of time for the teacher, for his students, and for me — the latter because I often needed to correct the teacher's assignments before allowing Cathy to work on them.

The principal insisted I must be mistaken about the teacher's having misspelled the words, and suggested that Cathy had copied them incorrectly. I showed him the teacher's assignment sheets. He suggested I take my complaints directly to the teacher. I told him I had done so, several times, and was less than satisfied. He said he would have to side with his teachers, on the assumption that they would not be teachers if they didn't know what they were doing.

A few days later, the principal wrote me a letter (so he could put a carbon copy in his office files), saying that the teacher we had discussed (but whom he didn't name) was a Trained Professional (his capital letters), and therefore must know what he was doing. The Trained Professional's qualification to teach, he went on to say, was proven by the fact that he had been hired by the school board.

Mark Twain once remarked that God made a fool for practice, and then made school boards. That's a harsh judgment, and may be extreme. Was the mistake Twain's or God's? As far as I know, neither was a Trained Professional, except that Twain had a license to pilot a riverboat.

Jesus told the sick man to pick up his bed and walk. Henry David Thoreau advised his contemporaries to throw down their beds and run. Anyone who is only a Trained Professional — that is, who has nothing more to offer than his Trained Professionalism — has little chance of doing either.

Since that time, we have taught our children at home and have seen no reason to try the public schools again, although the girls did choose to go for a year now and then.

The kids have all been active, according to their ages and interests, in ball games, 4-H, youth groups, dances, overnight slumber parties, national exchange trips, and jobs in town. They have been concerned about global problems, such as hunger, human rights, and the death penalty.

School at home wasn't always easy, but whenever problems arose, we tried to treat them not as interruptions of our education, but as parts of it. In facing problems and working with them, we have learned more about ourselves, each other, and the world.

We're increasingly convinced that education at home has made our children happier, healthier, and stronger — physically, mentally, and spiritually. Our children have remained bright, curious, and creative — and, we hope, have helped us to remain so, too.

# WHY THE MOVEMENT HAS GROWN AND WHY IT WILL CONTINUE TO GROW



Ten years ago the United States National Commission on Excellence in Education said, "For the first time in the history of our country, the educational skills of one generation will not surpass, will not equal, will not even approach those of their parents."

Unfortunately, this statement is as applicable today as it was ten years ago, with too many professional educators and public schools still trying to figure out what to do about it.

"To be culturally literate is to possess the basic information needed to thrive in the modern world," says E.D. Hirsch Jr. in his best-selling book *Cultural Literacy: What Every American Needs to Know*. As evidence that far too many school students are not learning this necessary knowledge, Hirsch offers the steadily declining verbal scores on Scholastic Aptitude Tests, and reports of the National Assessment of Educational Progress that student knowledge in key areas is shrinking.

A 1988 special edition of *Instructor,* a magazine for public school teachers, says, "Unfortunately, two recent surveys may back Hirsch up. The National Endowment for the Humanities assessed the study of history, literature, and languages in the nation's public schools and reported that 'America's elementary and secondary schools are failing to teach students about their shared past and culture.'

"In a related study [the article continues], Diane Ravitch, professor of history and education at Columbia University, and Chester E. Finn Jr., the U.S. Assistant Secretary of Education for Research and Improvement, analyzed a 1986 assessment of 7,812 high school juniors and gave them failing marks on their knowledge of literature and history."

This is also true for other subjects, and is as equally applicable to the Canadian school system as it is to U.S. schools. I have tutored a number of students and been amazed by the low standard of work that is considered acceptable to pass a test or to proceed to the next grade level. I find it scandalous that the billions of dollars spent on education produce such mediocre standards and ultimately handicap many young people.

The public schools throughout North America are failing, even by their own standards, which most critics agree are misguided and poorly conceived at best. Too many children are being labeled "learning-disabled" and put into special remedial classes with "high-interest, low-vocabulary" readers and textbooks. Too many tenth-graders are reading on a third-grade level. How did they get to the tenth grade without learning to read?

The past decade has seen increased publicity in national newspapers and educational magazines about North America's failing school systems. Yes, there are some good schools still in existence. Yes, there are some excellent teachers in the public school system. Yes, there are students doing exceptionally well in the public school system. But do you want to trust your child to this system that is openly confessing its massive failure to educate, that is witnessing an increase in drug usage and violence? Many parents have decided they can't wait any longer. As a result, there has been an average growth in home-schooling of about fifteen to twenty percent a year.

More and more people are teaching their own children in their homes. Home-schooling families are well over a million strong and growing. Some parents have no particular quarrel with the public schools, but simply feel that children shouldn't be taken from the family at an early age, if at all. A reason given more frequently is the steadily declining level of academic instruction in the public schools.

More and more parents are no longer accepting the weak promises and weaker excuses of the schools. They want their children to receive a proper education, even if it means removing them from the schools.

"Dear Mr. Reed,

"I hope you receive this and are still in business! I saw your ad in an issue of *Nurturing Magazine* that I borrowed from a friend. Today is the last day of school for our three girls. Yesterday, they brought home the year's "work" — what a pathetic example of wasted time! Six pages of a notebook for the entire year's effort for science; maybe twelve pages for social studies. The story my sixth-grade student wrote had no punctuation or proper grammar. I have told the girls of my dissatisfaction. They like the social aspect of school — but I have to look out for their welfare. I don't feel they are getting an education that will help them in years to come. They need something better!"

Yours truly,...

"Jean,

I'm desperate and frightened. The school wants to pass my son on to the sixth grade ... but I know he can't read well enough. They don't want to hold him back because of his self-esteem. I think he would feel better about himself if he were given the time to learn the basics before going on, but the school doesn't want to do it. Will you help me get started with homeschooling?"

From a conversation with the mother of a public school student who will remain in the public school: "Jean, will you please tutor my daughter? She doesn't really know her basic math. The teacher allows the class to use calculators in the classroom, but I don't think my daughter really knows her multiplication tables or how to do long division, and she is going on to high school next year."

Not very many years ago, a grade level lower than 70 was failing. In most schools today, any grade over 60, and sometimes 55 or even 50, is accepted as a passing grade — and often that "passing" grade is achieved by comparison with a class average, rather than with the overall requirements of a course. If the class average is 50, a passing grade need be no more than 25.

I find this alarming. As parents we have every right to expect better standards, but it isn't usually feasible to change a school policy. In the past it was common for teachers to defend the system, but with increasing frequency, I hear from teachers that they have to spend a great deal of time each year working to bring students up to last year's grade level before they can begin to teach them at their current grade level. Here are two increasingly common statements I hear from teachers: "If I weren't a public school teacher, I would teach my children at home," and "Now that I have school-age children of my own, I'm leaving my job to teach them at home."

Most school suppliers' catalogs have a high percentage of "high-interest, low-vocabulary" readers — books written on a reading level several years below the grade for which they are intended. In such catalogs, notations such as "Interest level, grades 11-12; reading level, grades 3-4" are common. There has always been some need for such books, especially in teaching remedial reading to the few students who somehow got behind, and in teaching adult illiterates, but now the failure of the public schools is making it necessary for nearly half of all textbooks, in nearly all subjects, to be written with "high interest" and "low vocabulary."

There are numerous reports of students not knowing the basic facts (e.g., not knowing that the United States fought against Japan in World War II, or not knowing who won the war). An important survey done by the National Assessment of Educational Progress in 1998 is very telling (check out their website: nces.ed.gov/index.html). This survey of high school seniors in seven major cities disclosed that in Dallas, 25 percent of the students tested couldn't identify the country that borders the United States on the south; in Boston, 39 percent couldn't name the six New England states; in Minneapolis-St. Paul, 63 percent couldn't name all seven continents; in Baltimore, 45 percent couldn't find the United States on a world map.

And it doesn't stop with the high schools. From speaking with college professors and from my own reading, I have learned that colleges are dumbing down freshman courses and offering remedial courses to incoming students just so they can keep up the flow of incoming students and the revenue they generate.

College students have similar problems. A journalism student at USC didn't know if Germany had been an enemy or an ally of the U.S. during World War II. A junior at UCLA thought Toronto was a city in Italy; another guessed that Stalin was the U.S. president just before Roosevelt; and another thought Lenin was a drummer with the Beatles before Ringo Starr.

"We have a situation," said the director of the U.S. National Council for Geographic Education, "where Johnny not only doesn't know how to read or add, he doesn't even know where he is."

A newspaper article written by a college graduate reported, "The body of a man found in the Saint John River last week is still trying to be identified."

A newspaper editor showed me a letter he had received from a recent high school graduate asking for a job as a "sprots writter."

What's the good news about public schools? They will still take your child off your hands for six to eight hours a day year after year, and are much cheaper than baby sitters.

Learning problems frequently come from prob-

*Nothing in education is so astonishing as the amount of ignorance it accumulates in the form of inert facts.* — Henry Brooks Adams lem teachers who seek to excuse their inability to convey knowledge to their students by saying the students are hyperactive, retarded, disturbed, disabled, or — more recently — have Attention Deficit Disorder.

One of the students in an adult literacy class I taught some years ago was a man with a measured IQ of 50. Previous teachers had tried briefly to teach him, but were quick to decide that he was incapable of learning, and therefore not worth the time it would take to work with him. He was living away from home, and the high point of each day for him was "writing" — dictating — a letter to his mother. One day, I typed the letter he had just dictated to me, then asked him to read it to me. None of the symbols meant anything to him, although I'd been working with him for several weeks. I pointed out the letters that spelled MOM, naming them and sounding them, then pronouncing the word again. "This is the word that means *your mom*," I told him. He repeated the sounds and the word after me, lovingly, wonderingly, studying the letters. I moved his finger, tracing the shapes of the letters as I said them. Then I guided his hand, with a pencil in it, to draw the letters. He printed **M O M** over and over for hours. With that word as his personal key, he progressed from total, "hopeless" illiteracy to a sixth-grade reading *and writing* level in less than six months. He could read comic books, magazines, newspapers, street signs, a driver's manual, and thousands of books. The psychologists and educators who had pronounced him incapable of learning decided their tests had been wrong, and were baffled when his IQ still tested at 50. Retarded? Disturbed? Attention Deficit? When I read those weak excuses for the schools' failures, I have a definite Belief Deficit.

Over the years we've heard many more disturbing tales from parents who took their officially diagnosed ADD children out of school, gave them more time and attention, and discovered the problem wasn't the children, but the system.

Teachers today are rated as much for their accuracy and punctuality in keeping attendance records as they are for their achievements in providing an environment in which students can learn. In most cases, the teachers themselves are not at fault, at least when they begin their careers. They have high ideals and higher hopes, but they are soon beaten down by the quasi-scientific theories of statisticians and pompous educational psychologists who can't get past the first four letters of analysis.

An article in the national home-school magazine *Growing Without Schooling* (December 1983) told of a Minnesota judge who ruled that a mother's actual ability to teach is unimportant if she isn't legally "qualified." The mother had offered her daughter's educational progress as evidence of the effectiveness of her teaching, but the judge ruled that if the mother doesn't have legal certification, then her being a good teacher in fact is irrelevant.

In the same state, according to an article in *Learning Magazine*, several teachers who had been out on strike were given up to thirty-three credits needed for the renewal of their teaching certificates, "on the theory that the teachers learned communication and political organization skills during the walkout."

*Time* reported in October 1983 that "when one-third of Houston's public school teachers took a competency exam last spring, some sixty percent failed the reading section."

A study titled "What's Happening in Teacher Testing," released in 1987 by Chester Finn Jr. of the U.S. Department of Education, says 28 percent of the applicants to teacher education programs are being rejected, and that 17 percent of teacher graduates who apply for teaching licenses are being turned down. In spite of this, says the report, passing scores are still set so low that many "incompetents" are being licensed and subsequently hired.

Joseph Weizenbaum, a professor of computer science at MIT, in an interview published in *Science Digest* (August 1983), said, "(F)ully half of all math and science teachers are operating on emergency certificates." That is, when there aren't enough qualified instructors to go around, unearned certificates are given to teachers whose training is in completely different and often unrelated fields.

The same school authorities who issue these "emergency certificates" would undoubtedly scoff at mail-order diploma mills that will sell a phony Ph.D. for a few hundred dollars. Is there really any difference?

Although the quotes above are dated, the problems still exist and are still unresolved. I believe the increased publicity about inadequate schools and incompetent teachers is helping some very dedicated people within the system to make changes, but slowly. How long can you wait?

> *My grandmother wanted me to have an education, so she kept me out of school.* — Margaret Mead

It's probably still true, as we've been told for so long, that high school graduates earn more money than dropouts, but it's not always because they're better educated. It's often because employers also have been taught that there is magic in the graduates' parchment coupons with the Olde Englishe lettering. Indeed, a few decades ago, there may have been some magic there, but today most of it is no more than clumsy legerdemain.

Thank goodness homeschoolers are no longer oddities. An increasing number of homeschooled children are now young adults. I have read their stories in *Home Education Magazine* and *Growing Without Schooling* and met many young adults who have had school at home and gone on to college or into the work force or created their own businesses. They are a very impressive group of self-assured young people. To the best of my knowledge these grown homeschoolers have not met with admissions or employment obstacles they could not overcome. As with everyone else, there are sometimes problems, but school at home has only extremely rarely been one of them, and that is rapidly changing. Colleges and employers are losing faith in the fancy pieces of paper given to those who spend their years in public education. More than ever, who you are and what you can do is what matters.

Public schools teach students how to pass tests — by memorizing facts and formulas, by guessing, or by cheating. If most teachers did not announce tests days and weeks in advance, then tell their students what to study in preparation, and even what questions to expect, and on what pages they should look for the answers, and then just as often give a "pre-test" for practice, many more students would fail. Even with all this rigorous coaching, most students would still fail if the test were unexpectedly postponed for two weeks, during which time everything would be forgotten again. It's only by such hocus-pocus that too many teachers are able to help most students "pass" their tests; the marks are duly recorded, and the year is considered a success. Next year, two or three months will be spent in "review" of last year's subjects before a new field or higher level can be introduced.

Sixty, forty, even twenty years ago, "average" students learned more and retained more than most of today's top students. "But we have more subjects to cover," protest the teachers. That's true, but so what? The larger range of subjects supposedly being pre-

sented is no excuse for dim mediocrity in all of them.

The academic failures of public schools are unimportant beside their much greater failure to provide an environment in which children can grow in moral strength and integrity. Most parents, whether or not they consider teaching at home, are worried about drugs, violence, sexual promiscuity, and teenage pregnancy.

Several magazines and newspapers have repeated a comparison of two surveys of public school teachers:

In 1940, the most serious problems they had to deal with were talking without permission, chewing gum, making noise, running in the halls, getting out of turn in line, and wearing improper clothing.

In 1980, their major concerns were rape, burglary, robbery, assault, arson, bombings, murder, suicide, vandalism, extortion, drug and alcohol abuse, gang warfare, pregnancies, abortions, and venereal disease.

These "problems" are the fault of society in general, not of the schools and teachers, but they are not doing enough to change them.

I find it interesting that none of the problems mentioned in either survey was academic. It's 2001. Have these problems been addressed? Are any of them under control? How many of these will you or your children have to deal with if you teach your children at home?

On an administrative level, the schools try to produce obedient, unquestioning citizens, good consumers, and productive (but not necessarily creative) workers.

On a social level — admittedly usually not through deliberate design — the schools promote religious intolerance, racial bigotry, drug abuse, sexual promiscuity, lying, cheating, emotional insincerity, philosophical skepticism, fake sophistication, and intellectual apathy.

When we began to homeschool, my parents were firmly opposed to our decision to do so. My father wrote to us, "Your lessons on morality are fine for your homeschool, but they have no validity in the real world."

Obviously we disagreed, but his statement seems to reflect the opinions of a disproportionate segment of society. Corporate advertising, popular music, television, and the majority of public schools are bombarding our society with the dictum "If it feels good, do it."

"You can't shelter your children forever," the self-appointed experts tell us. "They'll have to be exposed to these things sooner or later."

That's true, we answered; we can't shelter them forever — nor do we want to. We just want to shelter them until they are strong enough to face these issues by themselves without being overwhelmed by them. Most adults would have great difficulty in resisting a daily barrage of sex, drugs, and violence. How, then, can we expect our children — who are still learning to examine, evaluate, and judge — to put such "problems" into their proper perspective?

A distressed parent recently explained to me that she was taking her child out of public school because of the notes her daughter brought home from her teacher. These notes told the children to beware of pedophiles in the area and went on to detail personal descriptions and types of cars used. Her child became frightened of all men with blue cars. I do not believe we should have to define the word pedophile to our six- and seven-year-old children or that they should live with that type of fear unnecessarily.

Such issues and problems are facts of life, particularly in the cities, and our children need to be aware of them and to be prepared to deal with them, but they don't need — and should not have — daily or even frequent exposure to them. Such problems are symptoms of an unhealthy society, a society with an illness that, we hope and believe, isn't fatal, but is certainly dangerous and highly contagious.

"As any parent knows, teaching character is a

difficult task," William J. Bennett, former Secretary of Education, told the National Press Club in Washington, D.C., on March 27, 1985. "But it is a crucial task because we want all our children to be not only healthy, happy, and successful, but decent, strong, and good. None of this happens automatically; there is no genetic transmission of virtue. It takes conscious, committed effort. ... Not all teachers are parents, but all parents are teachers, the indispensable teachers. And, as teachers, parents always have had the first and largest responsibility for educating their children. ... And in some cases parents discover that their children are unlearning in school the lessons they have learned at home."

To protect our children from the harmful influences of a chaotic society until they are better able to handle them is not only our right, but our duty and responsibility — even if it means (although of course it doesn't) that they receive no academic education at all.

Hardly a day goes by without an article about home-schooling in a major newspaper or magazine. Publications that promote and celebrate family closeness are becoming much more numerous. There are now hundreds of home-school newsletters, organizations, and support groups.

Professional educators are beginning to realize that all their training and certification are not helping them teach, and that most parents could educate their own children far better, and in less time, than the schools can. The teachers may have to find other work — or throw out their schedules and formulas and remedial classes and get back to real teaching.

Drawing from our experience with our own children, the multitude of books with homeschooling stories, and the many articles in homeschooling publications and some national publications that have appeared in the last five years, it is now possible to make some general comparisons between public and home education. I clearly see that learning basic skills at home is done in less time, leaving more time for developing other interests, which creates a broader spectrum of learning. Learning at home is individualized, leading to a higher retention of material covered because the material is usually more creatively presented and related across the curriculum, linked to individual interests and to life itself. Homeschooling parents generally make a strong effort to involve their children with the community and activities outside the home, thereby giving homeschooled children the ability to relate well to all ages (and not just their peer groups). Many homeschoolers are going on to college, and according to the Home School Legal Defense Association, are generally scoring higher on the SATs and other tests then the average student in public school. Other homeschoolers have created their own businesses or followed their creative interests into the arts. Best of all, I see children developing with a deeper sense of themselves as individuals, maturing into responsible, caring adults, pursuing their own goals with a great respect for those around them and the world at large.

# "WE WOULD BETTER WAIT AND SEE"

"We would better wait and see," our provincial Minister of Education was quoted as saying, referring to the possibility of closing the public schools if 3,000 janitors, secretaries, and bus drivers decided to strike.

A staff writer for the *Telegraph-Journal* of Saint John, New Brunswick, went on to tell his readers about the Treasury Board's efforts to ensure that many non-teaching employees would be forced to work in the event of a strike: "The board has been only successful in having 132 non-teaching employees designated essential."

Did he think the board should have been more than successful? Wasn't success enough? Perhaps the adverb was meant to be an adjective, to modify the number of employees, "only 132," rather than to diminish the board's success.

The 132 employees whom the Treasury Board designated as "essential" should have been congratulated. Apparently, it wasn't their jobs that were essential, but the 132 employees themselves. Kings, queens, prime ministers, and presidents will all be replaced someday, so even they are not essential, but the writer brought to our attention 132 people with a sinecure greater than that of the Twelve Disciples — at least in the opinion of the Treasury Board.

Part of the problem, according to the chief negotiator, was that for more than six months the Treasury Board "constantly refused to negotiate in a serious tone."

According to all of my several dictionaries, "constantly" means "happening or continuing all the time; happening repeatedly." Those Treasury Board members must have been as busy as naughty schoolboys writing their penances on the chalkboard: "We will not negotiate in a serious tone, we will not ..." and so on, over and over, for six months.

The chief negotiator didn't say that the Treasury Board had refused to negotiate, but that it had refused to do so "in a serious tone." Did the board make flippant remarks? Giggle during meetings? Make faces at non-essential employees?

"The only reason Charlie got to be Minister of Education," a neighboring farmer told me recently, "is that he sat behind me in grade school and copied all my answers."

Another question pops up constantly, in a serious tone: If the school employees, whether essential or non-essential, go out on strike, and the schools are all closed, and the students spend the day watching *Sesame Street* and cleaning their fingernails, will it make any appreciable difference in the education of tomorrow's writers, educators, and politicians?

We would better wait and see.

# PERMISSION TO TEACH AT HOME

*Alice began to feel very uneasy. To be sure, she had not as yet had any dispute with the Queen, but she knew that it might happen any minute. "And then," thought she, "what would become of me? They're dreadfully fond of beheading people here."* — Lewis Carroll

Homeschooling is now permitted in all U.S. states and throughout Canada. Requirements and conditions vary from extremely lenient to very strict, with the majority in between but leaning toward the more permissive.

Information, suggestions, and advice about dealing with education laws were very difficult to find fifteen years ago, or even ten, but now such information is easily obtained.

Just a few years ago Donn suggested that you begin with a copy of the Education Act for your state or province, which your public library would have or be able to get. Now that homeschooling is more widespread I think it's more practical to contact the nearest group, whose members will be familiar with the state or provincial laws and be able to advise you about the best way to deal with those laws. Your local group also will know if your local officials are easy to deal with, what they will expect from you, and what you can expect from them. Many groups have detailed "legal packets" with both general and specific information and suggestions. If you're unable to find local support, write or call a statewide group. The advantage of starting with a support group instead of the Education Act is that you will avoid having to interpret the legal jargon. Your local group will know with whom you should speak and how to deal with the formalities. (Information about support groups is in the next section.)

You can also ask your Department of Education for a copy of all laws regarding home education, but don't get into a lengthy dialogue, and don't take the word of teachers, principals, or education officials as infallible. Sometimes they don't know the laws, but will gladly offer opinions or even guesses as if they were facts. Sometimes, they have been known to lie. (A couple in one state was told that home-schooling is allowed only in the first four grades, and another couple in the same state was told that home-schooling is allowed only *after* the first four grades. In fact, it's allowed there on all grade levels.)

The best single source for legal information and advice for most home-schoolers is **Holt Associates, Inc.**, 2380 Massachusetts Ave., Suite 104, Cambridge, MA 02140-1226. If you are in a hurry you can call (10 a.m.–4 p.m., EST), not collect, 617-864-3100. This organization, founded by John Holt in 1970 and continuing his work since his death in 1985, publishes the bimonthly magazine *Growing Without Schooling*.

John Holt's *Teach Your Own*, the only one of his books specifically about home-schooling, has many invaluable suggestions for dealing with officials and the law, as well as extensive information, with examples, about many other aspects of home-schooling. (See "Homeschooling and Education" for more detail.)

Another excellent source of general information is **Home Education Press**, P.O. Box 1083, Tonasket, WA 98855, which publishes the national bimonthly *Home Education Magazine* (see review in "Homeschooling and Education") and offers a free Resource Guide. Write them or e-mail HEM@home-ed-press.com, or find it online at www.home-ed-press.com.

An appendix in Ted Wade's ***The Home School Manual*** (see "Homeschooling and Education") lists the requirements of each state and all the Canadian provinces; the book is updated regularly.

The **National Home Education Network** (NHEN), P.O. Box 41067, Long Beach, CA 90853, is a group representing all homeschoolers. NHEN is creating a giant database with listings of audio and video recordings, books, online and distance learning schools, curriculum and resource distributors, e-mail lists, events, magazines and newsletters, speakers, websites, support groups, and more. A group to represent and help us all. Online at: www.nhen.org; you can e-mail them at info@nhen.org.

**TAKING CHARGE THROUGH HOME SCHOOLING: Personal and Political Empowerment**, by Larry and Susan Kaseman, is one of the most informative and interesting books about dealing with the legal aspects of home-schooling. Our right to home-school is established in all states and provinces, but the right to do it our own way is something we will have to guard continually. Larry and Susan have some excellent ideas for maintaining this freedom. (See "Homeschooling and Education.")

**Two of the cardinal points in our home-schooling are that individuals are always more important than government, and that individuals can effect meaningful changes in society**. Might does not make right, and we want our children to know it. We tell them that freedom is a very fragile and elusive condition. We agree with Thomas Jefferson that eternal vigilance is the price of liberty, not only in a broad, political sense, but also in our immediate, personal lives; not only against foreign governments, but against soft-drink ads, religious fanatics, and repressive forces in our own government, including a few education authorities.

If the government has particular rules and regulations regarding subjects taught or hours observed, we'll try to meet them — if such compliance doesn't interfere with the education of our children. If the government comes to us to discuss, negotiate, or offer a compromise, we're willing to listen and participate and consider. We don't want broadside confrontation with school officials. But if the government comes to us with orders and demands, as if it is right simply because it is stronger, then we resist. That which is demanded may be right, but the demand, as such, is wrong.

**We are convinced — not by anyone's scripture, but by observation and reason — that teaching our own children is not merely a privilege to be granted by the government, but is an intrinsic right**. Whether that right is God-given or a sine qua non of natural, universal law (not forgetting that they may be one and the same), the instruction to render unto Caesar only that which is Caesar's is completely pertinent, both literally and symbolically. As Emerson wrote in "Self-Reliance," "We cannot consent to pay for a privilege where we have intrinsic right."

**We never asked for permission to teach at home. A request for permission would imply a willingness to abide by the response, whether positive or negative**. The request might be denied, and then where would we be? We have no such willingness, so we usually just go about our business, and expect the government to do the same.

But people who build their home in the woods and don't put their children on the rural school bus don't blend into the woodwork, even if they dress conventionally and drive an ordinary eight-year-old car. Word gets around, although it's often like the old game of Telephone, in which the players sit in a circle and a message is whispered from one to the next and finally back to the one who began it, usually becoming considerably distorted as it passes through one head after another.

Although the following correspondence is dated, it is typical of what can be expected from educational authorities:

**OFFICE OF THE**
**SUPERINTENDENT OF SCHOOLS**
**Frederickton, New Brunswick**
October 27, 1980

Dear Mr. Reed:

It is my understanding that you have recently moved to this area from British Columbia. It has been brought to my attention that you have four school-age children for whom you are responsible. The Province of New Brunswick requires any person from seven to fifteen years of age inclusive to be in attendance at school. I have included the appropriate sections for your information.

59(1) In sections 59 to 66 inclusive "child" means any person from seven to fifteen years of age inclusive.

59(2) Except as provided in this section, every child shall attend school in the school selected by the school board in that school district provided for in section 5.

59(3) Where

(a) in the opinion of the Minister, a child is under efficient instruction elsewhere,

(b) a child is unable to attend school by reason of his own sickness or other unavoidable cause,

(c) the child is officially excluded from attendance under sections 45, 46, or 53,

(d) the child has completed the course prescribed for grade twelve, or

(e) the Minister certifies in writing to the school board that the child should be exempt from school attendance, the child shall not be required to attend school.

59(4) A school attendance officer shall examine every case of non-compliance with subsection (2) within the district for which he is employed.

59(5) When the examination warrants it, the school attendance officer shall notify in writing the parent of a child of the fact and the consequence of non-compliance.

59(6) Upon receipt of the notice mentioned in subsection (5), unless the child is excused from attendance as provided by this Act, the parent shall cause the child to attend school forthwith.

59(7) A parent who violates subsection (6) is guilty of an offense and on summary conviction is liable to a fine of twenty dollars for the first offense and forty dollars for each subsequent offense and in default of payment is liable to imprisonment in accordance with subsection 31 (3) of the Summary Convictions Act, or to both fine and imprisonment. 1966, c25 s.47.

Unless you receive special permission from the Minister of Education to exempt your children from the public school system, you must enroll them without further delay.

Yours truly,
Garth Hathaway

When the superintendent wrote, "It has been brought to my attention," he didn't say by whom. Certainly not by us. In these days of neighborhood watchers and satellite surveillance, there seems little need of our volunteering to the government what our intentions are.

Not knowing what kind of nut he might have to deal with, the superintendent let loose with both barrels, sections and subsections, including the penalties of fines and imprisonment for non-compliance with the rules. With the exception of 59(3) (a), "in the opinion of the Minister, a child is under efficient instruction elsewhere," there was no mention of the child receiving an education, but only of his obligation to attend school, or, rather, my obligation to cause him to do so.

The superintendent offered no arguments about the need of learning or the general advantages of dispelling ignorance, only the potential threat of losing my money or my freedom — or both — if I didn't comply without further delay.

"Thus the State never intentionally confronts a man's sense, intellectual or moral, but only his body, his senses," wrote Henry David Thoreau. "It is not armed with superior wit or honesty, but with superior physical strength."

My visceral inclination, held in check by reason, was to write back that I feel the government has no business interfering in the education of my children, and to refuse to answer questions or entertain an assessment of our books and program. However, we must refrain from the satisfaction of self-righteous paranoia. Government isn't always bad, nor are the public schools. Whether or not the school authorities are right, most of them sincerely believe they are. To challenge their beliefs or their authority is no better than waving the seat of one's pants at a mad bull.

We've known parents who have responded to such reminders of the government's strength with counter-threats, accusations, and ultimatums. Usually, it's fruitless. What would we have gained? Nasty letters, more threats, and probably loss of the one thing we wanted most — the opportunity to teach our children at home.

We were certain that our children were "under efficient instruction elsewhere," so the next step was to convince the Minister of Education. Since he and I were not yet on speaking terms, I wrote back to the superintendent, with extensive details of our kids' previous education, including specific courses and books, to indicate that we were taking the matter seriously, and listing many of our educational materials — "more than 2,000 volumes, including an encyclopedia, various reference books, dictionaries, and atlases; non-fiction works on art, music, philosophy, psychology, medicine, astronomy, history, literature, religion, science, botany, and biology; novels, short stories, and essays; posters, charts, flash cards, records, cassette tapes, a microscope, chemistry sets, and electronics kits; models of the human body, vital organs, and the solar system; and a world globe and a moon globe" — to point out that we had spent a great deal of money as well as thought, and also implying that our school's inventory, per capita, was superior to that of most public schools.

In closing, I wrote, "I hope this information will be of use to you. If you have any further questions about Brook Farm School, please do not hesitate to write or to visit us at any time. Thank you again for your concern, and for any help you are able to give us."

I didn't "request permission" to teach at home, but neither did I underline that omission.

I used the name "Brook Farm School" frequently in the letter (and earlier had had letterheads printed) to impress upon the Minister and his representatives that ours is a "real" school, not just a home with books. Subsequent letters from school authorities were addressed to Brook Farm School, and authorities usually used the name in referring to our educational program.

Many home-schooling parents are "invited," in a peremptory manner very like a court summons, to present their case in person before a school official or board. Failure to comply may mean automatic dismissal of the request for exemption. Those in this situation should prepare themselves with as much material as possible — laws, precedents, examples, educational theory, etc. — and proceed cautiously, a step at a time.

Some home-school writers feel it's best not to

invite officials to one's own home, but in our experience it has always worked out well. We think it's almost always best, if possible, to invite the superintendent or examiner to our home — and to get the jump on him, by inviting him before he invites us. "To look over our materials" is a good pretext, and not untrue. It has saved us the bother of collecting material, leaving home, tapping our feet in a waiting room, and facing the lion in his own den. People, like most other animals, are usually more at ease on their own territory; we feel more comfortable in our own homes. The visiting official is aware that he's a guest, and even if his basic attitude is hostile, he'll be less antagonistic than if we were in his office.

Not all school officials are suspicious or opposed to home-schooling. Most of those who have come to examine our materials and our children have been curious, friendly, and cooperative, and our visits have been genuinely friendly, with no need for verbal fencing. Officials in person are often much more human than in their letters or on the phone. They never know when their letters may be taken from the file, or by whom, so in their letters they'll be careful not to depart from the most conservative and official position. If they know they're speaking off the record, they may be freer and more helpful. (Two visiting officials admitted to us that if they were not working for the school system they would definitely teach their own children at home.)

In *The Power of Non-Violence*, Richard B. Gregg refers to disarming an antagonist with love and sympathy as "moral jujitsu." True peacefulness is not a tactic, but an attitude of being, so inviting an official to our home is not really equivalent; however, the changes in our relationship can be so marked that it might certainly be a kind of psychological jujitsu.

On the few occasions we were visited by an officious Mrs. Grundy and a suspicious Mr. Crabapple, we invited them in graciously. We introduced our children to them, and included the children in our discussions. Sometimes the officials wanted to talk with the children, to see if they could speak with some semblance of knowledge and intelligence; other times, they suggested that we might talk more freely if the children were excused. We explained that the children found adult conversation, particularly about education, stimulating and informative, and that they might as well stay. Besides, we said, we had to get back to our studies soon, which let the officials know that they were interrupting a serious school. We invited them into the kitchen (less formal than the living room and therefore more relaxing), offered chairs, and put examples of the kids' work on the table. Without asking, we served tea or coffee, and one of the kids passed a plate of cookies. The informality and the homey warmth was somewhat contagious. We stood by the visitors' shoulders occasionally to point out something in the material in front of them, causing them to look up at us — the eternal pose of a student with a hovering teacher, to reawaken a little of their own childhood conditioning toward authority. We tried to keep them slightly off balance — "jujitsu" — but not uncomfortably so. If they relaxed, then we did, too, but we stayed on guard, not wanting to lose any psychological advantage we had gained.

We seldom attacked the school system. It would only have made them more defensive and then more offensive. We just told them of our own materials, methods, and objectives. We knew we'd never convince the officials that our standards were superior to theirs, so we didn't try; instead, we tried to help them see that our educational program was good, not only by our standards, but also by theirs.

We read books and magazines about public education so we can talk the officials' language, use their terminology, and relate to their frames of reference. We can win and let them think they have won, but not by lying or deceit. Being imprisoned or having our children kidnapped by the state would certainly defeat our purpose, but avoiding either of those circumstances by deceit and subterfuge might defeat our larger purpose.

As the officials talked, even if they were telling us that we were depriving our children of all the advantages of life, we remained friendly (outwardly, at least), which confused them. Anger, no matter how thoroughly provoked it might have been, would have been taken as a sign of weakness, and as cause for a stronger position on their part. If they began a long harangue, we excused ourselves to get more of the children's work, and talked about it as if we hadn't interrupted a speech about something else.

We felt an attitude of firm commitment was of prime importance. If we had any doubts or reservations about our methods or materials, or about our ability to teach, we didn't let them show. Our manner exuded self-confidence and calm determination. Usually, school officials were as desirous of avoiding a serious confrontation as we were. Once they realized we wouldn't change our position, even under heavy pressure, they always gave in.

This approach won't work all the time, for everyone, but it has worked well for us, and many readers have said it worked well for them.

**DEPARTMENT OF EDUCATION**
**Office of the Minister**
February 3, 1981

Dear Mr. Reed:

I have arranged for the Coordinator of Elementary School Programs in my Department and the School Supervisor in Districts 30 & 31 to conduct an assessment of the instructional programs that you are providing in your home for your four children. It is my understanding that the Supervisor has discussed these programs in some depth with you and that he has communicated this information to the Coordinator.

It is reported to me that the instructional programs that you are using with your four children are adequate and that you have a good supply of books and materials.

In light of the positive report that I have received, I am willing to approve the exemption of your four children from attendance at public school for the current school year. You should make an application to me during the coming summer before the opening of school in September.

Yours very truly,
Charles G. Gallagher
Minister of Education

**BROOK FARM SCHOOL**
**Glassville, New Brunswick E0J 1L0**
August 15, 1981

Dear Mr. Gallagher:

As you requested, we are informing you of our intention to teach our children at home again this year.

Thank you for your attention and consideration.

Yours truly,
Donn Reed

**OFFICE OF THE SUPERINTENDENT**
September 30, 1981

Dear Mr. Reed:

You will recall that the School Supervisor came to visit the Brook Farm School to determine the suitability of your curriculum for your four children. You were subsequently given permission by the Minister of Education to teach in your home-school instructional program for the school year 1980-81.

Unless you plan to enroll these students in the school system, approval from the Minister of Education must be received for exemptions covering the 1981-1982 school year.

Please enlighten me with respect to your intentions relative to the education of your children for the 1981-1982 school year.

Yours truly,
Garth Hathaway
District Superintendent

**BROOK FARM SCHOOL**
**Glassville, New Brunswick E0J 1L0**
October 10, 1981

Dear Mr. Hathaway:

Thank you for your concern.

We wrote to the Minister on August 15, informing him of our intention to teach our children at home again this year, but have not received a reply.

Yours truly,
Donn Reed

**OFFICE OF THE MINISTER**
November 17, 1981

Dear Mr. Reed:

I have been advised that a follow-up assessment of the instructional programs that you are providing in your home for your four children has been conducted by the District School Supervisor. He has been in touch with the Coordinator of Elementary Education in this Department, and there is general agreement that the instructional programs that you are using with your four children are adequate and that you have a good supply of books and materials.

In light of the positive report that I have received, I am willing to approve the exemption of your four children from attendance at public school for the current school year ending June 30, 1982.

Should you wish to continue this arrangement beyond the current school year, you should make an application to me before the opening of school in September, 1982.

Yours very truly,
Charles G. Gallagher
Minister of Education

The following August, I wrote again, telling the Minister that we intended to continue teaching at home. We received no answer, nor any more letters from the Superintendent asking us to enlighten him with respect to our intentions relative to the education of our children. Although my letter had been one of declaration rather than of application, I felt it was close enough to the Minister's instruction to have fulfilled my obligation. No one had objected to my wording — not to me, anyway — so I assumed the absence of further inquiry was not because I had offended them.

The following year, feeling that the Department of Education was behind in its correspondence and owed me a letter, I wrote neither application nor declaration. There the matter stood for half a dozen years. We received letters from other home-schoolers in the province who were being harassed by the Department of Education or by their local school boards, but we received no more letters and no more assessments, and our children never had the privilege of being tested by school authorities.

We decided our file must have been misplaced, or the authorities had given up on us as a lost cause.

Then, after being ignored by the authorities for several years, we received a letter explaining that home-schoolers in the province were now in the charge of a new special branch, and asking us to fill out and return a long questionnaire that was enclosed. The questions seemed reasonable and non-threatening, so we answered them. A few weeks later, the administrator of the new special branch came to visit. We had many similar ideas about education, and she had no objections to our home-schooling, and she liked our homemade cookies.

Probably the cookies had nothing to do with the letter we received a few weeks later from the Minister of Education, granting exemption of our children from public school for the current school year, saying that our supplies seemed adequate, and telling us to apply again next summer if we planned to continue this practice.

We no longer felt ignored, but the renewed official stamp of approval didn't have any noticeable effect on the efficiency of our instruction elsewhere. Probably the department had been changing from human files to computer files, and it took six years for modern technology to bring us out of limbo.

Most of our experience has been limited to places where the grounds for exemption are not clearly or rigidly defined (as with New Brunswick's ambiguous phrase, "efficient instruction elsewhere"), or where home education is more or less well-accepted (such as British Columbia, where many people live more than several miles beyond any school bus line). Even in such areas, officials may bluster and threaten, and sometimes impede education, but they're not immovable obstacles.

In the past a few states made no statutory allowance at all for home-schooling. If we were in such a place, our approach might not work, but our attitudes would still be the same, so we'd probably try it anyway. I prefer not to wave flags (or the seat of my pants) at bulls, mad or not, but I also agree with Kahlil Gibran, who says in *The Prophet* that "if it is a despot you would dethrone, see first that his throne erected within you is destroyed."

"Unjust laws exist," wrote Thoreau in "Civil Disobedience." "Shall we be content to obey them, or shall we endeavor to amend them, and obey them until we have succeeded, or shall we transgress them at once?"

Across the United States and Canada, home-school support groups have lobbied and petitioned state and provincial governments with great success, causing restrictive education laws to be significantly modified, but many home-schoolers are still subject to laws they feel are too intrusive and demanding. "Men generally think," Thoreau said, "that they ought to wait until they have persuaded the majority to alter them. They think that, if they should resist, the remedy would be worse than the evil. But it is the fault of the government itself that the remedy is worse than the evil. ... As for adopting the ways which the state has provided for remedying the evil, I know not of such ways. They take too much time, and a man's life will be gone. I have other affairs to attend to."

So do we all.

We cannot change all the unjust laws, nor constantly risk our freedom even by resisting them all, but we must begin somewhere. Let us begin with those laws that affect us most personally and deeply.

Five of my ancestors were on the Mayflower, and twice that number dropped their hoes to join the fighting in Concord and Lexington. Maintaining the tradition of their spirit, I simply do not accept the authority of any person or government to force me into an action I believe is wrong. We would be very polite and tactful, but our final position would still be that no government has more right than we to determine our children's upbringing and education. If possible, without extreme danger of completely losing that for which we would be fighting, we would join Washington, Thoreau, and Gandhi in resisting the state's unwarranted demands. If necessary, we would emulate my Mayflower ancestors and go to another place where the demands were fewer and the restrictions more democratic. Exodus to escape persecution has several worthy precedents.

Home-schooling should never be just an avoidance of the problems in or created by the public schools. It should also be a positive contribution to the improvement of the society in which we live. By insisting upon our right to choose the place and method of our children's education, we are helping to prepare a slightly better world for them, and we are showing them, by our own example, how they can make similar contributions.

We must be clear, however, about the difference between moral right and legal right. Government, at its root and in its simplest form, is neither more nor less than a contract among individuals for their mutual benefit and protection. The need for some form of government, and the corollary need for some means of enforcing it, is obvious. However unjust or immoral an individual law may be, the basic principle of law per se is just. Disobedience of a law willfully or on a whim, simply because it is disagreeable or inconvenient, or because of greed or cowardice, strikes not only at the law but at the foundations of society itself. "Action from principle," wrote Thoreau, "the perception and the performance of right, changes things and relations; it is essentially revolutionary. ... Cast your whole vote; not a strip of paper merely, but your whole influence."

Your whole influence, and ours, will bring us all a little closer to true democracy, and beyond — to that time and place when people are governed not by the wishes of the majority or the dictates of the minority, but by what is right and true.

---

*To live outside the law, you must be honest.*
— Bob Dylan

---

**ANOTHER TYPE OF OPPOSITION**

You may or may not find school authorities opposed to your plans to homeschool. This type of opposition isn't always the hardest kind to deal with. When your parents or in-laws feel you are about to do something irresponsible and catastrophic to "their grandchildren," it's more personal and can put incredible strain on otherwise good and important family relationships.

Speaking from our experiences, I know how difficult this problem can be. If possible, strive to keep it from becoming a major issue that will destroy your relationships. Time is on your side. When your parents or in-laws see what your children are learning, and the kind of people they are becoming, they will eventually change their minds. Prepare yourself: It may not happen soon. For years some of our relatives would send fancy clothes, games, sports equipment, and toys, but they would not send needed educational supplies — not even good books. The family opposition we faced didn't really disappear until our kids were well into their teens. Only then did the attitudes change and become supportive. We all regret those missed years of closeness and harmony.

# SUPPORT GROUPS, ORGANIZATIONS, AND CORRESPONDENCE SCHOOLS

## GETTING CONNECTED

QUESTIONS?

ANSWERS

Some home-school support groups meet periodically to socialize and exchange views on home learning experiences, difficulties, and successes. Others have picnics, camp-outs, group tours, and regular meetings. Some have libraries, to be shared by members. Many have information packets that include resource guides and pertinent legal information useful to members and newcomers. Most publish newsletters with information and sometimes articles about home-schooling in their respective areas. Some groups are very active politically, presenting a unified front to legislators and school officials in seeking changes favorable to home-schoolers.

Many of the larger homeschool groups have initiated yearly conferences with speakers and workshops with special features for parents and specific programs for their children. Many groups (large and small) have yearly book fairs where you can peruse and purchase books and other learning materials. Some of these book fairs have a used book sale where you can buy, sell, and swap resources. These conferences are wonderful places to meet other homeschoolers and exchange ideas. This is one of the striking advances that have occurred since we began homeschooling.

We always lived in areas where there were few, if any, other home-schoolers, to say nothing of a support group. In fact, we had been teaching at home for a number of years before we learned that any support groups existed. We would have welcomed such a group, and undoubtedly would have joined, but at the same time we'd have been somewhat cautious about our identification with them. We might wear buttons proclaiming "I'm a home-schooler" when attending a support group meeting or camp-out, but never when visiting our neighbors or going to town. In relating to our neighbors, we have always been very casual about our home-schooling, wanting to be known as people who happen to be home-schooling rather than as home-schoolers. There's a big difference. Home-schooling, although interwoven throughout our lives, is still not the most dominant facet of our being. We also do many other things, none of which would be an adequate definition of our entire lives. Although we're glad to answer questions and to share information, we're not attempting to recruit converts to a new religion, and we carefully avoid any evangelistic stance that could easily antagonize people who would otherwise be friendly and interested (or not interested). We don't want our home-schooling to be a barrier between us and our neighbors. If the subject comes up, we're very open about our home-schooling, but we don't feel it's proper or even advantageous to answer our neighbors' comments about their children's problems in school with a smug reminder that our children don't have those problems. Self-righteous, proselytizing home-schoolers can quickly become as boring as recently reformed smokers and drinkers. Besides, the only home-schoolers who don't have problems of their own don't have children.

Most support groups invite all home-schoolers in their areas to join; a few insist upon agreement with certain religious doctrines or educational philosophies. If you don't agree with the requirements of the group nearest you, start another. Put a note on the supermarket bulletin board and a small ad in the local paper with your phone number, and you're bound to discover many others who share your views.

In rejecting the professional experts, we try to remember that amateur experts may not have all the answers, either. We read and listen, weigh and consider, and then take the course that seems best to us.

I urge you to keep in contact with at least one local, state, or provincial group to gain access to up-to-date information. Because the homeschooling laws are being challenged and changed, and because of the push for national standardized testing, in and out of the schools, it is imperative — for your own welfare and your freedom to homeschool in the manner of your own choosing — that you keep yourself informed and, I hope, involve yourself in the maintenance of homeschooling freedoms for everyone.

Below is a list of the largest national support groups and organizations. There is also a list of correspondence schools that offer either complete educational programs by mail or act as "umbrella" schools, which allow you to design your own program yet be protected legally in some states by being part of a "school."

**NOTICE!**
**A HOMESCHOOLING FAILURE**

There seems to be one outstanding, widespread failure within the homeschooling community. It's frequently very frustrating to find out who is homeschooling in your area and how to get in touch with them. The following listings were compiled from our own research with great assistance from Holt Associates in Boston and *Home Education Magazine* and are used with their permission. Many people refer to our publications to find help and support, yet very few groups contact publications like ours to notify us of address or contact changes for their support groups. We can't help you if you don't help us. We can only apologize for any inconvenience caused by inaccurate information, but not for the inaccurate information itself. If you find inaccuracies in the information below, please let us know so that it can be corrected. If you would like your group listed in the future, please contact *Home Education Magazine*, Holt Associates, or us. When writing to these groups for information, it is helpful to them if you include a #10 SASE.

## NATIONAL ORGANIZATIONS

**Alliance for Parental Involvement in Education** (AllPIE), P.O. Box 59, East Chatham, NY 12060-0059; 518-392-6900; allpie@taconic.net; www.croton.com/allpie. A non-profit group with resources for public, private, and home schools. Great catalog!

**Alternative Education Resource Organization**, 417 Roslyn Rd, Roslyn Heights, NY 11577; 516-621-2195. Extensive information source for alternative schooling options.

**National Home Education Network** (NHEN), P.O. Box 41067, Long Beach, CA 90853; info@nhen.org; www.NHEN.org. A new proactive group with a very solid base of long-time homeschoolers, leaders in the field, individuals, and many other homeschooling groups. NHEN's mission statement says it wants "to encourage and facilitate the vital grassroots work of state and local homeschooling groups and individuals by providing information, fostering networking, and promoting public relations on a national level. Because we believe there is strength in a diverse network of homeschoolers, we support the freedoms of all individual families to choose home education and to direct such education." NHEN is creating a giant database of all resources related to homeschooling. This is a group to represent and help us all. Write for information or check out their website.

**Unschooling.com** offers message boards, a free monthly newsletter, an e-mail discussion list, weekly online essays, a library, resources, and more. Sponsored by *Home Education Magazine*.

**Holt Associates, Inc.**, 2380 Massachusetts Ave., Suite 104, Cambridge, MA 02140; 617-864-3100; www.holtgws.com. Founded by John Holt in 1970, and continuing his work since his death in 1985. A national clearinghouse for unschooling information, maintaining files of current laws, recent decisions, and successful proposals to school districts; updating and publishing lists of homeschoolers willing to correspond with others, a list of correspondence schools, and homeschool support groups; and much more. Publishers of *Growing Without Schooling*, the bimonthly magazine begun by John Holt in 1977; call 888-925-9298 to subscribe to GWS. (See "Homeschooling and Education" for more information.)

**Home Education Magazine Press,** P.O. Box 1083, Tonasket, WA 98855. Publisher since 1983 of the national bimonthly *Home Education Magazine* (see "Homeschooling and Education" for review and phone number). A top-notch staff of regular columnists, plus articles by parents with information and ideas to share. Many other online and offline services at www.home-ed-magazine.com. Their e-mail is hem@home-ed-magazine.com. HEM's free *Pocket Field Guide to Homeschooling* answers most major questions about homeschooling. Write to HEM to request single copies or enough for your group, or download from www.home-ed-magazine.com/hem-guide.pdf. ***New*** networking and message boards at www.home-ed-magazine.com/wlcm_brds.html, where you'll find support and new resources and can ask questions about most of your homeschooling concerns.

**Homeschool Associates**, 116 Third Avenue, Auburn, ME 04210, puts out a brief newsletter; their best service is selling used textbooks — walk-in, mail order, and a cross-country bookmobile. Call 800-882-2828.

**National Association for the Legal Support of Alternative Schools** (NALSAS), P.O. Box 2823, Santa Fe, NM 87504-2241. Information and legal service center. Several functions and services. Send a #10 SASE for information

**National Home Education Research Institute**, Western Baptist College, 5000 Deer Park Dr. SE, Salem, OR 97301-9392; 503-375-7019.

## OTHER RELATED NATIONAL ORGANIZATIONS

**EVAN-G**, 977 Keeler Ave., Berkeley, CA 94708. Against corporal punishment.
**La Leche League International**, 1400 N. Meacham Rd., P.O. Box 4079, Schaumberg, IL 60168-4079; 800-LA LECHE. Promotes breastfeeding.
**Liedloff Continuum Network**, P.O. Box 1634, Sausalito, CA 94966. People interested in the "continuum concept."
**National Center for Fair and Open Testing** (FairTest), 342 Broadway, Cambridge, MA 02139; 617-864-4810.
**National Coalition of Alternative Community Schools**, P.O. Box 15036, Santa Fe, NM 87506; 505-474-4312.

## STATE AND PROVINCIAL SUPPORT GROUPS AND ORGANIZATIONS

### *** IMPORTANT!***

Homeschooling is legal in all states and provinces. Although the Department of Education is listed for each state, we strongly urge you to seek information and help with your questions about homeschooling from your local support group first. They will have up-to-date information about legalities. They will know the best way to deal with the formalities involved in meeting homeschooling requirements. Experience over the past years has shown (as Donn stated earlier in this book) that some professional educators and some people at the Department of Education do not thoroughly understand the regulations, and many people have been given incorrect information.

## UNITED STATES

### ALABAMA

**Alabama Home Educators Network**, 3015 Thurman Rd., Huntsville, AL 35805; Lisa Bugg.
**East Lake UMC Academy**, 1603 Great Pine Rd., Birmingham, AL 35235. Acts as a cover school.
**North Alabama Friends School**, P.O. Box 2183, Huntsville, AL 35802.
Dept. of Education, Gordon Persous Bldg., 50 Ripley, Montgomery, AL 36103; 205-242-8165.

### ALASKA

**Alaska Homespun Educators**, P.O. Box 798, Girdwood, AK 99587.
**Anchorage Home Spun Educators**, 7421 Tangle Ct., Anchorage, AK 99504.
**Homeschoolers Unlimited**, 392D Kenal Ave., Ft. Richardson, AK 99505-1227.
**Sitka Home Education Association**, 506 Verstavia St., Sitka, AK 99835.
Dept. of Education, Correspondence Study, P.O. Box GA, Juneau, AK 99811; 907-465-2835.

### ARIZONA

**Arizona Families for Home Education**, P.O. Box 2035, Chandler, AZ 85244-2035; 800-929-3927.
**Bethany Home Educators**, 2720 S. Flint Cir., Mesa, AZ 85202.
**East Valley Educators** (Phoenix/Metro area), 602-983-5660.
**Phoenix Learning Alternatives Network**, 8835 N. 47th Pl., Phoenix, AZ 85028.
**SPICE**, 10414 W. Mulberry Dr., Avondale, AZ 85323.
**TELAO Home Educators**, 4700 N. Tonalea Tr., Tucson, AZ 85749; 520-749-4757.
Dept. of Education, Research Unit, 1535 W. Jefferson St., Phoenix, AZ 80078; 602-542-3759.

### ARKANSAS

**Home Educators of Arkansas**, P.O. Box 192455, Little Rock, AR 72219; 501-847-4942; HEAREPORT@juno.com.
**Home Educators of Arkansas Voicing Excellence Now** (HEAVEN), 8 Glenbrook Pl., Sherwood, AR 72120.
Department of Education, State Education Bldg., Little Rock, AR 72201; 501-682-4252.

### CALIFORNIA

**All Ways Learning of San Jose**, 408-226-1518.
**Bayshore Homeschoolers**, P.O. Box 13038, Long Beach, CA 90803.
**California Hi-Desert Home Education Association**, 15185 Cactus St., Hesperia, CA 92345.

**California Home Education Conference**, P.O. Box 231324, Sacramento, CA 95823.
**California Homeschool Network**, P.O. Box 55485, Hayward, CA 94545; 800-327-5339; mail@cahomeschoolnet.org.
**Central California Homeschoolers**, 7600 Marchant Ave, Atascadero, CA 93422.
**East Bay Family Educators**, 1090 Mariposa Ave., Berkeley, CA 94707.
**Esparto Homeschoolers**, P.O. Box 305, Esparto, CA 95627; 916-787-3613.
**Family-Centered Education of Los Angeles**, 818-766-8914.
**Family Village Support Group**, 510-528-6510.
**Guild of Learning**, P.O. Box 90638, Industry, CA 91715.
**High Desert Homeschoolers**, Victoriaville, Apple, Hesperia, and Lucerne Valleys; 760-956-1588.
**Home Education League of Parents**, Suite 131, 3208 Cahuenga Blvd. W, Los Angeles, CA 90068.
**HomeSchool Association of California** (formerly Northern CA Homeschool Association), P.O. Box 2442, Atascadero, CA 93423-2442; 888-HSC-4440; info@hsc.org.
**Homeschooling Coop of Sacramento**, 15 Moses Ct., Sacramento, CA 95823.
**Humboldt Homeschoolers**, P.O. Box 2125, Trinidad, CA 95570; 707-677-3290.
**Lompac Valley Home Educators**, Chris Tykeson, 805-733-2710.
**Los Angeles Homeschoolers**, P.O. Box 1166, Malibu, CA 90265.
**Marin Homeschoolers**, 905 Tiburon Blvd., Tiburon, CA 94920.
**Monterey Bay Christian Home Schoolers**, 1558 Flores St., Seaside, CA 93955.
**Mountain View Park Homeschoolers**, 6603 Mammoth Ave., Van Nuys, CA 91405-4813.
**NorthBay HomeScholars**, P.O. Box 621, Vineburg, CA 95487.
**North Santa Clara Valley Homeschoolers**, 795 Sheraton Dr., Sunnyvale, CA 94087.
**Peninsula Homeschoolers**, 4795 Lage Dr., San Jose, CA 95130; 408-379-6835.
**Riverside Area Home Learners**, 731 Mt. Whitney Cir., Corona, CA 91719.
**Rose Rock Inclusive Global Homeschool Network**, 805-942-4465.
**San Diego Home Educators**, 210 Copley Ave., San Diego, CA 92116.
**San Francisco Homeschoolers**, 41 Eastwood Dr., San Francisco, CA 94112.
**School of Home Learning Support Group**, 1904 Flora Vista St., Needles, CA 92363; 619-326-2107.
**Sonoma County Homeschoolers**, P.O. Box 82, Santa Rosa, CA 95403.
**South Bay F.R.E.E. Scholars**, Cupertino area; 408-554-9014.
**South St. Centre**, P.O. Box 261, Boulder Creek, CA 95006. Resource center. Also P.O. Box 227, Boulder Creek, CA 95006; 831-338-2540 for information.
**SPICE**, P.O. Box 282, Wilton, CA 95693
**Tri-City Homeschoolers**, 39195 Levi St., Newark, CA 94560.
**Tri-Valley Explorers**, 925-556-3522.
**Valley Home Educators**, P.O. Box 4016, Modesto, CA 95352.
**Venture Home Schoolers Resources**, 231 Market Pl., #328, San Ramon, CA 94583.
**Whittier Homeschoolers**, 7432 Duchess Dr., Whittier, CA 90606; 310-695-7646.
**Wildflower Homeschoolers**, 1557 Vancouver Way, Livermore, CA 94550; 510-455-0465.
**Yosemite Area Homeschoolers**, P.O. Box 74, Midpines, CA 95345.
Dept. of Education, P.O. Box 944272, Sacramento, 94244; 916-675-2453.

## COLORADO

**Boulder County Home Educators,** c/o Berg, 1495 Riverside, Boulder, CO 80304; 303-449-5916.
**Colorado Home Educators Association**, 3043 S. Laredo Cir., Aurora, CO 80013; 303-441-9938.
**Colorado Home Schooling Network**, 1247 Harrison St., Denver, CO 80206; 303-369-9541.
**Colorado Home Schooling Network,** 7490 W. Apache, Sedalia, CO 80135; 303-688-4136.
**Colorado Springs Homeschool Support Group**, P.O. Box 26117, Colorado Springs, CO 80909; 800-532-7011.
**Concerned Parents of Colorado**, P.O. Box 547, Florissant, CO 80816.
**Fall River Homeschool**, P.O. Box 3322, Idaho Springs, CO 80452.
**Home Educators for Excellence of Durango**, c/o Gring, 315 Timberline Dr., Durango, CO 81301.
**Homeschool Support Network**, 3110 Pony Tracks Dr., Colorado Springs, CO 80922.
**Independent Network of Creative Homeschoolers**, 19062 E. Mansfield, Aurora, CO 80013; 303-699-9130.

**Mesa Verde Homeschoolers**, P.O. Box 134, Mancos, CO 81328; 970-882-7802.
**Rocky Mountain Education Connection**, 20774 E. Buchanan Dr., Aurora, CO 80304; 303-449-5916.
**Secular Homeschool Support Group**, Colorado Springs; 719-634-4098.
**West River Unschoolers**, 2420 N. 1st St., Grand Junction, CO 81501.
Dept. of Education, 201 East Colfax, Denver, CO 80203; 303-866-6678.

## CONNECTICUT

**Connecticut Home Educators Association**, P.O. Box 306, New Hartford, CT 06057; 203-781-8569.
**CT's Cure**, P.O. Box 597, Sherman, CT 06784; 203-355-4724.
**Home Educators of the Northwest Hills**, 22 Chatham Ct., Goshen, CT 06759.
**Unschoolers' Support**, 22 Wildrose Ave., Guilford, CT 06437; 203-458-7402.
Dept. of Education, Box 2219, Hartford, CT 06115.

## [D.C. AREA — see LEARN in Virginia]

## DELAWARE

**BVHERO**, P.O. Box 117, Claymont, DE 19703.
**Delaware Home Education Association**, Box 1003, Dover, DE 19903.
**Tri-State Homeschoolers Association**, P.O. Box 7193, Newark, DE 19714-7193.
**Unschoolers & Others**, Wilmington, DE; unschoolers-andothers@juno.com.
Dept. of Education, P.O. Box 1402, Dover, DE 19901

## FLORIDA

**Family Learning Exchange**, 2020 Turpentine Rd., Mims, FL 31754.
**Florida Parent-Educators Association**, P.O. Box 1193, Venice, FL 34284; 877-275-3732.
**H.E.L.P.S.**, info@helpsonline.org.
**Home Education Resources & Information**, 711 St. Johns Bluff Rd., Jacksonville, FL 32235.
**Home Educators Assistance League**, 3343 Shoal Creek Cove, Crestview, FL 32539.
**Home for Our Children**, jarnette2@juno.com or draper@bestnetpc.com.
**Homeschool Alternatives**, 7030 32nd Ave. N., St. Petersburg, FL 33710.
**Homeschool Network**, 548 N. Lake Pleasant Rd., Apopka, FL 32712; 407-889-4632.
**Independent Homeschoolers' Network**, sparrow@brevard.net.
**Parkland Home Educators**, 2045 Houndslake Dr., Winter Park, FL 32792; 407-677-1891.
**Tallahassee Homeschool Group**, 5227 Wild Olive Way, Tallahassee, FL 32310; 904-575-7091.
Dept. of Education, 544 Florida Education Center, Tallahassee, FL 32399.

## GEORGIA

**Athens Area Homeschoolers**, 1855 Jot-Em-Down Rd., Danielsville, GA 30633.
**Atlanta Alternative Education Network**, c/o Sheffield, 1672 Cody Cir., Tucker, GA 30084.
**CFEG** (Christian Family Educators of Georgia), 770-516-2624.
**Cobb County Homeschoolers**, 813 Wyntuck Dr., Kennesaw, GA 30144.
**Coweta Home Educators' Association**, 9 Ashley Oaks Ln., Newnan, GA 30263.
**Douglas County Home Educators**, 3855 Jims Ct., Douglasville, GA 30135.
**Free to Learn at Home**, 4439 Lake Forest Dr., Oakwood, GA 30566; 770-536-8077. A teen group.
**Georgians for Freedom in Education**, 7180 Cane Leaf Dr., Fairburn, GA 30213; 770-463-1563.
**Harvest Home Educators**, P.O. Box 1756, Buford, GA 30518; 770-455-0449.
**Home Education Information Resource Center**, P.O. Box 2111, Roswell, GA 30077.
**LIGHT**, P.O. Box 2724, Columbus, GA 31902.
**North Side Atlanta Homeschoolers**, c/o Jane Kelly, 4141 Wieuca, Atlanta, GA 30342.
**Parent Educator's Association for Children at Home**, P.O. Box 430, Buford, GA 30515.
**Robins Air Force Base Homeschool Network**, P.O. Box 563, Lizella, GA 31052.
**Southern Unschoolers Network**, c/o Jordan, 4617 Stewart Reilly Dr., Acworth, GA 30101.
**Spectrum Homeschoolers**, 3426 Williams Pl., Conyers, GA 30313.
**Thomasville Home Education Network**, 1717 Norias Rd., Thomasville, GA 31792.
**Valdosta Area Homeschooling Association**, 912-249-0809.
Dept. of Education, 1662 Twin Towers E., Atlanta, GA 30334; 404-656-2446.

## HAWAII

**Hawaii Homeschool Association**, P.O. Box 3476, Mililani, HI 96789.

**Hawaii Island Home Educators**, 808-968-8076 or 808-965-9002.

**Kauai Home Educators Association**, 808-245-7867.

**The Tropical Homeschooler** (newsletter), c/o Pinsky, 220 Waipaiani Rd., Haiku, Maui, HI 96708; 808-572-9289.

Dept. of Education, P.O. Box 2360, Honolulu, HI 96804.

## IDAHO

**Family Unschooling Network**, 1809 N. 7th St., Boise, ID 83702; 208-345-2703.

**Home Educators of Idaho**, 3618 Pine Hill Dr., Coeur d'Alene, ID 83814; 208-667-2776.

**Palouse Home Learning Alternatives**, 802 White Ave., Moscow, ID 83843.

**Southeast Idaho Homeschool Association**, 1440 Eastridge, Pocatello, ID 83201.

Dept. of Education, Len B. Jordan Office Bldg., Boise, ID 83720.

## ILLINOIS

**Evanston Home Educators**, Maureen O'Grady, 847-676-2440; 102723.2764@compuserve.com.

**Homeschooling Families of Illinois**, 630-548-4349.

**HOUSE**, 9508 Springfield Ave., Evanston, IL 60203; 847-675-3632 or 708-758-7374. Statewide.

**Northwest Chicago HOUSE**, 773-637-9085.

**Rockford Area HOUSE**, 2317 10th Ave., Rockford, IL 61104.

**Spectrum Homeschoolers**, 10859 S. Longwood Dr., Chicago, IL 60643; 773-779-7608.

Dept. of Education, 100 N. First St., Springfield, IL 62777; 217-782-5270.

## INDIANA

**Families Learning Together**, 1714 E. 51st St., Indianapolis, IN 46205; 317-255-9298.

**Homefront**, 1120 W. Whiskey Run Rd., New Salisbury, IN 47161.

**Indiana Association of Home Educators,** 1000 N. Madison, #S2, Greenwood, IN 46142; 317-638-9633.

**Kentuckiana Home Educators** (Kentucky-Indiana area) — see Kentucky.

**L.E.A.R.N.**, 9577 E. State Rd. 45, Unionville, IN 47468; 812-336-8028.

**Life Education and Resource Network**, 9998 West State Rd. 43, Bloomington, IN 47404.

**Wabash Valley Homeschool Association**, 914 Barton Ave., Terre Haute, IN 47803.

Dept. of Education, Rm. 229, State House, Indianapolis, IN 46204; 317-232-6614.

## IOWA

**IDEA**, 3296 Linn-Buchanan Rd., Coggon, IA 52218.

**Iowa Families for Christian Education**, R.R. 3, Box 143, Missouri Valley, IA 51555

**Iowa Home Educators Association**, P.O. Box 213, Des Moines, IA 50301.

Dept. of Public Instruction, Grimes State Office Bldg., Des Moines, IA 50319; 515-281-5001.

## KANSAS

**Central Kansas Homeschoolers**, c/o Susan Peach, R.R. 1 Box 28A, Rush Center, KS 67575.

**Christian Home Educators Confederation of Kansas**, P.O. Box 3564, Shawnee Mission, KS 66203.

**Circle of Homeschoolers and Unschoolers**, R.R. 1 Box 28A, Rush Center, KS 67575.

**Heartland Area Homeschoolers' Association**, 823 West St., Emporia, KS 66801.

**Konza Homeschooler Association**, 7675 Jinkins Rd., St. George, KS 66535.

**Lawrence Area Unaffiliated Group of Homeschoolers**, c/o Michener, R.R. 1 Box 496, Perry, KS 66073.

**Teaching Parents Association**, P.O. Box 3968, Wichita, KS 67201; 316-945-0810.

Dept. of Education, 120 E. 10th St., Topeka, KS 66612; 913-296-3142.

## KENTUCKY

**Bluegrass Home Educators**, 600 Shake Rag Rd., Waynesburg, KY 40489.

**Home Educators Resource Center**, 9127 Galene Dr., Suite E, Louisville, KY 40299.

**Kentuckiana Home Educators**, 6906 Timber Ridge Ct., Prospect, KY 40059; 502-228-6906.

**Kentucky Home Education Association**, P.O. Box 81, Winchester, KY 40392-0081.

**Kentucky Independent Learners Network**, P.O. Box 275, Somerset, KY 42501.

**Madison County Homeschool Association**, 239 Reeves Rd., Richmond, KY 40475.

Dept. of Education, 500 Metro St., Frankfort, KY 40601.

## LOUISIANA

**Homeschoolers Learning From Mother Earth**, 14189 Ridge Rd., Prairieville, LA 70769.

**Homeschoolers Organizing for Progressive Education**,

5229 Hwy. 3276, Stonewall, LA 71078

**Louisiana Home Education Network**, lahmednet@usa.net.

**Southwest Acadiana Homeschoolers**, 507 S. Arenas, Rayne, LA 70578; 318-334-2812.

**Wild Azalea Unschoolers**, 6055 General Meyer Ave., New Orleans, LA 70131; 504-392-5647.

Dept. of Education, P.O. Box 94064, Baton Rouge, LA 70804; 504-342-3473.

## MAINE

**Central Maine Self-Learners**, 36 Country Acres, Monmouth, ME 04259.

**Home and Unschoolers Group**, R.R. 1 Box 925E (Biscay and Pinkham Rds.), Damariscotta, ME 04543.

**Homeschoolers of Northern Maine**, Julie Tornquist, 207-476-8904.

**Maine Home Education Association**, P.O. Box 9715-199, Portland, ME 04988.

**Maine Homeschool Association**, P.O. Box 421, Topsham, ME 04086; 800-520-0577.

**Peninsula Area Homeschooling Association,** P.O. Box 235, Deer Isle, ME 04627.

**Sebago Lake Homeschoolers Support Group**, R.R. 2 Box 54, Sebago Lake, ME 04075; 207-642-4368.

**Southern Maine Home Education Support Network**, 76 Beech Ridge Rd., Scarborough, ME 04074; 207-883-9621.

**Western Washington County Homeschoolers**, RFD 1 Box 93, Harrington, ME 04643.

Dept. of Education, State House Station 23, Augusta, ME 04333; 207-287-5922.

## MARYLAND

**Educating Our Own**, 686 Geneva Dr., Westminster, MD 21157.

**Glen Burnie Home School Support Group**, c/o Whetzel, 6514 Dolphin Ct., Glen Burnie, MD 21061.

**Maryland Home Education Association,** 9085 Flamepool Way, Columbia, MD 21045; 410-730-0073.

**Maryland-Pennsylvania Home Educators** — see Pennsylvania.

**Montgomery Home Learning Network**, 14220 Denington Pl., Rockville, MD 20853.

**North County Home Educators**, 1688 Belhaven Woods Ct., Pasadena, MD 21122.

**Prince George's Home Learning Network**, 3730 Marlborough Way, College Park, MD 20720.

Dept. of Education, 200 W. Baltimore St., Baltimore, MD 21201; 410-767-0300.

## MASSACHUSETTS

**ALOHA** (A Loosely Organized Homeschool Association), c/o Hazelton, 24A Calamint Rd., N. Princeton, MA 01541; 508-464-7794.

**Alternative Ways of Learning**, P.O. Box 1274, Charlton City, MA 01508.

**Apple Country Homeschooling Association,** P.O. Box 246, Harvard, MA 01451; 508-456-8515.

**Berkshire Homeschoolers Group**, 217 Old State Rd., Berkshire, MA 01224; 413-443-1770.

**Cape Ann Homeschoolers**, 108R Main St., Rockport, MA 01966.

**Family Resource Center**, P.O. Box 308, Salem, MA 01970.

**Franklin County Home Learning Families**, 72 Prospect St., Greenfield, MA 01301.

**Greater Boston Home Educators**, 781-246-2059.

**Groton-Dunstable Home Educators**, c/o McLeod-Warrick, 663 Townsend Rd., Groton, MA 01450.

**The HOME Club**, 19 Florence St., Cambridge, MA 02139.

**Homeschoolers of Massachusetts Education Club** (Boston area), Phoebe Wells, 617-876-7273.

**Homeschooling Together**, 24 Avon Pl., Arlington, MA 02474.

**Lowell Area Group**, Debbie Finch, 508-458-3896.

**Massachusetts Home Educators**, 22 Garland St., Lynn, MA 01902; 617-599-6267.

**Massachusetts Home Learning Association,** P.O. Box 1558, Marstons Mills, MA 02648. In western Mass. contact Loretta Heuer, 508-429-1436. In eastern Mass. contact Kathy Smith, 508-249-9056.

**Medway/Mills Support Group**, 508-359-5910.

**Merrimack Valley Homelearners Group**, 13 Ashdale Rd., N. Billerica, MA 01862; 508-663-2755.

**Newburyport Area Homeschool Network**, 32 Columbus Ave., Newburyport, MA 01950; 508-462-5680.

**North Shore Support Group**, 508-468-4663 or 508-658-8970.

**Pathfinder Learning Center**, P.O. Box 804, Amherst, MA 01002.

**Plymouth Pals**, Eileen Fortunato, 508-747-0297.

**Shadows on the Shore/Cape Cod Homeschooling Network**, P.O. Box 533, Harwich, MA 02645.

**Southeast Massachusetts Homeschool Association,** P.O. Box 4336, Fall River, MA 02723-0403; 508-672-0248.

**Wakefield Area Group**, Lucia Jenkins, 617-246-2059.

Dept. of Education, 350 Main St., Malden, MA 02148.

## MICHIGAN

**Ann Arbor Homeschooling and Unschooling**, 734-332-7832.

**Belleville Area Homeschool Association**, 17719 Odyssey, Belleville, MI 48111.

**Benzie Home Educators**, P.O. Box 208, Benzonia, MI 49616.

**Families Learning and Schooling at Home** (FLASH), 21671 B Dr., N. Marshall, MI 45068; 616-781-1069.

**HELP-Michigan**, 125 E. Lincoln, Nagaunee, MI 49866.

**Heritage Home Educators**, 13339 Firestone Ct., Fenton, MI 48430.

**Hillsdale Area Homeschoolers**, 5151 Barker Rd., Jonesville, MI 49250.

**Home Educators' Circle**, 1280 S. John Hix, Westland, MI 48186; 313-326-5406.

**Homeschool Support Network**, P.O. Box 2457, Riverview, MI 48192.

**Older Homeschoolers Group**, c/o Linn Family, 9120 Dwight Dr., Detroit, MI 48214.

**OWL** (Oakland, Washtenaw, Livingston) **Homeschool Support Group**, c/o Debra Cohn, 6036 Seven Mile, S. Lyon, MI 48178; 810-436-8931.

**Sault Home Education Association**, 1102 Ashmun, Sault Ste. Marie, MI 49783.

**Sunnyridge Alternative Learning Center**, HCO 1 Box 134, Pelkie, MI 49958.

Dept. of Education, P.O. Box 30008, Lansing, MI 48909; 507-775-6622.

## MINNESOTA

**Families Nurturing Lifelong Learners**, 2452 Southcrest Ave., Maplewood, MN 55119.

**Fargo-Moorehead Homeschool Association**, 1909 8th St. S., Moorehead, MN 56560.

**Home-Based Educators Accrediting Association**, Rte. 1 Box 381, Cambridge, MN 55008.

**Minnesota Homeschoolers Alliance**, P.O. Box 23072, Richfield, MN 55423; 612-288-9662. Statewide.

Dept. of Education, Rm. 710, Capitol Square Bldg., 550 Cedar St., St. Paul, MN 55101; 612-296-6595.

## MISSISSIPPI

**Coast Military Home Educators**, 9212A Givens Cir., Biloxi, MS 39531.

**Home Educators of Central Mississippi**, 102 Hollow Hill Dr., Florence, MS 39073; 601-366-9218.

**Oxford Homeschool Network**, 21 County Rd. 3024, Oxford, MS 38655.

**Walter Valley Homeschoolers**, P.O. Box 1709, Oxford, MS 38655.

Dept. of Education, Sillers Bldg., Suite 306, P.O. Box 777, Jackson, MS 39205; 601-359-3598.

## MISSOURI

**LEARN**, P.O. Box 10105, Kansas City, MO 64171; 913-383-7888.

**Ozark Lore Society**, c/o Eisenmann, HC 73 Box 160, Drury, MO 65638; 417-679-3391.

**St. Louis Homeschool Network**, 4147 West Pine, St. Louis, MO 63129; 314-537-1171.

**Springfield Home Education**, P.O. Box 1412, Springfield, MO 65801; 417-862-0520.

Dept. of Education, Box 480, Jefferson City, MO 65102; 314-751-7602.

## MONTANA

**Bozeman Homeschool Network**, c/o Dalton, 201 S. 6 Ave, Apt. A, Bozeman, MT 59715; 406-586-3499.

**The Grapevine** (statewide newsletter), P.O. Box 3228, Missoula, MT 59806; 406-542-8721.

**Mid-Mountain Home Education Network**, P.O. Box 2182, Montana City Station, MT 59634.

**Montana Coalition of Home Educators**, P.O. Box 43, Gallatin Gateway, MT 59730; 406-587-6163.

**Montana Home Educators**, P.O. Box 95, Ulm, MT 59485.

Office of Public Instruction, 1227 11th Ave., Helena, MT 59620; 406-444-4402.

## NEBRASKA

**LEARN**, 7741 E. Avon Ln., Lincoln, NE 68505; 402-488-7741.

**Nebraska Independent Homeschoolers Network**, 8010 Lillibridge St., Lincoln, NE 68506.

**Omaha Project for Education and Nurturing**, 9218 Leavenworth, Omaha, NE 68114.

Dept. of Education, Box 94987, Lincoln, NE 68509; 402-471-2783.

## NEVADA

**Homeschool Melting Pot**, 1778 Antelope Valley Ave., Henderson, NV 89012.

**Home Schools United/Vegas Valley**, P.O. Box 93564, Las Vegas, NV 89193; 702-870-9566.

**Northern Nevada Home Schools**, P.O. Box 21323, Reno, NV 89515.

Dept. of Education, SCA Team, 700 E. 5th St., Carson City, NV 89701; 702-687-9134.

## NEW HAMPSHIRE

**Derry Area Homeschoolers**, Christine Pollina, 603-898-0828.

**Homeschooling Friends**, 204 Brackett Rd., New Durham, NH 30855.

**New Hampshire Alliance for Home Education**, 17 Preserve Dr., Nashua, NH 03060.

**New Hampshire Home School Coalition**, P.O. Box 2224, Concord, NH 03304; 603-539-7233.

**Orchard School Homeschooling Support Group**, Kathleen Burch, HC 63 Box 52, Alstead, NH 03602; 603-835-6086.

**Support Alternative Family Education**, P.O. Box 15, Plaistow, NH 03865; 603-382-3839.

Dept. of Education, 101 Pleasant St., Concord, NH 03301; 603-271-3453.

## NEW JERSEY

**Central Jersey Homeschoolers**, 23D Franklin St., South Bound Brook, NJ 08880.

**Educational Excellence—School at Home**, P.O. Box 771, Summit, NJ 07901.

**Families Learning Together**, P.O. Box 8041, Piscataway, NJ 08855.

**Homeschoolers of Central New Jersey**, 116 Mountain View Rd., Princeton, NJ 08540.

**Homeschool Playgroup**, Phillipsburg; 908-454-4574.

**New Jersey Homeschool Association**, jerseyhome@yahoo.com; www.geocities.com/jerseyhome.

**North Jersey Home Schoolers Association**, 44 Oak St., Hillsdale, NJ 07642; 201-666-6025.

**South Jersey Homeschoolers**, 1239 Whitaker Ave., Millville, 08332; 609-327-1224

**Unschoolers Network**, 2 Smith St., Farmingdale, NJ 07727; 908-938-2473. Statewide.

**Unschoolers Support Group of Central New Jersey**, 116 Mountain View Rd., Princeton, NJ 08540; 609-333-1119.

Dept. of Education, 100 Riverview Plaza, CN 500, Trenton, NJ 08625; 609-984-7814.

## NEW MEXICO

**East Mountain Family Educators**, P.O. Box 369, Tijeras, NM 87059.

**Enchanted Families**, 7415 Menaul NE, Albuquerque, NM 87110.

**Glorieta Family Educators**, Star Route 1 Box 404, Glorieta, NM 87535.

**Home Educators of Santa Fe**, 21 Frasco Rd., Santa Fe, NM 87505; 505-466-4462.

**Homeschoolers of Dona Ana** (HEDA), 2022 Rubina Ct., Las Cruces, NM 88005

**Homeschooling PACT**, Box 961, Portales, NM 88130; 505-395-1618.

**New Mexico Family Educators**, P.O. Box 92276, Albuquerque, NM 87199-2276; 605-275-7053. Newsletter and very active program. New scholarship program. Great idea! Everyone could learn something from this group.

**Unschoolers of Albuquerque**, 8116 Princess Jeanne NE, Albuquerque, NM 87110; 505-299-2476.

Dept. of Education, Education Bldg., Santa Fe, NM 87501; 505-827-6515.

## NEW YORK

**Albany Area Homeschoolers**, 46 Pershing Dr., Scotia, NY 12302; 518-346-3413.

**APPLE** (Attachment and Positive Parenting and Lovingly Educating) **Family and Homeschool Group**, P.O. Box 2036, N. Babylon, NY 11703.

**Columbia County Homeschooling Mothers' Group**, 29 Kinderhook St., Chatham, NY 12037.

**Families for Home Education**, 3219 Coulter Rd., Cazenovia, NY 13035; 315-655-2574.

**Fingerlakes Unschoolers Network**, 201 Elm St., Ithaca, NY 14850; 607-273-6257.

**Fingerlakes Unschoolers Network**, 5331 Heverly Rd., Trumansburg, NY 14886; 607-387-3001

**Greater Southern Tier Homeschoolers**, 1560 Red School Rd., Corning, NY 14830.

**Homeschoolers Network of the Mid-Hudson Valley**, R.D. 2 Box 211P, Ski Run Rd., Bloomingburg, NY 12721; 914-722-1002.

**Kids Place of Choice**, S. Nassau Home Educators' Resource Room, Freeport, Long Island; 516-868-5766.

**Lake to Lake Homeschoolers**, 1399 Maryland Rd., Phelps, NY 14532.

**Long Island Homeschoolers Association**, 4 Seville Pl., Massapequa Park, NY 11762; 516-795-5554.

**New York City Home Educators Alliance**, 8 E. 2nd St, New York, NY 10003; 212-505-9884.

**New York Home Educators Network**, 2255 Algonquin Rd., Niskayuna, NY 12309. Statewide.

**New York State Home Education News**, P.O. Box 59, E. Chatham, NY 12060; 518-392-6900. Newsletter.

**Oneida Lake Area Home Educators**, P.O. Box 24, Sylvan Beach, NY 13157.

**Oneonta Area Sharing in Homeschooling** (OASIS), P.O. Box 48, Gilbertsville, NY 13776.

**Rochester Area Homeschoolers Association**, 275 Yarmouth Rd., Rochester, NY 14610; 716-271-0845.

**Tri-County Homeschoolers**, c/o Hofer, P.O. Box 190, Ossining, NY 10562; 914-941-5607.

**Tri-Lakes Community Home Educators**, P.O. Box 270, Raybrook, NY 12977.

**Ulster County Home Ed Resource Person**, Yvonne Aspengren, 914-255-1870.

**Western New York Homeschoolers**, Gloria Aemer, 18 Maple Ave., Portville, NY 14770.

**Woodstock Home Educators Network**, 12 Cantine's Island, Saugerties, NY 12477.

Dept. of Education, Room 481-EBA, Albany, NY 12234; 518-474-3879.

### NORTH CAROLINA

**Caldwell County Home Educators**, Lenoir; ryearwood@twave.net.

**Families Learning Together**, 1670 NC Highway 33W, Chocowinity, NC 27817.

**The Home Education Association**, 300 Brown Cir., Rolesville, NC 17571; 919-554-1563.

**Lunch Bunch Learners**, P.O. Box 5715, Greensboro, NC 27435.

**North Carolinians for Home Education**, 419 N. Boylan Ave., Raleigh, NC 27603-1211; 919-834-NCHE.

Dept. of Education, Division of Non-Public Education, 530 N. Wilmington St., Raleigh, NC 27603; 919-733-4276.

### NORTH DAKOTA

**North Dakota Home School Association**, P.O. Box 486, Mandan, ND 58554; 701-223-4080.

Office of Private Education, State Capitol, 600 E. Boulevard Ave., Bismarck, ND 58505; 701-328-2295.

### OHIO

**Families Independently Schooling at Home**, P.O. Box 266, Polk, OH 44866.

**Families Unschooling in the Neighborhood** (FUN), 4132 Spring Flower Ct., Gahanna, OH 43230.

**Families Unschooling in the Neighborhood**, Mid-Ohio, 5668 Township Rd. 105, Mount Gilead, OH 43338.

**Families Unschooling in the Neighborhood**, 3636 Paris Blvd., Westerville, OH 43081.

**Growing Together**, c/o Nancy McKibben, 1676 Trendril Ct., Columbus, OH 43229.

**HEART** (Medina Co. area), 7979 Greenwich Rd., Lodi, OH 44254.

**Heights Homeschoolers**, 2065 Halsey, S. Euclid, OH 44118.

**HELP** (Central Ohio), 4132 Spring Flower Ct., Gahanna, OH 43230.

**HELP** (N. Ohio), 10915 Pyle-S. Amherst Rd., Oberlin, OH 44074.

**HELP** (N.W. Ohio), P.O. Box 98, Perrysburg, OH 43552; 419-478-9729 or 419-843-7179.

**Home Education League of Parents**, 3905 Herr Rd., Sylvania, OH 43560; 419-843-7179. Statewide.

**Home Education Resource Organization**, 170 W. Main St., Norwalk, OH 44857.

**Home Educators Advocacy League**, 26140 Yearsley Rd., Raymond, OH 43067; 513-358-2450.

**Home School Network of Greater Cincinnati**, 2115 Harcourt Dr., Cincinnati, OH 45244; 513-683-1279.

**Learning in Family Environments**, P.O. Box 2512, Columbus, OH 43216.

**Ohio Home Educators Network**, P.O. Box 23054, Chagrin Falls, OH 44023-0054; 216-786-8001 or 330-274-0542.

**Ohio's Uniquely Challenged Homeschoolers** (OUCH), 30213 Robert St., Wickliffe, OH 44092.

**Parents and Children Together**, 8944 Weiss Rd., Union City, OH 45390.

**Parents Enriching Alternative Childhood Education**, 9520 Co Rd., Delta, OH 43515; 417-337-4810.

**Youngstown Home Learners**, 266 Outlook Ave., Youngstown, OH 44504.

Dept. of Education, 65 S. Front St., Room 408, Columbus, OH 43215; 614-466-2937.

### OKLAHOMA

**Cornerstone**, P.O. Box 459, Sperry, OK 74073; 918-425-4162. Tulsa area.

**Fellowship of Shawnee Home Educators**, R.R. 1 Box 23681, Tecumseh, OK 74873.

**Green Country Home Ed Resource Organization**, 183 Fox Run Cir., Jenks, OK 74037.

**Home Educators Resource Organization of Oklahoma** (HERO), 302 N. Coolidge, Enid, OK 73703; 580-438-2253. Statewide.

**Oklahoma Central Home Educators Consociation**, P.O. Box 270601, Oklahoma City, OK 73137; 405-521-8439.

**Oklahoma Home Educators' Network**, P.O. Box 1420, Blanchard, OK 73010.

Dept. of Education, Oklahoma City, OK 73105; 405-521-3333.

### OREGON

**Greater Portland Homeschoolers**, P.O. Box 82415, Portland, OR 97282; 503-241-5350.

**The Learning Connection**, P.O. Box 1091, #196, Grants Pass, OR 97526; 541-476-5686; janemj.tic@ junocom.
**Mid-Valley Secular Homeschoolers**, Salem area; 503-362-1203.
**Online Support Group for Oregon Homeschoolers**, Christine Webb, Retromom@aol.com.
**Oregon Home Education Network**, P.O. Box 218, Beaverton, 97005; 503-321-5166.
**Willamette Homeschoolers**, 245 W. 27th Ave., Eugene, OR 97405.
Dept. of Education, 225 Capitol St. NE, Salem, 97310; 503-378-5585.

## PENNSYLVANIA

**Blue Mountain Homeschoolers**, 636 Almond Rd., Walnutport, PA 18088.
**Bucks County Homeschoolers**, 125 Mountain Oaks Rd., Yardley, PA 19067; 215-428-3865.
**Center City Homeschoolers**, 2203 Spruce St., Philadelphia, PA 19103.
**Central Philadelphia Homeschoolers**, vallone@drexel.edu, LMKenney888@cs.com, or AileenBth@gateway.net; cphomeschoolers.tripod.com.
**Chester County Homeschoolers**, 226 Llandovery Dr., Exton, PA 19341.
**Diversity United in Homeschooling**, 233 Bluebell Ave., Langhorne, PA 19047; 215-428-3865.
**Endless Mountains Homeschoolers**, c/o Kellogg, R.D. 3 Box 80, Columbia Cross Roads, PA 16914; 717-549-8179. (N. Central PA)
**Homeschoolers Association of Warren County**, R.R. 1 Box 87B1, Youngsville, PA 16371; 814-489-3366.
**Maryland-Pennsylvania Home Educators** (Mason-Dixon area), P.O. Box 67, Shrewsbury, PA 17361; 717-933-3603.
**McKeesport Area Homeschoolers**, Barb Page, 205 W. Virginia Ave., Munhall, PA 15120; 412-461-6788.
**Northeast Pennsylvania Homeschoolers**, P.O. Box 884, E. Stroudsburg, PA 18301; 570-476-9321.
**Pennsylvania Home Education Network**, 285 Allegheny St., Meadville, PA 16335; 412-561-5288.
**Pennsylvania Home Education News**, P.O. Box 305, Summerhill, PA 15958; 814-495-5651.
**Pennsylvania Homeschoolers**, R.D. 2 Box 117, Kittanning, PA 16201; 412-783-6512. Statewide newsletter and excellent resource catalog.
**People Always Learning Something** (PALS), 105 Marie Dr., Pittsburgh, PA 15237; 412-367-6240.
**Rolling Green Home Education Resource Room**, 2725 Aquetong Rd., New Hope, PA 18938; 215-862-2968.
**Southwestern Pennsylvania Home Ed Network**, 429 Union Ave., Pittsburgh, PA 15205. Gloria Molek: 412-922-8344.
**Valley Unschoolers' Network**, 565 Forgedale Rd., Barto, PA 19504; 610-845-8941.
**York Home School Association**, 717-292-5379.
Dept. of Education, 333 Market St., 5th Fl., Harrisburg, PA 17126; 717-783-3750.

## PUERTO RICO

**Western Home Education Association**, Lisa Rodriguez, Urb. La Monserrate #418, Calle Guadalupe, Moca, PR 00676.

## RHODE ISLAND

**Parent Educators of Rhode Island**, P.O. Box 782, Glendale, RI 02826.
**Rhode Island Guild of Home Teachers** (Home Spun News), P.O. Box 11, Hope, RI 02831; 401-821-7700.
**South County Homeschoolers**, 500 Carolina Back Rd., Charleston, RI 02813.
Dept. of Education, 22 Hayes St., Providence, RI 02908; 401-277-2031.

## SOUTH CAROLINA

**Carolina Superschoolers**, 777 Hillview St., Spartanburg, SC 29302.
**Home Organization of Parent Educators**, c/o Griesemer, 1697 Dotterer's Run, Charleston, SC 29414; 803-763-7833.
**Inclusive Network of Columbia Homeschoolers**, Shannon, 803-788-7110.
**Lancaster Area Homeschool Support Group**, 1528 Carmel Rd., Lancaster, SC 29720. Non-profit statewide. Newsletter. E-mail: ConnectSC@aol.com.
**South Carolina Association of Independent Home Schools**, P.O. Box 2104, Irmo, SC 29063.
**South Carolina Home Educators Association**, P.O. Box 612, Lexington, SC 28071-06121; 803-951-8960.
**South Carolina Homeschool Alliance**, 1679 Memorial Park Rd., Suite 179, Lancaster, SC 29720.
**South Carolina Homeschool Support Group**, 242 Weathers Farm Rd., Bowman, SC 29018.
**Teacher's Ink**, P.O. Box 13386, Charleston, SC 29422.
**Tri-County Educational Association of Community Homeschoolers**, 107 Prairie Ln., Summerville, SC 29483.
Dept. of Education, 1429 Senate St., Columbia, SC 29201.

## SOUTH DAKOTA

**South Dakota Home School Association**, P.O. Box 882, Sioux Falls, SD 57101; 605-335-1125.

Dept. of Education, Kneip Office Bldg., 700 Governors Dr., Pierre, SD 57501; 605-773-4770.

## TENNESSEE

**Home Education Association of Tennessee** (HEAT), 3677 Richbriar Ct., Nashville, TN 37211.

**State of Franklin Homeschoolers**, 494 Mill Creek Rd., Kingsport, TN 37664.

**Tennessee Homeschooling Families**, 214 Park Ln., Oliver Springs, TN 37840; 423-435-9644.

**Unschoolers of Memphis**, Margaret Meyer, 901-757-9859.

Dept. of Education, 710 James Robertson Pkwy., Andrew Johnson Tower 7th Fl., Nashville, TN 37242; 615-532-4705.

## TEXAS

**Austin Area Homeschoolers**, 510 Park Blvd., Austin, TX 78751.

**Heart of Texas Home Schoolers**, 1710 Vincent, Brownwood, TX 76801.

**Highland Lake Area Homeschoolers**, Route 1 Box 239, Burnet, TX 78611.

**The Homeschooling Center**, 1001 S. Allen Genoa, South Houston, TX 77587.

**Houston Alternative Education Alliance**, 12811 Ivy Forest Dr., Cypress, TX 77429.

**Houston Unschoolers Group**, 9625 Exeter Rd., Houston, TX 77093.

**Houston Unschoolers Group** (Southwest), 16426 Heatherdale, Houston, TX 77059.

**North Texas Self-Educators**, c/o Jordan, 150 Forest Ln., Double Oak/Lewisville, TX 75067; 817-430-4835.

**South Texas Self-Learners**, 1005 Delta Dr., Corpus Christi, TX 78412.

**Southwest Dallas Home School Association**, P.O. Box 1104, Cedar Hill, TX 75106.

**Tarrant Home Educators Association**, 6080 Hulen Dr., Suite 360-109, Fort Worth, TX 76132.

**Texas Advocates for Freedom in Education** (TAFFIE), 13635 Greenridge St., Sugar Land, TX 77478; 713-242-7994.

**Texas Homeschool Coalition**, P.O. Box 6982, Lubbock, TX 79493; 806-797-4927.

**Woodlands Area Innovative Scholastic Environments**, 130 N. Rushwing Cir., The Woodlands, TX 77381.

Dept. of Education, 1701 N. Congress, Austin, TX 78701; 512-463-9354.

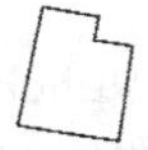

## UTAH

**FCLA Utah Spice Group**, 1510 W. 500 N., Provo, UT 84601; 801-377-4728.

**Salt Lake Home Educators**, 6522 Appomattox Way, Taylorville, UT 84123; 801-501-0344.

**Utah Home Education Association**, P.O. Box 57218, Sigurd, UT 84657-0218; 801-535-1533. Hotline: 888-887-UHEA.

Dept. of Education, 250 E. 500 S., Salt Lake City, UT 84111; 801-538-7743.

## VERMONT

**Center for Homeschooling**, 95 North Ave., Burlington, VT 05401.

**Ottaquechee Homeschoolers**, 1618 Westerdale Rd., Woodstock, VT 05091.

**United Homeschoolers**, R.R. 1 Box 47B, South Royalton, VT 05068.

**Vermont Association of Home Educators**, Marieken Volz, R.R. 1 Box 847, Bethel, VT 05032; 802-234-6804. Newsletter and resources.

**Vermont Homeschoolers Association**, R.D. 2 Box 4440, Bristol, VT 05443; 802-453-5460.

**Windham County Homeschoolers**, R.R. 2 Box 1332, Putney, VT 05346.

Dept. of Education, 120 State St., Montpelier, VT 05620; 802-235-2424.

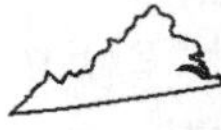

## VIRGINIA

**ALOFT** (Alternative Learning Options for Free Thinkers), 2120 Wiggington Rd., Lynchburg, VA 24502.

**BEACH** (Beech Educators Association for Creative Homeschooling), c/o Amy Birdwell, 255 Ipswich Pl., Charlottesville, VA 22901.

**Blue Ridge Area Network for Congenial Homeschooling** (BRANCH), 255 Ipswich Pl., Charlottesville, VA 22901.

**Children's Circle**, R.R. 1 Box 132A, Mouth of Wilson, VA 24363; 703-579-4252.

**Chincoteague Home School Newsletter**, 4288 Sunrise Drive Cir., Chincoteague Island, VA 23336.

**Coalition for Parent Educators**, 4151 Broad Street Rd., Gum Spring, VA 23065.

**Community of Independent Learners**, P.O. Box 16029, Alexandria, VA 22302; 703-998-9626.

**Fauquier Unschoolers Living Classroom**, P.O. Box 51,

Goldvein, VA 22720.
**Home Educators Are Restoring Their Heritage**, P.O. Box 69, Linden, VA 22642.
**Home Educators Assisting, Reaching, and Teaching**, 101 William Claiborne, Williamsburg, VA 23185.
**Home Educators Association of Virginia**, P.O. Box 6745, Richmond, VA 23230.
**Home Educators Network**, 3320 Waverly Dr., Fredericksburg, VA 22401.
**Home Instruction Group**, 217 Willow Terr., Sterling, VA 22170.
**Learning in a Family Environment**, 125G Clubhouse Dr., #2, Leesburg, VA 20175.
**Northern Virginia/D.C. Metro Group**, c/o Compton, 12310 Streamvale Cir., Herndon, VA 22070; 703-742-8597.
**Richmond Educational Alternatives for Children at Home**, P.O. Box 36174, Richmond, VA 23235.
**Virginia Home Education Association**, 1612 Columbia Rd., Gordonsville, VA 22942; 540-832-3578; vhea@virginia.edu; expage.com/page/folcfolks.
Dept. of Education, P.O. Box 2120, Richmond, VA 23216; 804-225-2747.

## WASHINGTON

**Clark Co. Home Educators**, P.O. Box 5941, Vancouver, WA 98668.
**Families Learning Together**, Box 10, Tiger Star Rd., Colville, WA 99114.
**Family Academy**, 146 SW 153rd, #290, Seattle, WA 98166.
**Family Learning Organization**, P.O. Box 7247, Spokane, WA 99207; 509-467-2552. Statewide.
**Fun Family Homeschool Group**, 421 N.E. 12th St., North Bend, WA 98045.
**Granite Falls Homeschoolers**, 3526 Robe Menzel Rd., Granite Falls, WA 98252.
**Home Educators' Cooperative of Mid-Columbia**, 41005 E. Hacienda, Benton City, WA 99320.
**Homeschoolers' Support Association**, P.O. Box 413, Maple Valley, WA 98038.
**Kittitas Valley Homeschool Association**, Ellensburg, WA 98926; 509-925-4033.
**The Learning Web**, 3209 Lorne St. SE, Olympia, WA 98501; 360-754-5536.
**Military Homeschool F.A.M.I.L.I.E.S. of Kitsap County**, P.O. Box 711, Keyport, WA 98345.
**Network of Vancouver Area Homeschoolers**, 162 Krogstad Rd., Washougal, WA 98671.
**North Central Washington Homeschool Co-op**, P.O. Box 147, Curlew, WA 99118.
**Palouse Home Learning Alternatives**, SE 405 Hill, Pullman, WA 99163.
**Peninsula Homeschool Exchange**, 419 Benton St., Port Townsend, WA 98368.
**Rainbow Way Playgroup**, c/o Bystrom, Kenmore, WA 98028; 206-522-4313.
**St. Thomas More Home Education**, 3853 76th Ave. SE, Mercer Island, WA 98040.
**Seattle Homeschool Group**, 819 N.E. 84th, Seattle, WA 98115; 425-402-9048.
**Teaching Parents Association**, P.O. Box 1934, Woodinville, WA 98072.
**Valley Home Educators**, 1413 Easthills Terr., East Wenatchee, WA 98802.
**Washington Homeschool Organization**, 6632 S. 191st Pl., Suite E100, Kent, WA 98032.
**Whatcom Homeschool Association**, 3851 Britton Rd., Bellingham, WA 98226.
Superintendent of Public Instruction, Old Capitol Bldg., P.O. Box 47200, Olympia, WA 98504; 360-664-3574.

## WEST VIRGINIA

**Morgan County Homeschoolers**, 1417 Fairfax St., Berkeley Springs, WV 25411.
**West Virginia Home Educators Association**, P.O. Box 3707, Charleston, WV 25337-3707; 800-736-9843.
Dept. of Education, Room 347, Bldg. 6, Capitol Complex, Charleston, WV 25305.

## WISCONSIN

**Families in Schools at Home** (FISH), 4639 Conestoga Trail, Cottage Grove, WI 53527.
**HOME** (Madison Chapter), 5745 Bittersweet Pl., Madison, WI 53705; 608-238-3302.
**Home Scholars of Sheboygan County**, W5607 Highway W., Adell, WI 53001.
**Milwaukee Area Home Learners**, W260 N7751 Jay Ln., Sussex, WI 53089.
**Ozaukee Explorers**, 4410 Bittersweet Ln., Cedarburg, WI 53210.
**Spooner Area Home School Group**, P.O. Box 343, Spooner, WI 54801.
**Unschooling Families**, 1980 N. Clark St., Appleton, WI 54911; 414-735-9832.
**Wisconsin Parents Association**, P.O. Box 2502, Madison, WI 53701.
Dept. of Education, P.O. Box 7841, 125 S. Webster. St., Madison, WI 53707; 608-266-5761.

**WYOMING**

**Laramie Home Education Network**, 429 Hwy. 230, #20, Laramie, WY 82010

**Unschoolers of Wyoming**, 429 Hwy 230, #20, Laramie, WY 82070.

Dept. of Education, Hathaway Bldg., 2nd Fl., 2300 Capitol Ave., Cheyenne, WY 82002; 307-777-6268.

**The Adventist Home Educator**, P.O. Box 836, Camino, CA 95709.

**At Our Own Pace**, c/o Jean Kulczyk, 102 Willow Dr., Waukegan, IL 60087; 847-662-5432. Newsletter for families with special needs.

**Catholic Homeschoolers of Scranton**, 1317 St. Ann St., Scranton, PA 18504; 717-344-8866.

**Catholic Homeschool Network of America**, P.O. Box 6342, River Forest, IL 60305-6343.

**Celebrating Home Under Rome** (Catholic), 517-349-6389.

**CHEF of Oklahoma (Christian Home Educators' Fellowship)**, P.O. Box 471363, Tulsa, OK 74147-1363. Requires signed statement of faith.

**Christ-Centered Home Educators**, 3601 Plank Rd., PMB 323, Fredericksburg, VA 22407.

**Christian Home Educators of Michigan**, P.O. Box 2357, Farmington Hills, MI 48333.

**Christian Home Educators of Ohio**, P.O. Box 1224, Kent, OH 44240.

**Christian Home Educators of Vermont**, 214 N. Prospect, #105, Burlington, VT 05401.

**Christian Homeschoolers Involved in Learning Development**, P.O. Box 94652, North Little Rock, AR 72118.

**Christian Homeschoolers of Hawaii**, 910824 Oama St., Ewa Beach, HI 96707; 808-689-6398.

**The Drinking Gourd**, P.O. Box 2557, Redmond, WA 98073. Homeschoolers of color.

**Family Education for Christ**, P.O. Box 16619, Savannah, GA 31416.

**Homeschool Education Network for Muslims**, 241 Meadowbrook Dr., Bolingbrook, IL 60440

**Home Educators Computer Users Group**, 26824 Howard Chapel Dr., Damascus, MD 20872-1247; 301-253-5467.

**Home School Association for Christian Science Families**, 445 Airport Rd., Tioga, TX 76271.

**Homeschoolers for Peace and Justice**, P.O. Box 74, Midpines, CA 95345.

**Homeschooling Unitarian Universalists and Humanists**, 3135 Lakeland Dr., Nashville, TN 37214-3312; 615-889-4938.

**Home School Legal Defense Association**, Box 3000, Purcellville, VA 20134. Conservative Christian organization. Sells legal insurance. I don't think insurance is necessary at this time. If you are considering joining HSLDA I strongly suggest you find out more about it at www.expage.com/page/folchslda.

**Homeschool Support Network/Home Educator's Family Times**, P.O. Box 1056, Gray, ME 04039; 207-657-2800.

**Illinois Christian Home Educators**, P.O. Box 261, Zion, IL 60099.

**Information Network for Christian Homes**, 4150 Ambrose NE, Grand Rapids, MI 49505.

**Islamic Homeschool Association of North America**, 1312 Plymouth Ct., Raleigh, NC 27610.

**Jewish Home Educator's Network**, 2122 Houser, Holly, MI 48442.

**Jewish Home Educator's Network**, c/o M. Lowe, 1295 Marshall Dr. SE, Salem, OR 97302; 503-362-1203; marilyn.lowe@chemek.com.

**Jewish Home Educator's Network**, P.O. Box 300, Benton City, WA 99329.

**Jewish Homeschool Association of Greater Chicago**, 773-764-5137.

**Jewish Homeschoolers of Massachusetts**, fernReiss@aol.com.

**Latter-Day Saint Home Educators' Association**, 2770 S. 1000 W., Perry, UT; 801-723-5335.

**Minnesota Association of Roman Catholic Home Educators**, 7211 Sherwood Echo, Woodbury, MN 55125.

**Muslim Home-School Network and Resources**, P.O. Box 803, Attleboro, MA 02703.

**National Association of Catholic Home Educators**, P.O. Box 787, Montrose, AL 36559.

**National Association of Catholic Home Educators**, P.O. Box 420225, San Diego, CA 92142.

**National Association of Mormon Home Educators**, 2770 S. 1000 West, Perry, UT 84302.

**National Challenged Homeschoolers Association (NATHHAN)**, 5383 Alpine Rd. SE, Olalla, WA 98359; 206-457-4257.

**National Handicapped Homeschoolers Association**, 814 Shavertown Rd., Boothwyn, PA 19061; 610-459-1035.

**Native American Home School Association**, P.O. Box 979, Fries, VA 24330.

**New Mexico Christian Home Educators**, 5749 Paradise Blvd. NW, Albuquerque, NM 87114; 505-897-1772.

**Simon of Cyrene Association** (African-American Homeschoolers of Christian Faith), P.O. Box 26357, Rochester, NY 14626.

**South Fort Worth Christian Home Educators**, P.O. Box 16573, Fort Worth, TX 76133.

**Uniqueness Twice-Gifted, Gifted Network**, 804-883-6757; UniGift@aol.com.

**Wharton County Christian Homeschool Organization**, P.O. Box 1411, El Campo, TX 77437.

## CANADA

For all Canadians with computer access, I recommend that you consult the Canadian Home Based Education site online for resources and legalities at www.flora.org/homeschool-ca.

**Canadian Alliance of Homeschoolers**, 272 Hwy. 5, R.R. 1, St. George, ON N0E 1N0; Wendy Priesnitz, 519-448-4001.

**Canadian Homeschooler: A Magazine of Canadian Content and Curriculum**, c/o Shannon, R.R. 3, Marmora, ON K0K 2M0.

### ALBERTA

**Alberta Home Education Association**, Box 3451, Leduc, AB T9E 6M2.

**Alternative Education Resource Association**, 11 Mosely Close, Red Deer, AB T4N 5S8.

**Calgary Home Educators Encouragement and Resource Society**, R.R. 6, Calgary, AB T2M 4L5.

**Community Connections**, BJ Smith, 225 37 St. NW, Calgary, AB T2N 4N6.

**Homebased Learning Society of Alberta**, 8754 Connors Rd., Edmonton, AB T6C 4B6.

**Homeschoolers Association of N. Alberta**, 6311 14th Ave., Edmonton, AB T6L 1Y1.

**Alberta Distance Learning Centre** (ADLC), Box 4000, Barrhead, AB T7N 104; 403-674-5333. Offers distance learning, both print- and computer-based, in and out of the province. ADLC covers grades 1 to 12. They have about 3,000 home education students. In Alberta tuition is covered through school principals and supervisors. Out of the province you'll have to investigate tuition.

### BRITISH COLUMBIA

**Canadian Home Educators Association of British Columbia**, 4684 Darin Ct., Kelowna, BC V1W 2B3.

**Canadian Home Educators Association of British Columbia**, 6980 Marble Hill Rd., Chilliwack, BC V2P 6H3.

**Cowichan Valley Christian Homelearners Support**, 1050 Marchmont Rd., Duncan, BC V9L 2M7.

**Cowichan Valley Homelearners Support Group**, R.R. 7, Duncan, BC, V9L 4W4.

**Education Advisory**, 2267 Kings Ave. W., Vancouver, BC V7V 2C1.

**Fraser Delta Homelearners**, 604-538-8163.

**Greater Vancouver Home Learners**, 604-228-1939 or 604-298-6710.

**Heritage Home Learners**, #16-10585 153rd St., Surrey, BC V3R 4H8; 604-582-1613; ebus08@uniserve.com.

**Home Education News**, Box 39009, Pt. Grey RPO, Vancouver, BC V6R 4P1.

**Home Learning Resource Centre**, Box 61, Quathlaski, BC V0P 1N0.

**Mid-Island Home Learners**, 5776 Kerry Ln., Nanaimo, BC V9T 5N5; 250-751-0337.

**North Shore Home Learners Group**, 212 West Windsor Rd., North Vancouver, BC V7N 2N1.

**Salt Spring Unschoolers Network**, 132 Bullock Creek Rd., Salt Spring Island, BC V8K 2L3.

**Tri-City Home Learners Network**, Port Coquitlan, BC; 604-464-1056.

**Victoria Home Learning Network**, 106-290 Regina, Victoria, BC V8Z 6S6.

**Wondertree Education Society**, Box 38083, Vancouver, BC V5Z 4L9.

### MANITOBA

**Manitoba Association for Schooling at Home**, 89 Edkar Cres., Winnipeg, MB R2G 3H8.

### NEW BRUNSWICK

**New Brunswick Association of Christian Homeschoolers**, R.R. 1 Site 11 Box 1, Hillsborough, NB E0A 1X0.

**Home Educators of New Brunswick**, P.O. Box 4574, Rothsay, NB E2E 5X3.

### NORTHWEST TERRITORIES

**Inuvik Homeschooling Group**, Box 2285, Inuvik, NT X0E 0T0.

### NOVA SCOTIA

**Christian Homeschoolers of Nova Scotia (CHONS)**, provincial group and newsletter.
Antigonish and eastern region: 902-386-2054
Halifax: 902-462-2759
Kingston: 902-765-4907
Pictou: 902-485-8516

**Nova Scotia Home Education Association**, R.R. 1, Rose Bay, NS B0J 2X0.

**Nova Scotia Support Group**, Laura Uhlman, R.R. 1, Pleasantville, NS B0R 1G0.

Amherst: 902-661-3202
Annapolis Co.: 902-765-4119
Bridgewater: 902-543-0160
Halifax: 902-464-0068

### ONTARIO

**Edcare: Homeschooling News**, Box 23021, Woodstock, ON N4T 1R9.

**Joy Center of Learning**, 140 Muriel St., Shelburne, ON L0N 1S1. Primarily but not exclusively Christian-based. parson@hurontario.net; www.joycenter.on.ca.

**National Capital Region Home Based Learning Network**, 136 Aylmer Ave., Ottawa, ON K1S 2Y2

**Ontario Federation of Teaching Parents**, R.R. 1, 145 Taylor Rd. West, Gananoque, ON K7G 2V3.

**Ontario Homeschoolers**, Box 19, Gilford, ON L0L 1R0.

**Orillia Homeschoolers' Group**, 45 Albert St. N, Orillia, ON L3V 5K3.

**Rideau Valley Home Educators Association**, c/o Dubuc, 1144 Byron Ave., Ottawa, ON K2B 6T4.

**Villa Villekula Homeschool Resource Group**, 1250 Gladstone Ave., Windsor, ON N8X 3H3.

### PRINCE EDWARD ISLAND

**HomeSchool and More**. Gertrude DeBoer, 29 Donald Dr., Charlottetown, PEI C1E 1Z5. Catalog of Canadian resources.

### QUEBEC

**Montreal Homeschoolers' Support Group**, 5241 Jacques Grenier, Montreal, PQ H3W 2G8.

**Quebec Association for Home-Based Education**, 3449 Peel St., Montreal, PQ H3A 1W7. Great bilingual support group and newsletter.

**Western Quebec Home School Association**, Jeff Schultz, R.R. 1, Shawville, PQ J0X 2Y0.

### SASKATCHEWAN

**Saskatchewan Home-Based Educators**, 116A Idylwyld Dr. N., Suite 13, Saskatoon, SK S7L 0Y7; 888-233-7423 or 306-545-3532.

### YUKON

**Yukon Home Educators Society**, P.O. Box 4993, Whitehorse, YT Y1A 4S2.

### AUSTRALIA

**Alternative Education Resource Group**, P.O. Box 71, Chirnside Park, Vic. 3116.

**Brisbane Homeschooling Group**, Lot 2, Caboolture River Rd., Upper Caboolture 4510.

**Canberra Home Education Network**, Drew Corrigan, 23 Bardolph St., Bonython, ACT 2905.

**Homeschoolers Australia Pty Ltd.**, P.O. Box 420, Kellyville 2153, NSW.

**New Central Coast Homeschool Group**, RMB 6346 MacDonalds Rd., Lisarow, NSW 2250.

**Sunshine Coast Homeschooling Group**, 40 Browns Rd., Belli Park via Edmundi, 4562, Queensland.

**Yarra Valley Homeschoolers**, 9 Salisbury St., Warburton.

### EGYPT

**Ma'adi Homeschoolers**, 25 Road 213, #3, Ma'adi, Egypt.

### ENGLAND

**Education Otherwise**, P.O. Box 7420, London N9 9SG; 0891 518303. Has local contacts throughout the U.K.

**Home Service**, 48 Heaton Moor Road, Heaton Moor, Stockport SK4 4NX.

### FRANCE

**Les Enfants d'Abord**, c/o Shosha, 4 rue de Lergue, F-34800 Brignac.

**Grandir Sans Ecole**, B.P., F-68480 Ferrette; +33 389 40 48 34.

**Homeschooling Bulletin**, c/o Sophie Haesen, 7 rue de la Montagne, F-68480 Vieux Ferrette.

**L'Ecole à la Maison**, c/o Nadine Stewart, 6 Grande rue, F-38660 Le Touvet.

### HONG KONG

**Discovery Bay Homeschoolers of Hong Kong**, General P.O. Box 12114, Hong Kong, China.

**Venture HomeSchooling Society of Hong Kong**, P.O. Box 70461, Kowloon Central Post Office, Kowloon, Hong Kong.

### IRELAND

**Home Education Network**, Knockroe, Borris, Co. Carlow; +353-1-282-9638.

### JAPAN

**Kanto Home Education Association**, PSC 477, Box 45, FPO, AP 96306-1299.

**Otherwise Japan**, P.O. Kugayama, Suginami-ku, Tokyo.

### NETHERLANDS

**Netherlands Homeschoolers**, Raadhuisiaan 31, 2131 Hoofddoorp.

### NEW ZEALAND

**Ezra Group**, 35d Salisbury Rd., Birkdale, Auckland 10.

**Home Educators' Network of Aotearoa**, P.O. Box 11-645, Ellerslie, 1131 Auckland. Newsletter.

**Homeschooling Federation of New Zealand**, P.O. Box 41-226, St. Lukes, Auckland.

**New Zealand Home Schooling Association**, 5 Thanet Av., Mt. Albert, Auckland.

### SOUTH AFRICA

**National Coalition of Home Schoolers**, P.O. Box 14, Dundee, 3000; 0341 23712.

### SPAIN

**Aprender Sin Escuela**, c/o Szil-Norberg, Apartado 45, Alfaz dil Pi 03580, Alicante.

### SWITZERLAND

**Vereinigung Freier Schulen der Schweiz/Association Suisse des Ecoles Nouvelles**, Davids-bodenstrasse 63, CH-4056 Basel; +41 61 322 50 30.

## CORRESPONDENCE SCHOOLS

**Alberta Distance Learning Centre**. They serve more than 3,000 homeschooling families, and you don't have to be in Alberta to use this program for grades 1 to 12. They also offer some adult courses, so why not set an example for your kids? Write to: ADLC, Box 4000, Barrhead, AB T7N 1P4, or phone 403-674-5333, for more information.

**Calvert School**, 105 Tuscany Rd., Baltimore, MD 21210. K to 8 home-study programs and some enrichment courses offered independently. All books and other materials supplied. Excellent (pricey for some) and structured. Children's work can be sent for evaluation and grading, if you want, for a fee. Many use Calvert for a year or two, to gain confidence, then design their own studies.

**Cambridge Academy**, 1111 SW 17th Street, Ocala, FL 34474. Grades 6-12, accredited diploma, grading, and record-keeping, toll-free tutoring, free catalog, and video.

**Canadian International Correspondence Schools**, 9001 Avon Rd., Montreal West, PQ H4X 2H2.

**Clonlara School**, 1289 Jewel St., Ann Arbor, MI 48104; 313-769-4511; clonlara@delphi.com; www.clonlara.org. Clonlara is an accredited, private, K-12, fully operational campus and distance-learning school. They will help with curriculum, certified contact teacher, resources, interaction with your local school officials, and much more. You can use your own curriculum if you wish. They have a computerized high school program using the Internet. Work from previous schools accepted. Transcript from Clonlara will fulfill graduation requirements. When you write for more information, please include a #10 SASE. Very supportive.

**CyberSchool**. Based in Oregon but open to all high school students, CyberSchool offers complete, interactive, full-credit courses online. You are invited to visit their website: CyberSchool.4j.lane.edu.

**Home Study International**, 12501 Old Columbia Pike, Silver Spring, MD 20904. Preschool through college courses with Christian content.

**Keystone National High School**, School House Station, 420 W. Fifth St., Bloomsburg, PA 17815. High school program, single course or complete program.

**Moore Foundation**, P.O. Box 1, Camas, WA 98607; www.moorefoundation.com. Many options available.

**North Atlantic Regional High School**, 25 Adams Ave., Lewiston, ME 04210; www.NARSdiploma.com. State-recognized private school. Parent-elected, parent-directed studies. Start any time, from anywhere.

**Oak Meadow School**, P.O. Box 740, Putney, VT 05346. K-12 correspondence courses. Waldorf-inspired, but now with considerable differences. Interesting.

**Oregon State University Outreach Program**, High School Outreach, OSU, 110 Kerr Administration Bldg., Corvallis, OR 97330; 800-375-9359; statewide.orst.edu. Offers college-level credit courses via distance learning over the Internet and video lectures.

**Phoenix Special Programs and Academies**, 1717 W. Northern Ave., Suite 104, Phoenix, AZ 85021-5469. Offers print and computer courses for diplomas with distance learning.

**Pinewood School**, 122 Road D, Pine, CO 80460. An affiliate of Clonlara.

**Santa Fe Community School**, P.O. Box 2241, Santa Fe, NM 87504-2241. Will help you develop your own educational program, keep records of reports you send in, record credits, send transcripts to schools or agencies at your request, and/or provide an "umbrella" service for those who want to follow their own curriculum but need legal status for state acceptance. Send a #10 SASE for information.

**The Sycamore Tree**, 2179 Meyer Place, Costa Mesa, CA 92627. Homeschool program and other services. Write for catalog.

**University of Nebraska, Lincoln**, Independent Study Program, Dept. of Distance Education and Continuing Studies, 269 Clifford Hardin Center, Lincoln, NE 68583-9800. College courses by correspondence and computer. Open for some high school courses too.

**West River Academy**, 2420 N. 1st Street, Grand Junction, CO 81501; 970-241-4137 or 800-400-1528, ext. 2848. Umbrella school. Contact Peggy Nishikawa.

# HOMESCHOOLING AND EDUCATION

## CHANGING THE WORLD, ONE HOMESCHOOLED STUDENT AT A TIME
## DEVELOPING YOUR LONG-TERM GOALS
## IDEAS TO THINK ABOUT — RESOURCES — LEGAL ISSUES

*If your plan is for a year, plant rice.*

*If your plan is for a decade, plant trees.*

*If your plan is for a lifetime, educate children.*
— Confucius

I firmly believe we are changing the world, one homeschooled student at a time. With every young adult who goes from homeschool to college, work, or other pursuits, we are broadening the definition of "meaningful education" and challenging the existing attitudes about the efficacy of standardized public schooling.

Whether we are consciously aware that our homeschooling creates pressure on the public educational system to change, or are doing so only to meet our personal goals, we are influencing the way people think about education now and in the future. What we do today, with our children, is changing and challenging the community around us and society at large. As we quietly go about the daily business of raising and educating our families, we should be aware that our actions have repercussions beyond the immediate goals we have for our families.

We are changing not only some attitudes about education, but also attitudes regarding parental responsibility and parenting. At a time when many feel it is important for women (in particular but not exclusively) to get out of the house and "make something" of themselves, we are living the "family values" that too many people just talk about. We are creating strong foundations for our children and ourselves.

There will always be those who are resistant to change or actions that vary from the norm. If you are new to homeschooling and find resistance or skepticism, remember that you are not alone. There are hundreds of thousands of parents just like you enjoying the time and privilege of sharing the learning adventure with their children.

★☆★☆★☆★☆★☆★☆★☆★☆★

*Never doubt that a small group of thoughtful citizens can change the world. Indeed, it is the only thing that ever has.* — Margaret Mead

★☆★☆★☆★☆★☆★☆★☆★☆★

Don't be dismayed at the lack of regulation textbooks in this book. You won't find many of them. Our kids never liked them. We never liked them. They reminded us of commercial baby food — they fill a need but on the lowest possible level. At best, some make reasonable reference books. You will find books you and your children will enjoy that will transform your learning into a creative adventure.

---

*It is good to have an end to journey toward; but it is the journey that matters, in the end.*
— Ursula K. Le Guin

---

Before considering resources it's important to think about where you want your homeschool journey to take you and your children. You need some idea of your long-term goals or you'll waste time and effort and encounter more obstacles than necessary. **THE QUESTION IS COLLEGE**, by Herbert Kohl, will stimulate and help clarify your thinking. Kohl is more concerned with the attitudes toward living that you would like your child to have at the end of your educational journey together than about academic skills and college attendance.

This book is not against college, but questions whether there is a genuine need for it. This book was written primarily for high school students, not parents, but in a homeschooling family, the concerns of one affect the other. This book was not intended to be used by parents of young children, but reading it while your children are young will help you create a philosophy about learning and living that will be of enormous benefit.

The preface to Kohl's new edition begins: "What do I want to do when I grow up? For many people that childhood question persists throughout life. At five it can lead to wild fantasies and lifelong dreams. ... And in middle age, it has the sadness of an incomplete life. Yet the question persists as long as the imagination is alive. What, of all the possible things that people do, would I love to do?" Donn and I have always felt that the journey from childhood through adulthood should be enjoyed in and of itself, progressing into a satisfying way of life and personally meaningful work. The skills we teach our children are, all too often, a reflection of what we think we needed to succeed in life. We should remember that our children's needs will be different. To fulfill their dreams we should strive to give them the most versatile tools possible along with the confidence to know they can learn whatever is necessary along the way. Our culture equates a college degree with success. Kohl's book will give you good reasons to look beyond the common equation: college = success = money = happiness. Kohl does not accept the premise that your life's work need be dull. Therefore, in homeschooling, we should seek out the greatest opportunities for exploration and discovery possible. I think a copy of this book should magically appear with the birth of every first child. Code HMN, $15.95. More about this book in "College and Alternatives."

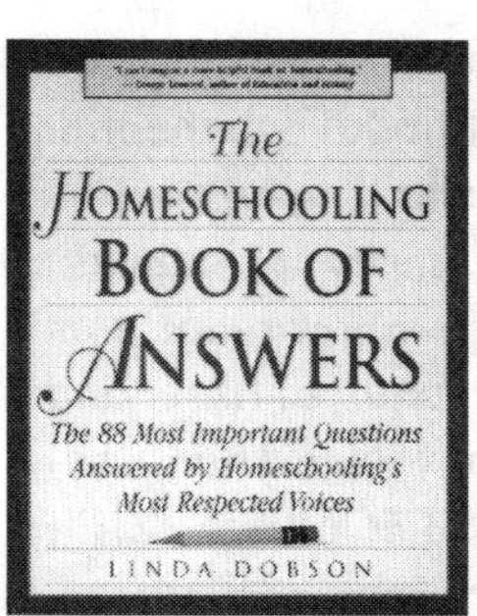


**THE HOMESCHOOLING BOOK OF ANSWERS,** by Linda Dobson. Finally! A book with more answers than questions. How can that be? Read on! Drawing from years of experience homeschooling her own family, time spent helping other homeschoolers through workshops, and her written work about homeschooling, Linda has posed more than 80 of the most important, most frequently asked questions about homeschooling and asked more than 35 of homeschooling's most respected voices to contribute answers. Issues of structure, expense, socialization, dealing with officials, resources, and many more are all answered here. Reading this book is like attending a homeschooling forum and hearing the most experienced people in the field express their ideas and opinions. Best of all, each question is answered by at least two people so you can consider differing points of view and form your own conclusions. I found it interesting to see where contributors agreed (without any consultation) and where they differed. The greatest value of this book lies not in the number of questions that are answered, but in the rich diversity of answers. You will come away from this book knowing that there are as many ways to homeschool as there are homeschooling families. These "expert" answers come from a combined total of more than 500 years of personal experience, experimentation, observation, and the courage to pursue personal dreams and values. This is a book for all homeschoolers. Reading it will empower you as you experiment and find the best learning style for you and your family. Code PP, $16.95.

In Linda's *Homeschooling Book of Answers* she asked several of us to address the following frequently asked question: "I hated school! How can I possibly teach my child?"

This was my answer, slightly altered to fit this book.

Homeschooling is a fantastic challenge! If you didn't want a challenge I don't think you would be homeschooling or considering it. It is also one of the most fantastic opportunities. The obvious answer to this question is to learn right along with your child or find someone willing to teach a particular subject for you.

I can't think of one valid reason we should know everything we would like our kids to learn before starting to homeschool. Some things we can learn about before beginning to actually do them. Some things are learned best by doing them. Some things require a combination of approaches. I believe homeschooling needs the combination of both approaches.

Only very young children believe their parents know everything, but kids ask the craziest questions, and by the time they are five or six they certainly know we don't have all the answers, and they love and respect us and have learned from us anyway.

Except for the time I attended public school, I've never felt that admitting ignorance about something was shameful or wrong. One of the most important things we wanted our kids to learn was that the only really stupid thing you can do is *not* ask a question when you don't understand something. In our homeschooling we found that admitting we didn't know something put us on equal footing with our kids and they respected that answer; then we could search for the answer together. Whenever you search for tools or materials so you can learn something together with your children you double your rewards. By saying, "Let's find out," you'll have the fun of doing something important together and you'll have learned something new.

I hated school. Period. I was a terrible student. The idea of teaching our kids scared me just about witless. But I never wanted our kids to go through the humiliation and fear I experienced, and that gave me courage. At the other end of the spectrum, Donn did well in school, found it an all-right experience, but felt it could have been much better. From opposite ends of the spectrum we had a common goal. We wanted something better for our children.

In the first month that Donn and I were together we met a family using the Calvert School correspondence program. Whenever we went to visit, the kids met us at the door bubbling over with excitement, immediately wanting to show us what they were learning and doing. Their excitement was tangible. It was our first glimpse of something that would shape our future.

Since that time hundreds of parents have written and told us that they've felt homeschooling gave them a glorious second chance to go back and learn many things they had missed in school. You may be challenged if you were a poor student in some subjects and you take your whiz-kid teenager out of school, but there are numerous great books to help you. If the material your child needs to learn is important, then you'll find the resources you need. You may just get more education in the process!

---

*The secret of education lies in respecting the student.* — Ralph Waldo Emerson

---

*Revised edition* — **LEARNING AT HOME: A Mother's Guide to Homeschooling**, by Marty Layne, mother of four homeschooled young adults. *Learning at Home* is a personal book. Marty's insights about interacting with her children can be well used by all parents and teachers even though it was written primarily for homeschooling parents. What makes this book outstanding are Marty's observations about the interaction between parents and children. She has an acute awareness of how children learn best and how to help them. Marty shares her insight into how to see and work through the conditioned responses we all subconsciously carry from society, our own upbringing, and our schooling in order to create a harmonious homeschool environment. The book begins by taking a close look at the answer to the very common question "Can I do this — teach my child at home?" You'll find Marty has the unique capacity to help you sort out your inner thoughts and motivations and recognize your fears (and learn how to deal with them), and to impart confidence. You'll find numerous comments and suggestions for creating a learning environment to suit yourself and your children, and the emphasis is always on how to relate and respond to your children, and how to best meet their needs and your own. Yes, Mom and Dad, you have to take care of your needs too; that's a strong part of Marty's message. Being a good mate and parent presents many challenges. Add teaching (working with, guiding, whatever you want to call it), and you've added to those challenges exponentially. Unless you're superwoman or superman you're going to find your life, at times, more stressful than is reasonable. Marty's chapter on burnout — how to recognize it, what to do about it, and (most constructive of all) how to prevent it — is the best I've seen. This is a book designed for real people. She recognizes that parents as well as kids have times when they are grumpy, that there are times when the kids get bored or are unhappy, and she offers some interesting observations about why these times happen and some ideas for improving the situation.

Along with all this sagacious writing about critical issues, you'll find chapters about helping your child learn to read, write, and do arithmetic; the importance of including the arts (music, art, dance, and drama); and using all of life as a curriculum. Many of us have read about homeschoolers becoming accomplished musicians at a young age, going to prestigious colleges, or doing other remarkable things. Marty makes the important point that homeschooling can "allow time to pursue an interest and reveal talent but can't create it." Thankfully, Marty recognizes that not all children develop remarkable talents or abiding interests, and points out that there are important talents our society does not recognize: "We tend to recognize only outstanding gifts that fall in recognized categories like art, music, drama, or sports. We are not willing to recognize talent for something like happiness, listening to others, being a warm person, taking delight in a rainy day." I particularly value this observation because more important than any talent or recognition, living well with ourselves and those around us is one of life's true goals and rewards. There is so much depth to this book that it's worth reading and rereading.

I highly recommend this book to all homeschoolers. If you are considering homeschooling it will help you decide if this is really what you want to do and how to do it successfully. This book also has great value to those who have been homeschooling for a while, because Marty has given so much thought to issues that frequently cause problems in daily homeschooling, and clearly states ways to help you deal with them.

The end of the book contains several very useful appendices, with a list of read-aloud books, a bibliography, help in setting goals, and addresses for U.S. and Canadian support. Code SC, $13.95.

*There's no way to be a perfect mother and a million ways to be a good one.* — Jill Churchill, *Grime and Punishment* (Bantam)

**THE BIG GIANT DECISION**, by Penni Reneé Pierce. This book has just been revised and expanded. What stands out about Penni's book is the focus on deciding whether or not to homeschool. Penni's personal story and the pictures of her family make this book feel more personal than many others. She makes reference, in her daily schedule, to Bible studies, but she's not on a soapbox trying to sell religion to you; it's just a part of her life. She uses a schedule, but makes it clear she is also very flexible. I think her examples of scheduling and flexibility are one of the essential techniques for successful homeschooling. She shares her insights into working with more than one child, approaches to subject matter, and a lot more. There are many very helpful sections: a getting-started checklist, a resource list, a book list to take to your library, information about college entrance and college, a new section with resources for working with learning disabilities, and a contribution by her husband. My only disagreement with Penni is with her suggestion that the Home School Legal Defense Association (HSLDA; see "Support Groups and Organizations") is the best place to check homeschooling legalities. I think you're always better off finding a local support group that knows the law and your school district. Write: Penni Pierce, 1234 Cypress, Richardson, TX 75080, for price and ordering, or for more information. E-mail: penmar@ev1.net.

HOW TO BEGIN HOMESCHOOLING
A Parent's Guide
by Judy Garvey

**HOW TO BEGIN HOMESCHOOLING: A Parent's Guide,** by Judy Garvey. This is a small but very useful booklet with some of the most sensible advice and observations I've seen. Excellent thoughts about beginner's doubts, the "flushing out" of kids who have been in public school, developing a non-restrictive curriculum, and much more. Highly recommended. $5 postpaid from Judy Garvey, R.R. 1, Box 3215, Blue Hill, ME 04614; 207-374-2437; bluehill@ctel.net.

**Ask Me Again About Socialization** — "Schoolyard Bullying and Victimization," a 28-page booklet to help educators, parents, and students understand and respond to schoolyard bullying. Write: National School Safety Center, 16830 Ventura Blvd., Suite 200, Encino, CA 91436 for ordering information.

*A teacher who is attempting to teach without inspiring the pupil with a desire to learn is hammering on cold iron.* — Horace Mann

**HOME SCHOOL: TAKING THE FIRST STEP**, by Borg Hendrickson. A very detailed, step-by-step guide for anyone planning to teach at home and not sure how to go about it, with chapters on frequently asked homeschooling questions and answers, your homeschool plan (partly to satisfy school authorities, partly to keep you on track toward your own goals), key components of teaching at home (curriculum, materials, planning, records), an extensive survey of state requirements, support groups, suggested reading material for children and adults, appendices (teaching methods, effective teaching, and lesson planning), glossary of terms, and several work and record sheets you can copy. Code MM, $18.95.

**THE THREE R'S AT HOME**, by Howard and Susan Richman. This is one of my favorites for its detailed but informal description of a family learning and growing together. The Richmans' approach to reading, writing, and arithmetic — and, through those subjects, all the rest — is the best example I've seen of family learning in a semi-structured environment. *The Three R's at Home* has no lesson plans, no step-by-step directions, but it will help readers gain the confidence to work out their own approach, fully assured that they don't need experts and authorities. $7.95 postpaid from Pennsylvania Homeschoolers, R.D. 2, Box 117, Kittanning, PA 16201.

**HOME SCHOOLING FROM SCRATCH**, by Mary Potter Kenyon. Mary begins by telling you about her own decision to home-school and goes on to discuss a variety of curriculum options that can save you money. The emphasis of this nice little book is on how to teach your children the way you want to without spending more money than necessary. Mary's done a lot of research. She lists and explains how to get the most for your time and money so you can concentrate on the important things — your children. 127 pages packed with good, sound ideas and sources. You'll save much more than you'll spend on this book by using her advice. Code GZ. $10. With more resources available today than ever, this book will help you choose wisely.

**HOMESCHOOLING: The Early Years**, by Linda Dobson. Linda is a longtime homeschooler and advocate of homeschooling. She's written columns for *Home Education Magazine* for many years and written many homeschooling books. Linda's enthusiasm about homeschooling is contagious. This book is a good basic reference for parents homeschooling children ages 3 to 7. It contains basic information (without overwhelming the reader) about getting started, tackling different subjects, and various problems you may encounter, and it lists some resource material. Code PRI, $15.

**HOMESCHOOLING: The Middle Years**, by Shari Henry. Another longtime homeschooling mom, Shari is currently the editor of *Homeschooling Today* magazine. In many ways this book is more valuable than the one listed above. Young children, unless spoiled by experiences in the public schools, are generally enthusiastic learners, innately curious and interested in whatever is at hand. The "tween years," ages 8 to 12, bring special challenges as children begin to develop a stronger sense of their own identity and need to be strongly supported as their special interests begin to take shape. Like the book above, it has good suggestions for covering various subjects and has lists of resources. Code PRI, $16.

**HOMESCHOOLING: The Teen Years,** by Cafi Cohen, follows the same format as the books above. Cafi has very good ideas for addressing the particular concerns of parents and teens as they search for alternatives to traditional graduation time and the challenges of moving on to college, work, and other options. Code PRI, $15.

I want to homeschool; how do I do it? I've homeschooled for a while; where can I find some fresh ideas? What do other families do during a homeschooling day? **HOMESCHOOLING: A Patchwork of Days,** is edited by Nancy Lande. This is a book of human resources — an intimate look at the way 30 families go through a typical day of homeschooling. It will help new homeschoolers, old-timers looking for fresh ideas, and the just plain curious to understand that homeschooling is a unique experience for each family and that there are many ways to succeed. You'll read about large and small families, families living in the city and the suburbs and the country, Christian-based and non-religious homeschooling, liberal arts approaches, very strong structuring, no structure, and combinations of styles. Just like the patchwork quilt featured on the book cover, this eclectic collection of homeschooling experiences is representative of homeschooling around the world. Code WC, $16.95.

**HOMESCHOOL: An Open House**, also edited by Nancy Lande. This second book is a follow-up to the first book, and much more. The emphasis is more on the thoughts and reflections about the past five years of homeschooling by the original contributors, with the addition of about 30 new families. This book provides in-depth support for homeschooling as well as a realistic look at the reasons some families stop homeschooling. 500 pages. Code WC, $19.95.

**THE HOMESCHOOL READER, Collected Articles from *Home Education Magazine*, 1984-1994** (revised), edited by Mark and Helen Hegener, editors of *Home Education Magazine* and parents of five homeschooled children. A wonderfully diverse collection of outstanding articles from HEM, offering a variety of perspectives about the major concerns prospective and long-term homeschoolers share. There are more than 50 articles by experienced homeschoolers sharing the lessons they have learned. Topics covered: why homeschool?, getting started, teaching and learning, approaches to basic fields of learning, special-education needs, advanced learning and higher education, networking, personal family stories, resources, and more. Code BT, $14.95.

**HOME EDUCATION MAGAZINE**, P.O. Box 1083, Tonasket, WA 98855. If I had to choose only one homeschool magazine to read, this would be it. The content is representative of the diversity within the homeschool movement. You'll find articles by parents and homeschool leaders pertaining to all facets of homeschooling, book and product reviews, regular columnists, support group information, pen pals, legal news (if you'd like to overlook legal issues, you have a lot of company, but we will not be able to maintain our hard-won freedom to educate our children at home if we ignore them), and much more. Fun to read and full of ideas to think about. 6 issues per year, $32; 2 years/12 issues, $64. Single issue $6.50. Call 800-236-3278. Visa/MasterCard and American Express accepted. HEM's website: www.home-ed-magazine.com. HEM's online newsletter is free on request. HEM also has a free e-mail information service you can use. Visit their website for more information. HEM also has a terrific resource and networking board on the web at www.home-ed-magazine.com/DSC/discus/messages/board-topics.html.

**HOMESCHOOLING IN OREGON**, by Ann Lahrson-Fisher. ***WAIT!* Don't go away if you live outside Oregon!** Ann starts with a Homeschool Emergency Kit that says "RELAX" on the first page, and that's just what you should do. Whether or not you live in Oregon there is a wealth of information about "how to do it" the best way for your family, including commonsense answers to common questions and concerns, resources listed by subject, and a special chapter on students with special needs. Each chapter begins with helpful commentary. This is a great resource for those new to homeschooling, and the resources will be a boon to those who have been teaching at home for a while. Ann has put together a first-class resource guide for the state, and you shouldn't miss it if you live there. Absolutely everything you need to know about homeschooling regulations and how to deal with them. Resource guides abound: Many are only lists, many are copycat books — but this book is special. 400 pages. Code OB, $18.95.

---

*Education is not the filling of a pail, but the lighting of a fire.* — William Butler Yeats

---

**AND THE SKYLARK SINGS WITH ME: Adventures in Homeschooling and Community-Based Education**, by David H. Albert. David's astute observations and comments about modern educational methods used in the public schools are important, but they aren't what impressed me most. More than the families in any other homeschooling accounts I've read, the Alberts integrated their freestyle homeschooling with people and resources within their surrounding community. This called for a change in lifestyle, and David calls that "hard work." Their striving to connect their children with people who were passionate about what they were doing, and who were willing to share and foster the interest of young children, demanded that they expand their network of friends and acquaintances and explore options through newspapers and by calling strangers. This was not always easy, but the results were immensely rewarding. The children's interests were respected, and their horizons expanded. Their intellectual growth flourished, and because this learning took place within the family and expanded into the community at large, the children formed relationships with people of all ages based on common interests and needs, as opposed to the public school standard of peers based solely on age. Many books emphasize "values," but mostly as they pertain to the family. David and his wife talk about imparting the values of community interaction — not just for social contact with people outside the family, but because this interaction makes activities outside the family more than just isolated incidents: They become a foundation for the future.

While David is cognizant of the precocity of his own children (and you will be well aware of this too), you will quickly see that the most important aspect of his story is how he and his wife labored to observe, respect, encourage, and only occasionally direct their children. The observations, ideas, and suggestions given for encouraging personal and intellectual growth will be useful to everyone.

You'll find many insightful comments about how children learn throughout the book. I heartily endorse his suggestion that you read James Loewen's *Lies My Teacher Told Me* and Howard Zinn's *People's History of the United States* (both reviewed in "History and Biography") so that you can incorporate varied perspectives about history and its depiction into your own presentation of the subject. I agree with his idea of repeatedly making math relevant to young children, thereby enabling them to discover its usefulness in making sense of their world. I particularly liked his statements about encouraging early reading and the use of phonics: "Having kids read at ever-younger ages may be high on the agenda of parents with heady images of escorting their sons and daughters off to Harvard, but given the content of most young children's reading material, learning to read is small potatoes compared with the fascination of an anthill." He goes on to point out that the choice of whether to use a whole-language or phonics approach to reading should be determined by each child's need at the time — and that this may change over time. He points out that his daughter Meera was not interested in having a word sounded out phonetically, but wanted the word said and explained (if necessary). She would then memorize it if it was useful. "What I am cautiously suggesting is that heavy emphasis on phonics *might* get *some* children to read earlier, but not necessarily better, provided 'late' readers are not stigmatized and their self-confidence damaged for not reading on someone else's time schedule. The problem with either phonics or whole-language approaches to reading is that they are each all too often tied to both a timetable and a content not of the child's own devising."

I concur with David's statement that "the [public] system fails far too often, and we all know it. The emperor has no clothes. Administrators hope, against all evidence, that by micromanaging the line through testing, confidence in the enterprise can be increased. Now, not only are children compared with each other, but schools pitted against schools. ... We are all taught to want to know how our kids measure up, but only against kids of exactly the same age and controlled experience, and only at skills related to data retrieval and symbolic manipulation, a bare fraction of a child's true humanity in the present moment or her human potential. Knowing how our kids measure up is, ultimately, no substitute for knowing, really knowing, our kids, and for our kids to know themselves."

David faults using E.D. Hirsch's cultural literacy and Core Knowledge books as standards for yearly content, and while I feel strongly that a common cultural knowledge is important, I agree that these books can become simply another set of artificial standards with emphasized data unrelated to a child's life, which makes the content just something to be regurgitated, not an integrated relevant set of useful knowledge.

At the end of the book he concludes that "to educate a child well is to enable her to find her destiny as well as our own. This can only be accomplished successfully, I am persuaded, by allowing her to find the freedom to listen to and be exhilarated by the harmony of her own inner voices and those of the world around her so that, like Blake's schoolboy, she comes to know that 'the skylark sings with me.'"

This is a book to inspire you throughout your homeschooling journey. An added bonus is a list, at the end of each chapter, of resources the Alberts found most useful. Code NSP, $16.95.

**THE BEGINNER'S GUIDE TO HOMESCHOOLING**, by Pat Farenga. Covers what homeschooling is like and how it works. It has good ideas for planning your curriculum — structured or unstructured; basics of record-keeping and its importance; and information about testing, college admissions, and more. Extensive lists of helpful organizations and resources. $10.95 from Holt Associates (see *Growing Without Schooling* below).

**GROWING USE OF "UNSCHOOLING"**

"According to the National Home Education Research Institute in Salem, Oregon, the fastest-growing approach to homeschooling elementary education is called "unschooling." The Institute estimates that 1.3 to 1.7 million, or about three percent of all 53 million school-age children, attend school at home. The numbers of these children are growing 7 to 15 percent a year." — Peter T. Kilborn, "Learning at Home, Students Take the Lead," *The New York Times,* May 24, 2000, A1

I think it's nice that the *New York Times* thought this news important enough to report. I do wonder if it was the National Home Education Research Institute or the *Times* that thinks *all* those home-schoolers are "unschooling." Unschooling is growing, but the majority of people, even those who consider themselves unschoolers, are using some type of structure.

The piece above was delivered to me by e-mail by the Computer Curriculum Corporation, www.CCClearn.com, which publishes Ed.Net Briefs, a free education newsletter sent to subscribers via e-mail each week from September through June. For a free subscription, visit www.edbriefs.com.

*"Did you have a happy childhood?" is a false question. As a child I did not know what happiness was, and whether I was happy or not. I was too busy being.*

— Alistair Reid

**The Works of John Holt.** For more than 20 years, until his death in 1985, John Holt was regarded internationally as one of the foremost educators striving for radical reform of the public school system. Two of his earlier books — *How Children Fail* and *How Children Learn*, published in the '60s — helped Jean and me form a great deal of the educational philosophy that led us to teach at home several years before John himself turned his back on the public system. His introduction to *Teach Your Own* describes his conversion to the idea of home-schooling. John seems to imply that the idea was originally his answer to the problems many parents had been having in trying to set up "private" schools. He makes no mention of the hundreds or thousands who had already been teaching at home for many years. *Growing Without Schooling*, his bimonthly magazine begun in 1977, and the publication of *Teach Your Own* in 1981 so easily established John as a knowledgeable thinker in the field of home education that it seems ironic it took him so long to carry his own philosophy to its logical conclusion. However, he caught up very quickly, and soon gained almost a cult following that regarded all his opinions and conclusions as established fact and educational gospel. Most of John's experience was with young children. He never had children of his own, so some of his observations may not apply as well to older children. John cared deeply about children, their rights, and their happiness, but readers should remember that being a theoretician and observer, however caring, doesn't include the hopes and fears and responsibilities of full-time parenthood, twenty-four hours a day for many years. All of John's thoughts are worth serious consideration, but those who regard him as an infallible saint are doing a disservice to him and to the children he cared so much about. Home-schoolers will get more use from some of John's writings than from others, but will find all his writing provocative and instructive.

**TEACH YOUR OWN**, by John Holt (new abridged edition 1997). Despite the many newer books now available, this is still a good introduction to school at home. Subjects include the reasons public schooling is bad for most kids, answers to some common objections to home-schooling, how to take kids out and keep them out legally, ways of living and learning with children that are not threatening or self-defeating, learning without teaching, and more. Much of the material is taken from John's letters published during the first few years of *Growing Without Schooling*, with John's responses, and covers many different aspects of learning at home. Now out of print. Try your library.

**HOW CHILDREN FAIL**, by John Holt (revised). When first published, this book sparked a whole era of educational reform, and soon was accepted as a masterpiece in the field of learning. This revised edition, written from the broader perspective John gained over the years, and in accordance with his newer home-school philosophy, discusses more deeply the ways children investigate the world, the pitfalls of classroom learning, grades, testing, trust, and authority, as well as mistakes many home-schoolers make and how to avoid them. Code HC, $13.

**HOW CHILDREN LEARN**, by John Holt (revised edition 1983). "Children do not need to be made to learn, told what to learn, or shown how. If we give them access to enough of the world, including our own lives and work in that world, they will see clearly what things are truly important to us and to others, and they will make for themselves a better path into that world than we could make for them." This new edition is almost twice as long as the first, with all additions and changes clearly indicated. All of John's original thoughts about the ways we learn to talk, to read, to count, and to reason have been expanded in several new chapters. Despite the title, I think much of the book could easily be applied to the ways in which anyone, of any age, learns. Whether we consider ourselves primarily learners or teachers, this book gives us an increased understanding of the learning process. Code HC, $13.

**INSTEAD OF EDUCATION**, by John Holt. The central theme of this book, which may mark the beginning of John's transition from public school advocate to a leading proponent of home-schooling, is that we learn to do things by doing them. John gives his playing of the cello as an example of learning by doing, pointing out that he does not first "learn to play" and then, once that mysterious process is completed, begin "to play." He just *plays*; the learning and the doing are the same. That seems to be an important distinction, but, as John also says, "Our language gives us no other way to say it."

Holt also discusses what real learning is, what schools are really for (or should be for), why school reform failed, what a healthy learning society might be, why learning and doing cannot be separated, and much more. John's proposals for more creative, practical uses of public school facilities are very sound, as are his arguments for "learning by doing" rather than "learning before doing." However, some of his suggestions, which at first glance seem surprisingly simple and practical, seem to miss the needs of many people in an increasingly complex society. His suggestion of matching skilled people with students who want to learn the same skills is an obvious choice for many, but students who haven't yet decided on a particular skill to learn, or those who want careers requiring more abstract skills and knowledge (astronomy, perhaps, or medicine, and many others), may have no option but to study and learn before doing.

Several years ago I went to Mexico and began learning Spanish. When I was asked by Mexicans if I spoke Spanish, after I had learned a dozen words, it would have seemed silly to say, "Yes," when the best I could have done with the rest of the sentence would have been to hold up my thumb and forefinger half an inch apart. I learned a fair amount of the language by listening, trying out my very limited vocabulary, asking to be corrected, and so on. This is a kind of apprenticeship, but I also learned a great deal by studying books and listening to cassette tapes. Learning processes may be very different for different kinds of knowledge and skills, and the method that is exactly right for one may be completely wrong for another. Some people learn better by doing, and some learn better by studying first. (I find it interesting that a baby learns language "by doing" but that an older person may find it more expedient to augment his learning through an immersion experience with textbooks.)

Our disagreement with the public schools' apparent insistence that everything must be "learned" before doing shouldn't become an equally obstinate insistence by home-schools that the opposite is always true. I might be content to get half-price haircuts at a barber's school, where the students learn by doing, and I doubt that I'll mind, when the time comes, if my undertaker is learning by doing. But if I ever need surgery, I'll hope the surgeon has had the opportunity to practice on cadavers and plastic dummies before he practices on me.

In *Instead of Education*, Holt's indictment of public education is far more general and sweeping than in many of his other books. It may be true, as John says, that compulsory education is one of the most dangerous of all mankind's social institutions, but for me it would be far down on a very long list. As much as I disapprove of most public school programs, I can't agree at all with John's statement that children are compelled to go to school simply because adults don't want them around.

I think this book will be of most interest to those who are curious about the evolution of John's opinions, rather than to those who are looking for practical advice to employ in their home-schooling. There is much of value, but if your budget is limited, I suggest you borrow it from the library and spend your money on some of John's other books that will be of more practical use. Now out of print. Try your library.

**SHARING TREASURES: Book Reviews by John Holt**, edited by Pat Farenga and J.P. Holcomb. This book, published five years after John's death, almost immediately has become one of my favorite collections of his writings — partly because I value his opinions (although I don't always agree with him) and partly because I enjoy good books and good reviews of good books. A good review, of course, is much more than a simple description of a book; it's a discussion of the book's ideas, balanced against the reviewer's own ideas. I looked right away for John's reviews of books with which I am familiar or that I particularly like, wanting to compare his opinions with mine; did he like them for the same reasons I do? Next, I read reviews of books I'd heard of, but hadn't read (and John's comments convinced me that I should read them soon), and then reviews of books I'd never heard of. Subjects include home-schooling, tests, history and geography, math, economics and work, health, poetry, art, records, and much more. If you like books and like to read about books, and if you agree even half the time with Holt, this book makes an ideal combination. From Holt Associates, $5.95.

**GROWING WITHOUT SCHOOLING**, a bimonthly magazine begun by John Holt in 1977, is primarily an informal open forum in which unschooling parents and children share their ideas and experiences, not as professional writers or certified experts, but simply as people who are actively involved in learning outside the school system. Each issue has articles about learning and teaching, up-to-date home-schooling news from around the world, resource reviews, legal information, support groups, suggested resources, a continuing directory of readers who wish to be listed, and much more. If you are thinking about using the unschooling approach to homeschooling, this should be one of your primary resources. This is also an excellent resource for the rest of us who homeschool, no "un" intended, for its creative resources and ideas. Subscriptions may be ordered from Holt Associates, 2380 Massachusetts Avenue, Suite 104, Cambridge, MA 02140. 6 issues per year, $26; 2 years/12 issues, $46. Write for overseas rates. Don't forget to ask for a current catalog of great books from John Holt's Books and Music Store.

3 booklets from Holt Associates (address above). $4.95 each, or all three for $12, shipping $5.

**TRANSITION FROM SCHOOL TO HOMESCHOOL** — The transition to homeschooling can be very easy for some children and more difficult for others. This handy reference with advice and suggestions from Susannah Sheffer can make this adjustment to living and learning differently much easier. If you're having problems — or anticipate some — this will help.

**UNSCHOOLING MATH** — Stories of kids ages 4 to 17 learning math their own way.

**LIFE AFTER HOMESCHOOLING** — Stories by grown homeschoolers who talk about college and finding the work they love. Included in this publication is a letter from a college admissions officer that is very useful for learning what a growing number of colleges expect from applicants.

**THE UNSCHOOLING HANDBOOK: How to Use the Whole World as Your Child's Classroom**, by Mary Griffith. This book kept me awake even at a very late hour. I enjoyed and learned from the creative ideas presented by her many contributors about how they help expand their children's knowledge and enjoyment in their learning activities. I liked her broad definition of a classroom. This book begins with suggestions and thoughts about unschooling that can help you decide if it's something you want to do — and can do. It continues on to cover all the subjects expected by schools and interesting unschooling approaches used by her contributors. The variety of approaches adds depth and interest and offers good suggestions. At the end of each chapter is an example of how that chapter's subject would be covered throughout an unschooling day, along with a list of very good resource books. Code PRI, $15.95.

**A SENSE OF SELF,** by Susannah Sheffer. Two of the questions parents, educators, relatives, and the just plain curious want answered are "How do homeschooled kids turn out?" and "What advantages, if any, do they have?" I admire the work Susannah has done with homeschooled adolescent girls. I completely agree with Susannah's conclusion that homeschooled girls have a much stronger sense of identity and self-confidence. I wish, however, that she had left the comparisons to Carol Gilligan's classic study of low-income, disadvantaged youth out of the book. I don't think the comparisons are valid. I realize there is not a large body of documentation about grown homeschoolers. Still, I would have preferred a larger, more diverse study. I met a number of unschooled young adults at the *Growing Without Schooling* conference in Boston in 1997. They were a very impressive group, with many accomplishments. You could feel their self-confidence, and that they had developed a strong sense of who they were. This book's greatest value is in boosting your own confidence that unschooling teens can be successful. Code HMN, $17.95.

---

*A sheltered life can be a daring life as well.*
*For all serious daring starts from within.*
— Eudora Welty

---

**HOMESCHOOLING FOR EXCELLENCE**, by David and Micki Colfax. Of all the homeschooling books that might have been chosen with which to test the public market, the one selected is a thoughtful, well-balanced description and examination of the subject. The publisher's blurb on the back cover seems to put the cart before the horse, by referring to "a prescription for excellence — Harvard educations for their sons," apparently missing the point that if the excellence hadn't come first, Harvard probably wouldn't have come after. A *Chicago Tribune* review, quoted on the cover, says the book is "a step-by-step guide," which also misses the mark. Readers who expect a manual of daily instructions may be disappointed. I think the Colfaxes deliberately avoided writing a step-by-step guide, recognizing that others must work out their own approaches according to their own needs and resources. The Colfaxes' book gives steady, calm reassurance and answers to many common (and some not-so-common) questions about home education, but leaves to the readers the ways of implementing their ideas. "The educational experience is simply much too complex, too varied, and too rich to be reduced to a neat formula or two, or a set of pat and trendy phrases," the authors say in their introduction. "We did not attempt to implement a particular educational philosophy, but ... attempted to respond to the evolving needs of the children more or less in an ad hoc fashion. ... [If we have a philosophy,] it is only that children *will* learn, *will* aspire to excellence, if we recognize and respect their different interests and abilities and give them a chance to develop them." A very important point, I think, is that the "ad hoc fashion" is a definite key to homeschooling for excellence. David and Micki list and discuss several of the materials they feel were most useful, not to pontificate but to suggest. Readers might use the same materials with similar satisfaction, or they might choose entirely different materials. The diversity of the materials listed suggests that the importance is not in what was used, but *how* it was used — with open-minded curiosity, self-assurance, and perseverance. The book isn't a blueprint for getting into Harvard, but an encouraging sketch of how others can find and pursue their own paths to excellence. As the Colfaxes say, acceptance by Harvard isn't the only "proof" of excellence in education. Their fourth son might become a boat-builder, which probably won't gain him national recognition but, if he's a *good* boat-builder, would be equal proof of educational excellence. Code WNR, $11.99.

Are you beginning to wonder what a normal homeschooler or homeschooling family is like? Linda Dobson asked the following question in her book *The Homeschooling Book of Answers* (listed above). "All I ever read about in the newspaper is exceptional kids doing exceptional things. Are there any 'normal' homeschoolers?"

This was my answer:

Normal! What's normal? Who is normal? Are you normal?

Exceptional people will make the headlines. Exceptional kids will make bigger headlines. Homeschooled children are essentially no different than children in public schools. Like people everywhere, we all have our strengths and weaknesses. If there are any significant differences it's because homeschooling can allow all children, gifted or not, to grow more freely and pursue an interest to the point of excellence.

Our four children may resent me for calling them "average, normal kids," but that's what they are. Just like kids all around the world they've argued and fought, played, failed at some things, and done some outstandingly great things. They're not geniuses, yet they have done some exceptional things because they had the freedom to investigate and follow their special interests. Susan, who never considered herself to be a great, or even good, writer, won a provincial writing contest because it centered around a subject she cared about. She's also been placed in an honors English class in college. Cathy spent hours studying dinosaurs in third grade and acquired an exceptional knowledge of the subject. Derek got hooked on sharks in about fourth grade and read everything we could find for him. He read through everything in the provincial library and we had to search the Library of Canada, and then enlist the aid of friends and relatives to find resources to help satisfy his insatiable curiosity. He began reading at high school and college levels because he really cared about what he was learning. Karen finished her entire high school studies in two years, tackling all twenty-eight subjects in *High School Subjects Self-Taught*, including some advanced courses we tried to dissuade her from doing. We couldn't see that she would need them. We were wrong, of course. She's used what she learned, and has been glad she did it all.

Not everyone needs to go to Harvard, or wants to. Not everyone can write a symphony at age eleven, win a national spelling bee, or be outstanding in a particular field of knowledge. Most adults don't make headlines; it's the exceptions who do. If we don't have exceptional kids, that's all right. The point of homeschooling is not to compete for headlines, but to give our children as much freedom and enjoyment as possible in their living and learning, and to help them prepare themselves for their own future.

**CHILD'S WORK: Taking Children's Choices Seriously**, by Nancy Wallace; foreword by Susannah Sheffer. In many ways a sequel to *Better Than School* (now out of print), this book is also a deeper exploration of the unschooling concept that some people say John Holt developed. (I'll go along with that, as long as "developed" doesn't mean "originated.") As in *Better Than School*, I was disturbed because the subject of "giftedness" is carefully brushed aside. In her foreword, Susannah Sheffer says "[S]ome readers may think this is a story about prodigies and consider it irrelevant to their own children. ... If we think of Vita and Ishmael as prodigies, we avoid having to think about what helped them become as competent as they are." To a small extent, I think she's right. When I taught adult illiterates, one of my students had an I.Q. of 50; it would have been silly (and self-defeating) for me to pretend that this was not a serious consideration in his learning. If a very low I.Q. is a factor in learning, then why isn't a very high I.Q.? Despite the frequent disclaimers, it will soon be obvious to most readers that Vita and Ishmael *are* prodigies. So what? Do we make Mozart or Edison more "relevant" to home-schoolers by pretending they were not prodigies? Whether a child is gifted or illiterate, we are referring to a special need that shouldn't be ignored. Vita and Ishmael achieved many great things — in part, because their parents recognized their need to learn in their own ways. I learned more from this book, but also found myself disagreeing more, and wishing Nancy would just come out and say, "Yes, my kids are prodigies. This is how they have developed their talents. These are the ways in which we have tried to help them, and many may be useful to you, too." Most of my lesser disagreements were about unschooling: How much, if any, should an adult "interfere" with a child's natural, innate learning process? Some of the problem, I think, may be that as soon as one adopts a particular philosophy, one's effort to be consistent will be tested continually. I find it a little ironic that the unschoolers' "non-interference" with children's learning would be construed as rude condescension if applied to adults. If I interrupt my son's woodworking to show him a way to start the saw-cut without nicking a finger, then I'm interfering with his ability to learn by himself; but if I withhold the same information from an adult, and he becomes aware of it, he'll wonder why I didn't offer him this useful advice. If someone shows me a way to get more leverage on a tire iron with less effort, I don't resent him for stunting my innate ability to learn. There are ways of using axes, saws, and knives that are completely or relatively safe, and I have no intention of letting my kids explore the various ways so they can learn by themselves which ways are safe and which are not.

Part of the idea of unschooling is to treat kids like adults, but this is almost constantly negated by unschoolers who withhold useful help from children on the theory that children should be allowed to learn at their own pace and in their own way. Waiting for the child to ask for help isn't the answer, either; if a child doesn't know or suspect there's a better way, then he has no reason to ask. Letting a child struggle with a task without offering advice that would make it easier is not showing respect — and, once he realizes that you could have helped, but chose not to, will not increase his respect for you. Any philosophy, carried to its "logical," consistent extreme, can easily become ridiculous and indefensible.

With all of these comments, and the many more I'm making myself not write, will you still believe me when I say *Child's Work* is informative, interesting, useful, and definitely worth reading? It is. If nothing else, it may challenge you to explore the philosophy of unschooling more deeply. I think you'll find many of Nancy's observations about learning relevant to most children, whether they are prodigies or not. From Holt Associates, see address above. $12.95.

**I LEARN BETTER BY TEACHING MYSELF and STILL TEACHING OURSELVES,** by Agnes Leistico. This new edition combines Leistico's previously separate books. Outstanding exploration of interest-directed unschooling, with lots of ideas and information for the older student (high school and college). Also the story of a family in which the children went in and out of public school and the effects. From Holt Associates. $19.95.

**SUMMERHILL: A Radical Approach to Child Rearing**, by A.S. Neill. The story of the remarkable school that began as an experiment and soon became a model for scores of others. Believing strongly in Freudian theory, Neill felt that social maladjustment, academic failure, and nearly all other problems were the result of artificial inhibition and repression; he therefore encouraged almost complete freedom, including deliberate violation of many of society's taboos. In a subsequent book, *Freedom Not License*, addressed primarily to numerous objections, Neill explained that students at Summerhill learned through their interaction that real freedom includes real responsibilities. The "experiment" had much greater success at Summerhill than at its imitators, which most critics agree was because of Neill's personal influence on his students. Whether liberal or conservative, readers will probably disagree with much of what Neill advocates. At the same time, *Summerhill* vividly demonstrates that freedom can work, although it needs guidance; that in an atmosphere of democracy and self-regulation, children can thrive, learn, and grow. Disregard the Freudian view of repression; disregard the impractical consistency of total freedom for all children of all ages; still, *Summerhill* is a refreshing, provocative book that will both challenge and encourage you. Code STM, $12.95.

***Revised, expanded, international edition* — THE TEENAGE LIBERATION HANDBOOK: How to Quit School and Get a Real Life and Education**, by Grace Llewellyn. Probably the best, most accurate review of this book was in *Bloomsbury Review*: "This is a very dangerous book. It contradicts all the conventional wisdom about dropouts and the importance of a formal education. It is funny and inspiring. Do not, under any circumstances, share this book with a bright, frustrated high-schooler being ground into mind-fudge by the school system. The writer cannot be responsible for the happiness and sense of personal responsibility that might come from reading this book." Grace Llewellyn has compiled a fantastic array of ideas and resources for a very comprehensive unschooling education, in all the standard subjects and scores of non-standard ones — science, math, social sciences, English, languages, the arts, sports and athletics, outdoor jobs and activities, travel — through books, personal contacts, jobs, apprenticeships and internships, volunteering, social and political activism, and more. She offers very encouraging advice throughout the book, and illustrates her arguments with dozens of real-life stories (many borrowed from *Growing Without Schooling*) of kids who have done it. Even a home-school with more structure than Grace advocates will find the numerous ideas and resources invaluable; for the truly unschooled teenager who is serious about doing more than watching TV, it will be an invaluable guidebook.

I have one major reservation, and a few minor ones. Like many unschoolers, Grace seems to think that any and all resources (people, places, etc.) are good — except the child's own parents. The first thing to do after making the decision to quit school, Grace advises the teenaged reader, is "celebrate your audacity with deep chocolate ice cream" and *then*, step two, "consult your parents." Some parents might feel they should have something to say about such a momentous decision, but Grace doesn't seem to have much sympathy for them. "You might get this over with after dinner tonight," she says, "or you might acclimate them slowly to the idea." At least she realizes that some old fogies may be a little slow. "Fortunately," she adds, "with a little care and planning, you will probably be able to help them see the light." Ah, yes, we remember it well — our kids, at the age of 13 or 14, suddenly wise and mature, trying to help us see the light — and we, stubborn and over-protective, always in the way of their freedom and happiness, trying to keep them from frying their brains or wrapping themselves around a tree. Our own "fortunately" is that *they* soon saw the light and grew out of this phase almost as quickly as they had grown into it, and we continued our lives together as friends and family. Over-protective or not, we still think that most kids of 13 or 14, and even some of 16 or 17, are not ready to take on the entire world on their own terms alone, with no consideration for their parents' opinions, guidance — and yes, even a few rules now and then. There are exceptions, of course, but even for them there is seldom any excuse for presenting parents with ultimatums and sudden declarations of independence.

My minor reservations about the book have to do with some of Grace's recommended reading for the newly liberated teenager. We happen to agree with most of her choices, but a few of them seem to encourage a "liberation" with which we cannot agree. Poe, Gibran, Thoreau, the Bible, Blake, Shakespeare — excellent choices. But Grace also recommends *Rubyfruit Jungle*, by Rita Mae Brown, with the parenthetical note that it's "sexually explicit, offends a lot of people," which is putting it very mildly. She recommends *The Color Purple*, by Alice Walker, without mentioning that it's largely about incestuous rape, sexual promiscuity, infidelity, and lesbianism. She does admit that Tom Robbins' *Even Cowgirls Get the Blues* is "rated R — some sex, some drugs," but her idea of some is a long way from the book's nearly total preoccupation with random promiscuity, lesbianism, and constant drug use. Grace's list of "poetry" looks okay, except "poetry by Sappho," which is explicitly lesbian. In what she calls "a short list especially tailored for searching teenagers," I think she could have made better choices than these.

These reservations are concerned with a tiny part of the book, and shouldn't keep you from buying it and using it, but keep in mind that the author has her own orientation and opinions, and you may not always agree with her. Code LH, $19.

P.S. A reader recently pointed out that Grace has no children of her own. Our reader wondered if Grace would be as liberal with her own children at the expense of parental judgment. Me, too.

## CANADIAN RESOURCES

**BROOK FARM BOOKS**, Box 101, Glassville, NB E7L 4T4. This is our Canadian address for *The Home School Source Book*. Phone: 506-375-4680; toll-free ordering: 877-375-4680. E-mail: jean@brookfarmbooks.com.

**SCHOOL FREE: Home Based Education in Canada**, by Wendy Priesnitz, founder of the Canadian Alliance of Home Schoolers. This book provides an overview and sampling of experiences of homeschoolers across Canada, plus basic legal information. 140 pages including index. Write for price and postage information: Canadian Alliance of Home Schoolers, 272 Highway 5, R.R. 1, St. George, ON N0E 1N0 altpress@netroute.net; www.netroute.net/~altpress.

**HomeSchool and More** is a very good catalog of Canadian resources. Gertrude DeBoer, 29 Donald Dr., Charlottetown, PEI C1E 1Z5.

**THE HOME WORKS**, 1760 Groves Rd., P.O. Box 340, Russell, ON K4R 1E1, provides resources by mail, many, but not all, Christian.

## MILITARY HOMESCHOOLERS

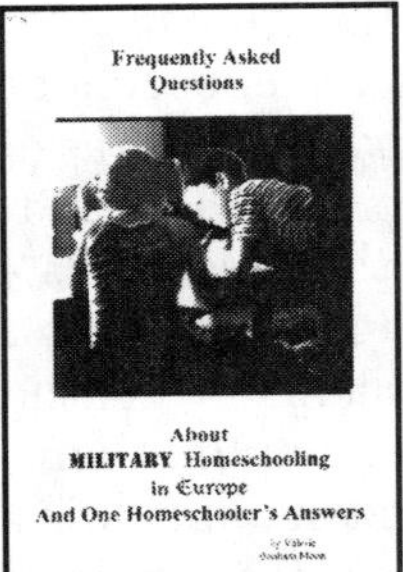


Here's a special resource just to meet your needs. Valerie Bonham Moon was raised as a military brat and then was zany enough to marry a career officer. As of this writing, Valerie has homeschooled three children while living in numerous places in Europe and the U.S. All three have gone on to college. Valerie still retains her incredible sense of humor. (I thought she should be decorated for that effort, so I sent her a decoration. She has promised revenge.) Valerie's large $8\frac{1}{2}$-by-11-inch 20-page booklet, **FREQUENTLY ASKED QUESTIONS ABOUT MILITARY HOMESCHOOLING IN EUROPE AND ONE HOMESCHOOLER'S ANSWERS**, will give you the information you need to incorporate and take advantage of homeschooling in your unique overseas situation. There is also a listing of addresses for getting helpful materials. For even more information, Valerie has put together a larger booklet, **ONE COMPULSIVE PACK-RAT'S ALPHABETICAL COLLECTION OF ASSOCIATIONS, SCHOOLS, MAGAZINES, BOOKS, CATALOGS, AND SCHOOL REGULATIONS.** Write: Valerie Moon, P.O. Box 1032, Belton, MO 64012. Each book $7 plus $1.50 shipping.

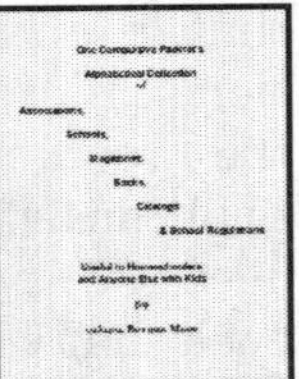

**ALMANAC OF EDUCATION CHOICES: Private and Public Learning Alternatives and Homeschooling**, edited by Jerry Mintz, is the best guide to the many national and international alternatives to normal public school education. More than 6,000 alternative schools and programs are listed and described but not evaluated, as that is a matter of personal choice. Essays on starting an alternative school; home-based education, Christian or otherwise; organic curriculum; charter schools; community-based programs; computer learning; and more. **Comprehensive listings for the U.S. and Canada**, plus international opportunities and alternative boarding schools. List of colleges that have accepted students with alternative backgrounds. $20 plus $3 postage (only $15 if you subscribe to *The Education Revolution*, formerly called *AERO*) from AERO, 417 Roslyn Rd., Roslyn Heights, NY 11577. Also from the same address: *The Education Revolution*, a newsletter with current information about alternative education around the world. $15.

What is education but a conditioning of the mind to a society and a way of life? There are many kinds of education, and often education closes as many doors as it opens, for to believe implies disbelief. One accepts one kind of belief but closes the mind to all that is, or seems to be, contradictory.

Louis L'Amour, *The Californios*

## CHRISTIAN RESOURCES

**HOME GROWN KIDS, HOME SPUN SCHOOLS, BETTER LATE THAN EARLY, SCHOOL CAN WAIT**, and other writings by Raymond and Dorothy Moore. One of the Moores' main premises, for which they give many well-researched reasons and arguments, particularly in *Better Late Than Early*, is that children shouldn't begin formal schooling before the age of 8 or 9, or even later. "We firmly believe," they say in *Home Grown Kids*, "that the greatest teaching talent in the world lies in the warm, responsive, and consistent parent whose love makes the needs of his children his highest concern. ... Parents' daily one-to-one example amounts to master teaching at the highest level." *Home Style Teaching* may be most useful for specific "how-to" suggestions and examples. The Moores are conservative Christians, but definitely not militant fundamentalists (and, in fact, are criticized by some fundamentalists for not being "Christian enough"). "From Christianity to Judaism to Confucianism and from Taoism or Islam to Zen, the Golden Rule threads through them all. And the home is its finest nest. It is the person who understands this well who is the most able creator of a family school." Much of their philosophy is very similar to the unschooling approach of John Holt and others. Of all home-school books by conservative Christians, the Moores' books will be most useful to the less-conservative or non-Christian; they often offer a good balance between the left and right extremes, and have many ideas that will be of good use to all home-schoolers, regardless of their religious beliefs. Write for more information and prices. The Moore Foundation, Box 1, Camas, WA 98607; www.moorefoundation.com. They've added *The Moore-McGuffey Readers*, a newsletter, and many other very useful publications you might want to consider even if you are not interested in using their program.

**7th updated edition — THE HOME SCHOOL MANUAL: Plans, Pointers, Reasons, and Resources**, by Theodore E. Wade Jr. *The Home School Manual* has grown and expanded over the years and continues to be a very valuable resource for new home-schoolers as well as old-timers. Ted and more than 40 other authors discuss in detail nearly every aspect of teaching at home. Subjects range from the three R's to moral and spiritual values (from a conservative Christian viewpoint), community resources, and introducing children to art. Several appendices include lists of home-school organizations, publishers, schooling laws, support groups, a typical course of study, and much more. *The CHRISTIAN Home School Manual* would be a more accurate title, but this book has scores, perhaps hundreds, of good ideas for everyone, and a great deal of extensive information not found elsewhere. Some of our less-conservative customers and correspondents have said they disagree with the highly structured approach, as well as the book's fundamentalism, but that they feel the wealth of ideas makes the book worthwhile anyway. We agree. "Yes, I advocate more structure than you do," Ted has written me, "but I see it as a servant, not as a master. Seeing character develop in my own children gives me confidence in certain principles." This book and the books by Raymond and Dorothy Moore are the only "conservative Christian" books we knowingly recommend to non-fundamentalists, and this is the only conservative Christian book we will sell; we wouldn't touch most of the others with a ten-foot rod or staff. Even if you don't agree with some of Ted's viewpoints (as we don't), we think you'll still find the book a valuable reference, worthy of a place on your home-school bookshelf. More than 500 pages including a good index. Code GZ, $30. Also available on CD-ROM: $24.

**HOME SCHOOLS: An Alternative**, by Cheryl Gorder. Most of this book is an examination of public schooling and the reasons so many people choose to teach at home, including educational controversies; social, moral, and academic failings of schools; legal aspects; origins and development of public schooling; state laws; and so on. Many home-school organizations and resources are listed. If you're already committed to home-schooling, the facts and statistics in this book probably won't surprise you. If you're undecided, or have friends or relatives who need convincing, this book should do it. Slight conservative Christian emphasis. $12.95 from Blue Bird Publishing, 2266 S. Dobson, #275, Mesa, AZ 85202; to order call: 800-888-4741.

**OUR REEDS GROW FREE**, by Karl Reed (no relation to us as far as we know). Warm, interesting, and informative story of Karl and Virginia Reed's homeschool, with suggestions, advice, and good examples. Conservative Christian, but not overly preachy. Illustrated with photos and drawings. Send a #10 SASE for information: Karl Reed, P.O. Box 100, Mammoth Spring, AR 72554.

**HOMESCHOOLING TODAY** offers unit studies and practical help for Christian homeschooling families. P.O. Box 1425, Melrose, FL 32666.

**THE BIG BOOK OF HOME LEARNING**, by Mary Pride, is really a collection of three volumes. Mary has written other books and columns for the fundamentalist magazine *The Teaching Home*. The first volume of this series appeared in 1986, blithely advertised as "the first resource guide of its kind." (That year I published the second edition of *The First Home-School Catalogue*.) About half the listings were very similar or identical to mine, although Mary's reviews and comments, as you'll see, are from a very different perspective. One newsletter said it was very good, "but you may wish Mary would get off her soapbox." At least a fourth of her listings are of conventional textbooks or materials, most of which I've ignored because they don't meet enough (if any) of my criteria — "fun, challenging, constructive, informative, and relevant to steady mental, physical, and moral growth." Many materials Mary recommends most strongly — for all areas of study, including history, science, and literature — are judged according to a strict, literal interpretation of the Bible. Most of the homeschooling books Mary recommends are by fundamentalists. Mary goes on to say a study of nature should begin with Genesis 1:1, before moving on to dinosaurs, which were part of the six-day Creation and became extinct shortly after the Flood ... and so goes Mary. Available from Alpha Omega Publications, 300 N. McKemy, Chandler, AZ 86226-2618. $24.95 per volume or $69.95 for the complete set, plus 10% shipping.

Regardless of your choices, you are always homeschooling.

## WHERE TO FIND CURRICULUM MATERIALS AND RELATED RESOURCES

We do not offer complete curriculum packages, but in the "Support Groups and Organizations" chapter we list a number of addresses for correspondence schools where you can find prepackaged courses. When you begin to look for resources you'll look at the world with new eyes — starting with yourself. You know much more about finding and using resources than you think you do. You've been showing your children how you live and learn in this world since they were born. You started the minute you first smiled and talked to your baby. Family unity, good values, curiosity, and learning to satisfy it aren't taught so much as shown by example. Some things you can't buy, and those are some of the most important gifts you can give your child.

Very young children use their immediate surroundings to explore and learn. You can start the same way. Your own house is full of resources! Your best tool is yourself — your love, playfulness, laughter, and encouragement.

Older children will need books and materials that may be harder to find. Successful homeschooling is not as much a matter of how much you spend as how creatively you use what you have. According to several surveys, the average spent per homeschooled child is $500 per year. I'm sure we never spent that much. Mary Potter Kenyon's *Home Schooling From Scratch* has a wealth of good ideas. Use your library card (and don't forget to check for library discards), visit yard sales, invest in cheap workbooks — and, occasionally, you can find good, inexpensive books at Wal-Mart.

It's amazing how much paper you'll use. Check your local newspaper office and print shop for rolls of newsprint and odds and ends left over from printing jobs. If you're part of a support group, make a list of books you'd like to borrow or are willing to lend, organize a book sale, or create a group resource library.

Look for homeschooling magazines and books, preferably by an author you know and trust, that review other books and products. Ask other homeschoolers who share your learning philosophy what they like. I also suggest you include either *Home Education Magazine* or *Growing Without Schooling*, because you'll find reviewed resources, how-to articles from different points of view, and news you should know about.

Donn did the very first of all the homeschool catalogs years ago (1982) because we learned by trial and some expensive errors that all that is hyped as educational *ain't necessarily so*, and he wanted others to benefit from our mistakes. Donn included a caveat concerning goods from "professional educators" in the last edition of our book, and it is more important now than ever. Commercial companies have discovered the "new" homeschool market, and some are working very hard to foist their standard material onto homeschoolers by changing their advertising. Brook Farm Books (the mail-order part of our business) is a known supplier for homeschoolers, and we have been inundated with promotional literature from publishing companies and suppliers of professional teaching materials urging us to carry their products. We don't take advertising and refuse to be influenced by any "special deals" these companies may offer. Many reviews in various publications are subsidized by the manufacturer or publisher of the product. It's called co-op advertising. A publication puts in an ad or sometimes writes a product review, and the publisher or manufacturer of the product contributes money toward the cost of publication or offers a better discount to the supplier if they sell the item. Caveat emptor. Some homeschooling publications will advertise almost anything to bring in revenue. Don't discount all paid ads — some of the books and products are excellent — but use your discretion.

When we began homeschooling, I felt very insecure and we used the Calvert School correspondence courses for a couple of years until I felt ready to follow our own course of study, guided by what we felt the kids should learn and what they wanted to learn. I know from corresponding with many of you that you would like to start with this type of security. Many of you also have to contend with periodic testing, which usually means you feel you must compromise between following your own path and satisfying officialdom. Therefore, if you want to compromise between a ready-made curriculum like the Calvert School and complete responsibility for all choices, there are several generally useful sources we recommend you use as guides — but not bibles.

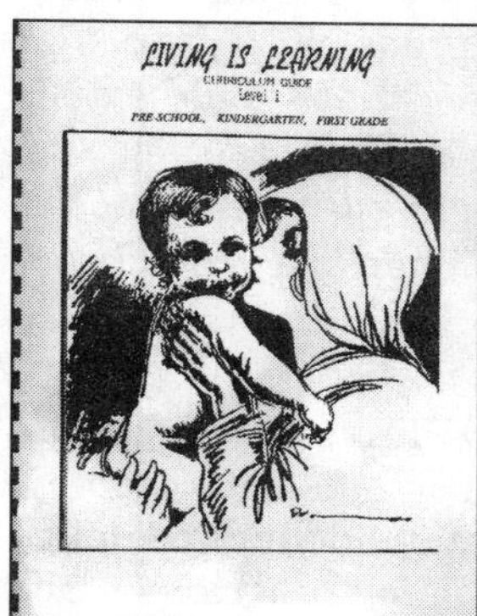


**LIVING IS LEARNING** curriculum guides are designed to be useful to all homeschoolers. These guides have all the basic information about what is usually taught for a particular age group. What makes them different from the World Book guides (free and listed below) is that Nancy Plent has included many good resources for finding the information you want to teach and special suggestions for unschooled learning, such as how to do it, how to keep useful records (for yourself and for school or state), and much more. Nancy offers a multitude of other good materials as well, so ask about her other products. From Nancy Plent, Unschoolers Network, 2 Smith St., Farmingdale, NJ 07727. $15 each for Level 1 (Pre-K, K, and 1st grade), Level II (2nd and 3rd grades), and Level III (4th and 5th grades); $22 for Level IV (6th, 7th, and 8th grades); $25 for the four-year high school guide.

**THE COMPLETE HOME LEARNING SOURCE BOOK: The Essential Resource Guide for Homeschoolers, Parents, and Educators Covering Every Subject From Arithmetic to Zoology**, by Rebecca Rupp. Rebecca has spent years finding resources and sharing them through her column for *Home Education Magazine* and in her earlier books. This is a mind-boggling collection of the good learning tools she's found. As Donn said in the last *Home School Source Book*, "It's a little difficult for the author of a resource guide to review someone else's resource guide, unless there are major disagreements in subject matter or philosophy. … I don't think I disagree with any of her choices, although only a small number of them appear in this book. That means you can consult both books with little chance of duplicated reviews." 865 pages, thoroughly indexed. Code RH, $29.95.

**HOW TO WRITE A LOW-COST/NO-COST CURRICULUM for Your Home-School Child**, by Borg Hendrickson. Step-by-step ideas and suggestions for designing a very formal, detailed curriculum, with short- and long-term goals, frequent assessments, and specific breakdowns of study areas and subjects for each grade, with particular attention given to keeping records that should satisfy the regulations of nearly any state. There are also suggested reading, sources, and a glossary. This book is now out of print, but it's worth checking your library to see if they have a copy.

**TYPICAL COURSE OF STUDY. Available for the U.S. and Canada.** This small booklet is not a step-by-step guide. It will provide general guidelines compiled from an analysis of many educational programs. Each grade level has a listing of general goals for social studies, science, language arts, health and safety, and mathematics. If you want more specifics see the Core Knowledge Series. This is free from World Book International, Educational Products Dept., 14333 Ash Ave., Flushing, NY 11355-2110, or World Book Educational Products of Canada, Georgetown Warehouse, 34 Armstrong Avenue, Georgetown, ON L7G 4R9. Online at www.worldbook.com/ptrc/html/curr.htm.

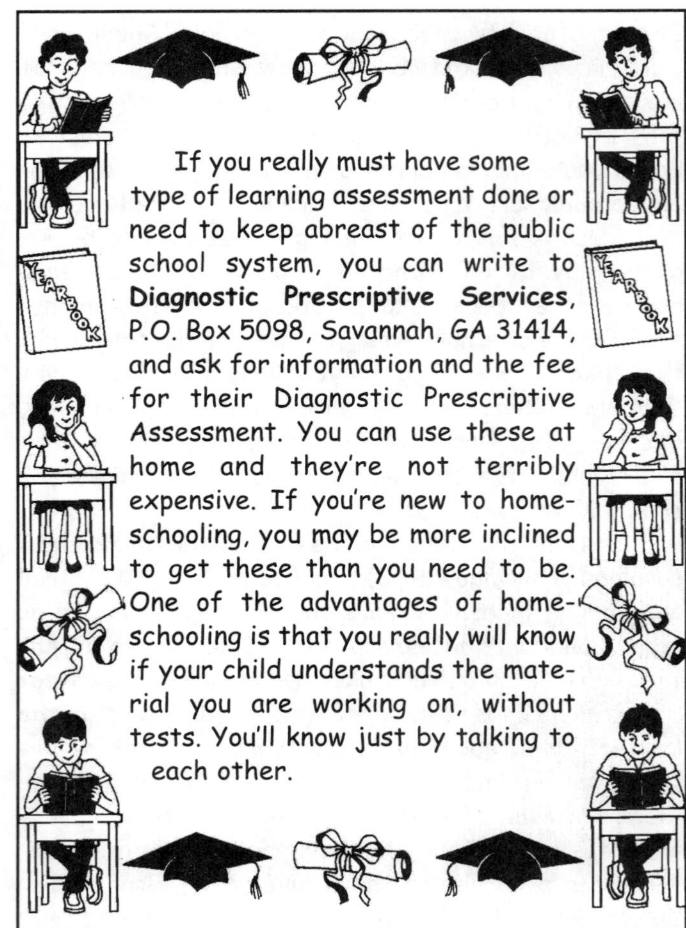

If you really must have some type of learning assessment done or need to keep abreast of the public school system, you can write to **Diagnostic Prescriptive Services**, P.O. Box 5098, Savannah, GA 31414, and ask for information and the fee for their Diagnostic Prescriptive Assessment. You can use these at home and they're not terribly expensive. If you're new to homeschooling, you may be more inclined to get these than you need to be. One of the advantages of homeschooling is that you really will know if your child understands the material you are working on, without tests. You'll know just by talking to each other.

**TEACHING WITH USBORNE BOOKS,** by Nancy Lotinsky. I'm sure you've seen the ads for Usborne books; if not, look for them in almost any homeschooling publication. They're great books! Parents and children find them fun to read and work with, but it can be very confusing trying to figure out in what order it's best to use them. I've reviewed and listed a number of them (the Usborne books all have the code EDC), but I've listed them by subject matter rather than sequentially. Nancy's handy book lists the books sequentially for all of us very nicely and concisely. Each chapter covers one particular subject, lists the book titles, the appropriate age group, and a short review of each book. The titles and age groupings are graphed, making it very easy to see what book will lead into the next. There's a handy quick-reference index in the back. I have no idea why the Usborne publishers haven't done this themselves, but I'm glad Nancy did. Thank you, Nancy. Code L, $5.95, and worth every penny.

**CHALLENGING PROJECTS FOR CREATIVE MINDS (Grades 1-5)**, by Phil Schlemmer, M.Ed. This set of projects helps children in grades one through five develop the ability to learn on their own in a creative and individual way. Projects are organized around four themes: Living Things, Numbers and Measurement, People and Places, and one theme created by the learner. Each project will give your child a chance to challenge himself and use his imagination, creativity, research skills, and more. This one book will provide ideas for 20 cross-curriculum projects, and you can use this base to suggest similar projects over a number of years. We can't teach our children *everything* they will need to know, but working with this book will help them acquire research and organizational skills that will become lifelong learning tools. There are forms for planning projects, which you may or may not want to use. I'd ignore the progress reports and evaluation material. Worth the investment. Can be adapted to family and small-group use. Code FS, $29.95.

**CHALLENGING PROJECTS FOR CREATIVE MINDS (Grades 6 and up).** Phil Schlemmer, M.Ed., has taken the above idea and added challenging elements for older learners to develop more advanced skills — such as preparing a biography or a time line, creating statistics, and acquiring more research skills. These projects are designed to be self-directed. A great chance to develop and showcase your learner's creative skills. As with the above book, there are planning suggestions and assessment material that you can ignore if you wish. Code FS, $34.95.

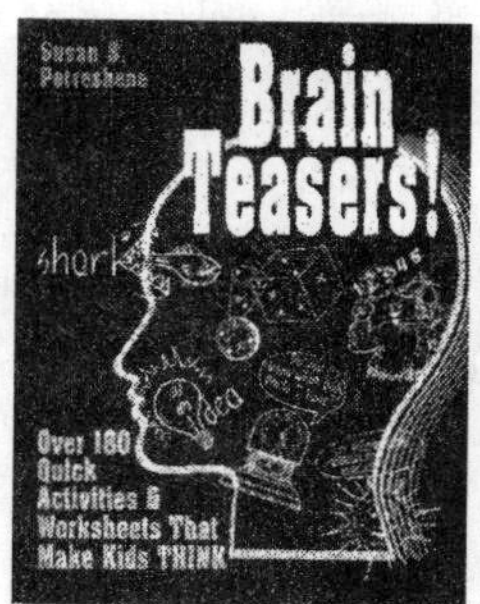


**BRAIN TEASERS!**, by Susan S. Petreshene, has more than 180 provocative yet quick activities and worksheets that will challenge your kids to think. No preparation is required. Materials involve pens, pencils, paper, and maybe a chalkboard. Each activity takes only 5 to 15 minutes. Covers thinking and reasoning skills, math, language and writing, listening, and memory. Easy-to-reproduce pages. Written for elementary grades. You'll be able to reuse many of these activities. Code PH, $27.95.

**Pennsylvania Homeschoolers**, R.D. 2, Box 117, Kittanning, PA 16201, has a small but excellent catalog of materials available for the asking.

**Calvert School** offers full-year K-8 home-study courses that arrive with books and all materials (paper, ruler, etc.). Calvert offers an excellent "classical education," if you can afford it and want or need a prepackaged curriculum. We used Calvert in the beginning, and I found it very reassuring to have a prepackaged curriculum, with suggestions about how to teach it, all planned for me. The kids loved it too. They still remember the mythology and history courses with affection. The math and science were very standard, with social studies a bit better, but it wasn't long before we felt we needed more freedom and fewer standard texts. You can use Calvert on your own, or use their advisory service to get a certificate for each grade. They do have high standards. Calvert now offers some materials for independent use, and reduced rates for families enrolling more than one child. Calvert School, 105 Tuscany Rd., Baltimore, MD 21210-3098.

**BOOKS TO BUILD ON: A Grade-by-Grade Resource Guide for Parents and Teachers**, edited by E.D. Hirsch Jr., author of *Cultural Literacy*. This book is designed to be a companion to the Core Knowledge Series (K-6) [*What Your First- (Second-, Third-, etc.) Grader Needs to Know,* see "Homeschooling and Cultural Literacy"]. If you're using this series, this book will be invaluable. If you need to write an impressive curriculum, I highly recommend this as a "guide" to resources you can use. Please remember that although it is written in a book, it is not written in stone. Use your own judgment. Allow latitude for following up areas of special interest. Keep in mind that if your child doesn't learn it all this year, there will be another chance next year or the one after. If I had to write a curriculum, I would use this book in conjunction with the Typical Course of Study listed above (which is free) as a guide. A word of caution: I'd use the book for writing a guide, but I doubt I would try to do it all within a school year. Although the material is good, I think there's just too much to reasonably do within a year. I'd stick with the most important elements.

The book is organized by subject and grade, with many good recommendations covering all phases of language arts, history, geography, visual arts, music, science, and mathematics through grade six. You are given the title, author, publisher, and age or grade levels, along with a written review of the book.

If you're not using any curriculum, this is an excellent reference book when your child wants information on a particular subject and you want to know what's available and appropriate for a certain age level. If you want books for an eight-year-old child interested in Egypt, this book will suggest titles, with reviews, and the approximate age or grade level of each book. This information is particularly useful if you are studying a subject with children of different ages. I think this is the best way to use this resource.

Hirsch lists the publisher's address and ordering information for some titles, but you may not save money by buying directly, because most publishers charge at least $3.50 for shipping. Your local bookstore will be the cheapest supplier. We have listed some of these books, but not all. If you can't find the books recommended by Hirsch at the library or in your local bookstore, we can probably get them for you. Please write and ask us. I think you'll find we charge less for shipping than most publishers. Code DD, $12.95.

Many used materials can be found online at the following site: www.vegsource.com/homeschool/.

**Textbook Tip From a Reader** — "Some of the major textbook companies won't sell teacher's editions or answer keys to individuals, especially those without teaching certificates. I found that if I send a photocopy of the education department's letter to me, granting permission to teach at home, the companies will keep the letter on file for a year, and will sell me the teacher's editions, answer keys, etc., at school prices. I've had no trouble receiving material I wanted." [Thanks for the tip, R.M.]

Using letterhead stationery helps too. You can create this on your computer, or see "rubber stamps" in the index to make your own.

**PETERSON'S SUMMER OPPORTUNITIES FOR KIDS AND TEENAGERS** (see "Family Living") is an incredible collection of summer programs for your average kid as well as for the gifted, talented, emotionally disturbed, hearing-impaired, physically or intellectually challenged, visually impaired, etc.

**BROOK FARM BOOKS** publishes *The Home School Source Book.* (That's our mail-order book service, and our addresses for the U.S. and Canada are in the front of the book). We can get almost any book that is in print if you send us the title, author, and (ideally) the name of the publisher and the ISBN. We've found and sent overseas special sailing guides as well as romance novels and Stephen King books as well as all the goodies in this book. We offer special discounts for reading groups and resource centers. Write to us for information.

*When making your choice in life, do not neglect to live.* — Samuel Johnson

## IDEAS AND EDUCATIONAL PHILOSOPHY

**GROWING UP ABSURD**, by Paul Goodman. Although not concerned only with education per se, this book of the late 1950s was among the few that helped people begin to examine the life and education of children in our "technological paradise." Its arguments about youth and complacent America may be more pertinent today than they were then. Write: War Resisters League, 339 Lafayette St., New York, NY 10012.

**"I LOVE MY FAMILY"** includes a poster, discussion guide, lesson plans, activities promoting the importance of strong family ties, the contributions children can make to their — Hey, how did this get back out of the wastebasket?

**Education Lectures and Discussions on Cassette Tapes.** For much less than the cost of taking your family to a movie, you can invite world-famous educators into your home to share their intelligent, thought-provoking discussions. These tapes are intended primarily for an adult audience, but we think they are also very good for bright and interested high school students, about 15 and older.

**THE DESCHOOLED SOCIETY**. Ivan Illich, the author of *Deschooling Society,* argues that the function of modern education is simply to produce consumers and workers in an industrial society — not necessarily by design on the part of individual educators, but by the very structure of public education. In the process, individual autonomy is sacrificed. He challenges the concept that true learning can occur only within schools, and suggests ways of educating people more effectively than in the school system. 33 minutes. Order by title and #729. Code AF, $12.95.

**THE RIGHTS OF CHILDREN**. John Holt (author of *How Children Learn*, etc.) and psychologist Richard Farson (author of *Birth-Rights*) discuss controversial changes in the treatment of children and suggest that young people should be enfranchised. 55 minutes, recorded in 1974 before John became a home-school advocate; from Heywood Hale Broun's "Avid Reader" Series. Order by title and #40067. Code AF, $12.95.

**CHILDHOOD**. Dr. Bruno Bettelheim analyzes the modern child's difficulty in forming his own identity, as contrasted with past generations. He discusses family structure and identity formation, his own criteria for "a happy family," and the need to make schools more human institutions. Two cassettes, approximately two hours; recorded 1974. Order by title and #S29622. Code AF, $31.95.

---

*We have to realize that for most men the right to learn is curtailed by the obligation to attend school.*

— Ivan Illich

---

**DESCHOOLING OUR LIVES**, edited by Matt Hern, foreword by Ivan Illich. There are many compelling reasons to read this book. The forward by Ivan Illich is a telling reflection on his earlier work, and brings questions to the reader's mind about the changes in our society and what will be pertinent and useful approaches to education for the future. Matt Hern's introduction is a stirring plea to think about what is currently accepted as "education within our society and its purpose," and what is most useful for all people learning at all ages. He writes, "I can see no real reason to distinguish between learning and living." Neither can I. The remainder of the book is broken into four sections with a very useful appendix. Part One, Looking Back, is a look at the roots of our modern deschooling, with sections by Leo Tolstoy, Vinoba Bhave, Ivan Illich, and John Holt. Part Two, Living Fully, is a more recent analysis, with contributions by Grace Llewellyn, John Taylor Gatto, Aaron Falbel, and other interesting thinkers. Part Three, Just Say No: Staying Home, contains writing by Donna Nichols-White, David Guterson, Susannah Sheffer, Seth Rockmuller, Katharine Houk, and others. Part Four, Schools That Ain't: Places That Work, is a clear look at Summerhill, the Albany Free School and Community, and other working alternatives to public schools. The appendix is a wonderful reading and resource list. Why read yet another book about alternative education? Because it will stimulate your thinking and provoke new attitudes and outlooks. This one will refresh your mind, clarify your ideas, and inspire you to reach for the best living and learning you can create within your family and community. Code NSP, $14.95.

**From *Newsweek*, Aug. 10, 1998**. Column by Robert J. Samuelson. "The United States spends more than a half-trillion dollars a year on education, counting everything from elementary to graduate school. We waste a lot of that. The ... latest evidence from Massachusetts, where — for the first time — applicants for new teaching jobs are being tested for basic competence in reading, writing, and a subject area ... [shows that] 59% of recent or soon-to-be college graduates failed. ... One of the most common failings in the written section was caused by phonetic spellings like improbly, corupt, bouth (meaning both), bodyes, and relif."

Samuelson says the common fix has been to throw money at the problem, and he feels this isn't the answer. He's right, of course, but he doesn't offer any realistic hope. He suggests that higher standards and better pay for teachers might help, stricter standards for passing each grade will help, and colleges reinstating decent admissions standards will make a difference. The problem, as he sees it, is from the top down, and he isn't optimistic. Colleges need the tuition revenues that students bring. If colleges have tough admissions standards, many students will go elsewhere. "Too many colleges chase too few good students. To survive, colleges scramble to get bad students (and their tuition). 'If you have a high-school diploma and tuition — and can walk and talk — you can graduate from college,' says Harvard's Murphy."

Samuelson's one constructive suggestion was to dismantle or reconstruct the teachers unions so that the incompetent can be fired. Even the best principal can't make a rotten apple a prize winner. He thinks the schools "result in huge wastage that is ultimately measured in lost human potential." Thank goodness for homeschooling!

> *The reasonable man adapts himself to the world; the unreasonable one persists in trying to adapt the world to himself. Therefore all progress depends on the unreasonable man.*
>
> — George Bernard Shaw, "Maxims for Revolutionists"

## THE "NOT SO DUMB" BOOKS

**"DUMBTH"**, by Steve Allen. Humorist, composer, author, actor, and lecturer Steve Allen has coined the word "dumbth" as a shorthand term for the muddle-headedness he believes has become characteristic of our society: education that fails to educate, airline mishaps, military errors, incompetence in private industry, and scores of similar cases that indicate that "the United States is suffering from a severe and worsening case of 'dumbth.'" The second half of the book is devoted to Allen's proposed solutions, beginning with the addition of "a fourth R" — reasoning — to the traditional reading, 'riting, and 'rithmetic. Then he offers 81 "rules" for good thinking, arguing that *thinking well* is a skill like any other, and must be studied, learned, practiced, and mastered. Code BT, $20.

**DUMBING US DOWN: The Invisible Curriculum of Compulsory Schooling**, by John Taylor Gatto. Several essays based on some of John's speeches about schools and education. A public school teacher for 26 years and three times named "Teacher of the Year," John's descriptions and criticisms of the public school system are wonderfully penetrating and scathing. In these essays, John doesn't speak of home-schooling, but he does advocate radical school reforms and a return to family- and community-centered learning. (His insight into the faults of public schooling is so clear, one can't help wondering why he stayed in it so long.) Code NSP, $9.95.

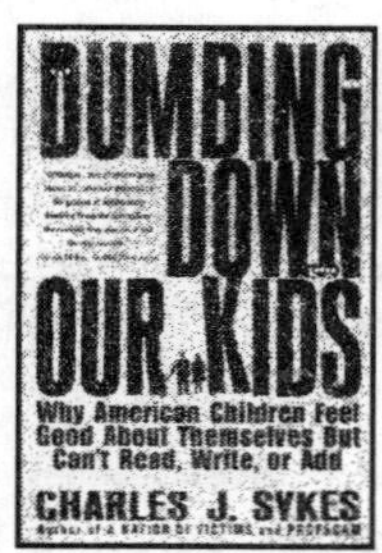


**DUMBING DOWN OUR KIDS: Why American Children Feel Good About Themselves but Can't Read, Write, or Add**, by Charles J. Sykes. This is not a book about homeschooling, but if you ever wonder why you homeschool, or are contemplating it but not sure if you want to, this book will put your mind at rest. An excellent analysis of why the public system is failing a large number of children, and some reasonable suggestions about what to do about it. Sykes attacks the religion of self-esteem and current math and language programs, and takes a critical look at the Goals 2000 program. Sykes argues that the implementation of national education standards would violate First Amendment rights. This critique of Goals 2000 is the reason I think every homeschooler should read this book. Code STM, $14.95.

## LEGAL ISSUES

I don't like politics. I don't like protests, meetings, lawyers, school principals (on principle), or school boards. Donn and I put years into being politically active, and we finally felt we had done enough. We just wanted to raise our family in peace and not deal with any more public issues, but we have always felt we have a responsibility to ensure the freedom of education for those yet to come. Like it or not, we all need to be constantly aware of what legal decisions are being made. There are a number of political groups working, within and outside the homeschooling community, to increase regulation of homeschooling. I feel it is our responsibility to understand what they are doing, and to ensure that everyone's freedom to homeschool in his own way is protected. We should all make a contribution. Those who invest nothing shouldn't be surprised if that's all they get.

**TAKING CHARGE THROUGH HOME SCHOOLING: Personal and Political Empowerment**, by Larry and Susan Kaseman. "Empowerment," say the authors, "includes identifying options and realizing that we can make choices and act on them, that we can take charge." Taking charge begins with making one's own choices about education (or anything else), which in itself is a political action, but the freedom to choose can be regained and held only by being politically active; i.e., by being aware of laws and lawmaking trends that affect homeschooling, and by taking an active part in influencing those laws. This is a very clear, comprehensive explanation of the many ways in which laws are made and how they can be influenced, and should certainly be read by anyone faced with legal or social opposition to home-schooling. Although the greater part of this book is concerned with political involvement, I think the Kasemans' suggestions regarding the everyday experience of home-schooling are just as important and useful, and make this a very valuable book even for those who don't feel ready to become politically active, or for whom just the decision to teach at home is sufficient challenge. $12.95 plus $2 shipping and handling from Koshkonong Press, 2545 Koshkonong Rd., Stroughton, WI 53589.

I think this book is more important now than ever. Although homeschooling is now legal across North America and there are more homeschoolers than ever before, there is also a stronger movement to regulate and control it than ever before. If you don't believe this or are just unaware of this move toward outside governmental regulation, read *Home Education Magazine*. Having won our freedom to teach at home, we now need to protect it.

➧ **THE TYRANNY OF GOVERNMENT SCHOOLING** is a 45-minute audiocassette by John Taylor Gatto on the advantages of alternative schooling and why compulsory attendance devastates our youth in public school. Call 800-326-0996 or write: Laissez Faire Books, Dept. C177, 938 Howard St., #202, San Francisco, CA 94103, for current price and shipping.

**In the Newspaper!**
August 1998. Hey, Wal-Mart has found us! Available only online or by phone. You can now get a five-piece homeschool curriculum set: complete book of phonics (ages 4-8), letters (upper- and lowercase), comprehensive curriculum (Grade 1), enrichment math/reading (Grades 1-2), and time/money flashcards. www.walmart.com; 800-966-6546. Sound good? Maybe.

**LUNO** — Learning Unlimited Network of Oregon. Literate, informative, confusing, sensible, outrageous newsletter with articles, news items, word puzzles, puns, book reviews, dialogues, monologues, etc. Send $1 for a sample to Gene Lehman, 31960 S.E. Chin St., Boring, OR 97009. Gene also has some great learning materials: phonetic building blocks (you can make yourself), English Taut or Naught, Grammar for Groanups, Limer-Ricks, and more. Ask him for more information.

***Revised*** — **ALTERNATIVES IN EDUCATION: Family Choices in Learning**, by Mark and Helen Hegener, publishers of *Home Education Magazine*. Capsule introductions to the philosophies and works of Rudolph Steiner, Maria Montessori, Jean Piaget, John Dewey, Herbert Kohl, A.S. Neill, Ivan Illich, John Holt, Jonathan Kozol, James Herndon, and George Dennison. Good reading and good ideas to stimulate your thinking. Code HA, $20.95.

---

*A mind, like a home, is furnished by its owner, so if one's life is cold and bare he can blame none but himself.*

— Louis L'Amour, *Bendigo Shafter*

## EXCELLENT MISCELLANEOUS RESOURCES

An excellent online site for resources and thoughtful writing is Karl Bunday's site: learninfreedom.org. Among many other interesting writings, you'll find a listing of colleges and universities that have accepted homeschoolers.

**Montessori World Educational Institute**, P.O. Box 3808, San Luis Obispo, CA 92403. Home-study courses, plus many other programs and materials. They have the **MONTESSORI AT HOME — COMPLETE GUIDE TO TEACHING YOUR PRESCHOOLER AT HOME**, by Heidi Anne Spletz. For information on consulting, write: American Montessori Consulting, P.O. Box 5062, Rossmoor, CA 90721.

I'm sure we're all aware that finishing "school" doesn't mean we stop learning. Bob Dylan said it very nicely: "He not busy being born is busy dying." The **SELF-UNIVERSITY NEWSLETTER** is dedicated to lifelong learning. Many interesting articles and book reviews on a variety of topics for the thoughtful reader and the perpetually curious. www.autodidactic.com/selfnews.htm.

I believe one of the changes we'll see in homeschooling in the coming years will be the growth of resource centers where children and adults can share resources, ideas, and the joy of learning together. The Coalition for Self-Learning has coordinated the writing of a new book, **CREATING LEARNING COMMUNITIES**, edited by Ron Miller. The book is brimming with creative ideas for starting this type of center, with examples of how it has already been done. Furthermore, the book presents ideas for making these centers into community learning centers, bringing together learners of all ages within a community, not just homeschoolers. Contributors include well-known homeschool experts, leading thinkers in the field of alternative education, and some people whose names you won't recognize but who have extremely valuable contributions and observations about exploring creative educational opportunities. A book with a vision for the future. $21.95 from The Foundation for Educational Renewal, P.O. Box 328, Brandon, VT 05733; call 800-639-4122 to order. The book can also be read online at www.CreatingLearningCommunities.org.

**CREATING A COOPERATIVE LEARNING CENTER: An Idea Book for Homeschooling Families**, by Katharine Houk, co-founder of The Alternative Learning Center and executive director of the Alliance for Parental Involvement in Education (AllPIE). This book is just off the press and the timing couldn't be better. Homeschooling is, for the most part, currently done in the isolation of our own homes. I hope this is going to change in the near future. As Katharine says in her book, "We are going to be moving from isolated individuals to support groups and conferences to learning centers, combining autonomy with connectedness." A learning center is a benefit to individuals of all ages, families, and communities. Katharine explains how these centers can combine flexibility, creativity, and a diversity of people with resources to make each center uniquely fit the needs of those using it. Katharine started her learning center with just a couple of families and "a dream of honoring the uniqueness of each person while creating vital connections between people of all ages." Think about it! It contains all the benefits of our individual learning at home and extends into the community at large, enlarging the possibilities and taking advantage of each community's special people and resources. What a marvelous opportunity for our children! And for us. The book includes all the information you need to start your own center. Don't just dream about it — do it. Katharine says, "If you build it, they will come!" She practically begs you to steal and redesign her ideas to fit your own needs. Included are practical suggestions for every step of the way and some useful forms. You'll find tips on organization, planning, decision-making, building a philosophy, money matters and financing, and much more. $16.95 plus $2.50 shipping from Longview Publishing, 29 Kinderhook St., Chatham, NY 12037. New York residents add sales tax.

Help for charter schools can be found online at www.uscharterschools.org. This excellent site has information and resources for those already involved in a charter school and for those seeking information about starting one. You'll find out how to start and run a charter school, a profile of existing schools, state information and contacts, a discussion group, and a resource directory.

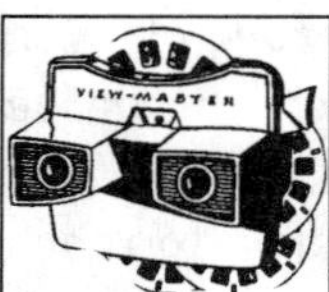

**VIEW-MASTER** is one of the cheapest, most enjoyable teaching aids. As you probably know, each View-Master set contains three disks, each with seven full-color stereo scenes, giving a very realistic three-dimensional view. Easily mastered, perhaps with a little help, by a two-year-old. Most subjects are of interest to all ages, including adults. Hundreds of subjects, including classical literature, Bible stories, history, nature, science, world travel, cartoons, TV shows, and many more. Most packets are $5 or less. The individual handheld viewer is about $5. With a View-Master battery-powered projector, pictures can be projected on a screen or white cardboard for group enjoyment, although the projected picture does not have the 3-D effect. Write for catalog: Worldwide Slides, 7427 Washburn Ave. S., Minneapolis, MN 55423.

**CHEEZ! UNCLE SAM**, by Ed Nagel. "The story of a long, brave, and resourceful struggle against an indifferent and often corrupt government, which all of us who care about children may have to wage one day, in one form or another." (John Holt) "The author ignores all the rules that stipulate serious education books must be boring, over-written, and void of useful content." (*The New Mexican*) "Moves fast, strikes deep, hits hard." (Jonathan Kozol) 220 pages. $10 postpaid from SFCS Publications, P.O. Box 2241, Santa Fe, NM 87501.

**AN "A" IN LIFE: Famous Home Schoolers**, by Mac and Nancy Plent. As a homeschool parent it's always nice to see what some outstanding homeschoolers have achieved. If you are encountering resistance to homeschooling from parents, grandparents, friends, or school officials, this book will give you information you can use when talking about the unlimited future homeschooling can offer. You'll find people listed here from many professions and differing ways of life. You'll also find out about many famous people you may never have known were homeschooled. Biographies are very brief, but make their point. As much as I enjoyed reading about all these people, I found the end of the book, where the Plents have pulled together the unifying threads among all these people and what we can learn from them, particularly interesting. Code UN, $8.50.

**REAL LIVES: Eleven Teenagers Who Don't Go to School**, edited and with an introduction by Grace Llewellyn. Yes, real lives. All 11 teens who tell their own stories in their own words are unschoolers and learning all the time, in their own way. An empowering book for kids who want role models in autodidactic learning. Not a story of genius, but of accomplishment through self-directed learning within and outside standard academic fields. Code LH, $17.

**PATHS OF LEARNING: Options for Families and Communities** is a new magazine with articles on schooling, unschooling, democratic schools, and much more. I found stimulating articles about living education from many different and interesting perspectives by some well-known authors, such as Ron Miller, Pat Farenga, Herbert Kohl, and Joseph Chilton Pearce, and other contributions from people I'd never heard of who had excellent ideas to contribute. To subscribe: *Paths of Learning*, P.O. Box 328, Brandon, VT 05733-9903. 1 yr./3 issues, $19.95; 2 yrs./6 issues $35. From their mission statement: "The purpose of this journal is to encourage an understanding of education as a means of nourishing holistic personal development and a sustainable, democratic, and peaceful community life." You can find their resource center on the web at www.PathsofLearning.net.

**MY LIFE AS A TRAVELING HOMESCHOOLER: In the Words of an 11-Year-Old**, by Jenifer Goldman. Jenifer shares her thoughts and feelings about her public and private school experiences before becoming a homeschooler. She also shares her thoughts about traveling with her uncle, Jerry Mintz (of *AERO* magazine, now titled *The Education Revolution)*, to various meetings about alternative schools and education. For current price write: Solomon Press Publishers, Education Division, 417 Roslyn Rd., Roslyn Heights, NY 11577.

**School Zone Publishing,** 1819 Industrial Dr., P.O. Box 777, Grand Haven, MI 49417; 800-846-5030; www.schoolzone.com. School Zone offers very good, inexpensive workbooks and materials, particularly for younger children.

One of our first purchases when we began teaching at home was a rubber stamp with our school name on it. It was almost a form of magic: Purchase orders with our name stamped on them often obtained sizable discounts from school supply companies, and the Department of Education treated us more seriously. When we loaned books, we'd stamp our school name inside the front cover, as a reminder to the borrower. A rubber stamp isn't an essential, but it's certainly a big help. The stamp we've been selling for several years is the highest quality ("hard" rubber that doesn't wear out) for the lowest price that we've found. This is approximately the actual size of the stamp:

**YOUR NAME IN ALL CAPS**
**Your Street Address Can Go Here**
**Your City, State, and Zip Here**
**Fourth Line Optional**

The stamp doesn't have to be your name and address, of course; you can add your school name, or it can be a bank endorsement stamp or a message stamp, with any wording you want. One year, we gave name-and-address stamps to our kids in their Christmas stockings. PRINT your name and address (or other wording) very clearly and carefully, including punctuation. Three lines, $12. Four lines, $13. Add $2 postage. Please allow three weeks for delivery.

Stamp pads, specify color: black, red, blue, green, or brown. $8 postpaid.

Replacement ink, specify color: black, red, blue, or green. $7 postpaid.

Donn had a good eye for detail and almost always succeeded in getting the stamp lined up neatly. I don't have his skill, and prefer a self-inking stamp that is easier to line up properly. Self-inking stamps: 3, 4, or 5 lines, $18. Specify black, red, blue, or green ink.

If you want a standard school textbook for any subject (pre-K through college), the best and cheapest source we've found is **Follett Educational**, 1433 Internationale Parkway, Woodridge, IL 60517; 800-621-4272. Follett cleans and reconditions used textbooks and resells them at reasonable prices. Name your school, then call them and request one of their catalogs.

## SELLING YOUR BOOK, CATALOG, MAGAZINE, OR OTHER HOMESCHOOL-RELATED PRODUCTS TO OTHER HOMESCHOOLERS

*Clues to what?*

**SELLING TO OTHER EDUCATIONAL MARKETS**, by Jane Williams, is a regularly updated guide for businesses that are interested in having their products sold or reviewed by home-school suppliers or other alternative educational businesses. It is published by Jane's company, Bluestocking Press, P.O. Box 2030, Shingle Springs, CA 95682-2030. Write for a free brochure if you're interested in buying or being listed in this book.

Brook Farm Books is listed in the book, inviting publishers and other businesses to submit material for possible review in *The Home School Source Book*. We receive hundreds of books and other items, and carefully consider them all. Sometimes the decision to review or not to review is difficult, but other times the material just doesn't impress us much. One such item was a 20-minute videotape (meant to sell for $24.95!) that didn't impress us at all, and it's not included in our reviews, but it gave us a chuckle anyway even before we opened the package. It was titled "**CLUES TO GOOD READING**," and was addressed to *Donna* Reed, *Bluestocking Press, in Bridgewater, Maine.*

---

*You can tell the ideals of a nation by its advertisements.* — Norman Douglas

---

## HOME SCHOOL, HOME-SCHOOL, or HOMESCHOOL?

Usually I prefer "home-school," with a hyphen, although "public school" doesn't have one. I haven't thought up any impressive etymological arguments yet. I try to be consistent in spelling and punctuation, but if my word processor insists that there are only ten spaces left on the line, I usually drop the hyphen and the intervening space rather than carry six letters over to the next line. I admit that's not consistent, but it's economical. I often hear or read "I home-school my children," but I've never heard "I public-school my children." I think the form with the strongest support so far is "homeschool" — one word, no hyphen. Would it surprise you to learn that some people take this problem very seriously? There are a lot of home-schoolers around, but I don't recall much reference to public-schoolers. A few people have written long arguments for one form or another, and I won't be very startled if some national organization soon puts it to a vote. The home(-)school movement may be divided by a hyphen more than by any other major issue. If you stare at the words long enough, none of them makes much sense. The same trick works with most of the arguments.

If you've noticed the variations in spelling home school, home-school, or homeschool, here's my explanation: Donn always preferred "home-school," and I've left his spelling in his work. I prefer "homeschool." It's just my preference, or maybe it's that I'm a lazy typist and leaving the hyphen out is easier. In quotes by other writers I've left the spelling the way it was originally written.

I'm curious — does anyone know if any group has voted on the proper way to spell home school/homeschool/home-school? I think the weight of common usage has decided the issue in favor of "homeschool," no hyphen, but I'm willing to hear arguments if someone is still inclined to belabor the point.

This attractive urn is for sale through the *Home Room* catalog for teachers. The ad suggests placing the urn "prominently in the classroom (to) serve as an amusing warning to parents, and encourage model behavior in students." Your choice of label: problem parents or problem students. Are you still debating with yourself about whether to homeschool or not?

Excerpts from **The Wit and Wisdom of Will Rogers**

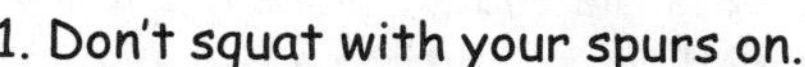

1. Don't squat with your spurs on.

2. Good judgment comes from experience, and a lot of that comes from bad judgment.

3. If you get to thinkin' you're a person of some influence, try orderin' somebody else's dog around.

4. After eating an entire bull, a mountain lion felt so good he started roaring. He kept it up until a hunter came along and shot him. The moral: When you're full of bull, keep your mouth shut.

5. If you find yourself in a hole, the first thing to do is stop diggin'.

6. Always drink upstream from the herd.

7. There's two theories to arguin' with a woman. Neither one works.

8. When you give a lesson in meanness to a critter or a person, don't be surprised if they learn their lesson.

9. When you're throwin' your weight around, be ready to have it thrown around by somebody else.

10. The quickest way to double your money is to fold it over and put it back in your pocket.

11. Never miss a good chance to shut up.

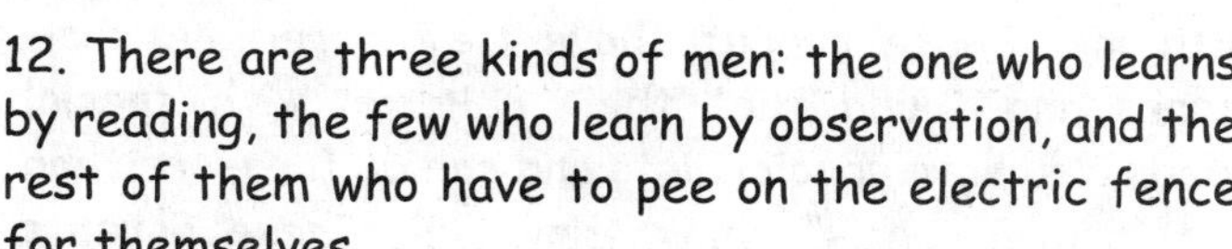

12. There are three kinds of men: the one who learns by reading, the few who learn by observation, and the rest of them who have to pee on the electric fence for themselves.

# SPECIAL EDUCATION

There are numerous resources for the gifted and disabled. You could spend a lot of time writing or investigating everything I've found and still wonder which items are really useful. I've limited the listings here to items and organizations I know and trust based on what have I learned from parents homeschooling children with ADHD, severe dyslexia, or other physical and mental problems.

First and foremost: If the "professionals" and "experts" give up on your child or tell you he will never read or learn independent skills, don't believe everything they say. I'm not suggesting you deny there is a problem. I'm simply passing on what I have learned from parents who have shared their special stories with me. These parents have met incredible challenges and found that their children with special needs also have special gifts and can do far more than the "professionals" think they can. These parents have found that they need to be more creative in their parenting.

These parents say patience — a lot of it — is essential. Also, children with special needs especially benefit from being read to. If these children can't read for themselves, you can read to them and open up a world they are unable to enter without your help. All children want to do the things they see other children doing. When you read to these special children, you are providing them with an example. Reading can become a goal for them, but without the pressure to perform. Many children who are unable to read on their own at the "normal" time learn to compensate with excellent memories, and can hear and retain incredible amounts of knowledge and information.

Along with patience, you will need imagination and flexibility to accommodate and stimulate these minds that march to their own drummers.

Don't give up. One mother wrote to me: "I have particularly noted over the years that what is impossible today comes magically later on. It has happened time and time again, and is a good plug for 'waiting until they're ready."

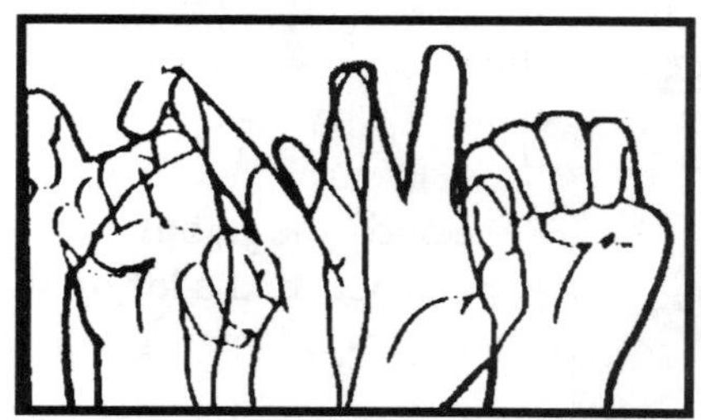

### RESOURCES FOR SIGN LANGUAGE AND THE HEARING-IMPAIRED

If you are hearing-impaired, I'm sure you know the difference between ASL (sometimes referred to as Ameslan), SEE, and PSE. If you're not hearing-impaired but you're interested in learning Sign Language, you should know that ASL (American Sign Language) is the standard. It qualifies as a foreign language in many school districts. The grammatical construction is unlike English. The books *Sign With Me* and *Joy of Signing* (below) are both ASL programs. SEE, which stands for Signing Exact English, is easier to learn, but is not used by the deaf community. PSE is referred to as Pidgin Signed English. It falls somewhere between ASL and SEE.

**Sign Language**. Our three girls began studying Ameslan — American Sign Language for the deaf — after reading about Helen Keller. They frequently told each other "secrets" with it, very pleased that Jean and I didn't know what they were saying. Cathy entered a 4-H speaking contest with the subject of Nim, a chimpanzee who signs to humans and other chimpanzees, and illustrated her speech with appropriate signs. (She won two first prizes and one second.) Since then, Cathy has been in several situations in which knowledge of Sign Language has been an asset: counselor in a girls' summer camp where one of the campers was deaf, working in a public library where several customers were deaf, and occasionally meeting deaf people in her travels who have been very glad to meet someone who could speak with them. More recently, Jean has studied Ameslan, and has had occasion to use it. Whether or not Sign Language will ever be of actual practical use to you or your children, it's fun to learn and to use — and it helps one to think of what it must be like to be dependent on Sign Language for communication.

I loved learning Sign Language. I studied it at a community college with a teacher who had lost her hearing later in life. Although she could speak English very well, the class was conducted in Sign Language only. Those first couple of classes were a real challenge! I made deaf friends, and the more I learned of their language the more fascinated I became. It may look simple, and much of it is, but don't be deceived. Sign Language is made up of many signs and, like all languages, involves more than simply spelling out words. The more you learn, the more complex it becomes: The grammatical structure is unique, and facial expression and body language play a complex role. If you or your kids have only a casual interest in learning Sign Language, much can be learned and enjoyed without getting into the complexities. There is a video of signed poetry (and I wish I could remember the name of it!) that is worth watching even if you're not interested in learning the language. Literally, it is pure poetry in motion, a true art form, and extremely moving — no poetry I know of in a spoken language is comparable.

**THANK YOU**

Move vertical fingers from lips forward to become "supine" hand.

The manual alphabet is not difficult to learn and is a good introduction to signing. **THE POCKET DICTIONARY OF SIGNING,** by Rod Butterworth and Mickey Flodin, contains the alphabet, along with numbers and simple signs, all presented in alphabetical form. There's a very good introduction to the basic hand shapes used. A good basic dictionary. 223 pages. Code BT, $6.95.

**THE PERIGEE VISUAL DICTIONARY OF SIGNING,** by Rod Butterworth and Mickey Flodin. The most comprehensive alphabetized guide to American Sign Language available. Includes history of signing, tips, inflection, synonyms, precise pictures of each sign, and much more. Organized by alphabet, not subject. 478 pages, Code BT, $15.95.

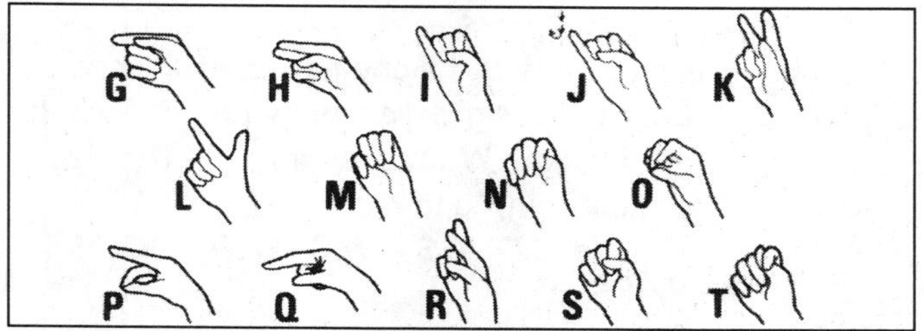

**MY ABC SIGNS OF ANIMAL FRIENDS**, by Ben Bahan and Joe Dannis. The authors graduated from Gallaudet University (for the hearing-impaired) and have years of experience working with both the hearing and deaf communities. The book begins with simple directions for learning the signs on the following pages. Each page shows one letter of the manual alphabet and one animal that helps to illustrate how to sign its name. The complete manual alphabet is illustrated inside the front and back covers. For young learners who are curious or parents learning to sign with a very young hearing-impaired child. Code GH, $8.95.

**MY FIRST BOOK OF SIGN LANGUAGE**. Slightly more advanced than the book above. Each page shows a letter of the alphabet and its sign, plus several pictures illustrating how to sign words that begin with that letter. Basic vocabulary: girl, boy, green, friend, man, woman, who, what, where, why, numbers 1 to 12, days of the week, thank you, happy, sad, etc. Code TRL, $3.50.

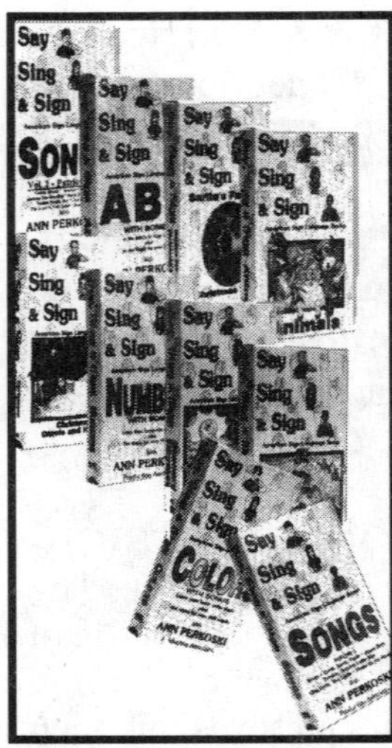

**SAY, SING, AND SIGN VIDEOS**. I don't know why there aren't more signing videos. There should be, because it's easier to learn to sign accurately when you can see someone do it. There are seven videos; they're entertaining and there are learning songs to sing and sign. A booklet accompanies each video. Ages 5 to 12 and all beginners. Code CS, $14.95 each except *ABC*, which is $19.95. Specify title.

**ABC** — Learn the alphabet and 50 basic signs.
**NUMBERS** — Learn numbers from 1 to 1,000. Lots of songs with signing activities.
**COLORS** — Learn colors and many new useful words.
**ANIMALS** — Learn the signs for many animals while you sing and sign "Froggie Went a-Courtin'," "The Bear Went Over the Mountain," and more.
Other titles include **SONGS**, **MOTHER GOOSE**, **NURSERY RHYMES**.

**SIGNS FOR ME**, by Ben Bahan and Joe Dannis. More advanced than their book above, this book introduces common vocabulary such as household items, family, emotions, safety, and more. Signs are organized by category: verbs, adjectives, nouns, pronouns, number signs, and manual alphabet. This book merits special praise because it introduces facial expressions, which are essential to signing accurately. It also shows signs clearly with the printed word to incorporate learning to write. A good bridge between beginning and advanced books. This book is also available in Spanish, Cambodian, Hmong, Lao, Tagalog, and Vietnamese. Well illustrated. Code GH, $12.95.

**THE JOY OF SIGNING**, by Lottie Riekehof. Excellent and well illustrated. Contains many useful signs for everyday conversation. I have this one and have used it a lot. Large paperback, 352 pages. Code BT, $21.99.

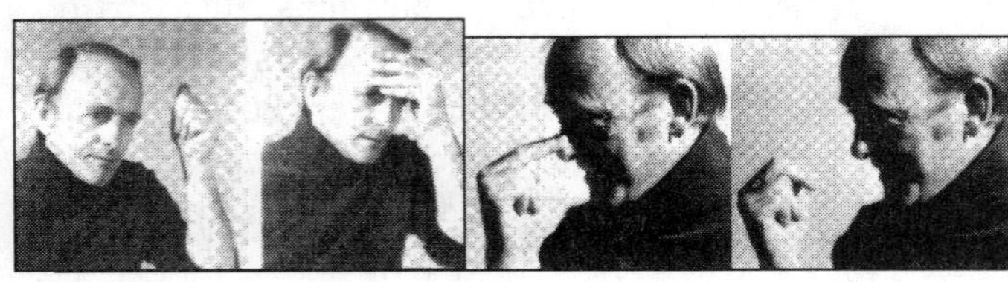

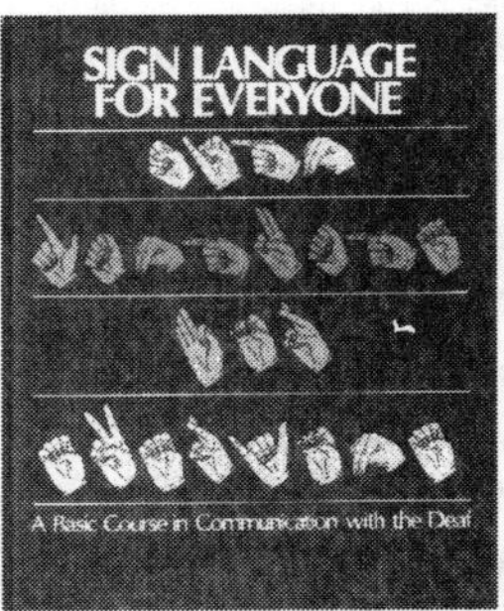


**SIGN LANGUAGE FOR EVERYONE,** by Cathy Rice. Nice introduction to signing. Rice begins by giving a general introduction to the language and goes on through 12 lessons to more complex signing. It's too demanding for a youngster who's simply curious, except for the nice, clear pictures of how to sign that are *not* in dictionary form but organized by subject and related signs. 171 pages. Code BT, $19.99.

**SIGNING MADE EASY**, by Rod Butterworth and Mickey Flodin. Complete program for learning Sign Language. Includes sentence drills and exercises for increased comprehension and signing skill. Another classic. The first part of the book teaches the basic concepts of Sign Language. The other half has thematic lessons. Excellent resource. Code BT, $12.95.

**Sign Language Materials**. Books, video and audio cassettes, teaching supplies, and more. Free catalog. Joyce Media Inc., P.O. Box 57, Acton, CA 93510.

**Sign Language Materials.** Free catalog. Garlic Press, 100 Hillview Lane, #2, Eugene, OR 97401.

**SAY IT BY SIGNING**. It's almost impossible to learn Sign Language properly without seeing it. This 60-minute video (VHS) will get you started properly with the basics. For older learners than the videos above. Code AF, $34.95.

**YOU CAN LEARN SIGN LANGUAGE!**, by Jackie Kramer and Tali Ovadia. More than 300 words in pictures. Organized by topics such as family, sports, your room, feelings, clothes, school, a party, and more. Ages 5 to 12. Code TRL, $4.95.

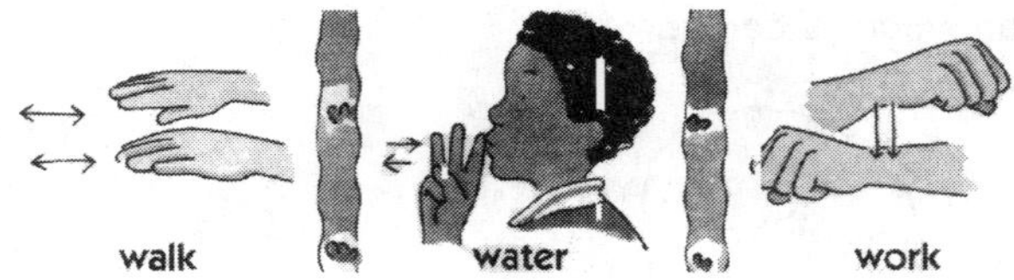


**For the Deaf and Hearing-Impaired**. Many books for all ages about deafness, Sign Language, parents with deaf children, deaf parents, signed English dictionary, sign/word flashcards, coloring books captioned with signs, first books using signs, children's fiction about children with deafness, and more. Gallaudet University Press, 800 Florida Ave. NE, Washington, DC 20002.

Microsoft's website for the hard-of-hearing is microsoft.com/enable.

Great help for **hearing parents of deaf homeschoolers** from Marilyn Agenbroad, 116 Jerome, Silverton, OR 97381; 503-872-8451; agie@ncn.com. There is a $6 charge for her newsletter.

**DEAF MOMS HOMESCHOOLING NEWSLETTER**. For deaf parents homeschooling hearing children. Write: c/o Vanessa Kramer, 602 S. West St., Carlinville, IL 62626-2110.

You can find various resources for learning Sign Language and an animated signing dictionary at www.deafworldweb.org/sl.

**Boys Town Press**, 14100 Crawford St., Boys Town, NE 68010 has a useful catalog that includes Sign With Me, a program that can help your whole family to sign and communicate with your deaf child.

## RESOURCES FOR THE BLIND AND DYSLEXIC

**Recording for the Blind and Dyslexic** offers recorded books: literature and educational material, including textbooks, on tape. 20 Roszel Road, Princeton, NJ 08540.

**FREE Braille and Audio Books** are available from the National Library Service for the Blind and Physically Handicapped. To apply, call and leave a message at the NLS: 800-424-9100.

**The Braille Institute** offers a publication called **EXCEPTIONS**, an anthology of literature produced annually in Braille. Also ask for the current Calendar of Facts. 741 N. Vermont Ave., Los Angeles, CA 90029-9988

The **National Association for the Visually Handicapped**, 305 E. 24th St., New York, NY 10010, offers an excellent series of free publications for the visually impaired (all ages) and free newsletters for youth (*In Focus*) and adults (*Seeing Clearly*).

## GENERAL RESOURCES

**NATHHAN** (NATional cHallenged Homeschoolers Associated Network) is a marvelous non-profit organization dedicated to providing encouragement to families homeschooling children with special needs. You will find help and caring support for yourself as well as for your children. NATHHAN publishes some of their own resources and lists many others. Families share their experiences. You will learn how to create a support system and discover new as well as tried-and-true methods of teaching and living well with disabled children. They even have a lending library! There is some Christian content, but if you are not a Christian please don't disregard this valuable resource. NATHHAN, 5383 Alpine Rd. SE, Olalla, WA 98359; 206-857-4257, fax 206-857-7764; NATHANEWS@aol.com; www.nathhan.com

**SUCCEEDING WITH LD**, by Jill Lauren, M.A. The common label LD can mean anything: learning difference, learning difficulty, learning disorder, learning disability. However, you will learn (from reading these 20 true stories by people, ages 12 to 62, who have overcome the labels and the difficulties) that it is possible for those with LD to live a satisfying and successful life. You will find straight talk about learning problems and the resulting emotional difficulties, and how these difficulties were overcome. Answers to common questions about LD plus a resource list for students, parents, and teachers. Inspiring. Code FS, $14.95.

See "Global Awareness" for the **Directory of American Youth Organizations**. There are some listings just for disabled young people, but a note at the front of the book says that many organizations feel disabilities do not present any barriers that would limit participation. If you don't ask, you'll never know.

**New Horizons for the Air Traveler With a Disability** describes accommodations, facilities, and services that are required to be available and accessible. 33 pages. Order #601D. Free from: R. Woods, Consumer Information Center-7B, P.O. Box 100, Pueblo, CO 81002.

**Center for Applied Research in Education** has a program called Sound Out to help special-needs students master letter/sound associations. P.O. Box 11071, Des Moines, IA 50380-1071.

**COMPUTER RESOURCES FOR PEOPLE WITH DISABILITIES**. $14.95 from the Foundation for Technology Access, 2173 E. Francisco Blvd., Suite L, San Raphael, CA 94901.

**LINC** (Learning Independence Through Computers) is a resource center that provides opportunities for children and adults with disabilities to use computer technology to achieve independence. LINC "is committed to the principle that every person with a disability should have access to the benefits of computer technology, regardless of ability level, age, income, or national origin." More than 40 affiliates across the country. LINC, 28 E. Ostend St., Baltimore, MD 21230; www.linc.org.

**TUESDAY'S CHILD MAGAZINE**. A magazine for parents of children with disabilities. Wonderful attitude and a wealth of useful articles and information. Advertising related to your needs. P.O. Box 270046, Fort Collins, CO 80527.

**Camp Wilderness**, for boys ages 10 to 17, is run by Talisman Schools, Inc. A full-time therapeutic wilderness program, which also has a summer camp for those specially challenged with learning problems. Contact Talisman, 601 Camp Elliot Rd., Black Mountain, NC 28711.

Camp opportunities for the disabled can be found in **PETERSON'S SUMMER OPPORTUNITIES FOR KIDS AND TEENAGERS**, reviewed in "Family Living."

On the Internet at www.homeworkcentral.com or www.nosweat.com (easy for kids to use) is the very best and most complete selection of resources for physical and learning disabilities. More than 700 carefully selected sites with links to more information. Homework Central provides this site free of advertising as a public service.

If you are looking for information about dealing with ADHD using alternative methods, check out this site compiled by Teresa Gallagher: borntoexplore.org. You'll find great support material here.

If you are working with emotionally disturbed kids — especially those showing great resentment coupled with a tendency toward violence — I recommend **GETTING THRU TO KIDS: Problem Solving With Children Ages 6-18**, by Phillip Mountrose. Mountrose is very perceptive and presents an excellent strategy for helping kids gain control and modify their own behavior (without resorting to power struggles or rewards). $11.95 plus $3 shipping from Holistic Communications, P.O. Box 41152, Dept. 2, Sacramento, CA 95841-0152; 800-644-KIDS. California residents add 7.75% tax.

If you would like to give someone you care about the opportunity to explore and enjoy music, *Sound Choices* in "Music" has resources for music therapy, and includes resources for the physically disabled and hearing- or sight-impaired.

Textbooks geared to children with learning disabilities are available from AGS (American Guidance Service), 4201 Woodland Rd., P.O. Box 99, Circle Pines, MN 55014-1796; 800-328-2560. Free catalogs.

**Learning disAbilities Resources** has a useful free catalog. P.O. Box 716, Bryn Mawr, PA 19010.

**NICHCY** (National Information Center for Children and Youth with Disabilities) has many good resources. P.O. Box 1492, Washington, DC 20013-1492.

## AUTISM

**Spectrum Children's Support** offers support for yourself and information to help you and your kids: resources, treatments, tutoring for autistic kids, and unique ways to make your life easier living with an autistic child. www.homestead.com/wholefamily/wholefamily1.html.

Tammy Glaser runs an e-mail list offering support for parents homeschooling autistic children. Write to her at tamglsr@sgi.net.

## RESOURCES FOR THE GIFTED

**YOU KNOW YOUR CHILD IS GIFTED WHEN ...**, by Judy Galbraith, M.A. This is a beginner's guide to help you decide if your child is gifted. Galbraith, who has had 20 years of experience working with the gifted, says, "If you think your child is gifted, you're probably right. You know your child better than anyone. ... In one study, a researcher found that parents were *better* at identifying giftedness than teachers." This basic guide explains the different ways in which children are gifted and offers many ideas for you to assist your gifted child. Done with honesty and a sense of humor. Code FS, $10.95.

**AMERICAN ASSOCIATION FOR GIFTED CHILDREN**, 1121 W. Main St., Suite 100, Durham, NC 27701. This non-profit organization based at Duke University publishes a free brochure, a newsletter three times a year ($3 per issue), and a homeschooling resource list ($3). In January 1996, they published "Homeschooling the Gifted Child," by Julie Stewart, and "Home Education: A Growing Trend," by Julie Blackwell. Ask about back issues.

**THE GIFTED KIDS' SURVIVAL GUIDE: For Ages 10 and Under**, by Judy Galbraith. This upbeat and informative perennial bestseller answers bright kids' questions about why they think and learn the way they do. Includes advice from hundreds of gifted kids. Illustrated, 72 pages. Code FS, $9.95.

**The GIFTED KIDS' SURVIVAL GUIDE: A Teen Handbook**, revised and expanded, by Judy Galbraith, M.A., and Jim Delisle, Ph.D. Contains a wealth of information and support for gifted teens. Galbraith and Delisle have spent years working in this field, and this book was written especially to help gifted teens sort themselves out and make the most of their potential. They write about what it means (and doesn't mean) to be gifted, how to have more control over your life, perfectionism, mistakes, goal setting, gender issues, stress, how to talk to parents, and much more. In this book, gifted teens have contributed their own thoughts about growing up, their education, and their choices (the good ones and the bad ones). At the back of the book is a useful listing of additional resources for parents and teens. This book is up-to-date and suggests web listings to explore. Highly recommended. 300 pages. Code FS, $15.95.

**THE SURVIVAL GUIDE FOR PARENTS OF GIFTED KIDS: How to Understand, Live With, and Stick Up for Your Gifted Child**, by Sally Yahnke Walker. The subtitle just about says it all! Authoritative information about giftedness, gifted education, problems, personality traits, and more. Friendly and inviting. You'll be glad you read this one. Code FS, $12.95.

**BOOKS FOR THE GIFTED CHILD, Part 2**, by Paula Hauser and Gail A. Nelson. A concise, annotated bibliography of intellectually challenging books for gifted children. Try your local or state library first, because the price is high. Code RRB, $49. (Strangely, *Books for the Gifted Child, Part 1*, is not available.)

# RESOURCES FOR LIVING WITH CHRONIC OR TERMINAL ILLNESS; DEATH AND DYING

**The Little Prince said, "It is only with the heart that one can see rightly. What is essential is invisible to the eye."**

Some may feel that this is an inappropriate chapter to include in a homeschool book. I haven't seen this type of information available for homeschoolers, which is precisely why it is here. We frequently read about celebrities who are dealing with serious illness or death, but the truth is that, eventually, everyone must learn to cope with these issues. We assume that old people will get sick and die. We expect that, but it isn't just old people who have serious medical problems. I hope with all my heart that you are not reading this because you have a child, a spouse, or another loved one with a chronic or life-threatening disease, but if you are, there is help and comfort to be found. Illness and dying are a normal part of all life cycles. It can be difficult, scary, and a great privilege to be a part of this passage.

To those of you who have had to deal with life crises, or are dealing with them now, I know the agony as well as the unbelievable and wonderful depth of relationship that can develop as you move through this experience together. I've seen relationships torn apart because of the stress this kind of crisis can create. You don't have to let this tear you apart. There is help and there is hope. It is possible to win all the battles and know you have been victorious in spirit — even in the face of death.

For those fortunate enough to have lived to this point in your lives without this kind of struggle, I hope you will find ways to help others less fortunate. There are many ways you can make a significant difference. You do not need to feel or act like a hero to be one. You can become someone's hero by being a friend, helping with errands, or doing seemingly small chores; sometimes being a good listener is all that is needed. Sometimes people who are sick have trouble asking for help. Don't wait to be asked to do something. Look and see what needs to be done. You can also volunteer time at your local hospital visiting with patients. Ask the staff and the patients what is needed. Sometimes all that's needed is a friendly visit. You could read to patients, or just talk. If you have a talent, share it. Make music in the halls, or put on a play in the pediatric ward. If you want to help, you will find a way.

Bill Moyers has done an excellent series of shows for PBS called *On Our Own Terms*. I highly recommend this series, which illustrates the many options that are available for end-of-life care. You'll see stories of the dying (of various ages) and their families that demonstrate the courage, beauty, and peace that can be achieved with the right care and support system. You'll also see medical professionals and volunteers working to improve the current system. Someday each of us must face and deal with these issues. Being as comfortable with death and dying as we are with birth should be natural, but in our society this isn't so. Watching *On Our Own Terms* as a family or with extended family can help you all learn to discuss these personal issues with more comfort.

About ordering the books in this section: For those of you dealing with chronic or terminal illnesses, if you can afford to pay full price for these books, that would be nice. If it will put a strain on your already overloaded budget, please let me know, and I will gladly get them for you at our cost. This is one of my ways to begin repaying the many people who helped us.

**THE PDR FAMILY GUIDE TO PRESCRIPTION DRUGS**. You don't need this book to learn about ordinary prescriptions; your pharmacist can provide standard information. If you are dealing with serious illness and prescription drugs, though, this book will be an invaluable guide to uses, abuses, side effects, conflicting medications, and more. Code BT, $23.

**THE FOOD PHARMACY**, by Jean Carper. I don't believe in miracles, but good nutrition, vitamins, and wise use of herbs and healthy food can produce nearly miraculous results. Carper's work describes commonsense use of healthy foods to improve our lives and heal ourselves. Donn found real relief and improvement by using her suggestions. Tastes good, too! Code BT, $15.95.

Need help with transportation to a consultation or treatment? If your insurance won't pay, contact the **Air Care Alliance** (800-296-1217; www.aircareall.org) or the **National Patient Travel Center** (www.patienttravel.org). There's a similar service for cancer patients called the **Corporate Angel Network** (914-328-1313; www.corpangelnetwork.org).

**YOUNG PEOPLE AND CHRONIC ILLNESS: True Stories, Help, and Hope**, by Kelly Huegel. Huegel was diagnosed with Crohn's disease at age 12. She tells us that her book deals only with chronic, lifelong illness and does not address terminal illness, but I think it offers a wealth of information about coping with serious illness, on a daily basis, that can apply to most young people with chronic or terminal illness. The first section of the book contains the personal stories of young people coping with hemophilia, diabetes, epilepsy, asthma, cancer, inflammatory bowel disease, juvenile rheumatoid arthritis, congenital heart defect, and lupus. You'll find honest talk about their reactions to diagnosis, their feelings of fear and isolation, their struggles and dreams, and their sometimes difficult relationships with family and friends. The second section has very straightforward suggestions for learning to manage your illness, working with your doctor, talking about your illness with friends and family, fear of hospitals, and more. You will find lists of support groups and organizations as well as places to find up-to-date information about your illness. Code FS, $14.95.

---

*When one door of happiness closes, another opens; but often we look so long at the closed door that we do not see the one which has been opened for us.* — Helen Keller

**WE ARE NOT ALONE: Learning to Live With Chronic Illness**, by Sefra Kobrin Pitzele. Harold S. Kushner, author of *When Bad Things Happen to Good People*, said, "This is the most practical book on chronic illness I know. It is clear, complete, personal, and extremely helpful. I highly recommend it." Although written for adults facing this difficult, life-altering problem, this book delves into the repercussions for the whole family and how to deal with them as constructively as possible. Contents: "Who Promised Life Would Always Be Fair?"; "First, There Is the Diagnosis"; "Grieving Is Normal"; "In Sickness and in Health"; "But Who Will Take Me to the Zoo?"; "Keeping Your Friendships Growing"; "Your Health Care Team"; "The Circle of Stress"; "Illness and Pain"; "Comments on Depression"; "Blessed Are the Caregivers"; "Resting"; "A Whisper in the Night"; "Bodywork"; "Adaptive Living Strategies"; "Practical Matters"; and an extensive appendix for finding helpful organizations, products, services, and financial help in the U.S. and Canada. I like Pitzele's frankness; there isn't anything she doesn't discuss. Her journal excerpts have depth and warmth; while personal, they express what many cannot put into words. Pitzele was diagnosed with lupus, but this book deals with the problems faced by everyone with chronic illness. Code WKM, $9.95.

---

*To laugh often and much; to win the respect of intelligent people and the affection of children; to earn the appreciation of honest critics and endure the betrayal of false friends; to appreciate beauty; to find the best in others; to leave the world a bit better whether by a healthy child, a garden patch, or a redeemed social condition; to know even one life has breathed easier because you have lived. This is to have succeeded.*

— Ralph Waldo Emerson

---

**LOVE, MEDICINE, AND MIRACLES**, by Bernie S. Siegel, M.D. Many doctors today rely increasingly on one or two of three ways of dealing with serious illness: drugs, radiation, and surgery. For many patients, none of these treatments works. Bernie Siegel tells about scores of "terminally ill" patients who gained partial or complete recovery after discovering the unity of their minds and bodies, an understanding that allowed them to heal themselves. He discusses the ways in which anyone can achieve the same understanding and healing. This is not a "new age," faith-healing message, but a sober examination of realities the medical establishment would rather not recognize. Reading Siegel will give you a different view of the medical profession. It can also awaken the healer within you. Donn used this book as a means to help himself, to take as much control of his situation as possible. I learned from this book how important it was to support his efforts and how I could best help him. It gave us the tools to work together. This book and the one below introduce new ways to heal yourself, while acknowledging the usefulness or necessity of conventional treatments at times. Code BT, $14.

**PEACE, LOVE, AND HEALING**, by Bernie S. Siegel, M.D. Further steps in the exploration of the mind-body unity the author discussed in the book above, continuing with many examples of "self-healing," and how anyone may live better, longer, healthier without conventional medicine. The most profound lesson I learned from this book is that it is possible to lose the battle for life yet win the war by living fully, deeply, with love and dignity. Code BT, $14.

**THIRD OPINION**, by John M. Fink. This is a comprehensive guide to alternative treatment centers around the world, everything from addresses, phone numbers, and contact names to philosophical approaches and methods of treatment. Also educational centers, information services, and support groups. It used to be a good idea to get a second opinion. If you're up against a killer disease, get a third opinion. Code BT, $16.95.

**Cancer Hotline**. For the latest information about cancer, causes, medical referral, consultation, support groups, and publications, call 800-4-CANCER (800-422-6237) or write: NCI, Cancer Information Service, NCI Building 31, Room 10A1B, Bethesda, MD 20205.

The **Bloch National Cancer Hotline** (800-433-0464) will put you in touch with someone who has had the same type of cancer and will help you deal with the initial fear and shock.

You can register to be a possible bone marrow donor. Call the American Bone Marrow Donor Registry at 800-736-6283 or the National Marrow Donor Program at 800-627-0690 for more information.

## DEATH, DYING, AND GRIEF

Elisabeth Kübler-Ross has written extensively on the subject of death and dying. She has extraordinary insights, and her books are well worth reading. They are found in almost all libraries and bookstores. If you can't find them, write to us for a list. We'll get them for you if you want them. *Dialogues on Death and Dying* and *Living in the Face of Death* are a couple of her titles.

The great need for healing and closure after losing someone you have loved deeply is an important part of continuing with your own life. There are various things you can do to help yourself and those around you. If death is not sudden, if you have some time to plan, visit this website: www.naturaldeathcare.org. This group sees death as a natural part of life. They feel strongly that care for the dying, whenever possible, should take place at home. You'll also find information about caring for the body after death, creating your own ceremonies, dealing with bureaucratic details, and much more.

**SOMETHING TO REMEMBER ME BY**. A very important book by Susan Bosak. I couldn't decide where to put this book. It's relevant here, but you need to see "Family Living" for details.

**FINAL PASSAGE: Sharing the Journey as This Life Ends**, by Barbara Harris Whitfield. I believe there is an existence beyond what we experience now. This book is about Whitfield's experiences working with the dying while observing and participating in the dying process. I offer it here in the hope that it will help ease the pain of this experience for someone else. This book will enable you to understand the process of dying, and what you can and can't do when faced with death — yours or that of someone you love. Understanding this process can bring some peace of mind and spirit. Code HC, $10.95.

**LIGHT ON AGING AND DYING**, by Helen Nearing. Nearing actually wrote only the forward of this book. The remainder is a variety of quotations and poetry she collected about aging, dying, and death, by some of the world's most profound writers from all religions, races, and creeds. Nearing speaks openly about the death of her husband, Scott (at the age of 99). Both Scott and Helen felt that the last stages of life are like all the other stages of life, a matter of choices that "can be a shiningness or shadowed. ... It can be a harrowing ordeal or a hallowed happening." You will soon realize, in reading this book, that as you contemplate aging and death you must also celebrate life; the two are inextricable. If religious content concerns you, you needn't worry; God is mentioned, but only in a universal sense. Most quotes make no reference to the word "God," and yet this is a book to be valued by the deeply religious, the agnostic, and the atheist alike, because it is a celebration of the human spirit. I particularly liked the following: "We are put on this earth to celebrate. You give it everything you have. Everything. That includes your death. The greatest thing you can do is possess your own death so that when it comes it is given, not taken. Honor your own death. It is a sacrament. ... Death renders life magnificent. ... Death walks beside one, and so does whatever one's sense of God is, or the sublime." (From an interview in *The Idler*, June 1989, by Scott Symons. Code TLB, $14.95.

**Hospice**. Do you know what hospice is and does? Here are some key points:

- Hospice concentrates on keeping patients free of pain and discomfort.
- Hospice offers more than just medical help. Patients and families can find help in spiritual, emotional, and practical matters.
- The patient is in charge of his or her care.
- Hospice involves the whole family as well as friends in end-of-life care and counseling before and after a loved one's death.
- Hospice offers advice and aid to caregivers.

For information write to the National Hospice and Palliative Care Organization, 1700 Diagonal Rd., Suite 300, Arlington, VA 22314; www.nho.org; or call the Hospice Helpline at 800-658-8898.

Related sites:
www.hospicefoundation.org. Information about how to select a hospice or how to be a hospice volunteer.
www.choices.org. Materials on advance directives and making end-of-life decisions.

**HELPING CHILDREN COPE WITH THE LOSS OF A LOVED ONE: A Guide for Grownups**, by William C. Kroen, Ph.D., LMHC; forward by Maria Trozzi, director of the Good Grief Program at Boston Medical Center. "To be able to grieve appropriately and cope with loss before, during, and after a death enables a child to grow up free of guilt, depression, anger, and fear. When we can help our children heal the pain of the deepest emotional wound — the death of a loved one — we are giving them important skills and understanding that will serve them the rest of their lives." Being empowered to help our children will also help us to grieve fully and to heal. This is the best book I've seen for adults who want to help children — from infancy through adolescence — cope with grief. Kroen answers our questions as parents, enabling us to help our children with their questions and emotions. Sensitive, with excellent suggestions for giving comfort and guidance. Code FS, $14.95.

**HOW CAN I HELP?**, by June Cerza Kolf. This is a very practical book with numerous suggestions for coping with grief and loss, whether in your family or that of a friend. Covers everything from how to talk to children, teens, and others about death to how to support others by taking on various tasks. Code FB, $12.95.

---

*If you would indeed behold the spirit of death, open your heart wide unto the body of life. For life and death are one, even as the river and the sea are one.*
— Kahlil Gibran

**HOW FAR TO HEAVEN?**, by Chara M. Curtis; wonderfully illustrated by Alfred Currier. Grandpa has died and a young girl discovers how close he really is, as she and her grandmother venture through an afternoon together. This poetic book will help forge new ties with the living and with those beyond this earth. Uplifting for children ages 4 and up and all adults. Hardcover. Code IA, $15.95.

**WHEN A FRIEND DIES: A Book for Teens About Grieving and Healing**, by Marilyn E. Gootman, Ed.D. Most books about grief are written for adults. This book, written especially for teens, is a welcome and needed addition to the field. Gootman speaks directly about the concerns of teens. She has included many quotes from teens about their feelings of loss, anger, guilt, and pain. If you have a grieving teen, this book will help. Gootman suggests to the teen reader that he share this book with others, including adults, so these others will have a better understanding of what he is going through. At the end of the book there are some excellent quotes about dealing with death and dying as well as inspirational quotes about living. Code FS, $9.95.

**ONE YOU LOVE IS DYING**, by James E. Miller. Nothing you read about coping with a loved one's dying will be easy. The radical adjustments in daily life in this situation create stress. The emotional upheaval you experience when someone you love is dying is like riding blindfolded on a roller coaster. This thought-provoking and sensitive book will not only help you, but be a valuable resource for the one dying. This is not a "how-to" manual; it is a "how-to-be" guide. There is some overlap with the above book; mostly they complement each other. Code WG, $5.95.

---

*That which dies in a man is only his five senses. That which continues to exist, beyond his senses, is immense, unimaginable, sublime.*

— Anton Chekhov

**GENTLE CLOSINGS: How to Say Goodbye to Someone You Love**, by Ted Menten. This book is a collection of true stories by a man who has dedicated his life to working with terminally ill and dying patients of all ages. There are hard-to-deal-with issues in this book, such as the difficulty of accepting that a child with AIDS is dying and how the child contracted AIDS, suicide, and unforeseen sudden death. This is a warm and gentle book with diverse suggestions about how to say goodbye to someone you love and don't want to lose. This book is about listening and learning, allowing laughter as well as tears, dealing with rage and anger, grieving and healing, making memories and talking, and learning to let go and move on. Menten doesn't set rules except to say there are no rules — to follow your heart and let the one who is leaving lead. Code RP, $14.95.

**AFTER GOODBYE: How to Begin Again After the Death of Someone You Love**, by Ted Menten. This book is about learning to grieve and learning to live again after someone you've loved has died. Again, there are no hard and fast rules for recovering, but there are things we can do to help ourselves, and to help others let go and work through the pain and back to life and living. This book is about pain and fear, meaning and understanding, and courage. Code RP, $14.95.

**WIDOW TO WIDOW**, by Genevieve Davis Ginsburg, M.S. Although written primarily for women, this book also addresses the problems faced by widowers. A compassionate guide by someone who survived the loss of a spouse and went on to found Widow to Widow Services. Ginsburg talks about real people, not clinical studies. She understands the shock, grief, and disorientation that come with losing a beloved. Drawing from her experience, and from that of those who have come to her for support, she offers practical advice for learning to live with grief and deal with mundane daily needs, and offers suggestions for moving on with life. She recognizes that everyone moves at his own pace through this process. A good book if you find yourself without your mate. There are special chapters for young widows, and other chapters for helping children. Code BT, $12.95.

Online support for those who are grieving is growing. The following sites are particularly helpful:
www.aarp.org/griefandloss is sponsored by the AARP. www.compassionatefriends.org is sponsored by Compassionate Friends, a group that supports families after the death of a child. All states have chapters of this organization. Call 630-990-0010.

**LOSING A PARENT**, by Fiona Marshall. This is an excellent guide to the emotions and realities of losing a parent. Marshall is extremely thorough in her coverage of a wide variety of situations viewed from a personal standpoint, as well as the changes in family dynamics that occur with the death of a parent. An excellent list of resources is included. Code BT, $12.95.

**ElderWeb** is devoted to the subject of caring for a parent or older loved one who lives far away. You can use this site to find out what type of services and care are available in a particular area. www.elderweb.com.

**THE CAREGIVER'S BOOK: *Caring for Another; Caring for Yourself***, by James E. Miller. This is an essential. Much has been written for those who are dying but not nearly enough for those who are caregivers. Miller's writing is simple, his perceptions personal and to the point. This book will help you explore your thoughts and feelings. It can be very difficult to allow time for yourself when someone you love needs you. Miller points out how essential this personal time is and how to be comfortable taking that time. There are many clinical books available on this subject. This one is practical and also speaks to the heart. Code WG, $14.99.

> *Death is the final stage of growth in this life. There is no total death. Only the body dies. The self or spirit, or whatever you may wish to label it, is eternal.*
> — Elisabeth Kübler-Ross, *Death: The Final Stage of Growth*

**Caregiver Survival Resources**. A comprehensive list of quality caregiving links on the Web. Includes general links as well as those for specific chronic illnesses. www.caregiver911.com

**COMFORT AND CARE IN A FINAL ILLNESS**, by June Cerza Kolf. This book has a good balance of suggestions for the one who is dying and for caregivers. Part one is written for the patient and deals with physical considerations, care options, emotional adjustments, and spiritual approaches. Part two is for caregivers. It will help you define your role as a caregiver and how to care for yourself at the same time so you avoid burnout. Good advice for dealing with your patient, listening and communication skills, physical care, suicide and euthanasia, dealing with anticipatory grief, final arrangements, and more. Code FB, $12.95.

---

> *May I try to tell you again where your only comfort lies? It is not in forgetting the happy past. People bring us well-meant but miserable consolations when they tell us what time will do to help our grief. We do not want to lose our grief, because our grief is bound up with our love and we could not cease to mourn without being robbed of our affections.*
> — Phillips Brooks

---

To every thing there is a season, and a time to every purpose under the heaven.

A time to be born, and a time to die; a time to plant, and a time to pluck up that which is planted;

A time to kill, and a time to heal; a time to break down, and a time to build up;

A time to weep, and a time to laugh; a time to mourn, and a time to dance;

A time to cast away stones, and a time to gather stones together; a time to embrace, and a time to refrain from embracing;

A time to get, and a time to lose; a time to keep, and a time to cast away;

A time to rend, and a time to sew; a time to keep silence, and a time to speak;

A time to love, and a time to hate; a time of war, and a time of peace.

---

This chapter is dedicated to Donn and Madge, who in their dying taught me many valuable lessons about living and loving. Thank you both. Death is the end of life as we've known it, but not of our relationship.

# HOMESCHOOLING AND "CULTURAL LITERACY"

Reflections on *Cultural Literacy: What Every American Needs to Know*, by E.D. Hirsch Jr.:

I went to school in southern Vermont in the 1940s and 1950s, and Jean went to school in suburban Illinois and a private high school in Colorado, just five years behind me. Three of our children — Cathy, Karen, and Derek — stayed at home with us through most or all of their "high school" education, and therefore have similar, if not superior, backgrounds. When we discuss key events in history or major works of literature, we usually understand each other very quickly; we learned the same basic information, and don't need to give each other long parenthetical explanations of our reference points before continuing a general discussion.

Our daughter Susan attended The Meeting School, a supposedly Quaker "alternative" boarding high school in southern New Hampshire, for two years. At least, it was founded by Quakers. She and I visited the school before her enrollment, and were very impressed by the informality, the large library, and the spacious grounds. The expectations Jean and I had of "alternative education" were that it would encompass most standard subjects, such as English, math, history, science, etc., but in a non-standard manner: i.e., without rote learning of dead facts without reflection, without quarterly exams, without grading of papers and performance, and so on. We soon realized, after Susan felt well established in the school and happy with many new friends, that the school's definition of "alternative," especially in some subjects, was very different from ours, and often depended largely on what the students felt like studying. Theoretically, that's the basis of "invited learning," and in theory I'm all for it. In practice, I need to see it working; if it isn't, I favor a little uninvited learning.

In one U.S. history course, Susan chose to concentrate on the role of women in U.S. history, which we thought was fine. A study of the important, but largely forgotten or ignored, roles of women in U.S. history should certainly give the student new perspectives on old concepts. Susan's final term paper on the subject, prepared with regular advice from a faculty adviser and awarded an A+, was an emotional defense of "rising feminism" through the ages, hardly touching any "historical" issues except that women have always been mistreated by a male-dominated society. Another student chose to study American history through its music, which we thought was a good idea; we suggested (through Susan) that he begin with Alan Lomax's *Folk Songs of North America*, which is almost a history course in itself. He began his "study" with Bob Dylan's later, "electrified" rock music, decided it was too tame, and devoted the rest of his time, including a four-week intercession, to being a Grateful Dead groupie, following the rock group from city to city, sleeping in his car and skipping meals so he could pay for rock concert tickets. And so on. All the students chose what we thought would be excellent behind-the-scenes approaches to history, and ended with little or no knowledge at all of even the most basic facts of U.S. history, such as the causes of the Civil War or of the two world wars, the significance or even the existence of the Monroe Doctrine, and relations between the United States and other countries. To the question, "Did you study U.S. history in school?" all the students will answer, "Yes," but their various impressions are more faulty and incomplete than those of the six blind men trying to determine what an elephant is.

And there are two more very good examples of the importance of Hirsch's message — that being "culturally literate" is to possess a large amount of shared knowledge of basic information about our world and our culture. Without that shared knowledge, says

Hirsch, communications fail, and then the undertakings; and that, he adds, is the moral of the story of the Tower of Babel.

Shared knowledge is neither more nor less than a kind of language that has evolved in our culture over many, many years; it provides a short-cut to effective communication.

If our family is sitting around the TV discussing a news item about some U.S. activity in the Middle East, someone may comment that it seems to be in violation of the Monroe Doctrine; for all of us, except Susan — through absolutely no fault of her own — many years of U.S. history and policy-making are summed up in that one reference, including many of the problems preceding Monroe's administration as well as more recent activities such as the never-declared Korean War. For someone unfamiliar with the Monroe Doctrine, a lengthy explanation may be necessary to make it relevant to the present discussion, and by that time everyone else has wandered off to play Ping-Pong.

The second example is my allusion to the six blind men. For most children of my generation, it's a familiar story; for many children growing up in the '70s and '80s, it's a mental blank. If you know the story, my point is made quickly and picturesquely with fewer than a dozen words; if you don't know the story, I must either tell it to you or use ten times as many words to communicate my thought to you.

Hirsch blames much of our society's decreasing shared knowledge on Jean-Jacques Rousseau and John Dewey, although he concedes that their ideas may have been carried to unreasonable extremes by their adherents. Until about 1960 or a little earlier, children's stories, literary heroes, and school subjects across the country were very similar, as were basic courses in secondary schools and universities, and such short-cuts in communication as I've described were easy and common. Then many leading educators decided that children were being made to memorize too many facts without being taught how to think about them. Public education changed almost overnight to emphasize "thinking skills" and "communication skills." At first, this seemed to be an important advance, but gradually people began to see that although children might have been learning how to think, they had nothing to think about. Publishers and teachers, not wanting to be accused of teaching dead facts, reduced history and science and literature to the bland consistency of vanilla pudding. Magazine articles complained that Johnny and Janie couldn't read, but no one seemed to realize that Johnny and Janie no longer *cared* about reading because their storybooks and textbooks were as exciting as yesterday's oatmeal. Today's students are still being taught "how to think," and are still being given very few facts or ideas to think about. They're absorbing their cultural knowledge from television and rock music because no one else is telling them anything of interest. There is very little on television about the Monroe Doctrine, and rock groups seldom sing about the Renaissance or the Reformation. Hollywood no longer makes movies about Joan of Arc or King Arthur or Lewis and Clark or Alexander Graham Bell or the Oklahoma Land Run. The people and events of the past that were a part of our everyday lives — in books, movies, radio programs, and even early television programs — are no more than blank faces and meaningless dates to most children today.

A friend in New Jersey wrote, "I told my husband I thought 'cultural literacy' was just what everybody knows. He just looked at me, and didn't say anything." That, of course, is the point: Cultural literacy *used to be* what everyone knew. Each day now, fewer and fewer people know the same things. "We have ignored cultural literacy in thinking about education," says Hirsch, "precisely because it was something we have been able to take for granted. We ignore the air we breathe until it is thin or foul."

Since reading Hirsch's book I encounter constant reminders of its truth:

In discussing our model of the solar system with a neighbor, an intelligent adult who finished the ninth grade of school, I discover that he doesn't know the planets go around the sun. Pointing at the model's sun, he thinks it's the moon.

Adult acquaintances in Vermont, learning that we once lived in British Columbia, say, "Really? Why did you go all the way to South America?"

Hirsch has been most seriously criticized for his book's 63-page appendix, an alphabetical listing of words, phrases, book and song titles, historical and geographical references, aphorisms, and quotations Hirsch says "literate Americans know." Critics ignore Hirsch's own disclaimer that the list is meant to be suggestive rather than definitive. Not every literate person, Hirsch says, is familiar with every item in his list, and, although he and two colleagues worked hard to make their list as complete as they could, Hirsch invites interested readers to suggest amendments and additions to the list. Although I haven't tried to "score" myself on his list — hardly his purpose in presenting it — I've looked it over, testing myself at random, and would guess that I am completely familiar with about half, somewhat familiar with another fourth, and completely ignorant of the other fourth. I can easily come up with several references I think he missed (or perhaps chose not to include).

Conversations and correspondence among educated, "literate" people are rife with references and allusions that often convey paragraphs or even volumes of meaning in a few well-chosen words. Much more than idle whim directs many authors to borrow from the Bible, Shakespeare, and other great literary works for their titles. Readers are given extra measures of meaning in the books if they are familiar with the chosen phrases in their original contexts. Derek recently wrote a very good book review of John Steinbeck's *Of Mice and Men*, not knowing that the title had been borrowed from a poem by Robert Burns. I sent Derek to *Bartlett's Familiar Quotations*, in which he read the words in their original context; he then rewrote his review, having quickly reinterpreted Steinbeck's book in light of his new understanding of the title. *East of Eden* is another Steinbeck title that comes to mind; a very good book, even if one doesn't recognize the origin of the title — but how much more meaning will be found by the reader who realizes that Steinbeck is drawing a loose parallel with the banishment of Adam and Eve from the Garden of Eden, along with the implicit implications of toil and shame and sorrow?

"Learning without thought is labor lost," said Confucius, seemingly in agreement with Rousseau and Dewey, but, he added, "thought without learning is perilous," which I think is Hirsch's contention. We want our children to know how to think, of course, but without the lessons of history, the examples of good literature, knowledge of other peoples and cultures, and basic information about the physical world around them, their ability to think won't help them emerge from a personal repetition of the Dark Ages. We don't want to teach our children *what* to think, but *how* to think, and to do that, we must help them find facts and information and ideas to think about. Word games and puzzles in logic are no substitute for information and ideas about the "real world" of the past and present and — if we're ready — the future.

In our home-school, we've tried to cover everything. It's a star we'll never reach, of course, but still worth aiming for. Just a few of the subjects we've entertained at Brook Farm School are reading, 'riting, 'rithmetic, geography, history, science, art, music, mythology, literature, languages, psychology, ethics, religion, philosophy, humor, home economics, physical education, civics, politics, government, citizenship, commitment, integrity, self-reliance, sympathy, empathy, responsibility, map reading, typing, biology, and physiology. We also toss in a little astronomy, physics, chemistry, botany, and woodworking. We discuss and evaluate astrology, palmistry, dream interpretation, and telepathy. We talk about marriage and divorce, birth and death, abortion, the death penalty, drugs, alcohol, and the world's health and hunger problem.

We occasionally refer to our home-schooling as "elementary and secondary education in the liberal arts." As immigrants to Canada but not forgetting our American background, and with two of our children born in each of the two countries, our home-schooling has included the history, literature, and culture of both countries, which are, after all, very similar and in many ways inseparable, having both sprung from Western Europe, bringing with them shared laws, history, literature, and tradition. As E.D. Hirsch makes us look back over the years, wondering if we have helped our children acquire "cultural literacy," we realize that his phrase is a more concise way of saying what we've been saying right along. Our children have, and are continuing to acquire, much of the basic information that used to be shared knowledge, and that Hirsch hopes will be restored not only to everyone's formal education, but also to everyone's thinking and communication.

One important omission in his list of "what literate Americans know" — which Hirsch could not have foreseen — is the phrase "cultural literacy" itself. Besides conveying a meaning far beyond a basic competency in reading and writing, the phrase now represents a new way of looking at education. In discussing educational theories and practices with other educators, I feel the conversation would be as difficult without a shared knowledge of Hirsch's ideas as it would be without a shared knowledge of the basic ideas of Rousseau, Dewey, and John Holt. "Cultural literacy" has become an important part of cultural literacy. **CULTURAL LITERACY: What Every American Needs to Know**, by E.D. Hirsch Jr. Code RH, $13.

**THE DICTIONARY OF CULTURAL LITERACY: What Every American Needs to Know**, by E.D. Hirsch Jr., Joseph Kett, and James Trefil. Expanding and augmenting the controversial list of "what literate Americans know" from the book *Cultural Literacy*, this book identifies the people, places, sayings, and ideas that form the common heritage of American culture. Twenty-three alphabetically arranged sections address major categories of knowledge with hundreds of entries that discuss ideas, events, and individuals, explaining their significance in our culture and placing them in context. Features 300 maps, charts, and illustrations. This book isn't a course in "instant cultural literacy," nor is it intended to be, but it will be a very useful skeleton guide to enjoyable productive reading and study: With the collection of ideas and information in this book as jumping-off points, the reader can become acquainted (or reacquainted) with vast areas of knowledge that may be vague or missing. Code HM, $27.50.

**A FIRST DICTIONARY OF CULTURAL LITERACY: What Our Children Need to Know**, by E.D. Hirsch Jr. This book is even more controversial than Hirsch's other two, but I think those who object that "Hirsch is telling us what to teach our kids" are like medieval kings who beheaded messengers who brought bad news. Would you rather have Clinton or a national committee tell you what your child should know? If we don't set some standards for ourselves (not values for everyone, just ourselves) we will not achieve our goals. Public educators agree more and more with the opinion home-schoolers have had for years — that today's kids are not being educated. Taking them out of school is no solution if they aren't being educated at home. This book presents Hirsch's concept of the core body of knowledge that has been (and should be) the framework of American society and culture, particularly for children through the sixth grade. More than 2,000 concise, understandable entries are presented in 21 sections, ranging from the Bible and mythology to geography, history, and mathematics to the sciences, health, and technology. Richly illustrated with photographs, drawings, charts, and maps. Like the lists in *Cultural Literacy* and *The Dictionary of Cultural Literacy*, this one is meant to be suggestive, not definitive, and readers can easily adapt it to their use. We think it's a very useful skeleton for all parents and teachers — especially home-schoolers — to use as a basic reference in designing a curriculum, in stocking a home library, or both before and after the children have learned to read. The suggestions in this book give children many things to think about while they're learning to think. Ages 9 to12. Code HM, $15.

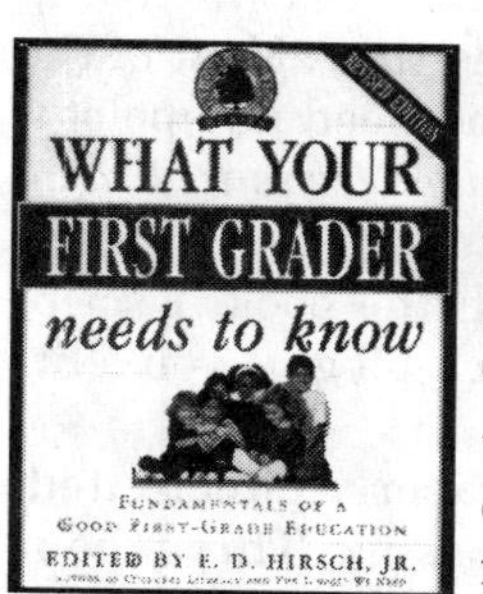


**The Core Knowledge Series**, edited by E.D. Hirsch Jr. There are six books in this series — **WHAT YOUR FIRST [2nd, 3rd, 4th, 5th, or 6th] GRADER NEEDS TO KNOW**, subtitled, "Fundamentals of a Good First- [2nd-, 3rd-, etc.] Grade Education." Each book is a very comprehensive, almost encyclopedic outline of basic information for each respective grade level in language arts, fine arts, history, geography, mathematics, science, and technology. The mathematics sections don't have "lessons" as such, but their very detailed summaries of all the basic facts, information, and skills that are most desirable will serve as excellent skeletons (or cores, as the series title suggests) around which to build your materials and activities. All the other subjects — such as nursery rhymes and Aesop's fables in the first-grade book through stories and poems and more advanced literature selections in the higher grades — are very good, but will need to be supplemented with other similar materials (more literature, more biographies, etc.). The series seems to be similar in some ways to Saxon's approach to math, using an incremental method of teaching, presenting very basic information at first, and then slowly building on this information, year by year, to give a more complete picture without bombarding the child with so much information that it can't be remembered or used. We have reservations about a few details, but in general we're very favorably impressed by the books. If they had been published when we were still teaching young kids, they would have made it much easier for us to design our own curricula. The arithmetic and math sections of these books — supplemented with some of the other early-learning books we recommend — can easily be all that's necessary to prepare for *Essential Mathematics* (or Saxon's Math 76, if you prefer a more academic program), with no need for the monotonous drill in standard school textbooks. Each book in the series is now in paperback. Code DD, $12.95.

# BUT—

Having praised and recommended the Core Knowledge Series, I have to remind you that the books were *not written* by E.D. Hirsch Jr., but were edited by him, and I sometimes wonder if he was watching *Sesame Street* at the same time. Most of the books in the series are well done and need no apology, but the first, *What Your First Grader Needs to Know*, is one of the most poorly written books of its type that I have ever read. As I read through the book, I scribbled out eight pages of notes, of which I'll give you a little sampling:

Many sentences are not properly punctuated; commas, in particular, are often missing. Throughout the book, many sentences begin with conjunctions (and, but), apparently to "simplify" the reading by dividing one sentence into two. The writer frequently jumps from third person to second person, then back again.

Several words and phrases need explanation; e.g., in a story about "Brer Tiger," the apostrophe is missing from "Br'er," and there is no explanation that the word is a colloquial abbreviation of "brother." There is no pronunciation guide for non-Hispanics of "Medio Pollito" (MAY-de-o po-YEE-to). There are several inane statements, such as "A written sentence starts out with a capital letter that says, 'Hey, a new sentence is starting'" and "A paragraph is made of several sentences *that talk* about the same thing" (my emphasis). "Rhyming words" are referred to as "rhyme words."

"Since it is a northern country, Canada is cold in the winter," says the book, ignoring the fact that many parts of Canada are warmer than some parts of the United States. Should the reader infer that Antarctica is warm because it's a southern continent?

World religions are tossed around as if they were cute nursery stories, with no mention of their place in world history, and with no regard for their real substance. Buddha "sat beneath a tree for 98 days! Don't you think that is a long time to keep quiet?"

People crossed from Asia to North America on a "bridge," the book says, with no explanation of a land bridge and how it differs from a man-made bridge.

"It may seem strange to you, but for thousands of years only a few ships from Europe had 'bumped into' North or South America." Most small children will take "bumped into" literally, like bumping into a table. Why not "found" or "discovered"?

"Some [of the Native Americans] wanted so much to be thought brave that they clashed [?] with the men of other tribes. They called it 'going on the warpath.'" Is that a direct translation from an Indian language? An old John Wayne movie?

"One reason that [sic] Mozart was so good at music was that his father's job was teaching music, so you might say that music was in Mozart's family." Does this idiocy need a comment?

In "The World of Plants," "a seed is a little plant in a box with its lunch." "Let's pretend you are a tree, to see how a plant works." Sure, and then let's pretend you're a typewriter, to see how an editor works.

"The Pilgrims were very religious people," says the book, and I don't disagree, but what does "very religious" mean to the average six-year-old? "They came to *our country* [my emphasis] to worship in a way that was not allowed in England." What way? Why not allowed?

"Even though [Washington] would have preferred to be at his home, Mount Vernon, with his wife, Martha, he agreed to become President and was in office for eight years. This is why he is called the Father of His Country." Whoops, lost me again. Because he left his wife for eight years? Because he was in his office for eight years?

Supposedly this book was written *for* first-graders and not *by* them, but how can you tell? If there were some other book I could recommend in its place, I'd do so, but I don't know of any. I still think it's a good core for a first-grade curriculum, but don't be surprised if you sometimes feel like throwing it on the floor and jumping on it.

# REFERENCE BOOKS FOR THE WHOLE FAMILY

Most encyclopedias will have the zillions of facts and bits of information you're looking for or will find fascinating when you bump into them by accident, zillions more you don't really care much about, and at least half a zillion *missing* bits of information that will prompt you to say, "Why on earth did they leave that out?" For most research subjects, and for most general information, a set that's ten years old will do as well as a more recent one, and can probably be found in a used-book store or garage sale for ten to twenty dollars. We have a set of the Britannica, which we bought new about twenty years ago, and usually we can still find most of the information we're looking for. When we can't, we look in various other reference books we have, or go to the public library.

If you're going to invest in a new set, your best choice is **THE ENCYCLOPEDIA BRITANNICA** or **THE WORLD BOOK ENCYCLOPEDIA**. Each has several advantages and disadvantages not shared by the other, so you'll want to compare them carefully before committing yourself. Write to the publishers, asking for a salesman — pardon me, "representative" — to visit you. The representatives will probably pressure you to sign up right away, but don't do it. Compare them first.

**THE ENCYCLOPEDIA BRITANNICA** has more in-depth articles, many written by world-renowned scholars. **THE WORLD BOOK** has an easier reading style and more illustrations, and is probably suitable for a wider age range. Both companies offer several other sets of books, such as **THE BRITANNICA JUNIOR** and **CHILDCRAFT**, respectively. The salesman's commission on an encyclopedia sale is fairly high — sometimes half the price of the set (several hundred dollars) — so, to get your signature, you may be offered additional sets of books at little or no cost, which will increase the value of your purchase and is another good reason not to make a hasty decision. Annual "yearbooks," supposedly keeping the sets up-to-date, will be offered (for about $35 each), but we found that these usually consist of windy analyses of "global trends" and have negligible value. Both companies offer monthly installment plans, with fairly low payments. Sometimes a "gift," such as a three-volume reference set (dictionary, thesaurus, and atlas) will be given to you just for looking at the salesman's samples.

Watch out: Entries in encyclopedias are almost as likely as those in school textbooks to be "modified" to reflect current trends in political thinking, "sexism," and omission of items that may offend special-interest or minority groups. For instance, whether you're Christian or not, you want the history of Christianity to be fairly accurate and truthful. Before buying, look up a few test items, such as the Pilgrims, the fall of the Roman Empire, and so on. Be prepared to accept the presence of writing attitudes you don't approve of.

**Encyclopedia Britannica, Inc.**, 310 S. Michigan Ave., Chicago, IL 60604. The Encyclopedia Britannica has made its 32-volume set available FREE online at www.britannica.com.

**World Book, Inc.**, Educational Services Dept., Merchandise Mart Plaza, Chicago, IL 60654.

If your child or you need to do research online and get frustrated by the number of sites with information, try www.inetlibrary.com. They've collected the information most useful to children K-12. They have 9,000 books, 2,000 magazines, 255 newspapers, 54 encyclopedias, and more, referenced for easy access. This site has a curriculum planner for all grades as well as help for college and scholarship searches. You can sign up for a two-week free trial and really check this site out before deciding if it's worth the fee. This is sold nationally for $89.79. At the moment it is on sale online for $49.79.

**USBORNE CHILDREN'S ENCYCLOPEDIA**. This book has 128 pages filled with well-illustrated information, although I wish they had photos and more realistic drawings for many of the items. Great for a first reference, and has many practical hands-on experiments. Ages 7 to 11. Code EDC, $14.95.

**OXFORD AMERICAN CHILDREN'S ENCYCLOPEDIA.** An outstanding reference set that can be used for an extended period of years, generously illustrated with color photos, maps, and charts. A pleasure to use and read. Volumes 1 to 7 contain 2,081 factual articles written especially with children in mind. The print is easy to read and the content has enough detail to provide a good understanding of the subject. Easy-to-use, cross-referenced format. Includes ideas for activities and experiments. Volume 8 is a special book with almost 500 biographies of prominent Americans and international personalities, painters, writers, composers, etc. Volume 9 contains a complete index and gazetteer (including a special feature on every country and its flag), as well as a timeline of world history to help put U.S. events in perspective. You don't have to sit at the computer to use this set. Computer CD-ROM encyclopedias may be cheaper, but you can't carry them from room to room. An even better reason to seriously consider this set is that sooner or later your kids will need to know how to do research using books. Books are not going to disappear. Ages 8 to 14. Code OX, regular price $300, but we can provide this set for the special price of $279.95 plus $4 shipping, UPS insured.

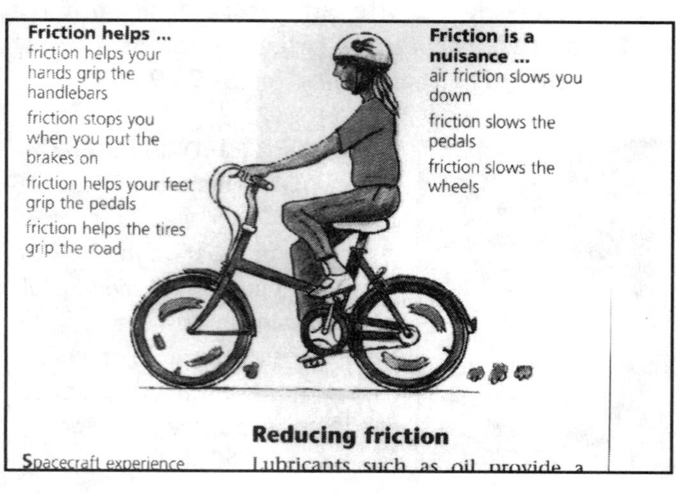

**THE CONCISE COLUMBIA ENCYCLOPEDIA** has more than 15,000 capsule entries. I've often found information I needed in this book when I couldn't find it elsewhere. Me too. Suitable for high school and adult usage. Code BT, $19.95 for the 973-page paperback; $59.95 for the 944-page hardcover.

**BARRON'S STUDENT'S CONCISE ENCYCLOPEDIA**. Subtitled "A Complete Reference Guide for Home and School," this is a single-volume encyclopedia of "essential information" for high school and college students. A review of all major subjects is presented in the form of A-to-Z entries within these general academic sections:

THE LIBERAL ARTS: Music, Art, Language and Literature, Philosophy, and Religion.

SOCIAL STUDIES: American and World History, Government, Geography, Economics, and Business.

MATHEMATICS and COMPUTER SCIENCE.

SCIENCE: Astronomy, Biology, Chemistry, Earth Sciences, Technology, Physics, and Psychology.

In general, the information presented is reliable and comprehensive. A notable disadvantage, however, is that most information (except in mathematics and a few other subjects) is arranged *alphabetically*, as in an encyclopedia, rather than chronologically or around a central theme. This makes study somewhat difficult with subjects such as history in which the chronological sequence of cause and effect is of major importance. However, these sections still serve very well as mini-reviews, refresher courses, and — the best use of this book — basic reference points and starting guides for more intensive study using other materials (library books, encyclopedia, etc.).

The mathematics section is very complete, from simple arithmetic to calculus and trigonometry, but is also very brief. For more detailed study, which you'll probably want, we recommend *Essential Mathematics* (the updated edition of *Survival Mathematics*) or *Arithmetic Made Simple* for high school math. (See "Mathematics.")

The U.S. history is fairly complete, but brief; world history is very skimpy.

Another section, "Study and Learning Workshops," provides advice and guidelines to help students make efficient use of study time and achieve their highest possible marks when taking tests. Detailed instructions are given for writing term papers and for making full use of library research facilities.

A section on "life outside the classroom" con-

tains information — some of it very useful — about basic health and nutrition, exercise programs, first aid, and practical tips for managing personal finances. The book also contains many excellent maps (including historical maps) and many charts and tables, including weights and measures, metric conversions, holidays, and time zones. Hardcover, approximately 1,200 pages. Code BE, $29.95.

**FIRST DICTIONARY**. See "Early Learning."

**MACMILLAN DICTIONARY FOR CHILDREN**. As kids grow away from their "first" picture dictionaries, I think this is the best step up (followed closely by a concise "adult" or college dictionary). Thousands of entries, definitions, and illustrative examples; 1,100 full-color photos; and more than 300 highlighted word histories and language notes. More illustrative sentences per main entry than any other children's dictionary. Illustrated timeline of world history. Updated atlas with maps of the world, the continents, the U.S., and Canada. Tables of weights and measures. Code MAC, $16.95.

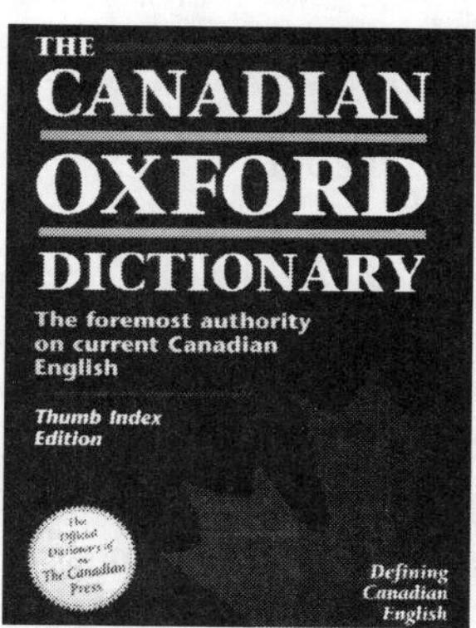


**THE OXFORD *CANADIAN DICTIONARY***. Yes! Finally! Not British or Australian. Not American. Truly Canadian and extremely well researched. I'll just bet there are terms in here you've never heard or thought you'd find in a dictionary. It's great! More than 2,000 distinctly Canadian words and meanings, covering all regions of the country; 130,000 total entries with Canadian spellings and pronunciations. Your favorite doughnut may be a jambuster, a bismarck, a Burlington bun, or the more prosaic jelly doughnut, depending on where you live in Canada. Find it all in one book. Hardcover. Code OX, $39.95.

**Dictionaries at Discount Prices**. I had planned to offer Webster's dictionaries for sale through Brook Farm Books, but we can't beat the prices offered by Follett Educational (see "Homeschooling and Education" for the address), and I doubt that anyone can. Follett Educational specializes in used, reconditioned textbooks, but these dictionaries are brand new, never used, yet at bargain prices.

**THE OXFORD AMERICAN DICTIONARY AND LANGUAGE GUIDE**. Our choice for a family dictionary. In its 1,330 pages you'll find all the standard features such as pronunciation guides, etymology, and examples of common usage. You'll also have a complete guide to weights and measures (including metric measures), signs and symbols, a periodic table, and much more useful and interesting information. Hardcover. Code OX, $35.

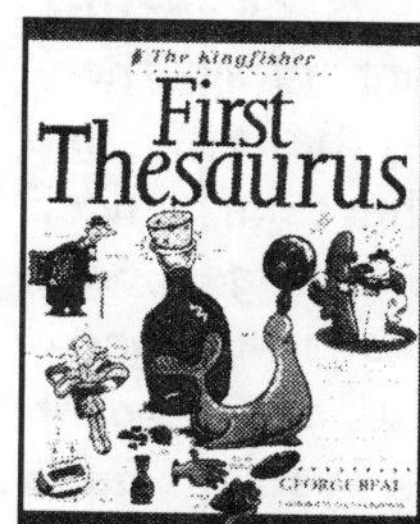


**FIRST THESAURUS**. An adult thesaurus can be intimidating to young learners. This one uses 100 key headwords that children commonly use, along with synonyms, homonyms, antonyms, and sample sentences. Easy to use. Ages 7 to 11. Hardcover. Code KF, $15.95.

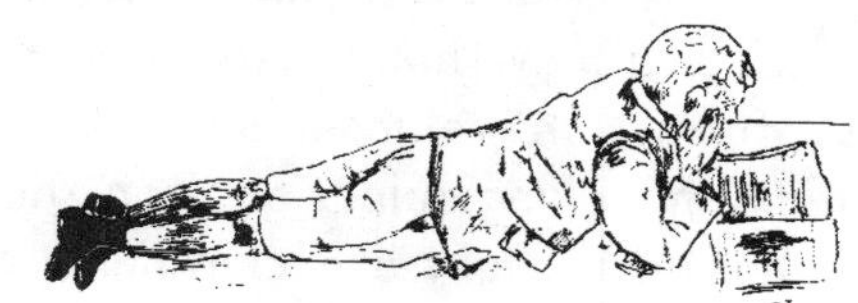

**THE HBJ STUDENT THESAURUS**. This easy-to-use thesaurus contains 800 main entries, with a group of two to five synonyms for each entry. An example sentence for each synonym shows how the word is distinct from others in the group, and illustrations are used to demonstrate subtle differences among related words. Each main entry is the most common word in its synonym group, with the more precise or sophisticated words following. An index lists all 3,300 words discussed in the book. Full-color illustrations. This is an excellent book to use with budding and developing writers who are just learning the subtle differences between words. Ages 7 to 12 (more or less). Code HBJ, $18.

**THE NEW ROGET'S THESAURUS IN DICTIONARY FORM**, by Norman Lewis. If you've used Roget's Thesaurus to find just the right synonym or antonym, or to avoid excessive repetition of words in your writing, you know how helpful and valuable it can be. If you've used the older, original version, with words grouped by concept — abstract, concrete, etc., etc. — then you know how fantastically frustrating it can be; after you've searched for the word you want for 20 minutes, you decide the one you had was good enough. This new edition does away with frustration. It's fully indexed, which means you can zoom in on the words you want right away. If you use a thesaurus — or should — this is the one. Ages 14 and up. Paperback, 496 pages. Code BT, $6.50.

**A WORLD OF IDEAS**, by Chris Rohmann. This one-volume reference is an A-to-Z dictionary of important theories, concepts, beliefs, and thinkers that have influenced mankind across the ages. Each listing discusses the significance of the idea in enough depth to give you a good understanding of the topic without flooding you with extraneous information. Rohmann says he was guided by two criteria in making selections for this volume: influence on human thought and continuing relevance in today's discourse. Here is a small sample of the 444 listings you'll find: affirmative action, balance of power, behaviorism, empiricism, fractals, and impressionism. This will be a tool to grow into for high school students and an asset to adults seeking cultural literacy in a broader sense than even E.D. Hirsch had in mind. Code BAL, $24.95.

**ATLAS OF THE 20TH CENTURY**. This book brings current history alive with interesting text that highlights the important events. Full of color maps, photos, and illustrations. Use this to cover topics across the curriculum. Ages 9 to 14. Hardcover. Code EDC, $12.95.

**Facts and Lists**. A series of books designed for quick reference. There are so many illustrations and interesting facts our kids often enjoyed just browsing through them. Better than that, at times when their minds seemed like unlimited sponges soaking up information, they really learned from these. Ages 8 to 12. Code EDC, $5.95 each.

**AMAZING FEATS**
**ANIMAL FACTS**
**BIRD FACTS**
**BODY FACTS**
**COUNTRIES OF THE WORLD FACTS**
**EARTH FACTS**
**OCEAN FACTS**
**PREHISTORIC FACTS**
**SPACE FACTS**
**WEATHER FACTS**

***COMBOS***: **NATURE FACTS AND LISTS**: Animal, Ocean, and Birds. Code EDC, $12.95

**FACTS AND LISTS**: Earth, Countries, Weather, and Space. Code EDC, $14.95.

See "Geography" for the very best children's atlas and a world geography reference book.

See "Science" for a science encyclopedia.

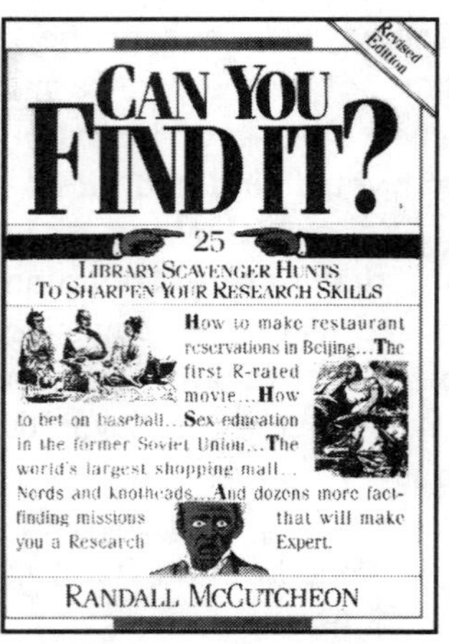

**CAN YOU FIND IT? 25 Library Scavenger Hunts to Sharpen Your Research Skills**, by Randall McCutcheon. Sooner or later all of us need to find an unusual piece of information and just don't know where to look. This book will take you to and beyond the usual reference books in search of answers to intriguing questions. Sections include tips for teachers, librarians, and parents; questions to be answered; clues (frequently in the form of cartoons and quotations); answers; resources; and more. I can't think of a better and more intriguing way to learn excellent research skills and have fun doing it. Ages 14 and up. Code FS, $10.95.

**ASIMOV'S CHRONOLOGY OF SCIENCE AND DISCOVERY.** A very impressive compendium — 775 pages! — encompassing development from 4 million B.C. to the present. The timeline linking historical and scientific discoveries shows how science and history have influenced each other. This book will help you synthesize various studies. A good source for research information. The relationship between the science and history notes was not always obvious, but the linking did put the developments in perspective, making for easier assimilation and understanding. I was also amazed to learn how long some knowledge had been around before it was finally utilized. Code BT, $30.

**ATLAS OF WORLD HISTORY.** Have we come a long way from our beginnings? In what ways? How could we improve? You can flip the pages and watch empires rise and fall. Full-color maps, diagrams, and good text show the dramatic changes in our history. Ages 9 to 14. Hardcover. Code EDC, $17.95.

**THE ILLUSTRATED HISTORY OF THE WORLD,** by J.M. Roberts. I was struck immediately by the extraordinarily rich color in the original artwork and illustrations. This series is visually captivating and makes for pleasurable browsing. This illustrated history — with its timeline, sidebars that feature key events, 190 maps, 2,200 photographs, detailed index, and excellent text — is a reference you'll enjoy just as much as your kids do. Although designed for about age 14, adults and younger children will be fascinated with the pictures (a good way to begin broadening horizons). 10-volume set. Code OX, regular price $275 plus $5 shipping, but we can get this for you for $249, UPS insured shipping included.

In "History and Biography" I recommend Roberts' *Short History of the World* as a guide for high school and college students. The *Short History of the World* is not illustrated and is written for college students and adults. *The Illustrated History of the World* is drawn from the that book, but is written for high school and junior college-level students.

**See "Geography" for a selection of globes.**

# FREE OR ALMOST-FREE TEACHING AND LEARNING AIDS

### "UNKNOWN" — "FORWARDING ORDER EXPIRED" — "RETURN TO SENDER"

For every inquiry that is returned to you with the above words, or an equivalent, I sincerely apologize. I've tried to ascertain the accuracy of all listings, but companies, like people, sometimes move and then seem to disappear. Usually, the best one can do in such a case is to look for similar services or materials from other companies.

This chapter lists scores of educational items that are free or almost free, just for the cost of a postcard, a postage stamp and an envelope, or sometimes a small fee. Suggestions: Be reasonable; don't request items you don't really want or need; when possible, be specific in your request. Although many of the following items are not necessarily intended for school use, it will often be helpful if you mention the age or grade level for which the material is intended. Many items can be requested on a postcard; others should be requested with a letter written in standard business form, by the teacher (not the students), preferably on a school letterhead. Usually, you can tell by the item listed which form of request will be appropriate. Please include an SASE (self-addressed, stamped envelope); a #10 (business size) envelope is usually best

I have tried to be sure that all offers are current and that the sources and other information are correct, but I can't guarantee either. Offers and prices change; companies move or, occasionally, go out of business. If an offer has been withdrawn, usually the company will send or offer another in its place. For all items no longer offered, and for all requests returned to you as "not forwardable," I apologize.

This chapter was done with the great assistance of Barb Merz; however, I am the one responsible for any and all errors. Please note that there are some addresses without an actual street name or number. These addresses do work!

The following sample letter is a good model, to be adapted to your own particular situation:

Address
Date

National Society for the Prevention of Blindness
79 Madison Avenue
New York, NY 10016

Dear Sir or Madam:

My sixth-grade health class is studying ________.
I would like to request your _______, and a list of any other charts or publications you feel would be of interest to us.

Thank you very much for your assistance.

Sincerely yours,

Mrs. Qurious

Note: All the following items are completely FREE unless otherwise noted (i.e., a small charge, usually less than $2, or an SASE, or other requirement).

## HOME, FAMILY, AND FOOD

**BABY SAFETY CHECKLIST** for ages 14 to adult. Great for babysitters and parents. U.S. Consumer Product Safety Commission, Washington, DC 20207.

**THE SUPER SITTER.** Baby-sitting booklet (booklet #052-011-00114-7). U.S. Consumer Product Safety Commission, Washington, DC 20207.

**SAFE KIDS ARE NO ACCIDENT.** Fire safety booklets, one for parents and an activity book for kids. National Safe Kids Campaign, 1301 Pennsylvania Ave. NW, Suite 100, Washington, DC 20004-1707.

**AQUA SMART.** Water safety program with 10 teaching units, an extensive guide, and an activity section. Specify grades K to 2, 3 to 5, or 6 to 8. Phaedra Bota, Education Analyst, Department of Boating and Waterways, 1629 S St., Sacramento, CA 95814-7291.

**Free circus ticket** to *any child born since 1993.* Ringling Brothers and Barnum & Bailey Circus will send you one free ticket (good at any time in the future). Send child's name, address, and date of birth to Ringling Brothers and Barnum & Bailey Circus, P.O. Box 39845, Edina, MN 55439.

**Free circus teaching unit**, poster, and more from Ringling Brothers and Barnum & Bailey Circus, Educational Services, Dept. A, 8607 Westwood Center Dr., Vienna, VA 22182; www.Ringling.com.

Can't decide if you should buy or lease a car? Request **A CONSUMER EDUCATION GUIDE TO LEASING VS. BUYING** from Heggen and Associates, P.O. Box 5025, Evanston, IL 60204. Include your name and address on a 3x5" index card and $1 for postage.

**MOTORIST'S TIRE CARE AND SAFETY GUIDE**, plus "Recreational Vehicle Tire Care and Safety Guide Care." Rubber Manufacturers Association, 717 W. Smith Rd., Medina, OH 44256.

**Know someone over 60?** Purina Pets for People (PPP) pays for pets from participating humane societies for people over 60. Covers adoption fees, neutering, initial shots, food bowl, and more. Purina Pets for People, Checkerboard Square, OCA, St. Louis, MO 63164.

**A GUIDE TO LEARNING AND DISCOVERING WITH TOYS.** Send an SASE to VTECH Smart Play Offer, 380 W. Palatine Rd, Wheeling, IL 60090.

**Looking for a suitable summer camp?** The American Camping Association, 5000 State Road 67 North, Martinsville, IN 46151, has a free booklet.

**FREE STUFF FOR KIDS.** Catalog from Meadowbrook Press, 5451 Smetana Dr., Minnetonka, MN 55343. There is about a $5 charge for this. Write for current information.

**Free Blistex samples**. Blistex Sample Offer, 1800 Swift Dr., Oak Brook, IL 60521.

**SKIPPY PEANUT BUTTER PARTY PLANNER**. Free ideas about children's birthday parties. Skippy Peanut Butter, Dept. SPP, Box 307, Coventry, CT 06238.

**Learn to bake**. Free and very inexpensive resources for kids. Send $1 to the Home Baking Association, HBA Resource Guide, c/o Nabeeha Kazi, 2405 Grand Blvd., Suite 700, Kansas City, MO 64108.

**FAVORITE POPCORN RECIPES**. American Popcorn Co., Box 178, Sioux City, IA 51102.

**Nutrition information**. The U.S. Department of Agriculture offers a variety of educational material. Ask for their food pyramid guide and a list of their other publications. Publications Div., Washington, DC 20250.

**Bison recipes**. Send $1 and a #10 SASE to the National Bison Association, 4701 Marion St., #100, Denver, CO 80216.

**PEANUTS!** Flash cards, lesson plans, worksheets, activities, comic books, a teacher's kit for grades 3 to 5, and more. Growers Peanut Food Promotion, P.O. Box 1709, Rocky Mount, NC 27802.

**BE A SMART SHOPPER**. Two-sided poster about nutrition facts on food labels. Del Monte Consumer Affairs, P.O. Box 193575, San Francisco, CA 94119.

**A 5-MINUTE COURSE IN NEW-TRITION** and a listing of other informational resources. Center for Science in the Public Interest, 1875 Connecticut Ave. NW, Suite 300, Washington, DC 20009-5728.

**FIVE A DAY LIVE**. Meet Bobby Banana, Lucy Lettuce, and Barney Broccoli in these educational materials and activities about nutrition. Write on school letterhead to Dole Nutrition Program, 155 Bovet, Suite 476, San Mateo, CA 94402.

**BREASTFEEDING GUIDE**. Medela Inc., P.O. Box 660, McHenry, IL 60051-0660.

## EDUCATION

**Free Canadian teaching resources** available through www.thecanadianteacher.com. A variety of books, CDs, catalogs, lesson plans, travel information, and more.

**TYPICAL K-12 COURSE OF STUDY**. World Book Educational Products, 14333 Ash Ave., New York, NY 11355-2110; www.worldbook.com/ptrc/html/curr.htm.

**OFFICIAL JUNIOR POLICE HANDBOOK**. An activity book with information about detecting strangers, dangerous and silly things, and more. National Exchange Club, 3050 Central Ave., Toledo, OH 43606-1700.

**DEPUTY FIRE MARSHAL KIT**. Seemore Smoke, Pueblo, CO 81009; 888-8-PUEBLO.

**NEWSPAPER CAREERS AND CHALLENGES FOR THE NEXT CENTURY**. Information about journalism careers and related fields. National Newspaper Foundation, 1010 N. Glebe Rd., Suite 450, Arlington, VA 22201.

**Transportation coloring book** and related materials. United Transportation Union, 14600 Detroit Ave., Cleveland, OH 44107-4250.

**FREE MATERIALS FOR SCHOOLS AND LIBRARIES**. Booklets published five times per year. Good, interesting resources on all subjects. In the U.S., $17 per year prepaid, $20 if billed. P.O. Box 34069, Dept. 349, Seattle, WA 98124. In Canada, $18 prepaid, $21 if billed. 101-1001 W. Broadway St., Dept. 349, Vancouver, BC V6H 4E4. International orders send $22 U.S. to U.S. address.

**Lettering charts**. Write beautiful calligraphy. Speedball Art Products Co., P.O. Box 5157, Statesville, NC 28677.

**Listing of Material From the Boston Ballet**. Boston Ballet Order Center, P.O. Box 9200, Waltham, MA 02154.

**Info about Canadian Indians**. Booklets, map, and more. Information Kiosk, Department of Indian and Northern Affairs Canada, Hull, PQ K1A 0H4.

**Info sheet about Indian arts and crafts**, American Indian and Alaska Natives fact booklet, and book list for young readers. U.S. Department of the Interior, Indian Arts and Crafts Board, MS 4004-MIB, 1849 C St. NW, Washington, DC 20240-0001.

**Information about Indians online**: www.doi.gov/bia/aitoday/more-info.html.

**BIODIVERSITY: WILD ABOUT LIFE!** Free video from Karol Media, P.O. Box 7600, Wilkes-Barre, PA 18773-9969. Compliments of Phillips Petroleum Co. Also available free: "A Home for Pearl" (about wildlife habitat) and "The Challenge of the Unknown" (math).

**STORY OF GRANITE**. Barre Granite Association, Box 481, Barre, VT 05641.

**COAL FACTS: THE STORY OF COAL FROM A TO Z**. National Coal Foundation, 1130 17th St. NW, Suite 2200, Washington, DC 20036.

**STORY OF ALUMINUM AND ALCOA**. Alcoa Corporate Center, 201 Isabella St., Pittsburgh, PA 15212.

**LEATHER IN OUR LIVES**. Leather Industries of America, 1000 Thomas Jefferson St. NW, Washington, DC 20007.

**Cotton facts.** Booklet: "Cotton From Field to Fabric"; brochure: "The Story of Cotton"; and poster: "Cotton From Field to Fabric." Ages 10 and up. National Cotton Council, 1918 N. Parkway, Memphis, TN 38112-5000.

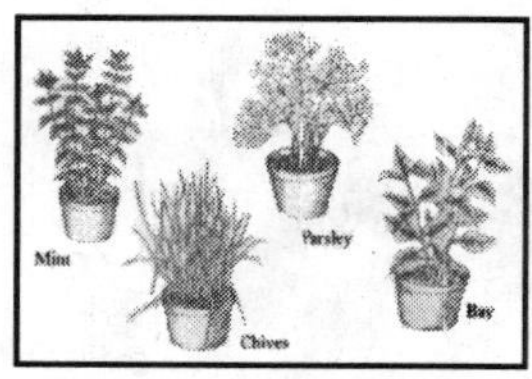


**HISTORY OF SPICES**. Send $2 to the American Spice Trade Association, Education Dept., 560 Sylvan Ave., P.O. Box 1267, Englewood Cliffs, NJ 07632; www.astaspice.org.

**WELCOME TO CITRUS COUNTRY**. Poster and information about healthy snacks. Florida Citrus Commission, P.O. Box 148, Lakeland, FL 33802-0148.

**Facts about bees** and honey, beekeeping, and recipes. Send a postcard to Dadant and Sons, 51 S. Second St., Hamilton, IL 62341.

**LEARNING ABOUT PORK**. Elementary-level activity/coloring book. Send 10 cents to the National Pork Council, Box 10370, Des Moines, IA 50306.

**CORN AND CORN PRODUCTS**. Corn Refiners Association, 1701 Pennsylvania Ave. NW, Suite 950, Washington, DC 20006-5805.

**STORY OF CHOCOLATE AND COCOA**, sample of unprocessed cocoa beans, nutrition info, and more. Hershey Foods Corp. Corporate Headquarters, 100 Crystal A Drive, P.O. Box 810, Hershey, PA 17033.

**HOW TO FORECAST WEATHER**. Gudebrod Inc., Old Reading Pike., #1H, Stowe, PA 19464.

**HURRICANES AND TORNADOES** and **OWLIE SKYWARN WEATHER BOOK**. National Logistics Support Center, 1510 E. Bannister Rd., Bldg. 1, Kansas City, MO 64131.

**TOPS IDEAS**. Free twice-yearly publications with ideas about hands-on science learning. Basically a catalog with a couple of sample activities. TOPS Ideas, 10970 S. Mulino Rd., Canby, OR 97013.

**PUTTING THE LIFE BACK INTO BIOLOGY**. Practical advice for students who object to dissection. Also two fact sheets: "It's Their World Too!" and "A Kid's Guide to Saving the Earth and Its Animals." Humane Services, P.O. Box 6560, Macon, GA 31208.

**HOW WE MADE THE FIRST FLIGHT**. A 20-page booklet about the Wright brothers. Also, a 259-page Aviation and Space Curriculum Guide for grades K to 3, and four resource packets: "Space Exploration," "Non-Powered Flight," "Aerospace and the Environment," and "Aerospace Communications." U.S. Department of Transportation, Federal Aviation Administration, Aviation Education Program, AHR-15, 800 Independence Ave. SW, Washington, DC 20591.

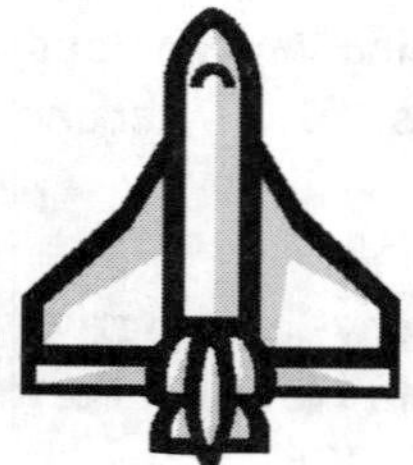

**NASA's education programs.** Information, posters, and online resources. Publications Section, Communication Affairs and Education Branch, NASA, Mail Code FEO-2, 300 E St. SW, Washington, DC 20546; education.nasa.gov/educators.html.

**NASA INFORMATION, SPACE SHUTTLE FACTS, STEPS TO THE MOON.** National Aeronautics and Space Administration, Kennedy Space Center, FL 32899; www.nasa.gov (NASA homepage); spacelink.msfc.nasa.gov (Spacelink, NASA's education site); www.ksc.nasa.gov (Kennedy Space Center home page).

**JOURNEY TO SPACE.** Free curriculum guide from NASA for grades K and up. Space Center Houston, Education Dept., 1601 NASA Rd. 1, Houston, TX 77058.

**SKYWATCHING.** Series of booklets with information about the sky and distant neighbors. Public Affairs Office, Harvard Smithsonian Center for Astrophysics, 60 Garden St., Cambridge, MA 02138.

**Astronomical Society of the Pacific**, 390 Ashton Ave., San Francisco, CA 94122, offers a wealth of information. Request a catalog.

**FREE EDISON TEACHING KIT.** Well, almost — $1 per kit for handling. Each kit contains how-to booklets with ideas for 66 experiments for grades 4 through junior high. Write as a teacher in your school. Send your name, name of school, and address (on a letterhead would be best) to the Charles Edison Fund, 101 S. Harrison St., East Orange, NJ 07018.

**STONE MOUNTAIN PARK TEACHING AIDS.** Stone Mountain Park, P.O. Box 778, Stone Mountain, GA 30086.

**GUIDE TO SCIENCE FAIR PROJECTS.** For ages 12 to adult. American Chemical Society, Education Division, 1155 16th St. NW, Washington, DC 20036.

**Free sample science project plan**, list of materials, and instructions. Includes a list of other projects available for a nominal fee. Send name and address label and two first-class stamps to The Mad Scientist, P.O. Box 50182, Knoxville, TN 37950.

**SCIENCE WEEKLY** will send a free sample of their newsletter for kids in grades K to 8. Specify grade level. Subscription Dept., P.O. Box 70154, Washington, DC 20088.

**CHEMISTRY ADDS DIMENSION TO YOUR LIFE.** Catalog from the American Chemical Society, 1155 16th St. NW, Washington, DC 20036.

**GEMS NETWORK NEWS.** Great Explorations in Math and Science offers inquiry-based math and science programs for kids pre-K through 12th grade. Information about GEMS is free but their materials all have a price. Matthew Osborn, GEMS, Lawrence Hall of Science, University of California, Berkeley, CA 94720-5200.

**SEISMIC SLEUTHS.** Interactive lessons about earthquakes, plus lots of other material. Specify grade level (7 to 12) and ask them what else they offer. Federal Emergency Management Agency, P.O. Box 2012, Jessup, MD 20794-2012.

**ALL ABOUT FLIGHT.** Historical and scientific information about flight, plus a booklet about the Wright Brothers. Send a postcard. U.S. Department of the Interior, National Park Service, Cape Hatteras, Rte. 1 Box 675, Manteo, NC 27954.

**Smithsonian resources.** Send $5 for a Resource Guide for teachers; includes many creative learning materials. Smithsonian Office of Education, Arts and Industries Bldg., Room 1163, MRC 402, Washington, DC 20560.

**PHOTO TOUR OF THE WHITE HOUSE, THE HOUSE OF THE PEOPLE**. Free photo-book tour and history. The White House, Washington, DC 20500.

**Lincoln's birthplace**. Get information, a booklet, and a list of videos for loan. Abraham Lincoln Birthplace, National Historic Site, 2995 Lincoln Farm Rd., Hodgenville, KY 42748.

**NEWSPAPERS IN EDUCATION: A GUIDE FOR WEEKLY NEWSPAPERS**. Free book with activities involving language arts, social studies, math, science, and more, for grades K to 12. One free copy (more for $1.50 each) for teachers (you are one). National Newspaper Association, 1525 Wilson Blvd., No. 550, Arlington, VA 22209.

**Money facts**. Information about how currency is designed, printed, circulated, and destroyed. Federal Reserve Bank of Atlanta, Public Affairs Dept., Atlanta, GA 30303.

**TEACHING YOUR CHILD HOW TO SAVE AND SPEND**. Free guide to money management for teens. Send an SASE to Consumer Federation of America, 1424 16th St. NW, Suite 604, Washington, DC 20036.

**Finance publications**. "The Story of Money," "The Story of Checks and Electronic Payments," "The Story of Inflation," "The Story of Banks," "The Story of Foreign Trade and Exchange," "A Day at the Fed." All from the Federal Reserve Bank of New York, Public Information Dept., 33 Liberty St., New York, NY 10045.

**SILVER VALUE CHART/GOLD CHART**. Numismatic News Weekly, 700 E. State St., Iola, WI 54990; www.krause.com/coins/.

Request a free sample of coin collectors newspaper, Numismatic News Weekly, Iola, WI 54990.

**GUIDE TO RECOGNIZING COUNTERFEIT MONEY**. United States Secret Service, 1800 G St. NW, Washington, DC 20226.

**THE HISTORY OF THE OLYMPICS**. U.S. Olympic Committee, 1750 E. Boulder St., Colorado Springs, CO 80909.

**Interesting origins of English words**. Catalog of reference books and price list. Merriam-Webster, 47 Federal St., P.O. Box 281, Springfield, MA 01101.

**NEWSCURRENTS**. Newsletter about current events around the world, for grades 3 to 12. Send for a free issue; include name, grade, school name and address, city, state, zip, and school phone number (I doubt they'll call). Comes with lesson plan. P.O. Box 52, Madison, WI 53791-9438.

**EXPLORING MAPS** (posters, guide, and info) and **GLOBAL CHANGE** (poster and activity sheets). Also ask them what else they have. Distribution Branch, U.S. Geological Survey, Box 25286, Denver Federal Center, Denver, CO 80225; www.usgs.gov.

**Pen pals** in more than 30 countries. Student Letter Exchange, 211 Broadway, Suite 201, Lynbrook, NY 11563-3265.

**UNCOVERING MATH WITH YOUR FAMILY**. Free booklet with activities for grades pre-K to 6, plus a sample classroom activity and a free subscription to "It's About T.I.M.E.," a newsletter on classroom technology. Write: K-6 Material Fulfillment, Texas Instruments, P.O. Box 650311, M/S 3908, Dallas, TX 75265-9862.

2+7=?

For your parents and grandparents: **Elderhostel**, 75 Federal St., 3rd Floor, Boston, MA 02110-1941, has a free catalog of inexpensive travel and learning opportunities for seniors.

**EDUCATION AND CAREER ADVANCEMENT NEWS.** Testing resource and information kit tells about a website students can use to practice for the SAT, ACT, GMAT, and other tests. Kim Connolly, Media Relations Coordinator, test.com inc., 1300 E. 9th St., Cleveland, OH 44114. You can get the information online at www.test.com if you have a computer.

**C-SPAN IN THE CLASSROOM.** Free program for educators offers teaching guides for C-SPAN cable TV programming and info about grants and special programming. 400 N. Capitol St. NW, Suite 650, Washington, DC 20001; 800-523-7586.

**Free watch and calculator**. Five-function quartz sport watch with world time, and a full-function pocket calculator. All you pay is $2 each for shipping and handling. Limit five of each per person. Specify "free watch" or "free calculator." Dollar Stretcher, BFT-Special Free Offer, P.O. Box 125, Hartsdale, NY 10530.

**Flag folders**. Information and materials about flags. Send 50 cents to The Star-Spangled Banner Association 844 E. Pratt St., Baltimore, MD 21202.

**HOW TO RESPECT AND DISPLAY OUR FLAG.** Publications, U.S. Marine Corps, Department of the Navy, Washington, DC 20380.

**STAR-SPANGLED BANNER and GRAND UNION FLAGS**, plus posters and a sample magazine. National Flag Foundation, Flag Plaza, Pittsburgh, PA 15219-3630.

**BILL OF RIGHTS TODAY**. Request #489A from the Public Affairs Informa\tion Service, 521 W. 43rd St., Floor 5, New York, NY 10036-4302.

**Foreign study**. For free information about foreign study for ages 16 and up, see "High School."

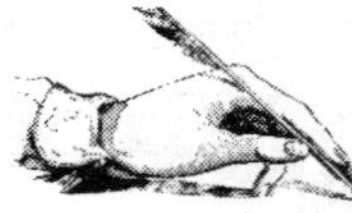

**HOW TO HELP YOUR CHILD BECOME A BETTER WRITER.** Specify English or Spanish. Send an SASE to the National Council of Teachers of English, Dept. C, 1111 Kenyon Rd., Urbana, IL 61801.

**A WAY OF TEACHING VALUES**. Send a stamp to the Language Press, P.O. Box 342, Whitewater, WI 53190.

**BEST FRIENDS TEACHING KIT**. Info about pet care, a poster, and more. Include school name and address. The American Kennel Club, Public Education Dept., Attn: Best Friends, 5580 Centerview Dr., Raleigh, NC 27606.

## ENVIRONMENT

**Animal facts**. Series of fact sheets about North American wildlife. Also a brochure: "Ten Fun Ways to Go Wild About Diversity." Defenders of Wildlife, 1101 14th St. NW, Suite 1400, Washington, DC 20005.

**Energy information for kids**. Excellent! Write CAREIRS, P.O. Box 3048, Merrifield, VA 22116. Request free information package.

**EARTH ANSWERS: WHAT YOU NEED TO KNOW.** Brochure series: #1, What's In a Tree?; #2, Is Using Paper Killing Trees?; #3, How Much Paper Can Be Made From a Tree?; #4, Are We Running Out of Trees?; #5, Why Recycle?; #6, How Is Paper Recycled?; #7, Why Do Some Paper Mills Have an Odor? Ages 12 and up. TAIPPI Public Outreach Dept., P.O. Box 105113, Atlanta, GA 30348-5113.

**Pack of 216 stickers** to reinforce character development. Example: "I respect others" and "I respect my environment." $3.50 plus 50 cents shipping. 888-381-9931; www.spotlites.com.

**MICKEY MOUSE AND GOOFY EXPLORE BUSINESS** and **MICKEY AND GOOFY EXPLORE THE UNIVERSE OF ENERGY.** Comic books. Request energy education/K-12 resource book. Exxon Public Affairs, Box 2180, Houston, TX 77252.

**Free pencil** made out of recycled newspaper. Request free resource packet from Tree Smart, P.O. Box 502, Lake Oswego, OR 97034.

**MICHAEL RECYCLE**. Comic book. Michael Recycle, Wise Recycling, LLC, Box 28737, Baltimore, MD 21240.

**THE STORY OF LEAD** and much more. Lead Industry Association, 295 Madison Ave., New York, NY 10017.

**LEARN ABOUT LIGHT**. Osram/Sylvania Products, 100 Endicott St., Danvers, MA 01923; www.sylvania.com.

**SCIENCE ACTIVITIES and ENERGY SERIES**. Technical Information Center, U.S. Department of Energy, P.O. Box 62, Oak Ridge, TN 37830.

**THE STORY OF MEASUREMENT**. Poster. Ford Motor Company, World Headquarters, The American Rd., Dearborn, MI 48121.

**LIBRARY OF CONGRESS INFORMATION BULLETIN** and more. Library of Congress, Office of Public Affairs, 101 Independence Ave. SE, Washington, DC 20540.

**Plant a tree.** Free materials resource guide with activities to promote tree planting and environmental awareness. National Arbor Day Foundation, 100 Arbor Ave., Nebraska City, NE 68410.

**Booklets on energy conservation**. "Energy Saver," "Solar Heating and You," and "Renewable Energy." Ages 14 and up. Energy Efficiency and Renewable Energy Clearinghouse, P.O. Box 3048, Merrifield, VA 22116.

**INVITE BIRDS TO YOUR HOME**. Soil Conservation Service, U.S.D.A., Box 2890, Washington, DC 20013.

**Newsletters about home safety, composting, the environment, recycling, and more**. Request a list of what they offer. Send a large SASE to Adam Nichols, Pennsylvania Resources Council, Environmental Center, 3606 Providence Rd, Newtown Square, PA 19073.

**RECYCLING STUDY GUIDE**. Grades 4 to 12. Department of Natural Resources, Education Section, P.O. Box 7921, Madison, WI 53707.

**Interested in renewable energy?** Write Renewable Energy Information, Box 8900, Silver Spring, MD 20907, and request information. Ask about related publications. Have a specific question? Call 800-523-2929. Want information on the Web? Go to www.eren.doe.gov.

**ENERGY SAVER BOOKLETS**. U.S. Department of Energy Technical Information Center, Box 62, Oak Ridge, TN 37830. Also information about nuclear energy and possible risks, and wind energy.

**DON'T TRASH IT!** Comic/activity book about how to minimize trash. Ask what else they offer. Environmental Protection Agency, National Center for Environmental Publications, P.O. Box 42419, Cincinnati, OH 45268.

**ENERGY EFFICIENCY/EARTH SHARE**. Information for kids about being more energy-efficient and helping the environment. Call 888-STARYES.

**ENERGY INFORMATION SERIES**. Facts about oil exploration and wind, nuclear, geothermal, and coal power. American Petroleum Institute, Publications Section, 1220 L St. NW, Washington, DC 20005.

**MAKING PAPER FROM TREES**. Forest Service, U.S. Department of Agriculture, Washington, DC 20250

**Information about redwoods**. Service Library, California Redwood Association, 405 Enfrente Rd., #200, Novato, CA 94949-7201.

**CANADIAN ECOZINE**. Ministry of Forests, Information Services Branch, 1450 Government St., Victoria, BC V8W 3E7.

**ALASKA'S FORESTS**. Alaska Forest Association, 111 Stedman, Suite 200, Ketchikan, AK 99901.

**THE KANSAS SCHOOL NATURALIST**. Newsletter about natural history and nature education — everything from snow flies to prairie fires. Ask to have your name added to the list. One theme per issue; ages 12 and up. Kansas School Naturalist, Emporia State University, 12 Commercial St., Emporia, KS 66801. Available to all.

## UNITED NATIONS

**BASIC FACTS ABOUT THE UNITED NATIONS**. United Nations Information Centre, 1889 F St. NW, Washington, DC 20006.

**UNICEF** (United Nations Children's Fund). Information about the world's children is available at no charge from Renny Lea, former representative to the U.N. and now a member of Citizens for Multicultural Education. Materials include a quarterly newsletter called "First Call for Children"; "Facts and Figures: 1994-95," the 1995 State of the World's Children summary report; the annual report of the U.S. Committee for UNICEF; and "The Progress of Nations," a report stating the achievements made. See address above.

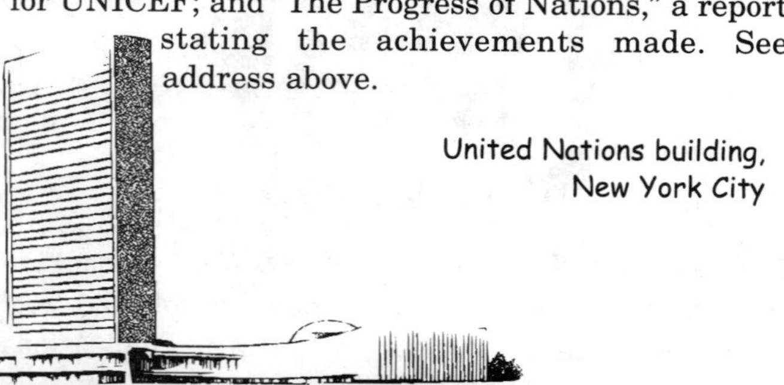

United Nations building, New York City

## TRAVEL

**Low-cost accommodations**. Call The Room Exchange, 800-846-7000 or 212-760-1000. Up to 50% off hotel rooms in the U.S., Canada, and the Caribbean. Or call Quikbook, 800-489-9887, for places in the U.S.

**Home exchange and rental club** brochure with listings in 37 countries. Worldwide Home Exchange Club, Box 21879, Washington, DC 20009

**www.homeexchange.com**. It's the only home exchange website that allows non-members to search and contact members, for free. This listing is from my marvelous copy editor, who has helped make this book so nice to read. She says her house is listed there, and they have been to Ireland and been offered homes in Italy, Australia, England, New York, and Florida.

**THE PEOPLE OF THE AIRLINES**. Pamphlets. The Air Transport Association, 1301 Pennsylvania Ave. NW, #1100, Washington, DC 20004-1707.

**ROAD ATLAS AND TRAVEL GUIDE**. Best Western International, Attn: Publications Dept., 6201 N. 24 Parkway, Phoenix, AZ 85016.

Cliff Palace
Mesa Verde National Park
Colorado

**Information about U.S. national parks**. You can request any or all of the following: Rocky Mountain National Park, Colorado; Mt. McKinley National Park, Alaska; Mesa Verde National Park, Colorado; Hot Springs National Park, Arkansas; Hawaii National Park; Yellowstone National Park, Wyoming; Carlsbad Caverns, New Mexico; free map of the whole park system. Department of the Interior, National Park Service, Washington, DC 20240.

**Thousand Islands**. U.S. and Canada tour information. 1) 1000 Islands, Box 428, Alexandria Bay, NY 13607, or 1000 Islands, Box 10, Lansdowne, ON K0E 1L0. 2) Kingston Bureau of Tourism, Box 486, 209 Ontario St., Kingston, ON K7L 2Z1. 3) Rideau Lakes Thousand Islands, P.O. Box 125, Perth, ON K7H 3E3.

**Argentine Embassy**, 1600 New Hampshire Ave. NW, Washington, DC 20009.

**Australian Consulate General**, 636 Fifth Ave., New York, NY 10020.

**Austrian National Tourist Office**, 500 Fifth Ave., New York, NY 10110. Austrian information package.

**British Tourist Authority**, 551 Fifth Ave., New York, NY 10110. British information package.

**Canadian Government Office of Tourism**, Ottawa, ON, K1A 0H6. Canadian tour information: where to go and what to see.

**Nova Scotia Information**, P.O. Box 130, Halifax, NS Canada B3J 2M7; 800-341-6096. If you take the ferry over, remember your Pepto-Bismol. My head loved the ride, and my stomach had grave second thoughts halfway there.

**Egyptian Government Travel Office**, 630 Fifth Ave., New York, NY 10111. Egypt information package.

**French Government Tourist Office**, 444 Madison Ave., New York, NY 10022.

**Lufthansa German Airlines**, 1640 Hempstead Turnpike, East Meadow, NY 11554. Welcome to Germany package.

**Greek National Tourist Organization**, Olympic Tower, 645 Fifth Ave., New York, NY 10022. Greece tour package.

**Hong Kong Tourist Information**, 590 Fifth Ave., New York, NY 10036.

**Consulate General of Hungarian People's Republic**, 8 E. 75th St., New York, NY 10021. Travel package.

**Information Service of India**, Embassy of India, Washington, DC 20008. India tour kit.

**Consulate General of Indonesia**, Information Section, 5 E. 68th St., New York, NY 10021. Information packet.

**For information about Ireland**, call 800-SHAMROCK.

**Israel Government Tourist Office**, 350 Fifth Ave., New York, NY 10118. Guidebooks and maps of Israel and the Holy Land.

**Italian Government Travel Office**, 630 Fifth Ave., New York, NY 10111. A Trip to Italy tour package.

**Japanese Tourist Organization**, 630 Fifth Ave., New York, NY 10111. Japan tour package.

**Mexican National Tourist Council**, 405 Park Ave., New York, NY 10022. Brochures about Mexico.

**Explorations Inc.**, 27655 Kent Rd., Bonita Springs, FL 33923. Information about Peru.

**Embassy of the Russian Federation**, 1706 18th St. NW, Washington, DC 20009; www.russianembassy.org and www.rian.ru. Information about Russia.

**Embassy of South Africa**, 3501 Massachusetts Ave. NW, Washington, DC 20008. Information about South Africa.

**Spain Office of Tourism**, 666 Fifth Ave., New York, NY 10103. Information about Spain.

**Swiss National Tourist Office**, 608 Fifth Ave., New York, NY 10020. Swiss tour package.

For travel information within the U.S. call 800-555-1212 and request the toll-free number for the Department of Tourism for the states you wish to investigate.

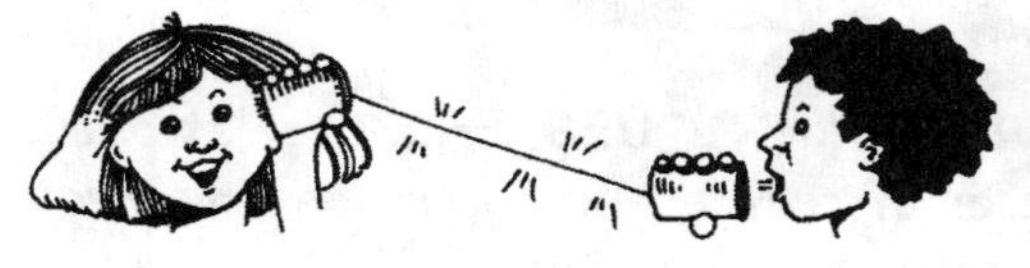

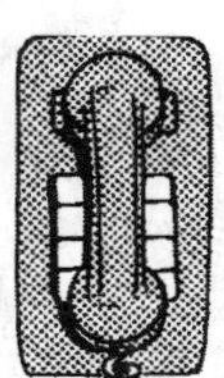

For general consumer problems, questions, and complaints and how to get action, call 800-664-4435 between 10 a.m. and 2 p.m.

**CONSUMER RESOURCE HANDBOOK**. The best source for information about making effective consumer complaints. It's free. Also available is a consumer information catalog. Consumer Information Center, Pueblo, CO 81009.

**ARTS — CRAFTS — GAMES — HOBBIES**

**Art lessons**. Request a list of their many interesting free lessons. American Art Clay Co., 4717 W. 16th St., Indianapolis, IN 46222.

**Art appreciation films**. Write for free reservation card and catalog. Your only cost is return postage. National Gallery of Art, Extension Program, Washington, DC 20565.

**EGGORY'S EGG CRAFT IDEAS**. Send $2 to Eggory, Georgia Egg Commission, State Farmers' Market, Forest Park, GA 30050.

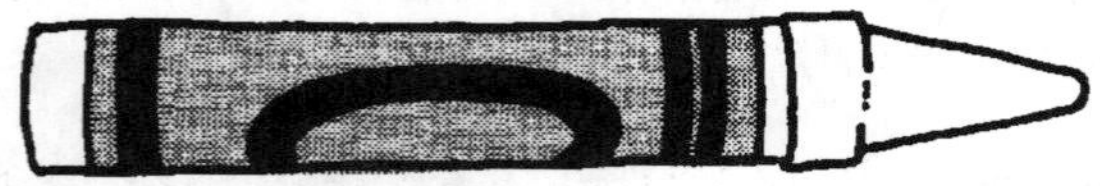

**CRAYOLA ART TECHNIQUES**. Free booklet about the various uses of crayons, pencil crayons, markers, and paints. Binney and Smith Inc., 1100 Church Lane, P.O. Box 431, Easton, PA 18042.

**HOT SHOTS WITH ANY CAMERA**. Free full-color book about taking excellent photos. 800-242-2424.

**ORIGAMI INFORMATION**. Learn to make flying birds, flowers, animals, and more. Send $1 to Fascinating Folds, P.O. Box 2820-235, Torrance, CA 90509-2820.

**HOW TO MAKE PAPER BY HAND**. Hammermill Papers Group, P.O. Box 1440, Erie, PA 16533.

**HOW TO MAKE PAPER**. Ages 10 and up. America's Forest and Paper Association, 1111 19th St. NW, Suite 80, Washington, DC 20036.

**HOW TO MAKE PLAY CLAY**. Send postcard to Arm and Hammer Consumer Relations, Division of Church and Dwight Co., Princeton NJ 08543-5297; 800-524-1328.

How about spending $3 for something called "Free Stuff"? The ad says, "Send $3 to Prime Publishing, Inc., 1954 First St., P.O. Box 663, Dept. CPPN131, Highland Park, IL 60035, for a copy of **FREE STUFF FOR CRAFTING, SEWING AND MORE**." Directory lists more than 400 free or postage-only offers of samples, kits, patterns, and more.

**Free newsletter and catalog** about beads and beading. Frantz Bead Company, 1222 Sunset Hill Rd., Shelton, WA 98584.

**YO-YO TRICK PAMPHLET**. Send an SASE to Duncan Toys Co., P.O. Box 5, Middlefield, OH 44062.

**CHOOSING TOYS**. Brochure. American Toy Institute, 1115 Broadway Suite 400, New York, NY 10010.

**Free maze**. PDK Enterprises, P.O. Box 1776, Boyes Hot Springs, CA 95416.

**TEN TIPS TO WINNING CHESS**. Send an SASE to the U.S. Chess Federation, Dept. 17, 186 Route 9W, New Windsor, NY 12553. Also ask about *Chess Life and Review*.

**Official rules for all sports.** Sporting Goods Manufacturers Association, 200 Castlewood Dr., N. Palm Beach, FL 33408.

**Learn to crochet**. Free instructions to make snowflakes and yarn ornaments. Lorraine Vetter-FT, 7924 Soper Hill Rd., Everett, WA 98205.

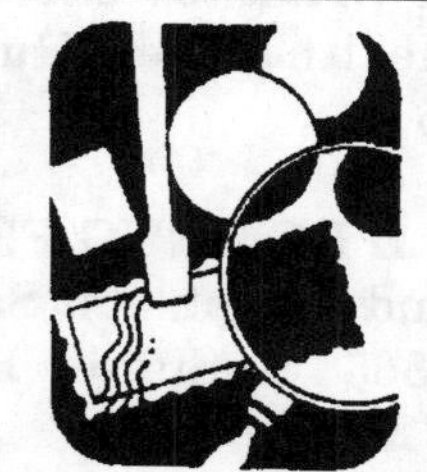

**Collection of mint United States stamps.** Remember to ask for the special stamp collector's information and price lists, along with other interesting offers. Send $2 to the Mystic Stamp Company, Dept. P259, 24 Mill St., Camden, NY 13316.

**INTRODUCTION TO STAMP COLLECTING.** Info packet, poster, resource guide, and more. Stamp Division, Postal Service, 475 L'Enfant Plaza SW, Washington, DC 20260-2435.

**Craft supplies.** Catalog of basketry, woodworking, stitchery, and macramé supplies. The Craft Basket, 117 Old State Rd., Brookfield, CT 06804.

**Catalog of etchings**, lithographs, and woodcuts. Association of American Artists, 20 W. 57th St., Floor 6, New York, NY 10019.

**Harmonica instruction**. Books and music for harmonicas. Hohner Inc., P.O. Box 9167, Richmond, VA 23227.

**MAGIC SALT CRYSTAL GARDEN**. Luther Ford & Co., 1700 W. 94th St., P.O. Box 201405, Bloomington, MN 55420.

**SEE HOW THEY RUN**. Info packet about batteries from Energizer. 800-383-7323.

**LET'S COLLECT SHELLS AND ROCKS.** Booklet. Shell Oil Co., 1 Shell Plaza, P.O. Box 2463, Houston TX 77252.

## PETS AND ANIMALS

**CARING FOR YOUR DOG** and **GUIDE TO HEALTH CARE FOR YOUR DOG**. Books with a brief history of dogs and tips on feeding, grooming, obedience training, and more. They will include some coupons too. Ralston-Purina, Dog Food Division, Checkerboard Square, St. Louis, MO 63164.

**Animal info**. Free catalog of publications with information about cats, dogs, horses, birds, and fish. American Humane Association, P.O. Box 1266, Denver, CO 80201.

**A IS FOR ANIMAL.** Sample issue of a teacher newsletter, plus a catalog of other materials and services. The American Society for the Prevention of Cruelty to Animals (ASPCA), Dept. LWI, 424 E. 92nd St., New York, NY 10128-6804.

**AMERICAN QUARTER HORSE**. Poster and other materials. American Quarter Horse Association, P.O. Box 200, Amarillo, TX 79168; www.aqha.org.

**THE AMERICAN BUFFALO**. Information sheet. U.S. Department of the Interior, Fish and Wildlife Service, Washington, DC 20240.

**WHY SAVE ENDANGERED SPECIES?** Request #589P from the U.S. Government Printing Office, Superintendent of Documents, Public Documents Distribution Center, Pueblo, CO 81009.

**ANIMALS ... IT'S THEIR WORLD TOO!** Bumper sticker. The Humane Society of the U.S., 2100 L St. NW, Washington, DC 20037.

**NATIONAL WILDLIFE WEEK KIT.** National Wildlife Federation, Leesburg Pike, Vienna, VA 22184.

**WOODSY OWL POLLUTION FIGHTER PACKAGE** and poster. Woodsy Owl, USDA Forest Service, P.O. Box 96090, Washington, DC 20090-6090; www.fs.fed.us/spf/woodsy.

## GARDENING

**HOW TO GROW AN ORGANIC GARDEN**. Organic Gardening and Farming, 33 E. Minor St., Emmaus, PA 18049.

**Interested in starting a community garden?** Write to the National Garden Association, 180 Flynn Ave., Burlington, VT 05401, and ask for their booklet "Growing Ideas."

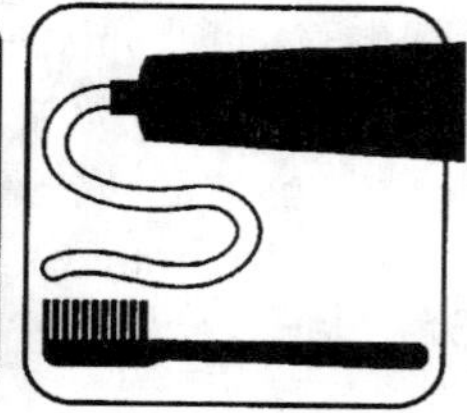

## SAFETY AND HEALTH

**HIDDEN HAZARDS II**. Information about child safety and hidden hazards. Send an SASE to the Coalition for Consumer Health and Safety, P.O. Box 12099, Washington, DC 20005-0999.

**Personal health record**, height and weight tables, family guide to safety, and more. Health and Welfare Division, Metropolitan Life Insurance Co., 1 Madison Ave., New York, NY 10010.

**Bicycle safety comic and booklet**. U.S. Consumer Product Safety Commission, Washington, DC 20207.

**TIPS FOR NEW DRIVERS**. Bridgestone/Firestone Inc., 50 Century Blvd., P.O. Box 1408900, Nashville, TN 37214.

**Information about prenatal care and children**. Department of Health and Human Services, Bethesda, MD 20205.

**HELP YOUR CHILD BE DRUG FREE** and related topics in booklets and pamphlets. Send $1 to Do It Now Foundation, 6565 W. Sunset Blvd., #417, Los Angeles, CA 90028-7206.

**PARENT'S GUIDE FOR EARACHES**. Learn causes, symptoms, and cures. Children's Tylenol, 1675 Broadway, 33rd Floor, New York, NY 10019.

**For your eyes**. Free information about eye care, selection of frames, correct lighting, sunglasses, and more. Send a #10 SASE to the Better Vision Institute, P.O. Box 77097, Washington, DC 20013.

**FACTS ABOUT SMOKING** package. Learn about your lungs. Also ask about their other free materials. Send a postcard to the American Lung Association, 432 Park Ave. South, 8th Fl., New York, NY 10116.

**Anti-smoking comic book**. Spiderman battles evil villain Smokescreen. American Cancer Society, 800-277-2345.

**FACTS ABOUT DENTAL HYGIENE**. Information about dental hygiene and career opportunities. Send an SASE to the American Dental Hygienists' Association, 444 N. Michigan Ave., Chicago IL 60611, Attn: Nutrition Dept.

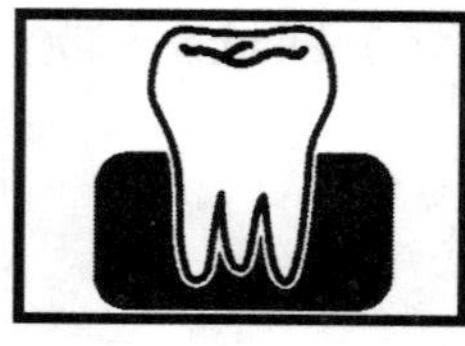

**Pamphlets about teeth and dental care**, plus a coupon. Chesebrough-Pond's USA Co., Consumer Services, 800 Sylvan Ave., Englewood Cliffs, NJ 07632.

**Mind-over-body information**. The Institute of Noetic Sciences, 800-628-4545.

**Catalog of books, brochures, videos, and posters about stuttering.** Stuttering Foundation of America, P.O. Box 11749, Memphis, TN 38111-0749.

**Free family health record log**, info on prenatal and postnatal care, drugs, and sexually transmitted diseases. March of Dimes, 1275 Mamaroneck Ave., White Plains, NY 10605.

**VISION AND THE VDT OPERATOR**. Information about reducing eye strain. Also **YOUR MIRACULOUS EYES** and a schematic chart of the human eye. Send an SASE to the American Optometric Association, 243 N. Lindbergh Blvd., St. Louis, MO 63141.

**Information about eyes and Seeing Eye dogs**. The Seeing Eye, Inc., P.O. Box 375, Morristown, NJ 07963.

**THE STORY OF BLOOD**. The history of blood and blood as medicine. American Red Cross National Headquarters, 17th and D Sts. NW, Washington, DC 20006.

**Help for alcoholics**. Alcoholics Anonymous, Box 459, Grand Central Station, New York, NY 10163.

**QUICK-REFERENCE FIRST-AID GUIDE**, plus coupons for first-aid products. Johnson & Johnson, 199 Grandview Rd., Skillman, NJ 08558.

**Health info**. Pamphlets about steroids, AIDS, marijuana, hallucinogens, inhalants, smoking, alcohol, crack, and cocaine. Ages 10 and up. National Clearinghouse for Alcohol and Drug Information, P.O. Box 2345, Rockville, MD 20847-2345.

℞

**Asthma information.** The Asthma and Allergy Foundation will answer questions. Call 800-7-ASTHMA.

**ABCs OF EYECARE**. Information about eye care, selection of frames, correct lighting, sunglasses, and more, for kids and adults. Send a #10 SASE to the Better Vision Institute, P.O. Box 77097, Washington, DC 20013.

**Free contact lenses**. Johnson & Johnson would like you to try their Acuvue contacts. They have made arrangements with many local optometrists. Ask your optometrist for a free pair. If he is not part of this arrangement, suggest he call Johnson & Johnson.

**HIKING SAFETY** booklet. Send an SASE to American Hiking Society, Dept. T, P.O. Box 21060, Washington, DC 20041.

**YOUR CHILD'S HEALTH RECORD**. An easy way to track illnesses, allergies, immunizations, family history, and more. Features the Peanuts Gang. Send a #10 SASE to Met Life Insurance (16UV), Box HR, One Madison Ave., New York, NY 10010.

**THE HOLISTIC HERBAL HEALTHCARE GUIDE**. A lot of information about holistic herbal health. Send four first-class stamps to Deborah Coble, 1420-E3 Steeple Chase Dr., Dover, PA 17315-378.

?
???
???????

**QUESTIONS TO ASK YOUR DOCTOR BEFORE YOU HAVE SURGERY**. Information about non-emergency surgery. This pamphlet is published by the Agency for Healthcare Research and Quality (U.S. Department of Health and Human Services). 800-358-9295. Also available at www.ahcpr.gov/consumer/surgery.htm.

For confidential help and information about **HIV** and **AIDS**, call the National AIDS Hotline of the Centers for Disease Control, 800-342-2437.

**ORDERING THE FOLLOWING INFORMATION FROM THE U.S. GOVERNMENT:** If you are ordering **up to 25 "free"** publications, enclose $1 for processing and send your order to: S. James, Consumer Information Center-7B, P.O. Box 100, Pueblo, CO 81002. If you are **ordering paid or both free and paid** booklets, send to: R. Woods, Consumer Information Center-7B, P.O. Box 100, Pueblo, CO 81002. Payment can be by check or money order payable to Superintendent of Documents.

**DEPUTY FIRE MARSHAL KIT**. Stickers, badge, and certificate. Ages 5 to 10. #504D. Free.
**HELPING YOUR CHILD LEARN GEOGRAPHY**. Ages 5 to 10. 36 pages, #372D. 50¢.
**HELPING YOUR CHILD LEARN HISTORY**. Ages 4 to 11. 50 pages, #307D. 50¢.
**HELPING YOUR CHILD LEARN MATH**. Ages 5 to 13. 64 pages, #308D. 50¢.
**HELPING YOUR CHILD LEARN TO READ**. Ages 10 and under. 65 pages, #309D. 50¢.
**ELECTRONIC APPLICATION FOR FEDERAL STUDENT AID**. Two 3.5" diskettes with Windows-compatible software, online instructions, and guide. You need a modem. #615D. Free.
**BABY SAFETY CHECKLIST**. #315D. 50¢.
**KIDS' VACCINATIONS GET A LITTLE EASIER**. #553D. Free.
**THE GED DIPLOMA**. #512D. Free.
**HEALTH INFORMATION ONLINE**. Suggestions about determining if a site is reliable. #613D. Free.
**DISCOVER AMERICA**. List of state tourism offices for free information, maps, and more. #379D. 50¢.
**PASSPORTS: APPLYING FOR THEM THE EASY WAY**. #364D. 50¢.
**THE U.S. AND THE METRIC SYSTEM**. #370D. 50¢.

**Your own private gold mine of information**. Ask for any of the following two-sided color posters: "Ground Water, The Hidden Resource"; "Navigation, Traveling the Water Highways!"; "Wetlands, Water, Wildlife, Plants, and People"; "Water Quality, Potential Sources of Pollution"; and "Watersheds, Where We Live." Also available is "Exploring Caves", a large poster and 58-page instructional book for grades K to 3, guide, and list of other resources about caves. Pamphlets offered include "Gold"; "The Big Five," some facts and figures about large U.S. rivers; "The Interior of the Earth"; "Finding Your Way With Map and Compass"; and "Landforms of the U.S." You can also request a very large poster called "Fossils Through Time." Ask for a list of their free publications for schools and individuals. U.S. Geological Survey Information Services, P.O. Box 25286, MS 306, Denver Federal Center, Denver, CO 80225.

**Free information** about many topics of interest is available from your local Extension Service, listed under County Government in the phone book.

**FREEBIES FOR KIDS, FREE STUFF FOR KIDS**, and **FREEBIES FOR TEACHERS**, $5 each or all 3 for $14; shipping included. Your choice of free gift with order: Memo Pad, Fun Activity Sheet, or Magic Window Toy. Mr. Rainbow's Neet Stuff, P.O. Box 908, Rio Grande, NJ 08242.

**A.D. Productions**, 3407-H W. Wendover Ave., Greensboro, NC 27407. Interesting and unusual calendars; about $12 each.

**Adventures in Cassettes**, 5353 Nathan Lane North, Plymouth, MN 55442. Old radio productions.

**Alpha Omega Publications**, 300 N. McKemy, Chandler, AZ 85226-2618. A Christian organization with religious materials and some very good non-religious materials.

**Anderson's Bookshops**, P.O. Box 3832, Naperville, IL 60567-3832. One of the best catalogs of children's books. Everything reviewed.

**Animal Town**, P.O. Box 757, Greenland, NH 03840. Great collection of toys, books, games, and more.

**Apple Garden**, P.O. Box 2666, Napa, CA 94558. Beautiful children's toys, books, and more.

**Applewood Books**, 128 The Great Rd, Bedford, MA 01730; 800-277-5312. Historical books about America's past. Perfect for reading and history. Good prices.

**Audio Literature**, 370 W. San Bruno Ave., San Bruno, CA 94066; 800-842-2665.

**Bits & Pieces**, One Puzzle Place, B8016, Stevens Point, WI 54481-7199. Puzzles from simple to complicated to unique.

**Books on Tape**, 800-548-6574. They say they have the largest selection of unabridged audiobooks. I don't know if that's true, but they do have a large catalog and some great titles.

**Carolina Biological Supply**, 2700 York Road, Burlington, NC 27215. Science materials.

**CBC Radio Catalogue**, General Distribution Services, 325 Humber College Blvd., Toronto, ON M9W 7C3. List of programs available to the public. They offer some interesting listening. Fortunately the recorded material is better than the PR letter I received, which had the following information: "The independent stores that decided to carry CBC Audio have done particularly well, and they indicated that audio did not sell well for them."

**Chinaberry**, 2780 Via Orange Way, Suite B, Spring Valley, CA 91978: 800-776-2242. Children's books sorted by reading level and books for adults, too, with marvelous reviews. Many other interesting items.

**Company of America**, P.O. Box 5026, White Plains, NY 10602-5026. Great catalog of math resources.

**Continental Press**, 520 E. Bainbridge St., Elizabethtown, PA 17022; 800-233-0759. Inexpensive workbooks and test prep books for grades K to 12 in all subjects, including special-needs.

**Creative Educational Materials**, 14650 28th Ave. North, Plymouth, MN 55447. Workbooks, stickers, and more.

**Curiosity Kits**, 11111 Pepper Rd., P.O. Box 811, Hunt Valley, MD 21031-1203. Lots of creative play and learning materials.

**Daedalus Books**, P.O. Box 9132, Hyattsville, MD 20781-0932. Book remainders. They say they try to choose books of lasting value. They also offer CDs.

**Delta Education**, Dept. TR385, P.O. Box 3000, Nashua, NH 03061. Good hands-on math and science materials.

**Dover Publications**, 31 E. 2nd St., Mineola, NY 11501-3582; 800-223-3130.. Hundreds of good books for children and adults at low prices. Ask for the juvenile catalog. Check with them about their shipping rates — it may be cheaper to buy these books from us. Anything you can order from Dover, we can get for you. Also **Dover Pictorial Archive Catalog**. More than 900 copyright-free illustrations and designs for artists and craftspeople. Also books of art prints.

**Edward R. Hamilton**, P.O. Box 5005, Falls Village, CT 06031-5005. Books: overstocks, imports, and reprints. Big discounts on many titles, some recent.

**Family*Fatherhood*Faith*Freedom** catalog from The Vision Forum, 8122 Datapoint Dr., #306, San Antonio, TX 78216. Henty and Dinsmore books; other Christian education books.

**Fas-Track Computer Products**, 130 Burrer Dr., Sunbury, OH 43074. Various software.

**Follett Educational Services**, 1433 Internationale Parkway, Woodridge, IL 60517; 800-621-4272; www.fes.follett.com. Used textbooks from most major publishers in very good condition at reasonable prices, plus teacher's editions, workbooks, dictionaries, reference books, and classroom paperbacks.

**Frank Schaffer Publications**, 23740 Hawthorne Blvd., P.O. Box 2853, Torrance, CA 90509-2853. A variety of inexpensive schoolbooks, workbooks, supplies, and more.

**Frostline Kits**, 2525 River Rd., Grand Junction, CO 81505. Patterns and kits for warm, insulated clothing, comforters, and more.

**The Global Classroom**, 12 Winter Sport Lane, Williston, VT 05495. A nice collection of books about character, service, coexistence, conflict resolution, and more. We review some of these titles. If you want some of their other books you can get them from us. Check shipping charges; ours may or may not be better.

**Harold Press**, 616 Walnut Ave, Scottdale, PA 15683-1999. Christian, Mennonite, and Amish books. Good children's section and books on peace.

**Hayes 2000**, 321 Pennwood Ave., Wilkinsburg, PA 15221. Teacher resources.

**Hearth Song**, 6519 N. Galena Rd., P.O. Box 1773, Peoria, IL 61656-1773; www.hearthsong.com. Creative and interesting toys and games. Decent prices. I'll be using this one for sure.

**Historical Products**, P.O. Box 604, Barre, VT 05641. Literary and musical T-shirts. I don't think I want to wear someone else's portrait in public, but I've toyed with the idea of getting a couple of these for night shirts. Or maybe barn shirts, and see what Mrs. Montgomery thinks of them. (Mrs. Montgomery is our Jersey cow.) Famous people, real and fictional, such as Bach, Einstein, Darwin, Newton, Twain, Verdi, the Marx Brothers, the Cheshire Cat, Bogart, Hemingway, Michelangelo, Thoreau, and many more. Or wear a quotation ("Common sense is not so common" — Voltaire) or a musical selection from Bach, Beethoven, or Mozart. The same designs are also available on linen calendars, aprons, tote bags, and sweatshirts.

**Home Again**, 1825 N. 183rd St., Seattle, WA 98133; www.home-again.com. Nice toys, books, games, and crafts.

**HomeSchool and More ...**, Gertrude De Boer, 29 Donald Dr., Charlottetown, PEI C1E 1Z5; shdeboer@auracom.com. Excellent **Canadian** home-learning resources. I like the materials except that I think the catalog is so Canadian that it's limiting.

**Instructional Fair Group**, P.O. Box 1650, Grand Rapids, MI 49501. Request Home Education Catalog. Cheap workbooks, some of which are worthwhile, but keep in mind that they have only recently discovered YOU, a homeschooler. You are being targeted with $$ in mind.

**Jackdaw Publications**, P.O. Box 503, Amawalk, NY 10501; 800-789-0022. Original documents including maps, letters, newspaper reproductions, and a lot more in unit-study groupings. Teachers complain because the students steal these. I take that as a recommendation. Wide variety of topics (e.g., Alfred the Great, American China Trade, American Revolution, Atomic Bomb, Blues in America, Computers, Charles Dickens, Tutankhamen and the Tomb, and a lot more). Now very expensive! Would be good for a group resource library.

**Johnson Smith Co.,** 4514 19th Court East, Bradenton, FL 34203. Request Novelty Catalog. Wacky, fun things, gadgets, and more. Scan as quickly as you can past the idiotic junk, such as the itching powder, the squirting camera, the safety pin through your nose, the dribble glass, the rubber cockroaches, and other "practical jokes," and watch for the relatively sane and useful things: an Indian bead set, an ant farm, 1,000 mini-magnets for $2.95, a Davy Crockett cap, foreign coins, a gemstone and mineral set, reproductions of early U.S. money, toy rockets, a crystal radio kit, a miniature steam engine that really works, and more.

**Kaplan**, P.O. Box 609, 1310 Lewisville-Clemmons Rd., Lewisville, NC 27023. A great variety of educational materials: toys, games, books, paints, and more.

**Key Curriculum Press**, P.O. Box 2304, Berkeley, CA 94702. High school math textbooks, computer software, and more.

**Kimbo Educational**, Dept. G, P.O. Box 477, Long Beach, NJ 07740-0477. Nice selection of musical resources I haven't seen before.

**Kits 'n Kaboodles**, 35819 Ramada Ln., Yucaipa, CA 92399. Hands-on learning kits.

**Knowledge Unlimited**, P.O. Box 52, Madison, WI 53701-0052; 800-356-2303. Very good learning materials.

**Kodansha America**, 114 Fifth Ave., New York, NY 10011. Japanese books and related material.

**Lighter Side**, 4514 19th St. Court East, P.O. Box 25600, Dept. LD, Bradenton, FL 34203-5600. Funny and unusual gift ideas.

**Mailbox Magazine**, P.O. Box 51676, Boulder, CO 80323-1676. Workbooks.

**Maple Ridge Books**, R.R. 6, Markdale, ON N0C 1H0. Canadian educational materials.

**Miliken Publishing**, 1100 Research Blvd., P.O. Box 21579, St. Louis, MO 63132. Good workbooks. Reasonable prices.

**Mr. Rainbow's Neet Stuff**, P.O. Box 908, Rio Grande, NJ 08242. Lots of cheap and interesting things, including books about more free or almost-free stuff for kids.

**More Than Books**, 146 McClintock Way, Kanata, ON K2L 2A4. A variety of books and resources, some of which are Christian-based. Many are in this book.

**Nienhuis Montessori USA**, 320 Pioneer Way, Mountain View, CA 94041-1576; www.nienhuis.nl. Montessori materials.

**Parenting Press**, P.O. Box 75267, Seattle, WA 98125. Lots of good books about raising kids. We've reviewed some of them.

**PBS Videos,** 1320 Braddock Pl., Alexandria, VA 22314-1698.

**Play Fair Toys**, P.O. Box 18210, Boulder, CO 80308. Very good toys, including three-foot dinosaur models, a human skull model, and Lincoln Logs.

**The Playstore**, 508 University Ave., Palo Alto, CA 94301. Beautifully made toys, games, costumes, and more.

**Radio Spirits**, P.O. Box 2141, Schiller Park, IL 60176. Old-time radio on cassette.

**Recorded Books, Inc.**, 800-505-8104 (this number works in the U.S. and Canada). Great literature on tape for kids. Book and cassette sets that can help encourage a reluctant reader or improve reading skills. Ask for the audiobooks complete and unabridged catalog.

**School Zone**, P.O. Box 777, Grand Haven, MI 49417; 800-253-0564. This company has some of the very few workbooks of which we thoroughly approve. They're clear and easy to understand, they stick to basic principles and explain them well, and they present exercises that make learning fairly easy and even fun. The books are graded, but most of the materials can be used without regard for the grade level intended by the publisher. Workbooks are available in math, grammar, spelling, reading, phonics, handwriting, number readiness, and several preschool activities. Prices are reasonable, and the service is prompt and efficient. They now offer CD-ROMs for young children and I'm sure they're good, but I don't think young children should be learning this way (see "Computers").

**Sky Publishing Corp.**, 49 Bay Street Rd., Cambridge, MA 02138. Books about astronomy.

**Social Studies School Service**, 10200 Jefferson Blvd., Room 17, P.O. Box 802, Culver City, CA 90232.

**Spilsbury Puzzle Co.**, 3650 Milwaukee St., P.O. Box 8922, Madison, WI 53708-8922. Puzzles, games, and more.

**Spizzirri Publishing**, P.O. Box 9397, Rapid City, SD 57709. Great science, art, and bilingual workbooks.

**The Strand Book Store**, 826 Broadway (at 12th St.), New York, NY 10003-4805. Art books.

**Tin Man Times**, P.O. Box 219, Stanwood, WA 98292. This small catalog of creative language arts material is promoted for the gifted, but I think it's good for everyone's kids.

**Treetop Publishing**, P.O. Box 08567, Racine, WI 53408-5567. Great blank books.

**Volunteer Energy Resource Catalog**, Energize, 5450 Wissahickon Ave., Philadelphia, PA 19144. Many sources for adults and organizations, with a few very good listings for children as volunteers. Some international resources.

**Whole Earth Catalog and Co-Evolution Quarterly**, 1408 Mission Ave., San Rafael, CA 94901.

**Zaner-Bloser**, Attn: Dianne Bradford, P.O. Box 16764, Columbus, OH 43216. Handwriting resources.

# USEFUL AND INTERESTING MAGAZINES

There's something special about a magazine that arrives addressed to a child; although it comes regularly, it's still a surprise.

Most magazines are cheaper than an equal weight in textbooks, and many are much better. These are some of the most helpful on the market today. We read some of them all the time, some of them occasionally, and some of them never. When subscribing, we try to order magazines at different times of the year, so the renewal notices don't all show up at the same time. Fortunately, a few subscriptions have been gifts from relatives. Magazine publishers will be glad to send advertising brochures; some will send samples or enter a trial subscription. Please send an SASE for price and subscription information whenever it is not given. We've done our best to list prices correctly, but they do change without notice. Many specialized magazines (science, history, etc.) are listed in those chapters.

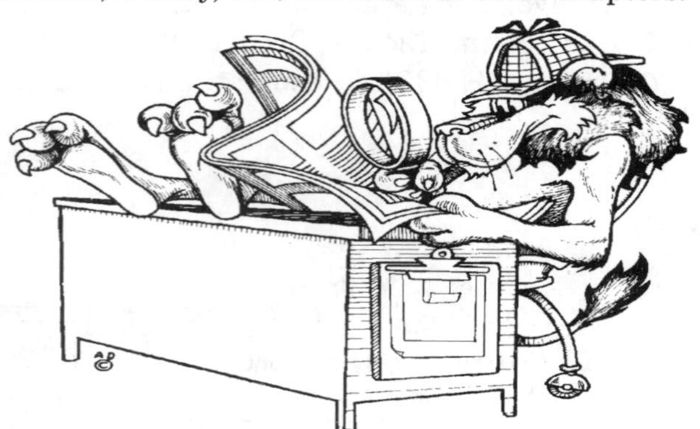

## EDUCATION AND EDUCATIONAL MAGAZINES

The two leading home-schooling magazines (*Home Education Magazine* and *Growing Without Schooling*) are listed with the books in "Homeschooling and Education."

**THE EDUCATION REVOLUTION**. Formerly called *AERO* (the Alternative Education Resource Organization). A magazine that will keep you abreast of major developments in alternative education around the world as well as covering major home-schooling news. Mentions camp opportunities; lists and describes related organizations and current activities, teaching jobs and internships, and conference news; and more. Subscriptions $15 per year U.S., all other subscriptions $20, in U.S. funds. Write to AERO, 417 Roslyn Rd., Roslyn Heights, NY 11577; jmintz@igc.apc.org.

**HOLISTIC EDUCATION REVIEW**. Quarterly magazine with articles, reviews, letters, and reader contributions on many aspects of alternative education; home-schooling; and Montessori, Waldorf, and other learning philosophies. I've seen the word "holistic" on dozens of bookstore shelves and in scores of publishers' catalogs, and still don't have a firm grip on it, but it probably doesn't matter. *Holistic Education Review* is far better than the cultish New Age publications with which its name might seem to make it belong. It gives me a better grip on the aims and methods of true education, and even a little more understanding of the word. The magazine's masthead says it aims "to stimulate discussion and application of all person-centered educational ideas and methods ... [and e]xplore how education can encourage the fullest possible development of human potentials and planetary consciousness. We believe that human fulfillment, global cooperation, and ecological responsibility should be the primary goals of education." Those discussions and explorations mean that *Holistic Education Review* covers a multitude of viewpoints, and will often intrigue, inspire, inform, surprise, entertain, and occasionally irritate you. You'll frequently gain new insights, encouragement, and food for careful reflection. 39 Pearl St., Brandon, VT 05733.

**CONNECT**. A publication dedicated to creative thinking, synthesizing science and hands-on math for grades K to 8. Articles about new products, ideas to investigate, multidisciplinary approaches, literature links, and excellent book reviews. Designed for classroom and group use, but you can adapt the material to suit yourself. Synergy Learning International, P.O. Box 60, Brattleboro, VT 05302; 800-769-6199; connect@synergylearning.org.

**CREATIVE CLASSROOM**. Articles, editorials, tips, suggestions, reproducible activity pages, holiday ideas and themes, useful ads, and book and product reviews. Citizenship, time, writing, maps, vitamin information, shadow plays, science, mini-books, logic games, math, plant projects, legendary heroes, and more. Early elementary levels. Written for classroom teachers, but most material is easily adapted to home-schooling. Box 863, Farmingdale, NY 11737.

**HOME EDUCATOR'S FAMILY TIMES**. Christian-based with a liberal view. Many good resources and articles. P.O. Box 708, Gray, ME 04739.

**THE LINK: The Homeschool Newspaper**. *Free* newspaper for homeschoolers. Lots of news, good book reviews, and resource ads. A wealth of information just for the asking. 587 N. Ventu Park Rd., Suite F-911, Newbury Park, CA 91320; hompaper@gte.net; www.homeschoolnewslink.com.

**HOMESCHOOLING TODAY**. Christian. Unit studies. P.O. Box 1425, Melrose, FL 32666.

**JOURNAL OF FAMILY LIFE: Empowering Young People**. See "Family Living."

**OPTIONS IN LEARNING**. An AllPIE publication. See address in "Support Groups." Very good.

**PATHS OF LEARNING: Options for Families and Communities**. See "Homeschooling and Education."

**F.U.N. NEWS**. Published by the Family Unschooling Network, edited by Nancy and Billy Greer, *F.U.N. News* is full of good commonsense ideas for all home-schooling families. It is written primarily for unschoolers, but there are too many good articles and reviews, relevant to all of us helping our children learn, to dismiss it as an "unschooling" and therefore useless publication to those using a more structured approach. Your kids will enjoy the special projects, and you'll definitely enjoy this upbeat newsletter. Computer information, timely articles, good resource page, book and magazine reviews, and more. Write for a free sample issue if you don't mind waiting until they do a bulk mailing; for $1 you get first-class service and two FUNBucks toward your subscription or order. Published quarterly. Also ask for their FUN Books catalog. Four issues per year/$8. F.U.N., 1688 Belhaven Woods Ct., Pasadena, MD 21122-3727; fun@FUN-Books.com; www.unschooling.org.

**CANADIAN HOMESCHOOLER**, c/o Rob and Kelly Shannon, R.R. 3, Marmora, ON K0K 2M0. A very nicely done bimonthly family magazine with articles, projects, unit study ideas, and more. $18 per year.

**GREAT IDEAS IN EDUCATION**. Articles and book reviews about changing and improving the current educational system through creative programs. Resource Center for Redesigning Education, P.O. Box 298, Brandon, VT 05733.

**BREEZY ACRES**. Bimonthly newsletter of government offices, private corporations, non-profit groups, etc., that offer educational materials at little or no cost. Write for subscription fee. 1728 Burtonville Rd., Esperance, NY 12066.

**LEARNING**. Our favorite "professional teacher's" magazine, intended for grade school use, but we have also been able to adapt much of it for high school use. Articles about teaching methods; frequently critical of testing, grading, etc. Strong recognition of the inadequacies of most textbooks; emphasis on hands-on approach to learning. Monthly calendar with daily bits of information about history, literature, ecology, conservation, and famous people. Reproducible activity pages. News of free or almost-free educational items and contests. Write for current price and introductory offer. P.O. Box 2589, Boulder, CO 80321.

**THE BLUMENFELD EDUCATION LETTER**. Monthly newsletter edited by Samuel Blumenfeld, author of *NEA: Trojan Horse in American Education*. He's a right-wing critic of public schools, who believes that "death education, values clarification, and lifeboat games" prove that the "humanistic progressives" have been deliberately leading America toward becoming a socialist society since early in the last century. Many of his examples and arguments seem valid enough, but I strongly question his conclusions. P.O. Box 45161, Boise, ID 83711.

**THE ECLECTIC HOMESCHOOL.** Always interesting and enlightening, with language notes, His Story Notes, websites, unit studies, and more. Christian. P.O. Box 736, Bellvue, NE 68005-0736.

**THE FAMILY LEARNING CONNECTION**. Bimonthly newsletter for homeschooling families. P.O. Box 12268, Oklahoma City, OK 72157.

**THE HOMESCHOOL EXCHANGE**. A newsprint publication for buying, selling, and exchanging homeschool books. Write for current subscription price. P.O. Box 1378, Boerne, TX 78006; hsxchange@aol.com.

**CHILDREN'S MAGAZINE GUIDE**. Directory of children's magazines now in print, with publishers, prices, and suggested readers' ages. Send an SASE for ordering information. International Reading Association, P.O. Box 8139, Newark, DE 19714.

## FOR KIDS

**BIRDS FLY FREE: Unschooling for Higher Education**. Produced by and for unschoolers, but an enjoyable and worthwhile contribution for all homeschoolers. Original artwork, poetry, and essays by kids. Kyce Bello, P.O. Box 1041, Questa, NM 87556; SkyDrum@aol.com.

**BOOMERANG!** A monthly "audio magazine," a 70-minute cassette tape with feature stories about geography, history, and current events; mysteries; letters to the editor; interviews; and jokes, for kids 8 to 12 (more or less), professionally written from a kid's perspective and reported on by kids. Each cassette is accompanied by related reading suggestions. Retail price in stores is $7.95 per issue, but an annual subscription is only $43.95, or just under $3.70 per tape. P.O. Box 261, La Honda, CA 94020; 800-333-7858 (credit card orders only); boomkids@aol.com; www.boomkids.com.

**KIDS FROM FOREIGN PLANETS: Unschoolers Living Around the World**. Randee Silverman, P.O. Box 138, Blacksburg, SC 29702, or Tola Cohia Brennan, c/o Bastiaan, Freira, 2000 Almoster, Portugal.

**Cobblestone Publishing** offers a variety of excellent publications targeting specific areas of interest, including some books for teaching with primary resources. A partial list: **CALLIOPE**, world history; **FOOTSTEPS**, African-American history; **APPLESEEDS**, social studies for younger kids; **CALIFORNIA CHRONICLES**, California history; **FACES**, world cultures and geography; **COBBLESTONE**, American history, and **ODYSSEY**, science.
The following are for a younger audience and also available from Cobblestone. Ask for free samples.
**BABYBUG** is for ages 6 months to 2 years. Sturdy cardboard format makes it easy to handle. Stories, rhymes, bright pictures.

**LADYBUG** is for ages 2 to 6. Stories, poems, songs, games, and more. Comes with activity sheet and special section for parents.

**SPIDER** is for ages 6 to 9. Stories, poetry, articles, artwork, and activities for independent young learners.

**CRICKET** is for ages 9 to 14. Lots to read: stories, folktales, fantasy, science fiction, history, biographies, poems, science, sports, and crafts — and, of course, humor.

**CICADA** is for ages 14 and up. Literary magazine with fiction and poetry.

Cobblestone Publishing Company, 30 Grove St., Suite C, Peterborough, NH 03458-1454; 800-821-0115; www.cobblestonepub.com.

**DRAGONFLY**. Science challenges, student artwork and investigations, scientific research, poetry, scientist interviews, and more. Ages 3 to 13. National Science Teachers Association, 1840 Wilson Blvd., Arlington, VA 22201-9778.

**ALL ROUND**. A radical "mag" for children ages 1 to 100+, as it states on the cover. Cartoons, feature articles, comics, stories, contests, and more about the environment and other issues of importance to kids. The free sample I'm looking at has in-depth articles, cartoons, puzzles, and more — all about trees. It's interesting and informative without being at all preachy, pushy, or bookish. I like their regularly featured cartoon characters, kittenish-type figures. The artwork is lively and fun to look at. A twice-yearly magazine for ages 1 to 100+. Honest! That's what they say. Call for a free sample issue. A Canadian publication with both Canadian and U.S. addresses! $11.50 U.S. per year, $14 Canadian. 400 McGill, 3rd Floor, Montreal, PQ H2Y 2G1, or P.O. Box 1783, Sedona, AZ 86339-1783; 888-938-3832; www.allroundmagazine.com.

**Children's Book-of-the-Month Club**, Book of the Month Club, Camp Hill, PA 17011-9850. Write for information. Mostly very good books for ages 6 months to 12 years. Shipping costs may be high.

**COUNTRY KIDS**. Bimonthly for and about rural children. Games, quizzes, puzzles, poems, crafts, and more. Reiman Publications, Box 572, Milwaukee, WI 53201.

**STONE SOUP: The Magazine by Young Writers and Artists**. Just what it says it is. Contributors through the age of 13 may submit stories, poems, and artwork. *Stone Soup* has been publishing quality children's art and writing for more than 25 years. Each piece published is accompanied by a picture of the contributor. A great gift for a child who wants to be a writer or artist. Write for current subscription rates. P.O. Box 83, Santa Cruz, CA 95063; www.stonesoup.com.

**THE GORILLA MAGAZINE**. You can make a contribution of $10 or $15 dollars and get this magazine about Koko and other gorillas who communicate with sign language. Fascinating studies about what animals can tell us with the use of sign language. Great poster! The Gorilla Foundation, Box 620-640, Woodside, CA 94062-9901.

**NATURE FRIEND MAGAZINE**, 2727 Township Rd., #421, Sugarcreek, OH 44681.

**ZILLIONS!** A magazine for kids from *Consumer Reports*. If you're not familiar with *Consumer Reports* for adults, look for a copy in the library. *Zillions!* is a gold mine of information about products for kids. The editors investigate a variety of products for children; products are tested and evaluated by adults and kids. They rate everything from bubble gum and videos to clothes and books. Everything is tested by kids and adults for safety, content, interest, and durability. Readers may write in with comments and questions. Ages 10 and up, but they test games and toys for younger children, so you might want it for yourself. Bimonthly. $16 U.S., $20 in U.S. funds (GST included) for Canadian delivery. Subscription Department, P.O. Box 51777, Boulder, CO 80323-1777. Allow 4 to 8 weeks for delivery; they give you a money-back guarantee. P.S. In *Zillions!*, I just learned that Patagonia recycles 25 one-liter soda bottles to make "fleece" for just one of their pullovers.

**U.S. KIDS**. Fiction, non-fiction, puzzles, and "Kids Helping Kids" advice column. 44 pages per issue. P.O. Box 16687, Columbus, OH 43216.

**HIGHLIGHTS FOR CHILDREN**. This is one our favorites. Creative writing, poems, and seasonal activities for ages 6 to 12. Sometimes they publish submissions by kids. Approximately $24 a year. 1800 Watermark Dr., P.O. Box 182340, Columbus, OH 43272-4710.

*Highlights* now has a couple of new publications for children ages 7 to 10 (more or less). Request information about **PUZZLEMANIA** and **MATHMANIA**, P.O. Box 5071, Clifton, NJ 07015-9872.

**KIDS AT HOME**. Written by and for home-schooled kids. P.O. Box 363, Astoria, OR 97103.

**YOUNGBIZ**. Magazine for ambitious young people to help them become successful entrepreneurs. Aimed at kids 8 to 18, this publication offers professional advice and many success stories to inspire and guide. They also have workshops in the U.S. and Canada. $18 per year; write for a sample issue. KidsWay, Inc., 5585 Peachtree Rd., Chamblee, GA 30341; 888-KIDS-WAY; www.kidsway.com.

**MATH CLUB**. Bimonthly magazine with lots of puzzles, games, art, history, and more. Sample copy $2. Tabletop Academy Press, R.R. 1 Box 114, Blue Mound, IL 62513-9709.

**READERS SPEAK OUT!** Free two-page quarterly publication in which teens write their opinions and discuss many controversial topics, personal issues, ethics, the arts, and more. Teens can write for a list of questions coming up for discussion or, I believe, simply write in about a pertinent topic for discussion with others. A good place for a budding writer to express his thoughts. I was impressed with the thoughtful responses by teens and the quality of the writing. Ron Richardson, 4003 50th Ave. SW, Seattle, WA 98116.

**SHOOFLY** is a quarterly audio magazine (on cassette) for ages 3 to 7. Lively and upbeat, *Shoofly* is the perfect vehicle for encouraging the imagination. These 50-minute tapes include classic fairy tales, old and new children's songs, and more by the regular staff and guests such as Jim Weiss. P.O. Box 70, Carrboro, NC 27510-0070; 800-919-9989.

**SKIPPING STONES** is the best multicultural magazine for kids that I've ever seen. *Skipping Stones* is full of excellent and exciting prose and poetry by and about children from every imaginable background. There are book and video reviews; contributions from city and country kids telling of their hopes and dreams, their living conditions, and the problems they cope with on a daily basis; pen pals from around the world; bilingual pages; photos by and about kids; and more. Exciting! Sample copy $5. Subscription $25 (and worth it). Ask for information on their low-income subscription allowance if you need it, or a multiple copy discount. P.O. Box 3939, Eugene, OR 97403-0939.

### GENERAL INTEREST

**NATURAL LIFE: Canada's Alternative Newsmagazine**. Articles and advertising related to living an alternative lifestyle. 272 Hwy. 5, R.R. 1, St. George, ON N0E 1N0.

**READER'S DIGEST**, Pleasantville, NY 10570, or 215 Redfern Ave., Montreal, PQ H3Z 9Z9.

**SMITHSONIAN MAGAZINE**. The Smithsonian Institution in Washington, D.C., has the greatest collection of "Americana" in the world and much more. The magazine covers everything from the far reaches of space to fossils. We've had the pleasure of a gift subscription from one of my aunts since the early '70s, and I always look forward to getting it. *Smithsonian* has provided a window into the world when we have lived in very isolated places. Strong focus on art and conservation. Intelligent articles and great photography. Smithsonian Institution, P.O. Box 420309, Palm Coast, FL 32142-9143. **MUSE** is a child's edition of *Smithsonian*. It offers a diversity of articles, puzzles, contests, and more just for kids ages 8 to 14. Box 7468, Red Oak, IA 51591-4468.

**THE WORLD & I** is put out by the Washington Times Corporation. I was fully prepared to dislike it — possibly intensely. I had just received a complimentary issue of the *Washington Times*, complete with propaganda, aimed specifically at homeschoolers, that I strongly resented. It's great that homeschooling is now so widely recognized that national publications feel we are a group worthy of a special approach, but the issue they sent had biased reporting, and the only thing I found specially aimed at me, a homeschooler, was the advertising — and I didn't like the products.

*The World & I* is a way to tour the world from the comfort of your own home. They say it's written for upper high school levels and college students. I would include adults wanting a broader view of the world. The writing is sophisticated, the articles are timely, and the subjects are covered in depth by knowledgeable people. Each issue has a "special section" that explores one topic in depth. The issue I'm looking at explores Islam, starting with the premise that too much of the media has substituted Islam for the Cold War threat of communism. Islam is introduced and the history and philosophy explained. I've seen a great deal of news coverage about the oppression of Islamic women. Reference is made to this oppression as well as to where changes are being made. The point is also made that, as with Christianity, there are different sects within Islam. Other regular sections include current issues, the arts, life, natural science, culture, book world, and currents in modern thought. Numerous color photos with a healthy diversity of articles. Request information (on a letterhead) about ordering a "classroom subscription" for a discounted price. Make sure you ask for the free teacher's guide. 3400 New York Ave. NE, Washington, DC 20078-0760; 800-822-2822 or 202-526-3497/832-5780.

**UTNE READER**. Articles, editorials, reviews, letters, and selections from more than 1,000 independent small-circulation magazines, journals, and newsletters. Offbeat, upbeat, politically aware. Bimonthly. Send an SASE to Subscriber Services, P.O. Box 1974, Marion, OH 43306.

**AMERICAN HERITAGE**. Lets you travel the country from your kitchen table or living room sofa. Articles include great color photos, notes of interest about historical places, and what's of interest in different geographical regions. Lots of free travel information. Subscription Dept., P.O. Box 5022, Harlan, IA 51593-0522.

**SMALL PRESS REVIEW**. For avid and voracious readers. Reviews of new books by small presses and publishers with news and notes of interest. Bimonthly; $25 per year. Dustbooks, P.O. Box 100, Paradise, CA 95967.

**BIRDS AND BLOOMS**. For those with flowers and birds, or those who would like more of them. Customer Service, P.O. Box 991, Greendale, WI 53129-1404.

**University Subscription Service**, 1213 Butterfield Rd., Downers Grove, IL 60615. Write for a listing of magazines at reasonable rates.

**NURTURING: The Journal of Motherhood.** Very good. 20 Paperbirch Dr., Don Mills, ON M3C 2E7.

**PRIORITY PARENTING**. Small but very useful and interesting monthly newsletter/magazine with articles, poems, pictures, pen-pal listings, problems and solutions, occasional cartoons, classified ads, letters, reviews, and recommendations. Good writing; good ideas. Sample issue, $2; subscription $14 per year. P.O. Box 1793, Warsaw, IN 46580.

**SKY AND TELESCOPE**. Sample issue. Specify you are a homeschooler. Send 8½x11" envelope with 55 cents postage to Sky Publishing Corp., 49 Bay Street Rd., Cambridge, MA 02138.

Having concluded before we started teaching at home that the loosely structured approach is definitely best, we were sometimes dismayed to find that it wasn't working, and it's hard to find an instruction manual for something that isn't supposed to have instructions. Until the kids were about six or seven, they were certainly eager to learn anything and everything around them. After that, sometimes they were eager to learn, and sometimes they'd go out to lunch for two or three weeks. We watched and waited, and told each other that they'd soon get tired of old Donald Duck comics or television and would return to doing something productive. Maybe they just needed a break. Usually, they did tire of their early retirement, and began reading, thinking, drawing, making things, and asking us twenty questions a minute about anything at all, but occasionally it looked as if they'd settled down for a long winter's nap.

"Hey, look, kids," we'd say, "we're having school at home. That means you're supposed to be learning something."

"Okay, Dad. What do you want us to learn?"

"What causes gravity? What makes the Aurora Borealis light up? Why was Mona Lisa smiling? What does x represent if five times x to the fourth power equals eighteen? How do you drive a nail without mashing your thumb? How can you collect a dozen eggs in the barn and deliver twelve eggs to the house? How high is up? Things like that."

"Dad, have you read this story about when Donald Duck and his nephews went to Yellowstone Park and —"

"Okay, then, where is Yellowstone Park?"

"You mean there really is a Yellowstone Park?"

"That's all, folks. Back to the drawing board. Notebooks, pens, pencils, eager minds, and smiling faces. Nine o'clock tomorrow morning. All drinks of water, toilet trips, and forgotten books to be remembered before then."

"Really? Okay, Dad! We were wondering if you were going to help us learn anymore, or if you were too busy."

"That's what I thought you were wondering. Is that about the time the Beagle Boys think Donald Duck has a buried treasure under a geyser? Let me borrow it when you're done with it."

So our unschool would become a home-school again, and we'd have fairly regular hours, and lots of discussions, and real Assignments For Tomorrow, and after a while we'd try the unschooling again. After all, how can I write a book about how well unschooling works for us if it doesn't? The kids just never realized what a responsibility they had to my readers.

School, as we all know, is a box or series of boxes in which children are required to sit for several hours a day, while government-inspected teachers attempt to transfer information out of books into the children's heads.

Home-school was around a long time before school, and often consisted of nothing more than a borrowed book and the light from a fireplace. Sometimes, just the fireplace. Some people did quite well with this arrangement, and went on to become president or to invent the phonograph. At that time, most of the

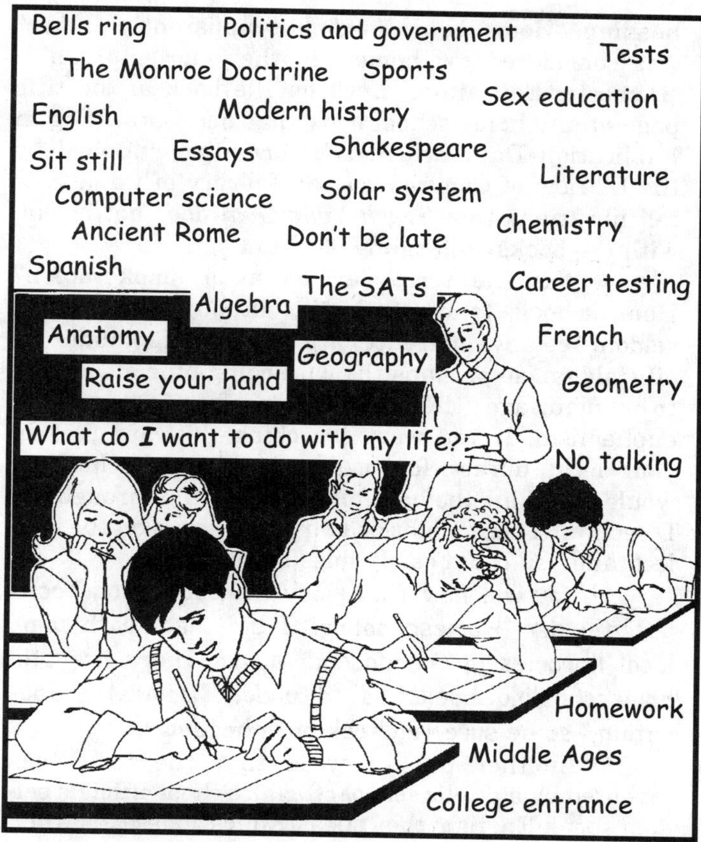


unschools were not different from the nonschools. Instead of spending years in preparing to learn how to make a living, people went out to make a living. Or stayed at home to make a living.

The industrial revolution reduced the number of job opportunities, so a different kind of child labor had to be invented. School was the answer. The government told parents they were too stupid and ignorant to teach their children anything, and the parents were too stupid and ignorant to realize the government was wrong, so the children tucked baked potatoes into their pockets and trotted off to school. A few people still became presidents and a few still invented things, and everyone had a piece of paper certifying that he had spent a lot of time behind a desk, so schools were considered to be Good Things.

Gradually the parents got smarter and noticed that their children were getting dumber. Although some were still growing up to be presidents or to invent things, most of the presidents were stupider, and so were the inventions, so a few parents reinvented home-schools. The children were taken out of school to be taught at home. Unfortunately, the parents had been taught in schools and thought school methods were the only methods, so the home-schools were not much different from the schools, except that fewer students were smoking dope or getting pregnant or both. They still learned to be almost as stupid and uninventive as they had in the public schools.

Most home-schools had a structure as rigid as that of most public schools, with the entire day planned in detail — so many minutes for spelling, so many for math, so many for standing in line, so many for getting out your books and sharpening your pencils, hold up two fingers when you have to go to the bathroom, and so on — with regular testing, grading, and even "homework" to be done in the evenings.

Many of the new home-schoolers were fundamentalists, who were usually very concerned with authority and obedience, which they felt couldn't be maintained without a rigid teaching structure and lots of what they called strict discipline. The fundamentalists frequently recommended an intricate system of rewards, bribes, punishments, and psychological games — not only for schoolwork, but even for such daily chores as making the bed. Punishments included spanking, forfeiture of meals, and withholding of play privileges; rewards included food treats, games, special trips, and even money. The fundamentalists didn't realize that such rewards and punishments not only undermined their goal of discipline, but usually indicated that discipline had already broken down. Or maybe it was too late, because now they had to try to maintain control over children who had unwittingly been taught that everything has its price. It must be discouraging to know that sinfulness has been a dominant characteristic on both sides of your family ever since Adam and Eve ate the fruit of the tree of knowledge.

A few public-schoolers and a few home-schoolers, who had read *Robinson Crusoe* or *Mowgli of the Wolves* and had heard of Jean-Jacques Rousseau, decided to chuck the whole works and have unschools. The unschools had no lesson plans, no assigned subjects, and no guided study, and the students could go to the bathroom without raising their hands. The unstudents unlearned several of the things they had learned in the schools and home-schools, and were allowed to sit at desks if they wanted to, to read books if they wanted to, and to get jobs as construction workers or hairdressers or magazine editors if they wanted to.

Sometimes unschooling is referred to as the invited learning approach. I think the idea is that when the kids decide they want to know something, they invite someone to teach them. Otherwise, they are protected by the First Amendment from any obligation to learn anything. Adults have no moral right to intrude on children's lives without invitation.

In New York City, parents don't have any legal control over their children who have reached the age of sixteen, but they are responsible for all contracts and crimes of their children who have not reached the age of eighteen. Many parents have found that this creates some very interesting situations.

Back to unschooling. The prefix "un" was

meant to communicate the unschooling parents' rejection of stiff structures and canned curricula. The term "unschool" has the drawback of saying what it is not, but not saying what it is. "Unhorsed" gives the impression of an impromptu flight from the back of a horse, but it doesn't say if the unrider is walking, dazed, or dead; only that he is no longer on the horse. When I stand up, am I unchaired?

Most home-schoolers are somewhere between these extremes, not requiring the students to hold up two fingers or sit still with their backs straight and listen, but also realizing that not all kids will learn reading, writing, arithmetic, history, geography, home economics, and penmanship just from sitting in the woods with a screwdriver and a pile of books.

Some people credit Thomas Mann* with starting public schooling in America. Others blame him for it. John Holt, very liberal, says public school is not a good idea gone wrong, but was a bad idea from the very start. Samuel Blumenfeld, very conservative and a fundamentalist, says we never needed schools at all. I went to school for twelve years and often tried to convince my parents I didn't need it, but some of my history lessons were about people two or three hundred years ago who surely could have used a little of it, whether they actually needed it or not.

There were books about schools before Moses left Egypt, and many more have been published since then. Now, there are also many books about home-schools, and even more than a few about unschools. Books about schools and schooling are usually cataloged under the heading of Education, which considering that a government agency does the cataloging, makes unexpected sense. When they began cataloging books about home-school, they could have used the heading "Home education," but apparently "home" was considered too homey, so they chose to call it "Domestic Education." Look on the back of the title page of any home-school book that has Cataloging in Publication Data, which is information supplied by the Library of Congress or the Library of Canada to tell librarians that *Teach Your Own* does not belong with the books on farming or plumbing.

Was the term devised as a smokescreen? Home-schools (and unschools, although authorities seldom see any difference) are not often applauded by officialdom, so perhaps the cataloging officials sought to camouflage their existence with a pedantic euphemism. If you were searching the card files in your local library for books about home-schooling, would you think (before I told you) to riffle through the D section? There might be two dozen books on the subject, and you could easily miss them all.

You will now find many homeschooling books listed under "Homeschooling." I did check with some local libraries in Canada and Maine. There are still homeschooling books listed under "Domestic Education," so be sure to check both headings.

Another possibility is that the term was invented by a public school official. School officials seldom speak English; they speak Educationese, as when the district superintendent wrote, "Please enlighten me with respect to your intentions relative to the education of your children for the approaching year." I divided both sides of the equation by the number of superintendents it takes to change a light bulb and reduced it to "Please tell me your plans for the year."

Educationese is one of the two foreign languages in which I have a little fluency, and sometimes I practice it when I correspond with school officials. Usually, however, Educationese is a lot like maple sap: It needs to be boiled down a great deal before it is of much use to human beings.

In my dictionaries, there are several definitions of "school" that don't refer to the formal institutions with which we usually associate the word. The problem, then, is not in the word, but in our associations with it. "A source of knowledge" is one of the definitions I think would be acceptable to even the most dedicated unschooler. But our conditioning is strong: When someone says school, we automatically think of report cards and corridors reeking of antiseptic. The word is lightened somewhat by the addition of "home," but some stigma remains. "Unschooling" has the disadvantage of adding a negative prefix to an already stigmatized word.

It's probably too late to coin a better term. "Home-learning" is used by some, especially those who want to make it plain that adults also can learn outside of school, but really is just as restrictive: It implies that learning takes place primarily in the

April 8, 1991

* Dear Donn,

Just received your delightful book today. I'm really enjoying it, but please correct [p. 69]. It's Horace Mann, not Thomas. Thomas was the great (greatest?) German novelist; Horace was the "father of the American public school system" — essentially to train the labor force of an industrial capitalist society. And the Socratic method [p. 70] is essentially the teaching of absolute syllogisms — it is only the appearance of conversation. A close and exhaustive reading of Plato (yuck — I was a philosophy student and teacher) demonstrates that. But your book is great!

[M.E.]
NYC

Apparently, M.E. is one of those who blame him, but she's absolutely right that it was Horace, not Thomas. I'm still blushing. DR

home, which is little better than the conventional assumption that learning takes place only in school.

Home-schoolers and unschoolers are well aware that a great deal of learning takes place outside of both home and school — in the streets, in the woods and fields, in fact, in any situation in which we're participants or spectators. *Being alive is learning, and the extent of our learning may depend upon the extent to which we are really living.* (Italics mine. J.R.)

John Holt's advocacy of very loose structure, and even of no structure at all, isn't new with his home-school book, *Teach Your Own*. Many similar ideas and arguments were presented in his *How Children Learn* and *How Children Fail* in the early 1960s. A few years earlier, A.S. Neill's *Summerhill* carried a similar message: If you leave kids alone, and let them study what and when they want to, they'll educate themselves. It worked for Mowgli and for Tarzan, and sometimes it has worked for us. Other times we've wondered why so few of the great educators have children of their own.

John Dewey, father of the "progressive education" movement of the first half of this century, encouraged teachers to be co-workers with their students rather than taskmasters, and to build their lessons around the students' natural interests. That was a compromise between schooling, which almost everybody had by then, and unschooling, which a lot of people had but didn't particularly want.

Before Dewey, Leo Tolstoy and Henry David Thoreau both felt that as much could be learned in the woods and fields as in the classroom. I don't think they meant that a walk in the woods would teach you the three R's, or that people didn't need the three R's; just that there's a lot to learn in the world besides the three R's, and some of it comes from doing and observing and thinking instead of listening to someone talk. Socrates and Confucius, nearly contemporaries 2,500 years ago, both used conversation as a learning aid, with the goals of discovering truth rather than teaching beliefs and of developing each pupil to his own highest potential. The approach of the modern schools differs only in that the teacher does most of the talking and then asks questions about something else, and nobody cares about silly abstractions such as truth and highest potential.

The rigid approach to teaching is repeatedly condemned by Maria Montessori, Ashley Montagu, Ivan Illich, Herbert Kohl, Paul Goodman, George Dennison, John Taylor Gatto, and many other knowledgeable educators, including John Holt. Some of them have kids of their own, and some practice on other people's kids. *Learning Magazine* frequently features articles questioning or attacking the concepts and practices of testing, grading, rigid structure, and tight curriculum. A lot of teachers read *Learning*. I don't know if any of them are allowed by their school boards to pay attention to it.

Among the growing number of books about home-schooling, the ones with a fundamentalist orientation are strongest in their recommendation of a strict curriculum. Ted Wade's *The Home School Manual* argues strongly for a planned structure, although he has written me, "Free time and exploring are important, [but] I feel it's important to work from a plan and to choose on the basis of goals rather than by what seems fun at the moment."

Most of the home-schoolers who argue against loose structure actually consider it to be synonymous with "what seems fun at the moment," and seem to rest their case primarily on a puritanical assumption that anything that is fun is automatically suspect, and is probably bad.

Advocates of loose structure repeatedly assert and sometimes demonstrate that most children are

eager to learn, anything and everything, and if not stunted by educational malpractice will follow their own interests and curiosity into ever-expanding fields of knowledge and skills. No child will prefer a steady diet of comic books any more than he will choose a constant diet of candy and cookies, although a child's appetite for junk food, both intestinal and cranial, can sometimes amaze even the most imaginative adult. Before long — that's "long" by his standards — he will have a craving for real nutrition, whether in food or knowledge. Many of those who favor rigidity are basing their arguments on observations of children who have never learned in a loosely structured situation. For the sake of argument, perhaps, they "try it" for a few days or weeks, and then announce that it doesn't work. Part of the problem is that they're dealing with children who are accustomed to having some form of knowledge or opinion poured into funnels that have been stuck in their heads, and part of the problem is that sometimes that's the only way to find out if the kids are awake. Like the parents and the teachers, the kids have come to believe that this is the only way to learn, and will sit around waiting for someone to teach them something. Sometimes, it's quite a revelation to them that they can learn something by themselves.

Ironically, the proverb "Virtue is its own reward" is promoted more by the so-called secular humanists than by many fundamentalists, who make virtue synonymous with obedience, and offer material rewards for both.

Perhaps a rigid structure depends upon such rewards and punishments. The more authority is asserted, the more it will be resented and tested, and the more it must be enforced, either by coercion or by bribery. It seems axiomatic that any program needing constant enforcement — whether with subtle bribes, rewards, threats, fear, punishment, or psychological games — must have several inherent weaknesses.

"Hey, Mom, I'll be good if you give me a dime."

"Now, son, why can't you be good for nothing, like your father?"

We have never used any form of punishment with our children, and they have never given us any "discipline" problems that couldn't be resolved with discussion. They do their share of our daily work — barn chores, housework, firewood, etc. — and spend each day learning hundreds of things. We often share a bowl of popcorn, a pot of cocoa, a game of cards or Ping-Pong, but never as rewards for obedience or accomplishment. Such pleasures are ordinary parts of our daily life.

Loosely structured learning isn't necessarily "what seems fun at the moment," but usually what is fun for a child (or an adult) in a creative environment will be interesting, provocative, and broadening — in other words, educational.

Another misconception of loose structure that is firmly held by many of its opponents is that there is little or no contribution by adults. The opposite is closer to the fact. With a loose structure, children and adults interact more often without regard for artificial barriers such as age differences, school walls, and honorific formalities. The parent plays several roles, the least of which is "teacher." The parent suggests, guides, converses, questions, supports, praises, encourages, and helps to obtain material. The parent is friend, mentor, confidant, and fellow student.

Throughout *Growing Without Schooling* are scores of readers' letters recounting their experiences with loosely structured learning. The factor most com-

mon to them all is interaction between adults and children in real-life situations, in which the children learn real skills and gain real knowledge. At an age when most kids are still working on how much Sally spent for three oranges if the price is 6 for $1.00, some home-school kids are earning money, putting it into their own checking accounts, and writing their own checks.

The Holt Associates conference in Boston in 1997, celebrating 20 years of publishing *Growing Without Schooling*, was impressive not only for the organization and the speakers, but for the families themselves. It was a treat for me to be around so many happy parents and children. I heard no crying or whining, no threats or bribes for good behavior, yet the children were having a good time. The teens who spoke at the seminars were prime examples of what self-motivated learning can produce. They were young adults with great self-confidence, definitive proof that structure is not a necessary ingredient for success in learning or growing up. The writings of other unschoolers in the *GWS* magazine that followed the conference reinforced this.

It may be that not all unschoolers are as impressively accomplished learners, but then not all public school children do poorly. So far, no one has found the perfect method for educating all children. Nancy Lande's book *Homeschooling: A Patchwork of Days* (see "Homeschooling and Education") provides excellent examples of the many ways learning can take place outside of the public school system.

The parents whose kids are less precocious, and even dislike studying and thinking, don't often write books or articles, although they sometimes write letters asking what's wrong with them or what they are doing wrong. The answer to both questions is "nothing." Wait a while, and try again. Some kids just don't like studying and thinking — whether they're in public school, home-school, or unschool. But they can sure fix cars or build birdhouses or catch fish. I know a lot of very nice people who fix cars and couldn't tell a noun from a nun. They have expensive homes and go to Florida for two weeks every winter.

In *Better Than School* (now out of print), Nancy Wallace tells of frequently chauffeuring her children to and from music and language lessons, and of the many hours she and her husband often spent reading to their children. The Wallaces' home-school program was as far from being only "what seems fun at the moment" as it was from the rigid structure of the public schools.

The older our kids got, the longer their lunch breaks became. Jean and I compared notes and concluded that the two who had had the most contact with other kids at an early age were the quickest to

lose interest in learning or creating. So much for the values of socialization.

Sometimes all four scurried through the day, learning and creating and discussing ideas, and sometimes one or two would sort of fade out and need a little jiggle, and sometimes all of them would just run down. After what we felt was a suitable break from straining their brains, we'd wind them up again.

By the time the kids were doing sixth- and seventh-grade work, we discovered a few flaws in Rousseau's, or whoever's, ideas about plunking a kid in the woods with a screwdriver and a pile of books. The biggest flaw was, then what? Once the kids have mastered the basics of language and arithmetic and nail pounding and cake making, will they go on to write and then discuss the Great Books and the History of Civilization all by themselves, or could they use a little more input from those who have gone before?

Does "invited learning" mean we shouldn't occasionally try to lead them into areas of which they aren't yet aware, and therefore can't invite us to help them in? Does "invited learning" mean the same kind of choppy, incomplete, fragmented learning that's going on in the public schools?

We never really figured out exactly what "invited learning" does mean, but we decided we couldn't always wait to be invited. Sometimes we just crashed the party, and amazed ourselves with the structure and organization we could devise. "Let's hope John Holt never sees this," we'd say to each other. "He'll stop selling our books." But the kids became so interested in Alexander the Great or the Renaissance or Martin Luther and the papal bulls that they forgot all about Donald Duck. They learned psychology and economics and world history and geography and where Yellowstone National Park is. They even began inviting us to introduce more subjects, or

help them with the ones they were on, and then we began feeling safe again. We always felt a little like renegades when we taught something without having been invited to do so.

When we were having unschool, the kids mostly set their own unschedules. When we were having home-school, it often went something like this:

6:45 — Jean and Donn get up with the alarm, feed fires, dress, etc. Feed dog, then let her out. Two cats in, growling at each other. Jean wakes Derek. Donn cleans and sharpens chain saw on Ping-Pong table.

7:30 — Jean wakes Cathy or Karen or Susan, who take turns daily setting the table, getting breakfast, and tending fires. Jean and Derek go to the barn; feed and water the pig, cow, calf, and 25 hens; clean the gutter; milk the cow; and collect eggs. Donn puts fuel in chain saw, then goes out to cut firewood. The one on breakfast duty calls the others, who are usually already awake and reading in bed.

8:15 — Breakfast: hot cereal, whole-wheat toast from homemade bread, homemade butter and apple jelly, honey, fresh milk, fresh eggs, peanut butter. Coffee for Jean and Donn.

9:00 — Jean and two girls clear the table, do dishes, and put them away. One girl sweeps the house and straightens odds and ends. Girls rotate these chores daily. Every fourth day, Derek sweeps. Donn goes out to split firewood.

9:30 — Derek and Susan or Cathy and Karen bring water, one dipping buckets into the brook (six feet from the corner of the house) and passing them in, the other carrying them to the kitchen and filling the 50-gallon can, stove reservoir, and large kettle on the stove. In warm weather, when the pipes aren't frozen, we have gravity-fed water from the brook directly into the house.

9:45 — Official school time, morning session, at the kitchen-dining table. Donn leading (or being led). (Jean listens, comments, sews, mends, plans meals, does laundry, plans her afternoon schoolwork, tends fires, bakes bread, etc.) Discussion of daily offering from Word-a-Day calendar ("saprogenic") and Quote-a-Day calendar ("A sharp tongue is the only edged tool that grows keener with constant use" — Washington Irving.). We pull the legs and wings off the words, examining roots, derivations, associations, usages, sometimes using the dictionary. We discuss the quotation and its author: Do you agree? Why or why not? What is his most-famous story? Does anyone know when he lived?

10:00 (this and other times given in Official School Time are approximate; we have no schedule) — Word play, dictionary and encyclopedia assignments from yesterday. Cathy: Tass, tacit, taciturn, apocrypha, anarchy, anachronism. Karen: cosmos, cosmic, wax, wane, flat, flatulent. Susan: awesome, awful, offal, Neapolitan, obese, obeisance. Derek: auk, gross, grosbeak, eject, elect. Words for tomorrow: faker, fakir, guild, gild, microcosm, macrocosm, zenith, nadir, anathema, spike, bolt, sally, dally. Each student gives definitions, uses the words in sentences; others take notes, discuss uses and usefulness, often making puns and other bad jokes.

10:30 — Yesterday's Detective Assignment, for encyclopedia and general book shelf research. True or false? Support your answers. Cathy: The Lutheran Church was founded by Martin Luther King Jr.. Karen: George Fox was an American Indian. Susan: Betsy Ross was a famous opera singer. Derek: "Doctor Livingstone, I presume?" was said by Sherlock Holmes. Students discuss and take notes on each other's research.

10:45 — Research assignment, to be worked on individually or together, your choice. Problem: A man lost in the woods can find no food except rabbits, which are plentiful and easy to snare. He has all he wants of rabbit meat, yet a few weeks later is found dead of starvation. Why? (Students had to consult several cooking and nutrition books before finding even a hint, and then had to brainstorm their findings to arrive at the answer.)

10:50 — Poetry: Read aloud the selection you found and practiced yesterday. Cathy: Ogden Nash. Karen: Carl Sandburg. Susan: Edna St. Vincent Millay. Derek: Robert Louis Stevenson. Tomorrow, bring one of your own choosing; practice reading aloud beforehand.

11:15 — Writing assignment: Discussion of more articles for our family newsletter; who will write what. To be done on your own time and submitted for discussion and refinement tomorrow.

11:20 — Self-image: Design and draw a button or T-shirt that would express The Real You.

11:40 — Discussion of ethics. How can we

know what is "right"? Do values change as society wants them to, or is there a constant right and wrong for all people and all times? How can we know? What is "conscience"?

12:00 — Donn reads excerpts from biographies, to be discussed.

12:30 — Research assignment for tomorrow: Find and read the story of the Prodigal Son. What does "prodigal" mean? What does "gospel" mean? Which are the "synoptic" gospels, and why?

12:35 — Discussion: Where do we get the common expression "I wash my hands of it." What does it mean? From last night's reading, what are some of the similarities between Christianity and Buddhism?

12:50 — History simulation. Karen, you are a prosecuting attorney at the Nuremberg Trials; your position is that anyone who contributed in any way to the persecution and murder of Jews should be punished very severely. Cathy, you are Franz Gruber; you were 17 years old, a railroad guard 60 miles from Auschwitz; you knew that Jews were in the train cars, but you had your orders; besides, you had been taught that Jews were a threat to your country. Susan and Derek, you are judges; you listen to each side as the defendant and the prosecutor argue their cases, then decide if Franz Gruber is guilty of "crimes against humanity," and, if so, what the sentence should be. Explain your decisions. (The students ad lib, with no attempt at drama or entertainment.)

1:30 — Lunch: sandwiches, milk, carrot sticks, etc. Free reading, Ping-Pong, walks outside.

2:15 — Official school time, afternoon session, Jean leading. (Donn works on business, orders and correspondence, or writing.) First aid, instruction and practice. Music: theory and practice; guitar, flute, clarinet, recorder, singing. Nutrition, health, anatomy. Work on individual electives, with help when wanted or needed. Cathy: Spanish, typing, history, literature, counseling, geography. Karen: French, typing, psychology. Susan: math, history, spelling, civics, French. Derek: math, handwriting, history, typing, art, Spanish, spelling.

3:30 — Official school time is over. The kids often continue working by themselves on their own electives or on morning assignments. Some go skiing or hiking. All four bring in firewood, usually five or six armloads each. The two who didn't haul water in the morning do so now. Reading. Ping-Pong. Visiting friends. Begin supper, sharing and rotating jobs.

6:00 — Donn goes to the barn for evening chores; milk cow, feed animals, etc.

6:30 — Supper. Sometimes with a history, literature, or entertaining cassette tape.

7:15 — Supper clean-up shared and rotated. Baking cookies, cakes, pies. Sometimes TV (powered by a car battery). Reading books and magazines. The girls sew, knit, tat, crochet, and, frequently, draw. Derek builds models of planes and spaceships. The girls have each made several articles of clothing — dresses, blouses, sweaters, etc. Small personal laundry. Letter writing, churning butter, square dancing (in town), skating, 4-H meetings, board games. Popcorn; maybe ice cream. Donn works in his office. Jean reads or plays the guitar.

10:30 — Bedtime. Cats out. Fires fed and shut down. All lights out. Goodnight!

One of my favorite dictionaries, the Oxford American, mentions several uses of the word "home" (as a noun, an adjective, a verb, and an adverb), but between "home-room" and "home-sick," where "home-school" should be, there is nothing. Even the third edition of The Random House Dictionary of the English Language, which weighs twelve pounds and is the most recent unabridged dictionary we have, with thousands of words I don't know and thousands more I don't care to know, somehow missed all references to home education, by that or any other name, when its compilers were combing the oceans of print in search of serendipitous fillers.

Nonetheless, I think "home-school" is becoming well established in the language, just as it is in society, and future lexicographers will have to make note of it.

Ironically, "unschooled" *is* offered by dictionaries, which claim it means "untrained, uneducated." Hardly accurate, of course, but I haven't time to write my own dictionary. Maybe next year.

In the meantime, we should recall the words of Shakespeare:

"What's in a name?
That which we call a home-school
By any other name would teach as well."

Not to mention the warning of Abraham Lincoln: "You can school some of the people all of the time, and all of the people some of the time, but you can't school all of the people all of the time."

# OBEDIENCE TRAINING VS. "INVITED LEARNING"

## or,

## HOME-SCHOOLING GOES TO THE DOGS

"Invited learning," as I understand it — and I'm sure some home-school theorists will be quick to say I don't — seems to mean that children intuitively know what they need to learn and when they need to learn it, and no one should presume to offer them information about anything at all until they ask for it. If they ask for it, of course, it's really invited *teaching*, but more people than you might suppose (unless you're one of them) get purple in the face over this, insisting that "teaching" is *doing something TO someone else* and is therefore a form of aggression — unless the students ask for it, and then it's okay, because then we can call it invited *learning*.

To Jean and me, the entire debate is slightly more exciting than the afternoon soaps or taking out the garbage, but "invited learning" is an intriguing concept, whether we understand it or not, and sometimes we like to play around with it and see what we can discover about it.

One of the things we've discovered about invited learning is that it often results in excessive barking, muddy paw prints on the sofa, missing or mangled shoes, and late-night festivities involving a mouthful of porcupine quills and a pair of pliers. With dogs, that is. Invited learning with children is another story, most of which can be told in polite language but isn't a part of this report.

We've had a few smart dogs over the years (usually one at a time), but we've never given much thought to leading them into any sort of Higher Education. Or even Lower Education. With our dogs, as with our children, we lean (not too firmly, I admit) toward a sort of invited learning, the biggest difference being that with the children it's usually more from conviction than laziness.

With dogs, it usually seems easier to brush mud off the sofa before sitting than to teach them to wipe their feet at the door, so we tend to excuse their poor manners by muttering, "Dogs will be dogs" (just as people used to say, "Boys will be boys" — another truism that, according to recent new magazines, is no longer the certainty we once thought it was, but that is also another story).

About a year and a half ago, Gus came to live with us, and almost immediately began challenging many of our favorite educational theories and convictions, including our smug assumption that dogs will be dogs.

Gus is about ninety percent German shepherd and ten percent something else. We found him (or vice versa) in January, at the SPCA sixty miles away, where he was being held in solitary confinement as a vagrant. He was a puppy, only eight months old, but already weighing 62 pounds, and it cost us more than a dollar a pound to spring him. When I brought him home, sitting beside me in our '84 pickup, he had the familiar dazed look of most ex-cons who have been in stir too long and didn't say much, but several times he expressed his gratitude by cleaning my right ear very thoroughly. He also made a few mechanical adjustments when my attention was elsewhere, and I finally had to explain to him — after the truck suddenly lost its oomph and nearly coasted to a stop before I found the cause of its unusual behavior — that he could move the rearview mirror all he liked but I would be in charge of the gear shift. He apologized by cleaning my ear again, and we got home with no more surprises.

Jean and I showed Gus the doors that connect Inside to Outside, and he signified his understanding by testing them all. We showed him his food and water dishes in the little nook in the hallway, and he tested them, too, giving no indication that the arrangement was less than satisfactory. We introduced him to Big Guy, our ferocious feline mouse, rat, grouse, and rabbit-killer, and said we hoped they would be friends. Gus, very pleased, offered to clean Big Guy's ears. Big Guy, who had once been chased up a very small tree by a very large dog, offered to clean Gus's clock, then ran upstairs to hide in the rafters until spring. (That turned out to be another lesson in invited learning, because for the next three months, at least once a day, we had to risk being torn to shreds by inviting Big Guy to go for a little walk outside, dog or no dog, and he soon learned to hide from us in places we couldn't reach.)

One evening about three weeks after he had come to live with us, Gus barked at the door, then at me, then again at the door. Making a natural assumption, I opened the door for him, but he stood and barked at me again. He wanted me to go outside to play toss-and-chase with his empty plastic milk jug.

"You're out of your mind," I told him. "It's ten below zero out there, with two feet of snow."

He still refused to go out by himself, so I shut the door and went back to my book and chair beside the woodstove, pretending to ignore the disgusted look he was giving me.

Just when I thought he had given up, Gus went to the hall closet and ran back with one of my snow boots in his teeth. He dropped it beside me, then returned to the closet for the second boot, which he dropped next to the first one.

"Gus," I managed to say, "dogs do this only in movies."

He put a paw on one of the boots and barked at me.

"Okay, okay," I said, pushing my foot into one of the boots. "You've made your point. But you should know that real dogs don't do this."

Putting the other boot on, I said to Jean, "Did you see what Gus just did? He's really smart!"

"It's a good thing one of you is," she said, as I went to the closet for my jacket and mittens.

Women tend to say things like that sometimes, so I pretended I hadn't heard her, but on the way out the door, I whispered to Gus, "See what I'm up against? You don't have to make it worse."

(It did get worse. Gus started bringing my jacket, too, and although I wouldn't have said it aloud, I didn't know how to say no to a dog that does all that, even at 15 below zero at 11:30 at night.)

A squeaky rubber football, about six inches long, became Gus's favorite indoor toy. Sometimes he just chews on it, daring it to squeak, then grabs it in his teeth and flips it into the air, then runs after it. Occasionally he loses it, and then spends twenty minutes or more searching for it — behind furniture, under pillows, down the hall, wherever a tricky rubber ball might be hiding. Usually he finds it, but sometimes he gives up and barks at Jean or me to find it for him — which eventually gave us the brilliant idea that he was inviting us to help him Learn something.

I called him to the end of the hall, then told him to sit and count to ten while I hid the ball. "Ten" is a very large number for a young dog, but I managed to get the ball behind a sofa cushion before Gus came galloping after me into the living room.

"*Find* the ball," I said, in that tricky way parents have of enlarging their children's vocabulary. "*Find* it."

Gus sniffed the air, which didn't help, then began searching, pushing chairs, poking his nose under magazines and into armpits, and flipping cushions around until he finally found the ball. He tossed it into the air, jumped and caught it, then dropped it in front of me and barked. This time, there was no doubt: He was definitely inviting me to help him learn something. (Some people might say he was inviting *me* to learn something, and others might say he was just inviting me to play a game, but I know better.)

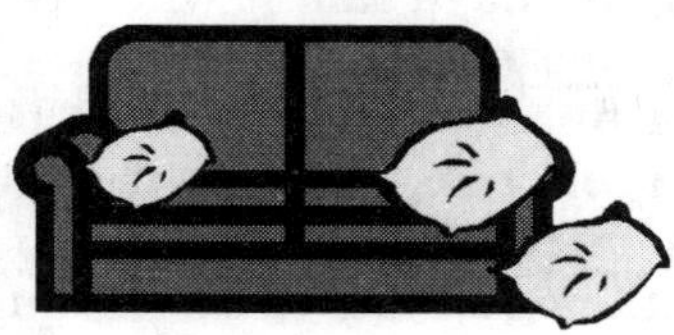

We did it several times that evening, and it became a daily game. I hid the ball in different places each time, and Gus always kept searching until he found it. At the same time, his vocabulary grew. Besides *find* and *ball*, he soon learned *sit, wait, stay, come, sofa, other sofa, chair, bed, wrong way, down, higher*, and *behind the pillows*. Some of the concepts seemed pretty abstract to us, but *abstract* was one of the words Gus hadn't learned.

One day Gus took his ball into our bedroom (which is downstairs, near the kitchen), stayed a few moments, then came out without it and barked at me. It had been quite a while since I had dismissed Gus's barking as mere random noise. If he was bright enough to tell me something but I wasn't bright enough to understand him, I'd have to fake it.

Stalling for time, I asked, "Lost your ball?"

"Woof," he said, wagging his tail.

"Is it in the bedroom?" I asked.

"Woof," he said again, still wagging.

"Can you find it?" I asked.

His tail stopped wagging. Gently but firmly, he took my hand in his mouth and pulled me toward the bedroom door. Releasing my hand, he said, "Rrowrrf!" and waited expectantly. Sometimes he seems to think I'm Learning-Disabled.

Searching my mind for possibilities, I made a wild guess. "You want *me* to find the ball?" I asked him, not really believing it.

"Rowf!" Gus exclaimed, wagging his tail again.

Feeling ridiculous, I went into the bedroom to look for the ball, which I quickly found on the floor beside the bed. Gus grabbed the ball from my hand and raced excitedly down the hall, then back to the living room, then back into the bedroom. He came out — no ball — and barked at me.

"Right," I said, still not believing; "Gotcha." I found the ball in the same place beside the bed. Gus grabbed it, ran around with it to celebrate, then hid it in the bedroom again. We went through the whole thing several times, and Gus looked at me with approval each time I found the ball. I hoped he could see that I may be slow sometimes but I'm not Learning-Disabled.

"Jean," I said, "is this possible? Is Gus really hiding the ball for me to find?"

"You said he's smart," she reminded me.

"Lucky for me," I said, "he's not smart enough to put the ball in different places. He always hides it in the same place."

I shouldn't have said it when Gus was listening. The next time he told me to look for the ball, it wasn't there. I finally found it on the bed, under my pillow. "Gus," I told him, "this invited leaning is going to your head. You're forgetting you're just a dog." It's hard to tell with dogs, but I think he laughed at me.

Gus likes Flavor Snacks — crunchy, bone-shaped dog biscuits I keep on the back of my desk so I can bribe him to go away when I'm working and he wants me to play with him. As usual, he's a step ahead of me. Bounding into my office, he bumps my elbow with his nose and says, "If you give me three Flavor Snacks, I won't bother you for a while." I don't know why he wants *three*. If I give him two, he demands another. If I give him four, he accepts them, but doesn't care much about the fourth one. So I give him three, and he goes away.

"Impossible," I told myself the first few times it happened. "Numbers are too abstract for a dog. Even a smart one. I'm going to prove it."

I broke a Flavor Snack in half, held one piece up for Gus to see, and asked him, "How many?"

He woofed, once, but that didn't prove anything because in Dog Talk "woof" is a homonym; like many English words, its meaning must be deduced from its context. It can mean "Please" or "I want to go out" or "I'm hungry." I wasn't convinced that it could also mean "one."

I gave Gus the Flavor Snack, then held up two pieces, one in each hand, and asked him, "How many?"

"Woof, he said, eyeing the piece in my right hand. When I didn't give it to him he looked at the piece in my left hand and said, "Woof."

"Coincidence," I said, giving him both pieces. "Accident." Holding up one, I asked him how many.

"Woof," he said. I waited. He waited. We both waited. Finally, suspecting that his attention span might be longer than mine, I gave him the Flavor Snack, and waited for him to eat it — *crunch-glumph*, like a boa constrictor. Then I held up two pieces, one in each hand, and asked, "How many?"

He woofed at the one in my right hand, then at the one in my left hand. I gave them to him. We did it again and again that evening, and several times in the next few days, always with the same result: a woof for each hand. I still didn't know if Gus was counting them or had only decided that I wanted him to woof for each one.

About a week later, I held up two Flavor Snacks and asked Gus, "How many?" He hesitated.

He looked at one, then the other, then at the first again, and then back to the second. Back and forth, several times. Then he looked at me and very distinctly said, "Woof-woof." Two syllables; one word.

Had he finally said "two"? We did it several times, sometimes with one, sometimes with two — and he answered correctly every time. He wasn't as certain, at first, about "two" as he was about "one" — he always took time to consider very carefully before saying "two" ("woof-woof") — but he obviously knew the difference. Gus could count!

So far, he hasn't mastered "three," a quantity that often excites him to the point of saying, "Nine! Fourteen! Six!" although he is always insistent on exactly three Flavor Snacks. Apparently he knows the quantity of three, but doesn't have a word for it. I've read of an aboriginal jungle tribe, purportedly unchanged since the Stone Age, whose entire numerical system is "One, two, three, plenty," meaning that any quantity over three is too much to count separately. Gus's numerical system — "One, two, plenty" — is only one digit short of Stone Age man's.

Since then, we've continued to be impressed by Gus's intelligence, but we're seldom surprised by it. When he's hungry, he brings his food dish into the kitchen. If he wants one of us to go out with him, he brings our boots (dirty sneakers, in the summertime), and then goes back to the closet to pull a jacket (usually the right one) off the hanger. If he wants his chest scratched, he pulls someone's hand down and leans against it. If we ask him to whisper, he makes a very soft, barely audible, *huff* sound. When he's riding in the truck and sees a stop sign or hears the click of the turn signal, he sits down and braces his front legs.

Early one spring, a sign in town announced registration for obedience training, bringing us face-to-face with the unexpected question of formal education. We discussed it. We hadn't wanted it for any of our kids, and all four of them have done very well without it, but maybe it would be different for Gus. "Different how?" we asked ourselves. Well, socialization, for one thing; he'd get to meet other dogs, learn to interact meaningfully with his peers. Broaden his cultural horizons by showing him part of the world beyond our rural homestead. Gus said he wasn't sure what we meant by "obedience" or "socialization," but anything involving a ride in the truck was okay with him.

We still weren't sure. Having devoted so much of our lives to home-schooling, it just didn't seem right to enroll our dog in public school.

On the other hand, we home-schoolers are a strange, perverse lot. I don't mean "we" meaning *us*, Jean and Donn Reed, personally; I mean we home-schoolers in general, generic home-schoolers or the home-schooling masses. We reject the standards and methods and results of public schools. We say we don't want our kids to meet public school standards, because those standards are empty and false. We say the world would be better off if public school had never been invented.

And then whom do we choose as our home-school heroes? John Taylor Gatto, honored as "Teacher of the Year" three times before he quit the public school system after twenty-six years. David Colfax, described on another author's book jacket as "father of three home-schooled Harvard graduates" — not even mentioning his fourth son who was also home-schooled but hasn't gone to Harvard. Grace Llewellyn, described on the cover of her book as "a former middle school English teacher." And, of course, John Holt, who worked in public and private schools for years before "discovering" home-schooling, which some of us had been doing for years.

We're like dying atheists asking a priest for absolution — not really believing in it, but hedging our bets, not taking any chances. A stamp of approval from professional teachers who have quit the public schools after ten or twenty years seems to mean more to us than the opinions of people who got out before they got in — that is, who never got involved in public schools at all.

Perverse or not, Gus and I registered for the

course. Each Tuesday evening, for eight weeks, we drove to the community recreation center and, along with about 30 other dogs and their owners, received instruction from a member of the American Kennel Club. Every day, at home, Gus and I diligently did our homework, most of which he thought was dumb and boring, but he was a good pupil, and more than willing to put up with such nonsense if it meant being outdoors with me. He even brought my boots and jacket to me two or three times a day, plainly Inviting me to help him Learn more.

We learned to Heel on Leash, which included Stopping or Starting on command, Right — and Left — Angle Turns, About Face, and promptly Sitting (Gus; not me) without command at each Stop. Gus didn't see the point of it, but he mastered it quickly and didn't argue about it.

Then came Heeling on Leash in a Figure 8, which Gus thought was one of the stupidest exercises he had ever heard of. At school, he wanted to make it a Figure 6 or 99 or 54, anything but Figure 8, and when we practiced at home during the week, he wrapped his paws around my ankle and chewed my foot.

The Long Sit (sitting and staying in place with minimal movement for at least a minute) and Long Down (lying down and staying in place for three minutes) were easy because he had already learned them at home when he was waiting for me to hide his rubber football.

Recall — sitting, staying, then coming on command — was also easy, for the same reason.

The final lesson, in preparation for exam night, was Stand for Inspection, and Gus thought it was dumber than the Figure 8. The idea was that he would sit beside me in Heel position, I would tell him to stand, and he would promptly stand; then I would walk away to the end of the leash, and he would stay, still standing, while the instructor walked up to him, ran a hand along his back, and walked away; and would remain there until I returned to his side. The whole exercise was a snap for him — all except the first part. Gus refused to stand on command. I had to nudge his belly with my toe, tug forward on his leash, and repeat the command several times, and then Gus would very reluctantly stand. Once he was standing, he did the rest of the entire exercise without a hitch, but after two weeks of practice he still refused to stand on command.

Graduation Night arrived. Gus and I discussed our test-taking strategy, and I told Jean before we left not to expect too much. Neither Gus nor I had taken the course very seriously, and I honestly expected us to score about 28th in a class of 30.

We started off with 100 points. On the Heel on Leash, we lost 3 points out of 20, for holding the leash too tight. On the Figure 8, we lost 1 point out of 10, for the same reason. On the Long Sit, no points lost, out of 20. On the Long Down, no points lost, out of 20. On Recall, 1 point was lost out of 15, for "handler error" (I tugged on the leash once when I shouldn't have). Gus was nonchalant, and I was amazed. But the worst was yet to come, and I knew it would be our downfall.

"Stand your dog for inspection," the judge said. "Stand," I commanded, knowing he wouldn't, and getting ready to sneak my toe under him. He stood immediately, without a nudge, and didn't move as I walked away from him. The judge walked up to him, ran his hand along Gus's back, then walked away, and Gus stood still as I returned to him. No points lost, out of 15.

Total points lost, 5. Final score, 95. Second place!

The next day, at home, I asked Gus to Stand. He yawned at me. I made it a command, and he chewed my foot.

There's a lesson in there somewhere, but I'm not sure what it is. Probably Gus was way ahead of us again, and just wanted to make a point about learning. Maybe about invited learning.

Gus has interrupted me several times while I've been writing this. He hid his football in the bedroom, then came to my office and told me to look for it. I knew he wouldn't leave me alone until I did, so I went to the bedroom. It wasn't beside the bed. Not under the pillows, which he had rearranged (probably just to mislead me). I finally found it under the covers, which he had pulled back, then pulled up over the ball. I told him to stay on the bed and count to 10 while I hid the ball. He's still not very good at numbers over 3, but I got the ball hidden under pile of sofa pillows before he came charging after me. He pushed pillows all over until he found the ball, then went to hide it again. Came to tell me to look for it. I went. Nowhere in the bedroom this time. I finally found it down the hall, just inside the bathroom door. Gus was laughing at me. Smart-alecky dog. My turn; I hid the ball under a folded blanket on the other sofa. Gus flipped pillows

around with his nose, then checked the other sofa, lifted the blanket with his nose, and got the ball. Hid it in the bedroom again, told me to look for it. I told him I'm busy writing a serious article about education. He sighed and looked out the window and woofed.

"Not now," I said. "Maybe later."

He woofed at the box of Flavor Snacks on the back of my desk. I took two out of the box and showed them to him. He counted them, then looked at the box and growled softly. I got another. He accepted all three, one at a time, and cleaned up the crumbs on the floor.

I went back to work. Gus jumped up on one of the sofas, rearranged the pillows, then lay down and looked at Jean, who was playing de Visée's "Suite in D Minor" on her guitar. I don't even know what D minor means, but Gus does, and he doesn't like it. He always growls — a very low rumble deep in his throat — whenever Jean plays anything in D minor. He growled and muttered, so Jean switched to Bach's "Gavotte in A Minor." Gus sighed contentedly, and went to sleep.

He sure is smart.

It's a good thing one of us is.

## Addendum

In the last five years Gus has matured. He can tell time better than I can. I'm frequently absent-minded about mealtime, but he knows exactly when it's five o'clock and time to eat. If I'm working here in the office, he'll come in and politely bump my elbow. I don't know why I ever think I can complete what I'm working on. If I ignore the gentle bump, he will do it again more firmly. If I'm talking on the phone, I have a tendency to drop it. If you call around 5 p.m., you may hear strange noises from either or both of us. The twice-yearly time changes are traumatic.

I occasionally tutor public school students. After we work for a while, we'll take a break, and one of my students' favorite break activities is playing games with Gus. One hot day I offered cookies and juice to a girl I'll call Jill. Naturally, Gus felt he should be included. Wanting to show off his talents I held up three pieces of a cookie and asked him to count. He said, "Woof-woof-woof." Very impressed, my student felt sure he could count more than three. I explained what I thought was Gus's philosophy about numbers, but my student felt I might be underrating him, so to humor my student, we tried four. Gus not only counted to four, but went on to count to five! No mistakes, no matter how I mixed up the numbers. When he got five I insisted we quit immediately, for two reasons (not that I couldn't think up five reasons!). The first was that I would have to put Gus on a diet if he learned any more. The other was that I'd soon have a dog taking my tutoring job.

I know some of you have bought this book only because you fell in love with Gus and want more Gus stories. Gus has worked hard not to disappoint you, and I'll try to tell the tales faithfully.

### Gus Becomes a Nanny

This story begins in 1994, when Big Guy (the cat that offered to clean Gus's clock) took a long walk one February day and didn't come back for nine months. I expected him back within a couple days, and then in the spring, but as time went on I had to admit that maybe the mighty hunter had met his match. I went into mourning and still looked and called for him when I went out. Donn had seen how much Gus enjoyed other cats when they visited the vet, and he and Gus made plans for introducing a dog-friendly feline into our house.

They chose an orange and white ball of fluff so small you could hold him in the palm of your hand. We all fell in love at first sight. Donn and I didn't have a name picked out, so we decided to wait a couple of days and see what type of personality this new addition to our family possessed. (We'd been too hasty in the past with one cat, and ended up having to change the name George to Georgina.) While we dithered about names, Gus named the kitty Ruff. Well, what did you expect a dog to call his cat?

At this time Donn was sick, and his condition varied from very good to not good. When we'd agreed to get a kitty for Gus, I hadn't taken into consideration that I would have to be the one to housebreak it and keep an eye on it outside — all the things the kids had always done with new animals in the family. By day two I was not as happy about Ruff as Donn and Gus were. In fact, I would have returned Ruff with hardly a second thought. Maybe Gus is psychic, and maybe not, but that afternoon he started taking Ruff out to use the bathroom. Imagine an 85-pound dog picking up a handful of fluff in his mouth and gently carrying it outside. Gus would set Ruff down and watch while he went to the bathroom, and bring him back in and groom him. Can you imagine a tongue the same size as you giving you a bath? With the housebreaking chores off my list, I settled back with Donn and enjoyed watching Gus bring Ruff up. They went for walks together. On a nice day, we could look out the window and see Gus trotting down the road with Ruff in his mouth. They'd be gone about 5 or 10 minutes and then come back. Gus was pretty tolerant of Ruff, but he did set some limits. Ruff was not allowed under the house and he was not to climb more than 18 inches off the ground. If Ruff went higher, Gus would pull him off the tree and take him inside.

All in all, I'd say Gus was a good nanny. There were, and still are, a few gaps in Ruff's education. Gus likes to play. He's definitely not a hunter in the same sense that most cats are, and he never completed the job of training Ruff to be a good mouser. In a country house like ours, it's an important job, worthy of great praise when well done. Big Guy is a hunter and he never fools around when on duty. He catches his prey, kills it, puts it in his dish, and then eats it. To be honest, I should say he eats it most of the time. Sometimes he will leave leftovers in his dish for later. Once, when Susan was home for a visit, he left a quarter of a rabbit by Susan's bed as an offering for her because he felt she was special. I'm glad Big Guy was unaware of how unappreciative Susan (then vegetarian) was when she woke up the next morning and put her foot right on it.

I've gotten sidetracked. My point was that Ruff never learned to be a proper hunter. He's very good at catching things but still hasn't learned to do more than play with the mice, moles, snakes, toads, bats, birds, ermine, and squirrels he has brought into the house to play with at one time or another. (What was the most exciting thing I did over New Year's for the new millennium? I watched Ruff's squirrel leap around my kitchen at a zillion miles an hour — but that's another story.) The first autumn after he learned to hunt, Ruff brought in enough mice to feed all the cats in the community — and he generally lost them somewhere in the house. By this time, Big Guy had reappeared, thank goodness, and we didn't have to buy food for him: He just cleaned up Ruff's escapees. Then came the day when we heard a commotion in the bathroom. Ruff had a bright idea: no more escapees! He discovered that if he put his playthings in the bathtub, they couldn't get away from him. (Well, most of them didn't leap out. The ones that did are in another story.)

Donn and I understood that cats hunt, and that many of them will play with their catch before killing it. It's a cat's nature to do this, and we knew we couldn't change that predisposition, but the idea of a mouse trapped in the tub with Ruff upset us. Ruff plays rough, so

Donn and I started rescuing the mice by putting a container over them to catch them. We'd take Ruff out of the tub, transport the mouse outside and away from the house, then let it go. Gus watched us each time we did this. Then came a day when we heard a BIG commotion in the bathroom. We looked at each other and went to investigate. We found Ruff in the tub with a mouse. Gus was climbing into the tub. He then nudged Ruff out of the way and picked up the mouse by the tail, climbed out of the tub, took the mouse outside, and let it go. He wagged his tail, and I swear he had a big grin on his face. Now, when I clean the tub (and mostly it needs cleaning even though no human has been in it), I clean up mouse tracks, cat tracks, and dog tracks. I don't know what all this has to do with homeschooling, except that someone wanted a good Gus story. Perhaps it's a lesson about the natural consequences of allowing unique talents to develop in freedom.

# DISCIPLINE

As I've said elsewhere, we have never used any form of punishment with our children, and they have never given us any "discipline" problems that couldn't be resolved with discussion. (No one's perfect; sometimes it takes a lot of discussion.)

Our children are generally honest, respectful of people and things, polite, and usually very well-behaved.

"If you don't punish your children, how do you discipline them?"

In one 1957 dictionary, "punishment" is not one of the definitions of discipline, although it's mentioned as a *colloquial synonym*. A 1973 dictionary lists "punishment" as the eighth definition, and in a 1980 dictionary it's third. The word has come a long way, baby.

"Discipline" is still used to mean "a branch of instruction or learning, such as 'an academic discipline,'" but that definition, once the first (and not really very long ago), is now fourth — coming *after* the meaning of "punishment given to correct a person or enforce obedience."

In verb form, "discipline" means first "to train to be obedient and orderly" and second "to punish."

When we watch other parents with their children, we think we may have many more rules of conduct than most — advice and suggestions and instructions covering nearly every situation — but our rules of conduct are more like social customs than laws, and nearly all of them could easily be expressed by the Golden Rule or a close parallel.

When our children began crawling and exploring, we placed limits only for their own protection or the protection of things that might be damaged by inexperienced handling. In our own home, we kept fragile or dangerous items out of reach. Our house has always been arranged for the presence of the kids. When visiting in other homes, which haven't been "child-proofed," we watch our kids closely but interfere with their movements, either physically or verbally, only when really necessary. We describe and explain the limits as briefly and clearly as possible. If the kids are curious about a fragile or dangerous item, we hold the item for inspection and discussion, and then set it out of reach. We never say, "Don't touch that; you might break it." Instead, we say, "Be very careful with this, because it's very fragile, and might break if it falls," or "I'll help you hold this, to make it easier for you to see." When prescribing limits, we stick to the facts, without exaggeration or threats.

Our kids always know that we expect only good behavior from them — not because of bribes or threats, but because we know they have no natural desire to break or lie or cheat or steal. Children, like adults, want to do what is right. They want to be liked, loved, and respected. They want to respect themselves.

Whenever one of our kids does something wrong or has made a mistake in judgment, we are quick to sympathize, to understand, and to forgive. Our expectation of goodness always includes the knowledge that mistakes will be made, that they don't diminish the child's inherent goodness.

A young child understands much of what is said to him, long before he can talk. When he is big enough to hold an object, he is old enough to understand directions about handling it.

The child is always more important than the object, even if actions toward it must be limited, and he must never be made to think otherwise.

In the relatively rare instances of "bad" behavior, we do our best to make it very clear that it's the behavior which is being rejected, not the child. We know parents who put their offending child out of the room, even out of the house, saying, "You're welcome to come back in when you're ready to behave the way you should." I don't think the child will make the desired distinction; no matter what the parent says, the child will feel personally rejected. Separation from the group or situation is often very effective, but if it's used as a punishment it just fosters resentment. "I'm not punishing you," says the parent. "I'm putting you outside to think it over." The child doesn't believe it. All he will think over is that he has been rejected, he is alone, he didn't mean to misbehave — or maybe he did, and as a parent you need to find out why. In any case, he's not big enough or strong enough to put his mother and father outside to think it over when they misbehave. He shouldn't be *put* outside; he should be *taken* out, and held closely, and talked with, not lectured.

For a young child, even with the most loving and understanding parents, the world is very often an incomprehensible and sometimes frightening maze of people and objects and rules. A parent who really tries to understand a child's feelings from the child's own point of view will be a much more positive influence on him than will a distant judge. We try to put ourselves in our children's places, really try to understand the situation as they feel it to be. We try to remember our own childhoods, the times we misbehaved, perhaps in the same way or worse, and how we felt about the people around us, how we felt about the ways we were punished.

We don't try to exact promises from our children, such as "Now, we'll go back inside if you think you can be nice." We talk about the problem, explaining why it is a problem, not expecting to reach solutions that will cover all future problems, and then drop it, perhaps even changing the subject. The situation may come up again, and we will deal with it in the same way, but the children never feel unloved or rejected. They don't resent us or feel a need to retaliate. Willful misbehavior is very rare. We are sure our children know we love them whatever they do.

We have never punished our children, in any way, for anything. We don't withhold privileges, or spank them, or send them to bed without supper. We don't threaten them with any kind of pain or suffering or deprivation — physical or psychological. If there is a problem in action or behavior, we discuss it; we consider it *our* problem. No one is "to blame"; it isn't "your fault" or "his fault." Fault and blame are irrelevant. Nearly every conflict between people is one of misunderstanding or lack of communication or an unfulfilled need. We discuss the problem — what led to it, how it might be avoided in the future. If something different should have been done or said, we discuss it, not to assign blame, but always to seek a better relationship in the future. Assigning blame creates defensiveness, which in turn creates barriers to understanding and progress.

We don't reward our children for good behavior, or for obedience, or for doing their work. We give praise for jobs well done, conflicts dealt with creatively and positively, or problems solved intelligently, but not as a reward. Such achievements deserve honest recognition.

Our children aren't paragons of peacefulness and harmony, but there is no physical violence between them, with the exception of occasional light slaps or pokes when they're very angry. They argue, complain, bicker, and sometimes call each other names. It's interesting that the kids who have had the most contact with public school kids at early ages are the ones most prone to name-calling and petty bickering.

In working to help the kids resolve their problems and conflicts with each other or with us, Jean and I sometimes lose our tempers right along with them. They shout at us; we shout back. When it's all over, we apologize to them for our having lost our tempers, and they learn from our example that even loving parents can get angry, can lose their tempers, and can apologize. They learn to apologize to us and to each other. They learn to accept apologies.

In examining disagreements, we search for the roots — away from issues of personality, always trying to avoid the concepts of fault and blame. The question is not *who* is wrong, but *what* is wrong, and what can be done to correct the present situation to avoid its recurrence.

Peaceful conflict resolution isn't easy. It takes far more time and effort, more introspection, more discussion, than would be taken by establishing blame and meting out punishment. But it works, and is well worth the effort. It also puts more responsibility on the kids for monitoring and controlling their own behavior, by not "releasing" them from past actions through having "paid" for them by receiving punishment. As the kids get older, we've seen them searching more and more for peaceful solutions.

The dual concepts of blame and punishment are rooted deeply throughout our culture — in its religions, its government, and its family life. The courts and churches insist that if you have done something wrong, you must pay for it. This belief has its roots in the pre-Mosaic code of "an eye for an eye," which may have acted as a deterrent but hardly worked as a correction, any more than such punishments do today. Jesus tried to overturn this rule but with little success, even within "his" churches. His doctrine of forgiveness is often preached but seldom practiced.

Parents who punish their children, either physically or psychologically, are using force and coercion to manipulate behavior. A child may not repeat an act for which he has been punished, but it's usually only because he fears the consequences, not because he understands the wrongness of what he has done. An ancient Hebrew said that the man who does not beat his son must hate him, and his cynical observation is taken by millions of parents to be a divine injunction to spank their children. Jesus didn't threaten children or adults with either a spanking or hellfire; he promised love and forgiveness. His lessons appeal to the conscience — realize what you have done, he said, and feel sorry about it, and don't do it anymore.

In our family, we have striven for discipline from within. We wanted our children to know and understand the difference between right and wrong, good and bad, and to choose the rightness and goodness because they want to, not because they're afraid of any external consequences or punishments.

The development of the conscience is sometimes difficult. Most of the people and institutions of our society are against it, although they often pretend otherwise.

Behavior codes are relaxing and eroding around the world, which is one of the proofs that morality cannot be enforced by laws or fear. It can come only from within each individual, from strong convictions about what is right and good, and the desire to live by those convictions. It comes from the strength and courage to go against the current — to do what is right because it is right, not because of hope of reward or fear of punishment. Those convictions and that strength constitute the only discipline, moral or social, that is lasting and real. We can't force it onto our children, or even give it to them. We can only try to help them find and develop it within themselves.

# KIDDING AROUND

The practice of referring to children as kids is thought by some to have begun as a tax dodge employed by slavers in the 1700s. Rather than declare their valuable and highly dutiable cargo, the righteous captains would insist they were importing goats and their kids, which even zealous customs officers admitted to be of little value.

Our daughter Karen would certainly agree with the customs officers, if not with the slave importers. Karen is a good kid and a great kidder, but she kids you not when she suggests that goats are not overly bright.

When one of our neighbors recently liquidated much of his barnyard stock, some of the flow ended up in our barn in the forms of five goats, four of whom keep our cow company and provide healthy exercise for our children's fingers and Karen's vocabulary.

(Digressing a little: We "water the cow," meaning we give water to her, and we "milk the cow," meaning we take milk away from her, and still we think English is a language that even young children can understand. Water and milk are both liquids, at least in their most common and desirable states, so could we say in either case, that we have liquidated the stock?)

(Digressing still further: Our little brook, central to our farm and our aspirations, is certainly a liquid asset, although financial reports usually reserve that term for money, as in "cash flow," as if even money might come from a spring up on the hill. Not *our* spring on *our* hill, I can assure them with satisfaction; what would our cow do with a bucket of money?)

Anyway, back to the goats. Derek cares for Shawna and Jingle, two young does who have not yet learned how to make milk. Susan milks Heidi and Karen milks Buffy, and they both care for their goats, although, playing with definitions, sometimes they say they don't very much.

The buck, we were told, was named Keyops by his parents, but a previous caretaker kept forgetting the name and decided to call him Fred. Fred went to live with a man named Fred, who called him Tyler. Then Tyler stayed with George, who continued to call him Tyler. Then Tyler moved in with us. His proud bearing, majestic horns, and strong odor reminded us of Egyptian mummies and other ancient artifacts, so we restored his earlier name, with the proper spelling Cheops.

At first, Karen and Susan and Heidi and Buffy took turns amusing each other when the former two attempted to extract milk from the latter two, and the entire operation was a splashing success. Heidi soon settled down and eventually gave Susan less trouble than milk, but Buffy continued to think milking time was circus time, and Karen developed very strong opinions about Buffy's intelligence.

Whenever Karen touched the faucets, Buffy became a rodeo queen — kicking, bucking, prancing, somersaulting, standing on her head, and sitting in the milk bucket. Karen was very impressed, and said so.

"Dumb goat," she muttered, over and over, as she tried to milk. At night, she had no need to count sheep jumping fences. "Dumb goat," we heard her mutter in her sleep.

I raided my toolbox and made a few quick installations in the goat pen.

"Observe," I instructed Karen and Susan. "This rope, with the loop in one end, attaches quickly to the goat's collar. The free end then goes through the eye-screw, down here, six inches from the floor. Notice how Buffy's head goes down as I pull the rope up. Now her collar is snug against the post, and so is her neck, and she is reluctant to practice gymnastics of any kind."

Karen and Susan nodded solemnly.

"Now," I continued, "Buffy is quite happy to wait patiently while you tie the remainder of the rope up here to this long screw. I recommend a clove hitch, which is made so — a loop, and another loop, and pull it tight. Some people call it a double half-hitch, but it's stronger if you call it a clove hitch. Any questions?"

"No," said Karen, "but you forgot two things."

"Two things?" I echoed. I looked over the entire arrangement — the taut rope, the perfect clove hitch I had learned in Boy Scouts, the waiting milk bucket, and the immobilized goat. "What did I forget?"

"A lever on the wall," Karen said grimly, "and a trapdoor under the goat."

A reader wrote to say that she and her husband (a math teacher) were disappointed by my comments about math. "Math literacy" — the understanding and enjoyment of all levels of math — are as important, she said, as reading literacy.

I wrote her a long letter, emphasizing that it certainly is not the study of mathematics I oppose, but the mandatory studying of math without enjoyment or purpose. I realize there are many people who really need math, and I'm even a little envious of those who enjoy it.

Our culture — in philosophy, history, and myth — is communicated much more through literature than through math, so I can't agree that a lack of math literacy is equal to a lack of reading literacy. A person who is well-read but non-mathematical will have a greater awareness and understanding of the world than a mathematician whose reading has been confined to mathematics. That doesn't preclude the possible desirability of being well-educated in both fields, but if I have to make a choice, I'll choose literature.

All four of our kids read a great deal, but none of them seems to have a natural bent for writing, so it's as unlikely that they'll be journalists as it is that they'll be astronomers. With writing, therefore, as with math, we encourage a general, basic competency that will be of use to them in areas they probably will pursue, and in most "real-life" situations: various styles of letters, basic reports (which may or may not be useful, but are easy to master and will probably be of good use someday), simplified research notes, and so on, along with basic spelling skills, grammar, sentence structure, and a few handshakes with parts of speech. If they ever need more advanced writing (or more advanced math), they have solid foundations on which to build.

The essential purpose of language — whether it consists of animal grunts and growls, human speech, mathematical equations, or computer symbols — is the communication of information and ideas. As the subject of this chapter, I'll consider writing to be human speech on paper. Its basic purpose is still the communication of information and ideas. Spelling is little more than a standardized system of encoding sounds and their meanings to facilitate that communication.

There's an old story, which you've probably heard, about a little boy who scribbled laboriously on a piece of paper and proudly told his mother, "Look, I'm writing."

"How nice," said his mother. "What does it say?"

"I don't know," the boy replied. "I haven't learned to read yet."

Like many apocryphal stories, this one may have some basis in fact, but most of us learn to read before we learn to write.

Ideally — except in modern schools that try to teach how to read without offering reading material of any substance, and how to write without asking that the writing be about anything of substance — the two processes soon overlap, each one contributing to the other. Spelling, principal parts of speech, and basic grammar are all learned simultaneously. The reading will be about subjects that interest the kids, and they will write about things or events that interest them. Printing is also learned at the same time, as well as the extension of meanings by the use of suffixes and prefixes, by different tenses, etc.

We never taught our children to read.

# READING OPENS THE DOOR TO THE WORLD

When they were very young, we read to them. When they were three months old, they gurgled happily as we read nursery rhymes, poetry, and even captions of "first interest" animal books. At six months, they smiled and pointed at interesting shapes and colors. When they were a year old, we read books with them, discussing the pictures and answering millions of questions. We often asked each other, "Where is the truck?" "Can you put your finger on the nose?" "Which flower is red?" and similar questions. The kids weren't reading words yet, but even picture books with no words involved verbal communication and a growing vocabulary, including concepts of space, size, color, action, and direction.

Between eighteen months and two years, each of them spent many hours each day with books, not yet recognizing many words, but studying the pictures. Despite the kids' early interest in books, we never pushed reading. We read to them every day, but they also chose to look at books on their own every day. It was unimportant to us if they learned to read at the age of two or six or ten. When we were reading to them we made a point of moving our finger along under the words we were reading. It wasn't long before the questions were about the letters and words as often as about the pictures. The kids were fascinated by the idea that the story was not only in the pictures, and were eager to decode the words. They asked us to identify specific words, especially nouns with which they were familiar (cow, horse, car, tree) and verbs, especially of movement (run, jump, fall). They'd point at a word (sometimes at random, sometimes deliberately) and ask "Cow?" If by chance, the "choice" was correct, the child felt such pride and delight that the word might never be forgotten. When the random choice was incorrect, we moved the pointing finger to the right word, saying, "Here's 'cow.'" If the child then returned to the first choice, wanting to know what it was, then we'd tell him; otherwise, we ignored it.

Their own curiosity about the pictures and the accompanying words we read to them taught them to read. They also saw us (whenever we had a chance) reading for our own pleasure.

Frequent positive reinforcement and absolute avoidance of negative corrections encouraged the kids, and they learned rapidly. None of them ever said, "I can't get it. It's too hard," because we never asked them to "get" anything. There was never any pressure to do something they hadn't yet learned to do.

The girls could identify and read several words before they knew the sounds of individual letters. We never had a definite plan of "how to teach reading," except to be sure it was always fun and interesting, so there didn't seem much point in interrupting their reading to teach them how to read.

## A LESSON IN PATIENCE

Derek learned in a different way. He had the same introduction to books, saw us and the girls reading, and asked all of us to read to him. He had a love affair with books, and it drove him (and us) nearly crazy for a couple of years. At age two he wished for a horse. At ages three and four he yearned for a horse and someone to read to him. After that he wanted a horse and he wanted to read. He would ask what a word was, but couldn't remember it a day later or even later that day. He frequently ad-libbed stories from books, some almost word for word. Sometimes he

made up his own stories to go with the pictures. When he realized that the letters had individual sounds he learned the alphabet and most of the sounds, but he still couldn't read on his own.

Derek's desire to read was not lacking, but something was. It made us wonder and sometimes worry. We didn't understand why, although he yearned to read, he couldn't do it. His frustration grew, even though we reassured him that he would learn. We had his eyes checked, even though we had never seen him squint at a book or the TV. He was given glasses, which he proudly wore. He went to get a book, almost tripping on the way, and sat down to read. He looked at the letters on the page and scrunched up his eyes and face so he could see better. The glasses were obviously wrong or not the answer at all. We had his eyes rechecked by another eye specialist who advised us to throw the glasses out, so we did.

No one really understands exactly what happens when the ability to decode the written word occurs. It's still a mystery. We do know that a certain amount of brain development must take place first, just as the muscles and nervous system must develop before a child crawls or walks. Studies have shown that linguistic and mathematical skills come easily at different times to different children.

All Derek really needed was time. When he was eight, "it" finally happened. After he made the first breakthrough on his own he was an insatiable reader, and within six months was reading way beyond

his grade level. Before he was able to read he would have been considered "slow," or worse, in a public school setting. I shudder to think what that would have done to this otherwise bright and happy child who went on to became a natural speed-reader with very high comprehension.

It was interesting to watch phonics and grammar grow naturally with the kids' learning to write.

We let the kids lead the way. Once the partial similarity of COW to CAR was noticed and questioned, it was very natural for us to discuss the alphabet and the different sounds of letters. Being able to "sound out" words phonetically is important, but it's just as important to be able to read entire words and even whole phrases without having to dissect them.

The conventional "sounding out" of "baby" is

buh-ay-buh-ee. Once the child can point to the letters in turn and make these sounds, we are supposed to say, "Very good! Now say the sounds faster; run them together." We are supposed to demonstrate the method, slowly and ponderously saying, "BUHay-buhEE," over and over, until the child finally hears — or guesses — the word "baby." "Now you do it," we say, with the reminder "Sound out each letter, then run the sounds together — and you have the word!"

It doesn't really work that way. For most beginning readers, it still comes out as buh-ay-buh-ee, but speeded up — buhaybuhee." The sounds trip over each other, but are not "run together." The trick is to condense four syllables into two — but then it's no longer a strictly phonetic approach; it's sight reading of syllables. The transition from four separate letter sounds to two syllables is less a matter of logic than of intuition. The conclusion may be accepted, but there is no logical transition to be understood.

Later, when we began using school readers, we made the mistake of also using the tests for "comprehension and retention" that invariably followed each story. We still hadn't learned to reject the methods of the "experts." Luckily, we soon realized that our kids' lessening interest in reading was the direct result of having to answer dumb questions about their reading, but it took us longer than it should have. We should have known better without even trying it.

I was reminded of those dumb questions many years later when I read Longfellow's "The Courtship of Miles Standish" to the family. It was in a book prepared for classroom use, and the poem was followed by about fifty questions, such as "The Pilgrims came to America on the (a) Atlantic (b) Mayflower (c) Titanic (d) Damascus." Like many test questions in the public schools, some of these were not only ridiculous, but intentionally tricky. Even if the student has been asleep throughout the entire poem, he isn't likely to answer either "Titanic" or "Damascus," even if he doesn't know what they are. But a conscientious student might easily suspect a trick in the first two choices. The Pilgrims came to America on the Mayflower, but they also came on the Atlantic. The teacher has the answer key and knows that the correct answer is *b*, which is what most students will answer. Does that mean that *a* is incorrect? The student who answers "the Atlantic" will be laughed at. The teacher, smiling condescendingly, will say, "The question is about the name of the ship." "But," the student might argue, "the question didn't say 'ship.' 'Damascus' isn't a ship's name." The teacher smiles tolerantly at the student's stupidity. The other students snicker — even those who answered "Titanic."

When Derek was nine, he became interested in sharks, and quickly exhausted the small amount of material we had on the subject. He borrowed books from the public library and requested more through inter-library loans. Relatives sent him books about sharks; he searched back issues of *National Geographic*. Except for helping him find material, we left him alone. We didn't try to direct his studies, or tie them in with any other subject, or test his "comprehension and retention." We knew that if he didn't understand the books, he wouldn't have chosen to read them. Soon he scoffed at popularized images of sharks, such as the movie *Jaws*, and could point out, in detail, the errors in them — not to impress anyone with his knowledge, but because he felt that both sharks and people were being wronged by the misconceptions and misrepresentations. His "retention," apparently, was excellent.

When Derek first showed an interest in sharks, we might have thought, "A-ha! Here's our chance. We can direct his study, so that it will include history, geography, oceanography, other aquatic life forms, sociology, anthropology, and psychology. We can expand his vocabulary."

We didn't; the thought never occurred to us. Had we assigned readings, followed by tests for comprehension and retention, I'm sure he would have lost interest in the subject very quickly. Such an approach to any subject is one of the quickest ways to kill interest in it. Derek studied sharks for two years because he wanted to, and learned a great deal about history, geography, oceanography, other aquatic life forms, sociology, anthropology, and psychology. His vocabulary certainly expanded.

Books have always been a prominent part of our lives. When Jean and I aren't busy with building, gardening, barn chores, housework, or working with the kids, we read. There are books in every room of our house. In providing books for our children, from the time they could first focus their eyes on a picture, we've always treated books as sources of pleasure, adventure, information, and discovery. Reading should never be a tedious chore; it should always be exciting and rewarding — as it will be, if we don't try to harness it, control it, pen it up, or direct it for our own purposes.

Educational distributors now offer innumerable books for "the reluctant reader." Because most children spend so many hours watching movies and television, publishers and teachers offer them countless books with "TV tie-ins" — i.e., stories based on popular shows and characters — with the hope that the tie-in will lead the kids from their mania for TV to a mania for reading; then, once hooked, they'll move on to better material.

Does it work? I doubt it. Early Christians, seeking to convert the heathens, incorporated non-Christian rituals, symbols, and even dates into some of their holidays (holy days) in an attempt to make conversion more palatable. Celebration of the springtime birth of Jesus was moved to more nearly coincide with the winter solstice. Painted eggs, chicks, and baby rabbits — once parts of pre-Christian fertility rites — are now popular parts of the Easter observance of many Christians. Who was converted — the pagans or the Christians?

Meaningless trivia on a movie or TV screen is not likely to become more meaningful or less trivial in a book. Why yield to the uneducated choices of the lowest common denominator? Are the antics of television soap operas and cartoons and sitcoms really more exciting and more meaningful than the writings of Dickens, London, Stevenson, Poe, Pyle, even Shakespeare? Granted that millions of high school students are still struggling with a third-grade reading ability, they have been deprived, by an incompetent school system, of the pleasures of reading.

The concerned teacher can read to them, helping them to feel the magic of words in books such as *A Tale of Two Cities, The Three Musketeers, Lost Horizon*, and *Shane*. Such books read, not for instruction but for the mutual enjoyment of both teacher and students, and without tests afterward for comprehension and retention, might in time overshadow the TV

tie-ins. Maybe not; maybe it's too late. But if the students can be helped to realize that the pleasure is worth the effort — that is, once they *want* to read — they will do so, just as much younger children can begin reading B-A-B-Y.

When I have taught adult illiterates, this approach was been successful in every case, as the basis for both reading and writing.

If the students will ever be led to better reading, it will be through the introduction of better literature to read, certainly not through low-vocabulary books about dirt bikes, teen romance, and the selfish cynicism of Garfield.

Teachers say, "My students will never be interested in the great authors, but at least they're reading. It's better to read about television characters than to read nothing at all."

Is it?

Is it better to write verses in restrooms than to write nothing at all? Is it better to listen to punk rock and thrash metal than to hear no music at all?

Whether the book is by an ancient great or a modern unknown, if it doesn't make at least a small positive contribution to the reader's life — his values, his knowledge, his understanding, his growth as a human being, his enjoyment of life — then it's not worth the time of reading. As an avid reader, I feel that illiteracy is a very sad handicap, but the cynicism, narcissism, and hedonism promoted by most television shows and their literary tie-ins, as well as a huge portion of other popular publications, are much greater handicaps.

It's hard for me to imagine my own life without books, but I know many people who don't read, yet are happy and successful — good neighbors, caring parents, and hard workers. Why should they clutter up their lives with books about puerile, melodramatic electronic images?

Just as Gandhi, probably the world's greatest proponent and practitioner of non-violence, said that violence is preferable to cowardice, I am sure that illiteracy is preferable to the exclusive reading of debasing or condescending trivia.

### WRITING

I think we taught our kids a little more about how to write than we did about how to read. Their writing, like their reading, seemed to grow by itself, with only a little help from us. We showed them how to make letters, what sounds the letters represented, and so on. In the beginning, we tried to follow standard schoolbooks, but we soon found that most of them followed logical sequences as much as the beginning readers did. Very little, that is.

Although a few schoolbooks are fairly good, we were soon much happier with the various activity books sometimes sold in toy departments, drugstores, and grocery stores. Now you can find them in Wal-Mart and similar stores and in some bookstores. These books include dot-to-dot pictures (which, besides being fun, teach number recognition and sequence), math and reading readiness, writing preparation, colors, shapes, sizes, and so on. Many are very good primers in natural science. Perhaps because these books are prepared and designed to appeal to parents rather than to school boards, they are often more attractive and interesting than schoolbooks. Future sales are largely dependent on the purchasers' satisfaction, so the books are both educational, which pleases the parents, and fun, which pleases the children.

We put printed alphabet cards on the kitchen wall, where they could easily be seen and copied. Usually the first written word they wanted to learn was their name. After that we followed their lead with their favorite words, names of friends, our names, siblings, names of our pets, and the all-time favorites: YES and NO. Besides pencil or crayons and paper, we used a wall-mounted chalkboard, magnetic letters on the refrigerator, and individual letters printed on cardboard. The kids sometimes spent hours printing letters, words, names, and eventually short sentences. Jean and I printed short messages to them on the chalkboard and the kids printed answers. We arranged the magnetic letters into words; the kids rearranged them into different words.

We agree wholeheartedly with John Holt's recommendation, in *How Children Learn*, that very young children be given access to a typewriter. As John points out, the kids will be fascinated by the machine's inner workings; they'll also want to learn correct spelling, capitalization, and punctuation — perhaps because typewritten material looks so neat, so official, so permanent, and so real. (There are now simplified keyboards for young children that you can use with your computer, but the typewriter mechanism — being able to see it and touch it — is still more fascinating. Also very cheap!) Just touch a key and see how many different things move, and the letter you want is printed right beside the previous letter. Yard and garage sales and pawnshops frequently have very good typewriters for $10 to $20. You can also put an ad in the paper for little cost. Most typewriters — if you can still find them (everyone wants you to buy a computer these days) — sold in toy departments, Christmas catalogs, and even by some educational suppliers, although they look solid enough and sell for as much as $150, aren't worth shelf space. They are too flimsy for the rough handling a child will sometimes give them; the parts, including the ribbons, are often a special size or brand you can't find anywhere; and, if there happens to be a breakdown or defect covered by the very limited warranty, the only "authorized service center" is ten thousand miles away and receives mail only by Camel Express.

Crossword puzzles for children, found in book and toy stores, increase spelling and vocabulary. The girls enjoyed them; Derek didn't.

The best preparation for writing is reading — anything and everything. The child (or adult) who gets little pleasure from reading will seldom see much purpose in writing.

If you have more than one child, you may discover, as we did, that the younger ones will learn a great deal by imitating older siblings. Karen watched Cathy learn to write, and understood the process enough to want to do the same. She spent a lot of time "writing" before she could write anything we could read. Then she spent a lot of time copying actual letters, but sometimes she must have invented her own writing code. We gave her an eight-by-ten-inch spiral-bound notebook with about a hundred pages in it, and she filled it up. Sometimes she would ask us to write a word for her to copy and sometimes she would just "write." Her writing looked to us like squiggles and curlicues, wavy lines and loops, but to her it was writing, and we never made fun of her efforts. Sometimes she would read what she had written, so we knew she was making up stories along with her writing. Sometimes she illustrated her stories. It was great creative fun for all of us.

When Derek was nine, he began reading the Tarzan novels, by Edgar Rice Burroughs. The first of these books was written in 1929, and Burroughs' style is very formal and often pedantic, as was the style of most writers in those days; the sentences are occasionally ponderous, with several subordinate clauses. The vocabulary is sometimes just as imposing: a friendly ape may be referred to as an amiable anthropoid. Try getting all that into the local school's curriculum! I read all of the Tarzan books (more than twenty) several times when I was a kid, and I still read them occasionally, so I knew Derek was starting out in pretty deep water. He asked for help with a few words, but soon figured out most of them from their context, and was soon sailing smoothly. Within two years, he had read all the books at least once, and some of them many times.

When he was ten, Derek started writing his own stories of Tarzan and his son Korak, with enthusiastic and bloodthirsty imitation of Burroughs' own style —

**KORAK, MAN OR BEAST?**
By Derek Reed

He swung silently through the lower branches of the trees. He stopped now and again to sniff the air. Now he stopped, thirty feet off the ground, for he was hunting, a beast among beasts, for this is Korak, son of Tarzan, and he is in Africa, the Dark Continent. You're probably wondering what he is hunting. Well, no matter, for you shall find out. For now, he swings into a natural clearing and sees what he has been tracking for about half an hour, but he does not know this. For he carries no watch, he just knows that he is terribly hungry and he is but a scarce eight feet from Bara the deer. He but broke upon the clearing when he launched himself full upon the buck's back. He fastened his teeth in Bara's neck and sunk his knife into his heart. Bara gave a little quiver and lay still. At that moment a wounded lion came upon them. He headed straight for Korak. Korak leaped high in the air, turned around in mid-air and came down upon the lion's back.

One bronze arm encircled the throat, while the two legs locked under the belly. The free arm drew the knife and drove it home into that savage heart. Again, he drives the knife home. Three times he drives it home. He feels the giant muscles relax. The body quivers and lays still. Korak leaps up, places his foot on the lion's neck and screams forth the victory cry of the bull ape twice. Once for Bara and once for Numa. He went back to Bara and cut a hole in his neck, this is so he will bleed and not be so messy. As he cuts a juicy steak, he finds himself wondering about his friends and if they could see him now naked except for a G-string. "I'm a man" thought Korak, "but I act like a beast." And then he took his kill to a tree and finding a comfortable place, fell asleep.

THE END

Derek usually disliked assigned writing topics, but seemed to be developing adequate writing skills without them, so we gave him very few. A thank-you note for a birthday or Christmas gift might take several weeks, unless we just laid down the law. But if he was writing about a subject that interested him personally and deeply — horses, sharks, Tarzan — he could fill pages in a very short time.

Cathy, Karen, and Susan have always enjoyed writing long, newsy letters to friends and relatives. When asked, we have helped them edit their spelling and punctuation. When Cathy was elected club reporter for her 4-H club, it was her job to write about club activities for a regional 4-H newsletter and for two local newspapers. Two years later, Karen received the job of 4-H reporter. Having their articles in print, with their own bylines, was rewarding, and gave them incentive for steady improvement. Both girls developed an easy writing fluency and wrote several papers for us on research subjects such as existentialism, William Penn, and a comparison of Leonardo da Vinci and Buckminster Fuller.

When Susan was eight, she asked to attend a public school for the entire year, mostly because she enjoyed the social life so much. Her teacher was a screaming bully and we saw several potential problems, but Susan never complained about the teacher, and we somehow convinced ourselves that any harm being done was superficial, and could be corrected easily. Early in the year, Susan lost all interest in reading to herself. When reading aloud, which she had been able to do smoothly and competently, she stuttered, coughed, covered her mouth, mumbled, mispronounced simple words, juxtaposed words, and missed words completely. Her spelling became so literally phonetic that it was almost incomprehensible: "Th tcher sed tak ot yr boke. I opnd it and b gen tu red." Her spelling hadn't been that bad since she was five. But she still seemed happy in school and did well in most other subjects. Her reading problems, we told ourselves, were superficial, and we could straighten them out next year.

We were wrong. It took us years to correct the damage, to rebuild the reading and writing skills that third-grade teacher had nearly destroyed in just a few months. Although Susan now reads avidly, for both pleasure and information, and can write and spell quite well, I'm sure that neither her reading nor her writing is as good as it would be if we had had the sense and courage to take her out of school when we saw the problems beginning. Susan's self-confidence took much longer to rebuild. "I can't do it, I just know I can't," was her standard response to any suggestion of writing. We continued to encourage her and she persevered. As a result, in April 1983, *Highlights for Children* magazine printed a prose-poem Susan had submitted when she was eleven:

**The Beauty of a Tree**
By Susan Reed

Can anyone see the beauty of a tree? The colors of light and dark in the summer? The leaves falling in the fall? What about the icicles hanging from the trees in the winter? Or the buds starting to grow in the spring? Some people may think a tree is just a thing to be used for firewood and building things, but it's not. A tree should be cared for, for just a square inch cut from the bark could end its life. What is the beauty of a tree? The beauty of a tree is life itself.

Her self-confidence leaped. Later that spring, she entered a 4-H club essay-writing contest, and in July 1983 two local papers, *The Woodstock Bugle* and *The Hartland Observer*, carried this story:

**Knowlesville Girl Wins Kings Landing Trip**

Susan Reed of Knowlesville is one of two winners in a province-wide 4-H Essay Contest, writing on the topic "Why I Would Like to Live at Kings Landing." Her prize: five days as a "Visiting Cousin" at Kings Landing.

Each year, 4-H Club members of New Brunswick are invited to submit essays about why they would like to live at Kings Landing. Only two entries are selected as winners — one in French, and one in English. The winners are each awarded five days as a Visiting Cousin at Kings Landing Historical Settlement, with all expenses paid.

Susan, twelve years old, is a member of the Glassville Co-Eds 4-H Club. She and her brother and two sisters attend school at home, taught by their parents.

"I'm very excited about the trip," Susan says. "It will be like going in a time machine to the past."

This will be the second time Susan's writing has gained public recognition. In April, "Highlights for Children Magazine" published a poem Susan had submitted last fall.

Susan will begin her visit at Kings Landing July 12, and return home July 16 — her 13th birthday.

"That's quite a plug for home-schooling," some friends told us.

Yes, we agreed, it was. But it was also much more. They would never know what a long, tedious, often frustrating journey it had been for Susan, and for Jean and me. They wouldn't know our fears and feelings of guilt about Susan's year in third grade, fears that were finally erased by Susan's achievement.

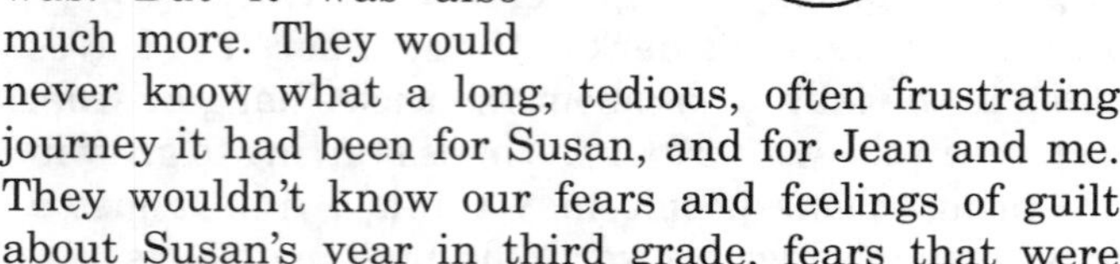

In September of that year, Susan wrote about her trip for our family newsletter:

"My trip back in time began at the Education Building, where I was fitted in a costume of 1849 and learned a little about the program I would take part in through the next week. I was assigned to the Killeen House, a square log cabin of an Irish immigrant. Besides cooking, eating, and other activities in 'my own' home, I spent time in several other homes and buildings, learning to make soap, candles, noodles, straw hats, crackers, and butter (which I already knew). I visited the blacksmith shop, spun flax, hooked a rug, learned about furniture making, and went to a quilting bee. Each day, I went to school with the other Visiting Cousins; at recess time, we played games of the 1840's. On Friday, I baked a crumb cake in the coals of the fireplace (we didn't have a stove for cooking), and on Saturday my cake and many others were served to the parents of the Visiting Cousins.

"I had a wonderful time and made many new friends."

Yes, it was definitely a plug for home-schooling. But, far more important, it was a plug for Susan, who had worked harder to reach that point than anyone outside our family would ever know.

It was also a strong lesson for us, although not a new one. It reinforced our conviction that children's learning should not be pushed. It can be encouraged, and should be, but always with care and patience and understanding.

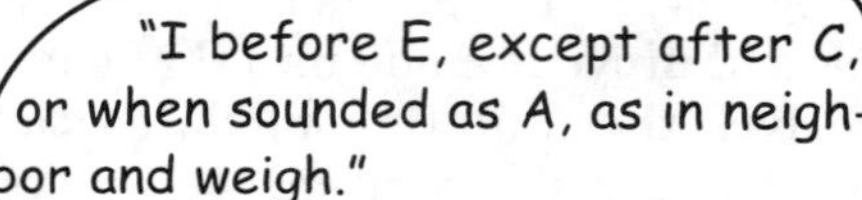

**SPELLING**

Rules such as these seem to be of some help to beginning spellers and readers, and sometimes we have tacked them up somewhere in the house. We never teach such rules, however, without a reminder that there are often exceptions to them. The first, for instance, has at least one weird exception. The second rule makes me cringe. The third rule is another form of grossness.

Try the word, we say, applying the rule; if it doesn't seem to work, then try the reverse of the rule. "When adding 'ing' to a verb that ends in 'e,' drop the 'e.' Oddly enough, that rule works for 'cringe,' but not for 'singe.'" "Oddly enough" is a phrase that helps the kids accept the idiosyncrasies of English. An attempt to learn spelling only by the rules will result in constant perplexity and frustration.

"That's the exception that proves the rule," some of my teachers used to say. I wondered where they had dug up such an illogical saying, and why they thought it meant anything. Years later, looking at reproductions of old English printing, I realized that some medieval monk must have forgotten his glasses when he was copying a manuscript. In some calligraphic lettering styles, the 'b' still resembles a 'v.' It's the exception that *probes* the rule, not *proves* it.

What makes a good speller? Why can some people spell correctly so easily, while others are forever turning to the dictionary (or should be)? I asked Jean. She is well-educated and has an above-average intelligence and a good vocabulary, but before she

mails a letter to a friend or relative, she has me look it over for spelling mistakes. There won't be many, but it's seldom that I don't find at least one. Her weekly shopping lists usually have at least one word misspelled, often one that is consistently misspelled week after week. She doesn't know why, nor do I. (I love her anyway.) (That's because my mistakes made him laugh.)

When I was in school, I usually got A+ for my spelling, and I almost always won school-wide spelling bees. Why?

I used to think that the ability to spell was nurtured most by reading, but Jean reads as much as I do.

I have a theory, which you're welcome to take or leave: I think that good spellers have, to some degree, photographic memories. Not to the extent that they could Amaze Their Friends With Astounding Feats of Memory Magic; not the kind, which a gifted few actually have, that enables them to read, from memory, a page they have briefly scanned. In most things, I have as much and as little difficulty in remembering as most people have — names, dates, numbers, lists, and so on. But when I'm in doubt about the spelling of a word, I close my eyes and try to visualize it; the word, usually printed, seems to float inside my eyelids. Have I called it up from a forgotten memory? If I can't visualize it that way, I write down several possible spellings; one will just "look right" to me, and it's almost always the correct one. Neither method is infallible, but usually one or the other works for me. Both methods work for Jean, too, but not very often.

I think it's related to sight-reading. The sooner a person learns to read whole syllables and words instead of "sounding out" the words letter by letter, the better his spelling will be. Maybe. That's my theory.

If he's right, it helps to explain my inability to spell. I think that having some photographic memory helps (Donn certainly had it). I also think learning to sight-read can make a big difference. I had a very hard time learning how to read in school. I hated the process, and the teacher made me feel even worse about it. Naturally, the worse I felt about myself and reading, the less I wanted to learn how to read. Not an auspicious way for a beginning speller to feel. If I were in school now, I would probably be labeled slightly dyslexic.

HELP!

What's more, at home, if I asked my mother for help spelling a word, almost invariably she would tell me to look it up in the dictionary. How do you look up a word you can't spell? Not only was this an interruption to my work, but I spelled so poorly that I could rarely find the word in the dictionary. I did learn a couple things from this experience. I learned not to ask my mother for help with spelling, and I learned that the dictionary was not my friend. Sometimes I'd get lucky, but more frequently, as time went by, I'd just make up the best spelling I could invent, and let the teacher correct it for me.

**But not if you are severely spelling disabled.**

My spelling has been a source of amusement for years. I was embarrassed when the kids asked me how to spell a word and I couldn't answer them. It was even worse when I'd ask Donn about the spelling of a word, and one of the kids would butt in and tell me. Once, in a desperate attempt to save face, I quoted Emerson, saying, "A foolish consistency is the hobgoblin of little minds."

We used to have the kids study lists of words, and then we tested them, just as the public schools do. The older the kids were, and the more reading they had done, the easier the spelling was. We discarded that approach, and then discarded all approaches. It made no difference in the kids' spelling abilities. When they wrote letters or essays, they sometimes asked us how to spell a word. If the word was short, we spelled it for them; if it was long, or didn't follow a neat rule, we wrote it down for them. Sometimes we'd suggest they look in the dictionary, but this was usually such an interruption of their train of thought that we didn't do it often. We didn't want to discourage their trying unfamiliar words by making the words a tedious chore. As they got older, they consulted the dictionary more often without our suggestion. If there was a catchy rule that might help them remember the word in the future, we'd give it to them. ("Write" ends with "e"; the paper we write on is stationery.)

If the word had interesting homonyms, derivatives, or second cousins, we often mentioned them, either at the time or later in general discussion. We helped the kids break words down, pull the wings off, tickle them, play with them. This builds vocabulary, spelling, perspective, and humor. Puns are excellent learning aids.

Reading, writing, and spelling (and even talking) are so closely related that trying to separate them is impractical and nearly impossible.

Another device we all enjoy is Tom Swifties. Remember them? They were a small fad way back when, parodies of the writing style of the Tom Swift series of boys' books popular during the 1920s and '30s — *Tom Swift and His Electric Submarine*, etc.

"I like camping in the rain," he said intently.

"I won't eat ham," he said pigheadedly.

"I won't be there," he said absently.

"I can't find the light," he said darkly.

"There's a hole in the tire," he said flatly.

It may take the kids a while to catch on to the kind of pun involved. The adverb must be related to the statement, it must be appropriate to the implied situation, and it must be a pun. The basic statement can be almost anything; the punch is the adverb.

I was writing about spelling and got sidetracked on to reading, writing, parts of speech, and vocabulary. Or is it a sidetrack?

"Does that make you feel like a dunce?" Jean asked pointedly.

"It's my typewriter's fault," I said mechanically.

"What are you driving at?" she asked automatically.

"It's gone with the wind," I answered rhetorically.

As you probably know, the worse the pun is (like my last one), the better it is; the proper response is a groan — unless you can top the pun with a better (worse) one. Once you get the hang of them, Tom Swifties are sort of like peanuts: you don't want to stop with just one. (I'll let you in on a secret. He got addicted. For about a week after writing about Tom Swifties he'd get up sometime in the night to make a note about a new one. Sometimes he'd make one up in his sleep and wake us both up because he was laughing.)

Back to spelling. Like all other learning, it can't be forced, but I have no doubt that a lot of reading will help it grow. Positive reinforcement definitely helps. When we're asked for the spelling of a word, we don't say, "Try to sound it out," unless the word really is phonetic and we think it can be sounded out easily. If we're not sure, either, we admit it freely, and get the dictionary.

When we spell a polysyllabic word for the kids, we do it by syllables — sometimes repeating each syllable as we go, then spelling it, then saying the whole word and spelling it all at once. Sometimes we ask to have the word spelled back to us — but only after the child has written it down. This helps to set the visual image. I think.

Trying to sound out a word that isn't fully phonetic results only in confusion, frustration, and random guessing, all of which can only reinforce incorrect spelling and a lack of confidence.

Can you sound out GHOTI?

It's "fish," of course. GH as in "tough," O as in "women," and TI as in "nation."

Probably there are some spelling books that will help, but if one doesn't read a lot and write a lot, memorization of rules won't do much good.

Here is a letter I received several years ago:

> "Der Don rede
>
> how ar you gud I hop. I am fin to. I hop I gettig ot frum thagt insttushn sun nd yu to. I m lrng rdng nd rtng pred gud. Thank yu fr techng me to red nd rte.
>
> Yur frend,
>
> —— ——."

The writer was twenty-two years old, serving three years in a federal prison for interstate car theft. When he joined my class for adult illiterates, six weeks before he wrote me that letter, he didn't know how to write his name.

I think he was lrng pred gud.

P.S.
More about Tom Swifties and a few other miscellaneous notes of equal importance.

In the spring of 1992, Teri Palazzolo, a customer and occasional correspondent in Sicily, sent me a photocopied entry form for an international "adverb contest" from *Practical English Teaching*, a British teacher's magazine. Teri said she was going to enter and hoped to win an unabridged Longman Dictionary of the English Language, which was offered for both the first and second prizes. The "adverb contest" consisted of what we have always called Tom Swifties, so I revised one of my earlier favorites — "Has he gone with the wind?' Scarlett asked rhetorically" — and mailed it off to England. The following November, long after I'd forgotten the contest, I received a letter of congratulations and a large, heavy package: second prize, an unabridged Longman dictionary, sent by airmail (which cost 18 pounds sterling, or about $40). Naturally, the dictionary had British spellings and usages — *kerb* instead of *curb, truck* meaning *barter*, and so on (not to mention *being on queer street*, which in the Mother Country means *being financially embarrassed*) — so it wasn't of much real worth to me. Since Teri had sent me the entry form that had given me this brief moment of fame, I wrote to her, offering to give the dictionary to her if she would pay the postage (only $6 by surface mail). She accepted, and wrote me that she had been a runner-up in the competition. How's that for irony and poetic (in)justice?

I don't subscribe to *Practical English Teaching*, and Teri hasn't sent me any more entry forms, but I'm preparing for the next contest by building my stock of Tom Swifties, usually in the middle of the night when Gus wakes me up to let him out. Rather than return to bed and be almost asleep when he woofs to come back in, I exercise my mind while I wait for him. As you probably know, some of one's greatest thoughts may come when one isn't quite awake. So far, Gus's untimely excursions have helped me produce the following:

"I can't think of the letter that comes after U," the boy said vehemently.

"Thanks for loaning me your pickup, Joe," he said truculently.

"I finally went to an exorcist for help," he said dispiritedly.

"That Kelly girl was delicious," the cannibal said gracefully.

"Oy, I don't think this food is kosher," the rabbi said judiciously.

"If I were a man, I wouldn't be a queen," Elizabeth said achingly.

"I'll show you the evidence again," the lawyer said reprovingly.

"I have to go home before sunrise," Dracula said cryptically.

"A good Tom Swiftie really wakes me up," Donn said dreamily.

**A child's world is not a simple place.**

Young children are naturally inquisitive about themselves and everything in their environment. Our job as parents is to provide a safe home and an environment conducive to learning. Even before children are able to explore the world outside our homes, we can begin to share this world with them through books. Reading is one of the most important and pleasurable activities you can share with your child. It is also one of the most important skills he will learn. I don't think you can do too much reading with your child. Well, maybe you could pick a book he doesn't care for, or read longer than he wants to sit, but I think you understand my point.

I hope you will keep in mind that early learning activities should be enjoyable for your child. Don't be in a rush to teach him anything. With time and patience on your part, a child who is slow in starting any of these activities will undoubtedly catch up. A child's brain grows in stages, and each child develops at a different pace. If your child isn't inclined to use these books when you first get them, be assured that he is busy developing other skills. Rushing your child into early reading or math before the necessary cognitive development has occurred will only create frustration, resistance, and other problems. The public school system is trying to make up for its failures by starting children in school at younger and younger ages. This leaves moms free to do other things and can solve a baby-sitting problem, but I don't think sending kids to school sooner — or trying too hard to teach them at home — will cure the academic failures.

From an article published in *Newsweek*, September 13, 1999:

> George W. Bush stated in his first major speech on education [that] he'd like to see children learning to read at three and cited National Institutes of Health research recommending phonics. The NIH commented after the speech that phonics is only one component of reading instruction.

I think *Newsweek* and the NIH both missed the obvious absurdity — that most children's brains are not ready to read at that age. I don't want this man near education reform. He scares me.

**ANIMAL PICTURE WORD BOOK.** Young children are fascinated by animals. This is another opportunity to casually demonstrate that there is a different word for each animal. A book a young child can "read" to you. Nice color pictures. Ages 2 to 6. Code EDC, $9.95.

**VERY FIRST WORDS.** A colorful, lively picture/word book with 100 familiar objects for kids to spot and name. Organized by category in two-page spreads: things to wear, animals, things that go, etc. Code EDC, $6.95.

**THE FIRST HUNDRED WORDS.** This picture book gives very young children (about 2 and up) pictures of objects, actions, and situations along with the words naming or describing them. Humorous illustrations and bold print soon give kids mastery of these common words (e.g., ball, boot, cat, etc.). Use with *Letters* (listed below as part of the First Learning series) to create an effective blend of phonics and sight-reading. Both this book and the accompanying sticker book (below) have double-page spreads where you'll have fun finding Stephen Cartwright's little yellow duck. Code EDC, $8.95.

**FIRST HUNDRED WORDS STICKER BOOK.** More fun! A companion to the book above. Code EDC, $7.95.

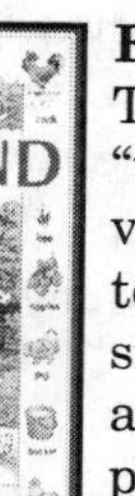

**FIRST THOUSAND WORDS.** Three levels of fun with words: "talk-about" words and pictures for very young children just beginning to speak and recognize pictures; simple words for beginning readers; and a source of ideas and spelling practice for those starting to write. Will work as a first dictionary too. Ages 2 to ? 6? 8? Hardcover. Code EDC, $12.95.

**THE FIRST THOUSAND WORDS STICKER BOOK.** A companion to the book above. Code EDC, $9.95.

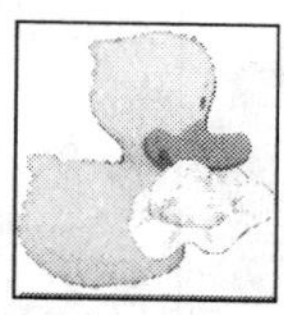

**THE ALPHABET BOOK.** Each page focuses on a letter. The complete alphabet is shown along the bottom of the page, with the featured letter in a contrasting color. All the pictures relate to characters in the Apple Tree Farmyard series of books. Kids will have fun finding the duck on every page. Ages 2 to 6. Hardcover. Code EDC, $10.95.

**1001 THINGS TO SPOT ON THE FARM.** An Usborne book with amusing fun-filled pictures. Each two-page spread has a list of things to be found (e.g., seven bales of hay, five mice, six seagulls, etc.). Lots to talk about while learning about numbers. Will you be able to find the duck? Ages 3 to 5. Code EDC, $6.95.

**GOODNIGHT MOON,** by Margaret Wise Brown; pictures by Clement Hurd. We began to get tired of some books after the first thousand requests, but not this one, which is still absolutely, positively one of our favorites. Warm, friendly pictures gradually darken as the little rabbit child prepares to go to sleep, saying goodnight to all the familiar things in his room. *He* doesn't notice the tiny mouse, but you and your child will. Whoops — where did he go? There he is, on the windowsill! Ages 2 and up. If your child is 5, it may not be too late. If he's older, have him read it with someone younger; or get it for yourself and save it for your grandchildren. The book is available in a thin paperback, which we have tried, but it didn't last. We prefer and recommend the hardcover edition, because it will surely get a lot of use. Code BT, $14.95 hardcover, $5.95 paperback.

**IF YOU WERE MY BUNNY,** by Kate McMullan. A classic. The combination of well-written text and illustrations will make you cuddle even closer as you read this bedtime story. This is about animal mamas tucking in their little ones for the night. You can sing the included lullabies to the tune of familiar melodies. This should go on the shelf next to *Goodnight Moon.* (If you don't have that, shame on you!) Ages 2 to 4 to 20 to 120. Code BT, $6.95.

**FUN IS A FEELING,** by Chara M. Curtis. What is "fun"? You can't see it or touch it. You can't smell it or taste it. You can't pick it off the shelf or buy it. It's not something you do, like a game, but just the same, it is something we all have inside us. Curtis's book will make it clear that it is something we feel inside us — and she includes clues for finding it. This book is bound to become a classic. It also belongs on the shelf next to *Goodnight Moon*. The good feelings you get when you read this book just bubble up inside you, and you want to share them with everyone. All our grandchildren will have a copy. Hardcover. Code IA, $15.95.

**MOVE OVER, MOTHER GOOSE!**, by Ruth I. Dowell, M.S. This won't replace the traditional Mother Goose stories, but it will find its own place in your daily play. Full of finger plays, action verses with body movements, and funny rhymes. There's lots of room for creative play; development of coordination and body movement; and an appreciation of language, rhythm, and rhyme. Some activities require moving around the room; others can be done while seated on the floor, in the car, or wherever you are. Also an amusing introduction to poetry. Ages 3 to 6. Code GH, $12.95.

**Early Childhood Music and Learning Activities.** Miss Jackie Music Co. publishes a catalog with a great variety of creative music, games, and other fun learning activities in book or cassette/CD format, especially designed for babies, toddlers, and children under 6. 10001 El Monte, Overland Park, KS 66207-3631.

Remember to check for resources in the "Music and Dance" and "Arts and Activities" chapters.

**Talkabout Books** explain basic concepts in pictures and simple text. Interesting illustrations. Ages 3 to 6. Code EDC, $4.95 each. Specify **THEN AND NOW** or **DAY AND NIGHT**.

**ENTERTAINING AND EDUCATING BABIES AND TODDLERS.** Hundreds of activity and toy ideas, all easy and inexpensive. Attractive and detailed drawings on every page. Sections cover things to look at and listen to, things to feel and hold, learning to talk, books and stories, energetic and messy play, imitating and pretending, things to fit together and take apart, walks and trips, and more. Code EDC, $7.95.

**ENTERTAINING AND EDUCATING YOUR PRESCHOOL CHILD.** Many constructive, easy-to-do activities you and your child will enjoy. Projects and games lead to pre-reading and beginning math skills. Code EDC, $12.95.

For hours of fun look for *Play With Boxes* in "Arts and Activities."

You will find the following Bible tales in "Philosophy and Religion," for ages 2 to 7: **Daniel and the Lions, David and Goliath, Jonah and the Whale, Joseph and His Amazing Coat, Moses in the Bulrushes, Noah's Ark,** and **The Christmas Story**.

**Sturdy Board Books.** Designed to last, this series features realistic machines. The pictures show what kind of work each does. Books are 7x8". Code EDC, $5.95 each. Specify **TRUCKS, RACING CARS, PLANES, DIGGERS,** or **TRACTORS.**

**NURSERY RHYME STICKER BOOK.** A collection of 20 best-loved nursery rhymes, each with a rebus puzzle that will allow your child to complete the verse with the appropriate sticker. You'll read this many times; then one day it will be read to you! 120 colorful stickers. Ages 3 and up. Code EDC, $6.95. Also see the *Nursery Rhyme Songbook* in "Music."

**Find It Kits**. Great fun! Each kit has a sturdy board book full of rhymes and includes a soft, cuddly, and cute pocket-sized stuffed finger puppet. The books have many amusing situations to talk about and objects to name. The challenge of looking for the duck, puppy, piglet, kitten, or teddy on each page will engage your son or daughter. The puppets make irresistible toys, and they will fit perfectly into your kids' pockets. If you get one of these books I think you'll find yourself

searching for these puppets in your kids' pockets before washing their clothes. Ages 12 months and up. Specify **DUCK, PUPPY, PIGLET, KITTEN,** or **TEDDY**. Code EDC, $10.95 each. If you'd prefer the individual board books without the puppets, the price is $3.95 each.

If you fall in love with the duck — or your child does — there is a set of three more board books for you. Includes: **DUCK ON HOLIDAY, DUCK AND HIS FRIENDS**, and **DUCK IN TROUBLE**. Ages 9 months and up. Code EDC, $14.95.

**LAND OF THE LOST TEDDIES.** Comes with a soft, plush teddy bear finger puppet (see above). Nice story line. Full of ways to encourage interaction and problem solving between parent and child. Ages 3 to 7. Code EDC, $12.95.

**Slot Activity Books**. Each book comes with a cute cardboard mouse or squirrel (with long tails), which your child can guide through the slots to follow the adventure story. A very good reading-readiness process. I discussed these titles with Gus and my cats, Big Guy and Ruff, and they didn't think I should include either story. We deal with country mice on an irregular basis. Ruff likes to put them in the bathtub and play with them. Gus thinks that's cruel and unusual punishment and will climb in the tub, take them outside, and let them go. He wags if they run away, and they become lunch if they die from shock. Squirrels, as we have discovered, don't stay in the tub to be played with. Watching a squirrel run around and leap through the trees outside is impressive. Seeing one up close in the kitchen doing the same thing with two cats and a dog in hot pursuit causes hysterical laughter on my part, but isn't funny (and no, I didn't have a video camera, and yes, I should have had one. Ruff did get a souvenir for me.). I guarantee that these books are more fun than the real animals in the house. Great fun for ages 3 and up. Code EDC, $10.95 each. Specify **A SQUIRREL'S TALE** or **THERE'S A MOUSE IN THE HOUSE.**

Ruff's squirrel trophy. The rest of the squirrel got away.

**THE GINGERBREAD BABY**, told and illustrated by Jan Brett. This hardcover edition will be a family favorite. I know you can get cheaper editions of this story or borrow the book from the library, but Brett's playful, colorful, original pictures make this book worth having in hardcover. It's one you'll be pleased to pass on to your grandchildren. Code PTN, $16.99.

**Then and Now Flip Flap Books.** Very cleverly done books that illustrate the history of homes, houses, travel, and transport, using a fold-out flap on each double-page spread. You'll explore a Roman apartment, an Egyptian house, and a medieval castle, and discover why Vikings kept animals in their homes. You'll look at the first cars, trains, boats, and planes. Ages 4 and up. Code EDC, $7.95 each. Specify **HOMES AND HOUSES** or **TRAVEL AND TRANSPORT**.

*I wish we'd had this one when the kids were little.* If we had had it, we would have had to replace it many times over. I love this book for nostalgic reasons. If you carry your child in a backpack, you will love this as much as your child will. **WALKING WITH MAMA**, by Barbara White Stynes. A warm, intimate tale of a mother and toddler on a nature walk — told from the child's point of view, first walking and trying to keep up with Mama, then from high up in the backpack. Ages 2 to ? Children who have been carried this way will enjoy reading this long after their backpack days are over. Code DN, $6.95.

**Board Books to Feel.** Simple text and bright illustrations carry the story. Ears, eyes, and paws have different textures for toddlers to explore. Code EDC, $7.95 each. Specify **THAT'S NOT MY TEDDY** or **THAT'S NOT MY PUPPY**.

I almost listed this book in "Arts and Activities," but I wanted to make sure you wouldn't miss it. **PRETEND SOUP: A Cookbook for Preschoolers**, is joyfully illustrated and written by Mollie Katzen and Ann Henderson. To use this book successfully, you must be willing to allow a role reversal between you and your youngster. Usually you cook and your child "helps." If you use this book it will be the other way around. If you have a large ego, save your money. You are necessary, but you are *not* the prime mover. Recipes are wholesome (though not fanatically so) and varied. (You will find white sugar as an ingredient in some recipes. Feel free to substitute honey — see note on page 167.) Directions for the adult helper are written, and directions for your child are clearly drawn. Great fun. Hardcover. Code TSP, $16.95.

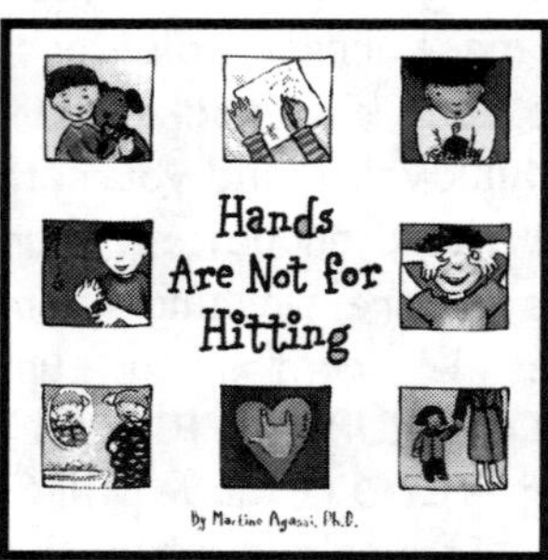


**HANDS ARE NOT FOR HITTING**, by Martine Agassi, Ph.D. A carefully crafted book with a positive message about all the wonderful things hands can do. The underlying message is that violence is never acceptable. It's designed to be read aloud, and the illustrations provide ideas for discussion. Included is a special section suggesting discussion topics and activities for parents or adults working with children. Ages 2 to 6. Code FS, $10.95.

**PAPERPLAY: You and Your Child.** Just right for young children. Introduction to concepts of size, shape, space, volume, and measurement. Only household items — and you — are required for activities. Ages 3 to 7. Code EDC, $6.95.

**EVERYBODY HAS FEELINGS — TODOS TENEMOS SENTIMIENTOS: The Moods of Children**, photographed by Charles E. Avery. This is a completely bilingual (English/Spanish) book about the moods we all experience. Simple text and many very expressive black-and-white multiracial photos to look at and discuss. Ages 3 to 7. Code GH, $8.95.

A child's first experience with a new situation sets the tone for all similar situations in the future. A child who understands, before going to the doctor, that a shot will hurt — but not for long — will generally accept this if you explain why he needs the shot. A child who understands what a dentist is going to do probably won't develop a fear of dentists. Before taking our children to a doctor or dentist, we spent some playtime with them pretending to go for these visits. First, we would pretend to be the doctor or dentist, asking the kids to open their mouths, breathe deeply, and do other things that would likely be asked of them. We would pretend to give shots. It was interesting that when we pretended to give shots, the kids objected when these pretend shots didn't hurt. They wanted something more realistic, so they suggested we give them a little pinch. Although Donn and I didn't think much of this idea, the kids were satisfied when we went along with the request. Then we would let the kids pretend to be the doctor or dentist. They didn't have a problem giving *us* a little pinch!

The following books are designed to help you discuss first-time experiences. The lively illustrations provide lots of things to look at, think about, and discuss. Simple vocabulary will allow beginning readers to read these books on their own. Ages 3 to 7. Code EDC, $4.95 each. Specify **THE NEW BABY, GOING TO THE DENTIST, GOING ON A PLANE, MOVING HOUSE, GOING TO THE HOSPITAL**, or **GOING TO THE DOCTOR**.

**GOING TO THE DOCTOR KIT**. Includes the book described above, toy stethoscope, thermometer, reflex hammer, mouth mirror, syringe, and more. Code EDC, $13.95.

**I CAN DRAW ANIMALS**. If your child can draw simple circles and squares, this book will show him how, with a few additional simple lines, he can draw many common animals. Clear, step-by-step instructions. Other books in this series provide good projects suitable for ages 3 to 6. There is nothing as sad as a child who tackles a project too difficult and feels discouraged when he's done. These books won't leave anyone unhappy. Each idea uses quick and easy techniques, ideal for little fingers. Code EDC, $4.95 each. Specify **I CAN DRAW ANIMALS, FUN WITH NUMBERS, I CAN ADD UP, I CAN COUNT, I CAN FINGER PAINT, I CAN CRAYON**, or **I CAN CUT AND STICK**.

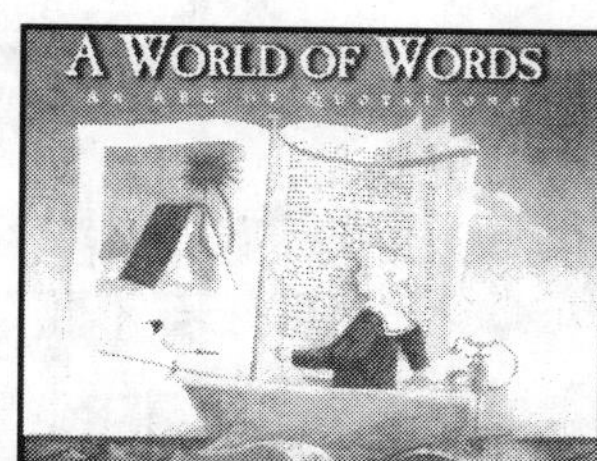


**A WORLD OF WORDS: An ABC of Quotations**, written by Tobi Tobias, illustrated by Peter Malone. If you just want to teach letters and phonics without frills there are better books available. This book is food for the imagination, from the introductory page — "The word is the making of the world" (Wallace Stevens) — to Animal — "In the very earliest time when both people and animals lived on earth, a person could become an animal if he wanted to and an animal could become a human being. ... All spoke the same language" (Inuit Eskimo) — to Zoo — "Human wandering through the zoo, what do your cousins think of you?" (Don Marquis). A book about creative thought and wordplay, with illustrations that are equally playful and imaginative. You can, of course, use it to teach the alphabet, but probably only as an afterthought. Hardcover. Code WM, $16.

## FIRST LEARNING SERIES

**First Concepts**. Developing thinking and observation skills comes before the ability to read, write, and do simple math. These books are fun to work with, and you and your child will find lots to talk about as you work through these together. Ages 3 and up. Code EDC, $4.95 each. Specify **COLOR, SHAPES, SIZES**, or **OPPOSITES**.

**First Words**. These three books are specially designed to help very young children develop basic skills and knowledge in learning to read, make letters, and begin putting letters together to form words, with "pre-reading" and "pre-writing" exercises in letter recognition, hand control, coordination, concentration, and awareness. Code EDC, $4.95 each. Specify **READY FOR READING, READY FOR WRITING**, or **LETTERS. REUSABLE LETTERS STICKER BOOK** — use again and again, $6.95.

**First Numbers**. With a handful of crayons or a pencil and an adult's playful guidance, these books introduce young children to various mathematical concepts. Code EDC, $4.95 each. Specify **NUMBERS, STARTING TO COUNT, COUNTING UP TO 10, STARTING TO ADD, STARTING TO SUBTRACT, STARTING TO MEASURE, ODD ONE OUT**, or **TIME. REUSABLE COUNTING STICKER BOOK**, $6.95. **TIME KIT**. Comes with clock with movable hands. $10.95.

**THE FIRST BOOK OF NUMBERS** was out of print, and I'm glad to see it back. This is a brilliantly illustrated introduction for kids 4 to 8 years old. How numbers were developed, how they relate to time and measurement, and many other fascinating facts. Puzzles and tricks extend the grasp of basic number concepts, including sets, sequence, shapes, size, and a world without numbers. This book brings together the concepts learned in the First Learning Series. Code EDC, $9.95. New large format — 19"x15", $14.95.

**Magnetic Letters and Words.** Kids enjoy having magnetic letters to play with and to make simple words with, but most letter sets have their limitations. How many sets of magnetic letters do you have to buy before it's possible to write a simple sentence? How much time does it take to use all those individual letters to make a word or a sentence? These magnetic words, numbers, and punctuation pieces are washable and color coded: green for nouns, yellow for pronouns, red for verbs, etc. There are periods, question marks, commas, exclamation marks, and even pieces with handy suffixes. You have a lot to choose from; specify item and price: **OBJECTS** (just the picture — apple, ball, etc.), $9.95; **LETTERS WITH OBJECTS**, $9.95; **BEGINNER'S WORD SET** (200+ pieces), $19.95; **INDIVIDUAL UPPERCASE LETTERS**, $12.95; **INDIVIDUAL LOWERCASE LETTERS**, $12.95; or Words Within a Theme (specify **OUR PLANET**, **CITY AND COUNTRY**, **PLANES AND TRAINS**, or **SPORTS AND GAMES**), $7.95 each. All code BC.

**Math Magnets**. (Illustration on opposite page.) For your refrigerator or magnetic board. Please specify **DOUBLE NUMBERS,** $9.95; **NUMBERS WITH OBJECTS,** $6.95; **MATH OPERATION SIGNS,** $6.95; **PATTERN BLOCKS,** $6.95; **TANGRAMS,** $9.95; or **PENTOMINOES,** $9.95. All code BC.

**Magnetic Boards**. Shaped like brightly colored trays, these are made to be used with the magnetic letters, words, and numbers above. You may find them handy for other types of play, and you can use them to serve lunch, too! You can use your magnetic letters and words on the refrigerator, of course, but it's hard to move that into another room or take on a trip. Code BC, $9.95.

**Learning Boards**. These 9x12" boards can be used with dry-erase markers for easy write-on, wipe-off use. These boards are also magnetic and can be used with the letters and words above. Code BC, $6.95. These can sometimes be found at Wal-Mart, office supply stores, and even some supermarkets.

## BEGINNING READING

Please take a minute to read the review of *Tending the Heart of Virtue* in "Literature." It will assist you in finding stories and books of enduring value.

**HELP YOUR CHILD LEARN TO READ,** by Betty Root. This is the only book of this kind I'd recommend. Most "help your child to read" books advocate impossible phonics, boring repetition of uninteresting words, and daily "practice." If you have any of these, throw them out the window or line the canary cage with them. This book has lots of sensible, practical suggestions and ideas that really will help you help your child learn to read, without taking any of the fun out of it for either of you. When to talk, when not to, what kinds of reading material to have on hand, and how to use it. Interesting illustrations and a wealth of good ideas. Code EDC, a bargain at $7.95.

**TEACH A CHILD TO READ WITH CHILDREN'S BOOKS: Combining Story Reading, Phonics, and Writing to Promote Reading Success,** by Mark B. Thogmartin. Similar to Betty Root's book (listed above) but with more detailed information about how and why this method works. Thogmartin advocates a combination of whole language and phonics skills, and includes beginning writing skills in a relaxed home atmosphere. A very helpful, readable book with suggestions for preparing your child to read long before you begin any formal lessons. Useful ideas for building a reading and writing program, and an extensive list of books to support each stage of learning. (If you can't find the books he suggests, let us know and we'll try to help you.) Designed for parental use, but I wish professional teachers would use it too. Code GB, $24.95.

**LEARN TO READ BOOK**, by Dr. Ernest Christman. A phonics-based approach that is very successful. I still think you need a combination of approaches, but adding this book to your learning-to-read resources will help you introduce various phonic skills. Used by many literacy groups for all ages. Code BBRD, $15.95.

**BOOKSTUFF: A Series**, by Patricia Reinold and Nancy Cross Aldrich. An individualized, personal approach to beginning reading. Too bad these books didn't come along until our kids were too old for them. These books begin by introducing basic pre-reading skills and then move on to simple sentences composed of words, pictures, and blanks — the blanks to be filled in with the child's own name, or the names of siblings, friends, parents, toys, or pets, thus making the books really personal. The child is instructed by pictures to copy words or pictures or answer (orally) a question. The books progress in difficulty and concepts. For information write: Bookstuff, 21534 St. James Place, West Linn, OR 97068.

**FAT CAT ON A MAT**. Sound familiar? The title mimics one of Dr. Seuss's titles, and the vocabulary is similar, but a variety of reading material is essential to developing and maintaining interest. This is an easy-to-read book co-authored by a language specialist to include helpful phonic development. A guide for parents is included. There are five books in the series, all phonics based. Funny stories, and some pages have a fold-out flap. Code EDC, $7.95 each, any three for $20, complete set for $35.

**TED IN A RED BED**
**BIG PIG ON A DIG**
**TOAD MAKES A ROAD**
**SAM SHEEP CAN'T SLEEP**
**FAT CAT ON A MAT**

**WORD AND PICTURE REBUS FUN.** Small 4x5" book with fun-filled picture-and-word story puzzles for parents to do with young children — and for beginning readers to do on their own. Code DV, $1.

**Little ABC Books to Color**. Child-sized books ($4\frac{1}{4}$x$5\frac{3}{4}$", 30 pages) with black-and-white line illustrations to color, plus a short caption on each page. Code DV, $1 each. Specify **DINOSAUR**, **FLOWER**, **ANIMAL**, or **ABC**.

**BEGINNING READERS**

These are some of the books our kids read over and over and requested from us over and over, as they were learning to read without lessons in how to read.

**HOP ON POP**, by Dr. Seuss. Sort of a combination of sight-reading and incidental phonics. Possibly the very first book the kids could read all the way through by themselves.

**ARE YOU MY MOTHER?** by P.D. Eastman. A long-time favorite. A funny but meaningful introduction to relationships and perceptions.

**GREEN EGGS AND HAM**, by Dr. Seuss. Tickles children's funny bones.

**FOX IN SOCKS**, by Dr. Seuss. Outrageous, fantastic tongue twisters. The kids may not read much of it for a while, but they'll try, and they'll be in hysterics as you try to read it to them without tongling your tangue.

Code RH, $7.99 each. You can borrow these from the library, but you'll be glad to have them around to read anytime.

The **Apple Tree Farmyard Tales** are a series of books for young readers, designed with the help of a language expert. These short stories are fun to read and humorous, and Stephen Cartwright's pictures give nice clues about the written content. You'll enjoy watching your child discover the little yellow duck on each page. Lots to discuss. A note in the front of each book says the book is written on two levels: "To help insure success, first read all the story aloud and talk about the pictures. Then encourage your child to read the short, simpler text at the top of each page. You read the longer text at the bottom of the page. This 'turn-about' reading builds up confidence and children do love joining in." Pretty soon they can read it all! Sturdy paperback. Ages 2 or 3 and up. Code EDC, $4.95 each.

**BARN ON FIRE**
**CAMPING OUT**
**KITTEN'S DAY OUT**
**THE NEW PONY**
**PIG GETS LOST**
**PIG GETS STUCK**
**SCARECROW'S SECRET**
**THE SILLY SHEEPDOG**
**THE SNOW STORM**
**TRACTOR IN TROUBLE**
**THE RUNAWAY TRACTOR**

**APPLE TREE FARMYARD TALES STORYBOOK**. A collection of eight popular single titles (some of which are listed above) in a sturdy hardcover book with Stephen Cartwright illustrations. A great read-aloud book for when the kids are very young; it will also serve as a beginning reader. Ages 3 and up. Code EDC, $19.95.

If you and your child enjoy the Apple Tree Farmyard Tales, here are some story-sticker books to go with them. Based on stories and characters from the series. 50 stickers in each book and a rebus puzzle activity in which sticker pictures replace words on each page. Ages 3 and up. Code EDC, $6.95 each. Specify "sticker book." **THE NEW PONY, PIG GETS STUCK, TRACTOR IN TROUBLE, THE SILLY SHEEPDOG.**

More sticker books featuring characters from Apple Tree Farm. These books introduce early-learning concepts. Activities include drawing lines and patterns, completing pictures, tracing, and copying letter shapes. Each book includes two wipe-clean activity pages for repeated use and two pages of stickers. Ages 3 and up. Code EDC, $6.95 each. **TIME, WORDS TO WRITE, STARTING TO READ, FIRST WORDS, STARTING TO WRITE, STARTING TO COUNT, LETTERS TO COPY, COUNTING TO TEN.**

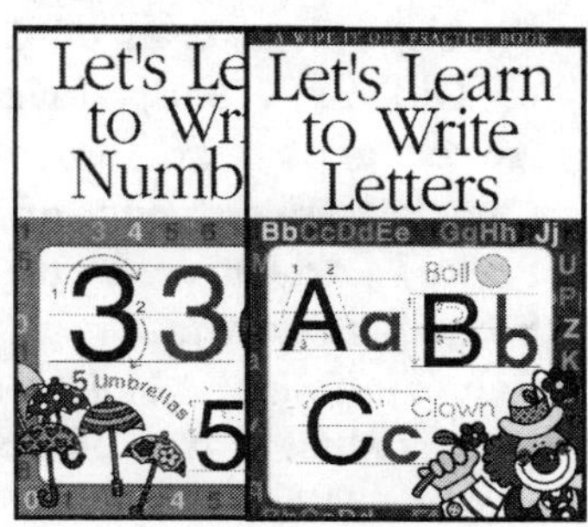


**Wipe-It-Off Practice Books**. One for learning to print, one for script, and one for numbers. Books have good examples and simple directions. Code TRL, $12.95 each. Specify **LETTERS, SCRIPT**, or **NUMBERS**.

**Reading on Their Own**. One of the most exciting steps you'll watch your child take is when he first begins to read on his own. Here is a series of books, with simple text and lively, full-color (and sometimes humorous) illustrations, that kids will enjoy reading. Ages 5 to 9. Code EDC, $4.95 each.

**BURGLAR'S BREAKFAST**
**THE CLUMSY CROCODILE**
**THE DINOSAURS NEXT DOOR**
**THE FAIRGROUND GHOST**
**THE INCREDIBLE PRESENT**
**THE MONSTER GANG**
**THE OGS LEARN TO FLOAT**
**THE OGS LEARN TO FLY**
**THE OGS DISCOVER FIRE**
**THE OGS INVENT THE WHEEL**

**GREEK MYTHS FOR YOUNG CHILDREN**. No, it's not too early to read these stories of brave heroes, monsters, gods and goddesses, battles, and great adventures. This collection begins with a brief introduction and contains 18 well-known myths and, fortunately for some of us, a pronunciation guide in the back. Brilliantly illustrated (not scary) and geared to ages 4 and up, this is a book to be enjoyed when first read aloud, and was written to be used as a reader for older children. Why not spark an interest in history through literature now? Hardcover, 128 pages. Code EDC, $18.95.

We never put our kids down for naps. They slept when they were tired and regulated themselves very well, just naturally adjusting to our living patterns, most of the time.

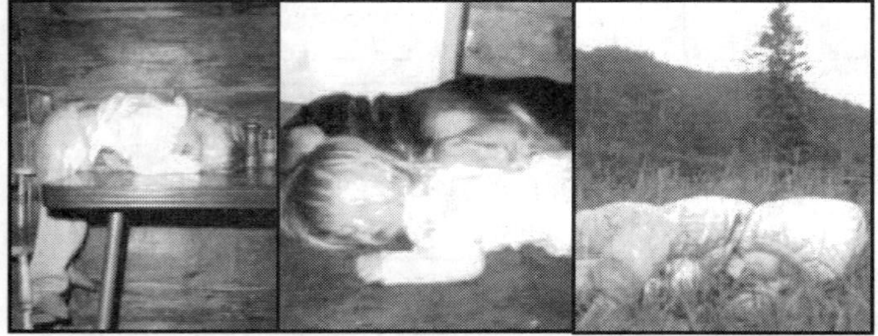

If you do put your kids down for naps, and they sometimes object or fuss, you could put on a quiet story for them to listen to until they fall asleep.

**Stories on tape or CD** for young children, by talented, vivacious, and captivating storyteller **Jim Weiss**. More than just entertainment, these tapes impart some of our cultural heritage. The use of tapes allows young children to develop listening skills, concentration, and, best of all, their imagination. You may get tired of hearing these stories, but your children won't. (Just remember whom you bought the stories for!) More Jim Weiss stories in "Literature." Code GH, $9.95 tape, $14.95 CD. Specify tape or CD.

**ANIMAL TALES** — "Three Billy Goats Gruff," "The Tortoise and the Hare," and many more.

**FAIRYTALE FAVORITES IN STORY AND SONG** — "Rapunzel," "Puss in Boots," and more.

**GOOD NIGHT** — Six quiet tales of safety and love.

**Thrift Classics to Read Aloud**. Code DV, $1 each.

**ADVENTURES OF PINOCCHIO**, by Carlo Collodi, abridged

**BEAR THAT WASN'T**, by Frank Tashlin

**BEAUTY AND THE BEAST**, by Mme. De Beaumont

**A CHILD'S GARDEN OF VERSES**, by R.L. Stevenson

**CINDERELLA AND OTHERS**, by Andrew Lang

**FAVORITE UNCLE WIGGILY ANIMAL BEDTIME STORIES**, by Howard Garis

**THE HAPPY PRINCE AND OTHER FAIRY TALES**, by Oscar Wilde

**LITTLE MERMAID AND OTHER FAIRY TALES**, by Hans Christian Andersen

**A LITTLE PRINCESS**, by Frances Hodgson Burnett

**PETER RABBIT AND 11 OTHER FAVORITE TALES**, by Beatrix Potter

**PICTURE FOLK TALES**, by Valery Carrick

**SLEEPING BEAUTY AND OTHERS**, by Grimm and Grimm

**SNOW WHITE AND OTHERS**, by Grimm and Grimm

**THREE BILLY GOATS GRUFF AND OTHERS TO READ ALOUD**, by Carolyn Sherwin Bailey

**THE UGLY DUCKLING AND OTHERS**, by Hans Christian Andersen

**UNCLE WIGGILY BEDTIME STORIES**, by Howard Garis

**THE WIND IN THE WILLOWS**, by Kenneth Grahame, abridged

**THORNTON BURGESS CLASSICS FOR YOUNG CHILDREN.** Stories to delight your youngsters. Line drawings for your child to color. You'll enjoy reading these many times. Code DV, $1 each. **Adventures of Bobby Raccoon, Adventures of Buster Bear, Adventures of Chatterer the Squirrel, Adventures of Danny Meadow Mouse, Adventures of Grandfather Frog, Adventures of Jerry Muskrat, Adventures of Jimmy Skunk, Adventures of Johnny Chuck, Adventures of Old Man Coyote, Adventures of Old Mr. Toad, Adventures of Peter Cottontail, Adventures of Poor Mrs. Quack, Adventures of Prickly Porky, Adventures of Reddy Fox, Blacky the Crow, Buster Bear's Twins, Lightfoot the Deer, Mrs. Peter Rabbit, Old Mother West Wind.**

**Boxed sets** at thrift prices. Code DV. Specify "boxed set."

**SIX FAVORITE THORNTON BURGESS ANIMAL STORIES**: "The Adventures of Buster Bear," "Chatterer the Red Squirrel," "Danny Meadow Mouse," "Grandfather Frog," "Peter Cottontail," and "Reddy Fox." $6.

**OLD MOTHER WEST WIND** and six others: "Bobby Raccoon," "Jerry Muskrat," "Jimmy Skunk," "Johnny Chuck," "Prickly Porky," and "Poor Mrs. Quack." $7.

**FIVE CHILDREN'S THRIFT CLASSICS**: "The Ugly Duckling" and more Andersen, "Peter Cottontail," "Sleeping Beauty," "The Happy Prince," poems, and more. $5.

**Thrift classics on cassette**, with a book that contains all the material on the cassette and more. Use these for rainy days while coloring, and at bedtime once you've started to fall asleep reading. Code DV, $5.95 each. All cassettes are 45 to 90 minutes. Specify "book and cassette," because otherwise we might get these confused with the boxed sets above.

**THE LITTLE MERMAID** and others, by Hans Christian Andersen

**THE UGLY DUCKLING** and three others, by Hans Christian Andersen

**PETER COTTONTAIL** and more, by Thornton Burgess

**UNCLE WIGGILY BEDTIME STORIES**, by Howard Garis

**A CHILD'S GARDEN OF VERSES**, by R.L. Stevenson

**FAVORITE POEMS OF CHILDHOOD**

**Games for Learning.** Lots of excellent activities for developing concentration and manual dexterity, using only normal household items. Introduce concepts of size, shape, space, volume, and measurement. Good fun. Ages 3 to 6, with parental guidance for 3- and 4-year-olds. Code EDC, $6.95 each. **NUMBER GAMES** or **READING GAMES**.

## BEGINNING MATHEMATICS AND ARITHMETIC

**HELP YOUR CHILD LEARN NUMBER SKILLS.** Lots of very good ideas for using materials in your home to help your child learn basic math. Well illustrated. Code EDC, $7.95. Also see *Numbers* under the First Learning Series.

**ONE, TWO, BUCKLE MY SHOE: Math Activities for Young Children**, by Sam Ed Brown. The introduction explains how even very young children begin mathematical explorations on their own as they investigate the world around them. This book has many good ideas for helping your child develop his sense of order and investigate basic concepts. Full of hands-on activities that parents and children can do together. Activities include counting, one-to-one correspondence, matching, measurement, shapes, sequencing, sets, ordinal numbers, very simple addition and subtraction, and more. Ages 3 to 6. Code GHS, $8.95.

**MATHARTS: Exploring Math Through Art for 3 to 6 Year Olds**, by MaryAnn Kohl and Cindy Gainer. *MathArts* has 200 interesting and enjoyable activities that help young children increase their awareness of math concepts they have already begun to develop. Young children naturally notice sizes, shapes, and patterns, and they enjoy sorting and counting. *MathArts* offers a wealth of simple creative activities (most of which require only common household materials) that will heighten your child's conceptual awareness. Teaching is neither necessary nor desirable at this age. Each activity begins with an explanation of the materials needed, the time involved, the optimal age, and whether or not assistance will be necessary. Hours of fun are contained within these 248 pages. Includes a handy index. Code GHS, $19.95.

**COUNT ON MATH: Activities for Small Hands and Lively Minds**, by Pam Schiller and Lynne Peterson. This book is full of beginning learning activities particularly suited to ages 3 to 7. This book is similar to the book above but has more advanced concepts because of its extended age range. There doesn't seem to be a duplication of activities. I asked myself if I would buy just one of these books or both. It must have been a reasonable question, because it took me a minute to sort out my thoughts — and I have both books in front of me, which you won't when you read this. I decided that if my kids were closer to 3 than 6 or 7, I would get *MathArts* and see how much we enjoyed it, then probably move on to *Count on Math*. If my kids were closer to 5 I'd definitely skip the first book. One reason for using both books is that through repetitive acts young children test the properties of the world. Using both books would offer a greater variety of approaches to the basic concepts. Code GHS, $19.95.

**BEGINNING SCIENCE**

**SANDBOX SCIENTIST: Real Science Activities for Little Kids**, by Michael Ross. A great guide for early science experiences. Numerous entertaining activities. Just do it — don't "teach" it. Ages 2 to 8. Code CRP, $12.95.

**SENSE-ABILITIES**. Michelle O'Brian Palmer understands that the first requirement of children who wish to explore and comprehend their bodies is to know their own five senses. Palmer has put together dozens of original science activities to explore taste, touch, sight, smell, and hearing as well as to tickle the funny bone in children ages 4 to 8. Perky illustrations and silly songs. Code CRP, $12.95.

**EVERYDAY DISCOVERIES: Amazingly Easy Science and Math**, by Sharon MacDonald. Your child's mind can grow with this book. Math and science go together; it's very hard to separate them completely. Here are dozens of activities — you could call them experiments — that you can do at home, mostly with what's on hand. You may have to purchase a few inexpensive items. The book was written to be used in a classroom, and there are sections you can easily ignore, but all projects can be done at home with one or more children. Projects are well organized, and I like the fact that MacDonald has included variations that can be used with slightly younger or older children; that makes the book very adaptable. Nicely put together with multiple activities for apples; birds, eggs, and feathers; bones; corn; crayons; ice; grains; rocks; shoes; wind; and more. Ages 4 to 8. Code GHS, $19.95.

**BITE-SIZED SCIENCE: Activities for Children in 15 Minutes or Less**, by John H. Falk and Kristi S. Rosenberg. Intriguing, playful, investigative ways for children ages 3 to 8 to explore the world around them. You won't need to buy anything. You can start in the kitchen with projects called Cupboard Talk, How Many Seeds?, Chewing Sounds, and Tangy Tongue. Sections include "High-Energy Activities," "Quiet Times," "Bedtime," and more. These activities engage the imagination, and you may be surprised at how much you'll enjoy doing them with your kids. Code CRP, $12.95.

Not to be confused with the Mudpies arts and activities books, **MUDPIES TO MAGNETS** is a preschool science curriculum by Robert Williams, Robert Rockwell, and Elizabeth Sherwood. Designed for classroom use, it is still well suited for use at home. In the introduction the authors state, "It must be remembered that acquisition of facts is not the goal of science for young children. Instead, we want the children to experience the success and joy that come from finding the answers to questions by doing things rather than by being told. In many simple ways, they can repeatedly be thrilled by their discoveries, particularly if the adults around them share their enthusiasm." Activities are designed in such a way that many can be completed by your child unassisted, while others are best done with an adult. Good ideas for indoor and outdoor exploration. More than 100 projects. Ages 2 to 5. Code GH, $14.95. There is a sequel to this in "Science."

**BUGS**. A play-and-learn kit from Philadelphia's Please Touch Museum. The kit comes with a large fold-out playboard, six bugs (made from heavy cardboard and easy to punch out), and a book for you to read with your child. The story tells of an ant finding a crumb and taking it back to the anthill. Along the way he passes many other bugs: ladybugs, a worm, a bee, and others, and the book tells us about each. There are many creative suggestions for play and for things to make with your child. Most children are fascinated by bugs; some are afraid. This kit will create a familiarity with fascinating everyday bugs that will help children set aside any fears they may have. (You too?) Ages 3 to 5. Code RP, $14.95.

**WHAT HAPPENS TO YOUR FOOD?** An ingenious interactive guide that answers many questions young children might have about their bodies. There are fold-out flaps that reveal a simple action or a cross-section. Simple explanations are brought to life by vivid cartoons. Ages 4 to 7. Code EDC, $7.95.

**BEFORE YOU WERE BORN**, by Jennifer Davis. This terrific interactive lift-the-flap book is for young children and parents to explore together. In full color, the main part of the page shows, month by month, what is happening inside Mommy's body, and lifting the flap you see how the baby is developing. Answers questions about the umbilical cord, baby's hiccups, and more. From conception through birth — "I pushed and pushed until your head showed a fraction." Ages 2 to 6. Code WKM, $10.95.

Some of the questions in these books are easy to answer, some more complicated. A book with good pictures can help you to explain and your children to understand. These three books are ingenious and interactive. Fold-out flaps reveal a simple action or a cross-section. Cartoons illustrate the text. Lots of good discussion material. Ages 4 to 7. Code EDC, $7.95 each. Specify **HOW ARE BABIES MADE?** or **HOW DO YOUR SENSES WORK?**

**Young Nature Series.** Each of these books is well-illustrated with large pictures and simple informative text for inquiring young minds. You will need to read these to your children, but they will enjoy the pictures all by themselves. Ages 4 to 7. Code EDC, $6.95 each. Specify **BABY ANIMALS, DINOSAURS, FARM ANIMALS,** or **HORSES AND PONIES.**
The next step in learning about nature is the *First Book of Nature* in "Science."

**First Science Books.** All these books are interactive, with flaps to open for discovering something new. Each book suggests to parents and children ways of exploring nature without disturbing it. Ages 3 to 6. Code KC, $6.95 each. Specify **A NEW DUCK: Life Cycle of a Bird, A NEW FROG: Life Cycle of an Amphibian, A NEW BUTTERFLY, A SEED GROWS: How Plants Grow,** or **HUNGRY ANIMALS.**

Please be sure to read about *Play Lightly on the Earth: Nature Activities for Children 3 to 9,* in "Ecology." It's just right for this age group.

**Starting Point Science** books answer hundreds of the questions your children will ask you. Thoroughly illustrated and visually interesting, with well-written text that gives clear answers. I'd start collecting these books when the kids are about 4. Although they won't be able to read the text, they will enjoy and learn from the illustrations. With 20 titles to choose from, I suggest you start with one or two, to see how much your kids enjoy them, and then go on to the collected volumes for a better buy. Ages 4 to 8, individual titles. Code EDC, $4.95 each. Because these books are good for such a wide age range, I've listed them in "Science."

**HUG A TREE: And Other Things to Do Outdoors With Young Children**, by Robert Rockwell, Elizabeth Sherwood, and Robert Williams. Many stimulating, environmentally friendly things to do with children ages 3 to 6. It also has a great list of resources: books for parents and teachers as well as books for children, suitable magazines of interest, places to find materials, ideas for field trips, places to write, and more. A section at the beginning of the book that is meant for teachers can be generally ignored. Be sure to check out the last few pages, which suggest a few more projects and some safety information about poison ivy and insect stings. Code GHS, $9.95.

## FIRST DICTIONARY AND ENCYCLOPEDIAS

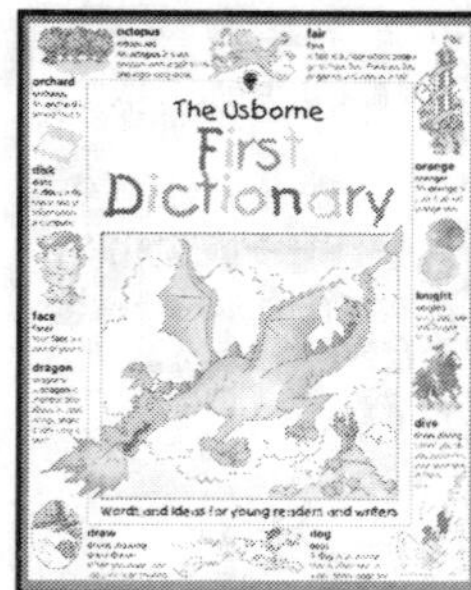


**FIRST DICTIONARY**. More than 2,500 carefully chosen words, clearly explained and illustrated, with lively pictures and photos. There are some spelling tips, writing ideas, word games, and puzzles for fun and to reinforce learning. Much more than just a dictionary. Fun just to look through. Ages 5 to 8. Hardcover. Code EDC, $19.95.

**First Encyclopedias**. These two 8½x11" full-color books are just right for sparking questions, exploring our world, and frequent browsing. I think you'll find you will enjoy looking through these books with your children and discussing the illustrations. I also think your kids will enjoy browsing alone. These are Usborne books with great color photos, illustrations, and clear text, wonderful books to explore with your young children. **FIRST ENCYCLOPEDIA OF OUR WORLD** explores geography, weather, climates, and ecology. **FIRST ENCYCLOPEDIA OF ANIMALS** contains separate sections on mammals, birds, water life, and creepy crawlies. Ages 4 and up. Code EDC, $9.95 each, $18 for both. Specify **FIRST ENCYCLOPEDIA OF OUR WORLD** or **FIRST ENCYCLOPEDIA OF ANIMALS**.

## ACTIVITIES

**Play Catch With Your ABCs**. A sturdy, inflatable 24" ball that comes with suggested games, but it's also easy to make up your own games. A **Time** ball is also available. Code ES, $10.95 each.

I like many of Montessori's ideas and learning tools, but I wouldn't use these computer learning/teaching programs with children under 8. (If you don't know what to think about this issue, refer to "Computers.") If you still want your young child to use the computer, you would do well to investigate Montessori Educational Computer Systems, 13008 Rover Ave. NE, Albuquerque, NM 87112; 800-995-5133; www.mecs-software.com.

**CHRISTMAS ACTIVITIES.** This is a very nice collection of activities and recipes that can be easily done by youngsters ages 4 and up. Includes more than 100 colorful stickers. Code EDC, $8.95.

**CHILD'S PLAY**. A catalog filled with books for learning through play. Excellent early learning books and games, beginning readers, and some inexpensive musical instruments. To request a catalog, send $1 to Child's Play, 67 Minot Ave., Auburn, ME 04210; 800-639-6404.

**Acid-Free Reusable Sticker Books.** Full-color background scene and reusable stickers. Kids can create and re-create their own versions of these fairy tales and everyday environments, or make up their own stories. All books $9\frac{1}{4}$x$11\frac{1}{4}$". Code DV. ***Important:*** Please specify title and that they are *sticker books* so we don't get confused.

**AIRPORT**, $4.50.
**CONSTRUCTION SITE**, $3.50.
**CREATE YOUR OWN FARM**, $3.50.
**CREATE YOUR OWN ZOO**, $3.50.
**GAS STATION**, $3.50.
**GOLDILOCKS AND THE THREE BEARS**, $2.95.
**LITTLE RED RIDING HOOD**, $2.95.
**THE OLD WOMAN WHO LIVED IN A SHOE**, $2.95.

**Early Learning Coloring and Activity Books.** Specially designed for preschool through first grade. Fun and good practice. Specify "Little Activity Book."All $8\frac{1}{4}$x11", 32 pages. Code DV, $1 each. Specify **ABC, A IS FOR ASTRONAUT, DINOSAURS, HIDDEN PICTURES, NUMBERS, OPPOSITES, SAME AND DIFFERENT, SEA ANIMALS, SHAPES, SPELLING FUN, WHAT'S WRONG?,** or **RHYMING WORDS.**

**WE CAN GET ALONG**, by Lauren Murphy Payne, M.S.W. This sounds so simple, but we all know that getting along with friends and family can be difficult at times. Conflict resolution is a skill everyone uses, and I'm sure all of us know some people who are better at it than others. There are times when we all feel hurt or have hurt someone else unintentionally. Sometimes we hurt others on purpose. This is a simple book for young children that will help you discuss ways to recognize feelings and deal with them constructively. Especially good for ages 4 to 7. Code FS, $9.95.

**WE CAN GET ALONG — A Leader's Guide**, also by Payne, is designed for everyone who works with young children, mostly in a public setting, but it can be used by parents at home. It's filled with suggestions for helping children recognize their feelings and know that they always have a choice about how they act on them. Lots of activities that work well at home or in a group setting. Code FS, $14.95.

**THE RIGHT TOUCH**, by Sandy Kleven, beautifully illustrated by Jody Bergsma. I've searched long and hard for a book suitable for young children that addresses sexual abuse. I don't think this is a prevalent problem within the homeschooling community, but our children are part of society and they need information that will keep them safe. I wanted a book that would open the door for discussing inappropriate touch and abuse but would not cause children to feel insecure or fearful. This is it.

In this book, Jimmy's mom explains the difference between touches that are loving and positive and touches that are secret, deceptive, or forced. This is accomplished in a completely non-threatening manner — through the use of a story. The story highlights how a child might feel under these circumstances. Kleven, with years of experience working with abused children, has included guidelines to follow if your child ever encounters such a situation. On the back cover, Bergsma presents us with a picture about feelings, which is great for discussions. If you really like it, you can obtain it in poster form. Age: whenever you feel your child is old enough. Hardcover. Code IA, $15.95.

---

* From page 156: For use with *Pretend Soup*, the general substitution of honey for sugar as given in *Joy of Cooking*, by Irma S. Rombauer and Marion Rombauer Becker: "As honey has greater sweetening power than sugar, we prefer to substitute 1 cup honey for $1\frac{1}{4}$ cups sugar and to reduce the liquid in the recipe by $\frac{1}{4}$ cup."

## SPELLING
## GRAMMAR
## VOCABULARY
## WRITING AND
## GETTING PUBLISHED

The technology has changed, but the message ...!

**WORDWORKS: Exploring Language Play**, by Bonnie von Hoff Johnson. This book contains knowledge as well as thinking challenges, and I guarantee it will make you and your kids laugh. When it first arrived here I meant to browse through it quickly and take a serious look at it later, but I couldn't put it down. I chuckled and read until Gus insisted on being fed — and he had to growl at me twice before I paid attention. The book is divided into ten chapters. Here are some brief descriptions. Chapter 1, Names: People — eponyms (was there really a Mr. Silhouette?), first and last names, plant names, and pseudonyms. Places — do you know or can you guess what a toponym is? Where is Easy Street? Things — unusual names for familiar things, word play in business names. Chapter 2, Hink Pinks: what they are and why they are more important than you ever dreamed they should be. Chapter 3, Idioms: getting down to brass tacks — a definition of "idiom." Nothing to sneeze at — writers who introduced common idioms. Not from this neck of the woods — idioms from other cultures. Chapter 4, Established Slang (nothing offensive): Not for Goof-offs — the study of slang. Oldies but Goodies: repeating slang and rhyming slang. Chapter 5, Multiple-Meaning Words: ambiguous headlines. Chapter 6, Proverbs: They never looked like this before! Chapter 7, Alike and Different: synonyms and antonyms at play. Chapter 8, Word Formation: affixes, abbreviations, and acronyms — to name just a few discussed. Chapter 9, Etymology: word origins and borrowings from *ampersand* to *zany*. Chapter 10, A Potpourri of Language Play: euphemisms, anagrams, slogans, and more. You'll have fun reading and learning, and you'll double your fun when you share it with your kids. Each chapter contains numerous activities and ends with a listings of references and children's books for further investigation. Recommended for grades 4 to 8, but you can stretch it either way; I think this material is good for kids up to 15 or 16. If you're not familiar or comfortable with wordplay, I suggest you read it just for fun. You could also use the activities in a group setting. Code FC, $17.95.

**DRAW WRITE NOW,** by Marie Hablitzel and Kim Stitzer. ***Rejoice!*** Finally, books for beginning readers, writers, and budding artists. Children love to draw, and beginning readers need encouragement and practice. Handwriting may require a bit of extra encouragement because there is a "right" way to do it, and writing neatly can seem more like work than play. Hablitzel and Stitzer have put together a series of books encouraging children to combine their writing and drawing skills.

The topic for each book is carefully chosen, and the drawing techniques are ones this age group

will easily master and use. These are colorful books, with easy-to-follow instructions. There is an amazing amount of good information about the core subject of each book that your child will absorb with no apparent effort. Your children will return to these books again and again to use the drawing tips, which are based on common shapes. I do wish we had had these when our children were learning to draw and write. There aren't many books or series I would call "must-haves," but this group of books belongs in that category. These books do not teach "handwriting" per se, but will encourage neat penmanship and creativity. These books are incremental and the depth of information and scope of the drawing techniques become more complex as the series progresses. A section at the end of each book provides more information about the subject matter, lists vocabulary, and includes teaching tips. Code BC, $10.95 each. Special discount when you buy two at the same time: $18.

Book One: **On the Farm, Kids and Critters, Storybook Characters**

Book Two: **Christopher Columbus, Autumn Harvest, and the Weather**

Book Three: **North America, Native Americans, and the Pilgrims**

Book Four: **The Polar Regions, the Arctic, and the Antarctic**

Book Five: **The United States, From Sea to Sea, Moving Forward**

Book Six: **Animals and Habitats, On the Land, Life in Ponds and Rivers, Oceans**

Book Seven: **Animals of the World, Part 1, Forests — Tropical, Northern, Down Under**

If your kids enjoy the *Draw Write Now* books they will also enjoy **MY DRAWING AND HANDWRITING BOOK!** by the same authors. This book includes more than 20 two-page spreads for drawing and story-writing, all neatly bound. Writing pages are lined. Code BC, $2.49.

## USEFUL TOOLS

**Magnetic Letters and Words** — See "Early Learning."

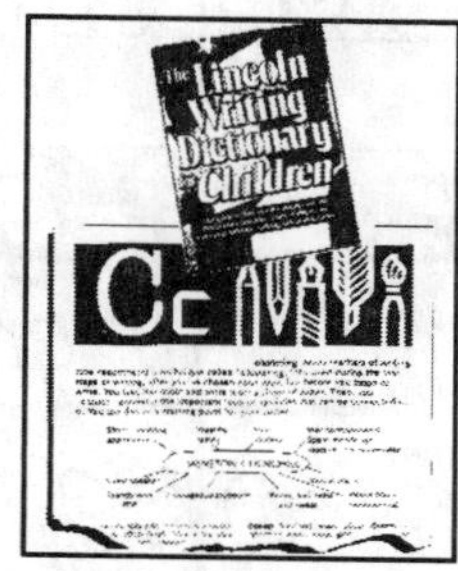


**LINCOLN WRITING DICTIONARY**. After the early childhood picture dictionaries, most kids' dictionaries aren't worth buying. Too many words are missing, too many definitions are incomplete, and the rules of grammar are ambiguous, confusing, or non-existent. This is one of the very few good kids' dictionaries, and is a useful bridge from early picture books to adult dictionaries. Besides being a clear and concise dictionary with more than 35,000 entries, the *Lincoln Writing Dictionary* really does have many features that will help any user — child or adult — become a better writer. There are 4,000 usage examples taken from more than 500 authors, and there are 600 short essays explaining writing techniques more fully. The 700 color illustrations include drawings and photographs. Reconditioned hardcover. Code F, $28.

**365 NEW WORDS A YEAR.** This page-a-day calendar is a painless way to increase vocabulary (and improve spelling). Each page has a word and its definition, origin, pronunciation, and sample sentence. Ages 14 to adult. Code WKM, $10.95.

**FOCUSING ON WORDS.** If you're interested in expanding your knowledge of English and its Greek and Latin roots, you can do it easily and painlessly by visiting John Robertson's Focusing on Words website (www.wordexplorations.com) or subscribing to his online newsletter. This site is just right for curious high school students and adults.

**MISS MANNERS' BASIC TRAINING: COMMUNICATION**, by Judith Martin. It may seem stuffy to some — and unnecessary or just not important to others — to learn the proper forms of communication, but there is merit to hand-writing a personal note on some occasions rather than sending an e-mail or fax. This book explains the proper technology to use for private, professional, and public messages, and tells you when to phone, when to fax, and when a handwritten note is obligatory, a form letter forbidden, and a chain letter out of the question. Examples of how to write a thank-you note and a letter of condolence, how to reply to various types of invitations and announcements, and a lot more. Believe it or not, this book is fun to read, and you'll notice a very subtle humor hiding in the examples. Code RH, $15.

Aa Bb Cc Dd Ee Ff Gg Hh Ii Jj Kk Ll Mm Nn Oo Pp

All letters written in one stroke unless otherwise indicated.

Aa Bb Cc Dd Ee Ff Gg Hh Ii Jj Kk Ll Mm

ana bnb cnc dnd ene fnf gng hnh ini jnj knk lnl mnm

abcdefghijklmnopq

abcdefghijklmnopq

*This is a sample of basic italic.*
*This is a sample of cursive italic.*

## HANDWRITING

**ITALIC HANDWRITING SERIES**. An attractive blend of manuscript and cursive. A number of readers have asked for this series, saying they prefer it to the standard Zaner-Bloser method of handwriting. It's fun to learn, it looks great, and the price is reasonable too. This italic handwriting series is based on the Dubay Getty method. It's easy to master, faster to write, more legible, and a delight to the eye when used. Complete courses for all ages. All code PS.

**Starter Set**: Comprehensive instruction manual, three student workbooks, three desk alphabet strips. Workbooks are illustrated to suit each level, with plenty of room for practice. The manual will help you teach this style of handwriting, improving yours too just in case you need it. It also has many projects that will showcase your child's new skills. Specify which three books (listed below) you would like. $23.

**Instruction manual only** is $5.75. Bought individually the books are $5.75.

**Book A**: Kindergarten. Introduces the complete alphabet and numerals. One letter per page. 72 pages.

**Book B**: 1st grade. For the beginning reader with short words and lively sentences. 64 pages.

**Book C**: 2nd grade. Considered a transition book. Introduces basic joins with interesting topics to write about. 68 pages.

**Book D**: 3rd grade. There's fun in this one, which includes tongue twisters and limericks. Covers all joins, vowel and consonant sounds, prefixes and suffixes, and the history of each letter, plus 12 rules of capitalization.

**Book E**: 4th grade. Lots of written practice using topics ranging from the solar system to plants and animals.

**Book F**: 5th grade. Lots of practice, with an introduction to figures of speech, synonyms, antonyms, analogies, metaphors, similes, idioms, euphemisms, and more.

**Book G**: 6th grade to adult. Practice extends to paragraphs; discusses the origins of our letters, from cave paintings to copperplate.

**WRITE NOW** is a self-teaching course for adult learners, but high school students can easily use this too. $12.95.

For standard handwriting books by MacMillan, Zaner-Bloser, HBJ, or Steck-Vaughn, refer to the Follett catalog listed in "Homeschooling and Education."

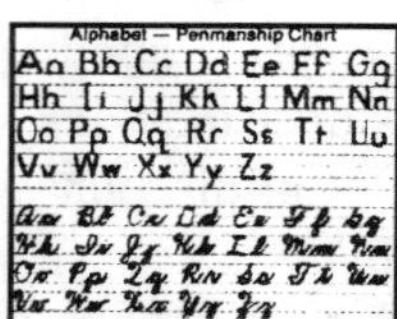


This **SMALL ALPHABET WALL CHART** is perfect for homeschooling. 8½x11". Shows manuscript and cursive upper- and lowercase letters. Code AO, $1.50, $1 with $10 order.

**ALPHABET TAPES**. 1x20" adhesive desk strips with the alphabet. Your choice: manuscript, cursive, illustrated manuscript, or illustrated cursive. Code ELP, $1.25 each or 75¢ with any other item ordered.

**ALPHABET ANTICS: Hundreds of Activities to Challenge and Enrich Letter Learners of All Ages**, by Ken Vinton. Abundantly illustrated with amusing cartoons. You'll learn a bit of alphabet history, increase your vocabulary, draw — or doodle, if you'd rather — and learn about the manual alphabet, the semaphore alphabet, flag code, Morse code, hieroglyphics, the Greek and Hebrew alphabets, and much more. Lots of ideas for creative minds to play with. Ages 8 and up. Code FS, $19.95.

## WRITING

**KIDS AT HOME.** You can't make an omelet without breaking eggs, and your child can't develop writing skills without writing and reaping the rewards. *Kids at Home* is a magazine for and about homeschooling kids. It's a forum for kids ages 4 to 13 to share their writing and art. P.O. Box 9148, Bend, OR 97708.

**WRITING**, by Amanda Lewis. A simple title and a fascinating book. A history of writing: Why do people brand cattle, sign paintings, or scrawl graffiti? Lewis tracks the history of the written word and writing tools, from pictograms to the computer. Many activities, the secret of secret codes, handwriting analysis, Braille, brush writing, paper-making, and a lot more packed in a book everyone will enjoy reading. I wish this book had been in print when our kids were home. I love the variety and creativity of the illustrations. One of my personal favorites. Ages 8 and up. Code KC, $6.95.

**Needed! Your Child's Imagination**. Each of these kits comes with everything essential for creating a unique book — except your child's imagination. Combine his imagination with this blank book, three pages of stickers to help illustrate the story and stimulate creativity (kids can add their own artwork too), and stencils. Along with the physical tools there are many good ideas for organizing a story. Your child can produce his own illustrated masterpiece! Ages 7 to 10. Code LB, $8.95 each. Specify **SPOOKY STORY, SPACE STORY, ADVENTURE STORY,** or **FAIRY TALE.**

**THE YOUNG PERSON'S GUIDE TO BECOMING A WRITER**, by Janet Grant. A practical and inspiring book for ambitious teens. How to prepare a manuscript, find a publisher, and maintain a writing career, plus tips from other young writers and more. Code FS, $13.95.

**THE ELEMENTS OF STYLE**, by William Strunk Jr. and E.B. White. This thin book, about 90 pages (including the index), is a complete guide to rules of grammar, spelling, usage, and concise but expressive writing. Probably best for high school age and older, but you can boil down its contents for your younger students. Whether you (or they) are writing articles, stories, essays, novels, or just letters to friends, you'll be glad to have this guide to the essentials of clear, sensible writing. Code MAC, $5.95. I've found it essential.

**BETTER SENTENCE WRITING IN 30 MINUTES A DAY**, by Dianna Campbell. A guide to sharpening your writing skills for letters, research papers, college, or career. You'll need to know basic grammar to make the best use of this book, which is more comprehensive than *The Elements of Style* and will help a writer learn proper and creative use of punctuation and sentence structure. High school age and up. Code CP, $9.99.

**WRITE WHERE YOU ARE: How to Use Writing to Make Sense of Your Life**, by Caryn Mirriam-Goldberg, Ph.D. The author says, "Writing gives you a place to save and savor memories and insights, your thoughts and wishes, your feelings and goals. Writing can help you create and re-create yourself. ... Writing can bring you hope, help you dream wide and deep." This book goes beyond creating a journal and offers suggestions for writing in many different styles, and tells you how to draw from your personal life to create poetry or characters for a story. It will encourage writing about the ordinary and the extraordinary. There are exercises if you want to use them, but they are not a major feature of the book. Constructive suggestions for proofreading and rewriting are included, along with suggestions for finding a mentor and tips and information about getting published. You can read this straight through or skip around; it's useful either way. For ages 14 and up. Code FS, $14.95.

**WRITING FOR SUCCESS**, by Alexandra and Francesca Swann. This book contains a sound review of all grammar and punctuation rules and moves on to creative writing skills. Very sequential, with well-organized lessons. Students can work on their own or with a parent. If I were using this book with my kids I'd let them work with it on their own, and now and then add a more exciting challenge using the skills they've mastered. Useful after kids have mastered basic writing skills and are ready and interested in improving them. Ages 8 to 16. $29.95 plus $3 shipping from Cygnet Press, HC 12, Box 7A, 116 Hwy. 28, Anthony, NM 88021.

**WRITERS.** An extremely well-written book about women writers, their lives, their difficulties, and their work. I think this would inspire any aspiring young writer ridden with doubts and fears. The section about Jean Little is truly remarkable. Glossary in the back of the book and a list of suggested reading. Ages 10 to 14. Code CT, $8.95. (Also see *Women of Words* in "Literature.")

**GHOSTWRITER**. Videocassettes, activities, books, and more. Produced by Children's Television Workshop. GPN, University of Nebraska-Lincoln, P.O. Box 80669, Lincoln, NE 68501-0669.

### GETTING PUBLISHED

**Raspberry Publications** (P.O. Box 925, Westerville, OH 43086-6925; 800-759-7171) is an established publisher of children's books. They are inviting K-12 students to submit manuscripts (with illustrations, if you like) for possible publication. If your child's work is accepted they will issue a standard book contract and royalties. They encourage young authors to invest their earnings in college trust funds. If you happen to be the parent of a child whose manuscript is accepted and need information about book contracts, the best place to get literary contract information is from the Authors Guild in New York City. For a $90 membership fee, you have access to their experienced contract lawyers. Well worth it. To contact the Authors Guild write to: 330 W. 42nd St., 29th Floor, New York, NY 10036; 212-563-5904; www.authorsguild.org.

**THE INKWELL** is a magazine forum for young authors to publish their short stories, essays, poetry, and art. The magazine is published quarterly for ages 12 to 19. Write c/o Dori Griffin, 920 Kennington Hills Drive, Hixson, TN 37343.

**MERLYN'S PEN** publishes an annual book of stories and poems selected through their annual contest, open to all students in grades 6 to 12. *Merlyn's Pen* also offers a mentoring program; there is a fee for the mentoring. Dept. DM98, 4 King St., P.O. Box 910, East Greenwich, RI 02818; www.merlynspen.com.

**CREATIVE KIDS** is a quarterly magazine looking for original writing (800 to 900 words), cartoons, songs, puzzles, artwork, games, poetry, and plays by children 8 to 14. Write for submission guidelines: Submissions Editor, Creative Kids, P.O. Box 8813, Waco, TX 76714-8813; www.prufrock.com/mag_ck.html.

### SPELLING

**BETTER SPELLING IN 30 MINUTES A DAY,** by Harry H. Crosby and Robert W. Emery. A lifesaver for those who consider themselves "spelling-disabled." Sensible approach: There's a diagnostic test at the beginning to pinpoint problem areas, and lots of practice. Tips for proofreading your own work. High school and up, but you could use it to help younger children. Code CP, $9.99.

**SPELLING THE EASY WAY**. A good way to learn to spell and increase your vocabulary at the same time. High school and up. Code BE, $12.95.

**SPELLING POWER**. This is a complete course with everything needed to master spelling for ages 8 and up, including adults. Designed to be used for 15 minutes a day, it combines deductive and inductive reasoning, dictionary skills, and multisensory activity task cards (sold separately). It's a big, intimidating-looking book, especially for those who have trouble spelling, but it's actually very easy to use. If you're looking for a "one size fits just about all" program, this is the best and most flexible. This course could make your life simpler, particularly if you don't spell well yourself.

On the other hand, if you spell well and are familiar with the general rules of spelling, you can create your own spelling lists from words the kids misspell. Or you could use one of the books designed for high school students, apply the spelling rules, redesign the exercises to fit the vocabulary of your student, and save your money. Another option would be to let your kids pick their own words from a dictionary, learning the definitions and spelling, and let them surprise you with their choices for the week. They are much more likely to really learn and use words they have picked themselves, and it eliminates work for you. In the course of looking for words they want to learn they will undoubtedly read a lot of other words, making the whole exercise very worthwhile and quite likely to increase their vocabulary.

You'll have to decide what will work best for you and your children. Code CM, $39.95 for the 300-plus-page book, $24.95 for the box of Activity Task cards. No shipping charge for the task cards if you buy them with the course.

**VOCABULARY**

**BUILDING A STRONG VOCABULARY: A Twelve-Week Plan**, by Carl B. Smith, Ph.D. The opening chapter of the book asks if you want to raise your child's IQ and then says the techniques in this book will increase the likelihood of your child doing better in school, getting into a better college, and eventually getting a better job — in other words, achieving the American dream. That's fine if that's your aim. I like the idea of increasing vocabulary because it increases the fun of reading and an appreciation of the nuances of our language. You can use this book as prescribed — in 12 weeks — but I'd take my time with it and just continue to use and reuse the ideas in it. I think your child will get more out of it that way and will be more likely to learn and to apply what he is learning to all his work. This book is designed for the middle grades; however, I see no reason why you couldn't take the principles involved and use them with younger children, or have older children use them to invent their own program with more advanced vocabulary. This book has excellent strategies to help you help your child, and help self-motivated learners help themselves.

Smith's use of multiple strategies makes this book a very flexible tool. You will be able to choose the approach best suited to your child from a variety of approaches that will create interest. Topics covered: synonyms, antonyms, homophones, base words and prefixes, meaning from context, an analogies game, creating word webs, dictionaries and thesauri, roots and affixes, Latin and Greek word families, and words from other languages. Designed for middle grades through high school (and still good for adults). Comes in a 8x11" loose-leaf binder. Code GB, $14.95.

**VOCABULARY**. This is a five-cassette and workbook combination, with recall cards that *will* increase your vocabulary. You won't be asked to learn isolated — and therefore meaningless — words. I found the first tape so interesting when I first listened to it that I forgot what I was doing and my dishwater got cold. Words are presented with clear but not strained diction. Hearing each new word repeated, in context, and in varied sentences, means you'll learn the correct pronunciation and be more likely to remember and use the word yourself.

Donn and I had a very intelligent friend who studied the dictionary in his spare time while he was stationed in France with the Air Force. He came home with an incredible reading vocabulary. He also didn't pay attention to the pronunciation guides. The first work he found when he returned home happened to be at a store called Plaidland. When he told us he was working at "playedland" we had a good laugh. Better us than his boss! Sometimes just knowing the word isn't enough; you need to be able to pronounce it and use it correctly.

Prefixes, suffixes, and usage are discussed in a conversational manner, and you'll learn why certain words are commonly confused. The vocabulary you are learning is used many times within each discussion. Writing a word and using the workbook will reinforce your aural learning. A sampling of the vocabulary: imply, infer, connotation, denote, expiate, cognizance, erudite, bellicose. High school and up. Code AF, $59.95.

**BETTER VOCABULARY IN 30 MINUTES A DAY**, by Edie Schwager. A 190-page book, more advanced than standard high school vocabulary, with a good section about word roots and a few word-matching games in the back to check your retention. High school and up. Code CP, $11.99.

Try letting your child pick a word or group of words for both of you to learn.

## GRAMMAR

**BETTER GRAMMAR IN 30 MINUTES A DAY**, by Constance Immel and Florence Sacks. A good study guide or reference book. All the information is there, examples are given, and only a little practice drill is provided. High school and up. Code CP, $11.99.

**CAUGHT'YA! Grammar With a Giggle**, by Jane Bell Kiester. Probably lots of giggles, which may be one of the reasons this method of teaching grammar, spelling, punctuation, and vocabulary is so effective. The basic idea, put very simply, is that the teacher makes the mistakes (on purpose), and the students correct him. Add to that a few minutes each day of a humorous soap opera with Hairy Beast, Wilfred Warthog, Bertha Boa, and other residents at General Animal Hospital, and you certainly have grammar with a giggle. Don't like the plot? Make up your own! There are lots of ideas for developing your own creative approach. This book came too late for us to try it on our kids, but the general approach is similar to the approach we often used ourselves. Easily adapted by *you* for different grade levels, from grade 4 through high school. Code MH, $17.95.

**CAUGHT'YA AGAIN: More Grammar With a Giggle**, by Jane Ball Kiester. More stories and lots more giggles. Code MH, $17.95.

**WORD DETECTIVE**. Young children increase their vocabulary and knowledge of basic grammar as well as learning the parts of speech from these humorous picture strips, in which a group of detectives — Inspector Noun; Sergeant Verb; and Detectives Adjective, Adverb, and Pronoun — are in pursuit of a bunch of incompetent crooks. Ages 5 to 12. Code EDC, $9.95.

> *Humor is the great thing, the saving thing. The minute it crops up, all our irritations and resentments slip away, and a sunny spirit takes their place.*
> — Mark Twain

**Fun With English Skills**. The activities of a prehistoric family help children gain basic or practice and skills in such an entertaining and amusing way that they won't regard the learning as a chore. Ages 7 to 11.Code EDC, $7.95 each. Specify **GRAMMAR, PUNCTUATION,** or **SPELLING PUZZLES.**

**Improve Your English.** The following grammar, spelling, and punctuation books are not just tests. They have all the basic information about each subject as well as practice sentences, puzzles, and games. It's all there, but I think you'll want to invent more of your own practice material (good for your imagination and creativity) for some of the concepts. These are not good "first books," but are excellent for the middle grades. Very well done. Ages 10 to 14. Code EDC, $5.95 each. **IMPROVE YOUR GRAMMAR, IMPROVE YOUR SPELLING, IMPROVE YOUR PUNCTUATION.** *All three in one volume*: **IMPROVE YOUR ENGLISH**, $14.95.

**HORIZONS GRAMMAR SKILLS.** Very "schoolish" but short and to the point. Each 24-page booklet teaches a different set of related language, grammar, and composition skills. Each has clear examples and practice drills, but not an overwhelming number of them, which is nice. You can always make up more if you feel a need for more practice. Each book includes an answer key. Grades 3 to 6. Code EDC. Available individually at $5.95 each, or the complete set of 15 (normal price $89.25) for a 10 percent discount: $80.35. *Shipping and teacher's guide included with set.*

**PERIOD, QUESTION MARK, EXCLAMATION MARK**
**APOSTROPHE, COLON, HYPHEN**
**QUOTATION MARKS, UNDERLINING**
**COMMA**
**ADJECTIVES AND ADVERBS**
**PREPOSITIONS AND CONJUNCTIONS**
**VERBS**
**NOUNS AND PRONOUNS**
**PREFIXES, BASES, SUFFIXES**
**FIGURES OF SPEECH**
**CONTEXT CLUES**
**SYNONYMS, ANTONYMS, HOMONYMS**
**CAPITAL LETTERS**
**DICTIONARY SKILLS**
**PARAGRAPH AND TOPIC SENTENCES**
**TEACHER'S GUIDE** — free with set, otherwise $1.

**HORIZONS CONCEPTS.** A set of 10 books to teach basic concepts. Best used after basic reading and writing skills have been established. There are two levels available. Booklets are 24 pages each, with good examples and some — but not too much — practice. Answer key included. Grades 3 to 6. Code EDC. Available individually at $5.95 each or the complete set of 10 (normal price $59.50) for a 10 percent discount: $53.55. *Shipping and teacher's guide included with set.*

**Each of the following is available in Level 1 and Level 2.** Please specify which level you would like.

**RECALLING DETAILS**
**FINDING THE MAIN IDEA**
**ESTABLISHING SEQUENCE**
**FOLLOWING DIRECTIONS**
**DISTINGUISHING BETWEEN FACT AND OPINION**
**DRAWING CONCLUSIONS**
**RECOGNIZING CAUSE AND EFFECT**
**PREDICTING OUTCOMES**
**RECOGNIZING PLOT, CHARACTER, MOOD**
**MAKING JUDGMENTS**
**TEACHER'S GUIDE** — free with set, otherwise $1.

---

My most embarrassing moment happened when ______ (GEOGRAPHICAL LOCATION). The bus was very ___ (ADJ) and held on to a/an ______ (NOUN). At the next stop get up, and I ran over to grab his ______ (NOUN), bu my ______ (PART OF BODY) into his ______ (PART OF B ______. And then, as I was apolog

vacation will stretch from the land of the midnight ___ the sunny ______ (PLURAL NOUN) of the Mediterranean. ______ (PLURAL NOUN) will stay in a luxurious private ___ (A RE You will dine in ______ (ADJECTIVE) surroundings in ou banquet hall on the ______ (NOUN) deck. Every ni

**THE ELEMENTS OF GRAMMAR**, by Margaret Shertzer. Explains the more advanced intricacies of English for those who wish to speak and write it properly. It's clear and concise. There are examples of each usage, but not enough if you are not used to hearing English spoken correctly. I've always thought my grammar was good enough. However, I listened to the tapes below and found I have speech patterns that are incorrect. If I were applying to a college (again) or writing a formal business letter — or writing for you — I would want my grammar to be correct. It does make a difference. I recommend this book as a text and the tapes below for ear training. High school and up. Code SS, $9.95.

**GOOD GRAMMAR MATTERS!** Four interactive cassettes which emphasize that we will speak and write what we have heard spoken. These tapes feature lessons about the proper usage of who and whom, pronouns used in comparisons, possessive adjectives with gerunds, and many other topics. (Don't let the proper grammatical terms deter you. You'll learn to feel comfortable with them or ignore the terms and learn the grammar anyway.) Each lesson begins with a simple, non-technical explanation and examples of incorrect usage, followed by a variety of listening and response-speaking exercises using the correct forms. I was surprised to find that I occasionally misuse who and whom and sometimes make other mistakes with other pronouns. My grammar has improved through using these tapes. I listen in the car, when I'm doing dishes, and at tasks that allow me to think about what I am hearing. High school and up. Code AF, $39.50.

**OK, THAT'S ALL OF THE SERIOUS STUFF!**

**MAD LIBS** is the funniest grammar game around. It doesn't really look like a game, just a pad of paper with stories written out and some blank spaces. The fun comes when you fill in the blanks. Under each blank space is written a part of speech: noun, verb, adverb, etc. Only one person sees the written story. That person calls out the part of speech written under the first blank space. Everyone else thinks of a word that matches that part of speech. When words have been given for all the blanks, the person with the story reads it out loud using the provided words. Stories don't come much sillier than these, and by the time you've done a couple of them, everyone remembers the parts of speech without working at it at all. Sometimes we laughed until we cried. When the stories had been used so many times that everyone remembered them, they were still fun because the kids worked to make them as silly as possible, and then sometimes they'd make up their own stories. Fun for all ages. Code PG, $3.99 each. Specify **MAD LIBS, CHRISTMAS MAD LIBS**, or **OFF-THE-WALL MAD LIBS.**

**PUN AND GAMES,** by Richard Lederer, illustrated by Dave Morice. Hours of pun for kids and adults. Sharpen your wits and prepare to giggle. A colossal collection of puns, jokes, riddles, daffynitions, tairy fales, and homographs at play. You'll find it's a "punderful life" as you read about "puns that Babylon." First you read about the multiple ways to play with words and then you are challenged to do the same. Code CRP, $9.95.

**FUN WITH PUNS**. This is an opportunity to have fun with language. Tickle your mind! There's an animal mobile to make, and room for lots of expression and fun. Ages 8 to 11. Code LW, $10.95.

**ENGLISH TRIVIA**. A game compiled by the Gamma chapter of the Michigan Delta Kappa Gamma Society International; 1,152 questions and answers in six categories: grammar and punctuation, spelling, research skills, literature, vocabulary, and quotations and idioms. Not-so-trivial trivia, I'd say. Level 1 asks, "What kind of reference book do you use to find the pronunciation of a word?" "Spell the plural of baby," and "Who wrote the Peter Rabbit books?" Level 2 is deeper: "Spell the words represented by the letters ESP," and "What part of a debate deals with refutation?" There are two sets of rules, competitive and non-competitive; a score pad; and six achievement certificates. $14.95 plus $3.20 postage from Country Concepts, c/o Pike Printing and Publishing, P.O. Box 57, Camden, MI 49232. (They also have a childbirth trivia game.)

**RHYMES AND NYMS**. This unique card game is one that almost the whole family can play. All that's needed is a basic understanding of rhymes, synonyms, antonyms, and homonyms (about the age of 8). An excellent way to introduce challenge and variety, increase and use your vocabulary, exercise the imagination, and have fun — all by playing with language. There are rules for several variations in play, so the game can be played by one or more players — even in teams. I've tested this game with family and friends and I thoroughly approve. It kept us on our toes and we had some good laughs. A reasonable price for the hours of fun and challenge you and your children will enjoy. For current price and ordering information write: Fireside Games, P.O. Box 82995, Portland, OR 97282-0995.

"Do you want to play Bethump'd With Words?"

"Bethump'd! Wazzat?"

"It's a game."

"Oh. I meant what's the word mean?"

"Bethump'd with words," to quote the explanatory paragraph in the game instructions, "is found in William Shakespeare's *King John*, Act II, Scene I, line 466. There, Philip, half-brother of Robert Faulconbridge — later dubbed Richard Plantagenet — responds to the wordy outburst of the Citizen of Angiers with: 'Zounds! I was never so bethump'd with words since I first called my brother's father dad.'"

The game Bethump'd With Words is about learning new words and is easier to play than reading Shakespeare — and much more fun. The Discovery Edition is designed for kids 9 and up with 2 to 8 players. There are a number of different game options, so

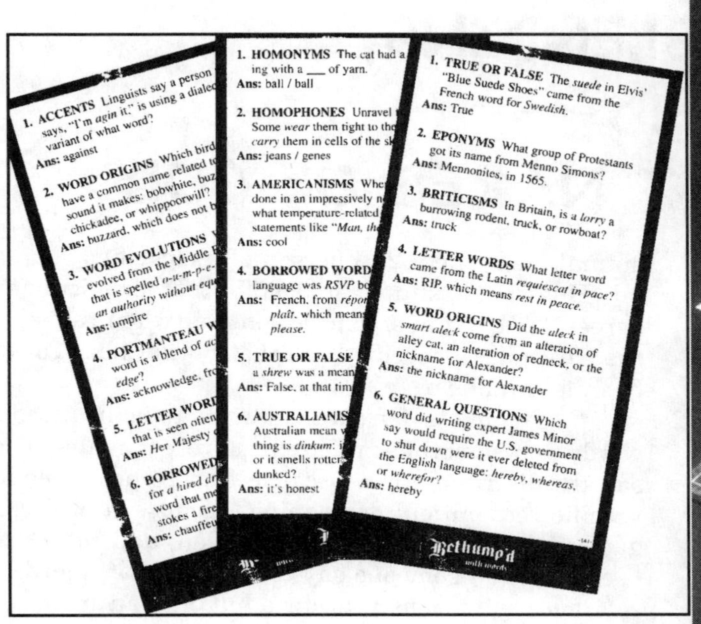

you can increase the difficulty after you get the hang of the game. Bethump'd will amuse and challenge you, but mostly you'll just have fun. You'll also end up feeling delighted with your newfound knowledge and appreciation of our language and its heritage. Scrabble and other word games intimidate me a bit. I like words and I like to play with words, but competing in that arena doesn't excite me, especially since I conceded the last game of Scrabble I played with Donn after he put down his first word. He used all his letters with the word "asinine" and I said, "You win!" Scrabble lets you play with the words you know. Bethump'd helps you learn more about what you already know and takes you further — with a chuckle. If you're wondering which "English" is used in the game, you'll be pleased to know that the words in the game come from American, Australian, British, and Canadian usage. You'll learn about accents, acronyms, calques, eponyms, euphemisms, history, idioms, spoonerisms, origins, and more. **BETHUMP'D DISCOVERY EDITION** is code MLR, $29 plus $3 shipping. For more advanced play — ages 13 and up — you want **BETHUMP'D SENIOR EDITION**. Code MLR, $40 (shipping included). Bethump'd Senior will be a challenge and a delight for many a dark and rainy night or for a congenial evening with friends.

Love the game? You'll love the **BETHUMP'D WITH WORDS BOOK EDITION** by Covey MacGregor, which is a portable version of the game with multiple levels of difficulty. The evolution of Englisc to English, as we should know it, is amusingly told in the first section. If you're thinking "boring yuck," you're in for a delightful surprise. The book contains many game options, and there's a lot more well-told information about the development of English. Code MLR, $15; shipping is free if you are getting any of the Bethump'd games (also see "History").

**Why watch television?**

# PESKY PRONOUNS, GENDER BLENDING, AND THE NON-SEXIST NAMES OF GOD

In 1850, the British Parliament — perhaps afloat on a sea of verbiage, as is often the fate of such bodies — enacted "An act for shortening the language used in acts of parliament," decreeing that "in all acts, words importing the masculine gender shall be deemed and taken to include females."

This is an example of "theoretical English," which tacitly stipulates that which is not explicitly stated, as in "Each student should open his book."

A few years earlier, when the Boston patriots symbolically dumped King George overboard and coffee suddenly became the national drink, those colonists who still preferred tea either escaped to Canada or were hanged. (To this day, the only Americans who drink tea are secret Loyalists. Britons and even Canadians have periodic tea-times, but real Americans never observe anything but a coffee break, even if it's only to nibble a Kit-Kat or sip a diet cola.) It's the nature of Americans, however, to be forgiving (with the exception of certain high executives, who are merely forgetful), and by 1850 sufficient détente had been regained to allow a few English words and speech conventions into the American language. One of the most significant conventions acquired — the generic pronoun, as it's called these days — although steeped in common English usage and further strengthened by Parliamentary edict, was prohibited by the belated First Amendment from a similar Congressional edict.

That Parliamentary edict is still upheld today by major dictionaries (although their editors are beginning to look warily over their shoulders). One dictionary says: "**he**, pronoun. 1. The male person or animal mentioned. 2. A person of unspecified sex, [as in] 'He who hesitates is lost.'" Another dictionary agrees: "2. Used in a generic sense or when the sex of the person is unspecified, [as in] 'He that hath ears to hear, let him hear.'"

Feminists don't want women to be included in words that sometimes refer exclusively to males. They say it's discriminatory, because they're not receiving specific recognition; demeaning, because it still relegates them to a subordinate position; and confusing, because when someone says, "Look at that man," the reference is obviously to an adult human male, but when someone says, "Man will go to the stars someday," they don't know if women will be invited. (People, men or women, who are so easily confused must have a hard time with homonyms. If they hear of someone telling a bare-faced lie, they'll expect to see an animal costume.)

I heartily approve of equal opportunity, equal liability, equal rights, equal everything, including equal pay for equal work, and if Jean seriously wants to shovel out the barn while I sweep the kitchen floor, I won't argue very hard. I realize there's still a long way to go before this fair and logical equality is fully achieved, but let's not get wound up in such a strictly literal interpretation of words and phrases that we lose sight of the real problems.

Many words and phrases in English certainly are "sexist" — that is, discriminatory against either men or women. Feminists claim that women are the targets more often than men, which may be true. They also claim that it's part of an age-old male conspiracy to demean and subjugate women, which is sexist hogwash. It's simply the way the language evolved. They claim that the changes they want in the language — right *now* — are just further steps in its evolution. More hogwash. It isn't evolution; it's erosion.

Attitudes, especially of multitudes, change slowly, and the changed attitudes will be reflected in a slowly changing language. But the feminists want to reverse the process; they want to change the attitudes by changing the language.

George Orwell's *1984* vividly illustrates how the feminists' strategy could easily succeed. The best way to control people's thoughts, he points out, is to control their vocabulary. If all the ways of expressing a certain concept are removed from people's knowledge, then it will be impossible for them to entertain the concept, except perhaps in vague circumlocution. Even that possibility can be eliminated by letting the words remain, but with all meaning removed, as in the slogan, "War is peace." Once people have been fully taught that war is peace and peace is war, how can they express a thought about the state of non-war?

(On the other hand, erasing words to express emotions — love, hate, fear — will not erase the emotions.)

Marie Shear, in an article about "Solving the Great Pronoun Problem," ho ho, complains that she heard a radio announcer refer to a wire-chewing squirrel as "he." "Had a reporter been to the morgue," she asks, "to check the corpse's sex?" Pausing only to start another paragraph, she answers her own question: "Of course not. Like lots of other organizations and individuals, the radio station had simply assumed that anything worth mentioning is male, until proved otherwise. That assumption creates The Great Pronoun Problem."

Turning a squirrel into The Great Pronoun Problem is giving him quite a big responsibility, and seems close to making a mountain out of a molehill. It even skirts pretty close to exactly the same sort of assumption Ms. Shear objects to. Did she check to see if the writer of the announcement was male or female, or did she simply assume that only a male would be guilty of such a sexist offense? Would her antennae have twitched any less if the reporter had referred to the squirrel as "she," or would Ms. Shear then have complained about the assumption that any mischief-making worth mentioning is female, until proved otherwise?

*Male* and *female, man* and *woman*, and *boy* and *girl*, say the feminists, refer to biological sex — the function of reproduction and (if the weather doesn't change) its attendant duties, such as breastfeeding. Period. The words should not be used in conjunction with any person or activity in which this specific function is not relevant. "Woman police officer" or "male nurse" are offensive because being a police officer or a nurse has nothing to do with being male or female. That's true, of course, and rightly so. But try to explain to the feminists that it has not always been so, and that those expressions are used not to reinforce stereotypes but to dispel them, and you'll get your lip buttoned. The next time you hear the word "nurse," feminists want you to picture a generic human being, neither male nor female, because that human being's reproductive functions have nothing to do with his/her/its ability to be a nurse.

This sort of discussion can easily engender — whoops — confusion, but I'm trying to make it as clear as I can.

When I was little, my grandmother told me that a dragonfly would sew up my lips if I told a fib. I don't think I fibbed any more than most little boys, possibly a little less, but whenever I saw a dragonfly I'd cover my mouth and go the other way, not knowing how fair the dragonfly's judgment might be. I tried to avoid fibbing, but I also avoided dragonflies, in case I'd slipped up without knowing it. When I say now that I try in the same way to avoid active confrontation with feminists, I don't mean to imply that feminists are like dragonflies. The problem is, the minute you let slip what you think is an innocent phrase such as "hired man" or "woman's work is never done," some Feminist Thought Police Person is ready to threaten you with something worse than dragonflies. You should say "hired person" or "worker," unless that person's biological sex is specifically involved in the work being done, in which case you're in a whole different kettle of fish, about which feminists are also very sensitive. I have always thought the old saying "A man works from sun to sun, but woman's work is never done" was either a woman's complaint or a man's tribute, or a little of both, or just a statement of unfortunate fact, but the feminists claim it shouldn't be said even if it's true, because it shouldn't be true. Sort of like hearing a noise at night; if you ignore it, maybe it will go away.

I don't know if all states have a position known as Revisor of Statutes, but there is one in Minnesota, and in 1984 that Revisor was ordered by the state legislature to remove "gender-specific language" from the state statutes. Without changing the meaning of the law, of course.

It was an excellent example of Your Tax Dollars At Work. The whole process took two years, and the Revisor and his staff must have been as happy as pigs in a mud puddle. They removed 20,000 "non-substantive gender-specific" pronouns. "His" was changed more than 10,000 times. "He" was eliminated 6,000 times. One hundred gender-specific nouns and adjectives (such as "chairman," "foreman," and "fisherman") were eliminated about 1,400 times. The Revisor reported to the legislature that a few gender-specific words, such as "manhole," were allowed to remain "because every proposed substitute has drawn so much bad press." (Well, yes, I can imagine a few editorial comments that might have been made, hee hee.) The Revisor's report ends with the humble opinion: "We are confident that the revised statutes are no worse than the originals. In many cases they are improved."

One down; forty-nine to go.

But feminists aren't happy attacking only generic pronouns and gender-specific work descriptions. They want to eliminate from the language *all* gender-specific references. Trying to keep abreast of feminist thought ("Forewarned, forearmed," Don Quixote advised), I've invested a few dollars in a couple of non-sexist dictionaries. I can entertain Jean for hours, without reading a single word aloud. She is not a feminist, and wouldn't dream of asking why I read the book and laugh and then read the book and cry and then read the book and bang my head on the wall and then read the book and throw it across the room.

— Let's rewrite Shakespeare: "The evil *people* do" instead of "the evil *men* do."

— Avoid "hysteria," which not only comes from the Greek word meaning "womb" (a female organ), but is almost always used (say the feminists) in referring to women.

— "Jack of all trades" uses a man's name. Sexist. Don't use.

— "Hit the jackpot." Another man's name. Substitute "strike it rich."

— "Hobson's choice." Ignore the historical basis for this phrase; it uses a man's name, so substitute a non-sexist phrase such as "No choice at all."

— "Jekyll and Hyde personality." *Two* masculine names! Substitute "split personality."

— "The patience of Job." You guessed it, Job was a man. Say instead "long-suffering," "very patient," or "uncomplaining."

— What about sexism in the barnyard? Feminists object to "Mad as a wet hen" (although many of them are), and want to substitute "Mad as a hornet." I've known several wet hens over the years, and have had a passing acquaintance once or twice with several mad hornets. Given a choice, I'll take the wet hens.

— "Man overboard!" is obviously sexist, unless you're sure it's a man, and even then, it wasn't his maleness that made him go over, so substitute "Person overboard!" and hope he or she or it doesn't drown while you get it right.

— Don't call a dog "man's best friend" because the only similar phrase referring to women is in the popular song of a few years back "Diamonds Are a Girl's Best Friend," which makes women seem greedy and materialistic, which isn't fair, so don't call a dog man's best friend. (Honest. I'm not making this up.)

— "Motherly," "fatherly," "sisterly," and "brotherly" are gender-specific, which makes them sexist, and should be replaced by more precise adjectives, such as "loving," "kind," "supportive," etc., which can be applied to anyone regardless of gender.

Those are probably enough examples to help you understand why Jean is so entertained by my reactions.

Wait. Let's not forget our Father in Heaven. Why not Mother in Heaven, the feminists indignantly want to know? In fact, since gender is an attitude learned from one's culture, God probably doesn't have gender, and is neither masculine nor feminine. God can't be male or female, either, because those words refer to biological function, and let's not get absurd. Therefore, the proper personal pronoun for God is "it." But calling God "It," even with a capital I, somehow doesn't sound right, so let's not give God a personal pronoun. Instead, let's search our little heads for other gender-fair, non-sexist, divine nouns and pronouns for God, such as Author, Being, Good Parent, Guide, God of Abraham and Sarah (we need Sarah, for non-sexist balance), Heavenly Parent, and so on. The Coordinating Center for Women in Church and Society (1400 N. 7th Street, St. Louis, MO 63106) has a report called "Inclusive Language Guidelines for Use and Study in the United Church of Christ," which explains the whole problem and lists 196 gender-free, non-sexist names, titles, and phrases referring to God. You can order a copy for a mere $2, postpaid.

"He or she who hesitates is lost" and "He or she that hath ears to hear, let him or her hear" are grammatically correct, and are acceptable to feminists, but they're awkward verbosities, as well as mangled corruptions of the originals.

"He or she," "him or her," "his or hers," and similar constructions always have at least three words for gender clarity where previously there was no doubt or confusion; hence, no need for clarification. The advantage, as with Russia's missiles in Cuba, is merely political, not strategic.

At first, some writers attempted compromise by putting "her" in parenthesis after "his," but feminists objected right away that this still included women only as an afterthought. Next came the slash, or diagonal, mark separating (or joining?) the two words, thus creating compound bisexual pronouns such as "his/her," "he/she," and so on. Sometimes the slash is called a stroke; sometimes it almost causes one. I'll return in a moment to the slash/stroke/diagonal.

Some hurried writers have harried us with another gelded pronoun, created by juxtaposing "he/she" and omitting the duplicated letters, thus arriving at "s/he," which can be pronounced aloud only as a sibilant hiccough; and can be read silently only with a slight mental back-flip, as one tries to define it: A split personality? A bearded lady? A gender-blender?

Many writers alternate the masculine and feminine pronouns from paragraph to paragraph, or even sentence to sentence, so they always have a fifty percent chance of being right, and the reader always has a fifty percent chance of being satisfied. Also a fifty percent tendency to skip every other paragraph. A book on parenting, for instance, is very disconcerting when the sex of your child keeps changing from male to female and back again.

I sometimes receive letters addressed to "Dear Sir or Madam," which is understandable and appropriate, since the writer doesn't know which I am, but many letters, third-class in particular, address me as "Sir/Madam," as if I might be half-and-half. That may be appropriate these days for some people, but it is definitely not for me.

In reading sentences such as "Each student must bring his/her book," some readers skip over the punctuation, reading it as "his her book," but with a slight pause between the pronouns to indicate an awareness that something isn't quite right; some supply the supplanted conjunction, as if the diagonal line were a grammalogue representing "or" — "his or her book"; and some others name the oblique punctuation as if it were a synonym for "or," thus: "Each student should bring his slash her book."

Apparently, not many people know that the tipsy line's real name is "virgule," which is just as well. Things are bad enough already. We don't need people saying, "bring his virgule her book." It sounds like a tropical fish. Why not stick to "or"?

Better yet, let's go back to one of the most intelligent enactments of the British Parliament. If men are gracious enough to allow the temporary emasculation of masculine pronouns, women should be gracious enough to accept their chivalry with dignity and even a slight smile of appreciation.

*Please*, before we all become he/shes and sir/madams.

Some readers write to me, "Dear Person," which solves the problem neatly and has little chance of being wrong.

Phantom conjunctions, bisexual pronouns, and conjunctive virgules are not the only language slashers lurking behind the bushes. Enter the plural singulars, rapidly increasing in popular usage. "Everyone should bring their book," "Each person should get their share," and "Everyone should watch their language." New math or not, "one" is singular and "their" refers to more than one — "of or belonging to *them*," which is also more than one — and never the twain should meet. Feminists say it's better to be wrong in quantity than confused in gender, but we could be correct in both if feminists didn't insist on redefining words to suit themselves.

The speech of radio and television announcers abounds with singular forms that suddenly become plural in the middle of the verbal stream. English teachers, without blushing, use this abrupt shift of number not only in their speaking, but also in their writing. They know it's grammatically incorrect, but, because it's in common usage, they say it's "permissible."

It shouldn't be. There are many speech and writing habits that are "in common usage," but shouldn't be. Sloppy English from a teacher makes us think he/she doesn't know their business.

In our home-school teaching, and in my book, I follow the edict of the British Parliament, although I'm not a loyalist, and I don't drink tea.

If anyone wants to write me about this, he/she is welcome to send their letter.

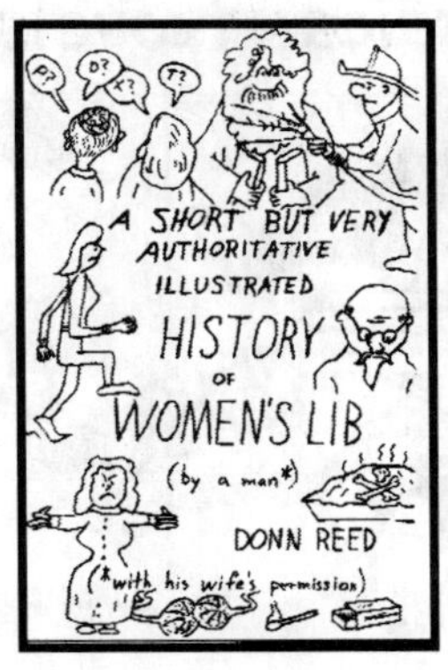


**A SHORT BUT VERY AUTHORITATIVE HISTORY OF WOMEN'S LIB (by a man*) (*with his wife's permission)**, by Donn Reed, is available from us. $5 postpaid.

**GENDER BLENDING: Confronting the Limits of Duality**, by Holly Devor. I haven't read this book and don't intend to. The publisher's description of it is enough to make me wander about muttering and bumping into things. A recent "Help Wanted" ad in our local newspaper said, with italic emphasis, that applicants *"must be either male or female."* At the time, I didn't think that would be too difficult, although I realize some people seem to be a little confused on the matter. Then along came this book, whose author, says the publisher, "interprets gender as a social distinction related to, but different from, biological sex. ... Gender is ... learned by displaying the culturally defined insignia of the gender category with which one identifies." The book is also about "fifteen women who have ... rejected traditional femininity, but not their femaleness ... [are] sometimes mistaken for men ... [and] minimize their female vulnerability in a patriarchal world by minimizing their femininity. ... Their gender identity does not fit either of the two roles socially and culturally defined as feminine and masculine." Hmmm. Let me see if I've got this, now. If you're dissatisfied with your gender but can't get a refund, you should homogenize yourself? Bob Hope once said the Old West was where men were men and women were women "— and I like it that way!" Me, too. You can buy this study of neutered neutrality from Indiana University Press. It's illustrated for the curious. Hardcover or paperback.

# LITERATURE

## Classics, Novels, Cassette Tapes

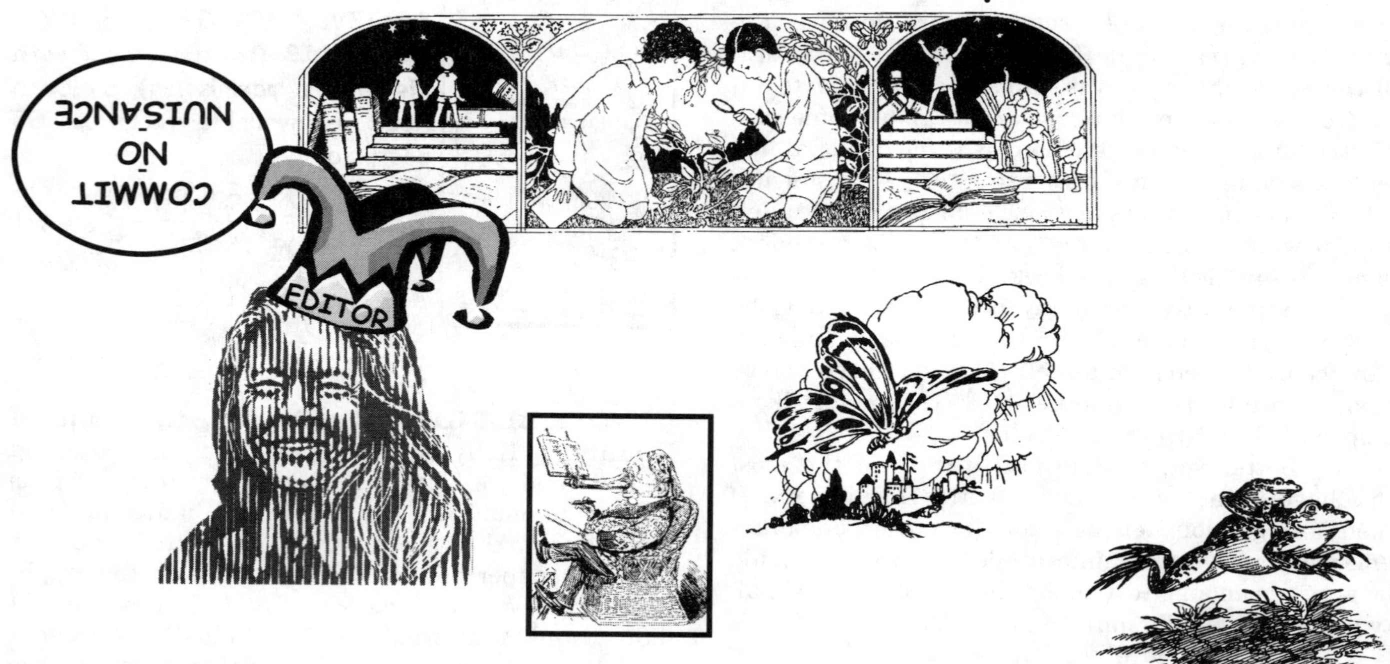

Many titles you would expect to find in this section aren't here, because I have put them in "History" or "Government" or some other chapter I think is just as appropriate. As the author, I put historical fiction in "Literature." As my own editor, I put it with the history. As editor, after all, I have the final word. As author, I must go along with the editor's decisions, and ask you to do the same.

Some titles certainly are hard to place. I won't fault Donn's logic, but as he would be quick to agree, I have my own logic, and some titles that were in this section are now in others. Using my prerogative as author I've moved *Help Your Child Learn to Read* from this chapter to "Early Learning" (along with the beginning readers). Wearing my editor's cap, I've included many classics for young children in this section. If you don't find a book listed where you think it should be, do as I have learned to do when stumped — look in the index!

Over the years Donn and I have done our best to make known and available to you the best of enduring literature. I'm sure we've missed many great books. There really are too many to list, but if you feel we have committed a great (or possibly unforgivable) error or omission, please write and share your thoughts with us.

**BARTLETT'S FAMILIAR QUOTATIONS** — See "Reference Books."

**NEW LIFETIME READING PLAN**, by Clifton Fadiman. This new edition includes all of the previous edition plus classic writers of the last century. It provides brief introductions to suggested readings of the best of the world's literature, from Homer to the present day. "The books here discussed," says the author, "may take you fifty years to finish. They can of course be read in a much shorter time. The point is that they are intended to occupy an important part of a whole life, no matter what your present age may be. Many of them happen to be more entertaining than the latest best-seller. Still, it is not on the entertainment level that they are most profitably read. What they offer is of larger dimensions. It is rather like what is offered by loving and marrying, having and rearing children, carving out a career, creating a home. They can be … a source of continuous internal growth. Hence the word *lifetime*. These authors are life companions. Once part of you, they work in and on and with you until you die. They should not be read in a hurry, any more than friends are made in a hurry." Hardcover, to last a lifetime. Code HC, $24.

---

*When you reread a classic you do not see more in the book than you did before; you see more in you than there was before.* — Clifton Fadiman

---

**The Classics — for Children Only?** It's interesting and curious that most of the books usually thought of today as "children's classics" were not written for children. Many, in fact, although enjoyable for children, are better suited to older readers, because the experience of younger readers is not yet great enough to help them understand many circumstances and situations. W.H. Auden, referring to *Alice's Adventures in Wonderland* as an example, said, "There are good books which are only for adults because comprehension presupposes adult experiences, but there are no good books which are only for children." A few years ago, I read *Alice's Adventures* aloud to the family, in daily installments, and Jean and I enjoyed it at least as much as the kids did. Not long ago, I reread *The Three Musketeers* and enjoyed it more than I did when I was 12; perhaps not "more," but in a different way, and on many more levels. I can read *A Tale of Two Cities* every five or six years, and browse in it occasionally, each time with a little more enjoyment, as if each reading earns compound interest. Classics are those books that endure, sometimes for centuries, not only because they tell exciting stories, or acquaint us with times and people of the past — but, more especially, because they tell us something of ourselves. At the age of 12, I enjoyed the excitement and intrigue of *The Three Musketeers*; a decade later, I could better appreciate the more subtle verbal exchanges; after another decade, I could also admire the writer's artistry and wit. Each time I read the book, I am able to receive more from it because I'm able to take more to it. Each time I read it, I bounce myself against it and come back amplified, like an echo rebounding in a canyon. Children will enjoy the classics, but their parents may enjoy them even more.

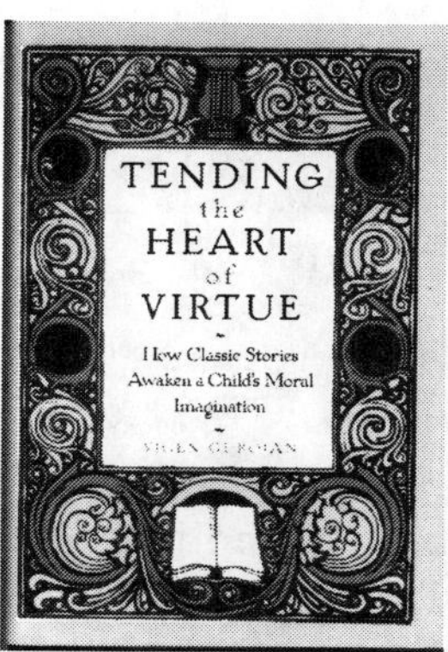


**TENDING THE HEART OF VIRTUE: How Classic Stories Awaken a Child's Moral Imagination**, by Vigen Guroian. An outstanding guide to and discussion of excellent children's books for those of us with the desire to inspire, as opposed to instill, a set of moral values to guide our children through life's dilemmas. Our children learn their values from us and others around them. They also can learn from what they read and what we read with them.

Guroian speaks about the need children have for guidance and moral road maps from adults: "Our society is finding it difficult to meet these needs. ... Some well-meaning educators and parents seem to want to drive the passion for moral clarity out of children rather than use it to the advantage of shaping their character. We want our children to be tolerant, and we sometimes seem to think that a too-sure sense of right and wrong only produces fanatics. ... Mostly we fall back on the excuse that we are respecting our children's freedom by permitting them to determine right from wrong and to choose for themselves clear goals of moral living. But this is the paean of a false freedom that pays misdirected tribute to a deeply flawed notion of individual autonomy. We end up forfeiting our parental authority and failing to be mentors to our children in the moral life." He has strong opinions.

We can tell our children that fire is hot, and some will learn from the telling. Many have to feel the heat before learning the lesson for life. We cannot expose our children to all of life's lessons, but through good literature they can steep themselves in another world, another character, and learn some of the lessons.

We tell our children it is always better to tell the truth, yet each must learn through trial and error that this is so. If we confront our children with a lie they have told, they generally become defensive. It is difficult to work with them when they feel this way. Yet through sharing a story about lying we can create an opportunity to discuss the value of telling the truth in a non-threatening atmosphere; for instance, children instinctively identify with Pinocchio's struggles and learn not only about telling the truth, but about the struggle to do so.

From the table of contents: 1) Awakening the Moral Imagination. 2) On Becoming a Real Human Child: Pinocchio. 3) Love and Immortality in *The Velveteen Rabbit* and "The Little Mermaid." 4) Friends and Mentors in *The Wind in the Willows, Charlotte's Web*, and *Bambi*. 5) Evil and Redemption in "The Snow Queen" and *The Lion, the Witch and the Wardrobe*. 6) Heroines of Faith and Courage: Princess Irene in *The Princess and the Goblin* and Lucy in *Prince Caspian*.

Guroian's book is a refresher course in using imagination as a teacher. This book is a pleasure to read. Hardcover. Code OX, $22.

**THE CHILDREN'S BOOK OF VIRTUES**, edited by William J. Bennett. There's an old joke about Preacher John, who was so excited about his new posting that although only one farmer came for the Sunday service, he just had to deliver his whole sermon. Afterward, Preacher John eagerly ran to the door to shake the farmer's hand and thank him for coming. When asked how he liked the sermon the farmer replied, "Well, it was just fine, but if I went out to feed the cows and only one showed up, I wouldn't give her the whole load."

I've heard a lot of praise for this book. I agree with everyone who says the stories included are excellent literature, effective, and beneficial teaching tools. The illustrations are beautiful. However commendable, though, a story or two each day with a moral or lesson is enough, in my opinion. More than this is gluttony. I'd gladly buy this book and use it, but with great restraint. Hardcover. Code BT, $19.95.

**INTRODUCING LITERARY GENRES: A Tapestry of Reading,** by Terry Zahniser McDermid. This book presents an excellent concept. It's too bad it was written for teachers. If you ignore the educational jargon and references to motivation and class work you can have a ball with this book. Beginning with the section about different types of media, this book has unit studies on biography, mystery, drama, fairy tales, romance, mythology, science fiction, and research. Clearly outlined goals, specialized vocabulary section, information about each genre, projects for individuals and groups, and suggested reading lists all make this resource easy to use. *Ages 9 to 14. Code HC, $10.95.*

**Children's Classics**. I don't want to get into a long tirade about cultural literacy for toddlers (not here, anyway), so I'll just say I'm glad most of these stories were a part of my early childhood, and, of course, we made sure not to deprive our own children of them. Each has large colorful illustrations. Ideal for reading aloud, pointing at things, and talking over details. Ages 3, 4, 5 to ?. Code TRL, $4.95 each. If you build a library in sets of ten we can give you a discount off the original price. Your choice of 10 for $40, plus $3.50 shipping.

**Aladdin and His Wonderful Lamp**
**Beauty and the Beast**
**Cinderella**
**The Elves and the Shoemaker**
**The Gingerbread Boy**
**Henny Penny**
**The House That Jack Built**
**Goldilocks and the Three Bears**
**The Hare and the Tortoise**
**Jack and the Beanstalk**
**John Henry**
**Johnny Appleseed**
**The Legend of Sleepy Hollow**
**The Lion and the Mouse**
**Little Red Riding Hood**
**The Nutcracker**
**Paul Bunyan**
**Rapunzel**
**Rumpelstiltskin**
**The Tale of Peter Rabbit**
**The Three Little Pigs**
**Thumbelina**
**Tom Thumb**
**The Town Mouse and the Country Mouse**
**The Twelve Days of Christmas**
**The Ugly Duckling**
**Odysseus and Cyclops**
**Pegasus the Winged Horse**
**Perseus and Medusa**
**Theseus and the Minotaur**

**REBUS TREASURY**, compiled by the editors of *Highlights for Children* magazine. I think technically I should put this with the early learning books, but I also think it should be used by beginning readers, so here it is. A collection of one-page stories with rebus pictures followed by the word written out. Very young children will quickly learn to read the pictures, and older children can read the words using the pictures to help them if needed. The illustrations are expressive and playful. *Ages 3 to 7. Code BMP, $4.95.*

**LEARN-TO-READ TREASURE HUNTS**, by Steve Cohen (with help from his son Peter, age 10). This is a great idea for kids ages 5 to 7, or for whenever your kids are beginning to read. 50 treasure hunts with helpful hints for parents. I don't agree with some of the information given in the introduction, but it's easily ignored. The games are fun and easy to do. Includes 50 reward stickers. Code WKM, $8.95.

**A FAIRY TALE UPDATED —**

**THE FOURTH LITTLE PIG**, by Teresa Celsi. Yep, there is a *fourth* little pig, and SHE shows the boys that hiding and cowering is a waste of time ...
**THE THREE LITTLE JAVELINAS**, by Susan Lowell. Three little Texican pigs, living in homes made of tumbleweeds and cactus ribs, escape the hungry wolf by hiding in their wise sister's strong adobe house ...

Where would you buy these? Beats me. I didn't read that far.

**BRER RABBIT**, collected from the stories of Joel Chandler Harris and retold by David Borgenicht; every page boldly and delightfully illustrated by Don Daily. In seven of these classic tales — full of fun, trickery, and laughter — you'll meet Brer Rabbit, Brer Fox, Brer Wolf, Brer Turtle, the Tar Baby, and more great characters. This is an oversized 10x13" hardcover book; a great gift, with a free color poster. The illustrations are as much fun as the stories. Ages 4 to 8, or maybe 80 or 180. Code RP, $9.98.

**UNCLE REMUS: His Songs and His Sayings**, by Joel Chandler Harris, with 28 original illustrations, in dialect as originally published in 1880. Like Disney's movie *Song of the South* (no longer available because of "political correctness issues"), this wonderful character — along with Brer Rabbit, Brer Fox, Brer Bear, and others — is almost impossible to find anymore. The spunky and quick-witted Brer Rabbit still has lessons we can learn from, and the tales have amused people for years. 256 pages. Code BT, $13.95.

**Fun With Words**. It's sometimes difficult to help children understand that English can be fun to use and that it's possible to play with it. These two wacky books have page-turning storylines and inventive meter and rhymes. Neither qualifies as great or classic literature, but they earn their place here for their success in combining playfulness with language. Ages 7 and up. Code EDC, $4.95 each. **PIRATE McGREW AND HIS NAUTICAL CREW** or **THE FANTASTIC ADVENTURES OF DRACULA'S DENTURES**



**GRANDMOTHER'S PIGEON**, by Louise Erdrich, illustrated by Jim LaMarche. This is a charming, poignant, magical tale to enliven the imagination. The colorful illustrations draw you right into this family story. Ages 8 to 10, but this will be a favorite for the whole family. Read it with pleasure to a 6-year-old, and older children will enjoy reading it aloud to younger ones. Code LB, $7.99.

**MORNING GIRL**, by Michael Dorris. Winner of the Scott O'Dell Award for historical fiction, this is great children's literature. It passes my test for being creatively written with language that excites the senses, creates images, elicits a new view of the world, and is thought-provoking for young readers and adults. This is a coming-of-age story of a brother and sister growing up on a Bahamian island at the time Columbus arrived. Ages 8 to 13 and you. Code LB, $4.99.

**SEES BEHIND TREES**, by Michael Dorris. I was even more impressed with this book than the one above. The language, even though written for children, evokes poetic images and probes deeply into the human psyche through the story of this boy's search for identity. *Ages 9 to 14 to adult. Code LB, $4.99.*

**DREAMBIRDS**, by David Ogden, powerfully illustrated by Jody Bergsma. The tale of a native boy in search of his gift from a dreambird. After many trials he finds it is the power of his own spirit. A book to grow with. Powerful story and incredible, beautiful, and symbolic illustrations. The book begins with a quote from Chief Seattle dated 1855: "And when your children's children shall think themselves alone in the fields, the shops, upon the highway, or in the silence of the pathless woods, they will not be alone." A favorite of mine. Ages 8 to adult. Hardcover. Code IA, $16.95.

**FUN IS A FEELING**, by Chara Curtis, illustrated by Cynthia Aldrich. I didn't get very far into this book before I said, "Wow!" A book for every child, young or old. What is fun? What about the times when nothing feels like fun? Where does this feeling of fun come from, and how can it be found? As you read the book you'll discover: "Fun isn't *something* or *somewhere* or *who*. It's a feeling of joy that lives inside of you." An exploration of feelings and perspectives that even young children will understand, with full-color illustrations that are extensions of the text and can take you beyond the written word. Okay! I know you read this in "Early Learning," but I couldn't help myself. I really love this book, and all my grandchildren have or will have copies of their very own. Hardcover (good thing, because this one will see a lot of use). Code IA, $15.95. (Also look for *All I See Is Part of Me* in "Philosophy and Religion.")

Publishers often have free bookmarks or posters to promote their books, particularly new titles. If you find a book you really enjoy, try writing to the Children's Book Marketing Department, care of the publisher, and ask if they have any related free material.

**I WAS BORN ABOUT 10,000 YEARS AGO**. Based on the song by the same title, this is a journey through time, simply written and creatively illustrated by Steven Kellogg. It will stimulate the imagination, tickle your funny bones, and bring a smile to your face. A treat for all ages. The music and words are in the back. I love it! (If you must be academic, then it is a good introduction to creative writing.) Ages 4 and up. Code WM, $5.95.

**CHARLOTTE'S WEB** and two other classics by E.B. White. Boxed set. *Charlotte's Web* is the wonderful blend of fantasy and reality in which Wilbur, a lovable and terrific pig, is rescued from a cruel and certain fate by a beautiful, intelligent spider named Charlotte. *Stuart Little*, an adventurous and heroic little mouse with very human qualities, searches for his lost friend, the lovely bird Margalo. Full of wit, wisdom, and amusement. *The Trumpet of the Swan* tells the eventful life of Louis, a voiceless trumpeter swan, from hatchling to contented fatherhood. Wonderful humor and beautiful depiction of nature, beauty, relationships, and the passing of time. Kids and adults! Wonderful Garth Williams illustrations. Code BT, $17.95.

**DADDY'S ROOMMATE, HEATHER HAS TWO MOMMIES,** and **ASHA'S MUMS**. No, you won't find these titles for sale in *The Home School Source Book*, but you can find them in many public schools that have banned *Snow White, Huckleberry Finn, The Wizard of Oz*, and the Bible.

---

*I don't know which is more discouraging, literature or chickens.* — E.B. White

---

**BEN AND ME: An Astonishing Life of Benjamin Franklin by His Good Mouse Amos**, discovered, edited, and illustrated by Robert Lawson. This remarkable manuscript is a children's classic, now 60 years in print. Amos's account doesn't exactly fit our accepted view of Ben Franklin, but then he has a very unique perspective. Fun to read aloud, and perfect for kids about 8 to read themselves. Generously illustrated with whimsical drawings. Code LB, $5.95.

**The Adventures of Tintin**, by Hergé. Humor, excitement, and touches of history and geography with Tintin, the world-famous boy reporter, and his dog, Snowy, as they face international bad guys of all kinds — pirates, jewel thieves, smugglers, and spies. Large colorful cartoons, with wonderful dialogue. For children (about 10 and up) and adults. They're comical books — but they're not "comic books." They're literate, intelligent, and imaginative. Code LB, $9.95 each, 3 for $27, 5 for $40.

**THE BLACK ISLAND**
**THE BLUE LOTUS**
**THE CALCULUS AFFAIR**
**THE CASTAFIORE EMERALD**
**CIGARS OF THE PHARAOH**
**THE CRAB WITH THE GOLDEN CLAWS**
**DESTINATION MOON**
**EXPLORERS ON THE MOON**
**FLIGHT 714**
**KING OTTOKAR'S SCEPTRE**
**LAND OF BLACK GOLD**
**PRISONERS OF THE SUN**
**RED RACKHAM'S TREASURE**
**THE RED SEA SHARKS**
**SECRET OF THE UNICORN**
**SEVEN CRYSTAL BALLS**
**SHOOTING STAR**
**TINTIN AND THE BROKEN EAR**
**TINTIN AND THE PICAROS**
**TINTIN IN AMERICA**
**TINTIN IN TIBET**

I like the Tintin books a lot. I like the Asterix books by Goscinny and Uderzo even better, but it's too late in the book production to do more than mention them now. Check them out at your library. We can get them for you if you find you can't live without them.

**Tarzan**. If you've seen Tarzan in the movies or Saturday-morning cartoons, but haven't read any of the original books by Edgar Rice Burroughs, then you don't know Tarzan. When Derek was ten, he wrote this review:

"The books about Tarzan are very good. I like the idea of a baby growing up with a tribe of apes and learning to swing through the trees. There is a big difference between the Tarzan in the books and in the cartoons. In the cartoons they make him look like an uneducated man. In the books he is very intelligent, and he can speak other languages besides that of the apes and English. His real name is John Clayton. Tarzan means Whiteskin in Ape language. The adventures he has are very exciting. He finds lots of lost civilizations, and sometimes he gets caught and has to figure out a way to escape. Sometimes he finds other people who want to escape too, and he helps them, unless they are burglars or something like that; then he just leaves them there."

Derek has enjoyed Tarzan as much as I did when I was a boy, and a few of our Tarzan books were my father's when he was a boy. I've reread a few of them recently, and I still enjoy them. The author never visited Africa, so you won't learn many "facts" from these books, but you'll enjoy the drama and adventure. Ages 10 to adult.

In case Donn and Derek haven't sold you on the idea of reading at least a few of these books, I'm going to add my two cents' worth. When Donn and I began our life together he introduced me to John Gould and his humorous and witty writing about "Down East" country living. Next he introduced me to Tarzan. Donn felt I would be uneducated if I had only the movie of Tarzan in my head. I found Burroughs very wordy sometimes, but fell in love with Tarzan and read all the books at the age of 19. If you enjoy the books, or would prefer listening to reading, write and ask about Tarzan on cassette tape. They're not listed here, but we have a lot of Tarzan stories on tape that we got for the kids to listen to at bedtime (or whenever), and we'd be happy to share them.

**TARZAN OF THE APES** (his origin). Code RH, $5.99.

**THE RETURN OF TARZAN**. Code RH, $5.99.

**THE BEASTS OF TARZAN and THE SON OF TARZAN** (available only as a 2-in-1 book). Code BAL, $5.99.

**TARZAN, LORD OF THE JUNGLE and TARZAN AND THE LOST EMPIRE** (available only as a 2-in-1 book). Code BAL, $5.99.

**TARZAN AT THE EARTH'S CORE and TARZAN THE INVINCIBLE** (available only as a 2-in-1 book). Code BAL, $5.99.

**TARZAN THE TRIUMPHANT and TARZAN AND THE CITY OF GOLD** (available only as a 2-in-1 book). Code BAL, $5.99.

**TARZAN**, retold by Robert D. San Souci, illustrated by Michael McCurdy. I wasn't going to include this book because I felt Burroughs' original should be read, but I made the mistake of opening the book just to take a peek. San Souci is a long-standing Tarzan fan, and it shows in his very careful retelling of the original story of Tarzan. All the essentials of the story are here — the circumstances of Tarzan's birth and his being raised by apes, learning to read and write, and discovering he is different from the apes — all without Burroughs' verbiage. Full-page illustrations on every other page complement the text. You can read this to an adventurous 5-year-old, and a 7- or 8-year-old reader can read this to himself. Interesting notes by the author on the last pages explain how he came to write this book and give some history of the original books. Hardcover. Code LB, $15.99.

**The Little House on the Prairie Books** — See "History and Biography" or the index.

**ALICE ROSE AND SAM**, by Kathryn Lasky. This is great fun to read. Alice Rose's mother dies, leaving Alice with a loving but rather neglectful journalist father in a mining boomtown during the Civil War era. Alice meets Sam Clemens and the plot quickens into an adventure story that relates to the Civil War, immigrant Chinese, crooked lawyers, bribery, and murder. This book isn't exactly a historical novel, but Sam Clemens, better known as Mark Twain, and many other characters are based on fact. Lasky makes advantageous use of Twain's own words, so although the story is mostly fiction, the reader comes away with a good picture of Twain as a person. Ages 9 to 12. Code LB, $5.99.

**ISLAND OF THE BLUE DOLPHINS**, by Scott O'Dell. A young Indian girl, stranded on a rocky Pacific island for 18 years, learns the art of survival — and more. This book was a winner of the 1960 Newbery Medal, and continues to attract fan mail thanking the author for the story. Exciting, inspiring, and thought-provoking for children and adults. Code BDD, $5.50.

**JACK AND JILL**, by Louisa May Alcott. Another story with all the charm of *Little Women* and Alcott's other stories. Two inseparable friends overcome difficulties that change their lives. Ages 10 and up. Code LB, $8.95.

**PETEY**, by Ben Mikaelsen. An exceptional book about a young boy's experiences when he moves to a new town and finds himself defending Petey, a withered old man, from bullies. It is also Petey's story: born in the 1920s with cerebral palsy and growing up misdiagnosed as mentally disabled. This is a story of friendship, self-discovery, and the triumph of the human spirit over physical obstacles. Ages 10 and up. Code LB, $5.99.

**THE GIVER**, by Lois Lowry. My granddaughter lent this book to me with high words of praise and made me promise to give it back. When it comes to books I always take her recommendations seriously; she's a voracious reader with excellent taste in books. This story of a young boy takes place in a community where there is no pain or fear. The setting sounds idyllic. At age 12 each person is carefully selected for his life's work — and given no choice. It all sounds so good, until Jonas is old enough to begin his training for his life's role and learns the truth. An exceptional book and one to grow on. Excellent for reading aloud and discussing or for private pleasure. I didn't want this book to end, and I wish there were a sequel. This book is a Horn Book Honor Book, an American Library Association Best Book for Young Adults, winner of the Regina Medal, and a Newbery Medal winner. Ages 12 to adult. Code RH, $5.99.

The **Nancy Drew mystery series** is now back in print with a new modern look, but with the same wholesome characters and reliably exciting reading. I read and enjoyed these books as a young teen, and our girls enjoyed them too. Good mysteries without the horror and gore that pervades too many modern adventure stories. Nancy and her friends solve mysteries that will intrigue and delight girls ages 10 and up. Code SS, $5.99 each. I have a list of 149 titles. If you want more than the five listed here, send a #10 SASE and request the list.

**THE BUNGALOW MYSTERY**
**THE HIDDEN STAIRCASE**
**THE MYSTERY AT LILAC INN**
**THE SECRET OF SHADOW RANCH**
**THE SECRET OF THE OLD CLOCK**

**Great Classic Literature Illustrated by N.C. Wyeth.** These familiar classics are all wonderful reading and deserve places in every family's home simply on their own merits as literature (and, sometimes, as historical fiction). The handsome bindings and beautiful paintings by famed illustrator N.C. Wyeth (1882-1945) make the books in this series handsome, heirloom additions to any home library, as well as excellent holiday and birthday gifts. They're a little expensive, but everyone in our family — including Mom and Dad — has read them at least twice and has browsed in them several times, making them worthwhile investments in lasting enjoyment, and I'm sure the books will be passed to our grandchildren with great mutual pleasure. (Incidentally, older editions, identical in every way except the date of publication, now sell in rare book stores for as much as $50 and much more if in very good condition.) Code SS, $27.95 each. Specify N.C. Wyeth edition with the title.

**THE BOY'S KING ARTHUR**, edited by Sidney Lanier from Malory's *Le Morte D'Arthur*.
**KIDNAPPED**, by Robert Louis Stevenson
**ROBIN HOOD**, by Paul Creswick
**ROBINSON CRUSOE**, by Daniel Defoe
**THE YEARLING**, by Marjorie Kinnan Rawlings
See "History and Biography" for *The Black Arrow* and *The Last of the Mohicans*.

**Young Reader Classics**, all unabridged reproductions of the originals by Howard Pyle, with illustrations. Code DV.

**ARABIAN NIGHTS**. $8.95
**CHAMPIONS OF THE ROUND TABLE**. $9.95
**ROBIN HOOD**. $9.95
**THE STORY OF SIR LANCELOT AND HIS COMPANIONS**. $9.95
**THE STORY OF KING ARTHUR AND HIS KNIGHTS**. $9.95
**THE STORY OF THE GRAIL and THE PASSING OF KING ARTHUR**. $10.95

**THE LEGEND OF KING ARTHUR**, retold by David Borgenicht; a young reader's edition of Howard Pyle's original classic. This edition will whet the appetite of adventurous youngsters. The tale is classic and the color illustrations on each page bring the text to life. Swords, sorcery, Merlin the magician, knights, and suspense — you'll find them all. Ages 9 to 12. Oversized 10x13" hardcover. Code RP, $9.98.

**Literature-related coloring books**. All 8x11", 48 pages. Code DV, $2.95 each. Specify that you want the coloring books, please.
**BLACK BEAUTY**
**KING ARTHUR**
**TARZAN**
**TREASURE ISLAND**

**LITTLE WOMEN PAPER DOLLS**. Reusable full-color stickers. Code DV-S, $3.95.

**Fantasy and Adventure.** Classic stories retold (abridged) for ages 10 and up. Well-written with dramatic color illustrations. Code EDC. (Write for current prices if you want a hardcover gift edition; they're either $16 or $17 each.)
**DR. JEKYLL AND MR. HYDE**. $9.95
**DRACULA**. $9.95
**FRANKENSTEIN**. $9.95
**KING ARTHUR**. $8.95
**ROBIN HOOD**. $9.95

**Great Horse Stories by Marguerite Henry**. More than "just horse stories," these books have themes relevant in many ways to everyday life, with interesting history, geography, nature, and animal lore woven into the stories. All four of our kids have read these books several times. Donn forgot to mention that I read them too — once when I was growing up and again when we got them for the kids. All for ages 12 and up, with the exception of *Brighty*, which is written for kids 8 and up. Code SS.
**BRIGHTY OF THE GRAND CANYON**. A story based on fact about a little burro who helped to catch a criminal. $4.99.
**JUSTIN MORGAN HAD A HORSE**. The true story of the first Morgan colt. $4.99.
**KING OF THE WIND**. Newbery Medal winner about the legendary Godolphin Aragon, forefather of Man O' War and other great thoroughbreds. $4.50.
**MISTY OF CHINCOTEAGUE**. An exciting story set on the picturesque island off Virginia. $4.99.
Boxed set: **MISTY OF CHINCOTEAGUE; STORMY, MISTY'S FOAL**; and **SEA STAR: ORPHAN OF CHINCOTEAGUE** (Stormy's foal). $13.50.

**THE CHRONICLES OF NARNIA**, by C.S. Lewis. Great entertainment and philosophy. Classic struggle between good and evil. Our kids have read and reread these books many times. (So has Jean.) Boxed set of seven titles: **The Magician's Nephew; The Lion, the Witch and the Wardrobe; The Horse and His Boy; Prince Caspian; The Voyage of the "Dawn Treader"; The Silver Chair;** and **The Last Battle**. Illustrated by Pauline Baynes. Ages 10 and up. Code HC, $34.65. Also available on tape. Code HC, $50.

**NOT A TAME LION: The Spiritual Legacy of C.S. Lewis**, by Terry W. Glaspey. A thoughtful look at a man whose series, *The Chronicles of Narnia*, has delighted young and old, and who inspired and influenced many with his other perceptive writings. The book has three sections: a biography, his thoughts in his own words with commentary by the author, and his legacy. Listings of Lewis's writings are at the end of the book. For astute teens and adults. Hardcover, 240 pages. Code HBSA, $14.95.

**THE DARK IS RISING**, by Susan Cooper. A classic series on par with the *Chronicles of Narnia*. Like C.S. Lewis, Susan Cooper writes about the age-old struggle between good and evil, the light and the dark forces of human nature. Cooper is a bit more open and obvious about the struggle, but it doesn't spoil this series even a little bit; it just makes its message easier to understand for early teens reading this on their own, and younger children being read to will need less coaxing to get the message and symbolism. A good introduction to reading for symbols and meaning. This series takes place in the British Isles and makes good use of English and Celtic myth, legend, and tradition. A pleasure for the whole family if you read it aloud. Suitable for the whole family but best for around 12 and up on their own. (I just reread the whole series this year and loved it. Somehow I missed reading it when the children were all home. Cathy remembers loving the whole series.) Set includes six books: **Over Sea, Under Stone; The Dark Is Rising; Greenwitch; The Grey King; Dawn of Fear**; and **Silver on the Tree**. Code SS, complete set $19.95, plus $2.50 shipping.

**TO KILL A MOCKINGBIRD**, by Harper Lee. A classic study of personalities, prejudice, and good and evil in a small Southern town in the mid-1930s, as seen through the eyes of a young girl. A book to grow with. I've read it three times and enjoy it more with each reading. Ages 14 and up. Code LB, $6.99.

**GREAT IDEAS THAT HAVE SHAPED OUR WORLD —** Excellent cassette programs presenting the ideas of Thomas Paine, Thomas Jefferson, Henry David Thoreau, William Lloyd Garrison, Adam Smith, John Stuart Mill, Edmund Burke, Alexander Hamilton, Thomas Hobbes, John Locke, Alexis de Tocqueville, and others. See "History and Biography."

**EARLY AMERICAN WRITING**, edited by Giles Gunn. Drawing material from journals and diaries, political documents, and religious sermons, this panoramic survey of early American life and literature includes such writings as Cherokee, Hopi, and other Amerindian genesis legends; narratives of discovery by Christopher Columbus and Amerigo Vespucci; and selections by John Smith, Anne Hutchinson, Chief Powhatan, Chief Tecumseh, Thomas Jefferson, Abigail Adams, and Phillis Wheatley. 720 pages. Code VP, $14.95.

*Back in print!* **MORE THAN HUMAN**, by Theodore Sturgeon. We recommend this novel to our kids as they reach the age of 16 or 17 — not just as a great story (which it is), but also for its moral and ethical implications. *Homo gestalt* seems to be the next step in human evolution, but is still in its infancy: a small group of social misfits, each with a certain psychic ability or power, including orphaned twins who can't talk but can disappear at will; the village idiot, whose strength seems to be in his eyes; a young girl who can move things with her mind; and a Mongoloid baby, whose computer-like brain holds them together. Together they are more powerful than any other being on earth — but, so far, *Homo gestalt* lacks the most human attribute — a conscience. Code VIN, $13.

Zenna Henderson wrote **THE ANYTHING BOX** years ago, and it is out of print. If you can find a copy you'll have a treasure chest of good science fiction reading. These short stories — on a great variety of themes — are delightful mind stretchers for everyone from 10 to 110. Our whole family loved this book, and our copy is falling apart. I've since found copies for everyone.

**Illustrated Classics**. Don't dismiss them because they're adaptations of the originals. Unlike most other "illustrated classics," such as those sometimes sold in stores along with other "comics," this series has very skillful abridgments of the original texts; the artwork is not obscured by fat speech balloons; and the text is not lettered by hand, but is printed in 11-point upper- and lower-case letters. They'll never replace the originals, of course — at least, we hope they won't — but they're good introductions and companions to the world's great literature, for adults as well as for children. For those who don't always have the time or inclination to read the originals, it's certainly better to read these illustrated, abridged versions than to dismiss them as "children's books" or "comic books," and continue through life without having much more than a vague idea of what the books are about. The artwork in the books is based on extensive research into the periods and locales. Because so many of the classic stories take place in periods and places with which most of us have little familiarity, it's often difficult to visualize the proper settings, no matter how skillfully the authors may have presented them; and, of course, many facets of everyday life were taken for granted at the time of writing, but have since become nearly forgotten. The artwork in these books gives us accurate images, adding a great deal to our understanding and enjoyment not only of these abridged versions, but also of the originals when we read them later. The pictures are black-and-white line drawings, on heavy opaque paper. Each book is about 64 pages, with a colorful cover, and has a short biographical note about the author. The reading level is approximately 5th grade, but our kids began reading them when they were about 8 years old, and still (many years later) enjoy reading them occasionally. Jean and I read them, too, and aren't offended by the simplified text. After all, at least 80 percent of the vocabulary most of us use daily is probably "5th grade." (And how many of these books have *you* been planning to read, and just haven't gotten around to it?) I have put an asterisk (*) in front of the titles that most particularly may be considered historical novels, whether or not they are based on actual incidents. To make a long, complicated story short, these books have changed publishers several times in the past couple of years, and the price has gone up each time. They are no longer $3 (their 1994 price). The current price is $4.95 each and you'll now get the best price buying from the publisher. Order from AGS (American Guidance Service), 4201 Woodland Rd., Circle Pines, MN 55014-1796; 800-328-2560; www.agsnet.com.

**PRIDE AND PREJUDICE**, by Jane Austen
**JANE EYRE**, by Charlotte Brontë
**WUTHERING HEIGHTS**, by Emily Brontë
**DON QUIXOTE**, by Miguel de Cervantes
**LORD JIM**, by Joseph Conrad
***THE LAST OF THE MOHICANS**, by James Fenimore Cooper
**THE RED BADGE OF COURAGE**, by Stephen Crane
**ROBINSON CRUSOE**, by Daniel Defoe
**A CHRISTMAS CAROL**, by Charles Dickens
***GREAT EXPECTATIONS**, by Charles Dickens
***OLIVER TWIST**, by Charles Dickens
***A TALE OF TWO CITIES**, by Charles Dickens
**CRIME AND PUNISHMENT**, by Fyodor Dostoevsky
**THE HOUND OF THE BASKERVILLES**, by Sir Arthur Conan Doyle
**SHERLOCK HOLMES**, by Sir Arthur Conan Doyle
***THE MAN IN THE IRON MASK**, by Alexandre Dumas
***THE THREE MUSKETEERS**, by Alexandre Dumas
**MUTINY ON THE BOUNTY**, by James Norman Hall and Charles Nordhoff
**RETURN OF THE NATIVE**, by Thomas Hardy
***THE HOUSE OF THE SEVEN GABLES**, by Nathaniel Hawthorne
***THE SCARLET LETTER**, by Nathaniel Hawthorne
**THE PRISONER OF ZENDA**, by Anthony Hope
***THE ILIAD**, by Homer
***THE ODYSSEY**, by Homer
***THE HUNCHBACK OF NOTRE DAME**, by Victor Hugo
**THE TURN OF THE SCREW**, by Henry James
***THE STORY OF MY LIFE**, by Helen Keller
**CAPTAINS COURAGEOUS**, by Rudyard Kipling
**THE CALL OF THE WILD**, by Jack London

**THE SEA WOLF**, by Jack London
**WHITE FANG**, by Jack London
**MOBY DICK**, by Herman Melville
***THE SCARLET PIMPERNEL**, by Baroness Orczy
**THE BEST OF EDGAR ALLAN POE**
**THE BEST OF O. HENRY**, by William S. Porter
***IVANHOE**, by Sir Walter Scott
**BLACK BEAUTY**, by Anna Sewell
**FRANKENSTEIN**, by Mary Shelley
**DR. JEKYLL AND MR. HYDE**, by Robert Louis Stevenson
***KIDNAPPED**, by Robert Louis Stevenson
***TREASURE ISLAND**, by Robert Louis Stevenson
**GULLIVER'S TRAVELS**, by Jonathan Swift
***THE ADVENTURES OF HUCKLEBERRY FINN**, by Mark Twain
**HEIDI**, by Johanna Spyri
***THE ADVENTURES OF TOM SAWYER**, by Mark Twain
**A CONNECTICUT YANKEE IN KING ARTHUR'S COURT**, by Mark Twain
**DRACULA**, by Bram Stoker
***AROUND THE WORLD IN 80 DAYS**, by Jules Verne
**JOURNEY TO THE CENTER OF THE EARTH**, by Jules Verne
**20,000 LEAGUES UNDER THE SEA**, by Jules Verne
***BEN HUR**, by Lew Wallace
**THE FOOD OF THE GODS**, by H.G. Wells
**THE INVISIBLE MAN**, by H.G. Wells
**THE TIME MACHINE**, by H.G. Wells
**THE WAR OF THE WORLDS**, by H.G. Wells
**SWISS FAMILY ROBINSON**, by Johann Wyss

Dad, you know these Illustrated Classics of Rudyard Kipling and Alexander Dumas and Jack London and James Fenimore Cooper? Those old writers sure could draw!

THRIFT BOOKS!

**Fairy Tales From Around the World**. Code DV, $1 each.
**The Boy Who Drew Cats and Other Japanese Fairy Tales**, by Lafcadio Hearn, et al.
**Chinese Fairy Tales**, by Frederick Herman Martens
**Favorite Celtic Fairy Tales**, by Joseph Jacobs
**Favorite Russian Fairy Tales**, by Arthur Ransome
**Irish Fairy Tales**, by Philip Smith
**Japanese Fairy Tales**, by Philip Smith
**Scottish Fairy Tales**, by Donald A. MacKenzie

**Young Children's Classics.** All unabridged unless otherwise stated. There are more stories for young children in "Early Learning." **NOTE:** A number of these titles have the same name and price. Therefore, **you need to state if the book you want is abridged or unabridged;** otherwise, we may send you the wrong edition. Code DV, $1 each.
**The Adventures of Pinocchio**, by Carlo Collodi
**Aesop's Fables**, by Aesop
**Aladdin and Other Tales of Arabian Nights**, by Philip Smith
**Alice in Wonderland**, by Lewis Carroll (abridged)
**Anne of Green Gables**, by Lucy Maud Montgomery (abridged)
**Beauty and the Beast and Other Fairy Tales**, by Marie Leprince De Beaumont and Charles Perrault
**Black Beauty**, by Anna Sewell (abridged)
**A Child's Garden of Verses**, by Robert Louis Stevenson
**A Christmas Carol**, by Charles Dickens
**Dog of Flanders**, by Ouida
**East O' the Sun and West O' the Moon and Other Fairy Tales**, by George Webbe Dasent, $2.
**The Elephant's Child and Other Just So Stories**, by Rudyard Kipling
**Favorite Poems of Childhood**, a collection
**Favorite Uncle Wiggily Animal Bedtime Stories**, by Howard Garis
**The Happy Prince and Other Fairy Tales**, by Oscar Wilde
**Heidi**, by Johanna Spyri (abridged)
**How the Leopard Got His Spots**, by Rudyard Kipling
**Huckleberry Finn**, by Mark Twain (abridged)
**Ivanhoe**, by Sir Walter Scott (abridged)
**Kidnapped**, by Robert Louis Stevenson (abridged)
**The Legend of Sleepy Hollow and Rip Van Winkle**, by Washington Irving
**The Little Mermaid**, by Hans Christian Andersen
**A Little Princess**, by Frances Hodgson Burnett (abridged)
**Mowgli Stories** (from *The Jungle Book*), by Rudyard Kipling
**Nonsense Poems**, by Edward Lear

**The Prince and the Pauper**, by Mark Twain (abridged)
**Robinson Crusoe**, by Daniel Defoe (abridged)
**The Secret Garden**, by Frances Hodgson Burnett (abridged)
**Selected Fables**, by Jean de La Fontaine (Aesop's fables)
**Sleeping Beauty and Other Fairy Tales**, by Wilhelm and Jacob Grimm
**The Story of Dr. Dolittle**, by Hugh Lofting
**The Story of Hercules**, by Bob Blaisdell
**The Story of King Arthur**, by Tom Crawford (abridged)

**The Story of Peter Pan**, by James M. Barrie and Daniel O'Connor
**The Story of Pocahontas**, by Brian Doherty
**Tarzan**, by Edgar Rice Burroughs (abridged)
**The Three Billy Goats Gruff and Other Read-Aloud Stories**, by Carolyn Sherwin Bailey
**The Three Musketeers**, by Alexandre Dumas (abridged)
**Tom Sawyer**, by Mark Twain (abridged)
**The Ugly Duckling and Other Fairy Tales**, by Hans Christian Andersen
**The Wizard of Oz**, by L. Frank Baum (abridged)
(More Thrift Classics listed in "Early Learning.")

**Thrift Editions for Young Adults and Adults.** Unabridged unless otherwise stated. Code DV, $1 each unless otherwise marked.
**12 Classic Ghost Stories**, by John Grafton. $2
**12 Classic Ghost Stories**, by Wilkie Collins, Henry James, Charles Dickens, Edgar Allan Poe, Robert Louis Stevenson, Rudyard Kipling, and more. $2
**5 Great Short Stories**, by Jack London
**6 Great Sherlock Holmes Stories**, by Sir Arthur Conan Doyle
**The Adventure of the Dancing Men and Others**, by Sir Arthur Conan Doyle
**Adventures of Don Quixote**, expertly retold for children, by Argentina Palacios
**Adventures of Huckleberry Finn**, by Mark Twain. $2
**Adventures of Tom Sawyer**, by Mark Twain. $2
**Alice's Adventures in Wonderland**, by Lewis Carroll
**Anne of Green Gables**, by Lucy Maud Montgomery. $2.50
**Around the World in 80 Days**, by Jules Verne. $1.50
**Beowulf**
**Black Beauty**, by Anna Sewell. $2
**Bulfinch's Greek and Roman Mythology**. $2.50
**Call of the Wild,** by Jack London. $2
**Captains Courageous,** by Rudyard Kipling. $2
**A Christmas Carol**, by Charles Dickens
**Civil War Stories**, by Ambrose Bierce
**Cricket on the Hearth and Other Christmas Stories,** by Charles Dickens
**Dr. Jekyll and Mr. Hyde,** by Robert Louis Stevenson
**Dog of Flanders,** by Ouida
**Dracula**, by Bram Stoker (abridged)
**Dracula**, by Bram Stoker. $2
**Favorite Greek Myths,** by Bob Blaisdell
**Favorite North American Indian Legends,** by Philip Smith
**Five Great Short Stories**, by Anton Chekhov
**Frankenstein**, by Mary Shelley (abridged)
**Frankenstein**, by Mary Shelley
**The Gift of the Magi and Others**, by O. Henry
**The Gold-Bug and Others**, by Edgar Allan Poe
**Great Short Stories by American Women**
**Gulliver's Travels**, by Jonathan Swift
**Heart of Darkness**, by Joseph Conrad
**Heidi**, by Johanna Spyri. $3.50.
**Hound of the Baskervilles**, by Sir Arthur Conan Doyle. $1.50
**House of Seven Gables**, by Nathaniel Hawthorne. $2
**Humorous Stories**, by Mark Twain
**The Hunchback of Notre Dame**, by Victor Hugo (abridged)
**The Iliad**, by Homer
**The Invisible Man**, by H.G. Wells
**The Island of Dr. Moreau**, by H.G. Wells, $1.50
**Ivanhoe**, by Sir Walter Scott (abridged)
**Jo's Boys**, by Louisa May Alcott
**The Jungle Book**, by Rudyard Kipling. $2
**Kidnapped**, by Robert Louis Stevenson. $2.50
**Little Men**, by Louisa May Alcott (abridged). $3
**Little Women**, by Louisa May Alcott. $3
**Lord Jim**, by Joseph Conrad
**The Man Who Would Be King and Others**, by Rudyard Kipling. $1.50
**The Marvelous Land of Oz**, by L. Frank Baum. $1.50
**The Moon and Sixpence**, by Somerset Maugham. $2
**North American Indian Tales**, by W.T. Larned
**Notes From the Underground**, by Fyodor Dostoevsky
**The Odyssey**, by Homer. $2
**O Pioneers!,** by Willa Cather
**Peter Pan**, by James M. Barrie. $2
**Portrait of the Artist as a Young Man**, by James Joyce. $2
**Pride and Prejudice**, by Jane Austen. $2

**The Prince and the Pauper**, by Mark Twain. $2
**The Railway Children**, by E. Nesbit. $2.50
**Red Badge of Courage**, by Stephen Crane
**The Republic**, by Plato. $2.50
**Rights of Man**, by Thomas Paine. $2
**Robin Hood**, by Robert Blaisdell. $2.50
**Robinson Crusoe**, by Daniel Defoe (abridged)
**Robinson Crusoe**, by Daniel Defoe. $2
**A Room With a View**, by E.M. Forster. $2
**The Scarlet Letter**, by Nathaniel Hawthorne. $2
**Sea Wolf**, by Jack London. $2
**The Secret Garden**, by Frances Hodgson Burnett. $2.50
**Sense and Sensibility**, by Jane Austen. $2
**Short Stories**, by Louisa May Alcott
**Siddhartha**, by Hermann Hesse. $1.50
**Silas Marner**, by George Eliot. $1.50
**Story of Hercules**, by Robert Blaisdell
**The Story of the Nutcracker**, by E.T.A. Hoffmann (abridged)
**A Tale of Two Cities**, by Charles Dickens (abridged)
**A Tale of Two Cities**, by Charles Dickens. $2
**Tales of Terror and Detection**, by Edgar Allan Poe
**Tarzan**, by Edgar Rice Burroughs (abridged)
**Tarzan of the Apes**, by Edgar Rice Burroughs. $2
**The Three Musketeers**, by Alexandre Dumas (abridged)
**Through the Looking-Glass**, by Lewis Carroll. $1.50
**Thus Spake Zarathustra**, by Friedrich Nietzsche. $2
**The Time Machine**, by H.G. Wells
**Toby Tyler**, by James Otis. $2
**Treasure Island**, by Robert Louis Stevenson. $1.50
**Turn of the Screw**, by Henry James
**War of the Worlds**, by H.G. Wells
**Where Angels Fear to Tread**, by E.M. Forster
**White Fang**, by Jack London
**Wind in the Willows**, by Kenneth Grahame. $2
**Wit and Wisdom From Poor Richard's Almanack**, by Benjamin Franklin
**Wonderful Wizard of Oz**, by L. Frank Baum. $1.50
**Wuthering Heights**, by Emily Brontë. $2
**The Yellow Wallpaper and Others**, by Charlotte Perkins Gilman

**BEST DEAL ON CHILDREN'S BOXED SETS AND BOXED SETS FOR OLDER READERS**

**BEST DEAL ON CHILDREN'S BOXED SETS**

All code DV.

**BEST LOVED CHILDREN'S STORIES**
*Hunchback of Notre Dame, Pocahontas, Beauty and the Beast, Little Mermaid, Pinocchio, Cinderella, Sleeping Beauty.* $7.

**BEST WORKS OF MARK TWAIN**
*Huckleberry Finn, Tom Sawyer, Humorous Stories, Mysterious Stranger and Other Stories.* $6.

**CLASSIC NOVELS FOR YOUNG READERS**
*Alice's Adventures in Wonderland, Treasure Island, Call of the Wild, Adventures of Huckleberry Finn.* $5.50.

**FAIRY TALES FROM MANY LANDS**
*Favorite Russian Tales, Irish Fairy Tales, Japanese Fairy Tales, Favorite Celtic Tales, North American Indian Legends.* $5.

**FAVORITE CHILDREN'S STORIES**
*The Secret Garden, Black Beauty, Aladdin and More Arabian Nights Stories, Story of Peter Pan, Beauty and the Beast and Other Fairy Tales.* $5.

**GREAT ADVENTURE NOVELS FOR CHILDREN**
*Tarzan, Tom Sawyer, Robinson Crusoe, Kidnapped, The Three Musketeers, The Story of King Arthur, Robin Hood.* $7.

**JACK LONDON: FAVORITE NOVELS AND STORIES**
*The Call of the Wild, White Fang,* and five others. 3 volumes, $3.

**5 CHILDREN'S THRIFT CLASSICS**
*Ugly Duckling and Other Fairy Tales, Favorite Poems of Childhood, Sleeping Beauty and Other Fairy Tales, Adventures of Peter Cottontail, The Happy Prince and Others.* $5.

**OLD MOTHER WEST WIND AND 6 OTHER STORIES**, by Thornton Burgess. Gentle lessons from the Green Forest about wildlife and the environment. $7.

**SIX FAVORITE NOVELS FOR GIRLS**. Classic stories about spunky girls. All abridged in $5\frac{1}{2}$x$8\frac{1}{4}$-inch format, illustrated. *Little Women, The Wizard of Oz, A Little Princess, The Secret Garden, Anne of Green Gables, Heidi.* A total of 576 pages! $6.

**BOXED SETS FOR OLDER READERS**

All code DV.

**5 PLAYS OF SHAKESPEARE**
*Macbeth, Hamlet, Julius Caesar, A Midsummer Night's Dream,* and *Romeo and Juliet.* 5 volumes, $5

**26 GREAT TALES OF TERROR AND THE SUPERNATURAL**
Sheridan LeFanu, Henry James, Edgar Allan Poe, John Grafton, Robert Louis Stevenson, H.G. Wells, and more. 6 volumes, $6

**36 SHORT STORIES BY AMERICAN WOMEN**
Louisa May Alcott, Willa Cather, Kate Chopin, Edith Wharton, and more. 5 volumes, $5

**47 GREAT SHORT STORIES**
Poe, Chekhov, de Maupassant, Gogol, O. Henry, Twain, and more. 6 volumes, $6

**GREAT AFRICAN-AMERICAN WRITERS**
Frederick Douglass, W.E.B. Du Bois, Washington's *Up From Slavery,* Johnson's *Autobiography of an Ex-Colored Man, The Narrative of Sojourner Truth,* and more. 7 volumes, $9

**GREAT AMERICAN NOVELS**
*Red Badge of Courage,* Stephen Crane; *The Scarlet Letter,* Nathaniel Hawthorne; *Ethan Frome,* Edith Wharton; *Adventures of Huckleberry Finn,* Mark Twain, *The Turn of the Screw,* Henry James. 5 volumes, $7

**GREAT MODERN WRITERS**
E.M. Forster, James Joyce, Franz Kafka, Thomas Mann, Gertrude Stein. 5 volumes, $8.50

**NON-FICTION THRIFT BOOKS**

Code DV, $1 each unless otherwise marked.

**The Devil's Dictionary**, by Ambrose Bierce

**Narrative of the Life of Frederick Douglass**, by Frederick Douglass

**Souls of Black Folk**, by W.E.B. Du Bois. $2

**Self-Reliance and Other Essays**, by Ralph Waldo Emerson

**Autobiography of Benjamin Franklin.** $1.50

**Totem and Taboo**, by Sigmund Freud. $2

**The Story of My Life**, by Helen Keller

**The Prince**, by Niccolò Machiavelli

**Meditations**, by Marcus Aurelius. $1.50

**Utopia**, by Sir Thomas More. $1.50

**Common Sense**, by Thomas Paine

**The Trial and Death of Socrates**, by Plato

**Civil Disobedience**, by Henry David Thoreau

**Walden, or Life in the Woods**, by Henry David Thoreau. $2

**The Narrative of Sojourner Truth**, by Sojourner Truth

**Up From Slavery**, by Booker T. Washington. $2

**Buying Books Cheaply Without Being Cheap** — Our home has thousands of books, and our car — I mean, our pickup, now that the girls have all moved out and Derek has his own car — is trained to stop at all lawn and garage sales, right next to the book tables. We usually live well below the poverty level, subsisting on a very small business income, occasional outside jobs, and our own home-raised food, so we're always alert for bargains. However, one of the reasons we're so poor in other kinds of material wealth is that we're rich in books. Mixed in with our 25-cent bargains are many books that have cost $10, $20, or $30, and a few at twice that price. If we see a book we want but wince at the price, we can: 1) wait for it to come out in paperback, and hope we still want it by then; 2) borrow it from the library and return it in two weeks; 3) go without; or 4) cut financial corners on something else and buy the book. Sometimes the corners have already been cut for some other purpose, but usually we're able to discover the money somewhere. Our kids have read and reread hundreds of books we own partly because they had easy access to them and partly because they, too, enjoy ownership of books. Just seeing a familiar, favorite book on the shelf can bring back memories of enjoyment. The classics with illustrations by N.C. Wyeth cost $20 to $25, and are good examples of our occasional extravagant purchases. They make great gifts, and are far more enjoyable than their cheaper counterparts. If you find one of these books at a garage sale, consider yourself lucky. My brother, who buys and sells antiques and rare books, easily sells older copies of them for $40 or more. The value of many things, including books, is often beyond price. We look for bargains, and try to buy what we want as cheaply as we can, but we don't want to become so fanatic about saving money that we miss the enjoyment or information in a few expensive books now and then.

---

*This will never be a civilized country until we expend more money for books than we do for chewing gum.* — Elbert Hubbard

---

If there is an out-of-print book you really want, write to David Reed Books, P.O. Box 635, Brattleboro, VT 05301; 802-257-4253; davereed@sover.net. (Yes, it's a plug for the rest of the family — Donn's brother. Service is great!)

**TWO THOUSAND AND TWO GREAT BOOKS FOR EVERY BOOK LOVER**, by Thomas Craughwell. Don't know what to read? What book to get on a particular topic for someone else? In this book you'll find 2,002 books reviewed and indexed by subject, title, and author. Good reference for grown-ups. Code WKM, $14.98.

**From the Modern Library and Everyman's Library**. Classic literature in well-made, attractive, hardcover books at moderate prices. When ordering, please specify "Modern/Everyman's Library" and the full title. Code RH.

**Anna Karenina**, by Leo Tolstoy. $22
**Arabian Nights**, by Richard Francis Burton. $20.50
**Basic Writings of C.G. Jung**. $19.50
**Basic Writings of Friedrich Nietzsche**. $21
**Basic Writings of Sigmund Freud**. $21
**Best Short Stories of O. Henry**. $20.50
**The Brothers Karamazov**, by Fyodor Dostoevsky. $21
**Bulfinch's Mythology**. $22
**The Canterbury Tales**, by Geoffrey Chaucer. $18.50
**Catch-22**, by Joseph Heller. $20
**City of God**, by St. Augustine. $21
**Complete Comedies of Shakespeare**. $21.50
**Complete Poetry and Prose**, by John Donne. $20
**Complete Tales and Poems,** by Edgar Allan Poe. $20
**Crime and Punishment**, by Fyodor Dostoevsky. $18.50
**Decline and Fall of the Roman Empire**, by Edward Gibbon. 3 volumes, $23 each
**Dr. Faustus**, by Thomas Mann. $18.50
**English Philosophers From Bacon to Mill**. $21
**European Philosophers: Descartes to Nietzsche**. $22
**Fire Next Time**, by James Baldwin. $14.50
**Frankenstein**, by Mary Shelley. $15.50
**Go Tell It on the Mountain**, by James Baldwin. $14.50
**Grapes of Wrath**, by John Steinbeck. $13
**Great Classical Myths**, by F.R.B. Godolphin. $15
**I, Claudius**, by Robert Graves. $13
**Interpretation of Dreams**, by Sigmund Freud. $16.50
**Introduction to Aristotle**. $19.50
**Invisible Man**, by Ralph Ellison. $19.50, paperback $12
**Leaves of Grass**, by Walt Whitman. $19.50
**Le Morte d'Arthur**, by Thomas Malory. $22
**Les Misérables**, by Victor Hugo. $22
**Life and Selected Writings of Thomas Jefferson**. $20
**Lincoln**, by Gore Vidal. $20.50
**The Magic Mountain**, by Thomas Mann. $19
**Maltese Falcon**, by Dashiell Hammett. Paperback $10
**Moby Dick**, by Herman Melville. $21
**Of Human Bondage**, by Somerset Maugham. $11.95, paperback $5.95
**Origin of Species and Descent of Man**, by Charles Darwin. $20
**Philosophy of Immanuel Kant**. $18.50
**Quiet American**, by Graham Greene. $13.50
**Selected Writings of Ralph Waldo Emerson**. $22
**Slaughterhouse-Five**, by Kurt Vonnegut. $22.95, paperback $6.50
**A Tale of Two Cities,** by Charles Dickens. $17.50
**Thus Spake Zarathustra**, by Friedrich Nietzsche. $15.95
**Tragedies of Shakespeare**. $22
**Ulysses**, by James Joyce. $21, paperback $17
**Uncle Tom's Cabin**, by Harriet Beecher Stowe. $20
**Varieties of Religious Experience**, by William James. $18.50
**Walden and Other Writings**, by Henry David Thoreau. $19.95
**War and Peace**, by Leo Tolstoy. $24
**Wealth of Nations**, by Adam Smith. $23
**Wisdom of Confucius**. $15.50
**Wisdom of Lao Tse**. $15.50
**Wuthering Heights**, by Emily Brontë. $16.50

Some other excellent classics in paperback.

**Animal Farm**, by George Orwell. Code PNG, $9.95.
**1984**, by George Orwell. Code BDD, $5.95.
**Brave New World**, by Aldous Huxley. Code HC, $11.
**Catcher in the Rye**, by J.D. Salinger. Code LB, $5.99.
**From Here to Eternity**, by James Jones. Code BDD, $13.95.
**The Great Gatsby**, by F. Scott Fitzgerald. Code SS, $11.
**Lord of the Flies**, by William Golding. Code PNG, $6.95.
**Native Son**, by Richard Wright. Code HC, $12.
**On the Road**, by Jack Kerouac. Code PNG, $12.95.
**The Sun Also Rises**, by Ernest Hemingway. Code SS, $11.

## POETRY

*There is no money in poetry, but then there is no poetry in money, either.* — Robert Graves

Do you feel you don't understand poetry? Can't wring the hidden meanings out of the words? Help is at hand. These tapes bring sense and meaning to an often overlooked source of enjoyment. Sometimes just listening to someone who understands the poetry reading it aloud can make it clear to you. Maybe you want to decode new poetry. These tapes will give you the tools to open a different form of communication. One cassette. Code AF, $12.95 each.

**SOUND AND SENSE IN POETRY,** by G.B. Harrison. The great importance of sound in understanding poetry is illustrated through the reading of well-known poems by William Shakespeare, John Donne, John Milton, Robert Browning, and others. Harrison adds commentary about each poet.

**OBSCURITY IN POETRY and COULD IT BE VERSE?** Two lectures so comprehensive that they are worth listening to several times (at least). Learn why some important and memorable poems are difficult to understand. Find out how to get the most out of funny poems and punning verses.

**THE CREMATION OF SAM McGEE and THE SHOOTING OF DAN McGREW**, two separate books by Robert W. Service, illustrated by well-known artist Ted Harrison. Kids love these two classic narrative poems, and Harrison's artistry brings them to life. The only thing better is hearing the recording of Hank Snow reading these poems, but I don't know where you'd find it. An unbeatable way to get kids involved with poetry. Ages 7 and up. Code KC, $5.95 each.

**EVERY TIME I CLIMB A TREE**, by David McCord. A touch of fun and modern poetry, with chuckles and thoughtful poems. The illustrations make me grin. Code LB, $5.95.

**A CHILD'S GARDEN OF VERSES,** by Robert Louis Stevenson, illustrated by Brian Wildsmith. This is a beautifully illustrated hardcover edition meant to be read over and over. A family heirloom. Code OX, $14.95. (You'll also find this in a $1 edition under Young Children's Classics.)

**I SCREAM, YOU SCREAM ...**, by Lillian Morrison. Do you remember that one? It was one of my favorite chants when I was growing up; I learned it from my grandpa. This book is a delightful collection of sayings and chants for young and old. You'll find fish flirt, dogs fish, and more to read, share, and smile about. Ages 4 and up. Code AH, $12.95. (All right! The last part of I scream, you scream is "we all scream for ice cream!")

**WHEN A CITY LEANS AGAINST THE SKY**, poems by Allan A. De Fina. I don't particularly like cities, but I like this collection of poems. It tickled my imagination and opened my eyes to things I hadn't considered. The imagery is vivid, imaginative, thought-provoking, and fun — all at once. Ages 10 and up. Code BMP, $8.95. Here's an example:

**Stories**

Only a city
has more stories
behind each windowed
shelf
than a library
can hold
or a storyteller
tell.

**THE OXFORD BOOK OF STORY POEMS**, compiled by Michael Harrison and Christopher Stuart-Clark. A perfect introduction to poetry. Children love stories, dragons, castles, knights, mermaids, witches, and magicians. 66 stories to ignite the imagination, enhanced with color and black-and-white illustrations. Perfect to share aloud or read in a cozy chair. Ages 8 and up. Code OX, $14.95.

**OXFORD TREASURY OF CLASSIC POEMS**. 93 classic poems you and your children will love and remember. Black-and-white illustrations. Ages 9 and up. Code OX, $15.95.

**A YEAR FULL OF POEMS,** edited by Michael Harrison and Christopher Stuart-Clark. A poem for every day of the year; by the time you finish you'll be ready to start again, because you will have enjoyed these so much the first time around. Funny and famous poems for all seasons and occasions with color illustrations. Ages 9 to 14. Code OX, $12.95.

**IMAGES OF NATURE,** compiled by Dr. David Booth. This book is a unique combination of Canada's Group of Seven artists and outstanding Canadian poets. Beautiful, sometimes stark pictures, together with the words of the poets, express and illustrate Canadian culture. A book to explore, ponder, and enjoy through the years. All ages. Hardcover. Code KC, $14.95.

**IMAGIST POETRY: *An Anthology***, edited by Bob Blaisdell. A look at early 20-century poetry. 180 selections from Ezra Pound, D.H. Lawrence, James Joyce, William Carlos Williams, and others. Good overview. Code DV, $2.

**Classic Poetry**. Code DV, $1 each (Emerson's *Concord Hymn* and Service's *Dan McGrew* $1.50 each)
**101 Great American Poems**
**Classic Tradition of Haiku**
William Blake, **Blake's Selected Poems;** and **Songs of Innocence and Songs of Experience**
Robert Burns, **Selected Poems**
Lord Byron, **Selected Poems**, $1.50
Samuel Coleridge, **Selected Poems**
Emily Dickinson, **Selected Poems**
John Donne, **Selected Poems**, $1.50
T.S. Eliot, **Waste Land and Others**
Ralph Waldo Emerson, **Concord Hymn and Others**
Robert Frost, **The Road Not Taken**
John Keats, **Lyric Poems**
Henry Wadsworth Longfellow, **Favorite Poems**
Edgar Lee Masters, **Spoon River Anthology**, $1.50
Edgar Allan Poe, **The Raven and Others**
Robert W. Service, **The Shooting of Dan McGrew**
William Shakespeare, **Complete Sonnets**
Percy Bysshe Shelley, **Selected Poems**, $1.50
Walt Whitman, **Civil War Poetry and Prose**
Walt Whitman, **Selected Poems**
William Wordsworth, **Favorite Poems**

**Boxed Sets**. Code DV.

**FIVE GREAT POETS**
William Shakespeare, John Keats, Edgar Allan Poe, Emily Dickinson, Walt Whitman. 5 volumes, $5.

**6 GREAT AMERICAN POETS**
Edgar Allan Poe, Emily Dickinson, Walt Whitman, Henry Wadsworth Longfellow, Robert Frost, Edna St. Vincent Millay. 6 volumes, $6.

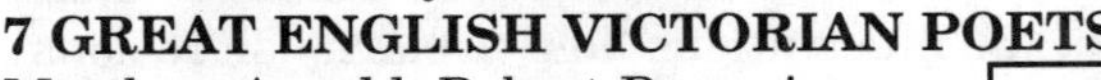

**7 GREAT ENGLISH VICTORIAN POETS**
Matthew Arnold, Robert Browning, Edward FitzGerald, A.E. Housman, Elizabeth Barrett Browning, Rudyard Kipling, Alfred Lord Tennyson. 7 volumes, $7.

**9 GREAT ENGLISH POETS**
William Shakespeare, John Keats, William Blake, Samuel Coleridge, William Wordsworth, Elizabeth Barrett Browning, Edward FitzGerald, Alfred Lord Tennyson, Rudyard Kipling. 9 volumes, $9.

**GREAT WOMEN POETS**
Elizabeth Barrett Browning, Edna St. Vincent Millay, Emily Dickinson, and Christina Rossetti. 4 volumes, $4.

SHAKESPEARE

It can be intimidating to tackle Shakespeare's works and help your kids understand the language and the subtleties that make his work great, but there is so much to be learned and enjoyed that it is well worth some effort. The best way to begin with your kids is to rent a video of one his plays, listen to a cassette, or watch a TV production. Watching takes little effort, the professionals do all the work, and it's amazing how easy it is to adapt to Shakespeare's English when you hear and see it in action. Just listening to a play on a cassette will help. The following materials will make your job much easier and more enjoyable.

**Illustrated Shakespeare.** These 12 plays have been edited and illustrated in a format similar to that of the Illustrated Classics (above), and are excellent introductions to Shakespeare not only for children, but also for adults who don't have the time or inclination to read the originals, and for all who think Shakespeare is boring or too complicated to enjoy. The reading level is about fifth grade, but as with the Classics, we find the excellent black-and-white drawings easily make up for the simplified text. Besides vividly showing the settings and costumes of the characters and their background, the illustrations help to clarify situations that are somewhat vague in the text, and will be appreciated even by those who enjoy reading the original plays in their entirety. $4.95 each from AGS (American Guidance Service), 4201 Woodland Rd., Circle Pines, MN 55014-1796; 800-328-2560; www.agsnet.com.

**As You Like It**
**Hamlet**
**Julius Caesar**
**King Lear**
**Macbeth**
**The Merchant of Venice**
**A Midsummer Night's Dream**
**Othello**
**Romeo and Juliet**
**The Taming of the Shrew**
**The Tempest**
**Twelfth Night**

**SHAKESPEARE FOR KIDS: His Life and Times**, by Colleen Aagesen and Margie Blumberg. This book has 21 interesting activities that help make Shakespeare's life and times come alive. The text is well written. Photos, drawings, and original artwork of the time make it easy to see what life was like. Activities include making a quill pen, learning to juggle, making a hornbook, playing Elizabethan games, making a sword and staging a fight, producing a scene from *Julius Caesar*, and more. Glossary and related websites included. Ages 9 and up. Code CRP, $14.95.

**THE BARD OF AVON: The Story of William Shakespeare**, by Diane Stanley and Peter Vennema. Excellent first biography. The authors likened themselves to detectives when they researched the material for this book. Shakespeare's life is the centerpiece of this book, with good supporting illustrations and information about life in and around London, Shakespeare's plays, and theater productions of the time. Very nice artwork on every other page. Good depiction of how Shakespeare staged scenes from Heaven and Hell and lots more. Ages 10 to 14. Code WM, $5.95.

**THE WORLD OF SHAKESPEARE** (an Usborne book). An essential guide for all ages. First-time readers and longtime fans will enjoy and learn about his world and his work. Covers Elizabethan London, Shakespeare's 38 works (synopses), the theater, the actors, different categories of plays, language, and a discussion of the qualities that make Shakespeare's works timeless. Good exploration of what motivates his characters. Illustrations feature classical and modern productions. Glossary of terms and phrases, words, and characters. Highly recommended to all who read Shakespeare and those who would like more enjoyment of his work. Ages 11 and up. Code EDC, $9.95.

**SHAKESPEARE ON STAGE MAKE-IT-YOURSELF POP-UP BOOK**. Build the theater and see the people.

A great way to see just how theater productions were put together. While you're creating the book you'll be amazed at the engineering involved in creating a pop-up book. Ages 12 and up. Code PW, $12.

**Oxford School Shakespeare Series**, edited by Roma Gill. An easy-to-use format for readers beginning to read Shakespeare. Unabridged plays are in easy-to-read type, copiously and clearly annotated. Your understanding of Shakespeare's sometimes very complex characters and plots will be clarified by character summaries and scene synopses, which are placed next to the text of the play so you don't have to constantly look for obscure footnotes. Topics for discussion, related essays, and a chronology of Shakespeare's life and work are found in the appendices of each volume. All this plus photos of the staged plays. Ages 11 to adult. Code OX, $7.95 each. **Antony and Cleopatra; As You Like It; Hamlet; Henry IV, Part I; Henry V; Julius Caesar; King Lear; Macbeth; Merchant of Venice; Midsummer Night's Dream; Othello; Richard II; Romeo and Juliet; Taming of the Shrew; The Tempest; Twelfth Night; A Winter's Tale.**

**Shakespeare's Plays.** Code DV, $1 each unless otherwise marked. **Anthony and Cleopatra ($1.50), As You Like It, Hamlet, Julius Caesar, King Lear, Macbeth, Merchant of Venice, Midsummer Night's Dream, Othello, Romeo and Juliet, Twelfth Night, The Tempest ($1.50).**
**SHAKESPEARE: A Book of Quotations.** 500 quotes arranged by subject.

Year-round Shakespeare classes are available online. E-mail Shakespeare_at_Home@usa.net. Three plays are covered, in-depth, per year by Dianna Mikulecky, J.D., who loves and understands Shakespeare. Mikulecky has had a lot of experience sharing her enjoyment with kids ages 12 to 17. Her methodology: "Follow at your own pace, and pursue your own interest." There is a three-month study of each play, alternating between the tragedies and the comedies. Students will be expected to do some writing. There is a directed one-hour online discussion each week. $30 per session.

Twelve of Shakespeare's plays are available on tape from DH Audio, 2221 Niagara Falls Blvd, Niagara Falls, NY 14304. In Canada: DH Audio, 3385 Harvester Rd., Suite 215, Burlington, ON L7N 3N2. Request a free catalog.

**Shakespeare**. A coloring book. Code BB, $4.99.

**Other plays**. Code DV, $1 each
**Antigone**, by Sophocles
**Lysistrata**, by Aristophanes
**The Mikado**, by William Gilbert
**Oedipus Rex**, by Sophocles

## MYTHOLOGY AND STORYTELLING

**BULFINCH'S MYTHOLOGY (and poster to color)**, retold for children by Steven Zorn, illustrated by Helen Driggs. 16 exciting tales with pictures to color in the book (separate from the poster) — all perfect for ages 6 to 10. Great introduction. Action and literary content all in one book. Book 8½x11". Poster 17x22." Code RP, $9.95.

**BULFINCH'S GREEK AND ROMAN MYTHOLOGY**. An unabridged republication of the original in a paperback edition. Everything you need for an exciting time — adventure, gods and goddesses, heroes, warriors, scoundrels, and romance. A great book to read aloud. 320 pages. Code DV, $2.50.

**THE STORY OF HERCULES**, by Bob Blaisdell. A fast-paced easy-to-read version tells of the immensely strong hero from birth to death, and brings him to vivid life with 25 illustrations. Code DV, $1.

**ADVENTURE OF HERCULES COLORING BOOK**, by Bob Blaisdell. Ready-to-color illustrations chronicle the adventure-filled life of this legendary Greek hero. 32 pages, $8\frac{1}{4}$x11". Code DV, $2.50.

**HERCULES STICKERS**, by Steven James Petruccio. Here's a way to let your child use his creative writing skills and illustrate stories about Hercules. 14 full-color stickers recalling this hero's life: wrestling the lion of Nemea, capturing the stag with golden horns, fighting the dreaded Hydra, diverting the waters of a river to clean the Augean stables, holding up the vault of the sky, and more. Code DV, $2.50.

**JASON AND THE ARGONAUTS**. The classic tale (abridged) of Jason's adventures to bring back the Golden Fleece is brought alive with dramatic artwork. Ages 9 and up (and younger children, if you read it to them). Code EDC, $10.95.

**ADVENTURES OF ULYSSES**. Fast-moving classic adventure (abridged). Ulysses returns from the Trojan War. Well illustrated. Ages 9 and up. Code EDC, $10.95.

**Myths and Legends**. Great color illustrations. A constructive way to satisfy a craving for adventure stories — monsters and such. Ages 11 and up. Code EDC.
**GREEK MYTHS AND LEGENDS**. $10.95
**NORSE MYTHS AND LEGENDS**. $7.95
Both books in one volume: **LEGENDS: GREEK AND NORSE**. $12.95

**A WONDER BOOK FOR GIRLS AND BOYS**, by Nathaniel Hawthorne, illustrated by Walter Crane, with an introduction by Ola D'Aulaire. Mythology at its best for young and old, with classic color illustrations. A treasury of old Greek myths and early American stories. A book to be treasured through the years and reread with much pleasure. This makes a beautiful gift. I just learned the hardcover edition will be going out of print soon. Ages 8 and up. Code OX. Hardcover, $21.95. Paperback, $15.95.

**THE STORYTELLER'S START-UP BOOK: Finding, Learning, Performing, and Using Folktales**, by Margaret Read MacDonald. This book is designed to give the pleasure of storytelling back to everyday people like us. MacDonald explains how to find, develop, and present a story and gives information about the historical tradition of storytelling. There is a fascinating chapter examining the values of storytelling. Think about it for a minute: Stories help us to understand ourselves and others; they give us exposure to other cultures and to different values. A storyteller can help children learn to listen carefully and enhance imagination and visualization, as well as entertain. Contains 12 stories for telling. Ages 14 and up. Code AH, $14.95.

**THE CELESTIAL RIVER: Creation Tales of the Milky Way**, by Andrea Stenn Stryer. Before the lights of cities dimmed our view of the heavens, anyone who looked up on a clear night could see the Milky Way. It reminded ancient peoples of common things around them, and they created myths that grew from each culture's fears, needs, and hopes. Glossary and bibliography included. Myths from Japan, Australia, Polynesia, Greece, Native Americans, and others. Ages 8 and up. Code AH, $7.95.

**WISDOM TALES FROM AROUND THE WORLD**, by Heather Forest. In her introduction Forest writes, "Since ancient times, people from diverse cultures have preserved and passed down homespun knowledge encased in stories. Wisdom tales are metaphorical. ... [P]lots can be simply enjoyed for the drama or ... [can] be a powerful teaching tool."

**Naked Truth and Parable**

Naked Truth walked down the street one day.
People turned their eyes away.
Parable arrived, draped in decoration.
People greeted Parable with celebration.
Naked Truth sat alone, sad and unattired.
"Why are you so miserable?" Parable inquired.
Naked Truth replied, "I'm not welcome anymore.
No one wants to see me. They chase me from their door."
"It is hard to look at Naked Truth," Parable explained.
"Let me dress you up a bit. Your welcome will be gained."

There is more to this poem, based on an 18th-century Eastern European Hasidic rabbi's tale, but I'm sure you get the point. More than 50 tales make reading this book a global experience. Ages 8 and up. Code AH, $17.95.

**HOW A BOOK IS PUBLISHED**, by Bobbie Kalman, explains the whole process. What does an editor do? How do you find the pictures? Research and book design are all explained. Well-illustrated with full-color pictures and photos. How do you get a book printed and sold? Reading this will give you an idea of what I've had to learn to put this book together. Maybe it will inspire you to write your own book. Ages 6 to 10. Code CT, $5.95.

---

*At Phillochry, in 1881, when Robert Louis Stevenson saw a dog being ill-treated, he at once interposed, and when the owner resented his interference and told him, "It's not your dog," Stevenson cried out, "It's God's dog and I'm here to protect it!"*

**THE NEW YORK PUBLIC LIBRARY'S BOOKS OF THE CENTURY**, edited by Elizabeth Diefendorf, illustrated by Diana Bryan. A book that spans this century's thoughts and deeds. 150 books are listed, with annotations, in categories reflecting predominant themes, including Mind and Spirit, Protest and Progress, Women Rise, Nature's Realm, and Favorites of Childhood and Youth. A worthy guide to modern literature. Just browsing through it makes me want to shut down the computer, pull the plug on the phone, curl up on the sofa, and read. Code OX, $8.95.

**WOMEN OF WORDS: A Personal Introduction to Thirty-Five Important Writers**, edited by Janet Bukovinsky Teacher. I found the dust jacket arresting, with its portraits of four women from different time periods. The artist for each is obviously the same, yet the details of each portrait, the expression on each face, are so personal I immediately wanted to meet these people. I can't, of course; many of them died long ago, but not all. I found as I read through the book that the biographical portraits were done with just as much care. Particular attention has been paid to the life of each. The biographies of these 35 women place them within the context of their times, and include examples of their work. Some were able to influence their world during their lifetimes; others weren't given recognition until after their deaths. All have influenced our times by their written words. For thoughtful mid-teens to adults. Hardcover. Code RP, $14.95.

**INSTANT AMERICAN LITERATURE**, by Laurie Rozakis, Ph.D. Covers 12 of the most influential writers and discusses, irreverently, their work and influence. Brief biographies, photos and drawings, excerpts from writings, and interesting notes about each author. Not a deep book, but a good outline for a self-made study. High school and up. Code RH, $10.

## AUDIO LITERATURE

**Jim Weiss**, a vivacious, captivating storyteller, brings these tales to life with great expression and excitement. Guaranteed: hours of happy listening, all the while enhancing your imagination and bringing some of our cultural legacy to life. If CD players had been around when our kids were still at home we'd have bought all our stories in that format. We wore out a lot of cassette tapes with our repeated listening! Code GH, tapes $10.95, CDs $14.95.

**ANIMAL TALES** — 9 classics from Aesop, Grimm, Chaucer, and others.

**ARABIAN NIGHTS** — Scheherazade and 3 more tales

**A CHRISTMAS CAROL AND OTHER FAVORITES** — "Gift of the Magi" and others

**FAIRYTALE FAVORITES IN SONG AND STORY** — "Stone Soup," "Puss in Boots," "Rapunzel," and other favorites.

**GOOD NIGHT** — 6 bedtime vignettes that take the listener into feelings of safety and love

**GREEK MYTHS** — King Midas, Hercules, Perseus and Medusa, Arachne

**HEROES IN MYTHOLOGY** — Theseus and the Minotaur; Prometheus, Bearer of Fire; Odin and the Norse Men.

**THE JUNGLE BOOK** — 3 Kipling tales

**KING ARTHUR AND HIS KNIGHTS**

**RASCAL** — Unabridged great classic of a boy and his raccoon. One of my favorite stories. 3 tapes, $23.95; with book $27.95.

**RIP VAN WINKLE and GULLIVER'S TRAVELS**

**SHAKESPEARE FOR CHILDREN** — *A Midsummer Night's Dream* and *Taming of the Shrew*. A perfect introduction to Shakespeare. Easily understood.

**SHE AND HE: Adventures in Mythology** — Psyche and Cupid, Pygmalion and Galatea, Echo and Narcissus, and more.

**SHERLOCK HOLMES FOR CHILDREN** — 4 tales

**TALES FROM CULTURES NEAR AND FAR** — 6 stories

**TALES FROM THE OLD TESTAMENT**

**THREE MUSKETEERS and ROBIN HOOD**

**Listen-and-Read Audio Thrift Classics for Children.** One 60-minute cassette with illustrated paperback book. Stories on tape stimulate each listener to re-create the story in his own mind, so imagination flourishes and the importance of literature and reading develop without effort. Code DV, $5.95 each.

**ADVENTURES OF PETER COTTONTAIL**

**ALADDIN AND OTHER FAVORITE ARABIAN NIGHTS STORIES**

**A CHILD'S GARDEN OF VERSES**

**A CHRISTMAS CAROL**

**FAVORITE IRISH FAIRY TALES**

**FAVORITE POEMS OF CHILDHOOD**

**THE LITTLE MERMAID**

**NORTH AMERICAN INDIAN LEGENDS**
**PETER RABBIT AND OTHER FAVORITES**
**THE UGLY DUCKLING AND OTHER HANS CHRISTIAN ANDERSEN FAVORITES**
**UNCLE WIGGILY BEDTIME STORIES**

**More Audio Thrift Classics**. One 60- to 80-minute cassette plus complete paperback edition containing all material on the cassette *plus additional selections.* Code DV, $5.95 each.
**BLAKE** — 45 poems come to life, including *Songs of Innocence* and *Songs of Experience*
**DICKENS** — *A Christmas Carol* (abridged), plus children's Christmas stories and poems
**EMILY DICKINSON** — 101 sensitively read poems come to life
**SHERLOCK HOLMES STORIES** — 6 of them
**THE MONKEY'S PAW AND OTHER GHOST STORIES**, by John Grafton — for a dark and stormy night.
**EDGAR ALLAN POE** — "The Raven" and other poems
**THE TELL-TALE HEART AND 3 OTHER HORROR STORIES**, by Edgar Allan Poe — for a very dark and stormy night.
**SHAKESPEARE SONNETS** — 61 favorites and book of the complete sonnets
**100 BEST LOVED POEMS** — 100 in the book; 36 are read aloud. Variety of classic poets.
**GREAT LOVE POEMS** — 66 of the greatest
**WHITMAN** — 9 poems from *Leaves of Grass.*

**More children's classics on tape**. From Durkin Hayes. In the U.S. call 800-962-5200, in Canada 800-269-5224, for a catalog or to order. About $16.95 each. **Alice in Wonderland, Anne of Green Gables, Black Beauty, Beauty and the Beast, Call of the Wild, The Emperor's New Clothes, Great Expectations, Gulliver's Travels, Moby Dick, Pinocchio**, and more.

**Even more children's classics on tape**. Excellent readings of these all-time favorites. Each tape 60 minutes. Code RH, $11 each. **Alice's Adventures in Wonderland, Black Beauty, Little Women, Peter Pan, The Secret Garden, Swiss Family Robinson, Treasure Island**.

**Children's Classics Library on tape**. 16 dramatized or narrated stories, plus 96 other fables, rhymes, and folktales by Mark Twain, Kenneth Grahame, Washington Irving, Robert Louis Stevenson, Rudyard Kipling, and others. You'll find yourself listening right along with your kids. You and your children will enjoy these again and again. Stories include *Huckleberry Finn, Treasure Island, The Legend of Sleepy Hollow, Rip Van Winkle, Youth, The Notorious Jumping Frog of Calaveras County, The Wind in the Willows, The Elephant's Child, Sleeping Beauty, The Rime of the Ancient Mariner, H.M.S. Pinafore, Aesop's Fables*, and more. You can't beat this price, and the tapes are well done with music and sound effects. 40 cassettes. Order from Newport Publishers, 100 North Lake Ave., Suite 203, Pasadena, CA 91101-1883; 800-579-5532; outside the U.S. call 626-796-4027. $49.95, shipping included. California residents add tax.

**Family Classics Library on tape**. Done with the same high quality as the tapes listed above but for an older audience. Well-read entertainment to enjoy anytime. Stories and books include *A Tale of Two Cities, A Christmas Carol, Great Expectations, The Scarlet Letter, The Pickwick Papers, The Tell-Tale Heart, Les Misérables, Call of the Wild, The Adventures of Don Quixote* and more. 40 cassettes. Order from Newport Publishers at the above address.

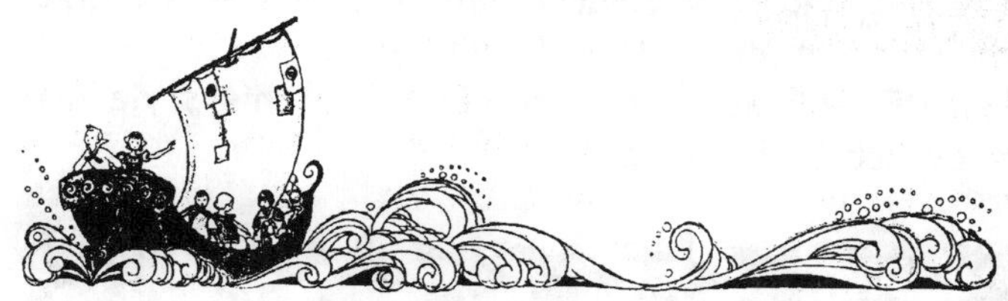

**KIDNAPPED**, a Robert Louis Stevenson classic. You'll follow the adventures of young David Balfour when he inadvertently gets caught up in the troubles of others as they try to restore Bonnie Prince Charlie to the Scottish throne in 1745. Abridged, but with 2 cassettes you'll get a lot of story, and the kids will listen again and again. Code AF, $17.95.

**THE RED BADGE OF COURAGE: A High School Study.** This audiocassette is a lecture about the book and the writing, symbolism, and philosophy in Stephen Crane's classic novel. It does not tell or retell the story. An excellent introduction to how writers use their skills to produce more than nice stories as well as an aid to help your student learn to look behind the printed words on the page. Code AF, $12.95. The book can be purchased for $1. See Thrift Books.

**THE GETTYSBURG ADDRESS AND AN INDEPENDENT AMERICAN**. Whitman's poem "Fourth of July" and others are read and discussed. Lincoln's famous Gettysburg Address is discussed. Find out what impression it made at the time and why it's memorable. Ages 16 and up. Code AF, $12.95.

**SIX AMERICAN AUTHORS**. Their philosophies, writing styles, and thoughts are discussed in lectures by Joseph Schiffman. Ages 14 and up. Code AF, $12.95 each.
**EMERSON, Idealist.**
**NATHANIEL HAWTHORNE** — his life, thought, art, and relevance
**SINCLAIR LEWIS, The Roaring '20s** — his life, thought, and relevance
**MELVILLE, The World a Ship** — his life, thought, and relevance
**STEINBECK, In Search of America** — his life, thought, art, and relevance
**THOREAU, Activist** — discussion of his style and relevance to our time

**Outstanding Radio Fiction and Science Fiction**. 60-minute tapes. You and your family will listen to these again and again — during a meal, at bedtime, in the car, or on a rainy day. Code AF, $12.95 each, 2 for $11.95 each, 3 for $10.95 each. If you want more than that write for a deal.
**THE PRAIRIE YEARS,** by Carl Sandburg. Gregory Peck is young Abe Lincoln. And **BERKELEY SQUARE**, with David Niven in a fantasy of past, present, and future all coming together.
**OF MICE AND MEN**. John Steinbeck's classic tale.
**BRAVE NEW WORLD**, by Aldous Huxley. Huxley narrates his story of the dehumanization of mankind and a prediction of 600 years in the future.
**THE LEGEND OF SLEEPY HOLLOW**, fantasy adventure by Washington Irving. And **THE THREE MUSKETEERS**, by Alexandre Dumas, with Howard Duff playing the leading role.
**GREAT EXPECTATIONS**. Rock Hudson plays the lead in Dickens' immortal tale of an orphan boy.
**STARBRIGHT,** by Jack Williamson. A father discovers that his young daughter is fantastically brilliant, And **CAVE OF NIGHT,** by James Gunn, about a space pilot in desperate need of a second ship.
**ALMOST HUMAN,** by Robert Bloch, about a robot so human-like it even begins to acquire human emotions. And **GREEN HILLS OF EARTH**. This is one of our all-time favorite stories by Robert Heinlein. Better than the written version. The story of a blind troubadour of the spaceways.
**TALE OF TWO CITIES**. Dickens' tale of the French revolution; the chaos and violence is the backdrop for a story of friendship and love.
**EDGAR ALLAN POE**. "The Tell-Tale Heart" and "The Black Cat," read by actor Jimmy Stewart. Outstanding thrillers.

Did you know that Edgar Allan Poe was expelled from West Point in 1831 for "gross neglect of duty"? Poe took literally the parade dress instructions for "white belts and gloves, under arms." Appearing on the parade ground, rifle balanced on his bare shoulder, Poe made his appearance wearing nothing but a smile, a white belt, and gloves.

**More Great Literature on Tape**. A wonderful way to share book treasures or encourage reluctant readers. Code RH.
**ANNE OF GREEN GABLES**. 2½ hours, 2 cassettes, $18.
**CHARLOTTE'S WEB**. 3½ hours, 3 cassettes, $22, CD $25.
**CHEAPER BY THE DOZEN** — family fun! Over 6 hours, 4 cassettes, $25.
**THE GIVER** — Newbery Medal winner. Spellbinding science fiction about the pain and pleasures of life. Not just for kids — I loved the book. Almost 6 hours, 4 cassettes, $25.
**HARRY POTTER AND THE SORCERER'S STONE**. Over 8 hours, 6 cassettes, $33.
**KING OF THE WIND** — classic horse story. 3½ hours, 4 cassettes, $25.
**LITTLE WOMEN**. Almost 5 hours, 4 cassettes, $25.
**SIX ADVENTURES OF TINTIN**, Vol. 1. (dramatized). 3 hours, 2 cassettes, $18.

**STORIES OF RAY BRADBURY** — read by the author (unabridged). 3 hours of fun, suspense, and imagination, 2 cassettes, $21.95.
**STUART LITTLE**. $2\frac{1}{2}$ hours, 2 cassettes, $18, CD $22.
**THE TRUMPET OF THE SWAN**. Almost $4\frac{1}{2}$ hours, 4 cassettes, $25, CD $28.
**A WRINKLE IN TIME** (unabridged). Over 5 hours, 4 cassettes, $25.

**BBC Radio Presents.** Full-cast dramatizations with music and sound effects. 2 cassettes. Code RH.
**PETER PAN**, $18.
**THE SECRET GARDEN**, $16.
**ALICE IN WONDERLAND and THROUGH THE LOOKING GLASS**, $16.
**THE WIND IN THE WILLOWS**, $16.
**THE JUNGLE BOOK**, $16.
**HEIDI**, $16.
**THE CHRONICLES OF NARNIA:**
**The Magician's Nephew**, $18.
**The Lion, the Witch and the Wardrobe**, $18.
**The Horse and His Boy**, $16.99.
**Prince Caspian,** $16.99.
**Voyage of the Dawn Treader,** $16.99.
**The Silver Chair,** $16.99.
**The Last Battle,** $16.99.
***Save $$*** — Complete Narnia Series $120.95 list; our price $99.95.

**Recorded Books, Inc.**, offers a free catalog of more than 2,000 unabridged audiobooks. 270 Skipjack Rd., Prince Frederick, MD 20678; 800-638-1304 (this toll-free number is good in Canada and the U.S.).

**Audiobooks Direct** offers a free catalog. P.O. Box 6309, Indianapolis, IN 46206-6309; on the web at www.AudiobooksDirect.com.

## FINDING MORE GOOD BOOKS

A report of **THE BEST CHILDREN'S BOOKS OF 1999** is available for $8 plus $2 for shipping and handling from the Children's Book Committee, Bank Street College of Education, 610 West 112th St., New York, NY 10025. This includes new editions of old favorites as well as new books. They also publish **BOOKS TO READ ALOUD FOR CHILDREN OF ALL AGES**, a 56-page annotated list of fiction and nonfiction, with almost 400 titles from classics to the newest books. Arranged by age and interest. $5 plus $2 shipping.

**THE NEW YORK PUBLIC LIBRARY GUIDE TO READING GROUPS**, by Rollene Sall. All the information you need to start and enjoy a reading group. Written for adults, but can be used for younger readers too. Tips for leading stimulating and well-balanced discussions. More than 35 annotated book lists categorized by interest. You can do this with your friends or maybe start a reading group within your support group. If you need books in quantity for your group we'll give you a discount. Code RH, $20.

For serious students of literature who are preparing for college exams, or college students at home or on campus, we highly recommend **CLIFFS NOTES**, a series of classic study guides covering written work through the ages. Reasonable prices. Request a catalog from Cliffs Notes, P.O. Box 80428, Lincoln, NE 68501.

### Books at Discount or Very Low Prices

**Edward R. Hamilton**, Falls Village, CT 06031. Free catalog of publishers' overstocks and bargain books. Many subjects.

**Dover Publications**, 31 East 2nd St., Mineola, NY 11501-3582. Without a doubt, one of the world's best sources of very good, inexpensive books — some original publications, many reprints of otherwise out-of-print books. Thousands of titles; most of them $6 or less. Free general catalog. We have a lot of these listed for you under code DV. Our shipping charges are less unless you are ordering a lot of them. You can get their catalog and order from us to take advantage of cheaper shipping, even if we don't have a particular title listed.

**Follett Educational Services**, 1433 Internationale Parkway, Woodridge, IL 60517, 800-621-4272. Free catalog of used, reconditioned textbooks — all subjects, all levels. Guaranteed to be 80% as good as the original, for much less than the new price.

**Quality Paperback Book Club,** Customer Service Center, P.O. Box 8840, Camp Hill PA 17012-8840; www.QPB.com. This is our favorite. After an initial order of several books for $1 each plus postage, there are no other required purchases. Lots of new books hot off the press with good reviews. Prices are lower than publishers' prices. Each purchase earns points that may be used toward the purchase of future orders.

**Children's Book-of-the-Month Club**, a division of the Book-of-the-Month Club, Camp Hill, PA 17011-9850. A good introductory offer is given, and the variety of books is consistently good. What better way to satisfy a child's love of getting mail and receiving good books?

**Intermediate and Middle Grades Book Club**, P.O. Box 6304, Indianapolis, IN 46209-8310. If you're looking for books for the middle grades, with pre- and post-reading activities and lesson plans, write for information.

**Bookspan**, 100 Armstrong Ave., Georgetown, ON L7G 5S4. Free catalog of fairly recent books at prices well below store prices.

**Conservative Book Club**, P.O. Box 97196, Washington, DC 10078-7197. They now have a homeschooling book club. It works just like many others. Buy 3 for $1 each, promise to buy 4 more at discount prices, etc. A few resources listed meet with our approval, but not the majority.

**A Common Reader**, 141 Tompkins Ave., Pleasantville, NY 10570; 800-832-7323, www.commonreader.com. Free catalog with more than 130 pages of literate, intriguing book reviews on a wide variety of subjects. All ages. A real pleasure just to read through every issue.

**Laissez-Faire Books**, 938 Howard St., #202, San Francisco, CA 94103; laissezfaire.org. Free catalog of thoughtful books on a wide range of subjects for adults. By "adult" I mean age group, not violent and/or sexual content. (What's happening to our language?)

Want more books? Write for a catalog from **The Strand Book Store**, 828 Broadway (at 12th St.), New York, NY 10003-4805.

The **MCGUFFEY READERS**, often recommended for a sound Christian classical education, have been revised for today's readers. Inquire about their study guide. Available from Hartline Marketing, 123 Queenston Drive, Pittsburgh, PA 15235; 800-677-2220. The series is also available from The Homeschool, 800-788-7887; www.thehomeschool.com.

If you live overseas you can receive a catalog and then order kids' books from **pro juventute**, Seehofstrasse 15, Postfach, 8022 Zürich, Switzerland.

**HOW TO STOCK A HOME LIBRARY INEXPENSIVELY**, by Jane Williams. This is a very useful little book, listing more than 100 sources of discount books, mail-order book suppliers, and remainder dealers. Williams also suggests many other sources of inexpensive books, such as used book sales (where to find them, what to look for), and ways of accumulating money to spend on books. 8½x11", 95 pages. $14.95 from Bluestocking Press, P.O. Box 2030, Shingle Springs, CA 95682-2030; 800-959-8586. Call for shipping charges and to order.

Someday I'm going to make a list of all the books the kids left behind and all our resource books that are no longer in use, and I'm planning to mail out a "used books" flier. If you would like to be notified, send an SASE. Fair warning — I may not get this list done for a couple of years!

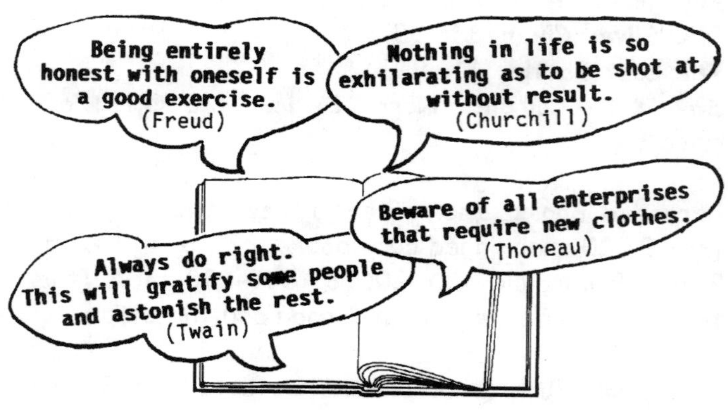


***I hate quotations.*** **— Ralph Waldo Emerson**

# HISTORY AND BIOGRAPHY

## Books, Coloring and Activity Books, Audio Cassettes, Reference Books, Historical Fiction, and Biographies

WHERE? WHY? HOW? WHO? WHAT? WHEN?

***Human history is in essence a history of ideas.* — H.G. Wells**

Yesterday, we played the cassette tape of an old radio program called "Battle Hymn of the Republic" that tells the dramatic story of Julia Ward Howe writing the words to go with the popular tune of "John Brown's Body." This morning, we started another tape, with a script written by Stephen Vincent Benét. We didn't get past the introduction. (We'll try again tomorrow.)

"That name sounds familiar," one of the kids said. "Don't we have some books by him?"

I stopped the tape and waited, as the kids looked at each other, searching their memories.

Seeing that they were all drawing blanks, I prompted. "It was mentioned briefly in the tape we heard yesterday," I said. "That is, something of the same name. A long poem, book-length."

"Hiawatha?" someone suggested, knowing better.

"What was the song in the story?" I asked.

"Battle Hymn! Of the Republic!"

"Right," I said. "Where did the tune come from?"

"Someone wrote it." (Always a wise guy.)

"Who?"

"Stephen Vincent Benét?" "Longfellow?" "John Brown?"

"'John Brown's Body'? Nobody knows who wrote it!"

"You win again. Perhaps it just grew, as people repeated the song. Who was John Brown? Did people really sing about his body?"

And so on. Sometimes the kids know the answers, or can brainstorm the answers. Sometimes we jog their memories with hints, riddles, puns, jokes, and related tidbits of information. Sometimes the subject or concept is new to them, and we tell them of our own ideas and experiences, books we've read, places we've seen. We bring out maps, posters, magazine articles, and more books. We help them collect miscellaneous pieces of information and ideas and tie them together — to relate the facts and ideas to each other, to the world, and to themselves.

This morning, John Brown led to states' rights, the Declaration of Independence, the Constitution, the Gettysburg Address, slavery, the Fugitive Slave Act, Thoreau, the Boston Tea Party, the Mexican War, democracy, *Uncle Tom's Cabin*, and several versions and usages of the word "yankee." The discussion that was interwoven with all these subjects was lively, with quick exchanges of ideas and opinions, and spiced with several puns, jokes, and wisecracks.

We like history, but there are very few history books we like. Browse through a public school's history books; notice how much they are concerned with wars. Not big wars, fought for principle, good against evil, but petty wars, fought for greed, money, power, and territory. See how little attention is given to the great thinkers, to inventions and discoveries, to works of art, music, philosophy, and medicine.

I received passing grades when I was in school, so I suppose I must have learned the answers to at least half the questions, such as Who fought the battle of Kickme? On what date did the commanding general lose his suspenders, and why? How did anteaters affect the outcome? Why was this battle important to the development of the fur trade in colonial Chicago? I have long since forgotten most of the answers, and I doubt that remembering them would contribute very greatly to my happiness or my worth as a person.

We learn more from historical novels than from textbooks. We listen to dramatized historical events on cassette tapes; we put up facsimiles of historical posters; we assemble models of historical buildings and castles and towns; we color pictures of great events and

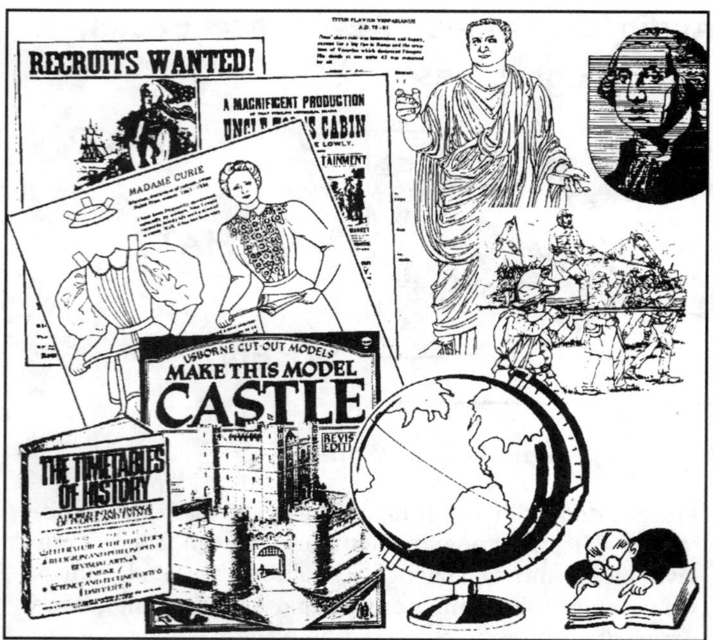


great people; we cut out and arrange paper dolls of great people and read their biographies; and we talk, talk, talk. We use history books, but seldom as intended by the authors and editors. Sometimes we immerse ourselves in an event or a period, collecting information about it from as many different sources as possible. Other times, we skip and bounce, skim and dive, reading aloud, discussing what we find, and relating it to other times and other events. We show the kids how to search out the highlights and the hidden undercurrents. We look for truly significant happenings in the development of humanity and human society. We look for "human interest" — unusual or humorous facts that demonstrate that the people of the past were real people, like us, who ate, slept, loved, feared, and hoped just as we do, not just shadows or silhouettes. We use maps — regional, national, historical, and world — and a globe. We point; we let our fingers do the walking over continents and over centuries.

Some scientists say humanity began here ... Biblical scholars say it began here ... Here is where agriculture is believed to have started ... Here, glaciers swept the continent ... How did people survive? Here was the first man to proclaim there is only one God ... Here, a new thought in philosophy ... government ... science ... medicine ... architecture ...

We look for the forerunners of democracy. We trace the evolution of human government — family patriarchs or matriarchs, tribal chiefs, religious leaders, monarchies, oligarchies. We discuss "good" kings and "bad" kings — what made them so, and what influence did they have on society's growth? We often brush over the names and usually settle for an approximate time, such as "about a thousand years ago." For our purposes, it seldom matters if an event occurred in the year 1169 or 1269. As the gap narrows, as the event is closer to us in time, we make finer distinctions.

Many facts of history stand by themselves; they have significance regardless of the time in which they occurred. Taking the history of mankind as a whole, very few individual names, dates, or happenings have any great significance. There is no reason to memorize most of them just for the sake of "knowing" them. For centuries, the little kingdoms and countries of western Europe were embroiled in countless wars, with heads of state shifting as fast as boundaries. Stevenson's *The Black Arrow* gives us a vivid picture of shifting alliances in medieval Britain. We can read about one or two "representative" wars and imagine the rest; there's no need to memorize all the dates and principals.

Other facts seem meaningless until they are put into perspective by relating them to their own time, their own place, and their own circumstances. Pivotal points and key figures in society's growth deserve a closer look. We have old radio programs on cassettes that take us back to Alexander's conquest of Asia, to Julius Caesar's victories and defeats, and to the signing of the Magna Carta, giving us front-row seats at some of the most significant events in history.

Besides knowing that Alexander the Great conquered a vast part of the world known to him, it's interesting and probably significant to know that he was taught by Aristotle, who was taught by Plato, whose teacher was Socrates. Was Alexander only seeking territory and power, or did he intend to promote a better form of government? What's the evidence? What would our society be like today if Caesar had not crossed the Rubicon? If Constantine, after pledging to spread Christianity if he won the next day's battle, had lost?

We feel it's important to have an understanding of the broad sweep of history — the long journey people have made from the caves and swamps to the moon. We believe it's important to know that we of today are not the first real people; that a hundred years ago, and a thousand, ten thousand, people got dressed and ate breakfast and worked for a living, and taught their children; they laughed and cried; when a boy of ancient Rome skinned his knee, it hurt and bled just as it would today.

We are not so greatly removed from our ancestors as we often think. Despite today's great advantages (and many disadvantages) in technology, industry, and medicine, we have changed very little over the centuries. That which makes us human — whether it's the size of our brain, the opposable thumb, or a share of divinity — is unchanged.

We marvel at the scientific discoveries and advances of the last hundred years. Technologically, why did mankind crawl for so long, and then suddenly walk, run, and fly? We marvel at our humanity, our self-healing bodies, our hopes and fears. The men who have walked on the moon have the same flesh as did the students of Socrates.

As we draw our fingers over the globe or map, and scan the centuries with our talk and our hands, we can back off into space for a broad overview or zoom in closely for a detailed picture. This big ball has been spinning through space for a long time, warmed and lighted by one of the dimmest stars. Down here a woman is preparing breakfast for her family. Is it charred mammoth, or corn flakes and toast? Here is a man digging a hole. A pitfall for a tiger? A hiding place for pirates' treasure? A city sewage line?

Men and women have always been concerned with good and bad, right and wrong. They have always striven for truth, for a good life, and for good government. Most of the best ideas in today's governments had their roots in very ancient times. Our social growth has not kept pace with our technological growth, but we are still advancing, moving from various forms of tyranny toward total emancipation.

A very few, here and there, such as the Hopi Indians of Arizona and the traditional Society of Friends, are models of what all humanity may one day achieve. Democracy, as visualized by Paine, Washington, Jefferson, and other architects of the U.S. government and by Lincoln — "government of the people, by the people, and for the people" — is the highest form of government yet achieved by any large society, but it's just a stepping-stone. Majority rule is better than dictatorship, but the majority is not always right, and the minority may still be misused and wronged. We wait, and strive, for the next development.

The next step in social government will be consensus and general agreement. Each member will seek what is right and good for all members, not only what is right for himself, or what is desirable for the majority or for those with the most influence and power. There will be no lobbying or filibustering or voting, only calm consideration and discussion until unanimity of opinion is reached.

"But that would take too long," many object. "People can never agree that much. Nothing would ever get done."

That's true, of course. As most of us are now, democracy is the best we can hope for. A thousand years ago, democracy was considered an impractical dream, when it was considered at all. A thousand years from now — who knows?

Our descendants will be living then, and we like to think that their society's conscience and spirit will have begun to catch up to the spaceships and computers. We hope the study of our yesterdays will help them have better tomorrows.

There are numerous creative ways to approach this subject. We particularly enjoyed using dramatized history (old radio cassettes and movies) and biographies to expand our knowledge of history. Sometimes we listened to tapes during our school time, sometimes during a meal. We found the kids enjoyed them as bedtime stories after we put speakers in their bedrooms.

Don't just read a book; discuss events and the people who created them. Every major event in history has at least two sides. It's important to discuss both sides. Investigate the people involved. Find pictures. They can be invaluable; without conscious awareness we learn a multitude of details from a picture. The action may be obvious, but the style of dress, furniture, architecture, and background action or scenery tell more. Many old movies are worth watching. Although many were fictional or historical (sometimes romanticized) fiction and fanciful, Donn and I grew up with vivid images of swashbuckling pirates and heroic knights in armor, and mental pictures of medieval times that made those parts of history alive and interesting.

Some people think you can't pass college entrance tests if you've taken this approach to learning history. If this concerns you, I suggest you first create an approach to history that makes it come alive. If a child is interested he will learn. Then as your child reaches high school age and expresses a desire to attend college, you can use other types of books to fill in facts related to passing college entrance tests. A good GED or SAT book will help you determine the areas you haven't covered. Before that time, make history as alive as it was for those who lived it.

**THOUGH GOD CANNOT ALTER THE PAST, HISTORIANS CAN. — Samuel Butler**

**LIES MY TEACHER TOLD ME,** by James Loewen. This may be the most important book about history that you've read in a long time — maybe ever. Most of the books in this section are for children. This book is for you. High school students may be interested too. This book will change the way you think about and teach history, even to your youngest child.

Loewen has studied and taught history on many different levels. He made an exhaustive study of history textbooks because he found his students bored, crammed with facts (many of which were untrue), and unable to separate the trivial details from the major events. His study revealed that conventional texts are based not on primary sources, but on other texts that have been adjusted to meet publishers' standards, which fluctuate according to current ideas of political correctness and what publishers think will sell. In other words, publishers instruct writers to write books that will sell, not books based on objective facts. The main issues that have influenced these decisions are race and religion. Many current history books leave out the influences of religion on migration to North America and have modified facts surrounding racial issues. This book explores and explodes the Columbus myth and gives a truer picture of Helen Keller, Woodrow Wilson, and many other historical figures. Unlike many other books, this one does not have a hidden agenda advocating separate ethnic studies; it strives to promote integrated studies. Toward the end of the book you will find guidelines for investigating and evaluating the history material you encounter in standard texts.

Loewen has practical suggestions for making history a living subject for teachers and students. He suggests you approach history as you do current news reports. Modern communication can show us in vivid colors the living detail of tomorrow's history. Human history is full of conflict. Scrutinize your history material as you should the daily news. Code BT, $14.

**EVERYTHING YOU KNOW IS WRONG: Common Fallacies, Mistakes, and Misattributed Quotations**, by Paul Kirchner, is full of interesting bits of information many of us erroneously believe to be true. Some of this will really surprise you! Put this book where it will be noticed, so everyone can browse through it. You'll have fun sharing what you've discovered. A good book for you to read so you'll avoid teaching misinformation in the first place. Ages 16 and up. Code RH, $5.99.

## REASONS TO AVOID STANDARD HISTORY TEXTBOOKS

### RELIGION IN HISTORY

*Learning Magazine* reported in November 1987 that the Association for Supervision and Curriculum Development encourages teachers to return to the inclusion of religion in their courses about history and society. *Learning* said the ASCD report, "Religion in the Curriculum," complained that "public school children aren't learning enough about the importance of religion in American history and society because educators and textbook publishers fear controversy."

### OMISSION OF RELIGION FROM TEXTBOOKS

U.S. District Court Judge W. Brevard Hand ruled on March 4, 1987, that 39 nationally distributed history and social studies texts and six home economics texts used in Alabama's 129 school systems "discriminate against the very concept of religion and theistic religions in particular, by omissions so serious that a student learning history from them would not be apprised of relevant facts about America's history. ... References to religion are isolated and the integration of religion in the history of American society is ignored."

### AND THEN

On August 26, 1987, the U.S. Court of Appeals for the Eleventh Circuit unanimously overturned Judge Hand's decision by ruling that the information in the books was "essentially neutral in its religious content." The fact that the texts *omitted references to religion* was "not an advancement of secular humanism or an active hostility toward theistic religion." Superior courts refused to hear further appeals.

### FREEDOM OF THE PRESS?

This information is from the American Library Association's *Banned Books Week '89: A Resource Book*, published for the use of booksellers in promoting the freedom to read. The American Library Association, the

American Booksellers Association, and other sponsors of Banned Books Week considered Judge Hand's ruling against the books to be an act of censorship, in that the charge of "promoting secular humanism" had been brought by fundamentalists, but the ruling that overturned Judge Hand's ruling was regarded as a righteous blow struck for freedom of the press.

The members of that Court of Appeals should be reminded that fictional history is not the same as historical fiction. Whether or not the omission of references to religion constitutes "active hostility toward religion," it certainly seems to indicate a disdain for truth and accuracy in history. Religion, Christianity in particular, was of unimpeachable importance in the founding and growth of the United States; the deliberate omission of the fact from school textbooks, along with supporting references throughout, is hardly "neutral." Such "neutrality" constitutes a censorship far more real and more malignant than Judge Hand's ruling against it.

Mark Twain said that God made a fool for practice, and then made school boards. I'd say that was for further practice; then God made the U.S. Court of Appeals that overturned Judge Hand's efforts to remove fictional history from the schools of Alabama.

**THE FUTURE OF HISTORY**, by Howard Zinn, contains very provocative material. In a series of interviews with David Barsamian, Zinn offers a reflection on history, a critical look at why history is written the way it is, and an examination of how social change happens. Included is material from Zinn's book *You Can't Be Neutral on a Moving Train*. Zinn, always an advocate of the people, speaks with humor and foresight. This stimulating critique will leave you with much to consider, and thoughtful readers will come away with critical tools for evaluating written histories. An excellent tool for those of us helping our kids develop critical thinking skills. Code CC, $13.95.

### Tools to Help You Through the Years

**COBBLESTONE, The History Magazine for Young People**. American history presented in a unique and exciting way — through original firsthand accounts, biographies, poems, maps, games, puzzles, cartoons, songs, and recipes. Each issue focuses on a single theme drawing from the political, business, scientific, artistic, and literary areas of life in the period covered. Ages 10 and up. Cobblestone Publishing, Inc., 30 Grove St., Peterborough, NH 03458; 800-821-0115; www.cobblestonepub.com.

**CALLIOPE, World History for Young People**. Very interesting and informative magazine about the myths, legends, history, and cultures from ancient civilizations through the Middle Ages and the Renaissance, for ages 10 and up. Excellent introduction to many of the roots of present-day civilization and the many ways in which modern society has grown from the thoughts and customs of older societies. Available from Cobblestone Publishing, listed above.

**ARCHAEOLOGY** is for young inquiring minds. This book is a good introduction to one of the fascinating ways we study the past. Clearly written with excellent and dramatic pictures, it offers safe and simple projects and experiments using household items. Written with the help of experts in the field. Ages 9 to 13. Code EDC, $6.95.

**ARCHAEOLOGY**, put out by Oxford University Press, is a more in-depth look at human history. I find the many color photos of archaeological digs absolutely fascinating. Through a timeline, maps, and photos this book will take you through the ages from 3.8 million years ago to the present. You'll see the past come to life, learn how archaeologists unscramble puzzles from the past, and travel all the continents of the world. High school students. Hardcover. Code OX, $25.

**ANTHRONOTES**. A free newsletter about anthropology and teaching it to kids. Three issues per year. Anthropology Outreach Office, NHB 363 MRC, 112 Smithsonian Institution, Washington, DC 20560. To receive by e-mail, e-mail your request to: kaupp.ann@nmnh.si.edu.

**THE WORLD'S GREAT SPEECHES**, edited by Lewis Copeland and Lawrence W. Lamm. This wide-ranging collection of 278 speeches from the early Greeks to 1970 presents a powerful, unique look at history. Code DV, $18.95.

**YESTERDAY'S HEADLINES, TODAY'S HISTORY**. Original radio broadcasts of world news events, including Lindbergh welcomed home, the crash of the Hindenburg, the Dempsey-Tunney fight, the Pearl Harbor invasion, the fall of Corregidor, the D-Day invasion, Truman announcing the dropping of the A-bomb, MacArthur at the Japanese surrender, the Nuremberg trials, the assassination of JFK, and much more. One cassette. Code AF, $12.95.

**VOICES OF THE PAST**. Actual voices of more than 40 famous people of history, including Florence Nightingale, Thomas Edison, P.T. Barnum, Enrico Caruso, Teddy Roosevelt, Woodrow Wilson, V.I. Lenin, Will Rogers, Billy Sunday, W.C. Fields, Calvin Coolidge, Herbert Hoover, Mohandas Gandhi, and Albert Einstein. One cassette. Code AF, $12.95.

**History Book Club**. For information, write to the History Book Club, Camp Hill, PA 17012-0001; www.historybookclub.com.

## WORLD HISTORY

**A CHILD'S HISTORY OF THE WORLD**, from the Calvert School, is now available to the public. This is the best book on world history for children that we've ever seen. It was originally presented for third grade, but we loved the book and didn't want to rush through it in one year. Instead, we stretched it out over more years than I can remember, taking our time and investigating everything that interested us. The paperback edition that we had fell apart and was repaired many times. When I recently discovered it is now available to the public I excitedly told our kids. All of them remember the book with affection. Now available in a hardcover binding that will last. $35, directly from Calvert School. Address in "Support Groups and Organizations."

**USBORNE BOOK OF WORLD HISTORY.** This book, combining five individual titles (*Dinosaurs; Prehistoric Mammals; First Civilizations; Age of Revolutions;* and *Crusaders, Aztecs, and Samurai*) and more, presents a concise but very comprehensive outline of the development of mankind from the Stone Age to World War I, covering great scientific discoveries, the evolution of the arts, the founding and spreading of the major religions, colonization, major revolutions, and the development of several civilizations. Key dates are given, along with a timeline for each major period. Alive with pictures, maps, and charts. Ages 8 and up, including adults, who will find it more fascinating and informative than any school textbook on the same subject. Code EDC, $24.95.

**TIME TRAVELER BOOK**. Combines four titles (*Knights and Castles, Viking Raiders, Pharaohs and Pyramids,* and *Rome and Romans,* listed separately below) into one volume, taking readers back in time for a very detailed introduction to fascinating aspects of daily life in four major periods. Colorful, detailed, well-researched drawings show the houses, social life, clothing, weapons, cooking utensils, farm equipment, schools, shops, markets, battles, feasts, and religious rites. Code EDC, $22.95.

**WORLD HISTORY THE EASY WAY**. These two volumes are not the most exciting books to read, but they have all that is essential for high school study and college entrance exams. Good as reference items, if nothing else. Code BE, $12.95 each volume.

**ESSENTIALS OF WORLD HISTORY**, by Jean Reeder Smith and Lucey Baldwin Smith. A concise reference book, with brief articles that outline ancient, medieval, and modern periods of major world areas: the Middle East, Europe, Russia, North America, Latin America, India and Southwest Asia, China, Japan, Southeast Asia, and sub-Saharan Africa. Bibliography and index. Very useful, but with definite limitations. In keeping with modern publishers' fear of controversy, *Essentials of World History* presents very bare facts with little mention of the political or sociological causes and effects, particularly if those causes or effects border on religion. For instance, the story of the Pilgrims being persecuted in England and eventually emigrating to America is told — but with no mention whatsoever of *why* they were persecuted or why they felt it necessary to emigrate. An excellent example of "neutrality" as defined by a U.S. Appeals Court (see Omission of Religion from Textbooks, above). Despite this serious shortcoming, this book can serve as an excellent skeleton upon which to build a good study program, simply by using the entries as guides to further research. High school and up. Code BE, $12.95.

**A SHORT HISTORY OF THE WORLD**, by J.M. Roberts. Personally, I wouldn't call 513 pages *plus* an extensive index "short," but considering that volumes have been written, this is an excellent condensation. It's written at a college and adult level; I would use this book to outline high school world history studies. I'd divide the book into a four-year project, read each chapter, and then write my own list of points to be studied and discussed. I don't think a high school student needs to try to absorb all the information, but I'd read it to gain a broad perspective and be able to help connect key events. I respect Roberts' approach because he isn't afraid to include the strong religious influences on our history. My only disagreement with Roberts is his statement that true history began when the written word made it possible to record it. Code OX, $15.95. Also see "Reference Books" for Roberts' *Illustrated History of the World* for younger learners.

For history essays at a high school level, the **CONCORD REVIEW** accepts exemplary student essays on historical topics from students around the world. Essays should be about 5,000 words, plus endnotes. Those chosen are eligible for the Emerson Prize of $3,000. For more information contact the *Concord Review*, P.O. Box 661, Concord, MA 01742; 800-331-5007; fitzhugh@tcr.org. A free sample issue is available upon request. Take a look at some samples of winning essays at www.tcr.org. The *Concord Review* also sponsors the National Writing Board (which reads and rates history papers) and will forward scores to college admissions officers, providing evidence that an applicant has gone above and beyond what is required. At the moment, they rate only history papers. Beginning in 2001, they will evaluate literature papers as well.

### History Atlases

**THE READER'S DIGEST CHILDREN'S ATLAS OF WORLD HISTORY**. The rise of the Roman Empire, great dynasties of China, Viking invasions, kingdoms of Africa, the age of exploration — every key period in the history of the world is vividly portrayed in this beautifully illustrated atlas. Young readers are taken inside all the great moments of the past — from the very first civilization in Mesopotamia through the Middle Ages, the world's great empires, and the age of industry and revolution — all the way up to the wars and scientific advances of the 20th century. Each important historic period is given its own two-page spread, with an easy-to-read introduction providing an overview of the time and putting it into context. A complete world map for each section shows major empires, centers of civilization, and nations of that time, and also includes such important information as trade routes, invasion paths, and voyages. A time chart puts major events into context; boxed features cover key people, places, and events; everyday life throughout history is shown in photographs of art and other illustrations. Special "Who's Who in History" and "The World Today" sections and a comprehensive glossary enhance the value of the atlas. This has been our favorite. Hardcover; full-color illustrations. Ages 7 to 14. Code BT, $22.

**ATLAS OF WORLD HISTORY**. An Usborne book with many clear maps and illustrations, time chart, glossary, map index, and index. Begins with the formation of the earth, discusses the first people, and shows the development of civilization around the world. Excellent, clear synopses of times and places. Covers main historical movements, including a few not usually mentioned, like the slave trade and right to vote. Hardcover. All ages. Code EDC, $17.95.

Both of the previous atlases are excellent. The Reader's Digest atlas has more information. You'll have to base your decision on your needs and budget.

**CONCISE ATLAS OF WORLD HISTORY**. A great family reference for teens and adults, with up-to-date, dramatic, easy-to-use maps and informative text. The many great changes brought about in civilization through exploration, wars, migrations, and other historic factors are clearly demonstrated. A useful book for dramatically showing your kids the sweep of world history. Paperback, 192 pages. Code HMD, $34.95.

## TRACKING DATES

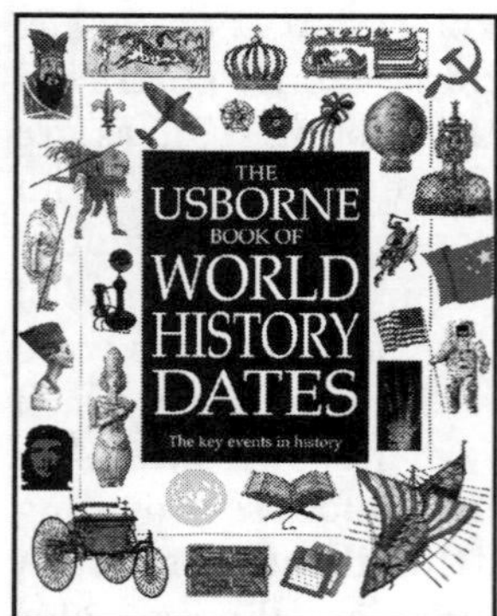


**USBORNE BOOK OF WORLD HISTORY DATES: From Stone Age to Computer Age.** An easy-to-read, profusely illustrated reference that combines detailed date charts with features highlighting important themes in world history, such as the First Farmers, the Provincial Wars in Japan, the Rise of the Manchu Dynasty, and the Great Depression. Each of the eight sections has feature articles on main events, a listing of important dates, many maps, and numerous illustrations. Some pages are divided into columns so you can easily follow simultaneous events occurring in different locations in the same time period. Glossary. Excellent reference tool for ages 10 and up, including teens. Code EDC, $22.95.

**WORLD HISTORY DATES** also comes in an abridged edition for easy reference. Facts covering the time between 9000 B.C. and the 1990s, quizzes, and activities. 32 pages; specify pocket-size. 7x4½". Ages 7 and up. Code EDC, $2.95.

*Revised* — **THE TIMETABLES OF HISTORY: A Horizontal Linkage of People and Events**, by Bernard Grun; based on Werner Stein's *Kulturfahrplan*. One of the most unusual books published, and one of our favorites. Look up any year from 4241 B.C. to the present and read the brief synopsis of the major events and accomplishments in seven areas: History and Politics, Literature and the Theater,

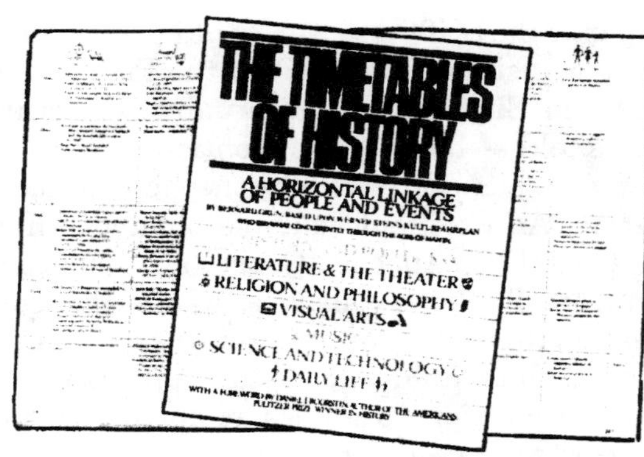


Religion and Philosophy, the Visual Arts, Music, Science and Technology, and Daily Life. For instance, in 1853, Franklin Pierce became U.S. president, the Crimean War began, Hawthorne published *Tanglewood Tales*, Vincent van Gogh was born, Wagner completed the text for "The Ring," and Samuel Colt revolutionized the manufacture of guns. Fully indexed. A resource for the whole family. Code SS, $21.

**PALEO PALS**. An interactive card game with a cassette and read-along book. Everything needed to absorb new information and have fun doing it. The cassette and book explain what life was like in the prehistoric age. There are puzzles to complete and four different games to play with the cards. Learning fascinating facts about the huge creatures that roamed the earth long ago will just happen as you play. Cards have excellent dinosaur pictures. 1 to 4 players, ages 4 to 8. Code A, $15.

**First Histories for Ages 6 to 8**. The following two sets of books are the best we've seen for this age group. These great introductory books to our past arouse interest, answer questions, and help young children make comparisons about life then and now. Well researched, with colorful illustrations.

**Starting Point History Series**. Ages 6 to 8. Code EDC, $4.95 each, or you can get the complete set for $25.95.

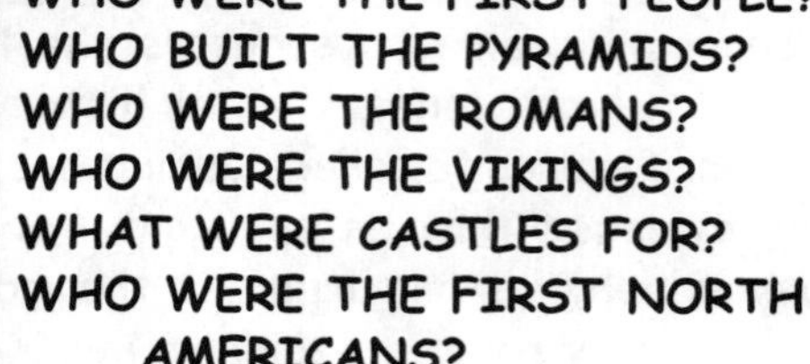

**WHO WERE THE FIRST PEOPLE?**
**WHO BUILT THE PYRAMIDS?**
**WHO WERE THE ROMANS?**
**WHO WERE THE VIKINGS?**
**WHAT WERE CASTLES FOR?**
**WHO WERE THE FIRST NORTH AMERICANS?**

FIRST HISTORY SERIES

**LIVING IN PREHISTORIC TIMES, LIVING IN ROMAN TIMES,** or **LIVING IN CASTLE TIMES**. Each book focuses on one central character, a child, to give a vivid picture of life in the different periods. Very detailed. Colorful pictures. A fantastic introduction to history for ages 6 to 9, Code EDC, $4.50 each, or all three in one volume, **THE USBORNE FIRST BOOK OF HISTORY**, $9.95.

**LIVING LONG AGO** is really four books in one: *Clothes and Fashion, Travel and Transport, Food and Eating,* and *Homes and Houses of Long Ago*. A colorful look at everyday life through the ages, including accurately detailed pictures of adults and children engaged in serious and sometimes funny activities. It's amazing how much you can learn just by looking at the pictures, and the text is great, too. Ages 7 to 10. Code EDC, $12.95.

**FIRST CIVILIZATIONS**, from 10,000 B.C. to 1500 B.C. Covers artwork, myths, religion, architecture, and daily life of the Sumerians, the ancient Egyptians, the Cretans, and the Babylonians, including children's games, cosmetics, cuneiform writing, bread and wine making, and much more. (Part of the *Usborne Book of World History* listed above). Ages 8 and up. Code EDC, $6.95.

EGYPT

***Revised* — PHARAOHS AND PYRAMIDS**. Shows construction of a pyramid, elaborate burial rites, the court of the pharaoh, an Egyptian temple with explanations of beliefs about the spirit world and afterlife, feasts, household structure, life on the Nile, and how hieroglyphic writing worked. Ages 8 to 11. Code EDC, $6.95.

**ANCIENT EGYPT**. A fact-filled coloring book with many of the line drawings taken from ancient Egyptian art. Its two-page spreads present one page with the information and the other with a related picture to color. You'll learn about the pharaohs, the Nile, food, architecture, fashion, education, daily life, mummies (who they were, how they were mummified, and what's been learned from them), and much more. 60 illustrations to color, plus a 16x20" poster to color. Ages 8 to 12. Code RP, $8.95.

**LIFE IN ANCIENT EGYPT**. A 48-page coloring book with pictures and captions that explain everyday life. Ages 8 and up. Code DV, $2.95.

**ANCIENT EGYPTIANS AND THEIR NEIGHBORS**, by Marian Broida. The ancient Egyptians didn't exist in a vacuum. This very interesting book presents Egyptian culture in context with the ancient Hittites, Nubians, and Mesopotamians, highlighting similarities and differences. Lots of activities are included: building a model Egyptian boat, writing cuneiform (and other forms of early writing), making a royal headdress, and more. Activities make use of household and other easily found items. Ages 9 and up. Code CRP, $16.95.

**SECRETS OF THE MUMMIES**, by Shelley Tanaka. When this book arrived with a pile of other books to be reviewed or given to the library, I first thought, "Oh, no! I need another book on ancient Egypt like I need another snowstorm." I'm glad I didn't follow my knee-jerk response, which was to donate it to the library. Not for the squeamish, although it isn't full of gore either, *Secrets of the Mummies* begins with an overview of what ancient cultures did with their dead. Tanaka then goes on to describe Egyptian mummies in detail, discussing the treatment after death of renowned as well as common people. Many wonderful color photos of mummies with up-to-date explanations of all that can be learned from them. Ages 8 to 12. Code LB, $16.99.

**EGYPTIAN PUNCH-OUT MUMMY CASE.** Simple directions and diagrams explain how to assemble a handsome model of a mummy case that once held the remains of a royal architect who lived during the reign of Ramses II (1304-1237 B.C.). Approximately 11" long, 3½" wide, and 4" deep, the brightly colored and ornamented sarcophagus, decorated with hieroglyphics, emblems of gods, and other artwork, comes complete with removable lid and gauze-shrouded figure inside the case. No scissors needed; just punch out, fold, and glue. Code DV, $3.95.

**NESTING EGYPTIAN PUNCH-OUT MUMMY CASES.** A set of three from large to small. Ages 7 to 9. Code DV, $4.95.

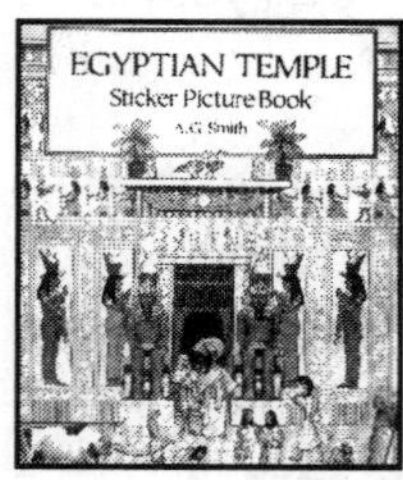


**Acid-Free Reusable Sticker Picture Books.** 9x12" book. The inside of the front and back covers becomes 18x12" background scenes. Ages 8 and up. Code DV.
**BUILDING THE PYRAMIDS**, $3.95.
**EGYPTIAN TEMPLE**, $3.50

**LEGENDS OF THE EGYPTIAN GODS.** Ages 8 and up. 352 pages. Code DV, $8.95.

**CUT AND MAKE EGYPTIAN MASKS.** Authentic reproductions. Decorative. Ages 6 and up. Code DV, $7.95.

## GREECE AND ROME

**ATLAS OF THE CLASSICAL WORLD**, by Piero Bardi. Brimming with colorful pictures, maps, and information about ancient Greece, Rome, Athens, the Minoans and Mycenaeans, and the Etruscans. Pictures and text are full of detail about daily life, social structure, religion, agriculture, trade, war, theater, science, literature and mythology, the arts, sports, and more. Learn about Alexander and the Hellenistic world, the influence of Christianity, the rise and fall of the Roman Empire, and the classical legacy we live with today. A book you can use for pleasant browsing and reference over many years. Written for an audience 10 and up, and the illustrations will fascinate younger readers. Outstanding! Code PB, $19.95.

**CLASSICAL KIDS: An Activity Guide to Life in Ancient Greece and Rome**, by Laurie Carlson. Great hands-on creative activities guaranteed to be fun. Make a star gazer, chisel a clay tablet, weave Roman sandals, create a Greek mosaic, and much more, while learning about life in Greek and Roman times. Ages 5 to 12. Code CRP, $14.95.

**LIFE IN ANCIENT ROME.** Coloring book with 41 captioned, finely detailed illustrations. Ages 8 and up. Code DV, $2.95

***Revised* — ROME AND ROMANS.** Shows a typical home, public baths, shops, markets, the Colosseum, temples, forums, aqueducts, gladiators, charioteers, and a Roman feast; covers life in the city, the country, at school, and in the army. Be a time traveler and visit Rome in the year AD 100. Good illustrations. Ages 8 to 11. Code EDC, $6.95.

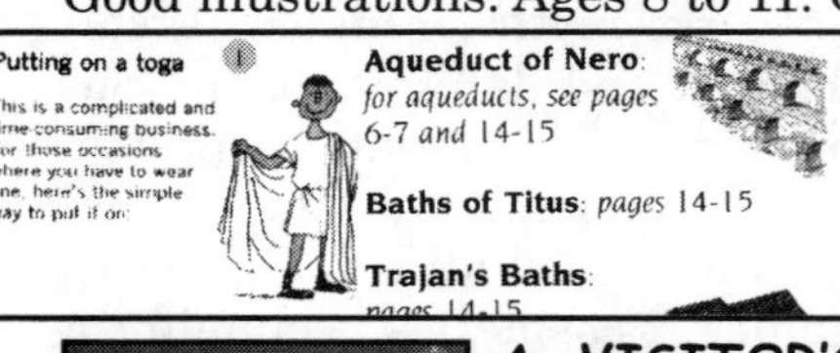

**A VISITOR'S GUIDE TO ANCIENT ROME.** If you were really going to ancient Rome, this book would be essential. It's well illustrated with color pictures and reproductions, and opens to a street map to help orient you (which also illustrates attractions, making them easy to find). Rome is at its height, and you will have to choose a place to stay, learn how to behave at a banquet, discover what to do if you're sick — in short, learn about everything to do with everyday life, religion, politics, and fashion. Lots of history in such a palatable format, with illustrations to capture the imagination. Lots of humor in the illustrations, too! A good companion volume to the book above. Ages 12 and up. Code EDC, $9.95.

**THE USBORNE ENCYCLOPEDIA OF ANCIENT GREECE.** You just won't find a more comprehensive guide to ancient Greece than this one. It covers the history from the first settlers to the great civilizations of Crete and classical Athens to the Roman conquest. This is all done through clear explanatory text and a wealth of color photographs, period artwork, detailed maps, and cutaways. Contains details of everyday life, wars, politics, and religious beliefs, plus a time chart, a glossary, and suggested references. If you're reading mythology to your children, they will be fascinated by the pictures in this book. Hardcover, 160 pages. Ages 9 and up. Code EDC, $19.95.

**ANCIENT MEDITERRANEAN VIEW OF MAN.** Arnold Toynbee analyzes man's knowledge of ancient Greek life, especially the contributions of the city-states to art, poetry, science, philosophy, and war. One cassette. Ages 14 to adult. Code AF, $12.95.

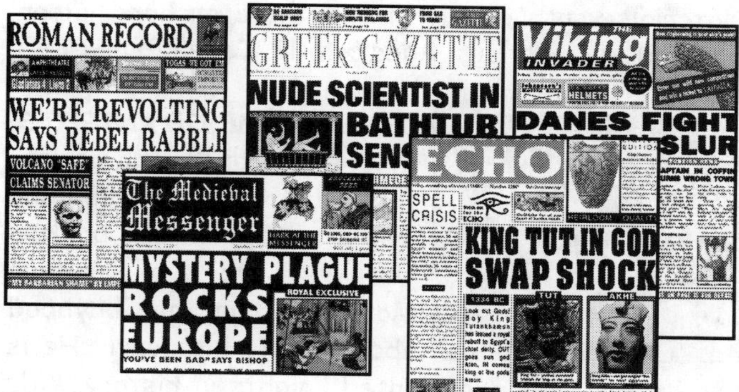


Add spice to history! Imaginative and *historically accurate*, these books look like tabloid papers you see on the newsstands. A real tongue-in-cheek look at the past. Great fun. Ages 10 and up. Code EDC, $6.95 each. Specify **STONE AGE SENTINEL, EGYPTIAN ECHO, GREEK GAZETTE, ROMAN RECORD, VIKING INVADER,** or **MEDIEVAL MESSENGER.**

Historical paper dolls are fun to play with — an easy way to absorb history. Each book is $9\frac{1}{4}$x$12\frac{1}{4}$", 32 pages. Code DV, $3.95 each. Specify **ANCIENT EGYPTIAN** or **ANCIENT GREEK.**

**Illustrated World History Series.** Each of the following books examines the everyday lives of people who lived long ago. Understanding how people from the past lived helps us to understand how today's complex civilization evolved. The artist's sense of humor makes the illustrations in these books come alive. Maps and diagrams too. Ages 11 and up. Code EDC.

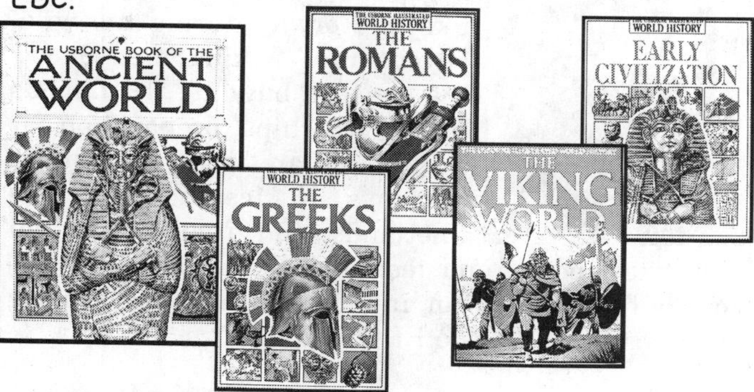


**EARLY CIVILIZATION** (96 pages), $12.95.
**THE GREEKS** (96 pages), $12.95.
**THE ROMANS** (96 pages), $12.95.
**VIKING WORLD** (64 pages), $11.95.
**THE ANCIENT WORLD** (combo of *Early Civilization, The Greeks,* and *The Romans*) 288 pages, $26.95.

**AND ON INTO THE MIDDLE AGES**

**The Living History Series.** Breathtaking photographs and a fact-filled text almost bring history to life in these books. This series re-creates scenes from various historical periods using an innovative computer technique to combine photographs of real locations with artifacts, costumed actors, and detailed miniature models. The books are edited by John D. Clare, a historian and teacher who has pioneered the use of computers in the teaching of history. To ensure accuracy, museum curators and historians have checked every detail of the text and photographs. Each book also has maps, timelines, and an index. Ages 8 and up. Hardcover. Code HB, $16.95 each unless otherwise marked. The lower prices indicate paperback editions.
**PYRAMIDS OF ANCIENT EGYPT**
**CLASSICAL ROME**, $9
**KNIGHTS IN ARMOR**, $10
**FOURTEENTH-CENTURY TOWNS**, $9
**THE VOYAGES OF CHRISTOPHER COLUMBUS**

*Revised* — **VIKING RAIDERS.** Be a Viking in the year AD 890. Find out what everyday life is like in Norway during the wild, adventurous Viking era. Shows the steps in building the famous Viking warships; preparation for a raid on an Irish monastery; journeys to Iceland and the Shetlands; and a winter festival of games, sports, and feasting. Great color illustrations of life on the farm, in a trading town, and on the sea. Ages 8 to 11. Code EDC, $6.95.

**VIKING VILLAGE.** Acid-free reusable sticker picture book, $9\frac{1}{4}$x$11\frac{1}{4}$". The inside of the front and back covers becomes an 18x$11\frac{1}{4}$" background scene for the 30 or more full-color, reusable stickers. Ages 7 and up. Code DV, $3.95.

**KINGS AND QUEENS: From Ramesses to Elizabeth II**. Filled with authentic details, charts, maps, diagrams, photos (when available), and color pictures. History will come alive as you read about the people who shaped it. Ages 10 and up. Code EDC, $8.95. (Part of *Famous Lives* in the biography section of this chapter.)

**CASTLES, PYRAMIDS, AND PALACES**. This book will satisfy the special fascination most children have with castles, pyramids, and palaces, and the life that goes on in them. Full-color maps and diagrams. Best of all, cutaway sections give a special look at what goes on in each room. Pictures show daily life, the serious and humorous. One of my favorites. Ages 7 to adult. Code EDC, $8.95.

**THE GREAT WALL OF CHINA**, by Leonard Everett Fisher. The story behind the building of the Great Wall of China, told with brief text and very impressive pictures — buildings, people, and animals seem almost three-dimensional in the large, colorful paintings. Ages 8 and up. Code MAC, $5.95.

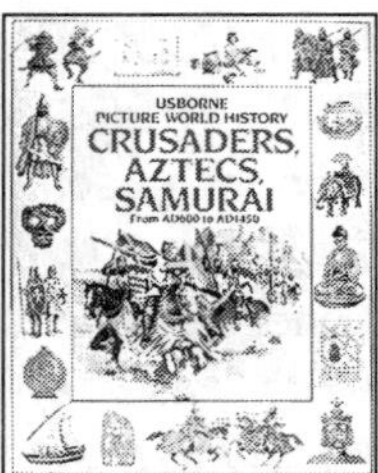


**CRUSADERS, AZTECS, AND SAMURAI**. Covers A.D. 600 to 1450, including the Dark and Middle Ages in Europe, the rise of Islam, life in Asia, Vikings, life in Europe (village life, the Church, knights, and castles), Genghis Khan and the Mongols, trade with China, the samurai of Japan, and life in Africa and the Americas (part of the *Usborne Book of World History*). Ages 8 and up. Code EDC, $6.95.

**DAYS OF KNIGHTS AND DAMSELS**, by Laurie Carlson. Outstanding book! Hours of creative play. Carlson really understands kids at play. A wonderful compendium of more than 100 activities to add magic and knowledge, based on historical fact, to everyday play. How to make a knight's armor, tiaras, garlands, basic foods of the time (that you can really eat), coats of arms, toys, games, magic tricks, candles, and much more, using materials you probably already have on hand. Clear, illustrated directions. Ages 5 to 12. Code CRP, $14.95.

**IN THE TIME OF KNIGHTS,** by Shelley Tanaka and beautifully illustrated by Greg Ruhl. The storyline in this book is the true story of William Marshal, from his boyhood abduction to his death. He is one of the best documented knights in history. Kids will enjoy his story by itself, but there's a lot more in this book. Through interesting sidebars, paintings, diagrams, and pictures of original artwork of the time you get a very good picture of what life was like. You'll pick up a bit of geography and learn about the traits needed for knighthood. This is part of a new series called "I Was There," and I hope to see many more of these in the future. Hardcover. Ages 8 to 12. Code LB, $16.99.

**KNIGHTS AND CASTLES** shows foot soldiers, serfs, squires, and stewards at work and play; detailed drawings of the castle courtyard, keep, and other buildings; outfitting a knight; jousting; and an attack on the castle. Great detail, intriguing illustrations. Lots of information. Ages 8 and up. Code EDC, $6.95.

**CUT AND MAKE A KNIGHT'S HELMET**. Code DV, $4.95.

**CUT AND MAKE A KNIGHT IN ARMOR**. Code DV, $4.95.

**MEDIEVAL TOURNAMENT**. Acid-free reusable sticker book, $9\frac{1}{4}$x$11\frac{1}{4}$". The book cover makes a backdrop for the 30 or more full-color, reusable stickers. Ages 7 and up. Code DV. $4.50.

**MEDIEVAL KNIGHT** and paper soldiers. Full-color figures, some on horseback. Well researched. Ages 10 and up. Code DV, $4.95.

**THE STORIES OF KING ARTHUR**, retold and illustrated by Howard Pyle. In 1902, Pyle undertook the retelling of the old Arthurian tales and eventually produced four volumes, which were published from 1903 to 1910. Other books have been written about King Arthur, but Pyle's works are the enduring classics, usually preferred over all others. The stories are packed with action, adventure, loyalty, bravery, romance, and heroism. Historians generally agree that King Arthur is fictional, but these stories can still be read as "historical fiction" because they portray fairly accurately the attitudes, beliefs, and political and religious issues of a short period of English history, many of which have carried over into our present society's legal and moral culture. Like millions of others, I grew up with these stories; we passed them on to our children, and we certainly hope our grandchildren will have them, too. Whether the stories are historically accurate or not, most of their ideas and values will always be valid and desirable. This is a volume to enjoy, give as a gift, or pass on to the next generation. Hardcover. Code MAC, $21.

**THE MERRY ADVENTURES OF ROBIN HOOD**, by Howard Pyle. Facsimile of the original 1883 edition, with 23 illustrations by Pyle. Code DV, $8.95.

**HISTORY OF THE SWORD.** A coloring book with 44 detailed and carefully researched drawings depicting swords and their bearers, from prehistory through the 17th century. Informative captions. Ages 8 and up. Code DV, $2.95.

**THE BLACK ARROW: A Tale of Two Roses**, by Robert Louis Stevenson. I read this book (for the first time, I admit) just a few weeks ago, and was fascinated by its vivid depiction of 15th-century Britain's conflicts — in this case, between York and Lancaster, in the 30-year War of the Roses. Besides being a tale of adventure and romance amid the country's shifting alliances, *The Black Arrow* is also a dramatic portrayal of the suffering war inflicts on all sides. Stevenson's re-creation of 15th-century English gives an insight into the evolution of our language. Originally published in 1888. This is a reprint of the 1916 edition, with 14 beautiful paintings by famed illustrator N.C. Wyeth. Hardcover gift edition, 336 pages. Code MAC, $28.

**LIFE IN A MEDIEVAL CASTLE AND VILLAGE.** A coloring book with 42 realistic, detailed drawings of farming, warfare, hunting, domestic life, crafts, tournaments, castle sieges, banquets, and more, all with good captions. Good introduction to this time period. Ages 8 and up. Code DV, $2.95.

**MEDIEVAL JOUSTS AND TOURNAMENTS.** A coloring book with 43 realistic drawings. Good detail and captions. Ages 10 and up. Code DV, $2.95.

**GARGOYLES AND MEDIEVAL MONSTERS.** A coloring book of dragons, winged dogs, demons, architecture, and more. Some drawings are from the Book of Kells. Good captions. Ages 10 and up. Code DV, $2.95.

## EXPLORATION AND COLONIZATION

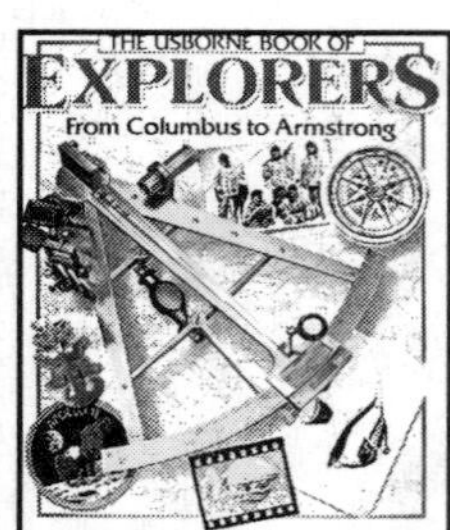


**EXPLORERS: From Columbus to Armstrong**. If you ask me, they missed the boat by not covering a longer time span, but they've done a great job of covering the time from Columbus on — with maps, charts, diagrams, and good illustrations. Ages 10 and up. Code EDC, $8.95. (Part of *Famous Lives* in the biography section of this chapter.)

**PIRATES**, by Gail Gibbons. A blend of fact and fiction, with a history of piracy on the high seas, short biographies of famous pirates, and nice color illustrations. A gentle introduction to geography too. Ages 5 to 8. Code LB, $4.95.

**PIRATES**. Bobbie Kalman and Greg Nickles have created a book that will capture the hearts of your scalawags and steep them in pirate history. Full-color illustrations and photos taken at pirate festivals (what a great idea!) show clothing, parts of a ship, flags, and maps with historic information. Learn about the life and duties of the crew, male and female pirates, how ships were captured, and punishments carried out. Ages 6 to 10. Code CT, $5.95.

**LAFITTE THE PIRATE**, by Lyle Saxon. Jean Lafitte was a romantic rogue whose den of pirates at Barataria Bay near New Orleans made him a terror throughout the Gulf of Mexico and the Caribbean. His battles with the law were legendary. When Louisiana Governor Claiborne offered a reward for his capture, Lafitte offered a larger reward for the capture of Claiborne. But when the British landed in Louisiana and threatened New Orleans, the pirate became a patriot and joined his band of outlaws with the army of Andrew Jackson to win the Battle of New Orleans. Illustrated, with a bibliography. 352 pages. Ages 10 to adult. Code PEL, $14.95.

**THE AGE OF REVOLUTIONS,** A.D. 1750 to 1914. Examines the effects of the agricultural and industrial revolutions; highlights of the French and American revolutions; the colonization of Africa, India, and Australia; Commodore Perry in Japan; and the impact of newly invented cars, steam locomotives, and airplanes. (Part of *The Usborne Book of World History*). Ages 8 and up. Code EDC, $6.95.

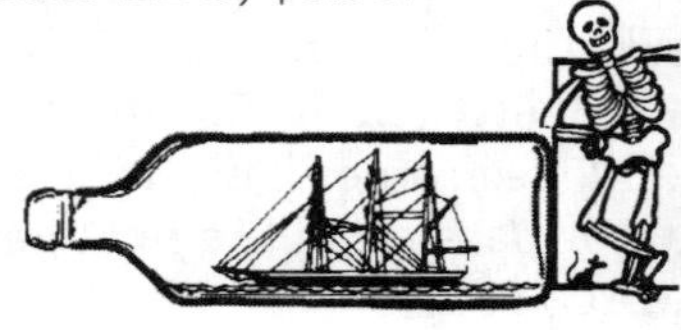

### U.S. HISTORY

Donn was so discouraged with all the U.S. history books he saw that he planned to write one someday. I despaired of ever finding one I could heartily recommend, with a focus on people, ideas, the arts, and inventions that changed the world — and yes, even on the wars (some of which had a major influence on the course of history), but we wanted the primary focus to be on people and issues.

Washington

Give me liberty or give me death.

I read the reviews for *A History of US* and thought the reviewers did a good PR job, but I didn't really believe what I read. I decided to take a look at the set anyhow — and was astonished! The series is terrific — just what Donn and I had been looking for.

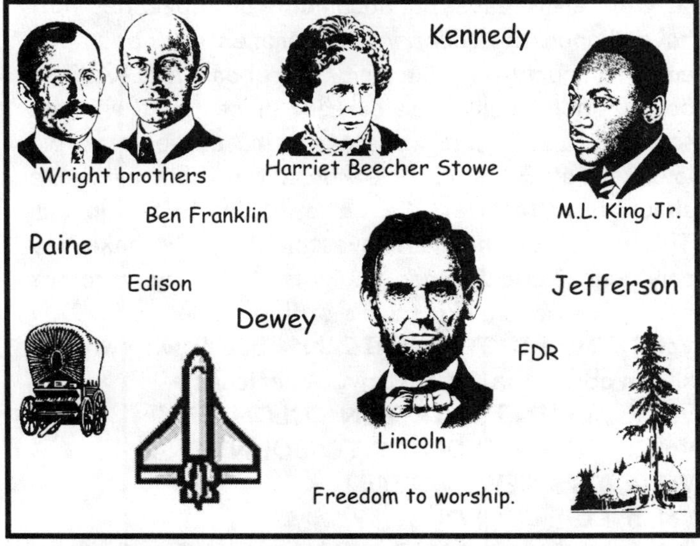


**A HISTORY OF US**, a set of 11 volumes, by Joy Hakim. These very readable books don't even resemble "schoolbooks" in spite of their having been written by a former teacher. Hakim presents history as the story of people, which is as it should be. You meet ordinary people, not just the presidents and well-known figures, and discover how they lived. These engaging books, with excellent color illustrations, ask the reader to think and form opinions. Hakim makes good use of original sources, newspaper excerpts, cartoons, diaries, drawings, maps, and the original artwork of the time. You'll find yourself spending more time thinking about the people and the issues

than memorizing meaningless names, battles, and dates. While this series of books is not cheap, it will be all that you will need from about third grade through junior high. If you have young children, I suggest that you can take your time going through the books, concentrating on one historical period at a time, or you can go through the books more quickly, returning for a more in-depth study when the children are older. Hakim's inclusion of an extensive list of related reading material in the back of each book is a real boon to those who like to explore in depth. While the original set was 10 volumes, the newly revised set is 11 volumes. This most recent addition to the set contains a complete index for the series, a good glossary of terms, essential documents and speeches that have shaped the country, and commentary about why each is important. The price per book is $13.95 if bought individually. The current price for the whole set is $153.45, but we are setting our price a bit lower — at $139.95 — because we think everyone should have this set. We'll also include UPS shipping. This is one of the best investments you'll make. My only regret about these books is that they were not available when our kids were still at home. Code OX.

Vol. 1, **THE FIRST AMERICANS** (begins with what is known about the first Native Americans)
Vol. 2, **MAKING THIRTEEN COLONIES**
Vol. 3, **FROM COLONIES TO COUNTRY**
Vol. 4, **THE NEW NATION**
Vol. 5, **LIBERTY FOR ALL?**
Vol. 6, **WAR, TERRIBLE WAR**
Vol. 7, **RECONSTRUCTION AND REFORM**
Vol. 8, **AN AGE OF EXTREMES**
Vol. 9, **WAR, PEACE, AND ALL THAT JAZZ**
Vol. 10, **ALL THE PEOPLE**
Vol. 11, Index, commentary, documents, and glossary

**TEACHING GUIDES**: one for each volume. You don't *need* these guides, but if you want to extract the most from these wonderful books you will find them useful. Each guide has more than 50 pages of chapter summaries, reading suggestions, vocabulary to learn, and — best of all — activities, projects, and ideas for discussion. The regular price for the guides is $4.16 each, or $41.60 for the complete set, plus $2.50 shipping. Our special price is $30 for the complete set of guides, with no shipping charged if you order these with *The History of US*. If you question the usefulness of the guides, send an SASE and I'll be happy to send sample copies of a few pages. Here's an example.

**7.** List some of the problems facing the nation at the turn of the century. If you had been a reporter working for S.S. McClure, which problem would you have chosen to investi gate? Why?

**8.** Study the map on page 129. Write a caption that John Muir might have prepared to accompany this map.

**9.** In 1832, Alexis de Tocqueville wrote:

*In Europe people talk a great deal about the wilds of America. But if you want to see this place in all its grandeur, hasten. . . . If you delay, it will have all been spoiled for you.*

What actions that Americans took to ensure that the "wilds" would not be "spoiled" were presented in Chapter 24?

**10.** ***Thinking about the Big Ideas:*** How do the writings of the muckrakers prove that the a free press has the power to bring about great changes? How can a free press also spur conflict or debate?

**Note from a happy mom:** "Wanted to let you know I got the books, personally I love the teaching guides. ... They help my son to focus in on what he will be reading, and the study guides ... will prove very useful for his end-of-the-year portfolio that I have to show the school system."

*** This series has extensive reading lists. If you can't find the books listed, write to us for help, even if the books are not listed in *The Home School Source Book.*

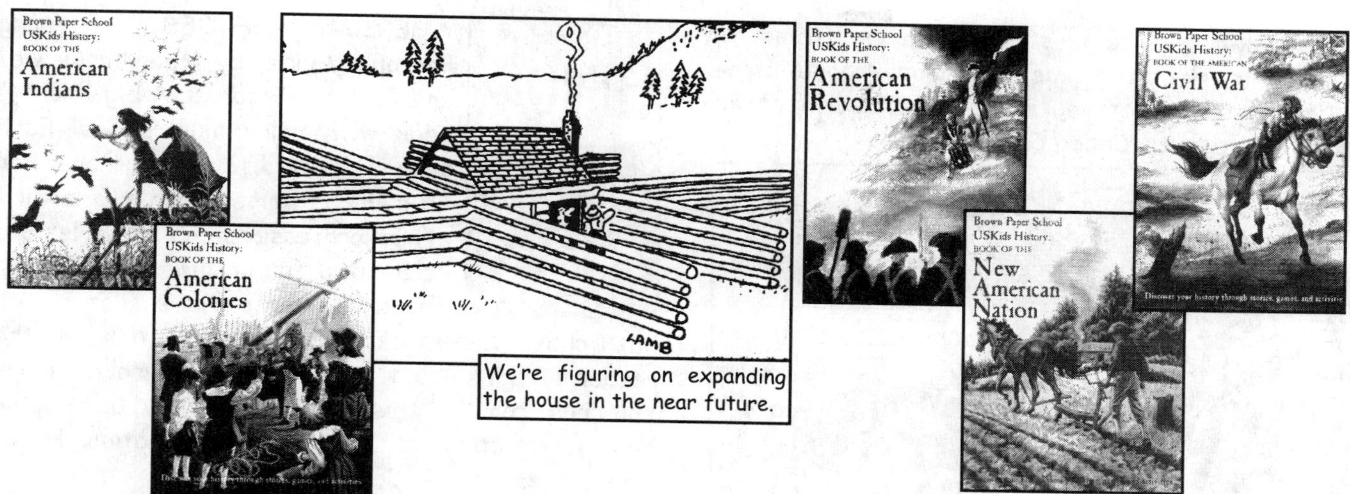


Having raved about *The History of US*, it almost feels inappropriate to mention another good series of history books. However, The Brown Paper School USKids History books are very good, and better for slightly younger children. Along with the engaging stories and exceptionally nice illustrations, you'll find games and a useful section at the back of each book with suggestions for related books, videos, activities, and more. Six-year-olds will enjoy the stories and absorb the information, but will need your help with the activities and projects. Eight- to 10-year-olds will be able to do more, but may still need some assistance. I like the variety of projects (and you will, too), but you will need to plan ahead to gather some of the materials or tools needed. Code LB, $14.95 each.

**BOOK OF THE AMERICAN INDIANS**. Organized by regions of the country, this book has well-researched, detailed text about daily life suited to this age group and at least one original Indian legend that helps to explain part of each different culture. You'll also enjoy the dramatic readings, poems, songs, speeches, and nice illustrations. Each section of the book includes activities based on the ideas, foods, customs, and crafts of this era.

**BOOK OF THE AMERICAN COLONIES**. This book begins with the exploration of North America by Norseman Leif Eriksson and continues through the time the colonies were well settled. This book (as well as the others) has a number of stories written from the perspective of young children that describe interesting facets of their daily lives. There's a fair amount of controversy about who did what to whom during this period. This book doesn't shy away from such issues, but doesn't make a big point of them either, which is very nice.

**BOOK OF THE AMERICAN REVOLUTION**. This book covers all the highlights of the times. Many stories are told from a child's perspective, which will certainly add to the interest your kids will naturally have in all these books. Good maps and illustrations will help capture the imagination as you read stories about colonists, pirates, and Loyalists. Interesting, easy-to-play games are included.

**BOOK OF THE NEW AMERICAN NATION**. Here you'll find fascinating and factual stories — both well-known and little-known — about the development and expansion of the new nation. Ideas and questions abound here as the characters, both real and fictional, ponder what kind of government will best serve the people, what rights should belong to the individual states, whether there should be slavery, and whether Native Americans had rights. Engaging text and creative games make this book exceptionally good.

**BOOK OF THE AMERICAN CIVIL WAR.** This book carries on the format of the previous four books, allowing you and your kids to discover your history through stories, games, and activities.

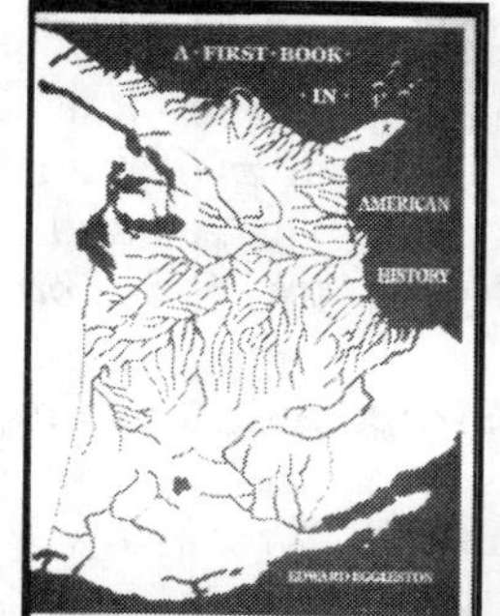


This book is part of a series for young readers. The publisher put some time and thought into considering what makes for interesting reading and constructive learning for this age group. Young people are far more interested in other people than in dates and facts. Following this reasoning, the publisher has republished **A FIRST BOOK IN AMERICAN HISTORY**, by Edward Eggleston, which draws an elemental framework of U.S. history through the biographies of people who shaped the nation, from Christopher Columbus to those involved in the Louisiana Purchase. A few history and geography lessons are thrown in, as well as some black-and-white illustrations (many from the original artwork of the time) and maps. A good introduction to a subject you will complete with other studies. Hardcover. Code LC, $24.95.

**DRAMATIZED AMERICAN HISTORY** brings it all alive. Narrated by Kenneth Bruce, a master storyteller and historian, with sound effects, music, and multiple voices. You will hear the excitement of the times — the problems, obstacles, and victories. You'll play these over and over because they'd be exciting to listen to even if you weren't learning something. These tapes make complex issues understandable.

#1. Pathway to Independence, The American Revolution, John Adams and the Undeclared War With France
#2. The Chesapeake Affair, Discovery of the Columbia River, Discovery and Settlement of California
#3. The Louisiana Purchase, The Era of Good Feeling, The Lone Star Republic
#4. The Lewis and Clark Expedition, The Era of Mountain Men, Manifest Destiny, The Oregon Trail
#5. The Rise of Sectionalism and the Monroe Doctrine, The Age of Jackson, Pathway to Destruction
#6. The Civil War, The Maximillian Affair
#7. The San Francisco Earthquake and Fire, The Race to the Pole by Hanson and Peary, The Titanic Disaster
#8. The Building of the Panama Canal, The Around-the-World Automobile Race, The Flight of *The Spirit of St. Louis*
#9. Prelude to World War I, The Struggle to Remain Neutral
#10. The Last Voyage of the Lusitania, The United States in World War I
#11. Background to World War II in the Pacific, Prelude to Pearl Harbor
#12. Day of Infamy, The Bay of Pigs
#13. The Cuban Missile Crisis

Order by number and title to avoid mistakes. All code AF, $10.95 each, any 6 for $55.95, complete set $119.95.

**AMERICAN HEROES: A Young Person's Guide**, by Mike Janulewicz and Richard Widdows. A big 10x13½" book with color illustrations. Each page is devoted to a hero. More than 45 men and women from a wide variety of professions and lifestyles are celebrated for unique achievements. There are numerous similar books, but I chose this one because the introduction asks the reader to think about the qualities that make a hero. You could combine this book with history, geography, historical fiction, etc. Use your imagination! Hardcover. Ages 8 to 12. Code RP, $9.98.

**AMERICAN HEROES**, by Morrie Greenberg. Greenberg presents 15 Americans who lived between 1735 and 1900 and were heroes in their day. They are potential role models for today's children. To make history come alive we need to feel involved. What better way than through reading about the lives of the people who set examples of courage and made important changes that influence the way we live today? You'll meet both famous and lesser-known people: Peter Zenger, George Washington, Benjamin Banneker, Dolley Madison, Dorothea Dix, Robert E. Lee, Clara Barton, Chief Joseph, John Muir, and more. Timeline included. The writing and discussion activities are schoolish; ignore them if you don't like them. Ages 9 to 13. Code BR, $9.95.

**AMERICAN ADVENTURES: True Stories From America's Past**, by Morrie Greenberg. Each story is preceded by a brief timeline and a summary of "what else was happening" and followed by writing and discussion activities. **BOOK ONE**: 15 stories of unusual and fascinating people and events between 1770 and 1870. "Moving North," "The Good Old Days of Medicine," "The Man Who Jumped to Fame," "The Orphan Train," "Camels of the Old West," "The Three-Hundred-Dollar Baby," and more. **BOOK TWO**: 15 more good stories from 1870 to the present. "The Woman Who Dared," "The Mysterious Cloud," "The Oklahoma Land Run," "Land Where the Buffalo Roamed," "The Girl Who Was Afraid," "Enough!," and more. Black-and-white illustrations. Ages 9 to 13. Code BR, $9.95 each. Specify Book 1 or Book 2.

**AMERICAN HISTORY THE EASY WAY**, by William O. Kellogg. The full sweep of American history is presented in clearly written narrative, covering events, trends, landmarks, and personalities from the arrival of aboriginal tribes across the Bering Strait through the Persian Gulf War. Discussion of each historical period is divided into brief sections that feature a summary of key points, quizzes, review material, and "links from the past to the present." Chapters begin with a discussion of historians' methods of gathering information to present a mosaic of the past. Index; illustrated with maps, charts, and editorial cartoons. Written for high school students. 8x11", 346 pages. Code BE, $14.95.

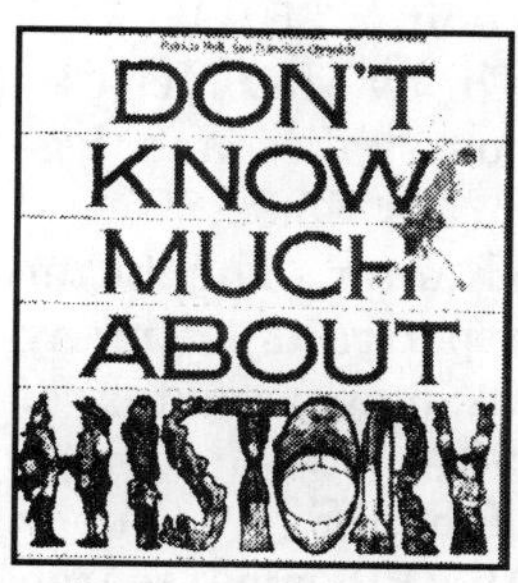

**DON'T KNOW MUCH ABOUT HISTORY: Everything You Need to Know About American History but Never Learned**, by Kenneth Davis. What did Franklin Delano Roosevelt know about the impending Japanese attack, and when did he know it? What was "voodoo economics"? Using an easy-to-follow question-and-answer format, sometimes irreverent but well-researched, this book explores the myths, landmark events, controversial issues, and colorful people of American history from the voyages of Columbus through the present. The book also has several mini-biographies, excerpts from notable speeches and writings, and informative chronologies. Not really "everything you need to know," but very interesting and informative anyway. An excellent supplement to other readings in U.S. history. Ages 14 to adult. Code BT, $12.50.

**AMERICAN HISTORY MAGAZINE** is for serious history buffs. Definitely for the serious history student. Full-color, with lots of illustrations and excellent, well-researched articles about well-known and little-known U.S. history. 6 issues $23.95, Canadian price $29.95 (U.S. funds), foreign price $47.95 (U.S. funds). *American History*, P.O. Box 420454, Palm Coast, FL 32142-9073.

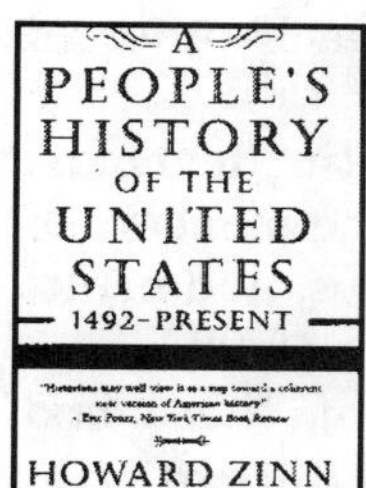

***Revised* — A PEOPLE'S HISTORY OF THE UNITED STATES**, by Howard Zinn. *Library Journal* says this is "a brilliant and moving history of the American people from the point of view of those who have been exploited politically and economically and whose plight has been largely omitted from most histories. An excellent antidote to establishment history. Stories of blacks, women, Indians, poor laborers, and war resisters of all nationalities." Since the "establishment" history books are unbalanced in the other direction, skipping over most of the exploitation and broken treaties in U.S. history, an "antidote" such as this is probably needed, but no one should regard it as a complete history in itself. It was used as the *main textbook* in one of Susan's U.S. history courses in the "alternative" school she went to for two years, and she came out of the course with justified sympathy for our society's underdogs, but draws a blank on most key events and people of U.S. history, such as the Federalist Papers, Paine, Jefferson, and most of the *positive* things in U.S. history. Unbalance is unbalance, regardless of its direction. 674 pages. Code HC, $18.

**Will you join us for a tea party?**

**UNITED STATES HISTORY: Notebooks for Families**, by Katherine Mehaffey. This study program comes in three distinct sections: 1. Mom (or Dad) savers, daily lesson plans that include reading suggestions, topics to cover, discussion ideas, writing suggestions, and more. 2. An extensive and impressive well-researched reading list. 3. Tests and answers.

My feelings are divided about this program. I'll think out loud for you. First, I liked the list of suggested reading, which includes biographies and historical fiction. It's thorough, extensive, and interesting. Second, the program is well organized and very flexible, and covers the required material for grades K to 12. Third, it is the only program I've seen that makes allowances for working with more than one age group at the same time using the same material. Fourth, it's all laid out with daily lesson plans. Fifth, you can't beat the price for a K-12 history package.

So what's not to like? First, I think it encourages too much dependence on the prescribed curriculum, which is geared toward getting good test results. Mehaffey says you don't need to bother with many of the details if you don't want to, but she wanted to include them for those who might be interested. *Notebooks for Families* has tests you can use or ignore (which I would); still, I think the main lessons are too centered around learning "test answers." If the convenience and ease of use of this resource is to your liking, then you could just ignore the nitpicky details. Second, and most important to me, it can't compare to Joy Hakim's *The History of US,* although some of Hakim's books are recommended. I think Hakim's books are just too good to miss. My conclusion: If your priority is to have a U.S. history program all planned out for multiple levels of study, that includes everything required in a public school, this is the resource for you. If, however, you want to be more creative, then invest in *The History of US* and use Hakim's reading list and guides for projects. Creating your own multilevel program really isn't that difficult.

To order *Notebooks for Families* send $75, plus $8 for shipping, to Notebooks for Families, 534 Ridgeway Dr., Metairie, LA 70001, or call 800-757-9712 with your credit card handy.

**UNITED STATES HISTORY ATLAS.** The ecological, social, demographic, and economic factors that have molded American history are shown in more than 100 maps, diagrams, and inset maps that range in topic from exploration, expansion, wars, growth, and the economy to modern urban problems. Full index. Hardcover, 9½x12½", 72 pages. Code HMD, $14.95.

**Landmark Books.** I think I had at least 30 of the Landmark books when I was a kid, and reread them often. They were exciting, dramatic, and informative. Several titles are once again available in paperback. Each book relates an important event in history with a lively, well-documented text featuring character portraits and anecdotes. Most volumes are illustrated with photographs and maps. For some reason, a few titles available just two or three years ago are out of print again, but new titles have been added to the list. I'm keeping my fingers crossed these are the ones now available. Ages 8 to 14. Code RH, specify Landmark book. (Ask about a discount for five or more.)

**ABE LINCOLN: LOG CABIN TO WHITE HOUSE**, by Sterling North. Lincoln's early years in Kentucky and Indiana; his frontier education; and his various jobs, from Mississippi flatboatman, farming, and carpentry to state assemblyman, lawyer, and president. $5.99.

**THE AMERICAN REVOLUTION**, by Bruce Bliven. Detailed account and examination of the major causes of the Revolutionary War, historic events, and battles from Lexington to Yorktown, with portraits in words of Washington, Howe, Greene, Cornwallis, and others. Many maps and photographs. $5.99.

**BEN FRANKLIN OF OLD PHILADELPHIA**, by Margaret Cousins. Lively record of Franklin's patriotic public life as statesman, adviser, ambassador, diplomat, inventor, printer, writer, and editor. $5.99.

**THE CALIFORNIA GOLD RUSH**, by May McNeer. Dramatic anecdotes about fabulous strikes and legendary characters of the mining camps. $5.99.

**GETTYSBURG**, by MacKinlay Kantor. The bitter three-day Civil War battle, with portraits of many brigades, townspeople, and generals; maps; and text of Lincoln's Gettysburg Address. $5.99.

**THE LANDING OF THE PILGRIMS**, by James Dougherty. Excellent account of the Pilgrims' search for religious freedom, dangerous ocean voyage, and hardships in establishing a colony. $5.99.

**PHARAOHS OF ANCIENT EGYPT**, by Elizabeth Payne. A clear and dramatic account of 3,000 years of Egyptian history, and of the soldiers, scholars, and grave robbers who rediscovered the ancient civilization's buried treasures. $5.99.

**PIONEERS GO WEST**, by George R. Stewart. Encounters with Indians and buffalo, near-starvation, and disasters encountered by an 11-wagon train from Iowa in 1844. Many maps. $5.99.

**THE STORY OF THOMAS ALVA EDISON**, by Margaret Cousins. I haven't seen this one, but I'm sure it's as good as the rest of the series. $5.99.

**THE VIKINGS**, by Elizabeth Janeway. Semi-fictional account based on Norse sagas, records of Eric the Red's discovery of Greenland, and his son Leif's voyages to North America 500 years before Columbus. $7.99.

**WITCHCRAFT OF SALEM VILLAGE**, by Shirley Jackson. The terrible time in the Massachusetts Bay Colony when pious villagers accused each other of devil worship. $5.99.

**THE WRIGHT BROTHERS**, by Quentin Reynolds. The boyhood and early experiments of the pioneers of aviation, who tinkered with sleds, bicycles, and printing presses — but their dream was to fly. $5.99.

I sometimes have secondhand copies of these and other Landmark titles. Send SASE for information.

**THE EARLIEST AMERICANS**, by Helen Roney Sattler; illustrated by Jean Zallinger. Convincing evidence of the most widely accepted theories about the origins of civilization in the Western Hemisphere. Ages 9 to 15. Code HM, $18.

**LOST TEMPLE OF THE AZTECS**, by Shelley Tanaka. In a book filled with color photos and illustrations, Tanaka tells how the lost temple of the Aztecs was found by workmen in the middle of Mexico City, and about the excavation and restoration that has been done. Better than that, she tells a very readable story of Cortés's expedition into Mexico, his meeting with Montezuma, and the destruction of Aztec civilization by war and disease. The fine illustrations, photos of artifacts, and informational inserts make this a superb resource. Hardcover. Ages 9 to 12. Code LB, $16.95.

## THE NATIVE AMERICANS

**THE WORLD OF NATIVE AMERICANS**, by Marion Wood. This large hardcover book is well-researched and informative. Wood recognizes that Columbus landed in the Americas by mistake, and that the land was already populated with a wide variety of peoples with long histories going back to the first settlers who came over the ice bridge in the Bering Strait. Wood makes it clear in the introduction that Native Americans had a multitude of lifestyles that changed over time, most drastically with the coming of the Europeans in the 15th century. Wonderful color illustrations with great attention to authentic detail. Ages 10 to 14. Code BT, $14.95.

**FIRST HOUSES: Native American Homes and Sacred Structures**, by Jean Guard Monroe and Ray A. Williamson; black-and-white illustrations by Susan Johnston Carlson. Native American creation myths include stories about the legendary "first houses" that the tribes used as patterns for their own homes and ritual structures. Many Native Americans considered their buildings — from the Iroquois longhouse to the Navajo hogan — to be constructed on cosmic patterns given by the gods. Their mythology is filled with exciting tales of the first houses and the beings that created them. Ages 9 to 15. Code HM, $16.

**WHEN THE GREAT CANOES CAME**, by Mary Louise Clifford. Seventy-five years after the settlement of Jamestown, Cockacoeske, the queen of the Pamunkey Indians, tells the adolescents of her tribe about the people, places, and episodes that were a part of American history before the Europeans arrived. This speculative fiction is based on tribal legends, history, and artifacts. Illustrated; with a map, chronology, genealogical chart, and bibliography. Code PEL, $12.95.

**THE DELIGHT MAKERS**, by Adolf F. Bandelier. A fictional reconstruction of prehistoric Indian culture in the American Southwest, by a 19th-century archaeologist. Code HBJ, $15.

**MANY NATIONS**, by Joseph Bruchac. A beautifully illustrated alphabet book to introduce the variety of Native Americans and their different cultures. Simply written for young children to enjoy. Ages 4 to 7. Code TRL, $5.95.

**INDIANS OF THE GREAT PLAINS**, by Lisa Sita. A good introduction to the numerous tribes who at one time inhabited the Great Plains from Texas to Alberta and from the Mississippi River to the Rocky Mountains. These are the tribes that most often excite youngsters, with their ponies, big war bonnets, and tepees. Not all tribes are mentioned in depth, but Sita gives the reader a good look at the variety of lifestyles among the various tribes that inhabited this vast region. Descriptions of daily life, religious practices, government, dwellings, the importance of horses and dogs, and more. Generously illustrated with many color photos and drawings. Any young aspiring Indian between the ages of 8 and 12 will appreciate this book. Code RP, $9.98.

**INDIANS OF NORTH AMERICA**. A 33x38" map by National Geographic. Illustrated ethnological color-coded map shows native locations of different tribes. Code MQ, $14.99.

**Acid-Free Reusable Sticker Books**. Acid-free reusable sticker books, $9\frac{1}{4}$x$11\frac{1}{4}$". The book cover makes a backdrop for the 30 or more full-color, reusable stickers. Ages 7 and up. Code DV.

**PUEBLO VILLAGE**, $4.50.

**TEEPEE VILLAGE**, $4.95.

**NORTHWEST COAST PUNCH-OUT INDIAN VILLAGE**. Some of the figures with small parts are best done with scissors, but are still relatively easy to do. Colorful communal house, three totem poles, boat, and many figures. Ages 8 and up. Code DV, $5.95.

**TWO PLAINS INDIAN DIORAMAS** to cut and assemble. Not suitable for small fingers. About age 10 is right. Includes shadow box, background scene, and figures. You need glue and patience. Finished product is satisfying. Code DV, $6.95.

**EASY-TO-MAKE PUEBLO VILLAGE.** Book is 9x12". Includes 3-D buildings, people, oven, and more. All you need are scissors and glue. Ages 6 and up. Code DV, $3.50.

**PLAINS INDIANS PUNCH-OUT PANORAMA**. Tepees, horses and riders, background, people doing daily chores. Ages 7 and up. Code DV, $3.95.

**CUT-AND-MAKE NORTH AMERICAN INDIAN MASKS**. Full-color, authentic masks are decorative and can be used in play. Ages 8 and up. Code DV, $6.95.

**Native American Titles.** Each of the following coloring books has accurate drawings of clothing and lifestyles, with informative captions. Code DV, $2.95 each.

**GREAT NATIVE AMERICANS**
**INDIAN LIFE IN PRE-COLUMBIAN N. AMERICA**
**INDIAN TRIBES OF NORTH AMERICA**
**NORTH AMERICAN INDIAN CRAFTS**
**N. AMERICAN INDIAN DANCES AND RITUALS**
**NORTHWEST COAST INDIANS (in the 18th, 19th, and 20th centuries)**
**PLAINS INDIANS (Apache, Pawnee, Blackfoot, Crow, and others)**
**SOUTHEAST INDIANS**
**SOUTHWEST INDIANS**
**WOODLANDS INDIANS**

**TOTEM POLES**. Three full-color models to punch out, fold, and glue. Historically accurate; easy to assemble. Ages 8 and up. Code DV, $4.95.

**INDIAN WHY STORIES,** by Frank Linderman; illustrated by well-known artist Charles M. Russell. Here are 22 entertaining, authentic tales gathered from the Blackfoot, Chippewa, and Cree tribes. Intriguing explanations of "How the Ducks Got Their Fine Feathers," "Why the Kingfisher Always Wears a War-Bonnet," "Why the Chipmunk's Back Is Striped," and more fine stories to read aloud to your 8- and 9-year-olds. Older kids can read them on their own. All interested adults will enjoy these too. I did. (He really did.) Code DV, $3.95.

**TRUTH IS A BRIGHT STAR: A Hopi Adventure**, by Joan Price. This gripping tale of courage, based on an actual historical event, tells the story of Loma, one of 14 children captured by Spanish soldiers from a peaceful Hopi village in 1832. The way in which 12-year-old Loma copes with a way of life completely foreign to her makes this a thought-provoking story that will stimulate understanding between people of different cultures. 156 pages, with a bibliography and glossary. Ages 8 to 12. Code TSP, $9.95.

Native American crafts and projects are in "Arts and Activities."

**MATERIALS**

Newspaper
Bathroom tissue tube
Small balloon
1 cup flour
1 cup water
¼ cup dried beans or small pebbles
Masking tape
Bowl
Tempera paints

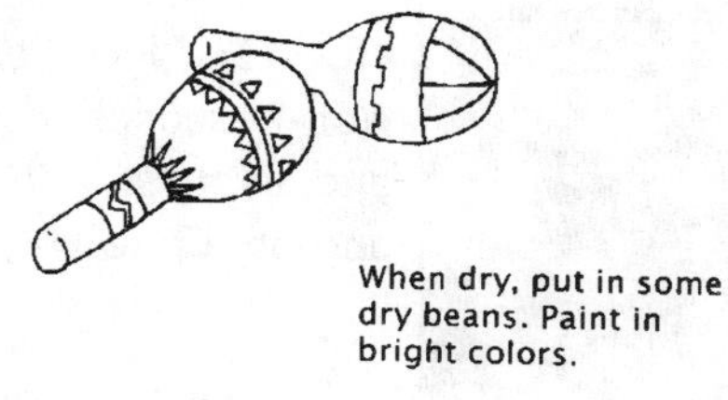

When dry, put in some dry beans. Paint in bright colors.

**MORE THAN MOCCASINS: A Kid's Activity Guide to Traditional North American Indian Life**. Laurie Carlson has written many excellent books for kids. I was really pleased to see this one. Great activities that combine information, creativity, and fun. Your kids will learn to make their own moccasins and much more. Indian games, traditions, foods (you can eat), and more. Ages 5 to 12. Code CRP, $12.95.

**Patterns for historic clothing**, western tools, and Indian crafts. Free catalog. Crazy Cow Trading Post, Box 314, Denison, TX 75020.

**Native American Biographies**. Four famous Indian leaders — Pocahontas, Sacagawea, Sequoyah, and Tecumseh — and their struggle to protect their land and freedom, with many details about the customs, beliefs, and cultures of the various tribes, and how the tribes were affected by the coming of the European settlers. 48 pages each, with full-color illustrations. Ages 8 to 11. Code TRL, complete set $14.

**QUANAH PARKER**, by Len Hilts. Son of a Comanche chief and a white woman, Quanah Parker became a great chief who valiantly led his people in an attempt to save their homeland. Both feared and respected by those he fought, he became a symbol of the Comanches. Photographs and map. Ages 10 and up. Code HBJ, $4.95.

**NATIVE AMERICAN SIGN LANGUAGE**, by Madeline Olsen; illustrated by Native American artist Ben Carter. A unique book teaching the hand signals the tribes used to communicate with each other. Learn to express the past, present, and future, and how signs relate to each other. You'll learn more than isolated signs. Ages 8 to 12. Code TRL, $4.95.

**INDIAN SIGN LANGUAGE**, by William Tomkins. There's no guarantee that giving this book to your Indians will make the house silent, but if they are dedicated they will learn enough to be able to tell secrets in front of you. Tomkins lived close to the Sioux Reservation in the Dakota Territory for ten years while he was growing up. He knew and worked with many Native Americans and learned to sign from them. Your young brave can use the simple signs. Older braves can read about the particular grammar and word construction. The book includes more than 870 alphabetically arranged words, sample sentences, small sections on pictography and ideography of the Sioux and Ojibwa, and smoke signals. Section for camp counselors, teachers, and parents with instructions on how to conduct a ceremony. Code DV, $3.95.

**Good Medicine Books**. Several excellent titles about Indian history, crafts, and culture by Beverly and Adolf Hungry Wolf. Also books about old trains. Free catalog. Canadian Caboose Press, Box 844, Skookumchuck, BC V0B 2E0.

**THE MOUNTAIN MAN AND THE FUR TRADE: Their Rocky Mountain World, 1820-1840** (a small book), western rubber stamps, wood-block prints and more, available from the Museum of New Mexico, Palace of the Governors Print Shop, P.O. Box 2087, Santa Fe, NM 87504-2087. Free catalog.

**GREAT SPEECHES BY NATIVE AMERICANS**, edited by Bob Blaisdell. Eighty-two compelling speeches encompassing three centuries of Native American encounters with non-indigenous peoples. Eloquent oratory. Well-researched notes about each speech and orator. High school and up. Code DV, $2.

**FROM THE EARTH TO BEYOND THE SKY: Native American Medicine**, by Evelyn Wolfson; black-and-white illustrations by Jennifer Hewitson. In 1535, French explorer Jacques Cartier and his crew were marooned on the frozen St. Lawrence River. Twenty-five men had died and the rest were close to death when Native Americans restored them to life with hemlock or pine-needle tea. It was 150 years later when Europeans realized the men had been dying from a lack of vitamin C, which is contained in the leaves and bark of those two trees. This is only one of the interesting things to be discovered in this account of the lore of Native American medicine men, who, from earliest times, had lived close to nature and learned many of its secrets. Ages 9 to 15. Code HM, $16.

## COLONIAL TIMES

**COLONIAL KIDS**, by Laurie Carlson, is packed with ideas to think about and projects to do. Good beginning history with hands-on activities to bring it all to life, plus a simple timeline and map for clarity. Do you know what a "groaning party" is? How to make a rag rug? A corn doll? Homemade ink? Carlson gives clear directions and recipes. You have most of the needed materials already on hand. You'll learn from and enjoy this book as much as your kids will. This book is terrific! Ages 5 to 12. Code CRP, $12.95.

**TWO LITTLE SAVAGES**, by Ernest Thompson Seton. When I was about 12, I borrowed this book from the public library and took it camping with me in my grandfather's back woodlot. Rain seeped into my tent, the book got wet, and the cover came off. The library charged my father a dollar and let us keep the book. In the next few years I probably read it 50 times. It's the story of Yan and Sam, two farmboys at the turn of the century, who "play Indian" whenever they're given a short holiday from farm chores. With the help of an old hermit, they (and the reader) learn to make authentic Indian clothing, drums, weapons, and a tepee, along with many bits of useful and interesting woods lore. Many illustrations. Code DV, $7.95.

**EARLY AMERICAN CRAFTS AND TRADES**, by Peter Stockham. A charming 1807 children's book that explains a variety of crafts and trades. A full chapter is devoted to each, including brickmaker, weaver, dressmaker, bookbinder, saddler, apothecary, and more. Quaint prose and 23 copperplate illustrations of early commercial art. Read it to your 8-year-old or let your older children read it themselves. You'll find it interesting too. Code DV, $4.95.

## REVOLUTIONARY TIMES

**STORY OF THE AMERICAN REVOLUTION**. Coloring book with 40 well-researched drawings of people and events. Good captions. Ages 10 and up. Code DV, $2.95.

**JOHNNY TREMAIN**, by Esther Forbes. A young apprentice silversmith in Revolutionary-era Boston becomes involved with Paul Revere, John Hancock, Sam Adams, and other rebelling colonists. While revolution takes shape around him, Johnny also learns important lessons about friendship, love, responsibility, and growing up. I first read this book when I was in the eighth grade, and it is still one of my favorite historical novels. Ages 12 and up. Code RH, $5.99.

Did you know that Paul Revere billed the Massachusetts State House 10 pounds and 4 shillings to cover the expenses for his ride?

**MY BROTHER SAM IS DEAD**, by James Lincoln Collier and Christopher Collier. Fictional reconstruction of how the Revolutionary War affects a non-partisan family in the Tory town of Redding, Connecticut. Gives readers a sobering, mature view of history and of war. Ages 12 and up. Hardcover. Code SS, $17.

**BLACK HEROES OF THE AMERICAN REVOLUTION**, by Burke Davis. The black soldiers, sailors, spies, guides, and wagoners who participated in the fight for American independence. Prints and portraits of the period. Bibliography and index. Ages 10 and up. Code HBJ, $5.

**THE COURAGE OF SARAH NOBLE**, by Alice Dalgliesh. Sarah and her father leave their family to build a home in the wilderness of colonial America. When they finish, Sarah's father goes away to bring the rest of the family, telling Sarah that "to be afraid and to be brave is the best courage of all." Sarah proves her courage while she waits in the care of an Indian family. A simple, dignified, realistic, and moving story. Illustrated. Ages 10 and up. Code MAC, $4.95.

**CALICO BUSH**, by Rachel Field. A moving novel of an orphaned French girl "bound out" in service to a family of settlers on the Maine coast in the 1740s. A close look at an aspect of pioneer life often neglected. Ages 12 and up. Code MAC, $4.99.

**THE LAST OF THE MOHICANS**, by James Fenimore Cooper. During the French and Indian War, adventure and tragedy befall two sisters as they travel through the wilderness near Lake Champlain to join their father, the British commander of Fort William Henry. Illustrated with several beautiful full-color paintings by illustrator N.C. Wyeth. Hardcover. Code MAC, *specify Wyeth edition*, $28.

**THE THOMAS PAINE READER**. Tom Paine was the first man to use the phrase "the United States of America," and, had it not been for him and his little booklet "Common Sense," there might never have been such a country. He was born in Thetford, England, in 1737. When he emigrated to the American colonies in 1774, his only asset was a letter of introduction and recommendation from Benjamin Franklin, whom he had met in London. Paine's life had been marked with constant failure and setback; Franklin had suggested that Paine try his luck in America. Soon after his arrival in Philadelphia, Paine became editor of the newly established *Pennsylvania Magazine*, and in that position he began crusading against slavery, advocating equal rights for women, suggesting international copyright laws, condemning cruelty to animals, criticizing the practice of dueling, and asking for the end of war as a means of settling international disputes. Following the battles of Concord, Lexington, and Bunker Hill in 1775, opinions in the colonies were still strongly divided between loyalty to the king and a feeling that war and separation were both necessary and inevitable. Sam Adams and John Hancock favored separation; Washington, Franklin, and Jefferson remained loyal to England. Paine spent the fall of 1775 writing down his thoughts; Dr. Benjamin Rush suggested the title "Common Sense," and Robert Bell of Philadelphia published the booklet.

"Common Sense" began selling on January 10, 1776 — 47 pages for two shillings. The price was high because the printer didn't expect many copies to be sold, and was afraid he wouldn't even break even on the cost of printing 500 copies. In three months, 120,000 copies had sold; total sales reached more than half a million in less than six months. Tradesmen, farmers, soldiers, and politicians carried copies in their pockets, and discussed the booklet's ideas heatedly and excitedly. Opinions changed rapidly, and on July 4, 1776, the Continental Congress proclaimed the independence of the United States of America.

This book includes "Common Sense" and excerpts from *The American Crisis, The Rights of Man,* and *The Age of Reason*. Code PNG, $13.95.

Democracy is the highest form of government most societies have yet attained. We give it a lot of thought at Brook Farm, for ourselves and for the world: how to achieve it, how to preserve it, how to keep it truly democratic. Democracy, after all, does not come from a government; "demos" means "people." It's up to us, and our children.

**LIFE AND SELECTED WRITINGS OF THOMAS JEFFERSON**. At a dinner honoring Nobel Prize recipients, John F. Kennedy remarked that his guests were "the most extraordinary collection of talent, of human knowledge, that has ever been gathered at the White House, with the possible exception of when Thomas Jefferson dined alone." Jefferson was a statesman, architect, scientist, naturalist, educator, and public servant; the main author of the Declaration of Independence and the Virginia Statute on Religious Freedoms; and governor of Virginia, secretary of state, ambassador to France, vice president, and third president of the United States. This 800-page volume is a comprehensive collection of his travel journals, biographical sketches of some of his notable contemporaries, important public papers, and a large selection of his letters on both public and private matters. Code RH, $20.

Did you know that when war with Great Britain seemed imminent, James Madison decided that it would be less expensive and easier to rent Portugal's navy than to build a navy from scratch?

**THE REAL THOMAS JEFFERSON: The True Story of America's Philosopher of Freedom,** published by the National Center for Constitutional Studies. Much has been written about Jefferson. Some writers have vilified him, others have deified him, yet all agree on the far-reaching influence of his life and work. This book is an attempt to give us a view of Jefferson through his own words, without interpretations. To that end the collaborators have divided this book into two parts. The first part is biographical, using as many of Jefferson's journal entries and excerpts from his correspondence as possible. The second is selected quotations arranged very conveniently in alphabetical order by subject. (This makes it very easy to reference Jefferson's thoughts on education, slavery, debt, truth, punishment, etc.) I was surprised and very pleased to find this 700-page book enjoyable reading, not dry and scholarly. Intended for adults, but any high school student researching Jefferson would also enjoy reading this book. Code NCCS, $14.95.

Replicas of the Declaration of Independence, the Mayflower Compact, and the Gettysburg Address (in Lincoln's handwriting) from Mr. Rainbow's, P.O. Box 908, Rio Grande, NJ 08242. About $1.50 each; write for current prices.

**Cornerstones of Freedom**. These books explore several important events and people in U.S. history. Many full-color photos and black-and-white engravings, with clear text, almost give readers a sense of witnessing history in the making. Each book is 8x9½", 32 pages. Reading level about 4th grade, interest level ages 8 to 12 or so. Code CP, $5.95 each, 5 for $25.95. **Assassination of Abraham Lincoln, Assassination of John F. Kennedy, Battle of the Alamo, Battle of the Little Bighorn, Bill of Rights, The Boston Tea Party, Chisholm Trail, The Constitution, Declaration of Independence, The Emancipation Proclamation, The Fall of the Soviet Union, The First Ladies, The Franklin Delano Roosevelt Memorial, The Gettysburg Address, The Great Depression, Impeachment, Industrial Revolution, John Brown's Raid on Harper's Ferry, Lewis and Clark, Lexington and Concord, The Liberty Bell, Library of Congress, Lincoln-Douglas Debates, The Louisiana Purchase, The Montgomery Bus Boycott, Oregon Trail, Panama Canal, Pony Express, Presidential Elections, Smithsonian Institution, The U.S. Holocaust Memorial Museum, Valley Forge, Women's Voting Rights, Women Who Shaped the West.**

**WE THE PEOPLE: The Story of the United States Constitution Since 1787**. See "Politics and Government."

## WESTWARD EXPANSION

**UNITED STATES TERRITORIAL GROWTH**. A 43x30½" map by National Geographic with seven sequential inserts charting the growth of the U.S. Code MQ, $14.99.

**A GATHERING OF DAYS: A New England Girl's Journal, 1830-1832**, by Joan Blos. A novel in the form of a diary kept by 14-year-old Catherine Cabot Hill of New England, recording in succinct journal entries changes and activities of daily life. Almost like short personal notes from a close friend. Ages 10 and up. Code MAC, $4.99.

**LEWIS AND CLARK FOR KIDS**, by Janis Herbert. I was fortunate to see this book when the publishers were still putting it together. If I'd had to wait for the finished product, it wouldn't be listed here. I'd feel bad, and you'd miss finding out about this exciting book. We owe the publishers a thank-you for the introductory "Note to Readers" that shouldn't be ignored: It explains the misspellings that occur in the original Lewis and Clark journals. (e.g., mosquito 20 different ways!). I was immediately reassured to know that this book would include original source material. Next comes a timeline of important events surrounding the expedition, putting everything into context. The timeline begins with the birth of Jefferson (1743) and continues until the death of Clark (1838). There is also a good map of the expedition. The people in this true drama are brought back to life through the telling of real incidents, making for very exciting reading. The 21 related hands-on projects seem like icing on the cake. This book includes many of the original drawings completed on the expedition; the reader (or even a casual browser) will come away with a vivid picture of what the country was like at that time. Ages 9 and up. Code CRP, $14.95.

**GIRL OF THE SHINING MOUNTAINS: *Sacagawea's Story***, by Peter and Connie Roop. Based on fact, this historical novel draws the reader into the personal aspects of Sacagawea's life. She tells her own story to her son, who, as a baby, made the journey with Lewis and Clark on Sacagawea's back. A very enjoyable reading experience. We first meet Sacagawea as a young Indian girl who was captured and enslaved to one man who then gave her to a slave-trader as payment for a gambling debt — all before she becomes a heroine in this amazing tale of exploration. Hardcover. Ages 8 to 12. Code LB, $14.99.

**LEWIS AND CLARK EXPEDITION**. Coloring book with 45 historically accurate drawings to color. Captions identify action and provide background information. Ages 10 and up. Code DV, $2.95.

**THE GOLD RUSH** is an outstanding book on the American West, a companion volume to the PBS documentary series *The West*. This book is designed for young readers, filled with pictures — either photos or drawings of the time. The text is drawn mostly from historical diaries and documents. These fascinating stories reveal that some people had an awareness of the historical importance of what they were doing, and others were just ordinary people seeking a better life for themselves and their families. Ages 9 and up. Code LB, $10.95.

**The Little House Books**, by Laura Ingalls Wilder; illustrated by Garth Williams. These warm and moving stories of one family's move westward mirror the growth of the nation. The close and happy Ingalls family struggles at times for survival as they move west during the 1870s and 1880s, but their troubles only make them closer. The first book, in which the story's children are quite young, is written on an easy reading level; the reading level becomes higher through each succeeding book, as the children grow older. Whether you and your children read these books as entertainment or as biography and history, you'll feel the closeness to the Ingalls family as well as a deeper understanding of the time in which they lived. Code HC, $4.95 each. **SPECIAL:** Boxed set of all nine books, $42.95.

**LITTLE HOUSE IN THE BIG WOODS**. The Ingalls family is snug in their Wisconsin cabin, in spite of blizzards, wolves, and the big forest.

**LITTLE HOUSE ON THE PRAIRIE**. Laura and her family journey west by covered wagon, only to find they are in Indian territory and must move again.
**FARMER BOY.** The boyhood of Almanzo Wilder, the future husband of Laura, on his father's farm in upper New York state.
**ON THE BANKS OF PLUM CREEK**. After moving to Minnesota, the Ingalls family encounters a terrible blizzard and a grasshopper plague.
**BY THE SHORES OF SILVER LAKE.** In Dakota Territory, Pa has a job in a railroad building camp, and Laura is now 13.
**THE LONG WINTER.** Almanzo makes a dangerous trip to secure wheat to save the village from starvation during the terrible winter of 1880-81.
**LITTLE TOWN ON THE PRAIRIE**. The little settlement becomes a frontier town, and Laura, at 15, receives a certificate to teach school.
**THESE HAPPY GOLDEN YEARS.** Laura is courted by Almanzo; they marry, and move to their own little house on a homestead claim.
**THE FIRST FOUR YEARS.** This book tells of Laura and Almanzo's Dakota homesteading in the 1880s and of the birth of their daughter, Rose.

Our whole family found long-lasting enjoyment in reading and rereading this set. We read them to the kids; then they went on to read the set themselves more than once. Although the kids are now grown, they still remember these books with affection, and will undoubtedly share them with their children.

Simplified versions of some of the Little House books exist, but you won't find them here. We think the original series is fine just the way it is.

**LAURA INGALLS WILDER AND ROSE WILDER LANE HISTORICAL TIMETABLE,** by Jane Williams. A timetable of important dates from books by and about Laura and Rose, along with other important American historical events, beginning in 1776 and continuing to the Vietnam War, when Rose was a war correspondent. An excellent way to naturally combine the wonderful Little House series with American history. Printed two-sided on $8\frac{1}{2}$x11" paper. Send $2 to Bluestocking Press, P.O. Box 2030, Shingle Springs, CA 95682-2030.

**THE LITTLE HOUSE COOKBOOK: Frontier Foods From Laura Ingalls Wilder's Classic Stories**, by Barbara Walker; illustrated by Garth Williams. More than 100 recipes introduce the foods and cooking of the pioneer childhood in the Little House books. Each recipe is prefaced with a short, well-researched essay on its origins, development, and characteristics. Lots of fun to read and look at, even if you don't try the recipes — but you will. Code HC, $7.95.

**WESTWARD HO! An Activity Guide to the Wild West.** Laurie Carlson has put together crafts, recipes, songs, and games with engaging text. Your kids will learn, but mostly they'll have fun. Clear illustrations and instructions for all activities. Ages 5 to 12. Code CRP, $12.95.

**CADDIE WOODLAWN,** by Carol Ryrie Brink. Wisconsin frontier life in the 1860s, through the eyes of Caddie (the author's grandmother) and her family and friends. Realistic portrayal of work, attitudes, and relationships, with interesting characters. Pen-and-ink drawings by Trina Achart Hyman, one of the best illustrators of children's books. Ages 10 and up. Code MAC, $4.99.

**Replicas of Historic Weapons**. "Toy" replicas patterned after rifles, muskets, and pistols that played important parts in U.S. history: Revolutionary War, Civil War, Kentucky long rifle, blunderbuss pistol, etc. Excepting a few carbine cork-shooters (called "popguns" when I was a kid), these guns cannot fire any kind of ammunition or projectile. As you will have gathered, I don't favor militarism, in reality or in play, but I think a few of these replicas might have a place in a family "hands-on" history study, perhaps a display. Wars *did* happen, for good or bad, and some have actually been fought for good purposes, even if we may wish those purposes could have been achieved peaceably. When I was a kid, my heroes included Roy Rogers, Gene Autry, Kit Carson, Daniel Boone, and others like them, who were always presented in movies, comic books, radio programs, and television shows as "the good guys" who never shot first, never shot to kill, and always protected the weak. Sometimes I reenacted various historic wars, always with the aim of defending freedom, and always with the principle that "good guys never shoot first." However inaccurate this may be, historically, it was a good principle to grow up with. The only modern gun-toting "heroes" seem to be Rambo-like psychopaths, so maybe there isn't any way for kids to play wholesome, moral games with guns anymore. Free catalog: Parris Manufacturing Co., P.O. Box 338, Savannah, TN 38372-0338; www.parrismfg.com.

## THE CIVIL WAR

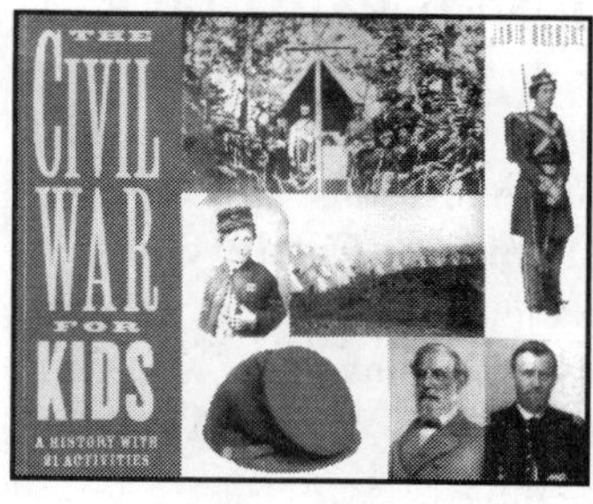

**THE CIVIL WAR FOR KIDS**, by Janis Herbert. An introduction to the issues leading up to the Civil War, the war itself, and the surrender at Appomattox. Twenty-one activities for hands-on learning and interest. You can make a butternut dye for a Rebel uniform, hardtack, and a medicine kit; learn drills and signals with flags, including learning to decode wigwag; and more. You'll read tales of the Underground Railroad, animal mascots, and friendships among enemies. Includes biographies of important figures from both sides of the war, maps, and photos, all of which give this book great kid appeal. All right — it appealed to me too. Ages 9 and up. Code CRP, $14.95.

**ABE LINCOLN GROWS UP**, by Carl Sandburg. The chapters on Lincoln's boyhood, from Sandburg's monumental *Abraham Lincoln: The Prairie Years*. More than 200 pages, and more than 50 drawings. Ages 12 and up. Code HBJ, $8.

**STORY OF THE CIVIL WAR**. Coloring book with 40 accurate, detailed illustrations of important people and historic moments: Ft. Sumter, Lee's surrender, Lincoln's assassination, and more. Ages 10 and up. Code DV, $2.95.

**STORY OF THE UNDERGROUND RAILROAD**. A pictorial history (1830-1860) with pictures to color. 44 scenes cover the main events, highlighting prominent people and providing interesting historical captions. Ages 12 and up. Code DV. $2.95.

**ABRAHAM LINCOLN**. Coloring book follows Lincoln's life from log cabin to White House. 40 pictures. Ages 10 and up. Code DV, $2.95.

**GRACE'S LETTER TO LINCOLN**, by Peter and Connie Roop. Based on fact, this is the story of 11-year-old Grace Bedell, who wrote to Abraham Lincoln because she wanted to help him win the election. She's the person who inspired him to grow whiskers. Ages 7 to 10. Code LB, $3.95.

**ABRAHAM LINCOLN: THE PRAIRIE YEARS AND THE WAR YEARS**, by Carl Sandburg. A one-volume edition containing the essence of the author's acclaimed six-volume biography. More than 750 pages. Various editions. Check your bookstore.

**CIVIL WAR POETRY AND PROSE**, by Walt Whitman. Code DV, $1.

**CIVIL WAR STORIES**, by Ambrose Bierce. Code DV, $1.

**LINCOLN'S GREAT SPEECHES**. Code DV, $1.

**CIVIL WAR FASHIONS.** Coloring book with 48 meticulously researched illustrations depicting men, women, and children in outfits for home and elegant evening wear, plus military outfits worn by Union and Confederate officers. Code DV, $2.95.

**THE LAST SAFE HOUSE**, by Barbara Greenwood. A wonderful, unique, and moving portrayal of slavery, friendship, cruelty, kindness, prejudice, and courage. A tale told from the perspective of two young girls, one an escaped slave from the southern United States and the other belonging to a Canadian family that offers refuge to escaped slaves. Each chapter is followed by background information and hands-on activities. Beautiful drawings complement the story perfectly. Ages 8 to 14. Code KC, $9.95.

**CIVIL WAR PAPER SOLDIERS**. 100 authentic, free-standing, Union and Confederate soldiers, cannon, flags, and more, in full color. Ages 10 and up. Code DV, $5.95.

Grover Cleveland, drafted into the Union Army during the Civil War, paid a substitute $150 to serve in his place while he stayed home to support his mother and sister while his two brothers were off fighting. This was completely legal under the terms of the Conscription Act of 1863.

**WITH LEE IN VIRGINIA,** by G.A. Henty, is an exciting tale of the Civil War as seen through the eyes of Vincent Wingfield, almost 16 years old. Vincent, raised in the South, spends four years in England only to return home to find many things different and very unsettling. War breaks out and Vincent fights for the South. This is not a pro-slavery book by any means, but one that remembers the many admirable parts of a lost way of life. An action-packed story that weaves together real people and events, teaching history without making a fuss about it. The glossary allows for quick reference without a great interruption to reading. It's great to see this book, originally published in 1900, back in print. The grammar and vocabulary have been updated, but the integrity of the story remains, along with the original illustrations. 410 pages. Ages 14 and up. Code LC, $19.95.

**MY BONDAGE AND MY FREEDOM**, by Frederick Douglass. Autobiography of a man born into slavery and later freed who became an outspoken force in the anti-slavery movement before the Civil War. Many detailed descriptions of slave life. Code DV, $8.95.

> *There is no king who has not had a slave among his ancestors, and no slave who has not had a king among his.* — Helen Keller

**CHILDREN OF STRANGERS**, by Lyle Saxon. This masterpiece of historical fiction, first published more than 60 years ago, tells the powerful story of life on a Louisiana plantation during the early decades of the 20th century, and the interactions among the plantation-owning whites, the black sharecroppers, and the half-breed mulattos. Famie, the heroine of the story, is a mulatto girl descended from free black slave owners, who rivaled the white planters in wealth and culture before the Civil War. Her dream is that her son, Joel, may someday escape the stigma of his black ancestry and be accepted by the whites. 312 pages. Ages 12 and up. Code PEL, $12.95.

## MOVING ON TO MORE MODERN HISTORY

**OLD-FASHIONED FARM LIFE**. A coloring book depicting the daily 19th-century activities on the Firestone Farm at Greenfield Village in Dearborn, Michigan. Finely detailed illustrations include churning butter, shearing sheep, plowing, making maple syrup, and many more activities. Code DV, $2.95.

**CARRY A BIG STICK: The Uncommon Heroism of Theodore Roosevelt**, by George Grant, Ph.D. An excellent way to absorb history through one of America's most interesting personalities. This book tends to insert more Christian lessons than I think are needed, but you can ignore the preachy parts and enjoy an in-depth look at Teddy Roosevelt and his life and times. Hardcover. Code CH, $14.95.

**THE PEOPLE, YES**, by Carl Sandburg. An epic poem using the myths, legends, tall tales, and popular sayings of America to create a beautifully unique cultural history. Code HBJ, $9.99. Lively. One of my favorites.

**THE HUMAN COMEDY**, by William Saroyan. An amusing, wise, engrossing story of the home front during World War II. Homer McCauley, 14, gets a job as "the fastest messenger boy in town" in San Joaquin, California, and learns about the joys of love, the pain of faraway death, and the modest greatness of ordinary human beings. Ages 14 to adult. Code HBJ, $15.95.

Did you know that the United States of America still owes money to General George Patton for parts he bought for U.S. tanks and other military vehicles? Apparently General Patton arrived at Fort Benning, Georgia, just as the U.S. was about to enter WW II — only to find that the tanks he was supposed to command had rusty and missing parts. The parts had been ordered but had never arrived. Many other vehicles were in a similar condition. Patton ordered parts from Sears, not only for the tanks but for many other vehicles, paying for them with his own personal checks; as far as I know, he's never been reimbursed.

## CIVIL RIGHTS AND INTOLERANCE

**CIVIL RIGHTS FOR KIDS**, by Mary C. Turck. Most history we present or share with our kids seems ancient to them even if we go back only to the 1920s or 1940s, 1960s, or 1970s — times when our parents were young or we were young. Most kids feel that anything before their birth is ancient history. I'm not bothered that they feel this way about much of history, but in the last century there were major civil rights issues, ones still present today, that have nothing to do with the usual historic battles — fighting for territory or political gain. These issues are important not only because they are still unresolved, but also because the fight for civil rights reintroduced non-violent confrontation — active non-violence as a means to bringing about needed changes to our modern society. We all want our children to grow up in a world that is safe and just. If we want to make this a reality then we must help our children understand what is important, how to achieve that goal, and, hopefully, how to use methods that do not create more violence and hatred. Working to end segregation and prejudice *can* be done non-violently. This book is the story of courageous men, women, and children who believed in equality for all and lived their lives accordingly, non-violently in the face of violence — some at the cost of their lives. It's not a pretty story, but it's real. These people changed our nation. All of us, young and old, can learn from them.

Interspersed with illustrations, true stories, and a chronology of events are activities your kids will find challenging and enjoy.

Chapter one, "Let the Children Lead," describes segregation in the U.S. before the civil rights movement. Chapter two, "Tired of Being Mistreated," introduces Rosa Parks, Martin Luther King Jr., and the bus boycotts. Chapter three: "Non-violent Resistance: Student Sit-ins 1960." Chapter four, "If Not Us, Then Who?" discusses the Freedom Riders. Chapter five, "Standing Up for Freedom," covers Birmingham, with its fire hoses, police dogs, murder, and police involvement — and non-involvement. Chapter six: "The March on Washington and 'I Have a Dream' Speech." There's a lot more, too. Ages 10 and up. Code CRP, $14.95.

**Note to Canadians:** This isn't about your history, but there are discrimination problems within Canada that need resolution. Learning about the non-violent methods used in the civil rights movement would be useful.

**US AND THEM: A History of Intolerance in America**, by Jim Carnes, with preface by Justice Harry A. Blackmun. This book (which should be required reading) provides us with a close look at issues too often overlooked in the history books — issues that are a strong comment on our past and present. If we ignore the shameful events in our history we will not learn how to recognize and prevent them from happening again. Contains 14 case studies, including the execution of Quaker Mary Dyer, Wounded Knee in 1890, the KKK in Alabama in 1981, and the Crown Heights riots in New York in 1991. Ages 10 and up. Code OX, $12.95.

**HERE I STAND**, by Paul Robeson (with Lloyd Brown). Robeson was the son of an escaped slave, an All-American football player, a scholar, an orator, an actor, an outstanding stage singer and performer, and a leader and pioneer in civil rights. Robeson, who was born in 1898, was one of this century's foremost black activists, even though you may not have heard of him. He was blacklisted during the McCarthy era, his visa was revoked, and his concerts were canceled, yet he continued to speak out in words and song. He was honored posthumously in 2000 with a lifetime achievement award at the Grammys. Although it is written for adults, teens interested in the fight for civil rights will learn from and enjoy this book. Code SYC, $12.

**NO PRETTY PICTURES,** by author and illustrator Anita Lobel. "I was born far, far away on a bloody continent at a terrible time. I lived there for a while. I live here now." The vivid and haunting story of Lobel's childhood and survival during WWII. A personal story, a survivor's story of uncertainty, hiding, capture, imprisonment, fear, and eventual freedom and reunification with her family. An emotional and stunning journey through the war, from innocence to coming of age in America. Ages 12 and up. Code WM, $16.

*I want to know what were the steps by which man passed from barbarism to civilization.*
— Voltaire

**THE SPIRIT THAT MOVES US: A Literature-Based Resource Guide, Teaching About the Holocaust and Human Rights**, Volume 1, by Laura R. Petovello, J.D., and Volume 2, by Rachel Quenk, both in association with the Holocaust Human Rights Center of Maine. Two very important books that can be used for exploring and learning about the Holocaust through literature. Why make a study of the Holocaust and human rights? The introduction provides us with a rationale, citing the words of survivors:

Dear Teacher,

I am a survivor of a concentration camp. My eyes saw what no man should witness.

Gas chambers built by LEARNED engineers; children poisoned by EDUCATED physicians; infants killed by TRAINED nurses; women and babies shot and burned by HIGH SCHOOL and COLLEGE graduates.

So I am suspicious of education.

My request is: help your students become human. Your efforts must never produce learned monsters, skilled psychopaths, educated Eichmanns.

Reading, writing, and arithmetic are important only if they serve to make our children more humane.

— Haim Ginott (*Teacher and Child.* New York: Macmillan, 1972, page 317)

And from another survivor:
We still feel the pain and we weep,
This nightmare will not let us sleep.
A page in history; one must learn,
Yesterday us, tomorrow your turn?
— Inge Auerbacher, author of *I Am a Star*

*The Spirit That Moves Us* provides a framework with many suggestions for studying not only the Holocaust, but our society, culture, and civic responsibilities. While it includes lesson plans, you are free to pick and choose what suits you and your children. Many books are recommended, with age guidelines enabling you to choose those appropriate to your reader. These books look deeply into the nature of culture, immigration, immigrants and refugees, and injustice and discrimination, and how we can react and choose our own path through the moral and ethical issues. You'll find chapters on the rise of Hitler, Jewish families living in Hitler's Germany, courageous acts of resistance, and how we can make a difference in the lives of others. Appendices at the end provide numerous resources for students and teachers looking for more material about the Holocaust and human rights. Excellent suggestions are given for using the material in these books in creative ways for many age levels. Take your time with these books. I suggest spreading out the reading over an extended period, allowing lots of breaks so that the horror is understood but isn't overwhelming. Although the main focus is on the Holocaust, there is also an ongoing theme: that prejudice and discrimination are still a problem in many places today. The books suggest actions we can take individually and as part of a community to tackle this issue. Volume 1 is for grades K to 4, Volume 2 for grades 5 to 8. Code TLB, $19.95 each.

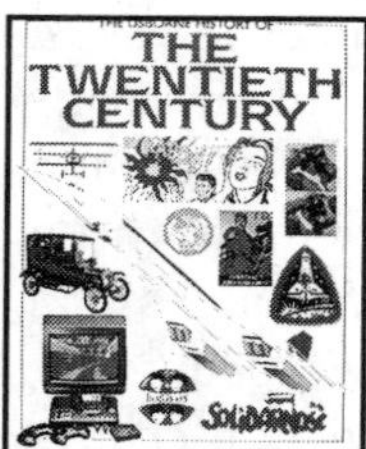


**THE TWENTIETH CENTURY**. A good reference and an excellent way to help put today's happenings into perspective. Well written with illustrations. Ages 11 and up. Code EDC, $10.95. While this book isn't as good as the next listing, it's still excellent and it is easier on the budget!

**THE CENTURY FOR YOUNG PEOPLE**, by Peter Jennings and Todd Brewster. Specially adapted from the adult edition. The photographs are spellbinding: Some gave me goose bumps, others smiles. The text is informative and enjoyable. The general format for the book combines period photos, historical text, and the personal story of a witness of the time in focus. This terrific modern history resource is a good look at where we've been — and perhaps, by looking back, an inspiration for what can be achieved in the future. Well worth the price. My only complaint is that it gives only us a U.S. perspective; still, it does cover major international events. Large 240-page hardcover. Ages 10 to adult. Code RH, $29.95.

**STEVEN CANEY'S KIDS' AMERICA**, by Steven Caney. Kids 4 to 14 and older explore American history through fascinating stories, anecdotes, toys, games, photographs, crafts, silly autograph sayings, and much more. A huge collection of fun and learning. Younger kids will enjoy the fun; older kids will enjoy the participation in history. Code WKM, $13.95.

**EDUCATIONAL SPECTRUMS CATALOG**. Very wide selection of U.S. history books, timelines, tapes, and other materials; extensive list of books by and about Laura Ingalls Wilder (author of the Little House books); economics; government; and many other subjects. They mail out catalogs through bulk mailings every four months; if you want one right away the charge is $3. Write: Bluestocking Press, P.O. Box, 2030, Dept. 98, Shingle Springs, CA 95682.

---

Did you know that North Carolina and South Carolina both claim to be the birthplace of Andrew Jackson, born March 15, 1767?

---

**AMERICA'S FIRST LADIES**. Coloring book of first ladies up to and including Hillary Rodham Clinton. Authentic settings; good introduction and captions. Maybe by the time you order this it will be completely up-to-date. Ages 10 and up. Code DV, $2.95.

**THE ROADSIDE HISTORY SERIES**. Based on current main travel routes, including photographs, maps, and stories that bring the past to life. These books make good reading for adults and high school students. Youngsters in the car will enjoy learning through the retelling of these stories. An excellent way to add pleasure to a trip by connecting the present with the past. I wish they had a book for each state. About 500 pages each. Code MPP. Arizona $20, Arkansas $18, California $18, Florida $18, Idaho $30 (hardcover), Montana $20, Nebraska $18, Nevada $20, New Mexico $18, Oklahoma $20, Oregon $18, South Dakota $18, Texas $18, Utah $18, Vermont $15, Wyoming $18, Yellowstone Park, $10.

**PORTRAIT OF AMERICA SERIES**. A book for each state plus one each for Washington, D.C.; Puerto Rico; and the Pacific Islands. Information about history, economy, culture, color map, photos, timeline of historical events, important sites, annual events, and vignettes of important people. Ages 9 to 13. Code RVS, $5.95 each. Request book by state name.

**Probing behind the events**. Very detailed discussions and analyses of such subjects as Kennedy's assassination, mind control, the CIA and narcotics traffic, Iran-Contragate, life in Germany during the rise of Hitler, and many more. Radio programs (from Radio Free Europe, Dave Emory, and others) on cassette tapes. Inexpensive. Send a #10 SASE and ask for a list of Dave Emory archive tapes. Archives on Audio, P.O. Box 170023, San Francisco, CA 94117; www.kfjc.org/emory.

### CANADIAN HISTORY
**for Canadians and Americans, because everyone should know his neighbors**

**THE KIDS BOOK OF CANADA**, by Barbara Greenwood. Finally, a good book of Canadian history! Ideal for the middle grades. Attractively done, good basic information, and easily used. A chapter is given to each province and territory, and one to Canada as a whole. Illustrations and text show the diversity of geography, industry, agriculture, and climate, with brief sections about the history, people, places, and events that shaped each province. I'd like to see a book just like this for older students, but this can be used as a base for further investigation. Highly recommended. Hardcover. Ages 8 to 13. Code KC, $17.95.

**Discovering Canada Series.** Meet the pioneer men and women who first came to Canada. Learn how they lived and how their achievements shaped the country. Nicely illustrated and informative without being dull and boring. Ages 8 to 10. Code SD, $7.95 each unless otherwise marked. Specify **Native Peoples, New France, The Vikings, The Railways, The Defenders (War of 1812), The Fur Traders,** or **The Loyal Refugees** (from the U.S. Revolution), $9.95.

**THE ILLUSTRATED HISTORY OF CANADA**, edited by Craig Brown and updated by Desmond Morton. This 592-page book contains pictures, engravings, lithographs, cartoons, maps, and photographs that chronicle the history of Canada from its earliest time to the present. Includes information about the Free (ha ha!) Trade Agreement, the Quebec question, and other contemporary issues. The text is provided by seven Canadian historians. This isn't a textbook. Very useful for older high school students and adults. Code FF, $19.95.

Donna Ward, Christian World Studies, 1048 Prince George Rd., London, ON N6H 4E1, has a small but nice catalog of Canadian history and geography materials.

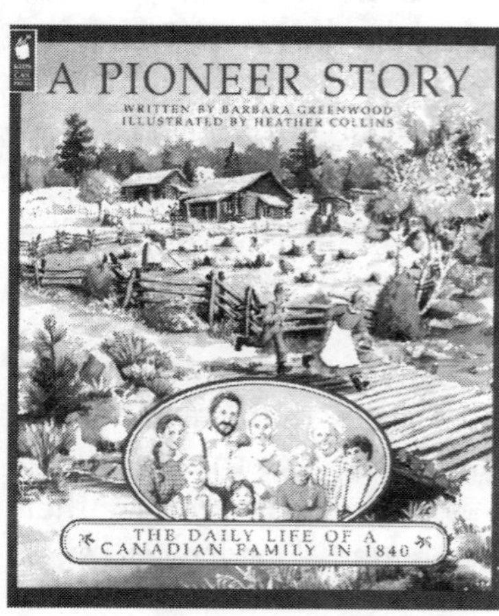


**A PIONEER STORY: The Daily Life of a Canadian Family in 1840**, by Barbara Greenwood; nicely illustrated by Heather Collins. Takes readers through a full year of family pioneer life in the backwoods. Includes free teaching guide. Hardcover. Ages 8 to 12. Code KC, $12.95.

Gertrude DeBoer has a nice catalog of Canadian resources. See "Support Groups and Organizations" for her address.

**A PIONEER THANKSGIVING: A Story of Harvest Celebrations in 1841**, by Barbara Greenwood. This companion to *A Pioneer Story* is historical fiction at its best. A chapter book enhanced by information about past harvest celebrations, superstitions, and hands-on activities. Ages 7 to 12. Code KC, $6.95.

**PIONEER CRAFTS,** by Barbara Greenwood. Complements the two books listed above, and will be useful for Canadians and Americans. Each craft has a historical introduction. A good way to add depth and variety to your studies on pioneering. Ages 8 to 12. Code KC, $5.95.

**CANADA'S MAPLE LEAF,** by Jane Yealland and Ann-Maureen Owens. This is a terrific book! A fascinating history of Canada's national flag and of all the colorful provincial and territorial flags. Learn about flag etiquette, flag-raising procedures, sending messages, related websites, and more. Ages 6 to 12. Code KC, $6.95.

**BOLDLY CANADIAN: Story of the Royal Canadian Mounted Police,** by Joann Hamilton-Barry. This book will help you separate fact from fiction. Fun to read, with surprising information about police dogs, undercover duty, the Musical Ride, crime labs, computer crime, famous Mounties, and more. Ages 8 to 12. Code KC, $10.95.

**WHY I HATE CANADIANS**, by Will Ferguson (a Canadian), is written with love and affection, great humor, and wit. It's funny and brash and I laughed until my sides hurt. If you take your Canadian identity *very* seriously and can't stand a good-natured poke in the ribs, don't read this. Code BT, $19.95.

## HISTORY THROUGH BIOGRAPHY

*There is properly no history, only biography.*
— Ralph Waldo Emerson

*Biography is the only true history.*
— Thomas Carlyle

**Easy Biographies**. An amazing amount of interesting information is packed into the short texts of these books, which concentrate on the childhood and early adulthood of these well-known men and women. Written for young readers, these books make history come alive. People are always more interesting than the plain reporting of an event. Ages 8 to 12. Code TRL. Minimum order of 5 books for $17.95, which gives you a bit of a break since the books are regularly priced at $3.95 each. For more than 5 books add $3.75 for each additional title. **Young Abigail Adams, Louisa May Alcott, Jim Beckwourth, Ludwig van Beethoven, Elizabeth Blackwell, Daniel Boone, Davy Crockett, Marie Curie, Young Frederick Douglass, Amelia Earhart, Thomas Alva Edison, Young Albert Einstein, Mohandas Gandhi, Patrick Henry, The Great Houdini, Young Thomas Jefferson, Helen Keller, Young Martin Luther King, Jr., Robert E. Lee, Abe Lincoln, Thurgood Marshall, Willie Mays, Wolfgang Amadeus Mozart, Rosa Parks, Paul Revere, Jackie Robinson, Eleanor Roosevelt, Young Eleanor Roosevelt, Teddy Roosevelt, Babe Ruth, Jim Thorpe, Harriet Tubman, George Washington, Wilbur and Orville Wright.**

Online you can find thousands of biographies at www.biography.com.

**DAUGHTER OF LIBERTY, A True Story of the American Revolution**, by Robert Quackenbush. Wyn Mabie is not a well-known hero of this turbulent time, but like her better-known contemporaries, she risked her life to help General Washington. This adventure starts when Wyn almost runs over Washington with her horse. Warmly told by one of her direct descendants. Ages 8 to 10. Code LB, $4.99.

**GREAT AFRICAN-AMERICANS IN HISTORY**. A collection of short biographies about people who have had a significant impact on our lives. Ages 10 to 14. Code CT, $8.95.

**JOAN OF ARC**, written and illustrated by Diane Stanley. An outstanding and thoroughly researched account of one of history's most notable young women. Brilliant color illustrations. Hardcover. Ages 10 to 15. Code WM, $16.

**LEONARDO DA VINCI FOR KIDS: His Life and Ideas**, by Janis Herbert. A four-color celebration of da Vinci's life, art, and science. Packed with splendid art and original drawings, plus 21 great related projects. Includes glossary, bibliography, timeline, pertinent museums, and websites. Wow! Ages 8 and up. Code CRP, $16.95.

**ALEXANDER GRAHAM BELL: An Inventive Life**, by Elizabeth MacLeod. Illustrated with photos, drawings, and Bell's handwritten notes. After he invented the telephone at age 29, he went on to invent many more interesting and useful items. He also became very annoyed with the people who gave him credit for inventing only the telephone! Ages 8 to 12. Code KC, $5.95.

**FAMOUS WOMEN: From Nefertiti to Diana.** Well-illustrated and chock-full of interesting detail about women who shaped their own destinies and events in their own lifetimes — most of which occurred before anyone had heard of a women's liberation movement. Each biography is set in historical context. The back of this book has a chronological list of things first done by women. Ages 10 and up. Code EDC, $8.95 (To enhance your investigation of this subject, see *Great Women* and *Infamous Women*, two books of paper dolls and clothes to be colored, with short biographies. See historical coloring books, below.)

**FAMOUS LIVES.** Five biographical books in one. Includes the Usborne books of *Inventors, Scientists, Explorers, Kings and Queens*, and *Famous Women* (listed separately elsewhere in this chapter). Discusses men and women who have changed the world. Charts, diagrams, and archival photographs. An excellent reference book that will be useful for years. 240 pages. Ages 10 and up. Hardcover. Code EDC, $24.95.

**SUSAN B. ANTHONY: And Justice for All**, by Jeanne Gehret. A very lively and readable biography of an outstanding personality. Ages 9 and up, Code VIP, $6.95.

**FRANK LLOYD WRIGHT FOR KIDS: His Life and Ideas**, by Kathleen Thorne-Thomsen. So much more than a biography that adults will find this very readable book as fascinating as their children. Besides learning about Wright's life, you will discover how his ideas about organic architecture developed. A multitude of projects are suggested: finding geometric shapes within everyday objects, comparing designs of different houses, reading plans, building a model of Fallingwater (using graham crackers!), designing a city, and more. 137 pages, with great illustrations. Ages 8 and up. Code CRP, $14.95.

These biographies bring history to life through the personal stories of people who have made a difference in our world. Ages 8 to 12. Code HBJ, $7.95 each. **Diana: The People's Princess, Wynton Marsalis: Musician, Mother Teresa: Saint of the Poor, Colin Powell, Luis Rodriguez: From Gang Member to Writer and Youth Activist.**

These beginning biographies have just the right amount of information to be interesting and informative without being overwhelming. Ages 6 to 11. Code HBJ, $5.95 each. **Kit Carson, Nelson Mandela, Rosa Parks, Diego Rivera, Booker T. Washington.**

**Real Lives Series**. This series combines a number of smaller individual books into one, at a much better price. Each anthology presents the stories of five extraordinarily inspiring people who have changed our world and made lasting contributions. Ages 5 to 8. Code TRL, each set normally $45, on sale for $39.95.

**BASEBALL GREATS**: Babe Ruth, Jackie Robinson, Lou Gehrig, Roberto Clemente, Willie Mays.

**HEROES AND IDEALISTS**: Sequoyah, Eleanor Roosevelt, Toussaint L'Ouverture, Marquis de Lafayette, Mohandas Gandhi.

**SEEKERS OF TRUTH**: Albert Einstein, Marie Curie, Thomas Edison, Benjamin Franklin, Louis Pasteur.

**GREAT ADVENTURERS**: Daniel Boone, Jim Beckwourth, Amelia Earhart, Francis Drake, Cabeza de Vaca.

**LEADERS OF THE PEOPLE**: Elizabeth I, Theodore Roosevelt, Benito Juárez, Sitting Bull, Patrick Henry.

**WOMEN OF VALOR**: Sacajawea, Elizabeth Blackwell, Clara Barton, Helen Keller, Rosa Parks.

**People to Remember Series.** A very good resource to use with reluctant readers, and a nice change in learning style for good readers. Each paperback book comes with a cassette with well-read identical text. Good for ages 9 to 14. Code JP, $9.95 each. **Clara Barton, Daniel Boone, George Washington Carver, Davy Crockett, Thomas Alva Edison, Nathan Hale, Helen Keller, Robert E. Lee, Abraham Lincoln, Francis Marion (the Swamp Fox), Florence Nightingale, Molly Pitcher, Betsy Ross, Sacajawea, Harriet Tubman, George Washington.**

**Presidential Read-Along Series** These four titles are in the same format as the People to Remember Series. Code JP, $9.95 each. **Andrew Jackson, Thomas Jefferson, James Madison, James Monroe.**

---

## DRAMATIZED HISTORY AND BIOGRAPHY FROM "OLD-TIME RADIO"

I was astonished at Donn's excitement when he discovered some old-time radio tapes for sale — and somewhat dismayed at the amount of money he sent off in the mail to get them — but then he went on to tell me about listening to the radio when he was growing up, and I realized that the difference in our attitudes was generational.

I grew up just as radio was being put aside in favor of television in middle-class homes. I remember watching *Howdy Doody, Captain Video, The Roy Rogers Show, Melody Ranch* with Gene Autry, and *The Lone Ranger* on our new seven-inch black-and-white

TV. I grew up having my entertainment presented to me. I didn't have to do anything more than sit passively and watch.

Donn's youth was strongly influenced by the end of the Depression and by living part time on his grandparents' farm. He vividly remembered his grandfather leaning against one of the cows he was milking and listening to a favorite show. He remembered sitting spellbound in the farmhouse kitchen with his parents and grandparents listening to the radio, his grandfather leaning his head on the polished wooden casing to ensure that he didn't miss a word of a favorite show. They listened to many of the shows listed below, as well as to mysteries, Westerns, science fiction, dramatized literature, and comedy shows. To enjoy a radio or a taped broadcast requires audience participation, because it engages the imagination. You have to create your own pictures. The body may remain still, but the mind is active.

I thought we would listen to these tapes once and then they'd gather dust, become part of the general clutter, and eventually be packed away in a box. Was I ever mistaken! Like favorite books, to be read and then reread, the tapes became a part of our way of life. We rewired the house so the kids could listen in their bedrooms. Although we continued to read to the kids every night, after a certain point (when we were starting to fall asleep) we asked for requests for tapes; the kids trundled off to bed, snuggled down under the covers with the lights off, and let their imaginations fly with stories from faraway places and different eras.

Old radio programs became one of our favorite learning tools. Besides being very entertaining, they give us a feeling of "being there" that is almost as good as actually being able to go back in time. Our kids frequently enjoyed coloring some of the related historical coloring books while listening.

Old radio has become a very popular form of time travel. These programs were produced on old radio's finest shows: *Lux Radio Theatre*, *Hallmark Hall of Fame*, *Screen Director's Playhouse*, *Favorite Story*, *Cavalcade of America*, *CBS's You Are There*, *Mercury Theatre*, and many others. Many of the voices you'll hear are those of the most famous actors of the time. Most are carefully researched dramatizations of actual events; others are historical fiction, interwoven with an authentic historical background. All have appropriate sound effects and musical background. Most of them have excellent sound, although a few are slightly muffled in places due to the recording techniques then used.

The following sets are each one hour, with either two 30-minute shows or one 60-minute show.

#1. *The Last Day of Pompeii. The Fall of Troy.*
#2. *Alexander: The Peace Offer From Persia. Alexander: The Battle for Asia.*
#3. *Alexander: Mutiny in India. Joan of Arc.*
#4. *Caesar Crosses the Rubicon. Assassination of Caesar.*
#5. *The Signing of the Magna Carta. The Execution of Captain Kidd.*
#6. *Death of Montezuma. Sailing of the Mayflower.*
#7. *The Count of Monte Cristo.*
#8. *Philadelphia, July 4, 1776. Ratification of the Constitution.*
#9. *A Tale of Two Cities.*
#10. *Les Misèrables.*
#11. *Napoleon Returns From Exile. Ireland Separates From England.*
#12. *1781: Mutiny in Washington's Army. Betrayal of Toussaint L'Ouverture.*
#13. *Colonel Johnson Eats the Love Apple. The Trial of John Peter Zenger.*
#14. *Sentencing of Charles I. Fall of Savonarola.*
#15. *Battle of Hastings. Hanging of Robert Emmet.*
#16. *Execution of Mary, Queen of Scots. The Dreyfus Case.*
#17. *Siege of Leiden. Trial of Samuel Chase.*
#18. *Lewis and Clark. (A few parts are muffled; still excellent.)*
#19. *Swanee River (biography of Stephen Foster).*
#20. *Impeachment of Andrew Johnson. Trial of Aaron Burr.*
#21. *Anna Karenina.*
#22. *Life on the Mississippi* (Mark Twain's youth on the river). *Ballad of the Iron Horse.* I love this!
#23. *Huckleberry Finn*
#24. *Abraham Lincoln* (played by Orson Welles).
#25. *John Brown. The Monitor and the Merrimack.*
#26. *The Prairie Years* (Sandburg's biography of Lincoln, played by Gregory Peck). *The Battle Hymn of the Republic.*
#27. *Battle of Lexington. I, Mary Peabody.*
#28. *The Red Badge of Courage.*
#29. *Battle of Gettysburg. Lee Surrenders to Grant.*
#30. *Mr. Lincoln Goes to the Play. The Capture of John Wilkes Booth.*
#31. *The Virginian* (Gary Cooper).
#32. *Viva Zapata!* (Charlton Heston).
#33. *Broken Arrow* (one of the few Westerns sympathetic to both whites and Indians).
#34. *Surrender of Sitting Bull. Oklahoma Land Run.*
#35. *Shane* (Alan Ladd, Van Heflin).
#36. *Greeley of the Tribune. Peary at the North Pole.*
#37. *The Ship the Nazis Had to Get* (carrying tanks to head off Rommel; great suspense!). *CBS Is There* (highlights of early radio—war news, abdication of King Edward, sports, more).
#38. *"I Can Hear it Now"* (the history of an era, 1933-1945, with the voices and actual sounds of the time: Roosevelt, Truman, Hitler, Mussolini, Stalin, newscasters; narrated by Edward R. Murrow).
#39. *The Grapes of Wrath* (Steinbeck's novel of the Depression; with Henry Fonda).
#40. *Alexander Graham Bell*
#41. *Young Tom Edison* (Mickey Rooney).
#42. *Madame Curie* (Greer Garson, Walter Pidgeon).

**"Mr. President"** series. Each 30-minute program dramatizes an important but little-known event or circumstance in the administration of one of the U.S. presidents. Play the tape without looking at the label and try to guess, along with the audience, who is the president.

#43. *George Washington. Thomas Jefferson.*
#44. *John Quincy Adams. Zachary Taylor.*
#45. *Andrew Jackson.* Two separate episodes.
#46. *John Tyler.* Two separate episodes.
#47. *Millard Fillmore. Franklin Pierce.*
#48. *Abraham Lincoln.* Two separate episodes.
#49. *Ulysses S. Grant.* Two separate episodes.
#50. *Grover Cleveland. Woodrow Wilson.*

Order by **NUMBER and FULL TITLE**. Each one-hour tape, $8. Postage: $1.50 for one tape, 25¢ for each additional tape. 10 or more tapes at one time, $7 each postpaid. All code BFB. If you'd like a list of some of our other old-time tapes: *The Lone Ranger*, *Roy Rogers*, *Gene Autry*, *Fibber Mcgee and Molly*, *Jack Benny*, *Edgar Bergen and Charlie McCarthy*, and many more, send $1 and an SASE.

**VOICES FROM THE PAST**. Actual recordings of more than 40 famous people in history, including Florence Nightingale, Thomas Edison, P.T. Barnum, Enrico Caruso, Teddy Roosevelt, Woodrow Wilson, V.I. Lenin, Will Rogers, Billy Sunday, W.C. Fields, Calvin Coolidge, Herbert Hoover, Mohandas Gandhi, Albert Einstein, and many others. One cassette. Code AF, $12.95.

**History-Makers in Your Home.** A series of dramatized biographical programs about some of the people who greatly influenced our history and the way we live today. Professional scriptwriters and actors make these worth listening to many times. Each cassette 60 to 80 minutes. Ages 12 and up. Code AF, $12.95, 2 for $11.95 each, 3 for $10.95 each. If you want them all, write for a deal.

**CHRISTOPHER COLUMBUS** — His obsession, struggles, triumphs, disgrace, and restitution.

**THOMAS ALVA EDISON** — An unschooler by any definition, who changed our lives as few others have.

**ALBERT EINSTEIN** — He changed our understanding in many fields of science.

**HENRY FORD** — Where would we be without him?

**V.I. LENIN** — A plotter, revolutionary, lawyer, writer, and anti-God prophet. How did he become a dictator and creator of chaos?

**MAO TSE-TUNG** — How did he become one of this century's most powerful leaders?

**GEORGE WASHINGTON** — The man who founded our democracy, assisted by the thinking of Jefferson and Franklin.

**THE WRIGHT BROTHERS** — From the humble bicycle shop, to inventors, to success and fame.

Historical novels, literature, and entertainment on tape are available from Durkin Hayes Publishing, 2221 Niagara Falls Blvd., Niagara Falls, NY 14304; 800-962-5200; www.dhaudio.com. In Canada: 3375 N. Service Rd., Unit B7, Burlington, ON L7N 3G2; 800-263-5224. Here is a partial listing. Request your own catalog for a complete listing of their titles, which include **The Red Badge of Courage, The Scarlet Pimpernel, Call of the Wild, Shane, Lust for Life, The Last of the Mohicans,** and **On Wings of Eagles,** to name just a few.

The works of classic thinkers throughout history are sometimes referred to as the "Great Conversation," because the authors respond to each other's ideas, although they may have lived thousands of miles or hundreds of years apart, and because, in various ways, they all address the most important and enduring questions and problems of humanity: What is truth? What is happiness? What is human nature? What principles should guide our actions? What authorities deserve our allegiance? These questions are as new — and as old — for us today as they were for Plato. The Great Conversation (or the Great Ideas) is not the useless ponderings of ancient, abstract philosophers. If we consider them in their historical contexts, we gain a better understanding of the past; if we apply them to our own time, they become powerful tools to help us better understand these times, our real nature, and our rights and responsibilities as human beings. Most of the Great Ideas were developed within the context of particular events of the past, and studying them will give us not only a better understanding of those events, but a higher value: that the basic principles are applicable to any period and circumstance, including our own.

When I first saw this cassette program advertised, I was very skeptical, expecting it to be no more than readings of condensed classics, which would be interesting and valuable, but of limited use. I requested a sample ("Civil Disobedience," by Henry David Thoreau, because I am especially interested in Thoreau's life and philosophy). I was very agreeably surprised and impressed.

The cassette tapes of **Great Ideas That Shaped Our World** are dramatized, with multiple voices portraying the author, contemporary observers, and critics, drawing on actual writings and quotations of the time, with an overview presented by a narrator. Each tape is about 90 minutes long, divided into shorter segments (about 20 minutes each) for more convenient study. The social and historical background of each work is presented, as well as the effects, both immediate and long-term, that the work had on contemporary and future society. There are numerous references to other works and historical events, demonstrating the continuing influence of the author's ideas.

The knowledge and understanding to be gained from each cassette program is easily equivalent to several hours of reading or high school- and college-level lecturing. These tapes won't take the place of the books presented, but they are very comprehensive introductions, and will definitely increase one's enjoyment and understanding of those works. For those who don't have the time or inclination to read the original works, these programs will make a very adequate substitute. After our complete satisfaction with our first tape, we bought several more, and are steadily adding titles to our library. We have listened to them several times, not only for "study" but for repeated enjoyment, just as we often browse through the Great Ideas in books.

Set 1. **COMMON SENSE**, by Thomas Paine. The little pamphlet that swept through the American colonies, converting thousands to the idea of independence. **THE DECLARATION OF INDEPENDENCE**, the announcement to the world of a new republic and the reasons for its inception.

Set 2. **CIVIL DISOBEDIENCE**, by Henry David Thoreau, one of the most influential essays in history, written after Thoreau was jailed for his opposition to slavery and the Mexican War, raising essential questions about law, conscience, and morality, and arguing that being a *person* must always come before being a *citizen*. **THE LIBERATOR**, the most outspoken abolitionist newspaper, edited by William Lloyd Garrison.

Set 3. **WEALTH OF NATIONS**, by Adam Smith, Part 1. In 1776, a shy professor from Scotland published this masterpiece on economics that changed forever what people thought of the role of government in the economy. Smith is suspicious of businessmen who say "a balance of trade" is in the national interest; such a proposal, he says, is motivated by a desire to restrict competition.

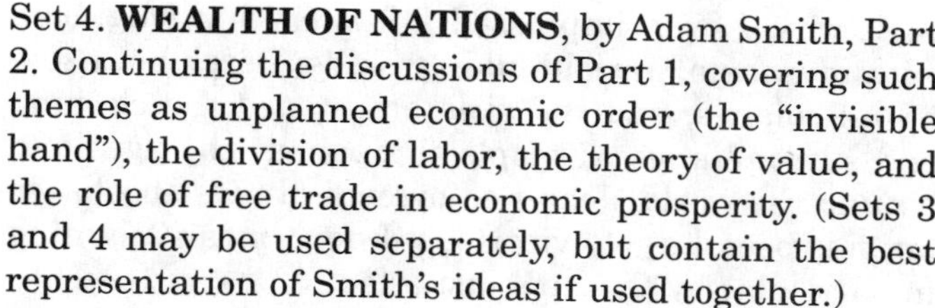

Set 4. **WEALTH OF NATIONS**, by Adam Smith, Part 2. Continuing the discussions of Part 1, covering such themes as unplanned economic order (the "invisible hand"), the division of labor, the theory of value, and the role of free trade in economic prosperity. (Sets 3 and 4 may be used separately, but contain the best representation of Smith's ideas if used together.)

Set 5. **ON LIBERTY**, by John Stuart Mill. A strong and well-reasoned defense of individual rights against the state. **VINDICATION OF THE RIGHTS OF WOMEN**, by Mary Wollstonecraft, considered by many to be the first declaration of "women's rights," written in 19th-century England, when women were excluded from universities and many professions, and could not bring a lawsuit, sign a contract, or vote.

Set 6. **THE PRINCE**, by Niccolò Machiavelli. A master politician who wanted to expand government power discusses the pros and cons of telling the truth, arguing that the end usually justifies the means. **DISCOURSE ON VOLUNTARY SERVITUDE**, by Etienne de la Boetie, who sought to limit government's power. The nearly opposite views of these two thinkers present an excellent dialogue of ideas.

Set 7. **THE COMMUNIST MANIFESTO**, by Karl Marx and Frederick Engels. One of the most famous, most misunderstood, and most misused documents in history, arguing that the best interests of the individual derive from merging with the greater social good; much of its reasoning is based on the economic struggle between the poor working class and the wealthy owners. **THE SOCIAL CONTRACT**, by Jean-Jacques Rousseau. Arguing more from a concern for civil rights and liberties than for economic or ownership status, Rousseau arrived at startlingly similar views about the precedence "the greater good" should have over the individual.

Set 8. **REFLECTIONS ON THE REVOLUTION IN FRANCE**, by Edmund Burke, is a heated condemnation of the French Revolution, and a passing criticism of Thomas Paine's roles in both the American and French Revolutions. **THE RIGHTS OF MAN**, by Thomas Paine, written in rebuttal of Burke's attack, argued further for the inherent rights of all individuals. The "debate" between these men produced two of the best-selling books of the 18th century.

Set 9. **THE FEDERALIST PAPERS**, by Alexander Hamilton, James Madison, and John Jay. During the bitter debate over the ratification of the U.S. Constitution, these articles were published in various newspapers as part of a campaign to swing the pivotal state of New York, and formed the basis of many aspects of the Constitution as it is today.

Set 10. **LEVIATHAN**, by Thomas Hobbes. Some of the most compelling arguments ever set forth in favor of a strong, centralized government. Although condemned by many political theorists, this powerful book continues to be fascinating, and some of its ideas will be found in even the most "liberal" of today's democracies.

Set 11. **TWO TREATISES OF GOVERNMENT**, by John Locke. Locke's ideas on individual liberty, government by consent, and the right of revolution helped set the stage for the English Revolution of 1688, the American Revolution of 1776, and the French Revolution of 1789.

Set 12. **DEMOCRACY IN AMERICA**, by Alexis de Tocqueville. Although written in the 1830s, this book is still considered by many to be the best examination of American democracy and the American character, and contains many provocative insights to help us evaluate democracy as perceived and practiced in today's America, and to see that many of our national concepts have changed radically, although we may use the same words.

EACH SET (two cassettes, approximately three hours), $17.95. Specify "Great Ideas," set number, and first title in the set (e.g.: "Great Ideas #5, On Liberty"). Code KP. Complete set for $175 with free shipping.

# MORE TOOLS TO MAKE LEARNING COME ALIVE GAMES, COLORING BOOKS, MODELS, AND MORE HISTORY!

**BETHUMP'D WITH HISTORY.** It's terrific! We've always felt history books overemphasized battles, dates, villains, dictators, and destruction (just like today's news media), while inventors, philosophers, scientists, politicians, and others who have made positive and enduring contributions received second billing. Bethump'd With History emphasizes people who have made our lives better and brings their deeds to our attention. The creators of this lively game say it is "devoted to the civilizing of civilization and, especially, to the civilizers of civilization." While playing this game you'll develop strategies and skills, and you'll learn about these fascinating people whose lives are every bit as interesting and adventurous as those of the leaders of destructive forces. Kids will love this game, and so will your adult friends. 2-8 players, ages 12 to adult. Code MLR, $40, plus $3 shipping. No charge for shipping if you are getting any of the other great Bethump'd games or book at the same time (see "English Language").

**History Alive Through Coloring Books and Activities**. Based on the art, sculpture, architecture, and costumes of the times, authentically reproduced, with explanatory text and captions. I didn't think I had much interest in old castles until I built the Chateau Gaillard of King Richard the Lionheart a couple of years ago, and then I became the family's Castle Authority. I even impressed a few visiting neighbors with my, ahem, model-building skills. Derek built several airplanes, and the girls brightened the clothing and surroundings of people throughout the ages and around the world. Jean's enjoyment of these books, so far, has been largely vicarious. I don't mean anything in particular by that; it's just a fact.

They talked about what they were doing, and I learned a lot of history while they all enjoyed coloring, constructing, and researching their projects. I guess I'd rather play my guitar, churn butter, sew, or try to catch up on the mending.

These are good tools for children who don't like to use regular textbooks or do a lot of research. Some younger children (under 8, more or less) may find there is too much detail in these books. They'll be happier with the history coloring books with the code DV. The cut-and-assemble projects here are also not for younger children. There are projects for them with the code EDC or DV. We found it enjoyable (and informative) to listen to either a related history cassette or literature on tape while working on these projects.

The following books are all code BB, prices as marked.

**13 COLONIES.** Coloring book with stories of their earliest settling and their flags and emblems. $4.95.

**A MEDIEVAL ALPHABET TO ILLUMINATE**. The intricate letters of medieval manuscripts are beautiful and elegant, and frequently contain the excellent humor of the 12th-century monks who labored over them for days at a time. $4.95.

**ACES AND AIRPLANES OF WWI**. Coloring book covering the earliest flying flivvers to the advanced planes at the end of the war, with the stories of the Great Aces of both sides. $3.95.

**ALEXANDER THE GREAT**. Coloring book illustrating the monuments of Alexander's life, along with the golden relics of the people he conquered. $3.95.

**AMERICAN INDIANS**. Coloring book including many different areas of American Indian art, and scenes by white men of Indians using their art, from prehistory to the present. Also masks to wear. $4.95.

**AMERICAN REVOLUTION**. Coloring book of political cartoons and caricatures from the age of the Revolution, offering an unusual glimpse at early American history. $4.95.

**ANCIENT AFRICA**. Coloring book from the art of Benin, showing the Oba, his warriors, and their costumes; his palace; and a noble queen of Benin. Some of the world's greatest portraits. $3.50

**ANCIENT CHINA**. Coloring book that is an excursion into Chinese art, from earliest paintings and ancient bronze animals to the famous painters of priceless scrolls and famous emperors and empresses. $4.95.

**ANCIENT EGYPT**. Coloring book including art from the earliest king through 3,000 years to Cleopatra. Animals at play, gods and goddesses, ships, dancers, and scenes of Egyptians at work and sport. $4.95.

**ANCIENT FACES TO CUT OUT AND WEAR**. Eight different masks, printed in full, authentic color, patterned after ancient relics in the Metropolitan Museum of Art. $5.95.

**ANCIENT GREECE**. Coloring book of all the Olympian gods and goddesses. Many scenes of daily life: music-making, dance, chariot and foot races, and more. Art from the finest ancient vase painters. $4.95.

**ANCIENT HAWAII**. Coloring book that offers an art history of Hawaii, including temple images, drawings by explorers, and portraits of early kings; some cutouts also. $2.95.

**ANCIENT INDIA**. Coloring book covering Alexander to the 12th century, including Sanchi, Barhut, and Sarnath and stories of Hindu gods and goddesses. $4.95.

**ANCIENT IRELAND**. Coloring book that offers a child's history of ancient Irish art, with amusing Celtic people and animals woven into ancient mazes and patterns. From 8th- and 9th-century artifacts and the Books of Durrow and Kells. $4.95.

**ANCIENT NEAR EAST**. Coloring book covering the art of Ur in 3,000 B.C. to that of the Babylonians, Assyrians, and Persians. Gods, goddesses, and great rulers. $4.95.

**ANCIENT ROME**. Coloring book covering all the Caesars, from Julius to Septimius Severus; chariot races; and more, in this collection of art from Imperial Rome, with text in both English and Latin. $4.95.

**BLACK COWBOYS**. Coloring book. There were many, and somehow our history books don't tell us about these hard-working men. $2.50.

**BLACK SOLDIERS OF THE CIVIL WAR**. Coloring book covers their recruiting, training, and fighting, and the contribution they made to the great effort. $3.95.

**CASTLES OF SCOTLAND** to cut out and put together. The greatest of Scot fortresses with their exciting history. $4.95.

**CASTLES TO CUT OUT AND PUT TOGETHER**. The Tower of London and King Richard the Lionheart's Chateau Gaillard, authentically drawn to scale, with full informative text. $4.95.

**CHRISTOPHER COLUMBUS**. Coloring book with great illustrations from 1493 and other early editions. Written in his own words, in English and Spanish, with easy-to-read type. $2.95.

**CIVIL WAR**. Coloring book. The interesting uniforms of different units were far more colorful than just blue and gray. $4.95.

**CIVIL WAR FLAGS TO COLOR**. Both sides had intricate, colorful banners. $2.50.

**CIVIL WAR HEROES**. Coloring book with stories of great generals from both sides. History every child should know. $4.95.

**CIVIL WAR HEROINES**. Coloring book with inspiring stories of the women in the Civil War. $4.95.

**COWBOYS**. Coloring book. From early vaqueros to the great settlers of the ranges, from Buffalo Bill to Hoot Gibson and Roy Rogers, each in his most magnificent garb. $4.95.

**COWGIRLS**. Coloring book. From the earliest working cow-women to those of Buffalo Bill's troop to movie queens and rodeo stars to Wild Horse Annie, who worked to save the mustangs. $4.95.

**DRAGONS.** Coloring book with great dragons, along with brief stories about each. $4.95.

**FAMOUS FIGHTERS OF WWII** to cut out, color, and fly. They really do fly well (with a careful thrust of the arm), but I recommend a soft lawn for the landing, or you'll have some extensive repair work to do. Accurately drawn. Somewhat challenging to assemble. $3.95.

**FRENCH REVOLUTION**. Paper dolls. Color and learn the stories and fates of these people. $5.95.

**GREAT AMERICAN AIRPLANES TO MAKE AND FLY**. Color, cut out, and glue together. The Wright Brothers' plane, Lindbergh's Spirit of St. Louis, the Bell XS-1 (breaker of the sound barrier), and Amelia Earhart's Lockheed Vega. $4.95.

**GREAT DOCTORS**. Coloring book with stories about Hippocrates, Galen, Avicenna, Elizabeth Blackwell, and many more. $3.95.

**GREAT DOGS**. Coloring book depicting heroic feats performed by dogs and their famous owners, in nearly every period of history and literature. $4.95.

**GREAT EXPLORERS**. Coloring book depicting Columbus, Balboa, Cortés, the Cabots, and many more. $4.95.

**GREAT INDIAN CHIEFS**. Coloring book with 50 portraits and brief biographies of Powhatan, Pocahontas, Hiawatha, Sitting Bull, Crazy Horse, Chief Joseph, and many more. $4.95.

**GREAT LAWYERS**. Coloring book (no it's not a joke book). Hammurabi, Moses, Demosthenes, Cicero, Portia, Coke, Blackstone, Marshall, Webster, Lincoln, Holmes, Darrow, and more. Interesting introduction to law. $3.95.

**GREAT WOMEN**. Paper dolls. Sappho, Cleopatra, Joan of Arc, Pocahontas, Susan B. Anthony, Florence Nightingale, Golda Meir, and others, each with appropriate costumes to color and a speech for her cause. $4.95.

**HENRY VIII AND HIS WIVES**. Paper dolls to color. Beautiful suits of armor, rich damasks, glittering jewelry, with full stories. $4.95.

**HEROES OF THE AMERICAN REVOLUTION**. Coloring book of pictures taken from old portrait engravings, with stories of the heroes who founded the United States. $4.95.

**HEROINES OF THE AMERICAN REVOLUTION**. Coloring book of stories with pictures to color about the women who helped us win our freedom. $4.95.

**HORSES AND RIDING**. Coloring book of fascinating historical pictures with explanations. $3.95.

**INCAS, AZTECS, AND MAYAS**. Coloring book depicting some of the finest art of these pre-Columbian civilizations: ballplayers, dancers, calendars, counting devices, and gods. $4.95.

**INFAMOUS WOMEN**. Paper dolls and costumes to color. Messalina Agrippina, Lucrezia Borgia, the Empress Wu, Catherine the Great, Catherine de Medici, Mata Hari, and many others, with their histories. $4.95.

**JAPAN**. Coloring book depicting the history of Japanese art, from the most ancient to Ho-kusai and Utamaro. Warriors, actors, dancers, children playing, and animals. $4.95

**KINGS AND QUEENS OF ENGLAND**. Coloring book. From the most ancient to the present queen, clothed in elegant garb requiring only to be brightly colored. $4.95.

**THE MIDDLE AGES**. Coloring book of little marginal figures from medieval manuscripts and full-size pictures of King Arthur, Sir Lancelot, Charlemagne, William the Conqueror, Richard the Lionheart, and more. $4.95.

**MODERN FIGHTERS** to color, cut out and fly. Accurate scale models of the F-15, the F-16, the MiG-25, and more. $4.95.

**MYTHS AND LEGENDS OF THE VIKINGS**. Coloring book with pictures of Norse heroes and sagas taken from ancient times. $3.95.

**OLD CARS** to cut out and put together. A history of automobile transportation. Text adds interesting highlights. $3.95.

**THE OLYMPICS.** Coloring book. The story is told by a boy at the games in 468 B.C., and the events illustrated are taken from beautiful ancient sources. $3.95.

**OUR FIGHTING MEN AND WOMEN**. Paper soldiers to color and learn about. $2.50.

**OUR PRESIDENTS**. Coloring book. They're all there to color and learn about. $4.95.

**PAPER SOLDIERS OF THE AMERICAN REVOLUTION**. A small army, complete with cannon, ready to color and cut out. Each soldier is on a stand that identifies his regiment. $4.95.

**PAPER SOLDIERS OF THE MIDDLE AGES**. Authentic figures representing several different stations in the Middle Ages, ready to color, cut out, assemble, and attack someone's castle. $4.95.

**PIRATES**. Coloring book with a full-page picture of each pirate at his work. Text on opposite page by authorities of the time, such as Daniel Defoe. $5.95.

**QUEEN ELIZABETH I.** Paper dolls to color. The queen and her gowns and Sir Walter Raleigh and his armor, with text by the queen. $4.95.

**RENAISSANCE**. Coloring book depicting fascinating scenes and people, including Cesare Borgia and his sister Lucrezia. $4.95.

**SHAKESPEARE COLORING BOOK.** A history of Shakespearean illustration, from the very old Peacham drawing to illustrations of Richard Burton as Henry V, Orson Welles as Othello, and more, $4.95.

**SOUTHWEST INDIANS BOOK #1**. Navajo, Pima, Apache. $4.95.

**SOUTHWEST INDIANS BOOK #2**. Hopi, Acoma, Tewa, Zuni. This book and the one above each briefly tell the myths of these people along with pictures of their original artwork to color. Carefully researched. $4.95.

**STORY OF OUR FLAG**. Coloring book. You can follow the history of our country as you color the flags of the past up to present time. $4.95.

**STORY OF SPACE AND ROCKETS**. Coloring book. Illustrated by a NASA artist, this is a history of rocketry from the beginning. $4.95.

**VIKING SHIPS** to cut out and assemble. Oseberg, Gokstad, and Skuldelev ships printed in full-color on heavy stock, with very authentic detail. $5.95.

**Historical Coloring Books.** These are better for younger kids. Detailed, authentic illustrations of many historical periods, people, and events, with informative captions. Very interesting and educational, even if you don't want to color them. We've found that colored pencils work best; crayons are too clumsy, and felt markers show through to the next page. Books are 8¼x11", 48 pages. Ages 8 to 16. Code DV, $2.95 each.

**ABRAHAM LINCOLN**. 40 detailed scenes from Lincoln's life: log cabin birthplace, debating Douglas, Gettysburg Address, and more.

**THE AMERICAN HOUSE**. Styles of architecture.

**AMERICA'S FIRST LADIES**. Pictures and wardrobes.

**CASTLES OF THE WORLD**. 31 medieval castles around the world, including Austria, France, Britain, Germany, Italy, Syria, and Japan.

**CATHEDRALS OF THE WORLD**

**CIVIL WAR UNIFORMS**. 21 Confederate and 24 Union uniforms of different ranks, states, and units, with historical figures — Grant, Lee, Farragut, and more — in color on the covers.

**COLUMBUS DISCOVERS AMERICA**. 41 drawings of shipboard life, the Spanish monarchs, storms at sea, arrival in the New World, and more.

**COWBOYS OF THE OLD WEST**. Detailed illustrations and informative captions about these symbols of the American spirit.

**EARLY AMERICAN CRAFTS AND OCCUPATIONS**

**EARLY AMERICAN TRADES**. Wigmakers, glassblowers, hatters, and 19 other craftsmen, accompanied on facing pages by their tools and products.

**EVERYDAY DRESS OF THE AMERICAN COLONIAL PERIOD**. Broomseller, farmer, wagoner, sailor, and more, accurately depicted with 14 color examples on the covers.

**EXPLORATION OF NORTH AMERICA**. Authentic dress and well-researched scenes to represent the people who first explored this land.

**FAMOUS BUILDINGS OF FRANK LLOYD WRIGHT**

**FOLK COSTUMES OF EUROPE**. 130 authentic costumes, male and female, in 45 pictures, from Italy, Spain, Central Europe, the Balkans, Russia, and more.

**FROM ANTIETAM TO GETTYSBURG**. 45 precise illustrations that document the battlefield action and many personalities of the Civil War.

**GREAT AFRICAN-AMERICANS**

**GREAT INVENTORS AND INVENTIONS**

**HISTORIC HOUSES OF NEW ENGLAND**

**HISTORY OF THE SWORD**

**JAPANESE COSTUMES**. Traditional.

**KING ARTHUR**

**KNIGHTS AND ARMOR**. Specify coloring book, because there are also paper dolls. Historically accurate depictions of knights in armor: Vikings, Crusaders, jousters, foot soldiers, Henry VIII, and more

**LEGENDARY OUTLAWS AND LAWMEN**. Authentic scenes of good guys (Bat Masterson, Wyatt Earp, etc.) and bad guys (Billy the Kid, Jesse James, etc.) with biographical captions.

**LEWIS AND CLARK**. 45 historically accurate illustrations of the high points of the expedition, with captions identifying the action and providing background information.

**LIFE IN A MEDIEVAL CASTLE AND VILLAGE**

**LIFE IN ANCIENT EGYPT**

**LIFE IN ANCIENT GREECE**

**LIFE IN ANCIENT MEXICO**

**LIFE IN ANCIENT ROME**

**LIFE IN OLD JAPAN**

**MEDIEVAL FASHIONS**

**MEDIEVAL JOUSTS AND TOURNAMENTS**

**THE MIDDLE AGES**. More than 50 woodcuts from German incunabular ("before 1501," my dictionary says) sources: knights, jousts, ships, maidens, medieval towns, battles, labors, and incredible beasts.

**OLD-FASHIONED FARM LIFE**. 19th-century life at historic Greenfield Village.

**PIRATES AND BUCCANEERS**. Morgan, Blackbeard, Anne Bonny, Mary Read, and others.

**POWELL'S COLORADO RIVER EXPEDITION**

**SHIPWRECKS AND SUNKEN TREASURE**

**STATUE OF LIBERTY AND ELLIS ISLAND**. 45 illustrations adapted from historic photographs and engravings detail Liberty's history, immigration at Ellis Island, and more.

**THE STORY OF THE AMERICAN REVOLUTION**. 40 finely drawn scenes of the Boston Massacre, Paul Revere's ride, the execution of Nathan Hale, and more.

**STORY OF THE CALIFORNIA GOLD RUSH**. 40 scenes, including Sutter's Mill in 1848, mining camps and boomtowns, old San Francisco, prospectors panning for gold, and more.
**STORY OF THE CIVIL WAR**
**STORY OF THE VIKINGS**. 38 detailed illustrations of the Viking saga: European raids, American and Russian presence, ship construction, weapons, art, literature, and more.
**STORY OF WHALING**
**UNIFORMS OF THE AMERICAN REVOLUTION.** 31 panoramas of military attire, with complete instructions for accurate coloring.
**UNIFORMS OF THE NAPOLEONIC WARS**. 45 full-page illustrations of combatants.
**WESTERN PIONEERS**
**WORLD WAR I UNIFORMS**. A Romanian infantry colonel, German flying ace, U.S. Marine corporal, and more.

**American Adventure Games** are among the least expensive yet most informative and enjoyable historical games available. They let *you* become a part of American history. Imagine your children riding with Paul Revere, following the North Star to freedom as a "passenger" on the Underground Railroad, or being present on the voyage of the Mayflower or at Bunker Hill. These games allow your children (and you, if you are lucky enough to be allowed to play too) to use and develop their imagination. These excellent games are in many museum stores. Each game comes with a colored game board. Game pieces are cut out by you; some are folded to create playing pieces. The rules provide interpretive information to help players understand the event portrayed in the game. Many of the games also include a historical essay and educator's notes along with other background information about the period. All games are about $10 — you can't go wrong with these. Why just read about the past? These games will inform as well as amuse you. You can learn while you play!
**BATTLE OF BUNKER HILL**. Based on the 18th-century game Asalto, players attack or defend the redoubt on Breed's Hill. 2 players.
**COUNTRYSIDE AND VILLAGE**. Live through all four seasons as part of an 1830s New England community. You'll be subject to all the ups and downs of tradition and fate while you work. Record your debts and credits. Will you be in debt at the end of the year? 2 to 4 players.
**DON'T GIVE UP THE SHIP**. American and British ships clash on Lake Erie, September 10, 1813. Lots of "what if" options in this game. 2 or more players.
**THE ERIE CANAL**. Travel through the Erie Canal in the 1830s. You'll have to cope with other passengers, cargo, locks, tolls, and unknown hazards! 2 players. (Available with audio cassette of songs.)
**NEW FLAMES ACROSS THE VALLEY**. Struggle with the Loyalists and the Indians on the colonial frontier during the American Revolution. Action and suspense! 2 or more players.
**FRIGATES!** Walk the quarterdeck of the U.S.S. Constitution or the U.S.S. Constellation as they sail into battle. Detailed sailing action. 2 or 3 players.
**HENRY FORD'S RIVER ROUGE**. Put on your coveralls, learn, and go to work building Model A Fords in 1928 Detroit. 2 to 4 players.
**THE MONITOR AND THE MERRIMACK.** Relive two days of battle in this game of dueling ironclads. Can the Monitor save the Union fleet from destruction? 2 to 4 players.
**THE "OLD PACIFIC."** Take the driver's seat in the Packard that made a spectacular transcontinental trip in 1903 from California to New York. 2 to 4 players.
**THE REDCOATS ARE COMING!** Ride with Paul Revere and William Dawes on April 18, 1775, as they gallop through the dark Massachusetts countryside to warn patriots of advancing British troops. 2 players.
**THAR SHE BLOWS!** Take command of a whaling ship in the 1820s and sail the icy, fog-bound waters off Greenland. You'll need luck to make a successful voyage. 2 players.
**THE UNDERGROUND RAILROAD**. Here's your chance to take slaves on the perilous journey north, surrounded by spies and slave catchers while you race through the night to freedom. 2 to 4 players.
**SPECIAL: THE UNDERGROUND RAILROAD** is also available as a Game and Music set with video and audio cassettes. With the game above you get a 25-minute cassette of powerful music associated with the Underground Railroad, performed in the context of narrative passages. The video is filled with songs, stories, historical images, and live-action re-creations.
**THE VOYAGE OF THE MAYFLOWER**. Sail with the Pilgrims in 1620, then decide if you are going to stay in the new-found country or return with the supply ships. 2 to 4 players. (Unique solo version of the game included.)
**THE WIZARD OF MENLO PARK**. Help Thomas Edison invent the light bulb in Menlo Park in the 1870s. 2 to 4 players.
**THE WRIGHT BROTHERS**. Travel the path of discovery and invention that led the Wright Brothers to succeed where so many had failed, in the development of a heavier-than-air "flying machine."
All games are available from Chatham Hill Games, P.O. Box 253, Chatham, NY 12037; 800-554-3039; CHGames@taconic.net; www.chathamhillgames.com.

**Easy-to-Make Historical Models**. All you need are scissors and glue. Books are 9x12". Ages 6 and up. Code DV.

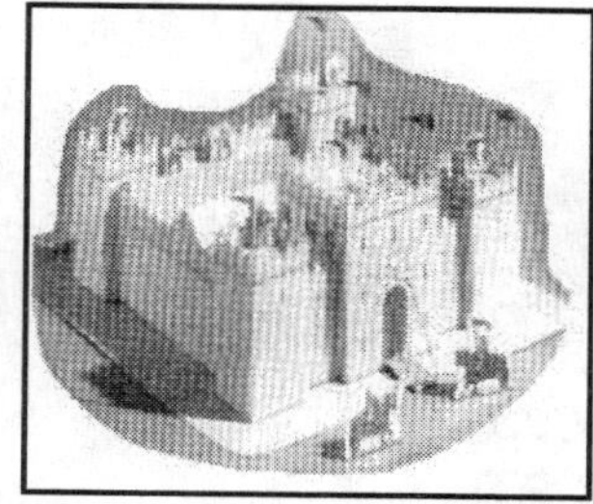

**COLUMBUS DISCOVERS AMERICA**. Sturdy full-color model, 25" long, includes paper models of Columbus's three ships, crew, natives, thatched huts, animals, and more. $3.50.
**EASY-TO-MAKE CASTLE**. Three-dimensional model of a medieval castle, with knights on horseback and more. $3.95.
**EASY-TO-MAKE HISTORICAL TOYS AND MODELS**. $3.95.
**PLAINS INDIANS TEPEE VILLAGE**. Five decorated tepees and 20 action figures (riding horses, cooking, hunting, dancing, playing lacrosse, and more). $3.50.
**WESTERN FRONTIER FORT**. Stockade fence encompassing three buildings; 17 soldiers on horseback, bugling, aiming rifles, walking, and more. $3.95.

**Acid-free reusable sticker books.** $9\frac{1}{4}$x$11\frac{1}{4}$". The book cover makes a backdrop for the 30 or more full-color, reusable stickers. Ages 7 and up. Code DV.
**FARM**, $3.50
**TEEPEE VILLAGE**, $3.50
**WILD WEST**, $3.95

**Historical Paper Dolls**. Our neighbors sometimes think parts of our lifestyle are a little strange, but so far no one has caught me playing with paper dolls. Don't be silly; I'm not playing with them, I'm arranging them in groups to illustrate the periods of history we're studying. It's very serious work. (How will I explain it after the kids have all grown up and moved away?) Oh, yeah, I guess I should mention that our kids like these paper dolls, too. A great way to have fun and an easy way to absorb history. Each book 9¼x12¼", 32 pages. Code DV.

**ABRAHAM LINCOLN AND FAMILY**. $4.95.
**AMERICAN COLONIAL FAMILY**. $4.95.
**AMERICAN FAMILIES OF THE CIVIL WAR**. $4.95.
**AMERICAN FAMILY OF THE PILGRIM PERIOD**. $4.95.
**AMERICAN PIONEER FAMILY**. $4.95.
**EMPRESSES AND QUEENS**. $4.95.
**FAMOUS AMERICAN WOMEN**. $4.95.
**GEORGE WASHINGTON AND FAMILY**. $4.95.
**HENRY VIII AND HIS WIVES**. $4.95.
**JOHN F. KENNEDY AND FAMILY**. $4.95.
**KNIGHTS IN ARMOR**. $4.95.
**MEDIEVAL COSTUMES**. $3.95.
**NOTABLE AMERICAN WOMEN**. $4.95.
**PRINCESS DIANA AND PRINCE CHARLES**. $4.95.
**ROYAL FAMILY OF BRITAIN**. $4.95.
**THOMAS JEFFERSON AND FAMILY**. $4.95.

**Coloring Books About Historic Transportation.** All books are $8\frac{1}{2}$x11" with some explanatory text. Ages 8 and up. Code DV, $2.95 each. **Antique Locomotives, Historic Sailing Ships, History of the American Automobile, History of Fire Engines, History of Flight, History of Space Exploration, Lindbergh and the Spirit of St. Louis, The Titanic.**

**Pop-Up Books to Make Yourself**. We didn't discover these until the kids were too old for them, but Donn was still young enough to work with them and ordered a couple right away. He said that most of the pop-ups were easy enough for children about age 9 or 10; a little help might be needed on the small cuts and folds of a few pieces. Besides learning about the subject in each book, you'll have the fun of learning about the engineering in a pop-up book, and the satisfaction of making it yourself. Each book contains six main scenes, with a number of mini-pop-ups built in, and brief text with interesting information and ideas. Code PW, $9 each. (List begins on next page.)

L'ARC DE TRIOMPHE

**THE EGYPTIANS POP-UP**. Black Land, Red Land, Kamak, the Great Pyramid, Tutankhamen, Abu Simbel, Cleopatra, and the Romans.

**THE GREEKS POP-UP**. Knossos, Mycenae, the Battle of Salamis, the Golden Age of Athens, the theater, Alexander the Great.

**THE MAYA, AZTECS, AND INCAS POP-UP**. Takai, human sacrifice, Teochtitlian, the struggle between the Aztecs and the Conquistadors, the Inca Empire, the Golden Enclosure.

**THE ROMANS POP-UP**. City of Rome, the Forum, a Roman house, the army, gladiators, Ostia, the port of Rome.

**POP-UP LONDON**. The Tower of London, St. Paul's Cathedral, Trafalgar Square, the Houses of Parliament, Buckingham Palace — a visitor's tour.

**POP-UP PARIS**. Notre-Dame, l'Arc de Triomphe, Montmartre, the Pompidou Centre, the storming of the Bastille. Text is in English and French.

**Cut-Out Models.** A tube of glue and a pair of scissors or a craft knife are all that are required to turn these books into superb models. Each model has been carefully checked for historical accuracy. Each includes full-color buildings, people, and baseboards. The baseboards of the village, town, cathedral (no longer available), and castle have been specially designed so they can be fitted together to make one large 12th-century model. More than 40 cut-out figures are included in each book. Most models are compatible with the 00/HO scale, so extra figures and accessories of the same scale are available in most hobby stores. Very satisfying to do and display. Each book 9½x12", 32 pages. Ages 9 and up. Code EDC, $9.95 each.

Donn thought it best to make some of these models before listing them, and he had a ball! He mounted his models on plywood, used some plaster of paris to make hills, streams, and contours in the land, and then painted the baseboard. He bought trees and shrubs from the hobby store. He sent me on errands (e.g., to find the right colored gravel for his roads. I finally found it in the aquarium department of Wal-Mart). It was great fun watching the models come together, and we learned a lot about the way people lived just by looking at the detail printed on each piece.

**MAKE THIS EGYPTIAN TEMPLE**
**MAKE THIS MEDIEVAL TOWN**
**MAKE THIS MODEL CASTLE**
**MAKE THIS MODEL VILLAGE**
**MAKE THIS ROMAN FORT**
**MAKE THIS ROMAN VILLA**
**MAKE THIS VIKING SETTLEMENT**

NEW LISTINGS *STILL $9.95*
MAKE THIS AMERICAN FORT
MAKE THIS CRUSADER CASTLE
MAKE THIS EGYPTIAN MUMMY
MAKE THIS GREEK TEMPLE
MAKE THIS MEDIEVAL CASTLE
MAKE THIS MEDIEVAL PORT

It took a while, but I figured out what to do with these once we were done with them. The local public library was very happy to display them. What they did with them after that I have no idea.

**Cut-and-Assemble Historic Models.** Our only problem with these is finding a place to display them all when they're done, so we usually rotate our displays according to how we feel and what we're studying. These models are fun, challenging, educational, and attractive. With scissors, a hobby knife, a straight-edge ruler, and some white glue, you can construct authentic replicas of historic buildings, villages, and ways of life. Except for the dinosaur dioramas, some of the small cuts and folds are a little tricky, and may be best for ages 10 or 12 and up, definitely including adults. Code DV.

**CRUSADER CASTLE**. The Krak des Chevaliers in Syria. A detailed, full-color 3-D model of one of the most powerful and imposing crusader castles, built in the 12th and 13th centuries on a towering precipice. $7.95.

**DINOSAUR DIORAMAS**. Two easy-to-assemble 3-D dioramas. Full color with 31 animals and plant cut-outs. $6.95.

**EARLY NEW ENGLAND VILLAGE**. 12 buildings in HO scale: Adams' home in Quincy, Massachusetts, Oliver Wright's house in Sturbridge, smithy, store, church, and seven others. $6.95.

**HISTORIC BUILDINGS AT GREENFIELD VILLAGE**. Full-color models of Henry Ford's Bagley Avenue Shop, Edison's Menlo Park Laboratory, William McGuffey's birthplace, the Wright Brothers' Cycle Shop, and many more. $7.95.

**MAYAN DIORAMAS**. Two pre-Columbian cities, Chichén Itza and Tulum, complete with temples; broad plazas; and cut-out figures of slaves, priests, children, traders, weavers, and more. Not suitable for small fingers. About age 10 and up. Includes shadow box and background scene. $5.95.

**THE MAYFLOWER**. Detailed 17" model of the reconstructed Mayflower at Plimouth Plantation. Challenging. $7.95.

**MEDIEVAL CASTLE**. Authentic, full-color model of Caenarvon Castle in Wales. HO scale. $6.95.

**NEW YORK HARBOR**. Beautifully illustrated, expertly designed panorama includes the Brooklyn Bridge, the Statue of Liberty, skyscrapers, tugboats, the Staten Island Ferry, the rivers, the bay, and much more. $6.95.

**PLAINS INDIAN DIORAMA**. Two dioramas, a buffalo hunt and a small camp, with many cut-out figures, illustrating the lost culture of the Plains Indians. $6.95.

**SOUTHERN PLANTATION**. HO scale model of an antebellum plantation, with authentic buildings and outbuildings. $6.95.

**VICTORIAN SEASIDE RESORT**. Nine buildings in HO scale: ice cream stand, bandstand, bathhouse and boardwalk, life-saving station, four cottages, and a tower. $6.95.

**WESTERN FRONTIER TOWN**. Ten full-color buildings in HO scale: opera house, sheriff's office, jail, Wells Fargo office, saloon, and more. $6.95.

**ZENGER VIDEO**, P.O. Box 802, Culver City, CA 90232. Free catalog of historical events, novels, dramatized literature, and more.

**OLD NEWS**. Tabloid-sized "newspaper" featuring items from history, with period photos and illustrations. My sample issue contains "Crewman Describes Wreck of the Titanic," "Presidential Candidate's Wife Accused of Bigamy," "Sitting Bull Predicts Victory," "First Shot Fired in American Civil War," and more. An interesting alternative for exploring history. Eleven issues per year; write for current price. 400 Stackstown Rd., Marietta, PA 17547.

For a catalog of old, used, rare, scholarly, and out-of-print books about American history, send $3 to Q.M. Dabney & Co., P.O. Box 42026, Washington, DC 20015.

***Up-to-date* WORLD HISTORY CHART**. A 6,000-year chronology of the world's people and events, 34" high and almost 8 feet long. (The history of the United States takes up only two inches!) People and events covered include politics, literature, theology, mythology, and archaeology. $29.95. (Add $15 for plastic lamination.) Shipping $5. VA residents add $4\frac{1}{2}$% tax. International Timeline, 2565 Chain Bridge Rd., Vienna, VA 22181; 800-886-4478.

**THE GREAT HISTORY SEARCH.** Forty-eight pages filled with accurately detailed pictures containing subtle or hidden images. Each page covers a different time period and place. Text on each page gives basic facts and an illustration about items to spot. Children about the age of 5 can look at the pictures and find the hidden items. Older children can read the text and learn more. Ages 5 to 9. Code EDC, $9.95.

**HISTORY QUIZBOOK**. A quiz book for those who like to know what they do and don't know. Thirty-two well-illustrated pages, with lots of background information and a basic point scoring system if you want to use it (easily ignored if you don't). Ages 9 and up. Code EDC, $7.95.

**MY BACKYARD HISTORY BOOK**, by David Weltzman (a Brown Paper School Book). History surrounds us in attics, on street corners, and in people's memories. Hundreds of projects, stories, and activities will plunge readers into a personal involvement with history (rather than wedging them between the dates and facts of a textbook). "Out on a Limb of the Family Tree," "Whashis Name," and "Friday Night at Grandma's" are a few of the chapters that will challenge readers to explore the history around them. Ages 10 and up. Code LB, $13.95.

# A WORLD OF FUN

"Right here is where your Grandma Betty lives," I told the kids as my finger dropped halfway to the equator on our world globe. "This is called Florida."

"Why is it green?" asked Karen, who was six years old.

"Because it's carpeted with money," I told her, firmly believing in telling children the truth. "This is Canada, where we live." I pointed. "And over here is Vermont, where we used to live."

"Wow," exclaimed Cathy, who was eight. "It sure took us a long time to drive just from here to here!"

"It's a lot farther than it looks on this globe, Cathy. You know the earth is like a ball. This globe is a little map of the world. Even a big city wouldn't —"

Derek, two years old, interrupted me. "Daddy, can I turn this ball?"

"Uh … just a little, Derek. A big city, Cathy, would be smaller than a tiny dot on this globe. Even a city with millions of —"

"Can I turn it more, Daddy?"

"Not now, Derek, please. Even a city with millions of people would be —"

"Daddy, I want to turn the ball!"

"Where was I? Oh, yes. Even a city with —"

"Do people live on the earth, Daddy?" asked four-year-old Susan.

"Sure they do. We live on the earth, and everybody —"

"But, Daddy, I don't see any people!"

"There aren't any people on this globe. This is a —"

"But, Daddy, you just said —"

"Daddy! I want to turn this ball!"

"Dad, where's our house on this globe?"

"Remember, Karen, Dad just said a million people —"

"Member-shmember! Dad said we live here, so our house must be here. But I don't see it! Dad, how come —"

"Whoa, kids, back up! Wait a minute! The real earth is much larger than this. This is just a … a toy. No, I don't mean a toy, not a toy to play with. I mean this is a pretend earth. Not real. Look, these big blue spaces are the oceans. This is Russia, here's Africa, here's Australia —"

"Dad," asked Cathy, "is this the place Columbus was looking for?"

"You mean India? Yes, you're right. He was looking for India. And China. But he found America instead. That's why the people he found were called Indians."

"You mean because they were in America?"

"No, I mean because Columbus thought he'd gotten to India."

"Too bad he doesn't have a globe like this," Karen said scornfully. "Then he wouldn't get losted like that if he did. Right, Dad?"

"Ah … right."

Cathy put her finger on India and asked, "You mean Columbus wanted to get here, Dad?"

"Right," I said again. "He was looking for a new way to the East."

Cathy nodded solemnly. "So he took his boat west. Isn't that a little strange, Dad?"

"He didn't know there was a big island in the way," I explained.

"Even so," Cathy said, "that would sure be a new way, all right, going west to get east. Are the people in America really called Indians?"

"Well, no, not most of them. Just the ones Columbus found when he first got there."

Karen's eyes got big. "You mean they're still alive?"

"No, no," I said quickly. "Not the same ones. I mean —"

"I know, Dad!" Susan said excitedly. "This is where we used to live, right?"

"Uh … right."

"And this is where Grandma Mary lives?"

"Right, Susan! Very good! You're really catching on."

Susan's eyes twinkled. She put her finger on Mexico and said, "I bet I know what this is!"

"Sure you do," I said proudly. "Tell us, then. What is it?"

She grinned, with pride matching mine, and said happily, "Our driveway!"

"Uh …"

"Daddy, can I please play with this ball now?"

# GEOGRAPHY

## It's more than just learning place names

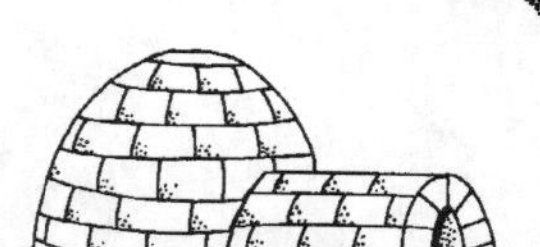

It's nice to be able to travel and learn about places firsthand, but it's not always feasible. When you study geography you can plan a trip anywhere you might like to go. You can begin by researching the route and places you want to investigate along the way to your destination. How far can or do you want to go in a day? What will you do when you get there? What's of interest in Chicago or Houston, Paris or Calcutta? Would it be more fun to fly around Europe or take the train, drive a car, or ride a bicycle? Are there hiking trails? What will you see? What languages will you need? Are there local customs you will need or want to observe? Ask your local travel agency for old travel posters and brochures.

**WORLD GEOGRAPHY**. An interesting, well-illustrated, up-to-date book about our world, with maps, charts, and diagrams. Includes sections on our changing world. Combines several other Usborne books: *The Seas, The Earth, Peoples of the World,* and *Houses and Homes,* with extra maps. Good beginner's book on geography. Hardcover. Ages 8 to 12. Code EDC, $24.95. (We're not listing all the individual books in this series because this is your best buy and *The Earth* is no longer available separately.)

**USBORNE GEOGRAPHY ENCYCLOPEDIA**. Profusely illustrated and arranged thematically with simple language for easy use by young learners. Includes many practical experiments. Ages 8 to 12. Code EDC, $14.95.

**THE READER'S DIGEST CHILDREN'S WORLD ATLAS.** Completely revised and updated to reflect the most recent political changes. Far more than just a collection of maps and color photos, this atlas uses colorful text to create a lasting picture of the character and culture of the world's continents, countries, and regions, and provide valuable information on every country's capital, largest city, currency, language, and chief products. This is a beautiful book! This has always been our favorite children's atlas. The information included covers far more than many atlases for adults and explains how to use an atlas, the basics of maps and map-making, earth's position in the solar system, the physical makeup of our earth and how it changes, weather and climate, living species, natural resources, a gazetteer of useful information (such as population, largest city, monetary unit, and religions), and much more. Other features include more than 3,000 illustrations and a multitude of activities. Besides providing fascinating information, this is excellent preparation for the complexity of an "adult" atlas. Hardcover, profusely illustrated in full color. Ages 7 to 15. Code SS, $22.99.

**NATIONAL GEOGRAPHIC MAGAZINE**. Accounts of anthropological travels around the world, visiting peoples, cities, cultures, climates, animals and their habitats, and the wonders of natural science with beautiful photographs. Subscription information: National Geographic Society, 1145 17th St. NW, Washington, DC 20036. The National Geographic Society has an education program called **UPDATE**. It's a newsletter with articles, lesson plans, and more. Write: National Geographic Society, Education Program, P.O. Box 37138, Washington, DC 20013-7138.

**WORLD MAGAZINE**. The National Geographic Society's children's magazine. We really enjoyed this for years. Interesting articles, great pictures, maps, and posters. Perfect for curious and growing minds. Subscription information: National Geographic Society, P.O. Box 64056, Tampa, FL 33664-4056.

**QUICK PIX**. A card game in which players match countries to various regions of the world. Country cards have the country's flag, name of the capital city, major language spoken, and a couple of other pertinent facts. Good game for beginners. Ages 8 and up. Code A, $10.

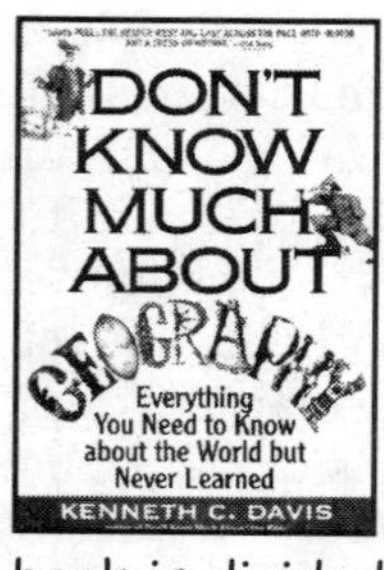


**DON'T KNOW MUCH ABOUT GEOGRAPHY**, by Kenneth Davis, is an amusing collection of facts about geography. If you're looking for something cohesive, staid, and sequential, this book will frustrate you, but the presentation is lively and there's a wealth of good, solid information. The book is divided into chapters: "The World Is a Pear," "What's So Bad About the Badlands?", "If People Were Dolphins the Planet Would Be Called Ocean," etc. I'd use the contents of this book to spark interest and create research projects. Ages 14 and up. Fun for adults too. Code AV, $12.50.

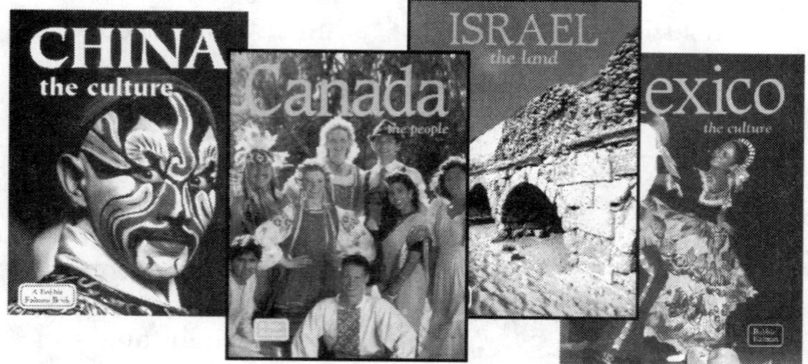

**LANDS, PEOPLES, AND CULTURES**. A great series of books to give you and your child an exciting, in-depth view of the featured countries. **The Land** books include physical characteristics, agriculture, transportation, history, industry, and special features. **The People** books explain unique customs of the featured country and what is shared around the globe, problems faced by minority groups, the role of women, and more. **The Culture** books describe modern and ancient festivals, processions, food, games, and much more. All books have 40 to 50 color photos, thought-provoking text, maps, diagrams, stories, and activities. Just right for ages 9 to 14. All books code CT, $7.95 each. Choose from this series of three books per country (unless otherwise stated): **CANADA** (there is a fourth book for Canada called **CANADA CELEBRATES MULTICULTURALISM**), **CHINA, EGYPT, FRANCE, GREECE, INDIA, ISRAEL, JAPAN, MEXICO, PERU** (only two books: **The Land** and **The People and Culture**), **RUSSIA, SOUTH AFRICA, TIBET** (only one book with everything in it — still $7.95), and **VIETNAM.** When ordering, state the country, then the particular volumes you want.

**EXPLORERS**. Arranged by region: Africa, Asia, the Americas, and Australia, with pages on Arabia, the Poles, mountains, circumnavigation, undersea, and space, and featuring the men and women who have explored the area. Good maps and illustrations accompanied by well-organized and interesting information, facts, and ideas. Ages 10 and up. Code EDC, $7.95.

**SEAS AND OCEANS**. Most of us are aware of abusive land-use policies. Our seas and oceans are even more important. Thought and study of our global water supplies will be getting more attention in the future. Excellent information, illustrations, and some hands-on activities. Ages 11 to 16. Code EDC, $6.95.

**WORLD FARMING**. An in-depth look at this essential process. I was glad to see someone look at this from more than a local or regional perspective. Well-illustrated book includes activities. Ages 11 to 16. Code EDC, $7.95.

**THE BOOK OF WHERE: How to Be Naturally Geographic**, by Neill Bell. Where in the world are you, anyway? You may think you know the answer, but don't be too sure. "Sitting on the floor at the foot of my bed next to my sneakers," is only part of the answer. The world is a pretty big place, and if you don't know where most of its parts are, you can't possibly be sure of your own location. If you think the Philippines is a rock group or the name of an all-you-can-eat vegetarian restaurant, then you need to look inside this book. If you aren't sure where the Andes are (or even what they are), look inside this book. And if you don't know that most of us live on big hunks of earth that move around like dinner plates, look in this book. It's a trip around the world in 199 pages. Code LB, $13.95.

**Geography Matters** has a free catalog of geography materials from K to 12, curricula and individual supplies. They stress the use of a timeline with your geography. A good idea. It's always better to know where and *when* you are in your studies. Write: P.O. Box 15855, Evansville, IN 47716; 800-426-4650. (If you think you're going to be buying a number of timelines, see *Timetables of History* in "History and Biography.")

**Geography Mysteries.** What a great way to intrigue budding map detectives! Each mystery provides geographical clues to follow using a map, globe, or atlas. Kids can make use of their map skills by decoding map symbols and interpreting directions, while sharpening their thinking skills and having fun. Ages 8 to 12. Code LW, $10.95 each. Specify **WORLD GEOGRAPHY MYSTERIES** or **MAP MYSTERIES** (which covers science, history, literature, and more).

**MAPWORKS**, by Pamela Amick Klawitter, Ed.D. Creative and challenging activities to help kids learn to use maps of the U.S. and the world. Ages 9 to 13. Code LW, $6.95.

**THE GREAT WORLD TOUR.** Travel the world in 48 pages of finely detailed (accurate) pictures of different places. Pictures are filled with hidden and subtle items to be found. Text explains each hidden item. Young children can look and find some of the hidden items; older ones will enjoy the text. Ages 5 to 9. Code EDC, $9.95.

**WILD PLACES.** A well-illustrated beginning geography book that offers a first look at three distinct regions of the earth (jungles, mountains, and deserts). Clear text about living things in each area and explanations of the characteristics of the geographical area. Ages 5 to 9. Code EDC, $12.95.

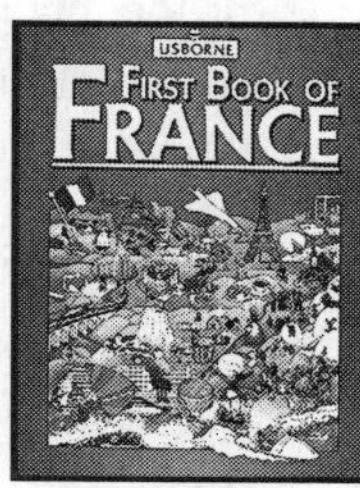

**Beginning Geography.** These first three books in a series (with more to come) are filled with entertaining information about people, places, and customs. Lively illustrations and good maps. Ages 6 to 10. Code EDC, $7.95 each. Specify **FIRST BOOK OF AMERICA, FIRST BOOK OF FRANCE,** or **FIRST BOOK OF GERMANY.**

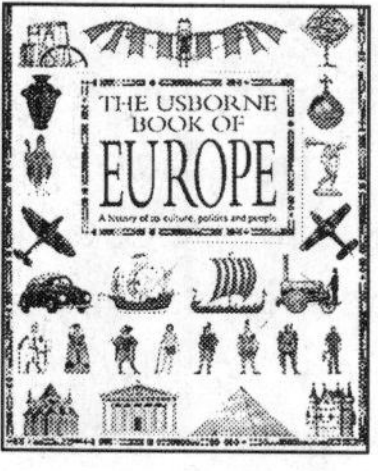

**USBORNE BOOK OF EUROPE.** A detailed exploration of the geography, history, and politics of the European community, with insight into issues in today's news. Useful facts are given country by country. Ages 10 and up. Code EDC, $9.95.

**PADDLE-TO-THE-SEA**, by Holling Clancy Holling. A young Indian boy carves a small canoe, names it Paddle-to-the-Sea, and sets off on a long journey. With brief text and large, wonderfully detailed, colorful pictures, the reader follows Paddle-to-the-Sea through the Great Lakes, down the St. Lawrence, into the Atlantic. Great art, geography, and history. Very enjoyable for almost any age, preschool through adult. A reader of my first edition recommended this book to us, and even sent her own copy (published in the 1940s) on loan, to convince me that it should be in my *First Home-School Catalogue*. I agreed immediately, and was glad to find that it's still in print, now in a large, inexpensive paperback. Code HM, $8.95. **Canadians**: You can borrow the film of this story from the National Film Board.

*It's a good thing our ancestors found their way to America, because today … one in seven can't even find the United States on a map of the world.* — Gilbert Grosvenor, president of the National Geographic Society

**UNITED STATES COLORING BOOK**. Color and learn at the same time. Map of each state with capital, major rivers, motto, flower, bird, tree, and more. One state to a page, with an inset of the U.S. map with the featured state highlighted. Ages 8 and up. Code DV, $2.95.

**Free maps and travel information for all states**. Call directory assistance (800-555-1212) to request the toll-free number of your state tourism department. Then speak to someone in the travel office and request their free information packet with maps.

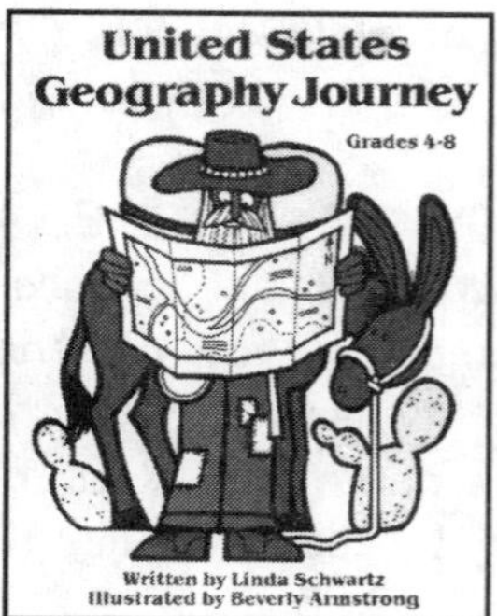


**UNITED STATES GEOGRAPHY JOURNEY**, by Linda Schwartz. A very nice introduction to the study and use of maps for grades 4-8. Schwartz cites a poll taken by the National Geographic Society revealing that half the people surveyed could not find New York within the U.S., and 14 percent could not even find the United States. This handy book will help remedy this appalling situation. Covers the different kinds of maps, common symbols, latitude and longitude, and time zones. It then goes on to help your student learn about the states by dividing them into sections of the country. Lots of activities, plus a section at the end with map-related questions to be researched. Upon completion of the book, you can fill out the Journeyman Geographer award for your child. Code LW, $6.95.

**TAKE OFF!** is a multilevel game that allows players to race around the world and absorb geography with hardly a thought. Lower levels of play race a fleet of jets from city to city. More advanced play will help everyone learn pertinent facts about the countries and cities of the world. "Geography is the unifying subject that describes our world. … If it's about our earth, geography is the key to relating what we learn to where we are," says the creator of this game. Country flags decorate the edge of the up-to-date game board. Ages 6 and up, Code RG, $29.95. $4 shipping.

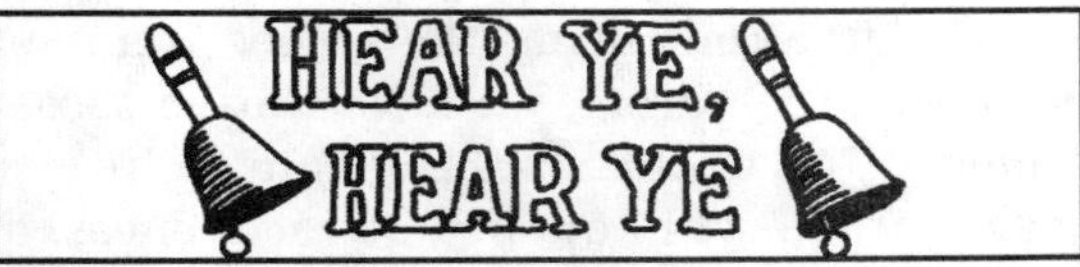


**The U.S. Geological Survey Information Service** has numerous resources (free unless otherwise stated). Send a letter of request stating what you want, including the number after the item and the age it's intended for, to Box 25286, Denver, CO 80225. Please limit your requests to one of each item; the USGS requests that you share when possible. Teaching packets are available on the web at: www.usgs.gov/education. Titles include:
K-3: **EXPLORING CAVES**, #97-0400; **MAP ADVENTURES**, #97-0300.
Middle school: **WHAT DO MAPS SHOW?**, #97-0250; **GLOBAL CHANGE**, #97-0200; **EXPLORING MAPS**, #97-0150.
High school: **LAND AND PEOPLE**, #97-0350.

Request a listing of "educational" paper models, posters, maps, booklets, and fact sheets. Some of these will have to be paid for, but the price is reasonable. Much of this information and a lot more is available online and can be downloaded.
U.S. Geological Survey: www.usgs.gov
National Mapping Information: geology.usgs.gov
Water Resources: water.usgs.gov
Declassified Intelligence Satellite Photos: earthexplorer.usgs.gov
Earthquake Information: quake.wr.usgs.gov
Earth Science Information Center: ask.usgs.gov
Energy Resources: energy.usgs.gov
Learning Web: K-12 Education: www.usgs.gov/education
National Atlas of the U.S.: www-atlas.usgs.gov

**WHY DON'T WE FALL OFF?**

The roundness of the world is a difficult concept for young children, and is a fascinating subject to consider and explore in many ways. We compare the land mass with the immensity of the waters. Using a flashlight and a baseball, we demonstrate the relationship of the sun, moon, and earth: sunrise, sunset, eclipses, quarters of the moon, earth's orbit around the sun, and the moon's orbit around the earth. When we begin working with maps, which are also fascinating, we show the relationship of the two-dimensional plane to the three-dimensional ball. What is "down"? Why don't we fall off? The earth is spinning rapidly, and the law of centrifugal force says we should be thrown off by the spin, yet we're not. Gravity? What is gravity? Scientists tell us it's the force that pulls objects toward the center of the earth — but that doesn't explain what it is, or how it works, or why; just that it does. Certainly there is not enough "magnetic attraction" between earth, wood, flesh, and water to counter the force and speed of our earth's movement through space. We introduce the mystery, and we never pretend it isn't a mystery.

**DISCOVERING GEOGRAPHY OF NORTH AMERICA WITH BOOKS KIDS LOVE**, by Carol J. Fuhler. This book has enough content to keep you and your kids busy for well over a year if you take advantage of all the suggestions, and Carol's program crosses over into other parts of the curriculum. Studies are organized by region of the U.S., plus sections to cover Canada and Mexico. The literature suggested is good, but I'd search the library to broaden it. Each section begins with an overview of the region. Lessons proceed to look at the region through themes of location and human/environmental interactions. Objectives are clearly stated, along with needed materials. All geographic map skills are covered and meet the National Geography Standards. Carol's activity lists are extensive and specific, and yet allow latitude to follow personal interests. Good bibliography, reference, and glossary section. Ages 8 to 12. Code FC, $17.95.

**DISCOVERING WORLD GEOGRAPHY WITH BOOKS KIDS LOVE**, by Nancy A. Chicola and Eleanor B. English. This book has the same approach as the one above. The world is divided into 12 realms, each studied through fiction and non-fiction. You'll find the same abundance of well-organized reading and activities, plus bibliography, reference, and glossary sections. Recommended for ages 6 to 12. I think it's better for ages 8 to 12. Code FC, $17.95.

# THE BEST WORLD GLOBES

After comparing the globes from several different manufacturers, we have chosen those made by Replogle, the world's largest manufacturer of globes, as being the best in quality, attractiveness, durability, accuracy, and price. They all have sturdy bases. All but the Moon globe and illuminated globes have raised relief.

If you're on a tight budget you can get a globe at Wal-Mart. Check to be sure it is up-to-date and not old stock. The only problem with their globes is you have to buy a new one to keep up with all the changes.

**All political globes listed below come with a half-price update certificate.** Whenever there is a major political change, such as the breakup of the Soviet Union, you can send your globe to Replogle and get an updated globe for half-price. All globes are code REP.

**THE ATLANTIS**. This is our favorite. Both raised and indented geographical relief enhance the globe's geographical features — and children love to feel the ups and downs. The political boundaries and names are clear and easy to read. We particularly like the coloring, which is light and has a subtle blending in with the realistic coloration of land and water areas, including deserts, mountain ranges, forests, and undersea physical features. The Atlantis most resembles the earth as it appears from space. 12" globe, 17" high, double-meridian gyrosphere mounting (which means you can turn the globe a full 360 degrees in any direction for easy viewing of any region). $49.99 plus $4 shipping.

**THE EXPLORER**. A 12" globe with bold colors and more than 4,000 political markings, with raised relief. Clear place names. Single-meridian mount that turns on the earth's axis. Specify blue or gold metal mounting. 16" high. $32.99 plus $4 shipping.

**THE FRANKLIN**. Identical to The Explorer, except that the oceans are "antique" (light tan parchment) instead of blue. Same price and shipping.

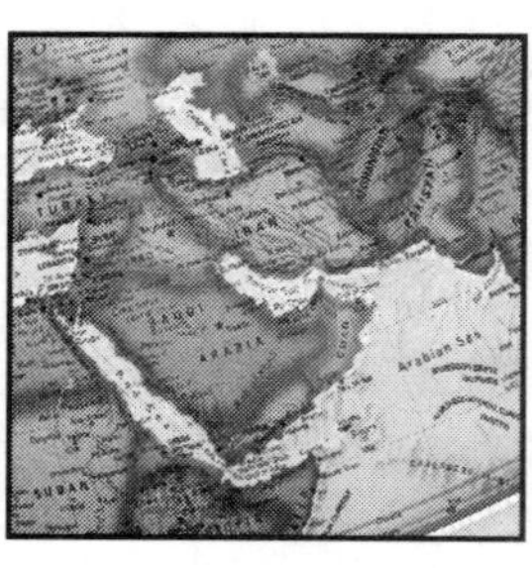

**THE DISCOVERY**. A 10" globe showing political boundaries until you turn on its light. When it's illuminated you see the earth's topography and undersea features. It's fascinating! $52.99 plus $4 shipping.

**THE LIVINGSTON**. A 12" single-meridian globe on a hardwood base. Two-way, raised-relief map of the physical world, or turn on its light and see political boundaries. Two globes in one! $69.99 plus $4 shipping.

**THE DOLPHIN**. I fell in love with the stand! A wooden dolphin holds the raised-relief 12" globe with political markings — the dolphin representing the need for us to balance the ecological needs of life on land and in the ocean. You can pick this globe up off the stand for closer viewing. $99.95. Free shipping. (It's on my Christmas wish list.)

**INFLATABLE GLOBES — LEARN WHILE YOU PLAY.** Your choice of a 16" political or topographical globe. Create your own games or just play with the ball and let the shapes of the continents and the countries sink in subconsciously. Code REP, $7.99 each. Specify political or topographical.

**GLOW-IN-THE-DARK GLOBES**. 16" inflatable globes with your choice of a star map or the stars with the constellation pictures of Orion, the Crab, the Big Dipper, and more. Code REP, $9.99 each. Specify star map or constellations.

**MY WORLD AND GLOBE**. An 18-inch inflatable globe is combined with a fully illustrated 64-page book that surveys all the continents, oceans, and major islands and rivers; where they are and how they were formed; and the weather, people, and animals there. The globe is printed with only the most basic features: water, land masses, and equator. Using a magic marker and more than 100 colorful stickers featuring people, places, cities, and blanks to fill in, kids make their own world of personalized knowledge. They can draw in boundaries, label the oceans, name the countries, and put the "I live here" arrow exactly where it belongs. Ages 5 and up. Code WKM, $13.95.

**THE MOON**. Accurately depicts the geographical features of the moon, including craters, "seas," and mountain ranges. NASA approved. 12" globe, 15" high on stand. Code REP, $46.99 plus $3 shipping.

When Susan was 16 she took part in an Outward Bound program in Maine, which borders the Canadian province of New Brunswick. She was glad to meet her fellow adventurers, most of whom were from big cities and all of whom attended public school. She was the only Canadian in the group. Around the campfire that first evening she was asked two serious and remarkable questions: "Do you still live in tribes?" and "Do you really live in an igloo?"

**DISCOVERING MAPS: A Young Person's World Atlas**. This unique book is intended for children up to the age of 12 or so, but is an excellent introduction to maps and other atlas features for students of any age, including adults. The first section contains descriptive explanations of symbols, scale, latitude, longitude, map indexes, projections, and time zones, using clear text, diagrams, maps, and full-color illustrations. The second section is a complete world atlas, with full-color political, physical, and special maps of the world, the continents, Canada, and the United States. The third section has about 16 pages of miscellaneous but very interesting facts and "trivia" about the world and its people, arranged in colorful chart form with many illustrations, followed by a glossary of important geographic terms and a digest of world statistics. Hardcover. Code HMD, $11.95.

**CITATION WORLD ATLAS**. The best all-around atlas for family use. In a large $8\frac{3}{4}$x$10\frac{3}{4}$" format with 368 pages of information. Easy-to-read maps with political boundaries, including individual country and state maps. Country facts, flags, topography, economy, agriculture, industry, vegetation, and climate on the same or adjacent pages. Gazetteer of useful information such as population, largest city, monetary unit, religions, and more. Paperback, but sturdy. Code HMD, $19.95.

**STUDENT'S NOTEBOOK ATLAS.** For those on a budget, 32 8½x11" pages with up-to-date information that will fit neatly into a three-ring binder. Full-color physical and political world maps, world flags, and reference guide with area; population; world statistics; chart about principal mountains, longest rivers, and major lakes; dimensions of the earth; and capital of each country. Code HMD, $3.95.

**NATIONAL GEOGRAPHIC ROAD ATLAS.** More than 400 detailed maps of the U.S., Canada, and Mexico, in 144 11x15" pages. Easy to read, with vivid terrain relief and other reference information. We'll send the most current edition (i.e., if you're ordering in 2001, you'll receive the 2001 atlas). Code MQ, $10.99.

<u>National Geographic Materials (next two items)</u>

**WORLD MAP MOUSE PAD.** You can read the names of countries and major cities easily on this 10x8" pad (a little larger than regular mouse pads, but a nice size for this world map). Its special finish allows you to clean it without fear of damaging the map. Non-skid backing. Code MQ, $12.99.

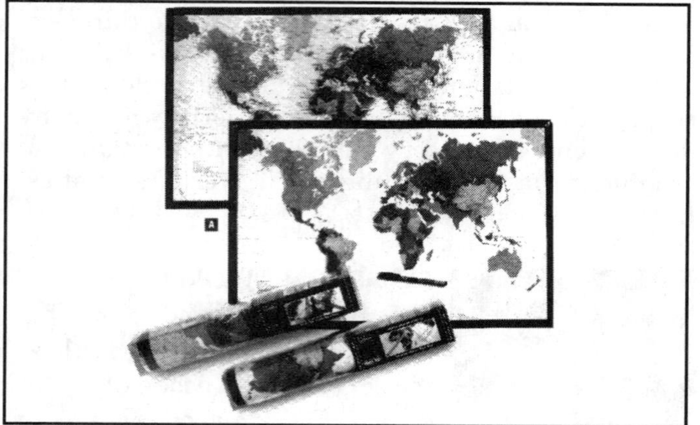


**Geography Fun.** Each map activity set includes two full-color poster maps, 28x17" (just the right size for home). One map is laminated with a heavy-duty write-on wipe-off finish, with a marker included. The other map is heavy paper that includes all reference points: countries, cities, river names, etc. Code MQ, $19.99 each. Specify **GUESS WHERE USA** or **GUESS WHERE WORLD**.

**CLEVER CATCH BALL.** Play catch with your states and capitals! 24" sturdy, inflatable ball. Comes with suggestions, and it's easy to make up your own games. Code CS, $10.95 each.

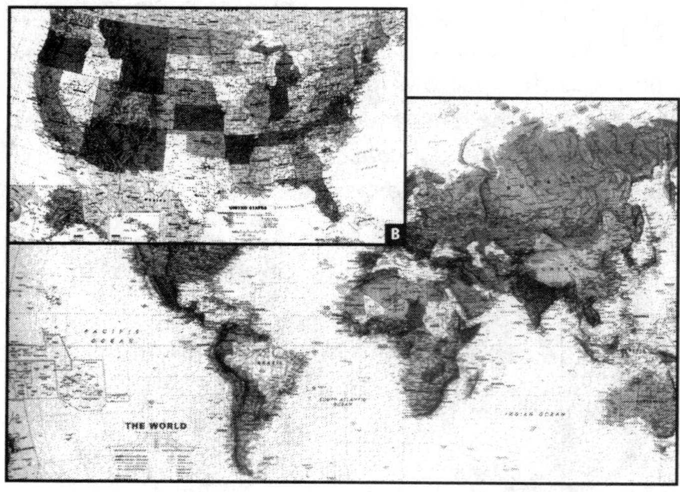


**National Geographic Maps**

**USA AND WORLD MAPS.** Full-color, showing states, major cities, mountain ranges, rivers, road networks, parks, railways, and more. 28x17½" (if you need something larger, write for sizes and prices). Code MQ, $9.99, laminated $12.99. Specify USA or World.

**CANADIAN MAP.** Includes the same information as above, but sorry folks, they price it higher. However, it is bigger (34x23") and is printed on both sides — one traditional and the other with various tourist attractions. Code MQ, $14.99.

**NORTH AMERICAN MAP.** Shows countries, states, provinces, cities, and geographical features. 23½x30". Code MQ, $10.99.

**HAWAIIAN MAP.** Beautiful full-color map with shaded relief. 34x22½". Code MQ, $10.99.

**ALASKAN MAP.** Political and physical features. An inset compares Alaska's size to the lower 48 states. 38x23". Code MQ, $9.99.

**WORLD MAP DESK PAD.** Bright colors and graphics on a durable, scratch-resistant pad. Wipes clean, which I think is an important factor, and has soft foam backing so it will stay in place. Matches the world map mouse pad. 26½x17". Code MQ, $29.99.

**Geography Coloring Books**. All books $8\frac{1}{2}$x11", with well-researched, detailed drawings with basic information. Ages 8 and up. Code DV, $2.95 each. Specify **AFRICAN PLAINS, ARCTIC AND ANTARCTIC LIFE, NORTH AMERICAN DESERT, RAIN FOREST, STATE BIRDS AND FLOWERS, STORY OF HAWAII, SWAMPLAND** (plants and animals), or **WETLANDS** (plants and animals).

**FLAGS OF THE WORLD STICKER BOOK**. *Reusable* colored stickers make this book more than just one-time fun. Maps on each page help your student learn the location of 200 countries. Ages 7 and up. Code EDC, $7.95.

**FLAGS.** Pictures, facts, quizzes, and things to do. Pocket-size for easy reference. 32 pages, 7x4$\frac{1}{2}$". Ages 7 and up. Code EDC, $2.95.

**FLAGS OF THE WORLD POSTER**. There are pictures of all the flags at the top and a map of the world with country names in English and native language at the bottom (cross-referenced with the flags at the top). Up-to-date and colorful. Code MQ, $9.99.

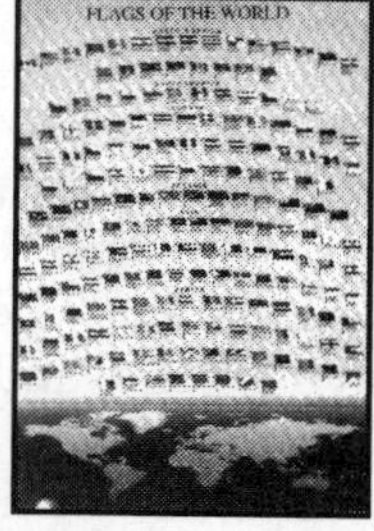

**GEOGRAPHY QUIZBOOK**. A quiz book for those who like to know how much they know. Thirty-two pages with questions and answers, plus lots of fascinating background information. There is a point scoring system you can use or ignore. Good pictures and lots to learn — especially if you can't answer all the questions. Mega-quiz in the back. Based on the Usborne geography books (code EDC). Ages 9 and up. Code EDC, $7.95.

---

*We are what we think. All that we are arises with our thoughts. With our thoughts we make the world.*
— The Buddha

**STICKER ATLAS OF THE U.S. AND CANADA,** by John Wright. An oversized sticker book packed with information about the land, wildlife, and people. Has a pullout poster-size wall chart of major cities, mountains, forests, wildlife, products, and flora. More than 130 color stickers. Guide included. Ages 6 to 10. Code TRL, $7.95.

**MAP OF AFRICA**. Acid-free reusable $9\frac{1}{4}$x$12\frac{1}{4}$" sticker book, with full-color stickers identifying countries and capitals. The inside front and back covers serve as a base map, and all stickers can be reused. Code DV, $4.95.

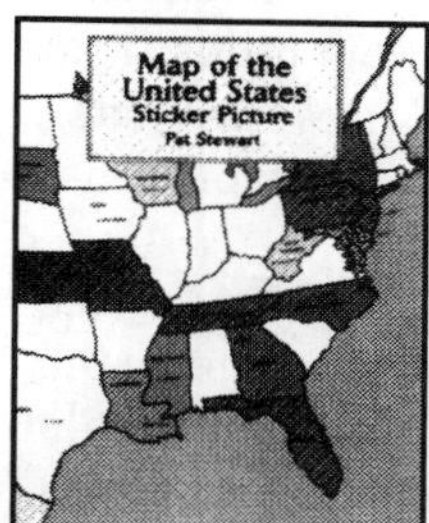


**Stickers and Seals.** Each book is eight $8\frac{1}{4}$x11" pages. Book includes identification information. All stickers and seals are in full color. Code DV, $4.95 each. **FLAGS OF THE WORLD STICKERS, MAP OF THE UNITED STATES** ($4.50), **STATE BIRD STICKERS AND SEALS, STATE FLOWERS STICKERS AND SEALS**

**THE DESERT**. Acid-free reusable sticker book, $9\frac{1}{4}$x$11\frac{1}{4}$". The book covers make a backdrop for the 30 or more full-color, reusable stickers. Ages 7 and up. Code DV. $4.50

# MORE EXPENSIVE BY THE DOZEN

Rural New Brunswick is very similar to the Vermont of my boyhood (in the '40s and early '50s), and Canada is pretty much what the United States would have become without the Boston Tea Party. The majority in both countries speak some form of English, and tabloids in both countries entertain us weekly with the latest adventures of British royalty. (It puzzles us sometimes that the longer we live in Canada the more American we feel, but we have a nice home and good neighbors, and we live just a few miles from the United States border, so we exercise our Americanism mostly on the frequent visits to our post office box in Maine.)

One of the more significant differences we've found between the two countries is that Americans still believe (or so they claim) in free enterprise, while Canada has "marketing agencies," which establish quotas and set prices and in many other ways regulate the production and sale of milk, eggs, lumber, and countless other consumer goods, all of which may be enterprising but is certainly not free. You don't cut costs by increasing the number of middlemen.

Government agencies often do funny things, but that doesn't mean their actions are humorous, and sometimes the public is severely taxed to find a single smile in a shovelful of government edicts. ("Shovelful," of course, isn't a metric term, and is therefore probably illegal in Canada now, but at present I can't think of a polite metric form of measurement to use for political excretions.)

Take for example, the Canadian Egg Marketing Agency.

We all know that Saudi Arabia is one of the poorest nations in the world, so no sensible person would have protested a few years ago when the Egg Marketing Agency sold that country millions of Canadian eggs for half the price Canadians had to pay. It was only fair, of course. After all, don't we always get their oil for half price?

When one of the Agency's shipments to Saudi Arabia of four million eggs (or 333,333 dozen, with four left over) got sucked into the twilight zone by high-seas hijinks, who could blame the Saudi Arabians for being reluctant to pay the bill? After all, the CEMA was charging them five cents per egg, or 60 cents a dozen. That was $200,000 for the whole kit and cockadoodle, which must be nearly half a week's wages for some of those middle-class oil dealers.

The Marketing Agency lost the eggs, and the Saudis refused to pay for them, so the Agency charged the Canadian public by raising the price of eggs sold at home. A neat solution to a problem that might have left the Agency with egg on its collective face.

According to one of its humorous — I mean, funny — press releases at the time, the purpose of the Egg Marketing Agency is the "orderly marketing of egg production at a fair price to both producer and consumer." In line with that purpose, the Agency offered farmers a price increase of one to three cents per dozen to help meet rising costs of feed and labor. (This was one of the points in the bill I sent to the Agency, which I'll explain in greater detail later on.)

Next, faced with more eggs than they could lose at sea, and fearing that the price per dozen on a glutted market might drop as low for Canadians as they had set it for the Saudi Arabians, the Agency's managers played with their pocket calculators and found another logical solution. They offered poultry farmers $2.07 per hen to kill off one and a half million laying hens, and to refrain from raising more hens for sixteen weeks.

My own calculator, which I wear under my hat, ran that through twice and came up with the news that the Agency was sticking taxpayers for $3,105,000 for eggs they would never eat, in order to make them pay more than 10 cents for each egg they did eat.

Naturally, I could see great possibilities in this for myself, and I went to discuss it with the Brook Farm Ladies Aid and Missionary Society, which lives in our barn and gives us an average of 20 eggs a day. The society has one rooster, named Hamlet, but he doesn't get out much, so I do most of the missionary work. Just to make it proper, I sent away $3 and received a card in the mail announcing that I am now fully ordained and should be addressed as "Reverend," and I have full authority to preside over marriages, baptisms, and funerals. So far, I have exercised that authority over 18 marriages (all bigamous, I'm afraid) and three funerals, all in my henhouse. I have yet to conduct a baptism, although I was surprised one day by a hen sticking her head into my boot, and I accidentally poured a bucket of water over two others.

When I told the ladies about the Marketing Agency's patriotic offer, they laughed so hard that one of them nearly turned inside out. Apparently it's difficult to live with a prolapsed intestine, which accounted for the first $2.07 I thought the Agency should pay me, and I went back to the house right away to prepare a bill, along with a letter to explain, itemize, and justify the total amount of $7.21 for which I finally billed the Agency.

I showed another hen, I wrote, what happens when the ax meets the chopping block, making another $2.07 the Agency owed me.

Matilda, with white flecks on her red feathers and beady black eyes, was a cute little thing, and Hamlet had had his gimlet eyes on her for some time. Whenever he tried to show his affection, however, she would glance shyly at the nest of eggs and say, "Please, dear, not in front of the children." So Hamlet took cold showers (not under my baptismal authority) and waited for us to collect the eggs.

One day, Hamlet fluttered up to the top roost for a midday nap and was perched there, like King Kong on the Empire State Building, when Matilda wandered in from the yard. Matilda perceived a delicious bug crawling on the floor, and Hamlet perceived an opportunity.

Hamlet has responded to countless magazine ads that promised to enlarge his biceps, triceps, forceps, and brain capacity. The courses have done wonders for him — all but the last. Nearly two feet tall at the shoulders and built like a ham, Hamlet is a 97-pound idiot.

He leaped off the roost, travelling eight feet out and six feet down, and landed squarely on Matilda's back. She surrendered meekly, and Hamlet bragged for weeks about his brilliant strategy.

What he didn't realize was that Matilda's neck was broken, making it a total of $6.21 the Agency owed me.

With an average of 20 eggs a day, our hens give us about 600 eggs a month. That's 50 dozen, believe it or not, with which we could help to glut the market if we didn't use them to glut ourselves. (I hasten to tell you that this was before our kids grew up and flew the coop.) By eating all our eggs — fried; scrambled; boiled; and in bread, cookies, and doughnuts — instead of selling them, we were doing our part to help the Agency inflate the market. This was a hardship we would gladly endure if it would help the national economy.

However, we still had to provide feed and labor, and here I called the Agency's attention to its offer of one to three cents per dozen.

My third-grade teacher used to insist that we can't multiply apples by oranges, but the government frequently proves that much of our education is worthless, so I cheerfully followed the Agency's example, as follows: The average of one and three is two, and two cents multiplied by 50 dozen equals 100 cents, which I rounded off to an even dollar.

"There you have it," I wrote. "My bill for this month: $6.21 for the demise of three hens, and $1.00 for grain fed to the remaining hens to help them produce eggs, which I promise not to sell — total, $7.21."

"Please remit promptly," I said, "as additional billing will increase my operating expenses, making me an even greater burden on the taxpayers."

You think the U.S. mail is slow sometimes? You should try Canada Post. I sent my bill to Ottawa six years ago, and I'm still waiting for a reply.

P.S. This story was written in 1991. It's now 2000 and still there has been no response. It seems Canada Post gets slower every year. Should I now bill the Agency for interest?

# MATHEMATICS

## Attitudes, Needs, Confession, and Resources

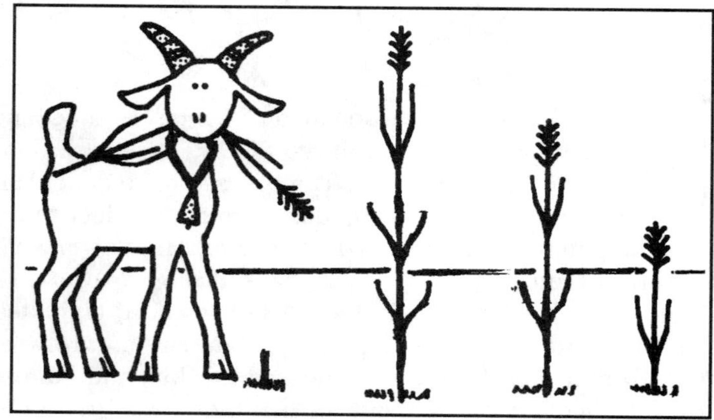

I planted a tree that was 8 inches tall. At the end of the first year it was 12 inches tall; at the end of the second year it was 18 inches tall; and at the end of the third year it was 27 inches tall. How tall was it at the end of the fourth year?

When I was a high school junior, in Brattleboro, Vermont, I wanted to take a course in auto mechanics.

"You can't," the guidance director told me. "That isn't part of the college prep course."

"But I don't plan to go to college," I said. "I plan to travel and work and study."

He chuckled. We argued. The guidance director had the final word, of course: "Your IQ and your aptitude tests indicate that you belong in the college prep program. I'm sure you'll come to your senses about college when the time comes."

Although I think college is fine for those who want or need it, I didn't change my mind. I traveled and I worked, and I have never attended college (except for a brief summer workshop at the University of Denver). When another institution asked for my high school transcript, the same guidance director wrote in the margin, "Too much a nonconformist to ever be happy." The split infinitive was his. I concluded that he knew as much about English as I knew about auto mechanics. The difference was that he was employed as an English teacher as well as a guidance director, and I have never been employed as an auto mechanic. I can change a tire, but I didn't learn how to in high school.

I did learn in school that a quadrilateral is a parallelogram if the diagonals bisect each other. I also learned how to find FH and DF if AB, CD, EF, and GH are parallel and AC and CE and EG and BD each equal 3. I've read that everything we ever learn or experience is tucked away somewhere in a dusty corner of the mind, and I don't doubt it, but you may be surprised to learn that since I graduated from high school I have had neither reason nor desire to find FH and DF. Most of the quadrilaterals I've encountered since then have been school officials, and their purposes are usually perpendicular to mine.

So much for at least half of the math I learned in twelve years of schooling. Hypnosis might revive my memory of it, just as it could help me remember the first time I fell off a bike, but I'm content to leave both memories buried in cobwebs.

If you like math, or expect to have a good use for it, then study it. We all use math in our daily lives, directly and personally; without it, our lives would be very different and probably difficult. We need math to bake a cake, plan a shopping list, or balance a checkbook. Jean and the kids and I built our own house, doing all the work ourselves, and we did a lot of measuring and calculating, both in building the house and in buying materials for it.

Most of the math we used, however, and most of that which I use daily, is no more advanced than simple long division, which is usually mastered in the fifth grade. I use a little plane geometry and, occasionally, some very elementary solid geometry (how big a hayloft do I need to hold three tons of hay?).

If I were suddenly confronted with a need to find FH and DF, I'm sure I could learn quickly how to do so, even if I had never once learned it. The desire to learn is the greatest incentive.

Most school students, if asked why they study math (or most other subjects), will answer, "It's required" or "So I can pass the exams." Neither reason is enough. Over a twelve-year period, first grade through high school, most students will spend an hour a day, including homework, for about 200 days of the year, trying to learn various forms of arithmetic and mathematics. That's 2,400 hours out of a lifetime. (See how easily I figured that out?) Will the information studied be used half that many hours after school? It's not a bad exchange if the information and skill are of real interest or use. Some people enjoy math, just as others enjoy word puzzles; others may not enjoy it, but know or expect that it will be of practical use to them in a chosen career, such as chemistry, astronomy, or architecture. I have no argument against studying advanced math for those who like it or need it, but to spend a hundred twenty-four-hour days studying something only to pass a series of tests is a ridiculous waste of time and energy.

A common argument in favor of math, with or without practical application, is that "it develops skills of reasoning" — that is, a logical approach to problem-solving. That's undoubtedly true, but is it the only exercise — or even the best — that develops reasoning? Mathematicians have no monopoly on the ability to perceive, consider, compare, evaluate, extrapolate, hypothesize, and reach conclusions. These processes are frequently related to math, but never limited to it.

Author Henry Miller once wrote, "Anyone can write; a writer can't do anything else." The same might be said of math and mathematicians. For those of us who need and use math only occasionally, just a few basics are necessary. If I need to calculate the stress of a certain weight on a ten-foot 2x4, I can easily find the appropriate formula, or even a chart or graph with the answer already given. An understanding of elementary mathematics is very desirable, perhaps necessary, in daily life, but tedious memorization of principles and facts that I'll probably never use, and in which I have no interest, is neither reasonable nor logical.

For many years, we tried several standard math textbooks, at all grade levels, and found partial satisfaction only after two of our children had grown up and left home. Most math books seem to have been written by people who know a great deal about mathematics but very little about children or about the learning process. Before we found a few existing books that make math enjoyable, understandable, and useful, we tortured our kids and ourselves with the same textbooks used in the public schools. Like most parents (and teachers), we believed that math was a necessary evil; that, no matter how unpleasant it might be, it must be mastered — "because someday you'll need it." The standard textbooks — being unpleasant, illogical, and monotonous — reinforced that belief. For more years than I want to admit, we didn't stop to realize that the only use Jean and I had for most of the math we had learned in school was to try to teach it to our kids. In the normal scheme of things, they would someday pass it on to their own kids, and so on. The sins of the fathers are visited upon the children.

I don't know why it took us so much longer to break away from conventional study of math than from most other forms of conventional study. Like many other home-schoolers, we believed the public system was wrong or inadequate, but we lacked enough confidence in ourselves to reject it; we were afraid that if our kids didn't measure up to the standards of the public schools, they would be at a disadvantage in later life. Gradually, we realized that just the opposite is true. By adhering to public school standards (not only in math), we were holding our kids back. We directed so much of their energy into the study of ordinary math — "to develop skills of reasoning" — that real reasoning skills were being stunted or warped.

"Laziness in doing a stupid thing," said the High Lama of Shangri-La in James Hilton's *Lost Horizon*, "can be a virtue."

Sometimes, the study of math became so frustrating and unpleasant, for all of us, that we just dropped it for a few days, or even weeks, and spent the time with other studies. We noticed that the kids were still using math frequently — in cooking, drawing spaceships, feeding the hens and cow, making dresses, calculating their babysitting earnings, or buying material for a new blouse. We stopped worrying.

Still, we thought, they had learned the basics of the math they were using very painfully, by being beaten over the head daily with standard textbooks. There must be a better way. Once we were open to better approaches, we found several — the best of which is the use of tools and materials of ordinary daily life.

The first step to a better approach was a change of attitude. We had to realize that a child's age has no bearing on the level or degree of math (or reading, or writing) he can or should master. If it doesn't come easily, there is no need to push and no need to worry; it will come sometime.

At age nine, Derek was bored and angered by his fourth-grade arithmetic book. We gave him a math kit — protractor, compass, and ruler — and turned him loose with a high school plane geometry book. He asked a few questions and we helped him sort out a few beginning principles. He drew spaceships, inside and out, with wonderful complexity and precision. Although he continued to bristle at the thought of the fourth-grade math, he could measure angles, bisect lines, and correctly construct complex geometric designs. He could also read and follow a cooking recipe, measure the pig's grain, and draw accurate plans of his room. We didn't push him, and we didn't worry. We knew that Derek might not go back to simple multiplication and division for many years, or he might return to them a week later. When he felt in need of them, he would study them, and learning them would be like learning to fry an egg after mastering soufflé. It was a number of years before he went back to the "beginning" and filled in the gaps. What was lost?

Suppose walking or talking were taught in the same way math and reading are usually taught: "Dear Parent, Your son/daughter is not achieving the level of Walking Competency that is expected for his/her age. He/she is now 13.8 months old and should have completed Level 7.9, but still crawls on Level 5.4. I am sorry to report that he/she may be Walking Disabled. I will place him/her in the Bluebird Section for Slow Walkers, but I think he/she may need Special Assistance. Sincerely, His/Her Teacher."

Children begin counting very early. They like to count — fingers, toes, cars, leaves, spoons, stones, steps, anything. By the age of three or four, most children will have gained several mathematical skills, and will enjoy using them. By the age of six, if they go to public schools, or if they are pushed too much at home, they will have lost much of their skill and all of their interest.

At sixteen, Cathy was taking a high school correspondence course, besides working with our own materials. She worked at her own speed, sending in completed lessons for grading. When she began algebra, it was clear sailing at first, but less than halfway through the course, it became increasingly difficult. Dad to the rescue, confident that he could recall enough from years ago to smooth out the wrinkles. Looking through her textbook, I quickly realized that this was an entirely different animal from the one I had struggled with for two years before going on to struggle for another two years with plane and solid geometry. I passed all four courses, and that was back in the days when students didn't pass unless they actually earned passing grades, but it was more through the patience and hard work of my teachers than through any great understanding on my part. Cathy's dislike of math was not acquired; it was in my genes, and she inherited it from me. (I studied biology, too!) It didn't help me that her book was titled *Modern Algebra*. What was wrong with the old algebra? I put myself through a quick refresher course, from the beginning, skimming and sorting until I felt I could handle it — with a lot of luck. Cathy and I worked together on the lessons and problems. It was still very difficult, for both of us. We weren't enjoying it, and were doing it only because it was a required subject in the college prep course. Cathy and I were both frustrated and bored by this modern algebra. One of the simpler problems ran something like this:

$$\frac{3a^3b^2 + 15a^3b^2}{2ab^2} + \frac{4a^6b^3 - 10a^6b^3}{2a^4b^3} = ?$$

I'm sure it's easy for some, and I'm even willing to admit that some people might enjoy playing with it. I'd rather split wood or shovel manure. If Cathy or we could anticipate any need for such math in her future, we would have continued struggling with it, but we knew she was very unlikely to pursue a career or way of life requiring the use of a subject that was so distasteful to her. Why waste so much time and energy? The only reason seemed to be that it was required as part of the college prep course; it was required because many colleges required it, and many colleges required it because they had always required it — or just because, that's why.

Math stretches the brain and gives you new reasoning skills. With the new reasoning skills I gained from this course, I came up with a brilliant solution: ask the school to change Cathy's course from College Prep to General High School. It was done, and with no arguments from the guidance director. In place of algebra, to obtain the necessary credits Cathy chose general math, more of the physical and social sciences, and more literature. She enjoyed them all. We both kept our sanity. It was an excellent exchange.

My mathematical aptitudes and attitudes embarrass me a little (but not very much). I think it's obvious that the universe and nearly all things in it (the exceptions include most math books) are constructed and governed by very precise principles, all of which can be or someday will be expressed in mathematical terms — which is, perhaps, a step toward understanding. However, I think it is just as true that mathematics is only one of many ways to view and understand the universe. A poet or mystic may understand as much as a mathematician; the biggest difference may be that it's easier for the mathematician to communicate what he has learned — but with the significant drawback that only other mathematicians can understand what he's saying.

There are a few fortunate exceptions.

Stephen Hawking, perhaps the most brilliant physicist and mathematician in the world's history, insists that even the most profound discoveries and theories about the universe can be expressed in non-mathematical terms. His book *A Brief History of Time* (see "Science") seems to be evidence of this.

We have found several basic arithmetic and math books that not only develop necessary skills and knowledge, but are actually fun to read and use, thus removing most of the drudgery. Unfortunately, a few things — e.g., basic multiplication tables, and deciding which procedures to use in solving word problems — may still need to be learned through boring repetition, but once they are learned, most of the rest will be clear and easy sailing, at least for all that's really necessary. Approaching math through a side door, the *I Hate Mathematics!* book and *Math for Smarty Pants* fool you into thinking math is fun, ha ha.

Fun or not, math seems to be here to stay. Waiting patiently while the cashier tries to figure the cost of half a dozen doughnuts if the price of a dozen is $1.99 has led me to realize that a little math won't hurt anyone, so we have come full circle to the point of telling our kids that they have to learn some of it whether it hurts or not. The important thing is to know when to stop. Let's consider carefully before we spend too much of our time or our children's time trying to learn facts and gain skills that will probably have little or no use in life. If the study is easy or fun or has a probable use, then carry on. If running headfirst into a brick wall would be more fun, force yourselves through *Essential Math*, then go for a walk or read a book or shovel manure.

## MY CONFESSION

My dictionary defines phobia as "a long-lasting abnormal fear or great dislike of something."

This embarrasses me, but you need to know that I am math-phobic. If I don't fight it, thinking about algebra produces narcolepsy.

There! I've said it. In theory — not a mathematical one, I assure you — confession is good for the soul and healing can begin. Do I feel better now? Not particularly, but now you have no illusions.

It doesn't mean I can't do the arithmetic. I can. I just don't actively enjoy the process.

I've heard from many of you that we share this problem in varying degrees. So how do we help our children find at least a comfortable competence in learning mathematical skills, preferably without inheriting our disability? First we need to understand why we have a problem with math. I believe it began because our teachers didn't understand the difference between mathematics and arithmetic.

I had never separated the two concepts until I started looking at the resources for this book. *Arithmetic* is the science of numbers and operations performed with numbers. It's what most of us had in school. This is the skill required for passing most tests. *Mathematics* is about patterns in numbers, shapes, and relationships. There are patterns in our daily life, such as the seasons, the symmetry in a flower or snowflake, and the ticking of a clock or the rhythm of our favorite piece of music. Most of us don't consider these things as part of mathematics, but they are the heart and soul of the field. If our children are to find enjoyment in math, those of us who grew up with only arithmetic must broaden our horizons.

About now, if I were reading this book instead of writing it, I would have to wonder how a math-phobe could produce a reasonable set of suggestions for learning math. It may not be an entirely fair test of the many materials I looked at, but I immediately dismissed anything that induced narcolepsy, made me want to take a walk, upset my stomach, or caused me to decide I'd rather clean the bathroom or see the dentist.

I think math games, hands-on exploration, and practical applications are among the best ways to give our children an enjoyment of numbers and math. I'm not saying there isn't a time and place for workbooks, or even textbooks, but first there should be an appreciation and enjoyment of the fundamentals. Sometimes it's useful to have a variety of small, inexpensive workbooks. A change of scenery can perk up your child's interest and outlook. If you're working with an older child who does not enjoy math I suggest using games that are at a level that will build confidence.

## Resources for Parents

**YES YOU CAN! Help Your Kid Succeed in Math Even if You Think You Can't,** by Jean Bullard and Louise Oborne. This book is for *you*, not your kids. Although written for parents of publicly schooled kids, this is a great resource for all math coaches. It's a confidence builder. If your child has been in public school and has developed a poor attitude toward math and his ability to do it, this book contains strategies that will enable you to help your child, including numerous suggestions for overcoming a child's resentment, embarrassment, and resistance. You'll find good advice about recognizing your child's best learning style. There's honest talk about most math curricula and textbooks; e.g., too much too soon is often expected from most children, and most math texts lack basic explanations on how to do the problems. There's a section about test-taking you can skip if it's not relevant to your situation. I don't agree with the reward strategies suggested, but I won't argue with their demonstration of the complexity of a division problem. They have a sensible attitude about the appropriate use of calculators. Illustrated with cartoons, tables, and charts. Resource list included. $18 from Bufflehead Publishing, 2400 N.W. 80th St., Suite 173, Seattle, WA 98117. Credit card orders call 888-937-7737, toll free in the U.S. and Canada. ***NO SHIPPING CHARGE if you mention you read about it in* The Home School Source Book.** You can also request their free catalog and curriculum index. The index has a distillation of the standard math curriculum used throughout the U.S. and Canada. A good tool for helping you plan your studies.

**OVERCOMING MATH ANXIETY,** by Sheila Tobias. A leader in research in this field, Tobias offers comfort and suggestions for those of us who feel seriously challenged by math. An excerpt from the blurb on the back of the book suggests we may call this anxiety many things: "math anxiety, math avoidance, fear of figuring, the defeat, even terror." Take comfort! First off, in reading this book I found I had a lot of company. Second, I learned that problems with math are most common in girls and women (although a lot of men feel the same way, but hide it or deal with it in better ways). Next, I found that there are constructive and productive ways to deal with this difficulty. Tobias talks about the many ways in which we develop problems in learning math, and why some classic methods of teaching it work better for some people but cause problems for others. Tobias points out the most common stumbling blocks in learning math: fractions, changing fractions to decimals and percentages, ratios, etc. She uses examples and demonstrates different methods for reaching an understanding of the process. There are strategies for dealing with these problems and there are courses you can take, although those of us working with our children at home will not need to take classes to overcome our fears. Tobias feels that because math is incremental, it is very important to understand one facet before going on to the next. If we are working with our children on a daily basis, we can do this for ourselves as well as our children. For adults. Code WWN, $12.95.

### In the Beginning

Many of the best books for beginning math are in "Early Learning," but I've included some here because some people start working with math when their children are older.

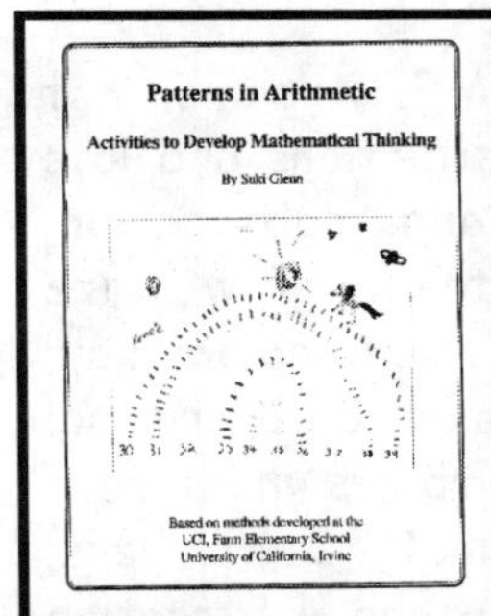


**PATTERNS IN ARITHMETIC,** by Suki Glenn, is the best introduction to mathematics and arithmetic I've seen. I like the Usborne math books (code EDC) and they are very good for children to work with, but I would start with this one first and use the Usborne books for practice and reinforcement if it's needed. This book was developed at the Farm School, a development and research school affiliated with the University of California at Irvine. The book is about the exploration of mathematical concepts. Its approach is to encourage the child to do the discovering, as opposed to the normal approach of "teaching" concepts. Glenn's method is very hands-on, and her excellent understanding of child development makes each lesson, game, or concept a process that happens very naturally. Her excellent ideas for exploring concepts with your child will make it fun for you too. You already have many of the materials needed, but you will need to purchase Cuisenaire rods (see the Institute for Math Mania, below) and a set of base-ten blocks. Ages 5 to 8. $21.50 from Pattern Press, P.O. Box 2737, Fallbrook, CA 92088.

**THE FIRST BOOK OF NUMBERS** was out of print and I'm glad to see it back. This is a brilliantly illustrated introduction, including how numbers were developed, how they relate to time and measurement, and many other fascinating facts. Puzzles and tricks extend the grasp of basic number concepts, including sets, sequence, shapes, size, and a world without numbers. New large oversized format: 19x15" hardcover. Ages 4 to 8. Code EDC, $9.95.

Online at CCClearn.com, you can find math manipulatives to print out, make, and use for grades K to 4.

**HOW MUCH, HOW MANY, HOW FAR, HOW HEAVY, HOW LONG, HOW TALL IS 1000?**, by Helen Nolan. Nolan has made great fun out of exploring the concepts of big, small, short, tall, distance, and more. Emphasis is on estimation rather than counting. Fun! Ages 5 to 9. Code KC, $12.95.

**DON'T BUG ME.** A game that uses real-life situations and lots of addition and subtraction. Players compete to grow prize crops, bugs must be kept at bay, and obstacles must be overcome. A game that combines an interest in nature with math. 2-4 players, ages 6 to whenever basic addition and subtraction have been mastered. Code A, $18 plus $3 shipping.

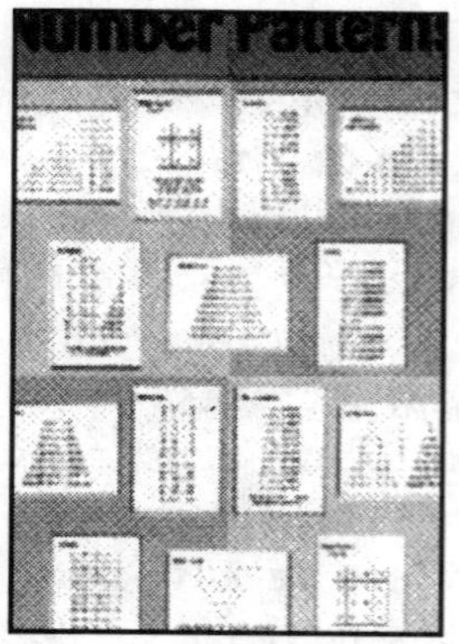


**NUMBER PATTERNS POSTER.** A vivid presentation of some remarkable addition, subtraction, multiplication, and division sums. Mathematics is about patterns in our world. This is a great way for your kids to see numbers in action and to stimulate curiosity about number patterns. Code PW, $10.

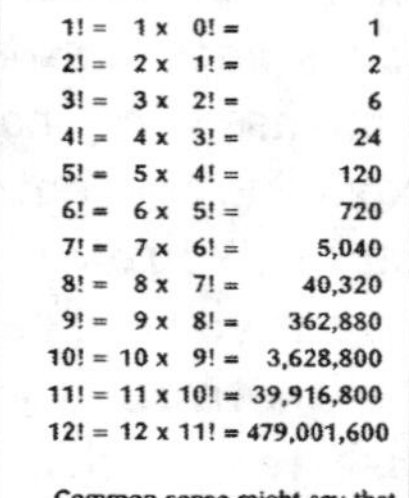

Factorials

| | | |
|---|---|---|
| 1! = | 1 x 0! = | 1 |
| 2! = | 2 x 1! = | 2 |
| 3! = | 3 x 2! = | 6 |
| 4! = | 4 x 3! = | 24 |
| 5! = | 5 x 4! = | 120 |
| 6! = | 6 x 5! = | 720 |
| 7! = | 7 x 6! = | 5,040 |
| 8! = | 8 x 7! = | 40,320 |
| 9! = | 9 x 8! = | 362,880 |
| 10! = | 10 x 9! = | 3,628,800 |
| 11! = | 11 x 10! = | 39,916,800 |
| 12! = | 12 x 11! = | 479,001,600 |

Common sense might say that 0! = 0, but in fact 0! = 1.

**MAKE YOUR OWN CALENDARS.** A great way to learn number sequence. 8x11" books with days of the week on one page and illustrations to color above. Ages 6 to 9. Code DV, $2.50 each. Specify Teddy Bears, Seasonal Pictures, or Jewish.

For another great way to learn number sequence, look in "Arts and Activities — Holidays and Gifts" for dot-to-dot books with different subjects to match your child's interests. Ages 4 to 7.

**CLEVER CATCH BALL**. Play catch with your math with a sturdy inflatable 24" ball. Comes with suggestions, and it's easy to make up your own games. Code CS, $10.95 each. Specify Fractions, Decimals, Percent, Money, Addition, Subtraction, Multiplication, Division, or Pre-Algebra.

Before you go very far into your exploration of mathematics, write for the **PIGOUT ON MATH** and **THE COW BARN PRESS** catalogs from the Institute for Math Mania, P.O. Box 910, Montpelier, VT 05601. Math manipulatives, Cuisenaire rods, and many other creative learning materials at reasonable prices.

For magnetic numbers and math symbol manipulatives, see Learning Boards in "Early Learning." For inexpensive workbooks get the School Zone catalog listed in "Free or Almost-Free Learning and Teaching Aids."

Practical Math

## Developing Skills

**Building Math Skills.** Five books that help kids develop basic math skills. Don't let the names fool you into thinking these are *regular workbooks.* Yes, there is math to do, but following the fortunes of a prehistoric family (the Ogs, from the early reading series), these books bring math into amusing everyday situations that help children absorb the rules of math in a way that clearly demonstrates their usefulness. Ages 7 to 11 (more or less). Code EDC, $7.95 each.
**ADDING AND SUBTRACTING PUZZLES**
**CHARTS AND GRAPHS**
**FRACTIONS AND DECIMALS**
**MULTIPLYING AND DIVIDING PUZZLES**
**TIMES TABLES**

Get a great free catalog of fascinating, colorful, inventive puzzles from Tessellations, 688 W. 1st St., Suite 5, Tempe, AZ 85281, or call 800-655-5341. Do it today; it's really good!

**MENTAL MATH.** I believe that for most children a hands-on approach is the best way to begin math. I read the introduction and instructions to one of these books and had a bad reaction. The approach sounded too regulated: Do this, do that — no variations, no leeway. I took a second look only because the game Fraction Mania (listed below), by the same company, is excellent. Each of these books is designed to give you five questions a day for first grade and ten questions a day for other grades, for the school year. Each daily set is meant to be a five- to ten-minute minute warm-up session. Questions are based on standard math programs and are to be done *without paper and pencil.* I'm not a visual person. I have great trouble visualizing words or numbers in my head. It could be that if I'd had practice when I was growing up I would be better at it, so maybe the no-pencil-and-paper rule is good. However, if I had a child who had trouble visualizing some of these problems, I'd ignore the "no-pencil no-paper" rule when necessary. The book has an incentive program that I might or might not ignore, depending on the child using it. I don't like bribes. All of us use mental math daily in one way or another, so I do like the idea of encouraging children to develop this skill. Code MC, $19.95. Specify grade level.

**HANDS-ON MATH!**, by Frances M. Thompson. This is a great book if your child learns best by "doing" or is having trouble mastering the basic concepts. It will require some time from you to make the manipulatives, but this is something you can do with your child, thus enhancing your experience. This hands-on approach will help your child understand the principles behind multiplication, division, fractions, etc. (If your child understands the concepts, and just needs practice with the basic tables, you don't need this book.) Complete instructions for creating manipulatives, clearly explained. Spiral-bound for easy use, 514 pages. Covers everything needed for grades 4 to 8. Code SS, $34.95.

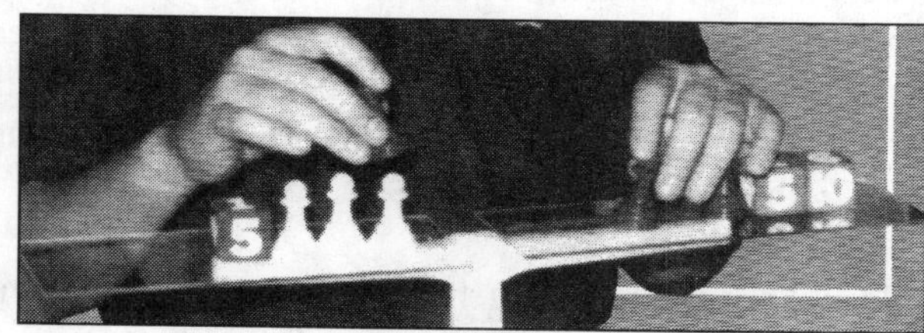

**HANDS-ON EQUATIONS: Making Algebra Child's Play!**, created by Henry Borenson, Ed.D. This is a truly wonderful set of lessons for learning *and mastering* essential basic algebraic concepts. Children about age 8 (and up, including adults) will experience success. It's easy, very intuitive, and fun to use. Although designed to be introduced to elementary-age students, it's completely suitable to use before beginning algebra with your older kids. The language used will not intimidate younger learners or seem to talk down to older students. It's also been proven to be very successful with gifted second-graders and with learning-disabled children working at about a fifth-grade level. Hands-On Equations comes complete with all the materials and workbooks necessary, including the answers to all problems. If we'd had these introductory lessons to algebra when the kids were home I think it would have changed everyone's attitude toward algebra — even mine. If you are interested in using this program with a group of students, please request information about their teaching video and classroom sets of materials. Borenson and Associates, 330 Schantz Rd., Allentown, PA 18106; 800-993-6284.

**NUMBER JUGGLERS MATH GAME BOOK,** written by Ruth Bell Alexander. I asked myself how an 80-page book and 74 cards could cover such a wide range of ages and abilities, and I smiled when I found the answer almost immediately in the introduction. Cards are numbered 0 through 10. Each card has dots underneath the number so that young children can visualize each number concept clearly. Odd and even numbers become immediately recognizable with this system. There are no +, -, x, ÷, or = signs. Players use their math skills and choose whichever symbol is needed to complete the equations for each game. There are 20 games *plus* variations, so you can do a lot of playing and avoid any chance of boredom. The same game can be played again and again and will be different each time. I recommend this as a way to help your child become very comfortable with basic number operations. This very versatile game can be played alone, in groups, or in teams. It is for kids of all skill levels from kindergarten through middle school — and you'll enjoy it too. Code WKM, $12.95.

**KRYPTO.** Another good math game, in some ways similar to Number Jugglers, above, but for kids 8 and up. There are variations with fractions. For price and more information write: MPH Games Company, P.O. Box 1125, Fairfield, CT 06432.

**Math Products Plus**. A lot more math products than you might think there could be: T-shirts, resource books, enrichment books, reference books, math diversions, math history, computer books, puzzles, postcards, manipulatives, games, and more. They have a very intriguing Children's Math Calendar — a daily math problem whose solution is that day's date, plus activities and puzzles. Write for a free catalog: Math Products Plus, P.O. Box 64, San Carlos, CA 94070.

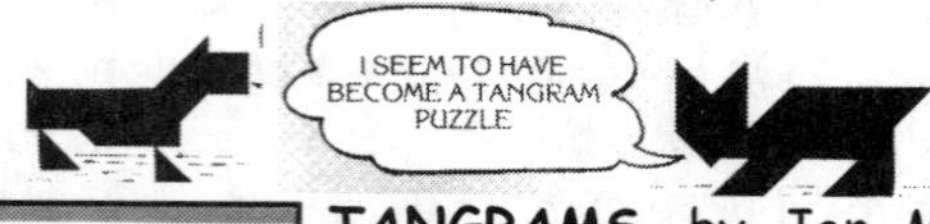


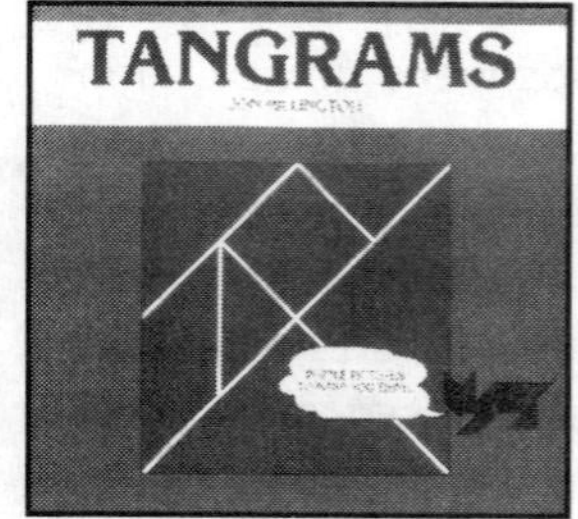

**TANGRAMS**, by Jon Millington. A colorful book with fresh ways to consider this very old puzzle. Included with logical thinking exercises are the materials to construct your own set of two tangram puzzles. Ages 7 and up. Code PW, $9.

**MATHNET MYSTERIES**. Videocassette mysteries, activities, and more based on *Square One TV*, produced by Children's Television Workshop. For information write: GPN, P.O. Box 80669, Lincoln, NE 68501-0669.

**Brain Benders!** Full-color puzzle books, full of spot-the-mistake puzzles, exciting mazes, humorous mixed-up pictures, and lots to think about. Good mental gymnastics. Clues at the end of the book if you get stumped. Ages 8 and up. Code EDC, $4.95 each.

**BRAIN PUZZLES**
**PICTURE PUZZLES**
**NUMBER PUZZLES**

All three in one volume: **BRAIN BENDERS** — $11.95.

**QUICK PIX**. An addition and subtraction card game for kids with beginning math skills, about age 7. The game is easy to learn and fun to play. This can be played slowly, giving beginning learners a chance to figure out the answers. The game goes faster as players learn their facts. Very enjoyable reinforcement for addition and subtraction skills up to and including the number 18. Code A, $10.

**MATH FOR SMARTY PANTS,** by Marilyn Burns (a Brown Paper School Book). Are you a mathematical whiz? If you answered no, this book has a surprise for you; you may be smarter than you think. If you said yes, the book may still surprise you. You may be smarter than you think and not so smart, too — because being smart at math doesn't mean being able to multiply fractions in your head at the speed of light. Numbers are only a part of math. Some people see shapes better than others; some can figure out logical problems better than others. There are many ways to be smart when it comes to mathematics, and this book will tell you about all of them. Many games, tricks, and interesting activities. For the curious who want to have fun with math. Ages 10 and up, certainly including adults. Code LB, $13.95.

**TIC TAC TWICE.** A game of logic, strategy, and pattern — all math skills, but this game has no "math"! To win this game, as in tic-tac-toe, you must place markers in a row, but doing so is not so simple: You must place four markers in a row while playing on two boards at the same time! 2 players, ages 7 and up. Code A, $12 plus $3 shipping. For variations with other subjects, see "Arts and Activities — Holidays and Gifts."

**METRIC WALL CHART.** It's 73 cm by 106 cm (if you're not sure how big that is, you need the chart!). Shows metric length, volume, mass, area, and temperature. Ages 7 and up. Code AO, $4.95.

**MATH BY KIDS,** edited by Susan Richman. This isn't just for kids! You'll have fun with it, too. It will be an inspiration and challenge from the time you and your children begin math. The problems were written by kids, for kids. I think your child will feel challenged, not intimidated, by this book. You'll find a surprising variety of problems to solve. This book challenges the user to write his own problems. Before you can write a problem you have to be able to analyze it and understand it enough to figure out the answer. A great way to help your child understand and use basic principles. You'll find many suggestions to help you make good use of this book. Write for price and shipping: Pennsylvania Homeschoolers, R.D. 2, Box 117, Kittanning, PA 16201.

**FRACTION MANIA.** Mention a fraction game and the most common reaction is "You've got to be kidding!" According to the research done by the manufacturer of this game, 80 percent of parents and teachers do not like fractions. I wasn't excited about trying this game. However, I felt compelled to try it because *you* are relying on me to make a judgment about math materials. I was pleasantly surprised when this game made me feel better about fractions! You can choose from five different playing levels, so the game is flexible and your kids won't outgrow it for a while. Ages 6 to adult. Code MC, $22.95, plus $3 shipping.

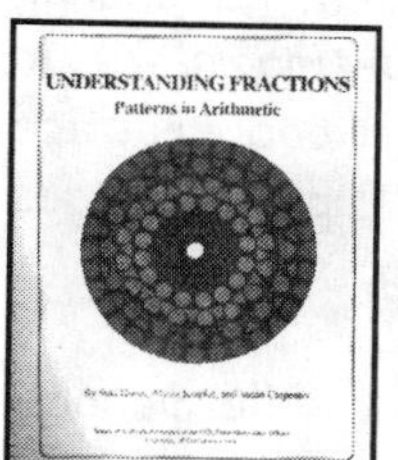


**UNDERSTANDING FRACTIONS,** by Suki Glenn, Alysia Krapfel, and Susan Carpenter. This book has the same approach as *Patterns in Arithmetic*, page 277, but is geared toward slightly older children and is specifically about fractions. This book has 103 pages of activities: cooking, building (Legos and other common toys), games, and worksheets. Includes a 51-piece fraction set. Ages 7 to 10. $17.50 from Pattern Press, P.O. Box 2737, Fallbrook, CA 92088.

**THE I HATE MATHEMATICS! BOOK,** by Marilyn Burns (a Brown Paper School Book). What does mathematics have to do with schemes to get rich quick; games called Creep, Pig, and Poison; or getting a vest off your grandfather without removing his coat? Are you a permutation ice cream cone eater or a combination ice cream cone eater? What offers you many new riddles, sidewalk games, things to do when you have the flu, and a sneaky way around drying the dishes? Answer: this book, which is about changing from a mathematical weakling to a mathematical heavyweight. Does it use tricks? Fancy talk? Threats? Fun and games? Yes! But there's a secret to it: You are a mathematical genius in disguise! Code LB, $13.95.

**MATH GAMES AND ACTIVITIES FROM AROUND THE WORLD,** by Claudia Zaslavsky. Zaslavsky combines math, history, art, and world cultures (so you can include geography, too) in this delightful, sometimes challenging collection of more than 70 games, puzzles, and activities. No boredom here. Every game is a hands-on activity. Clear instructions for making game boards and necessary playing pieces. Most materials are common household items. There's nothing intimidating about these activities. The talented as well as the reluctant math student will have fun (and learn). Ages 8 and up. Code CRP, $14.95 and well worth it.

**MONEYWISE KIDS.** This fast-paced game makes learning money skills fun. Using addition, subtraction, and multiplication, players must learn to make change and use budgeting skills in order to win. Good practice and good fun. 2 players, ages 7 and up. Code A, $15 plus $3 shipping.

**MATH GAMES: For Middle School,** by Mario Salvadori and Joseph P. Wright. This makes a nice change from regular book work. Challenges and skill builders cover all parts of the math curriculum, from addition and subtraction to plane and spatial geometry, graphing, and probability. There's something for every student here. Answers are in the back of the book for easy reference. Included are some hands-on experiments and realistic problems to solve. Code CRP, $16.95.

**Key Curriculum Project**. "Non-threatening" workbooks on fractions, decimals, geometry, algebra. Request catalog from: 1150 65th St., Emeryville, CA 94608.

**MATHEMATICAL CURIOSITIES**, by Gerald Jenkins and Anne Wild. All models are in full color and, when cut out and glued together, have curious properties. Some rotate, some fold and unfold, some twist, some fit together in unexpected ways, and all demonstrate amusing and interesting mathematical ideas. The book includes nine models, or sets of models, and a mini-book that provides more information and suggestions for further investigation. Using this book will help you take your math out of a book and into your imagination. Ages 9 and up — adults will find this fascinating. Code PW, $10.

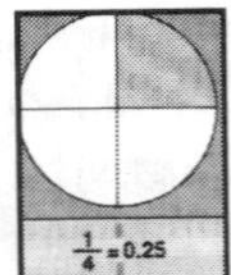

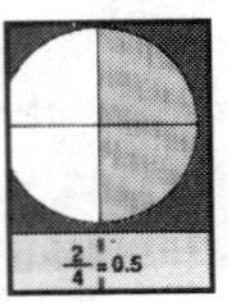

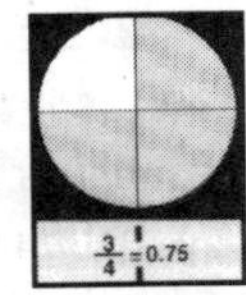

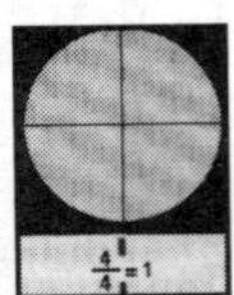


**FRACTIONS AND DECIMAL EQUIVALENTS POSTER**. Combines methods of representing a fraction as a sector of a circle and as a proportion of a bar of constant length. An interesting way to view relationships between fractions (up to twelfths) and corresponding decimals. Code PW, $10.

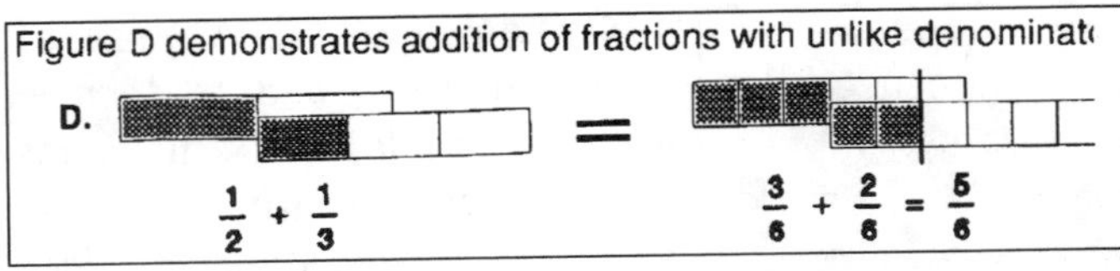


**Fraction manipulatives** and many other valuable math tools are available from Scott Resources, P.O. Box 2121, Fort Collins, CO 80522. Write for a catalog.

**MATHAMAKITS**, by Mutiara Buys, Ph.D. and Linda Weiss-Malik, J.D., is a unique hands-on exploration of geometry. No teaching manual is needed; everything you need to know is in the book. Using paper, scissors, protractor, compass, and a few other easily gathered materials, you'll explore the concept of area in triangles, parallelograms, and the other common shapes associated with the normal study of geometry. You'll find games as well as easy, clear directions for constructing three-dimensional models that will encourage users to think creatively. You'll acquire a complete working vocabulary of terms, common formulas, and theorems. Comes in a handy comb binding so it will lie flat. Ages 9 to 15. Code AP, $24.

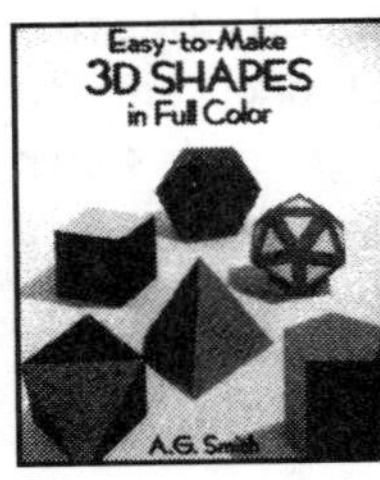


**EASY-TO-MAKE 3-D GEOMETRICAL SHAPES.** Six shapes. All you need are scissors and glue. Books are 9x12". Once you have the patterns from the book you can copy them and make more. Ages 8 and up. Code DV, $3.50.

**EXPLORING MATH WITH BOOKS KIDS LOVE**, by Kathryn Kaczmarski. This book has a wealth of interesting reading and related math activities. The combination of carefully chosen literature and math skills pulls math out of the sphere of theory and into the realm of real usage that makes it such a practical and useful skill. Kaczmarski recognizes that math should not be relegated to isolated exercises that are unconnected to practical applications. She says, "Life is not bundled up in tidy one-hour increments where we can handle one narrow facet of it before moving on to the next. Life itself is an integrated curriculum; it is impossible to tell where one discipline ends and another begins." This book uses novels, nonfiction, and a few poems to demonstrate lessons to be learned. Actually, you'll find that Kaczmarski takes you beyond literature to demonstrate the principles and usefulness of math, because she's incorporated art and architecture, history, sociology, geography, science, economics, and current events. This book contains all the lessons necessary to meet the standards set by the National Council of Teachers of Mathematics. So what more do you want from a math book? A good appendix? An extensive reading list? Well-organized, creative lessons? This book has it all. Ages 12 to 16. Code FC, $19.95. If you have trouble locating some of the reading material let us know, and we'll be glad to help.

### High School and Up

### THE QUESTION IS, WHICH HALF?

An official in the Department of Education told me one day that a certain school district was retiring 1.3 teachers. Another district would have no change in staff, but was hiring two new teachers. In another district, there would be 3.5 new teachers.

I scratched my head and murmured, "Pardon me?"

He said it all again, which didn't help, and I tried to visualize 3.5 teachers coming to work in the morning, but that didn't help, either.

It reminded me of the stage magician who asked another magician, "Who was that lady I sawed with you last night?"

"Oh, that was no lady," the second magician replied. "That was my half-sister."

I asked the official if he meant an average of 3.5 teachers. Say, two in one district and five in another. The average would be...

"No," he said, "not an average." He spoke slowly, to help me understand. "Three point five teachers."

In plain English, spelled out, that's three and a half teachers. Isn't it?

I'm still working on it. Just give me a little more time.

My cousin, who is a great editor, has two doctorate degrees, and teaches at a college in North Carolina, explained this to me, too. The explanation didn't help me either, so I think this must be some kind of new math or some new cognitive disease that's highly contagious, and hopefully confined within the educational system.

**ESSENTIAL MATH** (formerly titled *Survival Mathematics*). All the practical math skills and basic concepts most people will ever find useful or essential in everyday life, with a minimum of "abstract" math; with emphasis on skills and knowledge needed in bank transactions, stores, restaurants, tax forms, etc., and a full introduction to fractions, percentages, simple graphs, and elementary algebra. An excellent alternative to standard textbooks and more useful in daily applications even if you plan to study advanced math, too. Also covers the metric system. Grade 7 or 8 through high school and adult. 350 pages, 8½x11". Code BE, $13.95.

**ARITHMETIC MADE SIMPLE**, by A.P. Sperling and Samuel D. Levison. A complete guide to all the functions of arithmetic, beginning with the basic use of numbers and working through addition, subtraction, multiplication, division, fractions, decimals, percentages, money, measurement, simple plane and solid geometry, ration and proportion, graphs, signed numbers, and use of a calculator. Although the book begins with the simplest of arithmetic terms and usages, it's written for teens or adults who need to review (or learn for the first time), and isn't suitable for young children. See the Core Knowledge Series or Saxon math books for younger children. Includes answers to all problems and index. Code DD, $12.95.

**HANDS-ON ALGEBRA!**, by Frances M. Thompson. Better than a standard textbook for kids who master the concepts best through hands-on experience. I would use this book with a child who really needs these skills and requires more than textbook learning can provide. Ready-to-use games and activities plus complete instructions for creating manipulatives, clearly explained. 616 pages. Covers everything needed for grades 7 to 12. Code SS, $34.95.

**ALGEBRA I: Cliffs Quick Review.** Starting with a quick review of pre-algebra concepts, this book gives a logically presented review of the fundamentals. It is clearly arranged, with straightforward language and practical help in determining your comprehension of the subject. An excellent way to review core concepts before testing. Code BT, $7.95.

**MATH SHORTCUTS TO ACE THE SAT (NEW SAT) AND THE NEW PSAT/NMSQT**. An excellent supplement to Barron's and Peterson's SAT books. This book is not a complete review of materials covered by these tests, but for those taking these tests and those who wish to make math simpler, these shortcuts will save time on tests as well as effort in everyday usage. The 34 specific shortcuts and strategies presented should be part of every standard text, but they aren't. This book covers math (including fractions), algebra, geometry, and more, and is easy (even for me) to understand, providing clear examples and exercises. Ages high school and up. Code AP, $12.95.

For students who need a little extra help with regular math or trigonometry, write to PineBrook Academy, 1272 Marlborough Lane, Winston-Salem, NC 27105. Very reasonably priced courses for beginning trig, helping kids calculate carefully, multiplication tables, and more.

**MATH CLUB** by mail for high school students. Challenging publication with puzzles, strategy games, even a little relevant history, and more. Write for current prices: Tabletop Academy Press, R.R. 1, Box 114, Blue Mound, IL 62513-9709.

**RAPID MATH TRICKS AND TIPS: 30 Days to Number Power**, by Edward H. Julius. Sixty tricks and tips that will increase the speed of your calculations and decrease your dependency on calculators. Very useful for young adults facing timed tests. Extremely useful to those who use math daily. To make good use of this book, you do need to be comfortable with all the basic math operations, decimals, and fractions. Best used by older high school students and adults. Some of these tricks could be used by competent younger students. Includes good explanations, examples, and practice problems. Code JPW, $15.95.

**GUIDE TO EVERYDAY MATH: A Home and Business Reference,** by Brian Burrell. This is a handy guide for adults and advanced math students, covering all operations — basic, intermediate, and advanced — in capsule form: amortization, baseball statistics, balance sheets, construction, depreciation, gambling, GNP and GDP, taxes, interest rates, IRAs and 401(k)s, lotteries, maps, mortgages, stocks, tipping, and utility bills. Code MW, $14.95.

**G IS FOR GOOGOL,** by David Schwartz. A math alphabet book full of fascinating and entertaining facts and thoughts about mathematics. What's a googol? Something impressive: a 1 followed by 100 zeros! You'll discover that "P is for probability," and probability is explained in terms of weather and broccoli, and you'll learn about early measurements as well as rhombicosidodecahedrons (and how to pronounce it). A great book for increasing your appreciation and knowledge of math (or stimulating more interest in it) that's sure to put a smile on your face. Hardcover. High school students and adults. Code TSP, $15.95.

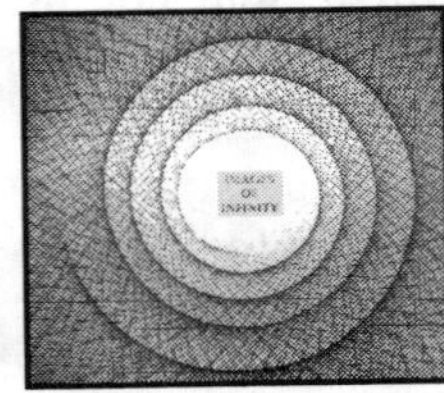

**IMAGES OF INFINITY**, compiled and written by Ray Hemmings and Dick Tahta. I don't understand most of this book, and yet I still find it, and many of the illustrations, fascinating. This book is filled with intriguing pictures, puzzles, and problems all dealing with the idea of infinity. A teaser and a mind-boggler — if you love math, you'll love this book. The pictures will fascinate everyone from the age of 10 to infinity, even if you don't understand it all. Code PW, $18.95.

**Saxon Math**. John Saxon's now-famous math books may be the only ones making full use of an "incremental" approach to learning — the introduction of topics in bits and pieces, which permits complete assimilation of one facet of a concept before the next is introduced, along with continuous review of all material learned previously.

We first learned of "the Saxon method" in 1985 from an article in *Reader's Digest*. We bought a copy of *Algebra ½*, tried it, and were very favorably impressed. Since then, we have used most of the other Saxon math books, with fairly remarkable results.

Two of our four children, who had seemed to have almost no mathematical aptitudes, gained a basic understanding (and even a little interest) in a very short time. On the other hand, the only "advanced" math studied by our daughter Karen, the only one of our children ever to be officially tested, was in an outdated, out-of-print copy of *High School Subjects Self-Taught*, and later she scored very high in the national SSAT (and was accepted by a college with only our high school diploma and no other official credentials).

For mastering advanced math, especially if it will have application in sciences such as chemistry (which is emphasized in some Saxon books), or if you're going to need a lot of math to get into college, Saxon's method may be the best — but many people are mastering math without ever seeing a Saxon book. A $15 book that covers all the basic math principles, with enough drill and practice to know whether or not you're going to be a nuclear physicist, may be sufficient; it's a lot easier on the wallet, and may be a lot easier on the student.

In the last edition of *The Home School Source Book*, Donn said we were no longer recommending or selling the Saxon math books. I've had second thoughts spawned by the tutoring I've done.

You can't explain math clearly to anyone if you don't understand it yourself. In an effort to educate myself enough to tutor students, I looked at a number of textbooks. I talked with math teachers and had to accord them a lot of respect; it seems some of them, too, are victims of the system. In search of the perfect textbook, schools frequently change textbooks from year to year. The methods of explaining math, if any, vary from text to text. As one teacher told me, many teachers have their own way of teaching various math concepts and prefer that math books be written without any specific methods of explaining math. Publishers, being well aware of the large profit margin in producing textbooks, are all too happy to accommodate these teachers.

I ordered some used Saxon books, and not only did I find them helpful, but they worked miracles for my students. Yes, we had to work at the basic tables. Boring? Yes, but within a short time my students were seeing progress as well as the reasoning behind learning the tables. The explanations and examples in the books were clear to me as well as to my students. Unfortunately, they were so good that I no longer have students paying to provide me with extra goodies for Gus.

Saxon's K-3 program, originally developed "especially for classroom use," was very difficult to adapt to individual use, but don't let that frighten you. The special "home study kit" for individual use in kindergarten comes with the hefty price of $55. Now add $85 for first grade, $87.50 for second grade, and $90 for third grade, and although you didn't grow up using Saxon math, you don't need a calculator, a degree in mathematics, or a special course in financial management to know that the Saxon folks must think homeschoolers have bottomless pockets! (Those prices do not include the recommended manipulatives.) Fortunately, the prices drop with the more advanced books.

I won't sell the Saxon K-3 courses because I object to the pricing, and because you can find cheap workbooks and make your own manipulatives. For the remaining grades I do suggest the Saxon books if you are trying to follow a prescribed school curriculum or if your own math skills are weak.

**Used Saxon Books** (Math 54, 65, 76, 87, and the algebra books listed below) can be ordered from Follett Educational Services, 1433 Internationale Parkway, Woodridge, IL 60517; call 800-621-4272 for a catalog. Prices are around $25 to $35. Books are in good condition. **They do not sell the answer keys.**

**New Saxon Home-Study Packets.** Includes texts, answer books, and test forms. Code CHB.
**SAXON 54**, $51.50
**SAXON 65**, $52.30
**SAXON 76**, $53.50
**SAXON 87**, $53.50
**ALGEBRA** $\frac{1}{2}$, $55.50
**ALGEBRA I**, $56.75
**ALGEBRA II**, $56.75
**ADVANCED MATH**, $60.75
**CALCULUS**, $67
**PHYSICS**, $61.95

# BUSINESS AND ECONOMICS

## ACCOUNTING, BOOKKEEPING, MONEY

### WHY WE CLOSED ONE OF OUR BANK ACCOUNTS

and discontinued business as our own ad agency

**BROOK FARM BOOKS**
GLASSVILLE, NB E0J 1L0

Assistant Manager
Bank of Nova Scotia
Florenceville, N.B. E0J 1K0

Sir:

In reply to your letter stating that my other business account, J-D Advertising Associates, is currently overdrawn 86¢, please find enclosed herewith a check from myself as a client of J-D Advertising Associates to myself as a partner in J-D Advertising Associates, in the amount of $1.00, which should restore said account to a state of solvency.

As I explained to the teller when setting up the account, it is not really a business. It is my left pocket, into which I put money I have taken from my right pocket. In the course of trying to make a living without robbing banks, I sometimes place advertisements in various publications, some of which allow discounts to advertising agencies. I therefore hired the printing of ad agency order forms, transforming myself into what the media call "a house agency" – meaning that I function as an ad agency in placing my own ads. These forms entitle me to a discount. So far, I have paid myself one commission of $6.00, the amount of discount allowed on a certain ad. That $6.00 was the deposit with which I opened an account in the name of myself as an ad agency, and was paid out of my regular account, which I maintain in my other guise as myself. Within a few days, I received a bank statement, noting that $1.50 has been deducted as a service charge, making my balance $4.50.

A few days later, I received some personalized checks that had been printed incorrectly. I returned them promptly to the bank, explaining the error. I assumed I would not be charged for these checks, which should indicate how naïve I am when it comes to matters of high finance. As I have written no checks on this account, and have not withdrawn any money from it in any other way, I am now assuming that I have already been charged for the incorrectly printed checks. Since my previous balance was $4.50, and you say the account is now in the red to the tune of 86¢, I compute the cost of the checks to be $5.36. Is that a penalty imposed on me for not accepting the checks? How much more will it cost me to have some checks printed correctly? Let me know quickly, before my account becomes overdrawn again, so that I can mail myself a check to cover the amount.

Incidentally, there is no use trying to get money from me as a partner in J-D Advertising Associates. The only money ever owned, even fleetingly, by me as an ad agency is in the account. The next time the ad agency's account slips down out of the black, you should write to me as myself and not to me as the ad agency. If your accounts say the ad agency is bankrupt, then it is really so. Write to me and I'll have a word with myself, and loan myself a little money to get over the hump. Which I am now doing, with the enclosed check for $1.00. That is not a commission for anything, so I have to regard it as a loan, which I will have to pay back to myself as soon as I pay myself enough commissions to do so. That may take quite a while, because so far I have put money into the account and have taken none out, but you have been taking money out of it faster than I can put it in.

I wonder if you have any little pamphlets explaining to me the benefits of a business account. So far, the only benefits I have noticed seem to be to the bank. How much more must I invest in the bank before some of the benefits come to me?

I hope some of my questions will be answered soon, unless such attention will result in more service charges, in which case I'll be better off if you leave me wondering.

Sincerely yours,
Donn Reed

P.S. Dear Canadian customers — The above letter, written some years ago, demonstrates the principles involved in maintaining a business account. This is why we now ask for payment in U.S. funds. We apologize for the inconvenience, but the bank doesn't.

**MAKING CENTS: Every Kid's Guide to Making Money**, by Elizabeth Wilkinson. A Brown Paper School Book. How can kids have fun making money in their spare time? By starting with this book, which gives a kid's-eye view of money, where it started, what it represents, how it's spent, and (best of all) how to earn it — all in a book the kids will enjoy reading. (Now out of print! Try your library. To protest the out-of-print status, write Time Warner/Little Brown, Attn: Linda Cook, 1271 Avenue of the Americas, New York, NY 10020.)

**INTRODUCTION TO BUSINESS**. Very detailed guide for absolute beginners, clearly explaining in simplified but accurate terms the development and major functions of money and business. Clear text is accompanied by detailed, colorful pictures. Hardcover. Ages 10 to adult. Code RW, $9.95.

**WHATEVER HAPPENED TO PENNY CANDY?**, by Richard J. Maybury, global affairs editor for *Moneyworld*. Highly acclaimed, clear introduction to the causes of inflation, recession, and wage and price controls. Topics include the origin and history of money, the economic behavior of government, investing, business cycles, recessions, depressions, and more as they relate to several areas of history, social studies, and even science. Ages 10 to adult. $12.95. The study guide, by Jane Williams, is actually a separate book based on *Whatever Happened to Penny Candy?*; it's $15.95. Add $3 shipping for the first book and $1 for each additional title. If you want to learn more about the complexities of modern economics, try **ECONOMICS**, by Jane Williams. All these books are from Bluestocking Press, P.O. Box 2030, Shingle Springs, CA 95682-2030. Request their catalog for complete listings.

**BOOKKEEPING MADE SIMPLE**, by Louis W. Fields; revised by Richard R. Gallagher. Complete accounting course, from journals and ledgers to merchandising accounts, depreciation, payroll records, partnerships, computer use, new financial regulations, and more. The most comprehensive basic guide available. Grades 9 to 12. Code DD, $13.95.

**A NOTICE RECEIVED FROM A PUBLISHER:**

IMPORTANT NOTICE

TO: All Retail Accounts

RE: Qualifying Discounts

The period for establishing your new qualifying discount will be from 5/1/98 through 8/31/98. During this time frame, your current qualifying discount will remain in effect. On 9/1/98, if you have not re-qualified, the old qualifying discount will be deleted from the system. The new qualifying discount will remain in effect from 9/1/98 through 8/1/99. For each product group, if the subsequent order is received within the fiscal year which carries a higher discount than the original qualifying order, it will receive the higher discount and become the new qualifying discount for that product group. The highest discount will remain in effect until August 31/1999. Please contact your sales representative or customer service regarding any questions on the above.

**Mathematics for Everyday Living**. A series of eight books with practical consumer math that most of us know (or should know). Each book covers a different topic in depth, with problems explained and practice exercises. These are not substitutes for regular math books. These books make fractions, percentage rates, algebra, etc. useful tools, not just abstract ideas learned for test-taking. For example, *The Mathematics of Buying* has a section on "promissory notes," explaining how to calculate the cost of borrowing money, including various fees involved; installment loans; financing a new car; home mortgages; different types of interest rates; and credit cards. Formulas are given to find the necessary information. The last section of each book focuses on a career using the skills learned. Each book contains the answers to odd-numbered exercises; answer keys for all problems are separate. High school students and adults. Code MG, $19.95 each book, $3.50 each answer guide. Each title begins with **The Mathematics of: 1) Buying 2) Saving 3) Borrowing 4) Taxes 5) Investment 6) Statistics 7) Insurance 8) Inflation and Depreciation.**

**THE STORY OF MONEY, A PENNY SAVED ..., and NEW DESIGNS FOR YOUR MONEY**. Two comic books and an information brochure. Free on request from the Federal Reserve Bank of New York. For access to a massive amount of *free* information about our banking and economic systems write and request their Catalog of Public Information Materials. There is a small charge for a few items, but not many. Worth doing, as you can find history as well as current policies. Federal Reserve, 33 Liberty St., New York, NY 10045-0001; www.ny.frb.org.

Get a free catalog of reasonably priced books, activity books, posters, coloring books, and more for elementary to middle grades from the National Schools Committee for Economic Education (NSCEE), 86 Valley Rd., P.O. Box 295, Cos Cob, CT 06807-0295.

**YOUNG MONEY MATTERS.** You can give your kids Wall Street smarts with the National Association of Investors Corporation's newsletter. $10 a year (5 issues) from NAIC, 711 W. 13 Mile Rd., Madison Heights, MI 48071.

**Online resources**: At www.smg2000.org, kids from grades 4 to 12 can pretend to invest in the stock market game. At www.investoreducation.org, kids can learn about compound interest.

**YOUNGBIZ.** A small magazine for and about teens starting their own businesses. True stories and many useful suggestions for those already in business and those thinking about it. $18 per year. KidsWay, Inc., 5585 Peachtree Rd., Chamblee, GA 30341; 888-KIDSWAY; www.kidsway.com.

**In a Nutshell**. "Omit needless words" is one of the rules for clear writing in Strunk and White's *The Elements of Style*. The Lord's Prayer has 56 words. The Gettysburg Address has 266 words. The Ten Commandments have 297 words. The Declaration of Independence has 300 words. A U.S. government directive on setting the price of cabbage has 29,611.

---

*Banking establishments are more dangerous than standing armies.* — Thomas Jefferson

# SCIENCE



## The Chapter of How and Why — The Chapter of Questions and Answers and More Questions

Science has not been one of the most popular fields of study in the last few decades. This is evident in popular polls and is reflected in test scores from high schools and universities around the country. I don't understand this lack of interest. The exploration of ourselves and the world around us preoccupies youngsters. I could spend a lot of time and waste space discussing what has happened to bring this about, but it's more to the point to give you a variety of exciting resources to stimulate and satisfy curiosity.

### THE BIG PICTURE

**EINSTEIN AND THE BUDDHA**. Dr. Fritjof Capra, lecturer and researcher at the Lawrence Berkeley Laboratories in California and author of *The Tao of Physics*, talks with Jocelyn Ryder-Smith. In the discussion of the parallels between modern particle physics and Eastern mysticism, Capra proposes that two themes — fundamental unity and interdependence of all phenomena, and the intrinsically dynamic nature of reality — are common to both views. He also suggests that physics and mysticism have much to offer to the fields of medicine, economics, and politics. (I think it may be significant that Eastern "mystics" might be more likely to say that physics and mysticism are not only parallel, but very probably the same phenomena expressed in different vocabularies. As physicists probe deeper into the mysteries of physical matter, they realize increasingly that material effects are influenced, and perhaps governed, by consciousness. The mystics have known this for centuries.) One cassette. Code AF, $12.95.

---

*The world embarrasses me, and I cannot dream that this watch exists and has no watchmaker.*
— Voltaire

---

Gy=c — If you agree with Albert Einstein's opinion that God does not play dice with the universe, you may be interested in this equation, which I found in *The Godwhale*, a science fiction novel by T.J. Bass. (It's now out of print. You might be able to find it with an Internet search or in the library.) The letters stand for "gravity times a year equals the speed of light." The kids and I spent several hours one morning playing with it, trying to prove or disprove it. Sure enough: The acceleration of gravity (32 feet per second per second) times the number of seconds in a year equals the speed of light (expressed in seconds). Try it. The speed of light is the one absolute constant fact throughout the universe. Does this have any real significance — or is it just the roll of the dice? A "coincidence"— or God's signature?

---

*That the universe was formed by a fortuitous concourse of atoms, I will no more believe than that the accidental jumbling of the alphabet would fall into a most ingenious treatise of philosophy.*
— Jonathan Swift

---

**POWERS OF TEN: About the Relative Size of Things in the Universe**, by Philip and Phylis Morrison. A fascinating, mind-boggling excursion through the universe, from the very smallest subatomic particles known to the farthest limits of space yet discovered, moving in 42 orders of magnitude, taking us one jump at a time to give us a breathtaking sense of the relative sizes within us and around us. A book to browse in, over and over, very slowly, with awe and wonder. All ages. Code WHF, $19.95.

**COSMOS**, by Carl Sagan. Based on the *Cosmos* television series, this book was on the *New York Times* bestseller list for 70 weeks. With more than 250 full-color illustrations and several in black and white,

*Cosmos* is about science in its broadest context, tracing the growth together of science and civilization. The book explores spacecraft missions of discovery of the nearby planets; research in the library of ancient Alexandria; the human brain; Egyptian hieroglyphics; the origin of life; the death of the Sun; the evolution of galaxies; and the origins of matter, suns, and worlds. Sagan retraces the 15 billion years of cosmic evolution that has transformed matter into life and consciousness, enabling the cosmos to wonder about itself. He considers the latest findings about life elsewhere and how we might communicate with the beings of other worlds. *Cosmos* is the story of our long journey of discovery and the forces and people who helped shape modern science, including Democritus, Hypatia, Kepler, Newton, Huygens, Champollion, Lowell, and Humason. Sagan looks at our earth from an extraterrestrial vantage point and sees a blue jewel-like world, inhabited by a life form that is just beginning to discover its own unity and to venture into the vast ocean of space. A beautiful, informative, exciting, reverent book. Code RH, $32.95.

**A BRIEF HISTORY OF TIME**, by Stephen W. Hawking. "[When] I decided to … write a popular book about space and time … there were already a considerable number of books about the early universe and black holes. … I felt that none of them really addressed the questions that had led me to do research in cosmology and quantum theory. Where did the universe come from? How and why did it begin? Will it come to an end, and if so, how? Modern science has become so technical that only a very small number of specialists are able to master the mathematics used to describe them. Yet the basic ideas about the origin and fate of the universe can be stated without mathematics in a form that people without a scientific education can understand. This is what I have attempted to do." If you've read my comments about math, you may be surprised that I'd read a book by the man who is considered by many to be the most brilliant physicist in the history of the world, and even more surprised that I understand it enough to enjoy it. I'll admit I've taken some of it in very small doses and I do a lot of ruminating, but it hasn't been as tedious for me as you might think. *Time* said of Hawking, "Even as he sits helpless in his wheelchair, his mind seems to soar ever more brilliantly across the vastness of space and time to unlock the secrets of the universe." *Astronomy* wrote, "The work of Stephen Hawking will be writ large in the annals of science." *Vanity Fair*: "Stephen Hawking has overcome a crippling disease to become the supernova of world physics. … He is leaping beyond quantum mechanics, beyond the big bang, to the 'dance of geometry' that created the universe." Large paperback. Code BDD, $14.95.

**A BRIEF HISTORY OF TIME**, by Stephen W. Hawking. Listening to this clear reading of Hawking's book is even better than reading it myself; I can close my eyes and imagine that Hawking is leading me through veils of human knowledge, a little closer to the nature of the universe. Four cassettes, six hours. Code PPD, $24.95.

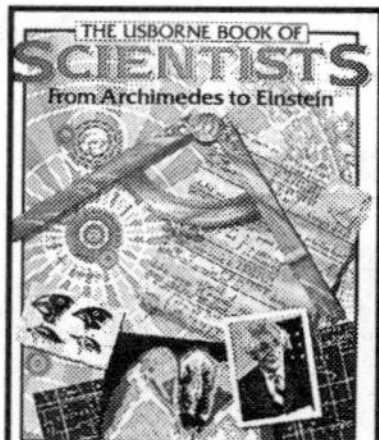


**SCIENTISTS: From Archimedes to Einstein**. How did "science" begin? What is a scientist? Great for inquiring minds and for inspiring an interest. Begins with the earliest scientific ideas and medical skills used in the ancient world; considers medieval Arab thinkers, Renaissance Europe, and the relationship between science and religion; and continues to modern times. A good look at the lives, and sometimes enormous obstacles, these scientists had to overcome. It should inspire kids to think about the world around them and to not be afraid to investigate and experiment. Chart of main events and highlights of women in science. Well illustrated with a quiz at the end if you want to use it. Ages 10 and up. Code EDC, $8.95.

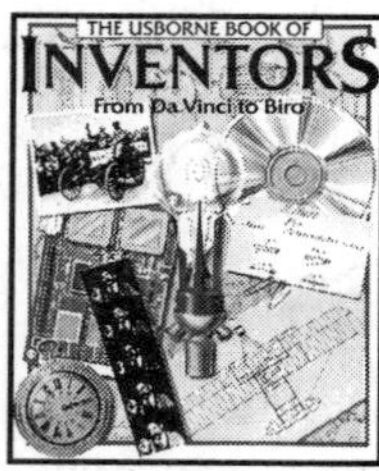


**INVENTORS**. Fascinating look at inventors and inventions throughout history, beginning with the wheel and examining architecture, writing, and money. Covers early inventions, measuring, observation, manufacturing, cars and transportation, printing, recording sound, medical inventions, computers, and the power of the imagination. Well illustrated with good cutaway pictures to expose internal construction. List of key dates and inventors quiz. Ages 10 and up. Code EDC, $8.95.

**FROM BUTTERFLIES TO THUNDERBOLTS: Discovering Science With Books Kids Love**, by Anthony D. Fredericks. A unique book. Fredericks recommends books for ages 5 to 12 that use award-winning books and other sources to teach science (e.g., biology, botany, and paleontology) in a cross-curriculum approach as integrated as our lives. Fredericks recommends books, poses questions about the books for kids to think about, and shares ideas to explore with lots of hands-on projects and activities, all based on the recommended books. You will have to get the books he recommends. If you can't find one of his recommendations please let us know and we will try to get it for you. Most should be readily available through any library or bookstore. There is a helpful list of recommended science periodicals and science supply companies listed in the appendix. Code FC, $17.95.

**FIRST GUIDE TO THE UNIVERSE**. Exciting pictures with brief text presenting a wealth of information about the earth, moon, planets, sun, rockets, and space flight. Ages 7 and up. Code EDC, $12.95.

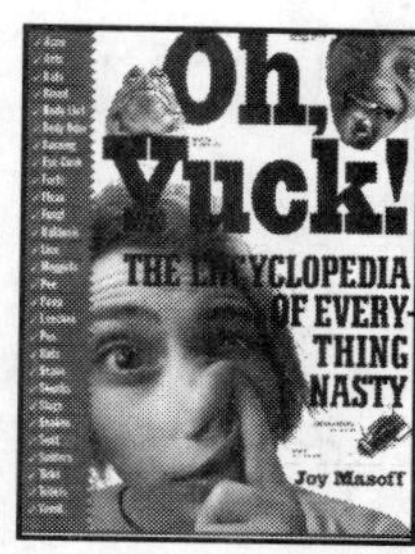

**OH, YUCK! The Encyclopedia of Everything Nasty**, by Joy Masoff. "Exhaustively researched and impeccably scientific, yet written with a lively lack of earnestness. ... An ants-to-zits encyclopedic compendium covering people, animals, insects, plants, foods, and more" is just part of the publisher's description. Here are all the things your kids are interested in that are never in the respectable textbooks and usually not even in most creatively written books. The book is filled with hundreds of cartoons and real-life photographs. It's here your kids will be able to learn about vampire bats, which sip blood and pee at the same time so they'll always be light enough to fly away; where dandruff comes from; why vomit smells; why maggots adore rotting meat; and probably a lot more you don't want to know. The book also features gross recipes, putrid projects, 10 foods that make you airborne, and more. Publishers always list a book as hardcover or paperback. This one is listed as "Paper over slime cover. A full-size, non-toxic slime-filled, plastic pouch is affixed to the front cover." Perfect for ages 8 to 12. Code WKM, $15.95.

**THE EVOLUTION BOOK**, by Sara Stein. Books such as this (one of the best) should be read, and perhaps discussed, with at least a little skepticism now and then, tempered with reason. Evolution within a species is obvious, even in the limited time and space of a barnyard. Evolution of one species to another is still without evidence of any kind. The missing link is still missing. This book offers scores of projects from preserving sea stars to making seaweed pudding, has hundreds of drawings and photos, and attempts to answer several important questions, such as How did life begin? What makes the continents move? The answers to such questions, says the author, can be discovered by reading the ancient messages left on the earth. Like Voltaire, I can't believe "the watch has no watchmaker," so I don't swallow the entire evolutionary theory, but neither do I believe "the watchmaker" is a white-bearded egomaniac playing with mudpies. Movement of continents is a measurable phenomenon. The beginning of life, supposedly from a chance collision of cosmic debris, is only a "scientific" doctrine, with no more to support it than corresponding religious doctrines. Most of this book deals with demonstrable facts, presenting them in very informative and interesting ways. The attempts to describe and define the greater mysteries, such as the beginning of life and consciousness, should be recognized as no more than current theory, with as little foundation as the divine creation theory. Lots to think about, observe, and discuss. Ages 10 and up, including adults. Code WKM, $12.95.

**ORIGIN OF SPECIES** and **THE DESCENT OF MAN**, by Charles Darwin. See "Literature."

## PREHISTORY AND DINOSAURS

**Prehistory**. Two books that form a brilliantly visual, continuous account of our world through the beginnings of the first civilizations. They have been prepared with the help of experts in each period of history, and are written and illustrated with great attention to detail and accuracy. Ages 8 to 12. Code EDC, $6.95 each. **Dinosaurs** or **First Civilizations: From 10,000 B.C. to 1500 B.C.**

**Coloring Books About Prehistoric Times**. All books are 8½x11" with detailed drawings and basic informative text. Ages 8 and up. Code DV, $2.95 each. **Before the Dinosaurs, The Dinosaur Coloring Book, Prehistoric Mammals, The Days of the Dinosaur.**

**DINOSAUR STICKERS AND SEALS.** 8¼x11" book with full-color stickers. Code DV, $3.95.

**Dinosaur Sticker Books**. Acid-free, reusable sticker books, 9¼x11¼". Background scene with lots of full-color stickers. The book cover makes a backdrop for the 30 or more full-color, reusable stickers. Ages 7 and up. Code DV, $4.50 each. **Cretaceous Dinosaurs** or **Jurassic Dinosaurs**.

**ALL NEW DINOSAURS** coloring book. There is nothing new under the sun, but this book concentrates on recent discoveries. Ages 8 and up. Code BB, $3.95.

**EASY-TO-MAKE DINOSAUR PANORAMA**. All you need are scissors and glue. 9x12" book has a large background scene and seven dinosaurs. Ages 6 and up. Code DV, $3.50.

**2 DINOSAUR DIORAMAS** to cut and assemble. Not suitable for small fingers. About age 10 is right. Includes shadow box, background scene, and dinosaurs. You need glue and patience. Finished product is satisfying. Code DV, $9.95

**CUT AND MAKE A DINOSAUR SKELETON**. For patient 10-year-olds and up. Code DV, $2.95.

**MAKE THESE MODEL DINOSAURS**. You need just glue and scissors or a craft knife. Five different dinosaurs with baseboard and backdrop. (Photocopy the patterns onto heavy paper and make more!) Ages 9 and up. Code EDC, $9.95.

**Dinosaur Book, Bones, Egg, and Poster Kits!** What kid could resist? What big kid could resist? I couldn't. 14x16½" full-color poster, plus a scientifically correct "fossilized" plastic egg, with snap-together dinosaur bones inside, all ready to be assembled. The book is full of information as well as instructions for putting the dinosaur together. The book is by Dale Russell, a renowned paleontologist with the Canadian Museum of Nature. The poster and book are illustrated by Ely Kish, who is known for his historically accurate scenic reconstructions. Code AMBT, $12.95 each. Specify **Triceratops**, **Stegosaurus**, **Tyrannosaurus**, or **Brachiosaurus**.

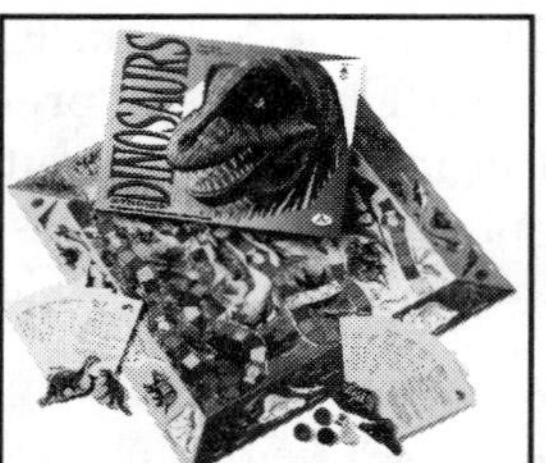


**DINOSAURS AND THINGS**. A board game to bring the prehistoric world and different geological ages to life. Learn life forms, and more, without noticing — because you're having fun! Game has several levels of play so it will grow with your family. 2 to 4 players, ages 4 and up, Code A, $25, plus $3 for shipping.

A note in the *Christian Science Monitor* (June 21, 1996) says, "French and Thai researchers announced they've discovered the granddaddy of all tyrannosaurs: *Siamotyrannus isanensis* is 20 million years older than the earliest known tyrannosaur and may prove the species evolved in Asia."

**NORTH AMERICA IN THE AGE OF DINOSAURS**. A National Geographic full-color map showing North America during the Mesozoic era. Pictures of dinosaurs, locations of fossil discoveries, and descriptions of the dinosaurs. Code MQ, $10.99.

## GEOLOGY
## WEATHER AND THE SEASONS

**DISCOVER THE SEASONS**, written and illustrated by Diane Iverson. This is a perfect introduction to the seasonal changes for young children. Much of the text is poetic yet informative, and pictures are detailed, giving space for lots of observation and discussion. Part of the text is written in large type for children to read if they are able, and part is for adults or older children to read. Some activities are deliberately designed to encourage parent and child interaction. Appropriate seasonal projects and recipes included. Resource list. Ages 4 to 10. Code DN, $9.95.

**SNOW WATCH**. Lots of interesting things to learn and special things to do with snow. A veritable delight for kids. Ages 8 to 11. Code KC, $7.95.

**THE WEATHER TRACKER'S KIT**. Contains everything needed to set up a weather station. Your meteorologist will get a full-color poster showing cloud formations, equipment for tracking wind direction and speed, a rain gauge, a thermometer, a wind-chill chart, and a handbook explaining how to use everything. Also notes about weather lore. Ages 10 and up. Code RP, $18.95.

**WEATHER AND CLIMATE**. What they are and how they differ. Well written and illustrated. Activities, experiments, and projects. Ages 10 to 16. Code EDC, $8.95.

**PLANET EARTH**. A good look at the physical makeup of this fascinating planet on which we live. Well illustrated. Activities, experiments, and projects. Ages 10 to 16. Code EDC, $8.95.

**STORMS AND HURRICANES**. More than just a look at the weather, this is an in-depth global look at this subject. Well illustrated with hands-on activities. Ages 11 to 16. Code EDC, $7.95.

**THE USBORNE ENCYCLOPEDIA OF PLANET EARTH**. A visually breathtaking, comprehensive introduction to all earth sciences, with maps, graphs, photos, a glossary, information about earth, scientists through the ages, useful online and postal addresses, and descriptive text. Great browsing, with pictures that will make you want to read. For instance, if you're reading about weather, you'll get all the better-known facts and then discover some amazing ones: Did you know that the heaviest hailstones on record fell in Bangladesh and weighed up to 2 lbs., 3 oz. (1 kg)? Or that the biggest snowflakes recorded — 38 cm/15 in. — fell in Montana? Or that the driest place in the world is Calama, Chile, where until 1971 there had been no rain for 400 years? Ages 9 and up. Code EDC, $21.95 and worth it.

**EARTHQUAKES AND VOLCANOES**. An in-depth look at the unpredictable actions of earthquakes and volcanoes around the world. This book covers growing areas of knowledge and study. Factual, with great color illustrations. Ages 11 to 16. Code EDC, $7.95.

**ROCKS AND FOSSILS**. Fully illustrated introduction to collecting, including basic skills for the beginner and information on choosing equipment. Lots of interesting background info and many helpful hints for enjoyment. Ages 10 and up. Code EDC, $6.95.

**ROCKS AND FOSSILS KIT** comes with the 32-page book listed above and eight rocks and minerals, mounted and labeled for quick and easy reference, plus a magnifying glass for field use. Ages 10 and up. Code EDC, $13.95.

**ROCKS AND MINERALS**. Pocket-size for easy reference. Facts, quizzes, and activities. 32 pages, 7x4½". Ages 7 and up. Code EDC, $2.95.

**SPOTTER'S GUIDE: ROCKS AND MINERALS**. Pocket guide, but with more detail and information than the book above. Full color. Ages 10 to adult. Code EDC, $5.95.

**ROCKS AND MINERALS STICKER BOOK**. More than 70 rocks and minerals described. Colorful stickers so that your child can easily tell a garnet from sandstone or limestone. Ages 7 and up. Code EDC, $7.95.

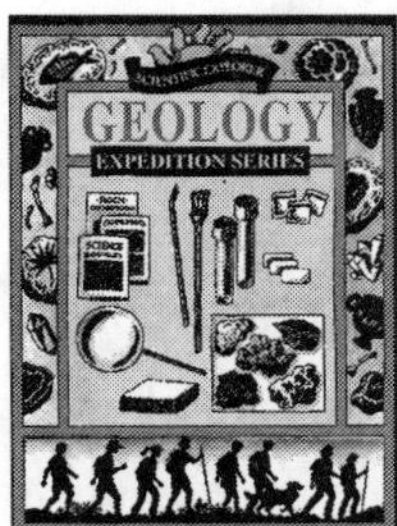

**GEOLOGY KIT**. This kit will provide hours of fun, information, and activities. Start your own rock collection, learn to perform streak tests, and try your hand at rock writing. You'll be able to identify many of your rocks with the ID charts, accompanied by a guidebook and experiment chart. Comes with a selection of interesting stones, tools for rock testing, a magnifier, and containers for collecting samples. Ages 6 and up. Code CS, $16.95.

**Ring-of-Fire**. Geology kits for curious kids. Great kits that come with everything needed, including a handheld microscope, rock or mineral samples, activities, and more. Kit #1, Igneous Rocks; #2, Sedimentary Rocks; #3, Metamorphic Rocks; #4, Minerals; #5, Rock and Mineral Identification. You can join their science club to get a monthly science kit. $24.95 plus shipping per kit. Five kits are available at this time; more will be ready soon. Send an SASE for more info. Ring-of-Fire, P.O. Box 489, Scio, OR 97274-0489.

**THE ROADSIDE GEOLOGY SERIES**. They say these books are designed to be read at 55 mph, but I don't recommend it. Based on well-traveled routes, these adult books with non-technical language, diagrams, and sketches will add interest to any trip. Unfortunately, there isn't one for each state. Code MPP. Available for the following states: Alaska, $16; Arizona, $18; Northern and Central California, $20; Colorado, $18; Hawaii, $20; Idaho, $18; Indiana, $18; Louisiana, $15; Maine, $18; Montana, $20; New Mexico, $16; New York, $20; Oregon, $16; South Dakota, $20; Texas, $20; Utah, $16; Vermont and New Hampshire, $12; Virginia, $12; Washington, $18; Wyoming, $18; Yellowstone Country, $12.

## OCEANS AND LIFE IN THE OCEANS

**UNDERSEA**. An introduction to a different world, yet one all Earth's inhabitants share. Clearly written, with dramatic illustrations and safe and simple projects and experiments (using household items). Ages 9 to 13. Code EDC, $6.95.

**SEA MAMMALS** coloring book. Children 6 and up will enjoy this. Short text about each mammal. Code BB, $4.95.

**THE INCREDIBLE CORAL REEF**, by Toni Albert. Tells you where to find coral reefs, what they are made of, who lives in them, and why they are a very fragile and special part of the ecosystem. Lots to learn. Lots to do. How to snorkel safely anywhere, list of environmental organizations, and other books on the subject. Many activities. Ages 10 to 14. Code TC, $10.95.

**DREAMS OF DOLPHINS DANCING** by Joan Bourque. Winner of the Best Children's Book award from the North American Bookdealers Exchange, this book is for everyone who loves dolphins, is concerned with the fate of our oceans, and is interested in the intricate global ecology. I've always loved dolphins, and I'm not sure if it was the sound of the title of this book or the illustrations that I fell in love with first. Because of the stories I've heard and reading I've done about dolphins, to my mind they are living legends. All dolphin lovers will want this book for their own. If you can't squeeze it out of your budget, borrow it from the library.

This is a beautifully illustrated book about a family trip to an ocean island, so thoughtfully written that it is about much more than just a trip. Between the covers, you will find reality and fantasy, ecology, a comparison of different lifestyles, and the strong message very quietly stated that one person can make a difference. Comes with an eight-page workbook. Ages 6 to 12. Hardcover. Code CB, $15.95.

**It gets better:** The publisher, Curtis Books, will send $1 from the purchase of each book to the environmental group of your choice. You will also receive an activity book with suggestions for discussions on the following topics: the environment, ecology, multicultural comparisons, the web of life and living things, recycling, conservation, and much more. Your child is invited to write to the author, and to think about and become involved in the future of our planet. Ages 7 to 12 will get the most out of the activity book, but younger children will certainly understand and appreciate the story.

**BIG BLUE OCEAN**, by Bill Nye (you know, the "Science Guy" on PBS). 12 experiments you can easily do at home, divided into four-page units. Each experiment is preceded by three illustrated pages of information. Topics cover salt in the ocean, the sense of smell in the ocean, sea jellies (invertebrates), what makes a fish a fish, currents, tides, and more. Ages 8 to 12. Hardcover. Code LB, $15.95.

**Coloring Books About the Oceans.** All books are $8\frac{1}{2}$x11" with detailed drawings and basic informative text. Ages 8 and up. Code DV, $2.95 each. **Coral Reef, Fishes of the North Atlantic, Seashore Life, Sharks, Shells of the World, Tropical Fish, Whales and Dolphins.**

**SEASHORE**. Illustrated pocket-size reference book. Facts, quizzes, and things to do. 32 pages, 7x$4\frac{1}{2}$". Ages 7 and up. Code EDC, $2.95.

**WHALES OF THE WORLD.** National Geographic map, 31x$22\frac{1}{2}$". Beautiful color painting. A description of each kind of whale is provided, along with both their common and scientific names. Code MQ, $10.99.

**ADOPT A WHALE**. When you adopt a humpback whale for a year you will get a quarterly newsletter called "The Whalewatch," a photo, and a biography of your whale. The fee is $18. For a teacher's curriculum kit on whales for grades K to 5, send $3. Ask for their Great Whale Order Catalog. Whale Adoption Project, 70 E. Falmouth Highway, East Falmouth, MA 02536; www.iwc.org/adopt/adopt.htm.

**A SWIM THROUGH THE SEA**, by 17-year-old Kristin Joy Pratt. An alphabetical look at many of the fascinating creatures that live in the sea, with information about how each lives. Well researched and illustrated by the author. Ages 6 to 12, but a good book for anyone beginning to explore sea creatures. Code DN, $7.95.

**Sea World**, Education Dept., 500 Sea World Dr., San Diego, CA 92109, offers a free catalog of books, posters, and videos. Items are reasonably priced.

## TREES
## GROWING THINGS AND GARDENING

**STARTING GARDENING KIT**. With this kit, all you need is a sunny window and an enthusiastic child. Comes with a variety of seeds — flowers and edibles — a small trowel, and a book that includes gift ideas. You will need to buy potting soil. Ages 5 and up. Code EDC, $10.95.

**GREEN THUMBS: A Kid's Activity Guide to Indoor and Outdoor Gardening**. Author Laurie Carlson created this activity book to encourage kids to acquire one of life's most satisfying skills. Whether your interest is flowers or vegetables, the well-written text, clear directions, and line drawings weave facts and fun together so kids can successfully create a garden indoors or outside. Ages 5 to 12. Code CRP, $12.95.

**GROW IT AGAIN**, by Elizabeth MacLeod. Don't throw it — grow it! Much more than a kids' gardening book. Learn how to grow a carrot top, apple seedling, or pea vine, and sprout avocado pits and garlic bulbs. Some fast and fun recipes and many ideas for creative activities related to gardening. You'll be surprised by the jokes and interesting sidebars. Ages 7 to 12. Code KC, $5.95.

**MY FAVORITE TREE: Terrific Trees of North America**, written and illustrated by Diane Iverson. If you're just curious about trees or are looking for information about a North American tree, Iverson's book will have the answers. Each two-page spread is devoted to one tree. There is a map showing where it grows; what trees it's related to; its habitat, height, bark, leaves, flowers, and seeds; wild companions; facts about how natives have used the tree; current uses; and what it's known for. The title is misleading. It's not about one particular favorite tree, but many favorite trees. Ages 8 to 12. Code DN, $9.95.

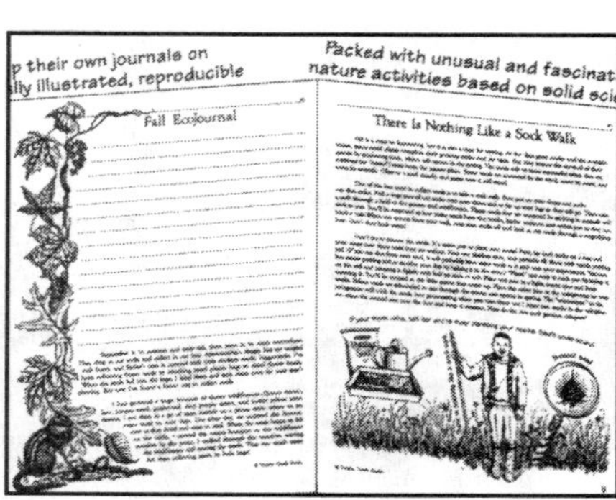

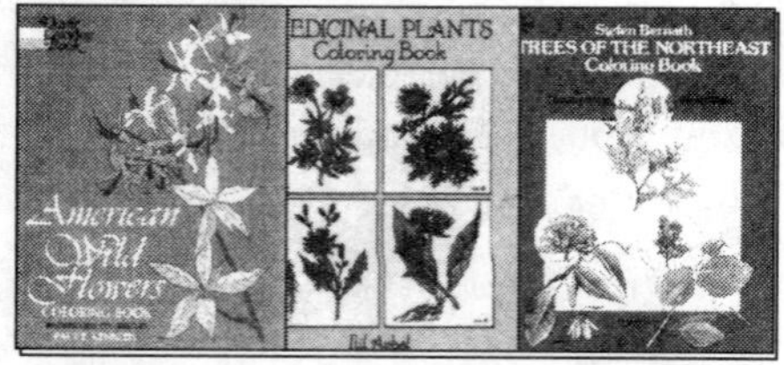


**Coloring Books About Plants**. All books are $8\frac{1}{2}$x11" with detailed drawings and basic informative text. Ages 8 and up. Code DV, $2.95 each. **American Wild Flowers, Medicinal Plants, Trees of the Northeast.**

**BEGINNERS' BOOK OF WILDFLOWERS.** This book has 32 full-color stickers: one for each page, with common and scientific names. Text gives info about habitat and size, and other remarks. Room for notes taken in the field. Code DV, $4.95.

**THE REMARKABLE RAINFOREST**, by Toni Albert. Where are the rainforests? What makes them special? Should we care about what happens to them? What one person — your child — can do to preserve them. An active learning book for ages 9 to 14. Full of interesting activities and information. Code TC, $10.95.

## SCIENCE IN YOUR BACK YARD AND BEYOND

**Ecojournals: With Nature Activities for Exploring the Seasons**. A year's worth of science, ecology, reading, writing, activities, and adventure. I take that back. Actually, this is a series to use and reuse over the years, since the faculties of observation, thought, and creativity change over time.

First you'll want **A KID'S ECOJOURNAL** (specify **Spring**, **Summer**, **Fall**, or **Winter**), by Toni Albert, beautifully and delightfully illustrated by Margaret Brandt. Each 56-page book is packed with a great variety of materials. The first couple of pages explain the basics for nature writing — making notes, observing to your best advantage — and suggest different ways to explore your special nature place. The remainder of the book is in two-page spreads. On the left-hand page Toni shares her writings and observations for a particular time of year, leaving space for your child's notes. The right-hand page has projects and information designed to increase understanding of various subjects. The hands-on activities are creative, inexpensive (or free), and fascinating.

Next you will want **ECOPRINTS**, a kit containing: 1) full-color seasonal prints by Margaret Brandt, with poems by well-known authors; 2) four beautifully illustrated (ready to color and/or photocopy) pages for your best writings of each season; 3) dozens of creative ideas for writing, tips from the author and artist, and a guide to nature writing; and 4) an excellent and extensive list of nature books for kids.

These materials are a great way to merge several subjects into an integrated, more lifelike paradigm. Ages 8 and up. Code TC, *EcoJournals* $9.95 each, *EcoPrints* $7.95.

**PLAY LIGHTLY ON THE EARTH: Nature Activities for Children 3 to 9**. See "Ecology."

**THE BACKYARD SCIENTIST**, by Jane Hoffman. Safe and easy science experiments children can perform around the house and yard, using common household materials, with step-by-step instructions; designed specifically for home-schoolers ages 4 to 12. Teaches critical thinking as well as scientific principles of chemistry and physics. Several books and kits in the series, all at reasonable prices. Send a #10 SASE for information. Backyard Scientist, P.O. Box 16966, Irvine, CA 92713.

**SANDBOX SCIENTIST** for ages 4 to 8. See "Early Learning."

**BACKYARD EXPLORER KIT**, by Rona Beame, has a great full-color, illustrated guide showing examples of all major leaf and needle shapes and matching them with the trees from which they come. Leaf collecting album included. Ages 5 to 10. Code WKM, $11.95.

**LIFE IN A BUCKET OF SOIL**, by Alvin Silverstein and Virginia Silverstein. This book has 96 pages packed with clear, accurate drawings filled with information about the abundance of life that can be dug up in most back yards. Fascinating facts about tunnel-building, methods of locomotion, feeding, defense, and more, along with suggestions for collecting specimens and how they can be preserved and studied. For grade school. Code DV, $4.95.

**YOUR BIG BACKYARD**. The National Wildlife Federation publishes this magazine full of eye-pleasing, kid-pleasing photos and illustrations with articles about our natural world. Crafts and activities along with notes for parents with suggestions for using the magazine with kids. Ages 3 to 6. Write for subscription information: P.O. Box 777, Mt. Morris, IL 61054; www.nwf.org/ybby.

**BACKYARD NATURE**. 8½x11" book with detailed drawings and basic information; well researched. Ages 8 and up. Code DV, $2.95.

## THE VARIETIES OF LIFE

**THE YOUNG NATURALIST**. A fully illustrated introduction for beginning naturalists. It teaches basic skills, offers guidelines for choosing equipment, and provides interesting background info and many helpful hints for enjoyment. Ages 10 and up. Code EDC, $6.95.

**YOUNG NATURALIST — A KID KIT**. Includes the above book; techniques of observation and how to collect specimens; paper for sun-prints; and a sturdy pocket tool that has a compass, magnifying glass, binoculars, and four other functions. Ages 10 and up. Code EDC, $18.95.

**THE URBAN NATURALIST**, by Steven D. Garber. Garber goes beyond rats, roaches, and pigeons to explore the inhabitants outside city and suburban doorsteps. He begins with a discussion of grasses, wildflowers, and trees, and moves up the food chain from insects to mammals. Practical tips on where to find things. 85 black-and-white illustrations. Ages 12 to adult. Code DV, $8.95.

**LIFETIMES**, by Michael Maydak. This book has a unique and special message. Maydak demonstrates that each life on this earth is different and has an important place within our ecosystem. Did you know that the life span of a mayfly is about one day? Do you know what it does with its day? How long does a whale live? An earthworm? A Venus flytrap? Bacteria? What does each do? Some of the values presented are cooperation among species, saving for the future, and the need to play.

Many books have teaching guides that seem unnecessary. The guide that comes with **LIFETIMES** is an extension of the main book, with activities, lesson plans (if you want to use them), things to think about, a list of more resources, and a thoughtful list of "skills for living" that is used by the Education for Life Foundation. Ages 8 to 10. Code DN, book $7.95, teaching guide $7.95.

**EVERYBODY'S SOMEBODY'S LUNCH**, by Cherie Mason. Finally! A sensible and sensitively written book about the food chain, and how everything fits into it with an intricate and perfect order. Many people, children in particular, think of animals as either good or bad, when in fact each animal does only what is natural. This is the story of a young girl shocked, saddened, and confused by the death of her cat. The girl gradually comes to understand the relationship between predator and prey, and finally makes her peace with natural law. Ages 8 to 12. Hardcover, with wonderful illustrations! The teacher's guide for this book is actually larger than the book it accompanies. A wonderful tool for teaching and learning about life cycles and the food chain, predators, and prey. Much to think about and many fun projects. Code TLB, book $16.95, teacher's guide $9.95.

**CREEPY CRAWLIES KIT**. This 32-page book has simple yet informative text and detailed illustrations about common invertebrates. Comes with 4-inch bug viewer that has a sliding magnifying glass. Ages 6 and up. Code EDC, $8.95.

**Minipets for the young naturalist!** The following books for curious kids explain how to find "minipets," make a nice home, and care for them. Nice illustrations and good information about life cycles, food, and habits. Ages 8 to 10. Code RSV, $5.95 each. **Caterpillars, Slugs and Snails, Spiders,** or **Worms.**

**CREEPY CRAWLY CATERPILLARS**, by Margery Facklam, with great color illustrations by Paul Facklam. Thirteen common caterpillars are illustrated, showing their life cycles from egg to cocoon and then to moth or butterfly, and their favorite foods so you'll know where to look for them. The four steps from crawling to flying are nicely explained. Ages 8 to 10. Code LB, $5.95.

**WHO'S AT HOME?** A game that takes players through eight habitats and helps them learn how animals survive. This can be played at two different skill levels. Highly recommended. 2 to 4 players, ages 8 and up. Code A, $25 plus $3 for shipping.

**ANIMAL BEHAVIOR** takes an in-depth look at animal behavior from a scientific point of view. Great illustrations; interesting and fascinating information. Ages 10 to 16. Code EDC, $8.95.

**CHICKADEE**. Very good nature magazine for preschool children. Send an SASE for a sample issue and subscription information. Young Naturalist Foundation, 59 Front St. E., Toronto, ON M5W 1B3.

**A PINKY IS A BABY MOUSE: And Other Baby Animal Names**, by Pam Muñoz Ryan, with beautiful watercolor illustrations by Diane deGroat. Kids are fascinated by baby animals, and this book introduces more than 100 of them with pictures and poetry. A real pleasure to read, with lots to discover and discuss in the pictures. Ages 6 to 10. Code HY, $5.99.

**THE NIGHT BOOK,** by Pamela Hickman. Staying up late is fun for kids. Add the activities, experiments, and information from this book and you'll create many nights to remember. Hickman explores the fascinating things that happen after dark. It begins with a good explanation of why it gets dark. Other topics explored include moon watching, how animals sleep, night prowlers, plants at night, how to make a star scope, basic constellations, why most plants grow at night, why cats' eyes glow, and more. Many of the activities suggested can be done during the day, but it will take the adventure out of some of them if you do them in daylight. Ages 7 to 11. Code KC, $6.95.

**ENDANGERED ANIMALS STICKER BOOK.** Acid-free, reusable sticker book, 8¼x11". The book cover makes a backdrop for the 30 or more full-color, reusable stickers. Ages 7 and up. Code DV, $3.95.

**Live Insect Kits**. Each of the following kits comes with all materials needed for a successful project. Included is a certificate to send in to receive your caterpillars (to grow painted lady butterflies), silkworm larvae, ladybugs, or worms. I like this convenient feature because you can buy your kit at any time of year, yet save it to use when it fits your plans. All code CS. Add $3 shipping each kit.

**LIVE BUTTERFLY BUNGALOW**. The fun begins when you color the cardboard butterfly habitat house with windows on both sides and on the top (crayons included). You'll receive a certificate for five caterpillars, feeding kit, fun-filled fact guide, and informational life-cycle fold-out to color. Ages 4 and up. $19.95.

**LIVE BUTTERFLY PAVILION**. This kit comes with a 3-foot-long cylindrical net butterfly house, certificate for 10 caterpillars, feeding kit, fun-filled fact guide, and full-color life-cycle poster. Ages 4 and up. $29.95.

**SPECIAL BUTTERFLY CURRICULUM**. Ready-made lessons to enhance your project. Code CS, $9.95 each. Specify grade level: K-2, 3-6, junior high, high school.

**LIVE SILKWORM CITY**. This comes with a complete silkworm habitat, certificate for three silkworms, special incubation tub, handling brush, and interesting fact guide. You'll be able to watch the transformation from larva to cocoon to moth. Ages 4 and up. $14.95.

**LIVE LADYBUG LODGE**. Unlike butterflies and silkworms, you can handle ladybugs, and there are suggestions for conducting gentle experiments with them. This kit comes with a brightly colored habitat box, certificate for 75 to 100 ladybugs (not available from March through May), activity and experiment book, magnifying lens, and feeding kit. Ages 4 and up. $14.95.

**LIVE WORM ACRES**. Watch and learn from nature's greatest recyclers! This kit comes with a composting bin, certificate for 250 live redworms, compost bedding and airflow filter, water sprayer, and experiment and study guide. Ages 6 and up. $29.95.

**THE MAGICAL INCREDIBLE BUTTERFLY**. From the National Audubon Society, this is a large calendar with 15 cut-out and punch-out butterflies and moths in true-life colors to hang on an easy-to-make mobile. The calendar is packed with information that's easy to assimilate, with puzzles, trivia, and games. Ages 8 to adult. Code WKM, $11.95.

**AFRICAN WILDLIFE DIORAMAS** to cut and assemble. Includes shadow box, background scene, and animals. Some tricky cutting and folding. Ages 10 and up. Code DV, $5.95.

**BEGINNING BIRDWATCHER'S BOOK**. Offers 48 pages with accurate, full-color stickers and all the information a new observer needs. Room provided for field notes. Code DV, $4.95.

**EVERYTHING YOU NEVER LEARNED ABOUT BIRDS: Lore and Legends, Science and Nature, Hands-on Projects**, by Rebecca Rupp, illustrated by Jeffrey C. Domm with full-color photos, drawings, and diagrams. Just because you never learned these interesting tidbits and facts about birds doesn't mean they aren't fascinating. Learn who flies the highest and the fastest, and what owls do in winter. (I doubt you'd ever guess the answer.) You'll learn about feeding habits and different types of beaks; how to build attractive, inexpensive birdfeeders (not with plastic milk jugs); why birds flock together; and a lot more interesting information. Good hands-on projects that kids and adults will enjoy doing. Ages 9 to 99 (it says that on the book — I didn't make it up). Code RH, $14.95.

**ORNITHOLOGY**. Not a casual guide, but an in-depth look at birds, their behavior, and their world. Ages 10 to 16. Code EDC, $7.95.

**BIRDS OF NORTH AMERICA KIT**. There are more complete guides available, but they frequently contain a lot more information than you need. This is well illustrated. Comes with a simple birdfeeder to put together (some kids may require help), natural paints, and sealing varnish. All you add is seed. Ages 8 and up, including adults. Code EDC, $15.95.

**Viewbird Observation Birdhouses**. Watch baby birds as they hatch in a variety of birdhouses with one see-through side that will easily attach to your window. Viewbird, 2858 31 Ave., P.O. Box 2351, Greeley, CO 80632, or Viewbird, Box 61110, Kensington Postal Outlet, Calgary, AB T2N 4S6; 900-730-4578; viewbird@rocketinc.com.

**WILDBIRD**. Monthly magazine about bird watching, field tips, equipment, and more. Also **BIRD TALK**, a magazine about pet birds. P.O. Box 52898, Boulder, CO 80322-2898; 800-542-1600.

**THE LANGUAGE AND MUSIC OF THE WOLVES**. Thrilling harmony and talking of wolves narrated by Robert Redford, on audiocassette, with notes. We used to live in the mountains of British Columbia's Central Interior, and often heard wolves howling to each other — an eerie, hair-lifting, but beautiful sound, very unlike the cacophony of coyotes or dogs. This tape is the next best thing, and you won't have to stand outside when it's 40 below zero. $9.95, but they ship UPS and you'll need to write for the exact shipping cost, or call 212-769-5150 and order with a credit card. American Museum of Natural History, Central Park West at 79th St., New York, NY 10024. (Our dogs have always been able to distinguish the sound of wolves from that of coyotes. They never liked the sound of wolves howling. They don't mind hearing coyotes.)

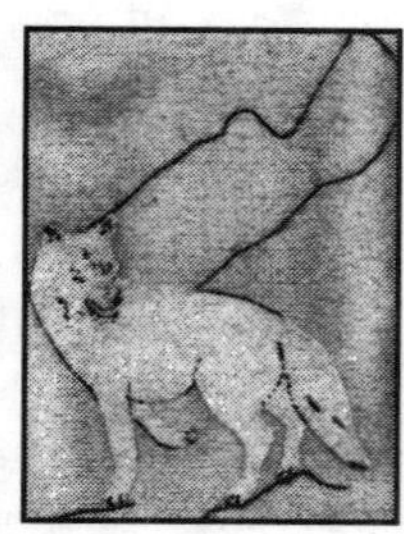

**TO THE TOP OF THE WORLD: Adventures With Arctic Wolves,** by Jim Brandenburg. Beautiful and enlightening photographs taken by the author during two months of living with an Arctic wolf pack, with comments about the wolves' nature and society. Ages 8 and up. Code WA, $7.95.

**WOLF SONG OF ALASKA.** Non-profit organization dedicated to awareness and protection of wolves. Adopt-a-Wolf program, newsletter, gift catalog. P.O. Box 110309, Anchorage, AK 99511-0309; www.wolfsongalaska.org.

**SPOTTER'S GUIDES**, for adults and children. Hundreds of fascinating facts and excellent pictures. Take them on a ride, trip, or walk and you'll learn something new every time. 64 pages, $5.95 each, two for $10.50, three for $15. If you want more than that, write for a deal! Code EDC. **Birds, Cats, Dogs, Horses and Ponies, Rocks and Minerals, Shells, The Night Sky, Weather, Trees, Wild Flowers**

**Spotter's Guide Sticker Books.** These sticker books have information about each subject, including varieties, breeds, and characteristics. Brightly colored stickers for each. Ages 7 and up. Code EDC, $7.95 each. **Cats, Dogs, Flowers, Horses and Ponies, Insects, Seashore.**

**Mysteries and Marvels**. Put a zoo on your bookshelf. Every one of these books brings a particular subject to life with color illustrations and enough detail to satisfy the curious. It will take a while to learn all that is in these books. Factual text, including some fascinating details not found in other books. Ages 8 to 12. Code EDC, $6.95 each. **Insect Life, Ocean Life, Plant Life, Reptile World**.

All four titles in one volume: **MYSTERIES AND MARVELS OF NATURE**. Code EDC, $26.95.

**RANGER RICK**. Published by the National Wildlife Federation, this magazine is filled with color pictures, articles, activities, and crafts related to our natural world. Derek read and reread each issue of this magazine. Ages 7 to 12. 8925 Leesburg Pike, Vienna, VA 22184; www.nwf.org/rrick.

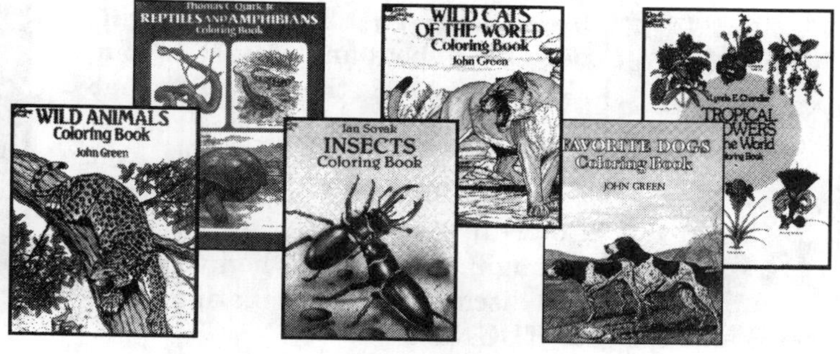


**Nature Coloring Books for Kids and Adults**. Very attractive, authentic, well-researched drawings with informative captions. Many of the books have the subjects in full color on the covers. Interesting reading and browsing, even when you're not in a coloring mood. *Specify coloring book when ordering*. Code DV, $2.95 each.

**AUDUBON'S BIRDS OF AMERICA**. 45 of Audubon's illustrations to color.

**BIRDS OF PREY**. 42 species from around the world: bald eagle, great horned owl, Andean condor, and more.

**BUTTERFLIES**

**FAVORITE DOGS**. 42 popular dogs: poodle, collie, dachshund, and more.

**FLORAL ALPHABET**. 26 attractive designs (one for each letter) contain flowers and plants beginning with the letter they decorate, from apples and artichokes to zucchini and zinnias.

**HORSES OF THE WORLD**. 42 accurate illustrations of horses in authentic settings around the world.

**INSECTS**

**MONKEYS AND APES**. 42 realistic pictures: chimpanzee, gibbon, orangutan, gorilla, lemur, mandrill, and many more.

**NOCTURNAL CREATURES**

**REPTILES AND AMPHIBIANS**. More than 70 alligators, snakes, lizards, frogs, etc. in 44 illustrations.

**SMALL ANIMALS OF NORTH AMERICA**. 45 accurate drawings of common and uncommon animals that share our continent.

**SNAKES OF THE WORLD**

**TROPICAL FLOWERS OF THE WORLD**. 45 exotic flowers.

**WILD ANIMALS.** 47 species: snow leopard, giraffe, tiger, rhinoceros, reindeer, gorilla, giant panda, and more.

**WILD CATS OF THE WORLD**. 41 drawings: lion, tiger, ocelot, Spanish lynx, and many more.

**LIVING WORLD ENCYCLOPEDIA**. This book has 128 pages of well-illustrated information about our living world, arranged thematically for easy use. Lots of in-depth explanations and practical experiments. Ages 8 to 12. Code EDC, $14.95.

## THE HUMAN BODY

**THE BODY BOOK**, by Sara Stein. DNA, chromosomes, and genes; how one sandwich can feed 40 trillion cells; tonsils, appendix, and the remnants of a tail; how the little bits of iron that color your blood red also flowed through the veins of dinosaurs; and hundreds of other facts, statistics, explanations, and fascinating illustrations that turn the science of the human body into a series of exciting discoveries. Ages 10 and up. Code WKM, $11.95.

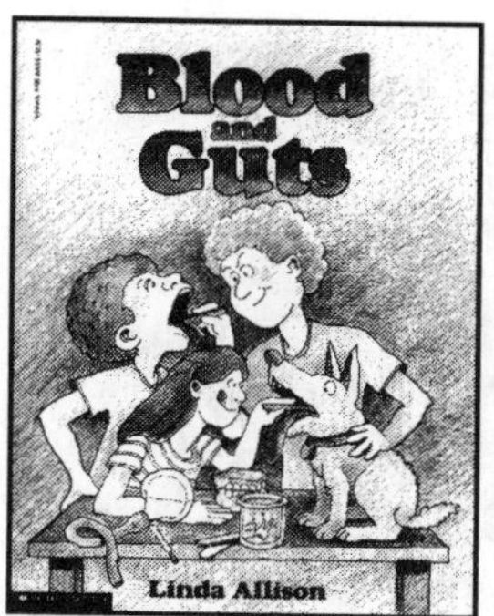


**BLOOD AND GUTS: A Working Guide to Your Own Insides**, by Linda Allison (A Brown Paper School Book). You are many things — miles of blood vessels, hundreds of muscles, many thousands of hairs. You are a furnace, filters, and a fancy computer with a huge memory bank. You are a finely tuned organism with more parts than there are people in New York. This book will help you explore the amazing territory inside the bag you call your skin. It will show you experiments to try, tests to take, and tools to make that will help you see and feel and hear what is going on inside. You'll amaze yourself. Ages 10 and up. Code LB, $13.95.

**HOW YOUR BODY WORKS**. Packed with lively illustrations, this book answers the highly original, sometimes amusing, and always insistent questions children ask about the human body. Ages 7 to 9. Code EDC, $8.95.

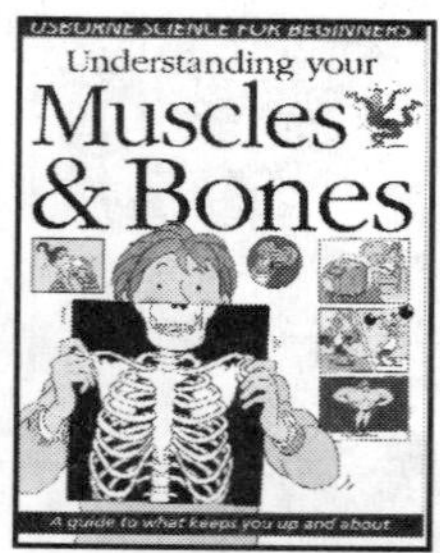


**MUSCLES AND BONES**. A beginner's book about anatomy. How your skeleton fits together, muscles that never stop working, how exercise improves your muscles, how you grow, and how broken bones mend. Colorful and just fun to look through; even better when you read and discuss all the fascinating facts. Ages 8 and up. Code EDC, $6.95.

**HUMAN ANATOMY FOR CHILDREN**. Organs, body areas, and major systems in straightforward, non-technical language, with several references and explanations of familiar, puzzling phenomena such as sneezing, curly hair, and more. Ages 8 to 10. Code DV, $3.95.

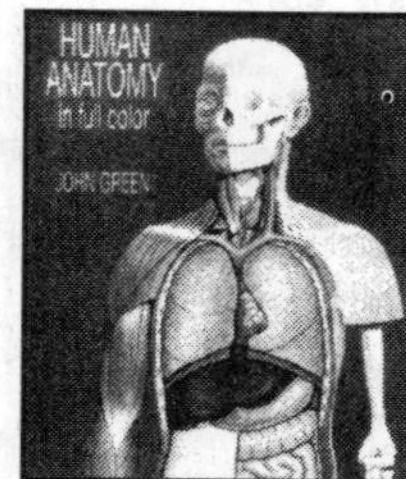


**HUMAN ANATOMY**, illustrated in full color by John Green with text written by Dr. John W. Harcup, Fellow of the Royal Society of Medicine. Detailed illustrations are absolutely accurate. Text was written to be easily understood by children, yet be thorough and precise for adults. Ages 10 to adult. Younger if you are willing to spend time explaining. Code DV, $5.95.

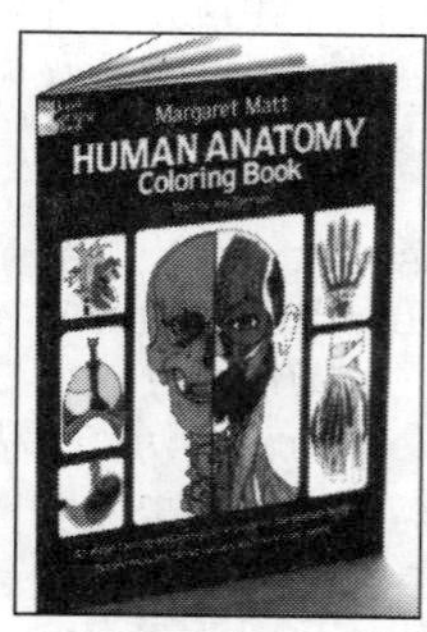


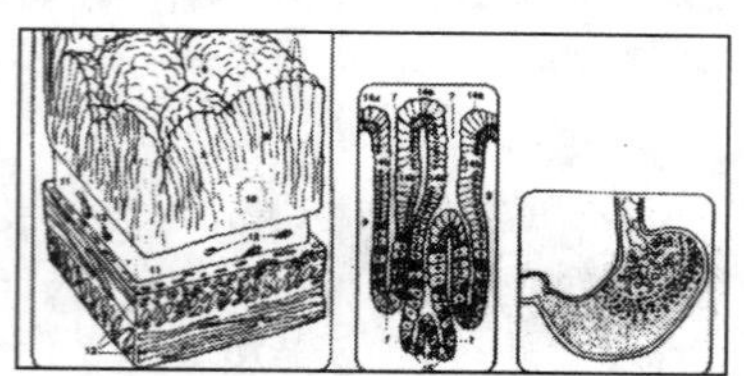

**HUMAN ANATOMY COLORING BOOK**, by Margaret Matt and Joe Ziemian. This book won't prepare you to take a medical exam tomorrow, but it's the best book we've found for beginners, teen to adult, and will give you a very comprehensive understanding of the basics of human anatomy. Forty-three scientifically accurate pictures of the body's organs and major systems, with numerous views, cross-sections, diagrams, clear explanatory text, and suggestions for coloring. Because the body's structures can't be understood independently of what they do, the functions as well as the shape and location of body parts and systems are described and explained, as well as their relationships to each other. You'll need a set of good pencil crayons with at least a dozen different colors. Jean began working in one of these books a few days ago, spending about an hour each evening reading and coloring, and she doesn't hear me when I speak to her. Code DV, $2.95.

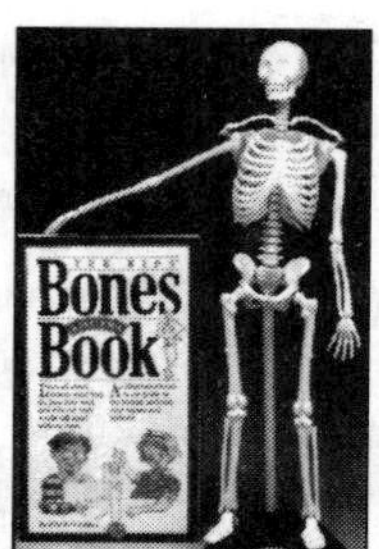


**THE BONES BOOK AND SKELETON**, by Stephen Cumbaa, illustrated by Kim La Fave. Shake those bones and become an anatomist! Then put them all together to get a good look at how your amazing bones form one of nature's most successful inventions — the skeleton. From maxilla and mandible to pelvis and patella, *The Bones Book* is a lively and informative head-to-toe account of how bones grow, fit, flex, and sometimes break. Learn how bones make blood, why people shrink during the day and grow again at night, and what the shape of bones may be in the future. *The Bones Book* also describes all the vital parts bones protect in the body, including the brain, digestive tract, and circulatory system. The accompanying plastic skeleton is the most accurate model available for children on the market today, sculpted by a professional prosthetist to the standards set by *Gray's Anatomy*. The skeleton's joints simulate the connections of real bones and move the way actual skeletons move. The 21-piece skeleton comes unassembled in a clear plastic cylinder, which may be used to display the assembled 11½" skeleton. Ages 7 to 14. Code WKM, $16.95.

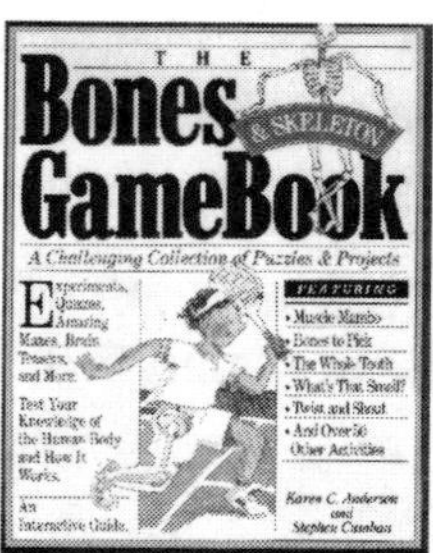


**THE BONES AND SKELETON GAMEBOOK**, by Stephen Cumbaa and Karen Anderson. A step beyond the fun and science of *The Bones Book* and skeleton, this workbook is a heavily illustrated, large-size collection of activities, quizzes, paper games, puzzles, and experiments to help kids (or adults) learn even more about the human body and how it works. Kids can solve mysteries of the body; make a working model of a lung with balloons, rubber bands, and a bottle; play "Meet Me at the Joint" to name the intersection of Humerus and Scapula streets; discover a trick to expand long-term memory; crack the Genetic Codes; and perform Aristotle's Illusion (suddenly, you have two noses!). Ages 8 to 14. Code WKM, $7.95.

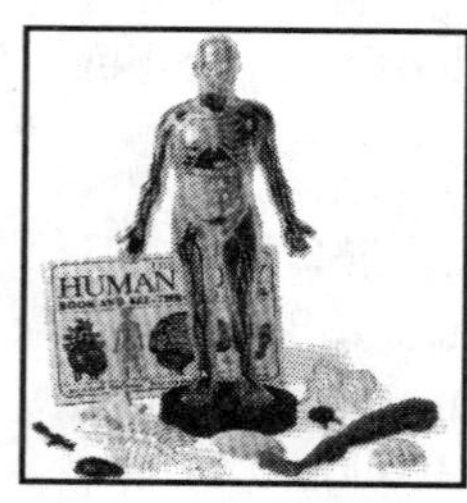


**THE HUMAN BODY BOOK AND MODEL**, by Luann Columbo. Much like the above listing, but a bit more and a bit less, depending on how you think about it. A bit less: You don't have to put all those bones together — they come as a set. A bit more: This see-through model includes all the other systems that make up the body. This 12" model is put together system by system, with a 64-page book to guide you. Code AMBT, $19.95.

**THE NEANDERTHAL BOOK AND SKELETON** by Stephen Cumbaa and Barbara Hehner, comes complete with a full-color book. Skeleton is 12" high assembled (25 pieces), and has a dome-covered stand for display. Fascinating comparison to the human skeleton. Ages 9 and up. Code WKM, $16.95.

**SOMEBODY: A Human Anatomy Game**. Actually five games in one package, with two different levels of play. Younger children will use Some Body as a puzzle activity; older ones can cooperate or compete in the games. All will learn to name body parts and their functions while they play. 2 to 4 players, ages 6 to 10 (more or less). Code A, $25 plus $3 shipping.

**CUT-AND-MAKE HUMAN SKELETON.** If you're not up to having a full-sized model around the house or the closet, try this one. Preteens, teens, and adults can put together this 16½" 3-D model that accurately represents the human skeletal structure. All parts are printed on heavy stock (some on both sides), in appropriate colors, and are easily assembled using scissors, glue, a hobby knife for a few small tricky pieces, and a needle and thread to connect some of the joints. Diagrams, introduction, and instructions include information about the skeleton and the medical terminology of its components. Can be mounted on a base and positioned in lifelike poses. Code DV, $4.95.

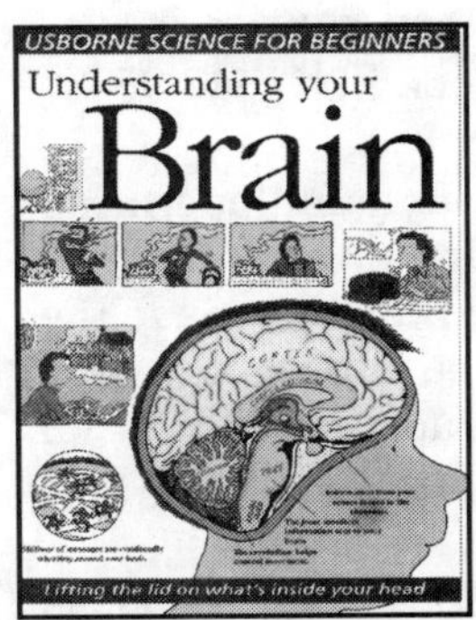

**UNDERSTANDING YOUR BRAIN**. This fascinating book is packed with information, good humor, great illustrations, and explanations. Were you born or bred to be the way you are? The many puzzles and questions (that do get answered) make this a very interactive book, providing plenty of food for thought and discussion. Ages 8 to adult. Code EDC, $6.95.

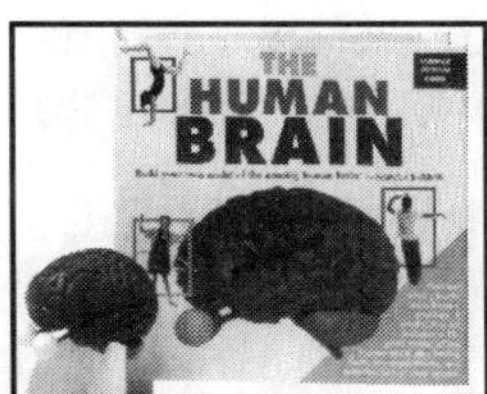

**THE HUMAN BRAIN.** Find out what's inside your head and how it works. Make your own model and mount it on the included display stand. No glue is necessary to put this 12-piece kit together. The 11x11" book gives an overview of different brain functions, brain surgery, the nervous system, sleep and dreaming, sensory perception, memory, and more. Comes with 3-D glasses to test your perceptions, plus experiments and activities to test your senses. Ages 8 and up. Code RP, $19.95.

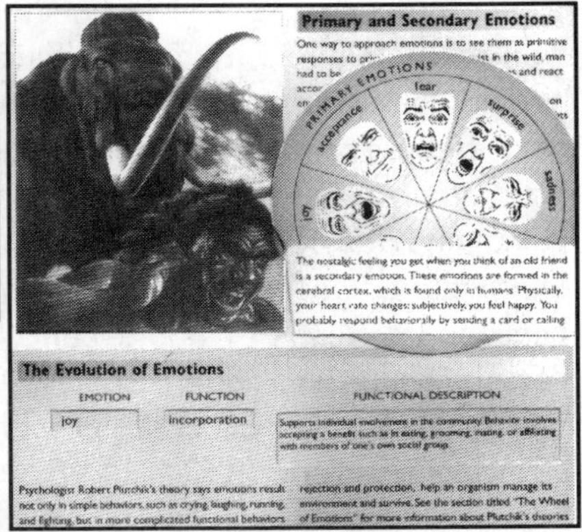

**THE BRAIN PACK,** created by Ron Van der Meer, text by Ad Dudink. The most incredible, fascinating interactive pop-up book I've ever seen — and the text is just as engaging and absorbing. Explore how we think, why we forget, how hypnosis works, and where emotions come from. You'll examine a 3-D model of your brain and see how and where information from the five senses is received and processed, trace the development of the brain from conception to infancy and through adolescence to adulthood, take a 15-minute recorded tour of the brain with the accompanying audiocassette, test your psychic abilities with the deck of psi cards, and much more. Filled with information, charts, diagrams, and interactive inserts to fascinate you. An investment, yes, but you'll spend hours with this book and come back to it again and again. Ages 14 to adult. Code RP, $40.

For a fascinating catalog of anatomy materials, write: Anatomical Chart Co., 8221 Kimball Ave., Skokie, IL 60076; 800-621-7500.

**BEFORE YOU WERE BORN**, by Jennifer Davis, is terrific for young children. See "Early Learning."

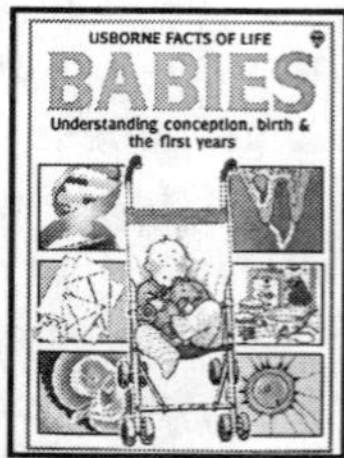

**BABIES: Understanding Conception, Birth, and the First Years** and **GROWING UP: Adolescence, Body Changes, and Sex**. These two excellent books use clear, accurate text with appropriate illustrations. Important aspects of the human body and reproduction are explained. Especially suitable for ages 10 or so and up. *Babies* traces the growth and development of a baby from conception to birth and during the first years of life. *Growing Up* describes the emotional and physical changes that occur during puberty, and includes sections on sexuality, contraception, and common problems of adolescence. Very well done and very informative. Code EDC, $7.95 each.

**FACTS OF LIFE**. A combination of ***Babies*** and ***Growing Up***. Code EDC, $14.95.

**40 WEEKS TO MOTHERHOOD**. A great poster to assist parents and kids who are learning about birth. I found it on the wall of my doctor's office and tracked it to a supplier in Canada. It's practically free. You pay only the cost of a fax to request this poster: 514-956-8775. You may get some propaganda about Similac, but the poster is worth it.

**NOW YOU SEE IT — NOW YOU DON'T: The Amazing World of Optical Illusions**, by Seymour Simon. I have no idea if this man's name influenced the writing of this book or his fascination with optical illusions. How can we see what isn't there? How can we see two distinctly different pictures in one drawing? Reading this book is like being shown how magic tricks are really done. The text is informative; you will learn how the eye sees and the mind interprets. The pictures include fascinating line drawings and some classic art. You'll learn how to create some of these illusions. This book could also have been called *The Art of Illusion*. Ages 8 and up. Code WKM, $5.95.

**RAINBOW GLASSES**. Cardboard spectacles with plastic lenses that change any light source — sunshine, electric light, a TV screen — into brilliant flashes of rainbow colors. Fun and fascinating for all ages. About $1 each. Write for catalog: Mr. Rainbow, P.O. Box 908, 3106 Shunpike Rd., Rio Grande, NJ 08242. Other great things at good prices, like Dinosaur Gliders.

**GOOD FOR ME! All About Food in 32 Bites**, by Marilyn Burns (a Brown Paper School Book). You have holes in your head. In one of them, you put plants and animal parts, you pour water and other liquids, and sometimes you chew on things too fierce to mention. We call that eating. If you have ever wondered why you eat things and what happens when you do, this is a book for you. You'll learn why you should drink that glass of milk, and why that triple-dipp-cream-filled-nutcrunch-winko might just gum up your works. You'll get acquainted with your pals, the vitamins and minerals. You'll learn what's good for you and why, and also what isn't; how the hot dog got its name; and about a man named Diamond Jim Brady, who some folks say ate himself to death. When you're through reading this book you'll be the food expert in your home. All that in 32 bites! (Out of print. Try your library or contact us. We have a few copies left. $12.)

(I may be wrong, but I doubt that homeschoolers have a strong need for a good book about teens, fad diets, dietary problems, and workouts, so I'm not including one. If you need one ask us about **THE RIGHT MOVES**, Code FS. For most of us, the following book has the necessary information about our food and digestive system.)

**FOOD, FITNESS, AND HEALTH.** Sensible, basic information in a readable format. Why we need to eat more than just hamburgers. Well illustrated, entertaining; experiments and puzzles included. Ages 11 and up. Code EDC, $12.95.

A secret Japanese radio station was found operating underground in Hollywood during World War II because of a report made by Lucille Ball. She made the report because whenever she walked close to the area involved, she picked up Japanese radio broadcasts on some temporary fillings in her teeth.

**GREAT DOCTORS** coloring book. See coloring books in "History and Biography."

## HOW IT WORKS AND WHY

*Revised — Better Than Ever —* **THE NEW WAY THINGS WORK**, by David Macaulay. From levers to lasers, cars to computers — a visual guide to the world of machines. Intricate, full-color illustrations and clear, explanatory text give a fascinating depiction of how machines do what they do, from the simplest lever to the space shuttle, including the building of the pyramids and many "simple" gadgets we use daily without thinking of them as machines, such as zippers. Difficult concepts are made easy, and common bits of technology we usually take for granted are shown to have greater significance. If this were no more than a textbook, to be skimmed or studied and then forgotten, I'd balk at the price; but it's a book that will draw readers of all ages back for frequent browsing, each time giving added knowledge and understanding of many key inventions that shape our lives. Children and adults — all ages. It will fascinate everyone. Absolutely worth the price. Code HM, $30. Now available on CD-ROM with a great kit for creating your own sail-powered land yacht, pneumatic earth mover, winch, hoist, and other materials to create 12 working models. Good instructions. All in a toolbox-shaped carrying case. Code DK, $39.95.

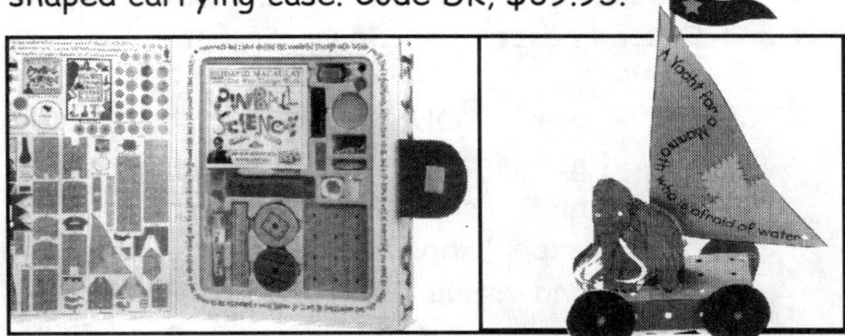


## DISCOVERY KITS

**INVENTOR'S WORKSHOP**. From the Boston Museum of Science. Create five incredible machines and learn the basic principles that make them work! When I opened the box, the contents looked like a collection of Donn's "possibly useful junk." I can't say I was disappointed, because Donn always used these odd bits and pieces to fix something, or make something useful; I just didn't expect it from the Boston Museum. Among the oddments are an electric motor, gears, and heavy-duty rubber bands. Your inventor can make a time-keeping machine, a music maker, a telescoping machine, and more. Comes with the Inventor's Handbook, which has clear instructions, explanations, and creative and critical thinking challenges. Who knows what your child will invent on his own! Ages 12 and up. Code RP, $18.95.

We always thought a "do it yourself" project was much better than buying something assembled and ready to use. With that in mind we supplied the kids with everything needed to make their own beds: 2x4's, boards, nails, hammer, and a tape measure.

**STEVEN CANEY'S INVENTION BOOK**. This book is bursting with ideas, illustrations, diagrams, and photographs; it's almost the ultimate book for the young inventor. The author covers everything from setting up a workshop and building the prototype to naming the creation, applying for a patent, and even marketing the final product — but it isn't as serious as it sounds. It's a great introduction to the world of inventing, and suggests how to get into an inventing frame of mind, with 20 projects (from fly catchers to back scratchers) to concoct from household items. Caney also tells the stories behind 35 landmark American inventions, and lists hundreds of invention possibilities. Ages 8 to 15 and up. 206 pages. Code WKM, $10.95.

**THINGS THAT FLY**. A kit containing everything needed to build and paint a model plane. Includes a book with clear, simple language that answers questions such as "How does a plane fly?" "How does a rocket work?" and "How does a helicopter hover?" Lots of good illustrations and cutaways. Ages 7 to 9. Code EDC, $14.95.

**KIDS' PAPER AIRPLANE BOOK**. Here's one for ages 5 and up. Includes 16 models, and there isn't a better way to introduce the basic ideas about aerodynamics. Code WKM, $12.95.

**PAPER PLANES KIT**. Comes with everything needed to make five colorful super flyers, from a small beginner's model to a 20-inch glider with a 15-inch wingspan. Insignia stickers and pilot's license included. Ages 8 and up. Code EDC, $9.95.

Much of what we call science is actually theory. On June 14, 1996, the *Christian Science Monitor* reported that "astronomers trying to calculate the age of the universe hit a snag: a galaxy that appears older than the cosmos. The find may force scientists to rethink the theory of how the universe was created."

## EXPLORING OUR SOLAR SYSTEM

**BUILD A TELESCOPE**. You'll make a telescope modeled after Galileo's 16th-century design, re-create the world's first thermometer, and investigate the motion of pendulums. Information and guidebook included. That's a lot for just one kit! Code CS, $24.95.

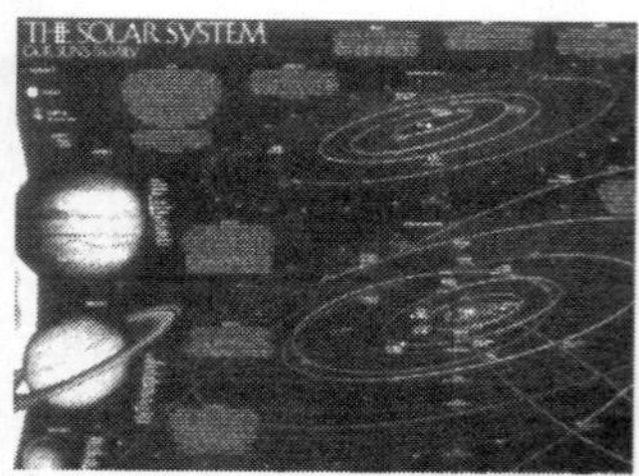

**MAP OF THE SOLAR SYSTEM**. This 24¼x18¼" map diagrams the positions and orbits of the planets, with illustrations of each planet and its moon(s) along with informative text. Comes in a tube. Code MQ, $14.99.

**EXPLORING THE SOLAR SYSTEM** or **HISTORY OF SPACE EXPLORATION**. Explore the solar system through these two 8½x11" coloring books, with pictures to color and facts galore. A great combination. Ages 8 and up. Code DV, $2.95 each.

**TAPES OF THE NIGHT SKY**. Great idea! Instead of shining your flashlight on your star map, then looking up at the sky and wondering what happened to your night vision, you listen to this audiocassette-guided tour of the heavens, which teaches you to locate and identify the major stars and constellations. The program includes two cassettes, which contain four half-hour tours (one for each season of the year), with clear instructions and brief pauses to give you time to get oriented; four star maps for additional reference; a suggested reading list; and an illustrated booklet. Code AF, $24.50.

**THE NIGHT SKY BOOK, An Everyday Guide to Every Night**, by Jamie Jobb (A Brown Paper School Book). This book invites you to learn the wonders of the night sky. You will get to know Pegasus, Andromeda, Hercules, and many other fascinating constellations. Stories from long ago will show you how people used the signposts in the sky to lead them through the darkest nights to home. Have you ever wanted to make a cross-staff or nadir-zenith finder? (Do you know what they are?) Do you know your longitude and latitude? Meteors, auroras, zodiacal light, and counterglow are just a few of the night sky events that will top any fireworks show. This book will keep you up all night! Ages 10 and up. Code LB, $12.95.

**Books About Space**. Four great books with great color photos and drawings. Lots of detail for the enthusiast. The space photos are terrific! Ages 7 to 10. Code CT, $5.95 each. **Cosmic Light Shows, The Moon, Satellites and Space Probes, The Space Shuttle.**

**THE YOUNG ASTRONOMER**. A good introduction to the fascinating night sky. Well illustrated with expert tips on choosing equipment and usage. Very practical for the beginner. Ages 10 and up. Code EDC, $6.95.

**FIRST ON THE MOON**, by Barbara Hehner. Part of the "I Was There" series of books, this is primarily written from the standpoint of Jan Aldrin, the young daughter of astronaut Buzz Aldrin. Lots of color photos that include every facet of the moon mission. As you read through the book, and Jan tells her story, you'll find numerous inserts with pictures of mission control, the spaceship, equipment, plus the moon and earth from space, with additional interesting bits of information. Sure to fascinate ages 8 to 14. Hardcover. Code LB, $16.99.

**ASTRONOMY**. Explains complex ideas with stunning pictures and illustrations. Fascinating facts and projects. Ages 12 to 18. Code EDC, $8.95.

**STARS AND PLANETS**. Pocket-size for easy reference. Facts, quizzes, and things to do. 32 pages, 7x4½". Ages 7 and up. Code EDC, $2.95.

**CUT AND MAKE SPACE SHUTTLES**. Eight full-color models to fly. Ages 12 and up. Code DV, $3.50.

**MOON EXPLORATION**. Acid-free, reusable sticker book, 9¼x11¼". The book cover makes a backdrop for the 30 or more full-color, reusable stickers. Ages 8 and up. Code DV, $3.50.

**Little Sticker Books**. 4x5" books with 18 full-color stickers each. Code DV, $1 each. **Solar System** or **Spacecraft**.

**SPOTTER'S GUIDE: THE NIGHT SKY**. Informative field guide with more than 100 illustrations. Ages 10 to adult. Code EDC, $5.95.

**Space Camp** for kids 7 to 11. An out-of-this-world experience! Locations in Alabama, California, and Florida. Call 800-63-SPACE for information. On the web at: www.spacecamp.com.

**NASA TEACHING MATERIALS**. Videotapes, slide programs, computer software, CD-ROMs, kits, and more from their free catalog for educators — and this includes homeschoolers. They will ship overseas. Very reasonable prices. NASA-CORE, Lorain County JVS, 15181 Route 58 South, Oberlin, OH 44074; core.nasa.gov.

**ODYSSEY**. Children's magazine that deals with basic concepts and principles of astronomy and other science topics. Write for ordering information: Cobblestone Publishing Company, 30 Grove St., Suite C, Peterborough, NH 03458-1454; 800-821-0115; www.cobblestonepub.com.

**Astronomy Book Club**, 3000 Cindel Dr., Delran, NJ 08075, offers a wide range of books about astronomy and related fields.

**Astronomical Society of the Pacific** offers a free newsletter on teaching astronomy for grades 3 to 12. Each issue contains articles about recent developments in clear non-technical language, practical classroom activities, and suggestions for other resources. Be sure to request this on *school stationery and identify the grade level you want.* If you don't have a computer, find a friend to manufacture your school stationery (or write to us). (Also see rubber stamps in "Homeschooling and Education.") Teachers' Newsletter, Dept. N, 390 Ashton Ave., San Francisco, CA 94112.

**Model Rockets**. Color catalog of rockets and related materials, with more than 100 flying models. Scale models of real rockets, space shuttle, gliders, and more. Send $1 to Estes Industries, Dept. 501, 1295 H St., Penrose, CO 81240.

**THE SPACE PRIMER** (satellites, rockets, shuttles, orbiting, life in space, and more) and **THE GLOBAL POSITIONING SYSTEM** (what it is, navigation, in satellites, ground control, and more). Both are free booklets available from The Aerospace Corporation, Dept. of Public Affairs, 2350 E. El Segundo Blvd., El Segundo, CA 90245-4691; www.aero.org.

**Books for the Future**. These books discuss current scientific applications and explore potential developments and problems that could have serious consequences for society and the environment. Good glossary of scientific terms and concepts. Great color photos and illustrations. Much to think about, discuss, and enjoy. Ages 8 to 12. Code CT, $8.95 each. **Alien Life Search, Artificial Intelligence, Cloning, Cyberspace.**

**Telescopes and More.** Catalog with a large selection of telescopes and other astronomy materials. Orion Telescope Center, P.O. Box 1158, Santa Cruz, CA 95061; www.telescope.com.

**Space Stuff**. Meteorites, books, jewelry, and other educational items. Send $2 for a catalog: Bethany Sciences, LLC, P.O. Box 3726-HSSB, Amity Station, New Haven, CT 06525-0726.

## ENERGY AND PHYSICS

**ENERGY AND POWER**. A good look at what we have and can have in the future — our children's future. It should be obvious to us all that in our children's lifetimes we will have to use less power, find ecological alternatives, or both. Our current system is abusive to the earth's ecology. The winds of change are blowing even when we can't see them. Activities, experiments, and projects. Ages 10 to 16. Code EDC, $8.95.

**ELECTRICITY**. Written with the help of experts, this informative book has safe and simple projects and experiments (using household items) to help young people understand electricity. In the not-too-distant future, society will have to find new and better ways to provide for the increased demand for power. A good understanding of the subject will help our future scientists in their quest for alternatives. Ages 9 to 13. Code EDC, $6.95.

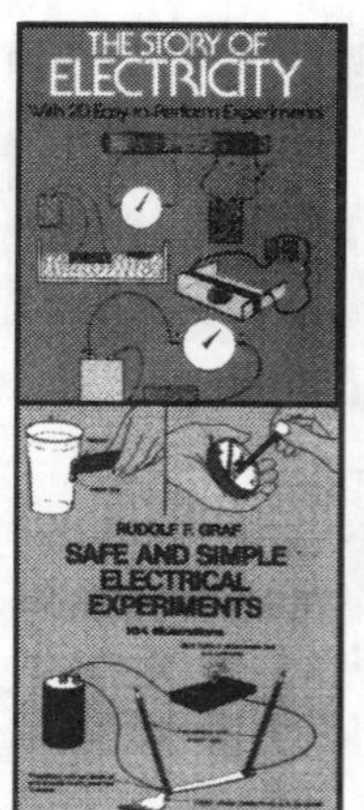


**THE STORY OF ELECTRICITY**, by George deLucenay Leon. The chronicle of significant discoveries in electricity and magnetism over 2,500 years, and instructions for repeating 20 famous experiments. Ages 10 and up. Code DV, $4.95.

**SAFE AND SIMPLE ELECTRICAL EXPERIMENTS**. 101 entertaining projects and experiments that teach basic principles of electricity. Ages 6 and up, including adults. Code DV, $6.95.

> **Side effects:** "[A] power plant in Toledo, Ohio, shut down after a swarm of bugs began conducting electricity from one component to another, causing transformers to shut down." "Efforts to clean Lake Erie have increased the mayfly population, experts say." — From the *Christian Science Monitor*

**ELECTRICITY AND MAGNETISM**. This book goes beyond the very basics with its great explanations, illustrations, experiments, and projects. Ages 12 to 18. Code EDC, $7.95.

**SCIENCE WITH MAGNETS KIT**. A book, three magnets, a compass, coated wire, corks, clay, and paper clips will produce hours of fun and fooling around. The book explains the experiments with easy-to-follow directions. When was the last time you fooled around with a couple of magnets? Ages 6 and up. Code EDC, $14.95.

**BATTERIES AND MAGNETS KIT**. Use the motor, propeller, battery holder, and wooden dowel to make a whizzing plane that really flies. The book explains how to have hours of fun using the pipe cleaners, magnets, paint brush, and your imagination. Ages 8 to 12. Code EDC, $19.95.

**THE WIND AT WORK: An Activity Guide to Windmills**, by Gretchen Woelfle. Includes an interesting history of design and function, and how windmills have evolved. More than 12 wind-related projects. Photos, line drawings, and charts. Ages 8 to 13. Code CRP, $14.95.

**PHYSICS EXPERIMENTS FOR CHILDREN**. 103 projects demonstrate the composition of objects; how substances are affected by various forms of energy, such as heat, light, sound, and electricity; and more. Ages 12 to 16. Code DV, $3.50.

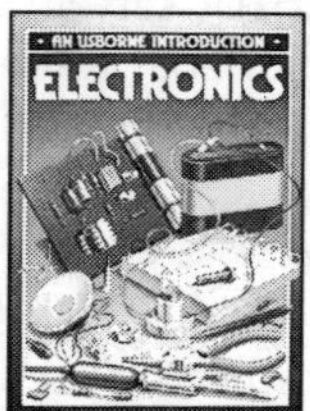


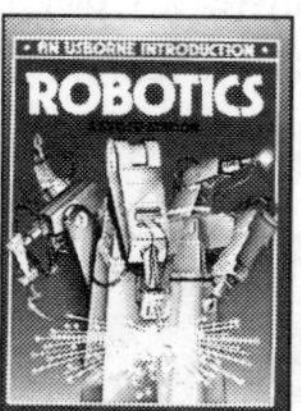


**Introductions to Science**. Ages 11 and up. Code EDC, $7.95 each.

**ELECTRONICS**. An excellent introduction to a fascinating and fast-growing field of study. Well illustrated with clear drawings and diagrams of how things work, explaining much of the sometimes confusing jargon. Includes experiments, puzzles, and games that help you use and enjoy what's been learned.

**LASERS**. For some of us, lasers were the stuff of science fiction. Now they're becoming an increasingly useful element in our lives. This fascinating field will become even more important in the future. You can explore laser technology with your kids, using the games and puzzles that come with the well-written text and clear illustrations.

**ROBOTICS**. You already have robots in your home. Find out what they are and how they work. Explore the possibilities for the future. Experiments, puzzles, and games.

**SCIENCE WITH AIR KIT**. Comes with everything needed (except a few common household items) to perform more than 30 experiments. Race a rocket balloon, construct a model winch, make a glider fly in various ways, and more. Comes with a tornado tube for making a bottle-contained twister. Good illustrations and instructions. Ages 6 to 9. Code EDC, $15.95.

**SOUND SCIENCE**. Etta Kaner's activity book is full of easy-to-do experiments about sound. More than 40 fun-filled experiments, and Kaner gives us some challenging questions to ponder. The directions are clear, and the illustrations are fun to look at. Ages 8 to 12. Code KC, $6.95.

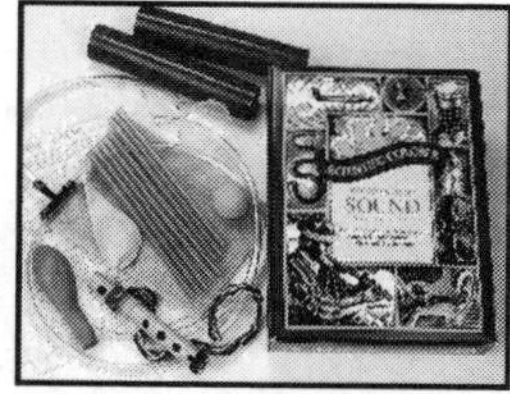

**THE SCIENCE OF SOUND KIT**. Design a model ear, build your own stethoscope, extinguish a candle with sound, and explore the connection between music and math. Your child will also have hours of fun playing your new flute, a replica of an ancient instrument. Activity and information book included. Ages 7 and up. Code CS, $24.95.

**CODE CRASH**. Learn Morse code in 25 minutes! Jerry Mintz (publisher of *The Education Revolution*; see "Homeschooling and Education") has developed this technique, demonstrated on a videotape of two 12-year-olds learning the method in less than 20 minutes. A letter to Mintz said, "My daughter learned the entire alphabet and all the numbers in a single sitting, then started sending me code faster than I could take it down." $20 plus $3 for shipping from Jerry Mintz, 417 Roslyn Rd., Roslyn Heights, NY 11577; 800-769-4171 to order with a credit card; www.edrev.org/catalog.htm.

**THE PHONE BOOK: Instant Communication From Smoke Signals to Satellites and Beyond**, by Elizabeth Macleod. The title conveys all except the lively illustrations. This book is designed to engage the reader. Learn why most area codes used to have a 1 or 0 in the middle, play a tune on your touch-tone phone, and find out why coming generations may be issued a PCN at birth. (If you don't know what a PCN is, you'd better read this book!) Ages 8 to 12. Code KC, $6.95.

**Essential Guides**. Pocket-size (but don't let that fool you; these books are packed with information) books with all major key facts, diagrams, charts, and illustrations. Good summary information; concise study guides. Ages 12 to 16. Code EDC, $7.95 each. **Essential Biology, Essential Chemistry, Essential Physics. Essential Science** (all three combined). Code EDC, $15.95.

## BIOLOGY

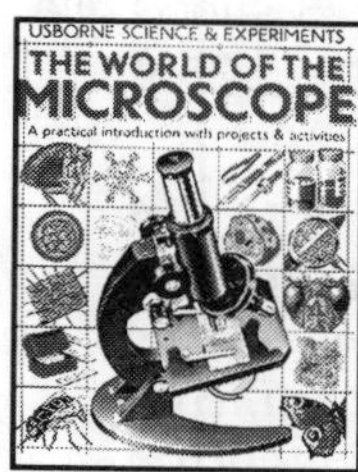


**WORLD OF THE MICROSCOPE**. Filled with facts about a part of our world we depend on and live with but don't see in our daily lives, this resource encourages readers to make their own observations and perform simple but effective experiments that will reinforce what they've read. Very clear text, with detailed and colorful illustrations. An excellent introduction to the microscope for all ages. Ages 10 to 16. 48 pages. Code EDC, $8.95.

**USBORNE COMPLETE BOOK OF THE MICROSCOPE** is the next step up from the above book. There are fewer hands-on activities, but more information and fantastic full-color detailed illustrations. Ages 10 and up. 96 pages. Code EDC, $14.95.

**BIOLOGY EXPERIMENTS FOR CHILDREN**. 77 experiments that include growing protozoa and bacteria, building a terrarium, growing seeds in a sponge, studying spider web formation, and much more. More than 100 illustrations. Ages 10 to 14. Code DV, $3.95.

**A WORLD IN A DROP OF WATER**, by Alvin and Virginia Silverstein. A fascinating 64-page adventure featuring one-celled creatures found in pond water. Perfect to go with a microscope project. Introduction to the life cycles of amoebas, paramecia, suctoria, and euglena. Ages 8 and up. Code DV, $3.95.

**FRESHWATER POND**. An information-packed coloring book with 43 accurately detailed drawings of a beaver pond, farm pond, mountain pond, and more. Denizens of these habitats are identified with common and scientific names, including information about flora and fauna. Ages 10 and up. Code DV, $2.95.

**POCKET MICROSCOPE**. This versatile 100X illuminated microscope with 8X magnifier will give you plenty of detail because the built-in light concentrates its strength on the object you are viewing. You can easily take this into the field with you, and it comes with a handy plastic base allowing you to view objects mounted on slides. 6 slides are included with a good user's guide. Code CS, $25.95.

---

*May the universe in some strange sense be "brought into being" by the participation of those who participate? ... The vital act is the act of participation. "Participator" is the incontrovertible new concept given by quantum mechanics. It strikes down the term "observer" of classical theory, the man who stands safely behind the thick glass wall and watches what goes on without taking part. It can't be done.*

— John Wheeler

---

## REAL HANDS-ON SCIENCE

**Design-a-Project**. The following kits will add depth to your science discovery activities, help you explore meaningful scientific facts, and relate them to health and environmental issues. Each kit comes with complete, easy-to-follow directions. Ages 8 and up. Code CS, $14.95 each, plus $3 shipping.

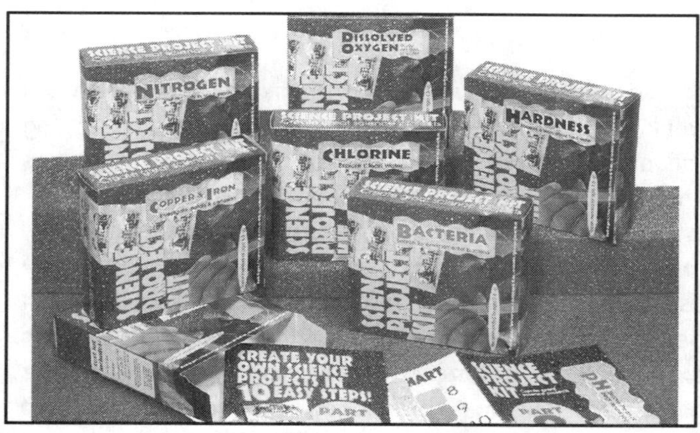


**CHLORINE — EXPLORE CLEAN WATER**. Discover how water is treated to make it cleaner for drinking and swimming. Measure for safe levels of sanitizers in swimming pools and other water samples.

**COPPER/IRON — INVESTIGATE METALS AND CORROSION**. Find out why corrosion causes damage to water systems and metal surfaces. Demonstrate corrosion and measure the amount of copper and iron in water samples. Includes 10 tests each for copper and iron.

**MEASURE AND LEARN ABOUT HARD WATER**. Find out the effects of water hardness and make tests to determine hardness in your samples. Investigate the causes of soap scum and its effect on water systems.

**NITROGEN — DISCOVERING SOIL AND PLANT NUTRIENTS**. Learn about plant nutrition, fertilizer, and water pollution. You'll design a soil test for nitrogen and demonstrate the effects of water pollution.

**THE pH OF THINGS AROUND YOU** lets you investigate acid rain, corrosion, acids, and bases. You'll create experiments to test household items.

**SEARCH FOR ENVIRONMENTAL BACTERIA**. Explore how water is tested to ensure that it's safe for drinking and swimming. Includes supplies for three water tests for coliform bacteria.

**STUDY OXYGEN IN WATER**. Discover why dissolved oxygen is important to a healthy aquatic environment. Perform dissolved oxygen tests on water samples and measure the effects of pollution.

## CHEMISTRY

**CUP AND SAUCER CHEMISTRY**. 38 safe experiments using common household items such as aspirin, paper towels, and vinegar. Easy instructions, illustrated. Ages 7 and up. Code DV, $4.95.

**CHEMISTRY EXPERIMENTS FOR CHILDREN**. Safe experiments with common materials. Well illustrated, interesting, and fun. Ages 10 to 14. Code DV, $3.95.

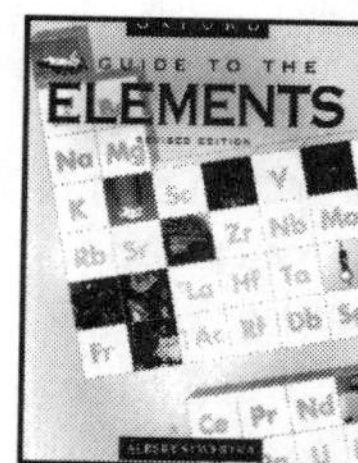


**GUIDE TO THE ELEMENTS**, by Albert Stwertka. An excellent Oxford University Press handbook for high school students. Begins with a short overview of the elements, the atom, and isotopes, then gives a history of the periodic table to modern times. The remainder of the book goes on to explain each element in order, with information about its discovery, atomic number, chemical symbol, and group, followed by detailed current data on where it's found, its uses, and much more. Illustrated. Code OX, $17.95.

**IT'S A GAS!**, by Margaret and Ruth Griffin. Explore a variety of gases in our bodies, homes, air, and outer space, and test principles of gases by baking pita bread, freezing water, and building a greenhouse. Ages 8 to 12. Code KC, $9.95.

**FRIENDLY CHEMISTRY: Upper-level science**, created by Lisa and Joey Hajda. I love it! Hands-on and easy to use, with clear explanations in language you and your kids will easily understand. After perusing several dull chemistry books and a computer program that almost crashed my computer, I was genuinely relieved to find this course. Friendly Chemistry is designed to provide all that's needed for high school studies and college entrance, and you'll have fun learning it all. Included are brief biographies of important scientists and many games, some with multiple playing levels to challenge you as you learn. This course is all you will need, but you could supplement the experiments with some of the inexpensive code DV chemistry books if you want more to do. $95 plus $5 shipping, with a 60-day money-back guarantee and free telephone or e-mail support. If you're feeling a bit insecure, the Hajdas have put together a guidebook for parents and group leaders. It includes more lab activities, group games and activities, and 32 pages of supplemental practice problems as well as a week-by-week presentation plan. There's also a week-by-week planner on a two-hour videotape. Guide and videotape $45 plus $4 shipping. If you buy Friendly Chemistry, the guidebook, and the video at the same time, the total is $130, shipping included.

For those of you lucky enough to have active support groups, I suggest you work with Friendly Chemistry as a group project. Your teens will enjoy the interactive learning.

**ATOMS AND MOLECULES**. Clear explanations and good illustrations of this increasingly complex field. Interesting reading. 32 pages. Ages 12 to 18. Code EDC, $7.95.

## TIME

**THIS BOOK IS ABOUT TIME**, by Marilyn Burns (a Brown Paper School Book). Time to read, time to think, time to do, time to wonder about time and you. When did people start measuring time? Why did they do it at all? What did they use to measure time? What does time have to with flowers, birds, bees, and the fiddler crab? Besides telling you the whole story, this book's activities will help you perk up your time sense, make a timepiece or two, understand time zones, and look at your own biological clock. When you learn about time, you learn about history, biology, biorhythms, and more — the Mayas, the ancient Egyptians, jet lag, and the Roman calendar. And you'll have the time of your life. Code LB, $13.95.

Every school-room needs an "old-fashioned" face clock! With a face clock, it's easy to convey the divisions of the day into hours, hours into minutes, and minutes into seconds. If you must have a digital clock or watch, show how the numbers relate to the positions of the hands on a face clock. A digital clock may tell what time it is, but it won't give any *sense* of time.

You might want two face clocks — one to learn about time and the other for hands-on fun. If it lands on the floor and breaks, it will provide another type of investigation! The internal works are fascinating.

"Mommy, where does lightning come from? Mommy, why do stars twinkle? Mommy, what are hiccups?" "Hey Daddy, why are bubbles round? Daddy, why are you yawning, and why does it make me yawn too?" "Mommy, why is the sky blue?" "Mommy!"

"Daddy!!" Sound familiar? **HOW COME?**, by Kathy Wollard, is for every kid who wants to know — and for every parent who almost knows, but isn't sure how to explain it all. More than 100 frequently asked questions *with the answers*. Ages 5 to 14. Code WKM, $12.95.

## AND A LOT MORE! KITS, HANDS-ON LEARNING, AND EXPERIMENTS

**GEE, WIZ! How to Mix Art and Science, or the Art of Thinking Scientifically**, by Linda Allison and David Katz (a Brown Paper School Book). This book is about science. It's also about art. Inside you'll find the Wizard (also known as Professor Bumble) and the Lizard (who is the Wizard's reptilian sidekick). You'll learn that science is more than test tubes, lab coats, and microscopes. Science is a way of thinking about the world. It's a way of finding out what you don't know by figuring out what you do know. This book will show you that scientists and artists share one very important trait — imagination. The absentminded scientist Wiz and his efficient, curious assistant, Art, will lead you to new answers to some old questions. One of the best things about science is that you don't need experts or books or magical hocus-pocus to get answers. All you need is a question and enough curiosity to find an answer. Code LB, $12.95. This is in short supply and about to go out of print. Don't procrastinate if you want your own copy.

**SCIENCE ARTS**, by MaryAnn Kohl and Jean Potter. Year-round projects that investigate and create at the same time. Crystal bubbles, dancing rabbits, stencil leaves, bottle optics, and a nature window are just a few of the many wonderful projects you'll find in this book. Picture icons at the top of the page indicate the best time of year, preparation time needed, appropriate age level, type of activity, and whether or not adult help is necessary. Clear instructions and facts about the science involved are provided. Ages 3 to 10 (a very versatile book). Code GH, $15.95.

**SCIENCE EXPERIMENTS**. More than 100 in one book! Chemistry, biology, and physics will come to life through practical, hands-on means, demonstrating the basic principles involved. Ages 9 and up. Code EDC, $9.95.

**SCIENCE EXPERIMENTS — KID KIT**. This kit includes the previous book and materials to perform some of the experiments. Any needed materials not included in the kit are common household items. You'll build an alarm with a buzzer, learn about air pressure using straws and an empty thread spool, create a signal light (light bulbs included), and have fun. Good, clear directions and illustrations. Ages 9 and up. Code EDC, $19.95.

**HANDS-ON SCIENCE**, by Dorothea Allen. I especially like this book and the activities described, and I like Allen's approach: She encourages kids to do the experiments, making their own observations and coming up with their own conclusions, with the parent or teacher acting only as a facilitator. Contains 112 mostly easy high-interest activities for grades 4 to 8. You may need to improvise some materials and buy other inexpensive items. The book is well organized with activities outlined according to the motivation (why each experiment is important or interesting), grade level, list of materials needed, and procedure. Illustrations are clear. Personally, I find that the explanations of the experiments require more scientific knowledge than I have, so I'd plan ahead so I'd have time to look up and understand some of the terms used (as there is no glossary). Code SS, $29.95.

**BIG BOOK OF EXPERIMENTS**. For slightly younger children. Organized thematically, this book has sections on chemical reactions, nature projects, and testing your own senses. Clear, concise instructions make each project easy to follow, providing satisfying — and sometimes surprising — results. Have fun while you learn! Some everyday household items and a few inexpensive purchases are required. Ages 8 to 13 (some use of matches and cooking involved). Code EDC, $14.95.

**SOAP SCIENCE**, by J.L. Bell. A book bubbling over with 36 experiments. Experiment with soap and light waves, surface tension, static electricity, and bouncing bubbles. (Honest! It really says bouncing bubbles.) Ages 8 to 12. Code KC, $6.95.

**47 EASY-TO-DO CLASSIC SCIENCE EXPERIMENTS**. These experiments using common household materials teach the principles of light, elasticity, perspective, gravity, air pressure, optics, and more. Ages 10 and up. Code DV, $3.95.

**SCIENCE EXPERIMENTS AND AMUSEMENTS FOR CHILDREN**. 73 safe and easy experiments that illustrate basic phenomena and simple chemical reactions, requiring only household materials such as candles, coins, and steel wool. Ages 8 to 12. Code DV, $3.95.

**ENTERTAINING SCIENCE EXPERIMENTS WITH EVERYDAY OBJECTS**, by Martin Gardner. 100 amusing tricks and experiments to delight you and your children while teaching the elements of astronomy, chemistry, mathematics, mechanics, geometry, and more. Ages 8 and up. Code DV, $3.50.

**SCIENCE RESEARCH EXPERIMENTS FOR YOUNG PEOPLE**, by George Barr. Illustrated collection of 40 experiments in electricity and magnetism, transportation, sound and light, the human body, weather, water, distance, insects, plants, time, and "Science in Your Home." Ages 10 and up. Code DV, $4.95.

**MORE MUDPIES TO MAGNETS**, by Elizabeth Sherwood, Robert Williams, and Robert Rockwell. This sequel to *Mudpies to Magnets* (see "Early Learning") is designed for ages 6 to 9, with 112 active projects that help children learn to classify, measure, and think about space, relationships, and communication. Chapters include "Chemistry Beginnings — Colors, Crystals, and Creations"; "First Physics — How Things Work"; "Earth Explorations — Digging in the Dirt"; "Weather Watchers — How Hot, How Cold, How Windy, How Wet"; "Flight and Space"; "Roots and Shoots"; and many more. Teaching tips included. You will need to purchase some inexpensive, easily found materials you won't have in the house. Some projects definitely need adult guidance. Code GH, $14.95.

**Experiment Books**. The following books all have a good variety of projects that require little beyond what you already have around the house (and a bit of work). The last two titles have more extensive experiments. Ages 9 to 14. Code DV. **Fascinating Science Experiments for Young People**, $3.95; **Fun with Science**, $4.95; **Science Tricks and Magic for Young People**, $4.95; **Sports Science**, $4.95; **Outdoor Science Projects for Young People**, $4.95; **Science Projects for Young People**, $4.95.

*New Edition* — **SCIENCE IS ...**, by Susan Bosak, working with the Youth Science Foundation of Canada. Here, in one book, are enough exciting and informative activities to help your child (and you) learn the basics in nearly all areas of earth science, under headings such as "Science Olympics," "Matter and Energy," "Humans," "Environmental Awareness," "Rocks," "Plants," "Weather," "The Heavens," and a lot more. This book will satisfy all learning styles, and I particularly recommend it for children who learn best when they are actively involved with their hands as well as their minds. Learn how to do a bee dance and how animals do yoga. Learn about the impossible-to-straighten cord, cookie concerns, soap bubble derby, shadow creatures, and the "plane" truth. Suitable for children around 6 to 14 working by themselves; also enjoyable for older kids, and for kids and adults working together. More than 500 pages, including a long list of other exciting and related resources. The book is divided into three major sections: "Quickies," short activities requiring few or no materials; "Make Time," activities requiring a little planning and using a few inexpensive materials; and "One Leads to Another," a series of activities related to each other. Interesting tidbits of information are scattered throughout the book in "Fact and Fun Circles" (e.g., "Are clouds really light? A mid-sized cloud can have the mass of five elephants!") *Science Is ...* is absolutely one of the best science books you'll find. Now available in sturdy paperback with a lower, more affordable price. Code CP, $19.95.

Knowledge Is POWER!

**TRUE SCIENCE**. This game was created by Aristoplay (maker of quality games) and the producers of *NOVA* (an award-winning PBS program). Their goal was to create an intriguing game that was fun to play and incorporated interesting questions and answers relevant to everyday science. They did a great job! There are 900 questions designed to help kids (and you) learn to think about science and our world. Did you know that the water you drink today was around when dinosaurs lived? Why does a clock on the top floor of a skyscraper run faster than one in the lobby? A great alternative to a textbook! 2 to 4 players, ages 10 and up. Code A, $25 plus $3 shipping.

## GENERAL INTRODUCTIONS AND BOOKS IN A SERIES

**Starting Point Science Books** answer hundreds of the questions your children will ask you. Thoroughly illustrated; visually interesting. The well-written text gives clear answers. I frequently suggest that parents start collecting these books when their kids are about 4, even though they won't be able to read the text. 19 titles in all. Start with one or two to see how much your kids enjoy them, then go on to the collected volumes for a better buy. Ages 4 to 8. Code EDC, $4.95 each.

**How Do Animals Talk?, How Do Bees Make Honey?, How Does a Bird Fly?, What Makes a Car Go?, What Makes a Flower Grow?, What Makes It Rain?, What Makes You Ill?, What's Inside You?, What's Out in Space?, What's the Earth Made of?, What's Under the Sea?, Where Did Dinosaurs Go?, Where Do Babies Come From?, Where Does Rubbish Go?, Where Does Electricity Come From?, Why Do People Eat?, Why Are People Different?** (my favorite), **Why Do Tigers Have Stripes?, Why Is Night Dark?**

Combos of *Starting Point Science* books: $13.95 each, 2 for $25, 3 for $35, 4 for $49.

**STARTING POINT SCIENCE #1** — *What Makes It Rain?, What Makes a Flower Grow?, Where Does Electricity Come From?, What's Under the Ground?*

**STARTING POINT SCIENCE #2** — *What's Inside You?, Where Does Rubbish Go?, Where Do Babies Come From?, Where Did Dinosaurs Go?*

**STARTING POINT SCIENCE #3**— *Why Do People Eat?, Why Do Tigers Have Stripes?, What Makes People Different?, What Makes You Ill?*

**Bigger combos** of the books listed above: $17.95 each, 2 for $32, 3 for $45.

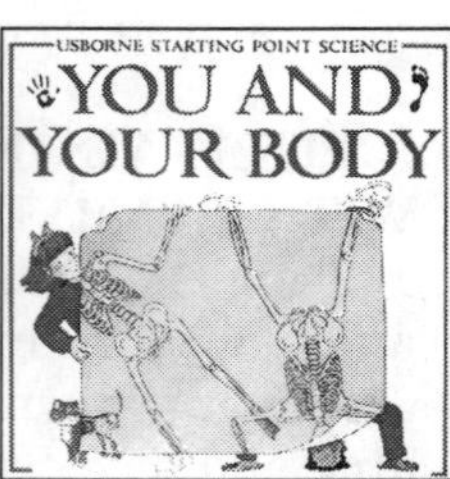


**EARTH AND SPACE** — *What Makes It Rain?, Why Is Night Dark?, What's Under the Ground?, What's Out in Space?, What's the Earth Made Of?*

**LIFE ON EARTH** — *What Makes a Flower Grow?, Why Do Tigers Have Stripes?, How Does a Bird Fly?, How Do Animals Talk?, Where Did Dinosaurs Go?, How Do Bees Make Honey?*

**YOU AND YOUR BODY** — *What Makes You Ill?, What Makes People Different?, Where Do Babies Come From?, What's Inside You?, Why Do People Eat?*

**Beginning Science for Ages 6 to 9.** Each of the following well-illustrated books explains clearly the basic scientific principles involved. They are chock-full of fun, interesting experiments and activities using everyday household items. I noticed a subtle but definite bias toward environmental responsibility. Code EDC, $4.95 each, or save money by purchasing the 3-in-1 *Science Activities* books at $12.95 each.

**Science with Light, Science with Magnets, Science with Water.** All three in **SCIENCE ACTIVITIES #1**

**Science in the Kitchen, Science with Air, Science with Plants.** All three in **SCIENCE ACTIVITIES #2**

**Science and Your Body, Science with Batteries, Science with Weather.** All three in **SCIENCE ACTIVITIES #3**

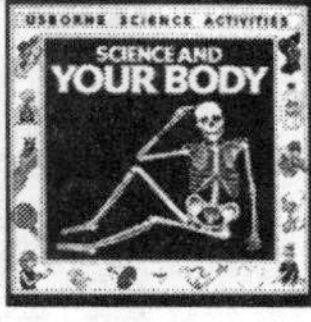


**A Canadian Wildlife Series**, all written by Deborah Hodge. Ages 5 to 9. Code KC, $5.95 each.

**BEARS.** Polar bears, black bears, and grizzly bears all lead fascinating lives in very different habitats. Excellent realistic illustrations and fascinating facts.
**BEAVERS.** Did you know some beaver dams are longer than a football field or that beavers have teeth that never stop growing? A good look at their natural habitat and how they raise their families.
**DEER, MOOSE, ELK, AND CARIBOU.** An intriguing look at these large herbivores. Do you know how much antlers can weigh? Find out what a moose shovel is and explore a cross-section of a deer. Realistic detailed illustrations.

**WHALES.** Lots to learn about these large mammals that inhabit our planet but in an entirely different environment. Learn how they communicate, how some migrate, how they raise their young, and much more.
**WILD CATS.** Learn how they are alike and how they differ from our household friends, where they live, and what they eat. Did you know they can eat up to 200 snowshoe hares in a year? Basic introduction to their anatomy.
**WILD DOGS.** Wolves, coyotes, and foxes are all part of the same canine family as our family dogs, but they live much different lives. This book will introduce their habitats, basic anatomy, and lifestyles.

The best introductions to science are books written for young children. They explain terms and concepts much more completely than do the books for older readers, without assuming prior knowledge the reader may not have, and they always have lots of clear diagrams and pictures.

**Introductions to Science.** How the stagecoach got its name, where cave people lived in summer, why the moon seems to change shape, how a telephone works, why ships float, how a skyscraper is built, where bananas come from, what gears are for, how glass is made, how big the earth is, why food is frozen, what plastic is made of, how planes fly, and much, much more. Superb introductions to science for ages 7 to 9. Code EDC. These books combine several smaller books. These collections are your best buy.

**EVERYDAY THINGS.** Combines: *Things That Go, Things in Our Homes,* and *Things Outdoors.* $14.95
**WILD PLACES.** Combines: *Jungles, Mountains,* and *Deserts.* $12.95
**WINGS, WHEELS AND WATER.** Combines: *Things That Fly, Things that Float,* and *Wheels.* Perfect for kids fascinated with trains, trucks, ships, and all kinds of transportation. $12.95

**THE FIRST BOOK OF NATURE** is 168 pages filled with interesting color illustrations, simple text, and appropriate vocabulary that will encourage young readers. Topics covered: birds, flowers, trees, wild animals, creepy crawlies, butterflies and moths, and fish. A basic encyclopedia of nature for ages 5 to 7. Includes puzzles, games, and activities. Simpler explanations and easier text than the Starting Point Science books listed above. Code EDC, $16.95.

**Science Quizzes**. Two well-illustrated quiz books for those who like to know what they do and do not know. 32 pages each, with lots of background information, lots to learn, and a basic point scoring system (if you want to use it). Ages 9 and up. Code EDC, $7.95 each. **Animal Quizbook** or **Science Quizbook**.

**Introductions**. Up-to-date informative text and illustrations. These are not complete studies of these subjects, but they do have experiments, puzzles, and games to intrigue your kids, give them basic knowledge of the subject, and (hopefully) inspire them to want to learn more. Ages 11 and up. Code EDC, $7.95 each. **Biology, Chemistry, Fitness and Health**, or **Physics**.
Save by getting three books (*Biology, Chemistry, and Physics*) in one: **BOOK OF SCIENCE**, $16.95.

Published by Barron's, these books for high school students will provide all the basics they would get in public school. They are designed for self-teaching and are easy to use. Code BE. **Anatomy and Physiology the Easy Way**, $14.95; **Biology the Easy Way**, $13.95; **Chemistry the Easy Way**, $13.95; **Electronics the Easy Way**, $13.95; **Physics the Easy Way**, $13.95.

**Science Kit Rental Program**, through the Museum of Science in Boston. Seventeen science project topics are covered for grades K-8. Each unit is available for you to rent with all the materials needed for students, including a teacher's guide. For a brochure and more information contact: Science Kit Rental Program, Museum of Science, Science Park, Boston, MA 02114-1099; 800-722-5487; www.mos.org.

**TOPS IDEAS** is a small catalog, published to promote hands-on learning, and full of great ideas for science and math you can do at home. There are some lesson-activities for various ages in almost all areas of science. They also supply unit study kits. TOPS Learning Systems, 10970 S. Mulino Road, Canby, OR 97013.

**SCIENCE ENCYCLOPEDIA**. This 128-page, comprehensive young readers' encyclopedia is arranged thematically with clear explanations. Hundreds of illustrations (both realistic and cartoon), quizzes, experiments, facts, lists, charts, glossary, and index make this an invaluable reference book for ages 8 to 12. Code EDC, $14.95.

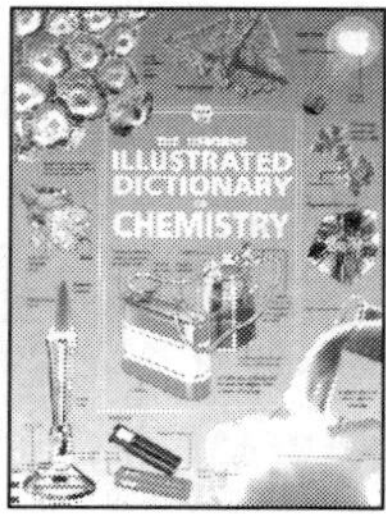

**Just Revised and Updated Illustrated Dictionaries**. Each of these books has just been revised to reflect the latest research and information. Full of interesting text and diagrams. Excellent reference books, with cross-referencing and links between related areas of study. Ages 11 and up. Code EDC, $12.95 each. **Illustrated Dictionary of Biology, ... of Chemistry, ... of Physics. ILLUSTRATED DICTIONARY OF SCIENCE**. Combines all three in one volume, $29.95.

**TOBIN'S LAB**. I really like this catalog. It's full of books, kits, science equipment, and more that's just right for those of us teaching at home. There's some duplication with our book, but they have much that we don't have, making it definitely worth getting. P.O. Box 6503, Glendale, AZ 85312-6503; 800-522-4776.

## PERIODICALS AND OTHER RESOURCES

**CURRENT SCIENCE**. An excellent school periodical that not only reports and discusses recent science findings and developments, but gives information to help readers understand how the news in science and technology affects their own lives and futures. Frequently reports new developments before major "adult" publications mention them. Each issue has a teacher's guide with extra background information, worksheets, and a summary of important articles. Reading and interest levels are for ages 12 and up, including high school and adult. 16 issues during the school year. Weekly Reader Corp., 3001 Cindel Drive, Delran, NJ 08370; 800-446-3355.

**SCIENCE NEWS**. A weekly magazine with articles about current discoveries and issues in the world of astronomy, behavior, biology, ecology, math, physics, and other sciences. Ages 14 to adult. 231 W. Center St., P.O. Box 1925, Marion, OH 43306-2025.

**SCIENCE WEEKLY**. Request a sample issue of this magazine for kids in K through 8th grade. Specify the grade level. Subscription Dept., P.O. Box 70154, Washington, DC 20088.

**SCIENCE NEWS BOOKS**. Free catalog with science books and project materials for all ages. Science News Books, Division of Science Service, 1719 N Street NW, Washington, DC 20036.

**POPULAR SCIENCE**. A well-known science and technology magazine for upper teens and adults. 457 Horner Ave., Toronto, ON M8W 4W9.

**SKULLDUGGERY**, 624 South B St., Tustin, CA 92780. Interesting catalog of realistic museum-quality reproductions for displays. Grizzly, saber-toothed tiger, gorilla, human, fossils, and more.

**P-3: The Earth-Based Magazine for Kids**. Games, cartoons, and environmental information for ages 6 to 12. P-3 Foundation Inc., P.O. Box 53, Montgomery, VT 05470.

**KIDS DISCOVER**. Science magazine for ages 6 to 12. Each issue is devoted to one topic with several articles and photos, plus puzzles, word games, and things to make or do. P.O. Box 54205, Boulder, CO 80322.
I found an interesting note among the PR material sent to me by *Kids Discover*: "No matter how good your child's school is ... [n]o matter how stimulating the classes ... [m]ost learning in life happens outside the classroom." They got that right!

**DISCOVER**. A monthly science magazine written for adults. Many short articles about what's happening out on the cutting edge, in the laboratories, in space, and around the world. Good feature articles. The moral and ethical implications of scientific advancement are also explored. Our older kids enjoyed this magazine. P.O. Box 37281, Boone, IA 50037-2281.

**The National Energy Foundation** is a non-profit educational organization that provides materials about electrical, nuclear, and renewable energy and energy conservation. 5160 Wiley Post Way, Suite 200, Salt Lake City, UT 84116.

**EUREKA!** A free catalog of books, toys, solar energy kits, universe maps, telescopes, microscopes, and more. Discovery Corner, Suzanne Krivoy, LHS Publications, Lawrence Hall of Science, University of California, Berkeley, CA 94720-5200; lhsstore@uclink4.berkeley.edu.

**More Science Supplies**. Don't overlook Sears, Radio Shack, your local hardware store, and other local and/or mail-order stores. The prices are often lower than those of school suppliers, and their products are as good or better.

**www.yucky.com** offers a wacky look at science, and posts various amusing experiments you may not find in science books. They offer a parents' guide, an online club, book suggestions, and more.

**Spizzirri Publishing, Inc.**, publishes a great free catalog of super fun learning materials, books, cassettes, posters, mazes, and plays. Good prices! P.O. Box 9397, Rapid City, SD 57709.

**CONNECTIONS 1: Learning About Science Through Literature**. A great way to learn for readers. Books are grouped by units such as flight, light and color, construction, and more. Also **LEARNING THROUGH LITERATURE**. Recommended books are offered for sale by the publisher of the listings. (If you can't find them, write to us.) Storytrain, 1510 Park Royale Blvd., Mississauga, ON L5E 2Z1.

**SCIENCE THROUGH CHILDREN'S LITERATURE: An Integrated Approach**, by Carol M. Butzow and John W. Butzow — a great book that covers life, physical, earth, and space sciences. Glossary, activities, and related books and references. Teacher Ideas Press, Libraries Unlimited, P.O. Box 3988, Englewood, CO 80155-3988.

**ATOM** is a science magazine for the middle grades (ages 9 to 12). A wide range of interesting articles, frequently tying in mathematics. Sometimes poster inserts are included. 6 issues per year, $25. P.O. Box 7216, Austin, TX 78713-9827.

**Forestry Canada Communications Program** has an activity book, posters, and general information about forestry. 351 St. Joseph Blvd, 19th Floor, Hull, PQ K1A 1G5.

**Scott Resources, Inc.** Catalog of science materials. P.O. Box 2121, Fort Collins, CO 80522.

**SCIENCELAND** is a quarterly magazine for the middle grades. $18 per year. Foreign orders write for information. P.O. Box 1177, Scarsdale, NY 10583.

**American Science and Surplus**. A cornucopia of bits, pieces, gears, gadgets, lights, switches, alarms, hinges, containers, unidentified technical artifacts, and other miscellaneous items for tinkerers. Catalog $1. Well worth it, even if you're just a browser. Listings are written with great humor, and there's a chance you'll see at least one item you've always wanted but didn't know it. 3605 Howard St., Skokie, IL 60076.

**Environmental Projects**. Project Learning Tree, Project Wild, and Project Aquatic Wild integrate environmental/forestry information into a curriculum. Although designed for classrooms, they are ideal for small groups, and can be adapted for individual use. A good opportunity for support groups to create a project that can involve everyone. All materials are free to facilitators; if you attend a workshop, you may or may not be charged a minimal sum. American Forest Council, 1250 Connecticut Ave. NW, Suite 320, Washington, DC 20036; www.plt.org.

**A CHILD'S GUIDE TO SOLAR COLLECTORS**. Information on renewable energy. Solar Energy Society of Canada, 15 York St., Suite 3, Ottawa, ON K1N 5S7.

**CREE (Conservation and Renewable Energy) Info Service** offers information on a variety of topics. CREE, P.O. Box 8900, Silver Spring, MD 20907; 800-523-2929.

**Free Stuff for Science Buffs**. Mostly for computer users, but there is still much good information about astronomy (in particular), weather, the earth, atoms, and more. The Coriolis Group, 7339 E. Aroma Dr., Suite 7, Scottsdale, AZ 85260; 602-483-0192; www.coriolis.com.

**Science Supplies**. Free elementary science and math materials catalog. Great kits! All the standard stuff plus earth sciences and more. You can request the "STC Update" newsletter, which has ideas and resources. Carolina Biological Supply Co., 2700 York Rd., Burlington, NC 27215-3398.

**Science Videos**. The Children's Television Workshop sells videotapes from the *3-2-1 Contact* science program ($19.95 to $29.95). Also ask about the Amazing Science series and the Architecture programs. 1633 Broadway, New York, NY 10019.

**Young Nature Company** offers kits about leaf, tree, and crop identification. Specify info for individual or classroom use. 1900 N. Main, Newton, KS 67114.

**WATER EDUCATION**. A new water education book for grades K to 6 about water, its physical and chemical makeup, its importance, background info, and more. $14 plus $2 postage from the Publications Dept., International Office for Water Education, Utah Water Research Laboratory, Logan, UT.

**ZOO BOOKS**. Outstanding, inexpensive wildlife books, with beautiful artwork and detailed information. Write for catalog: Wildlife Education Ltd., 9820 Willow Creek Rd., Suite 300, San Diego, CA 92131.

**NASCO SCIENCE 2000**. Complete catalog of science materials. 901 Janesville Ave., P.O. Box 901, Fort Atkinson, WI 53538-0901; www.nascofa.com.

**Nature Stuff**. Free poster and teaching guide with wildlife facts, games, list of books of interest, and more. Also Naturescope Books and the Earthsavers club for kids (leader's kit, with club certificate, membership cards, and quarterly newspaper and activity guide). National Wildlife Federation, 8925 Leesburg Pike, Vienna, VA 22184; www.nwf.org.

The **American Zoo and Aquarium Association** website lists the home pages of all accredited zoos and aquariums in the U.S.: www.aza.org.

**Edmund Scientific Company**. Free catalog of science kits, accessories, telescopes, and more. Great stuff. 101 E. Gloucester Pike, Barrington, NJ 08007; www.edmundscientific.com.

**Sargent-Welch**. Free catalog of science materials covering all fields of study for students of all ages. P.O. Box 5229, Buffalo Grove, IL 60089-5229.

# ECOLOGY

**We have not inherited the Earth from our parents — we have borrowed it from our children. (Native American saying)**

**EARTHWAYS,** by Carol Petrash, is perfect for young children to use with just a bit of help from you. Petrash has studied early childhood education (that's not always a recommendation, but it is this time) and has had experience working with Waldorf education. There's a wide variety of simple environmental activities you can do in a year. Some use common foods, others materials you can find outside: nature's people, cornhusk dolls, lanterns, and more. Organized by season. Nice list of reading resources included. Ages 4 to 8. Code GH, $16.95.

**GOOD EARTH ART: Environmental Art for Kids,** by Maryann Kohl and Cindy Gainer. Clear instructions for more than 200 easy and open-ended art activities using recycled and natural materials. Once you see the possibilities you'll think of your own projects, too. Ages 3 to 8. Code BRP, $16.95.

**PLAY LIGHTLY ON THE EARTH,** by Jacqueline Horsfall. A book full of activities for active youngsters. This book is divided into sections: "In the Plant World," "Among the Trees," "On the Earth," "In the Wildlife World," "Among the Birds," "In the Human World," "In the Sky," and "All Together as One World." Each section starts with a poem, then offers a number of related activities followed by some guided imagery play. There is also a section for adapting activities for indoor use, and a helpful section about how to teach when you don't know the answer. Creative play with a gentle message about eco-awareness. Ages 3 to 9. Code DN, $12.95.

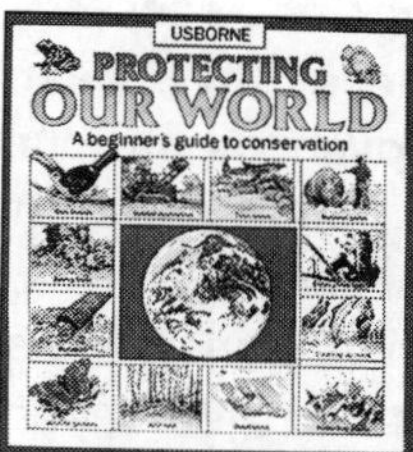


**PROTECTING OUR WORLD**. Although this book was written for children, we all need to be (or should be) aware of how to protect our world. You'll find good information about basic ecology and conservation issues, clearly presented, with lots of good illustrations. Plenty of food for thought and discussion, plus suggestions for how children can help in practical ways. Ages 7 to 10. Code EDC, $10.95.

---

*Our true home is in the present moment. To live in the present moment is a miracle. The miracle is not to walk on water. The miracle is to walk on the green Earth in the present moment.* — Thich Nhat Hanh

---

**TAKING CARE OF THE EARTH: Kids in Action,** by Laurence Pringle. A nice book with many stories and suggestions about what kids have done and what you can do to take care of our "spaceship earth." Many of the projects are intended for groups, but are easily adapted to individual use. A good section on where to get more information. Ages 7 to 12. 8x5½", 64 pages. Code BM, $7.95.

**EARTH BOOK FOR KIDS: Activities to Help Heal the Environment**, by Linda Schwartz. An amazing collection of kid-friendly information describing what kids can do to help heal the earth. This resource explains, without being preachy, the major problems we face and what can be done to clean up pollution, landfills, and acid rain. Good information about power sources and how they can be replaced with what are now considered "alternative" sources, and how to make better use of the power we do use. All this information is matched with arts and crafts projects, experiments, games, and projects large and small that can make a difference. Also tips on how to write a letter to the president, a local official, or a corporation to protest an action or express a concern. Includes a long list of organizations in the U.S. and Canada that will supply information on a variety of related subjects. Ages 8 to 12. Code LW, $9.95.

**ECOLOGY.** Facts about our intricate world, how the earth's ecosystem works, and what is necessary to maintain it. There have been great scientific advances in our lives, but this book points out that none should take precedence over the well-being of our planet. This well-written book contains experiments, projects, and activities that relate to current scientific and environmental issues. The activities help put the theories into practice. 48 large-format pages, profusely illustrated. Ages 10 to 16. Code EDC, $8.95.

---

*The path of civilization is paved with tin cans.*
— Elbert Hubbard

---

**YOUNG OXFORD BOOK OF ECOLOGY**, by Michael Scott. This book has everything the inquiring mind of a junior high or high school student needs. The text is interesting and full of well-known and unusual facts. The photos, illustrations, and maps are superb. The book explains the basic processes such as photosynthesis, food webs, and migration, and moves on a detailed journey through the habitats and ecosystems of the earth. I found it very easy to pick up and very hard to put down. Code OX, $16.95.

**SILENT SPRING**, by Rachel Carson. Two cassettes, approximately 2½ hours, read by Ellen Burstyn. This is the book that began to awaken Americans to the dangers of pesticide pollution. Rachel Carson eloquently evokes the specter of a barren land in which all the familiar voices of spring have been silenced, and documents the immediacy of the threat with shocking case histories. Far more important today than when it was written. Older teens and adults. $16.99. To order, call Durkin Hayes Publishing, 800-962-5200.

---

*A child's world is fresh and new and beautiful, full of wonder and excitement. It is our misfortune that for most of us that clear-eyed vision, that true instinct for what is beautiful and awe-inspiring, is dimmed and even lost before we reach adulthood.* — Rachel Carson

---

**ISHMAEL**, by Daniel Quinn. Very few books are unforgettable. This is one that will stay in your mind long after you finish reading it. It will change the way you view the world and the place of mankind within it. Quinn's aim was to challenge some of the basic precepts about our society, and he succeeded brilliantly. Through a fascinating philosophical discussion between Ishmael, who happens to be a gorilla, and his pupil, Quinn points out how our culture has grown to the point that it is consuming and destroying the world and itself in the process. His conclusion is one I hope you will embrace. This is an excellent book to read aloud and discuss with teens and other adults. Code BT, $14.95. The sequel, **MY ISHMAEL,** expands on the ideas discussed in *Ishmael*, and includes an interesting discussion of education from a perspective that I think will interest you. Code BT, $14.95. We liked these books so much we've given them as Christmas gifts.

**CLEAN AND GREEN**, by Annie Berthold-Bond. Complete guide to non-toxic and environmentally safe housekeeping. 485 ways to clean, polish, disinfect, deodorize, launder, remove stains, and more. Most ingredients are readily available. All recipes use non-polluting, renewable ingredients. Code CP, $8.95.

**BLUE AND BEAUTIFUL: Planet Earth, Our Home**, by Ruth Rocha and Octavio Roth. Beautifully illustrated book to help children of all ages understand the role each of us needs to play to keep our planet "blue and beautiful" for ourselves and for future generations. Based on the 1972 Stockholm Declaration on Human Environment. Order #E.90.1.15, from United Nations Publications, Sales Section, Room DC2-853, Dept. 202, New York, NY 10017.

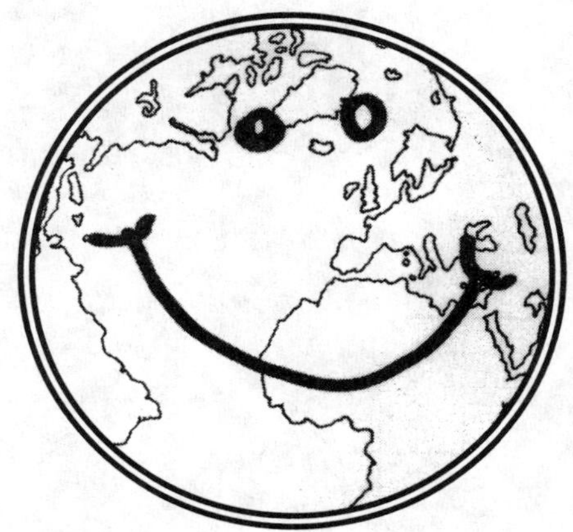

Did you know that "eco-safe," "Earth-safe," and "environmentally friendly" may not mean anything at all on labels? Check to see if there is any value to these words. Sometimes these words are added only as an advertising gimmick.

**ENVIRONMENTAL YOUTH ALLIANCE**, P.O. Box 29031, 1996 W. Broadway, Vancouver, BC V6J 5C2. Newsletter that discusses issues of interest to high school students.

If you'd like to incorporate more earth-friendly "green" products into your daily life, and be aware of the businesses that are not helping our environment, write **Co-op America**, 1612 K Street NW, Suite 600, Washington, DC 20006, for information about their National Green Pages book of products and services for people and the planet.

**The Kids' Earthworks Group,** P.O. Box 1117, Ashland, OR 97520. It's worth writing to see what they have to offer.

**E: THE ENVIRONMENTAL MAGAZINE**. Timely information about global and environmental issues, covering diverse topics such as solar-powered products, natural bedding, natural flu remedies, political issues, and more. Its advertisers promote appropriate products. If you buy from the original source you'll save money on products and books you can also find in the catalog from Real Goods (555 Leslie St., Ukiah, CA 95482). The Real Goods catalog is full of excellent ideas, but it can be more expensive. I was given a rechargeable flashlight from the Real Goods catalog for Christmas. When it broke, I looked for a replacement in the Real Goods and L.L. Bean catalogs. I found the item, but it was more than five dollars more than at the local auto repair shop. I really resent the mercenary approach many "green" companies seem to have written into their financial policies. E Magazine, Subscription Dept., P.O. Box 2047, Marion, OH 43305-2047.

Did you know that the recycle symbol doesn't necessarily mean a product has recycled content? The symbol may be there simply to remind you, the consumer, to recycle. And "recyclable" means only that the material *can be* recycled, which is meaningless if there are no recycling facilities in your community.

**Have you ever wondered what "predator-friendly" means?** "Predator-friendly" wool and woolen products are available and are produced by people raising sheep commercially who support the reintroduction of wolves into the habitat. They are currently using dogs and llamas to protect their flocks.

**Gaia Education Outreach Institute.** Courses that carry college credit and community outreach programs. Write for more information. R.R. 2, Box 793, Derbyshire Farm, Temple, NH 03084-9715.

A California newspaper reported finding 40 running shoes in a coyote den. Does this mean the running shoes (or the people leaving them outside their doors) are predator-friendly? And what about the report of a golf ball retrieved last week on a New Brunswick (Canada) golf course — by a fox?

*"One tree has the cooling effect of five air conditioners. ... One acre of growing trees will scrub clean the air polluted by eight automobiles operated for twelve hours."*

— From *The Washington Spectator*, quoting the Maryland Forest Service

The **Student Conservation Association** helps place teenage volunteers in national parks to work five to seven weeks during the summer. Students help to create trails, repair bridges, repair erosion damage, care for campsites, rescue wildlife, plant trees, and get involved in many other activities that help maintain the national parks. P.O. Box 550, Charlestown, NH 03603; 603-543-1700.

**Island Press**, a non-profit organization, has a wealth of information and news about ecosystems, community issues, global change, and economics. They publish many excellent books, too many for us to review or list here. I think we charge less for shipping, so get their catalog and if you want one of their titles, let us know. 24850 East Ln., P.O. Box 7, Covelo, CA 95428.

**The peoples are not the problems. They are the solutions.**

— Nichol VonHoufram

## TODAY'S HEADLINES, TOMORROW'S HISTORY

I don't think there are any really objective news magazines being published today. The news articles are riddled with opinions, pontifical analyses, and biased writing. I've almost learned to tolerate it with radio weather forecasts, so I don't mutter too loudly when the "meteorologist" says, "Well, folks, it's going to be another miserable day tomorrow, with lots of rain all day." Why should it be assumed that rain will make the day miserable for me? Perhaps my garden needs water, or maybe I like to walk in the rain. It's worse when the "reporting" is of national or international events. Just tell me what's going on, without what you and your team of experts think it "means." We'd like to boycott all the news magazines, but, for all their fluff and biases, they do tell us a little of current events, so we grit our teeth and try to read between the lines. We assume that half of the truth isn't being told and that half of what is being told isn't true or is being told in a slanted, misleading manner. If a magazine has a four-page car advertisement, costing thousands of dollars per inch, we don't expect the magazine to say much about the safety hazards of automobiles. If the magazine receives support from major oil companies, we don't expect it to dig very deeply into the causes of oil spills or the failures of oil companies to clean up their messes. If the magazine's demographic surveys show that 76 percent of its readers are suspicious of what the Russians, Cubans, Chinese, etc., are up to now, we don't expect it to risk six million cancelled subscriptions by telling the truth when the Russians, Cubans, Chinese, etc., actually do something good and right. We try to balance our understanding of the news by reading publications such as the *Nation* and the *Washington Spectator*, which don't depend on big corporations for their revenue. Since most of them tend to be somewhat or very left-wing, we don't believe all they say either, but at least their biases are more open and honest. We read both viewpoints, divide by the number of starving children in the world, multiply by the number of politicians it takes to change a light bulb, and hope thereby to arrive at some measure of the truth.

We tried *Time*, *Newsweek*, and *U.S. News & World Report*, all at one time, comparing them for a full year. *U.S. News* claims to have a higher percentage of "hard" news than the other two, but I think its extra margin is concerned primarily with the stock market. *Time* and *Newsweek* were neck and neck, but *Time* kept billing us for our subscription long after we had paid for it, so for several years we've subscribed only to *Newsweek*, and don't feel any great loss. You can't judge any of the magazines by their cover stories, which will be about real news one week (politics, wars, elections) and popular culture the next week (the latest movie craze or why Americans like to go to the beach). Inside, the magazine will always be the same mishmash of news and garbage and expert analyses of both. Lumping all such publications under one representative name, Thoreau said, "Read not the *Times*; read the eternities." *Reader's Digest* recently printed an anecdote about a vacationer in the woods of Wisconsin who told his guide, "It'll be interesting when I get back home to read the papers and see what's been happening in the real world." The guide replied, "I thought that was why you came out here."

I would truly like to be able to stick my head in the sand and forget about politics and foreign wars, droughts, and starving children. I don't enjoy reading about them. But something inside compels me to attempt to make a contribution toward making the world a better place, or at least to help it hold its own for my children and the children of the future. As PBS has said, "If we don't do it, who will?"

**WORLD MONITOR**. News magazine from the *Christian Science Monitor*, with world news, editorials, and analyses of the news, plus articles on art, music, film, education, science, technology, and more. Photographs, charts, maps. Edited somewhat from a global viewpoint, rather than that of a particular nation or region, but the view is still basically Western. Although I'm sometimes disturbed by the *Monitor*'s subtle (sometimes not so subtle) slanting of the news and by editorial comment woven into the reporting, the news coverage tends to be more objective than in most major news magazines, and more of the content is given to real news rather than trivial fillers on pop culture.

Donn reviewed the *World Monitor*, the weekly news magazine of the *Christian Science Monitor*. If you feel you need a daily paper, I suggest the daily edition of the *Monitor*. It's not perfect, but like the *World Monitor*, it does the best job I've seen in terms of unbiased reporting, and it does stay away from most of the pop culture covered by *Time* and *Newsweek*. There is one regular column concerning the church in each issue, but religion stays in that one spot and doesn't influence the rest of the reporting.

For subscription rates for *World Monitor* or the *Christian Science Monitor* call 800-456-2220. This number works in the U.S. and Canada. You can also get an online subscription that is much cheaper. You can also write: *Christian Science Monitor*, P.O. Box 37304, Boone, IA 50037-4304.

**THE WASHINGTON SPECTATOR**, edited by Ben A. Franklin. A very informative, politically aware four-page newsletter, published 22 times a year. Each issue usually focuses on a particular political, social, or environmental situation, with information, excerpts, and editorial comment from many different sources, such as the *Washington Post*, *Christian Science Monitor*, *Los Angeles Times*, recent books, and legislators. Background to many news items, frequently ignored by the mass media as too controversial and/or objectionable to corporate advertisers, is often disclosed in the *Spectator*. Each issue has half a page of "FYI, Items of Interest from *Spectator* Files," such as the following note: "The *Houston Post* has dug up a new angle on the savings and loan scandal. Four major borrowers of a Colorado S&L that failed also made deals with individuals and savings and loans that did business with organized crime or the CIA. Apparently, the Colorado S&L was used for money laundering." No matter what other publications I read, or how many, I feel I'm getting only half the news until I read the *Spectator*. For subscription information: The Public Concern Foundation, Inc., P.O. Box 20065, London Terrace Station, New York, NY 10011.

**THE NATION**. This monthly magazine is a very close second to the *Washington Spectator* as a publication without which we would feel we were missing at least half the news of the world, regardless of how many others we read. Somewhat left-wing sometimes, but not radical or rabble-rousing. Pokes sharp needles of inquiry into the pomposity of politicians, social incongruities, and the mass media. Uncovers hidden facts and motives behind the headlines. Write for current subscription rates: 72 Fifth Ave., New York, NY 10011.

Weekly Reader

Will ANTARCTICA Keep Its Treasures?

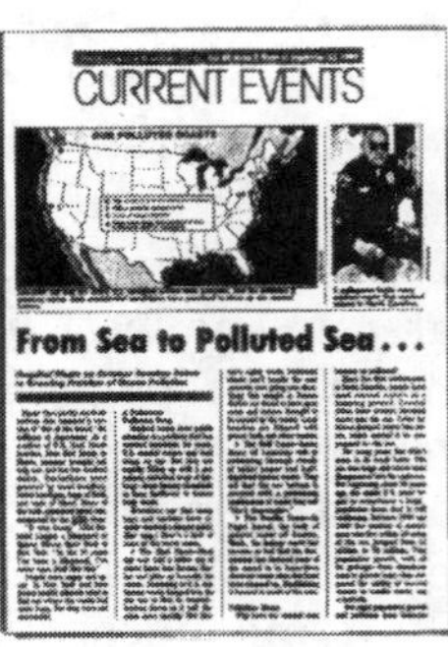

CURRENT EVENTS

From Sea to Polluted Sea . . .

**WEEKLY READER**. Student newspapers, with a different edition for each level from pre-K to 6. Varied subject matter, appropriate to the grade level: news, science, global issues, etc. Our kids always looked forward to receiving this newspaper, and Donn and I remembered enjoying it when we were in school. Inquire for current rates: 3001 Cindel Drive, Delran, NJ 08370; 800-446-3355.

**CURRENT EVENTS**. Student newspaper, 26 issues per school year. It does a competent job of reporting key issues, although from a very standard perspective. Includes photographs, helpful graphs, tables, and maps. Good variety of information, puzzles, vocabulary lists, and more based on current news. Grades 6 and up (the level of most adult publications). For subscription information: Weekly Reader Corp., 3001 Cindel Drive, Delran, NJ 08370; 800-446-3355.

**IT'S NEWS TO ME**. An exciting "un-bored" game that involves learning how to make the most of any newspaper. Great fun! There's also an activity book called **NEWS TO USE**. Newsline Publications, P.O. Box 8114, Pittsburgh, PA 15217.

For news from literally around the world, contact **Multinewspapers**, P.O. Box 866, Dana Point, CA 92629. You can subscribe to their service and they will send you local newspapers and magazines from around the world, all conveniently translated into English. These will give you another perspective on world events. You can personalize your service to a particular local area for special studies and even the number of mailings you receive.

**TIME FOR KIDS**. Subscriptions for grades 2 to 6, with free teacher's guide included. Price: $3.50 to $3.75 per student. They will do this for single homeschooled students. Call 800-777-8600.

**Newsweek Education Program** gives you the regular weekly magazine and all special issues at 57¢ per issue, plus a 130-page cross-curriculum teaching guide and a weekly guide and quiz (by e-mail, fax, or post). There is an associated interactive website at school.newsweek.com with more activities and links to follow items of particular interest. You can't beat the price. Schools can order this for 18, 26, 34 or 40 weeks. Homeschoolers must order for the year. You can order from the website; you will need to tell them how many students, their ages, and your name and address, and use a credit card. Or write: Newsweek Education Program, P.O. Box 59937, Boulder, CO 80322-9937, sending the above information and a check for $29.64. It's still a good deal for under $30.

**NEW INTERNATIONALIST**. No advertising here! It's just news with an international perspective to help you sort out what your national media are telling or not telling you. Comprehensive coverage of world events, in-depth articles by some very distinguished writers, thinkers, and activists such as Noam Chomsky, John Kenneth Galbraith, and Margaret Mead. A bit more expensive than many publications, but well worth it. P.O. Box 30000, Station BRM B, Toronto, ON M7Y 7A2.

**READERS SPEAK OUT**, for teens. See Magazines in "Free and Almost-Free Learning and Teaching Aids."

**THE AMERICAN PROSPECT**. Literate, informative, liberal quarterly. Free information. P.O. Box 383080, Cambridge, MA 02238-9810.

# GOVERNMENT

## STRUCTURE, PURPOSE, FUNCTION, POLITICS, CITIZENSHIP, BENEFITS, DANGERS, CENSORSHIP, AND CONSPIRACIES

**You can only protect your liberties in this world by protecting the other man's freedom. You can only be free if I am free.**
**— Clarence Darrow**

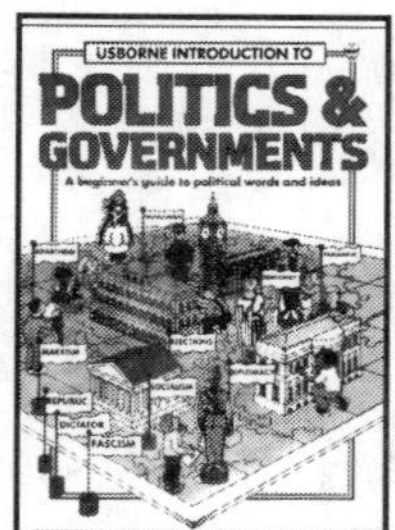


**INTRODUCTION TO POLITICS AND GOVERNMENT**. Very clear, detailed, *unbiased* descriptions of various forms of government, how they compare, and how they relate to each other, with historic and modern examples, including dictatorships, fascism, elections, republics, democracy, autocracy, Marxism, electoral systems, diplomacy, and summit meetings. Accurate information about Britain's parliamentary system, a presidential system, and a one-party system. Very well-illustrated hardcover with detailed, colorful drawings. Ages 10 to adult. Code RW, $9.95.

**GOVERNMENT 101**. An easy-to-use "nuts and bolts" course on how the federal government works. Presents the three branches of government, how each works, and how they interact to create a balance of power. Designed for homeschoolers, with a five-week lesson plan. No prior knowledge needed. Write Laurie Petrisin, P.O. Box 771, Trumansburg, NY 14886; lpetr14886@aol.com. Student book $3.50, teacher's guide with answer key, worksheets, and test, $5. Total $8.50. NY residents add 8% tax.

### HUMANS AND GOVERNMENTS

The following novels are considered classics and were written with an adult audience in mind. There is nothing objectionable in these books, but the concepts will be better understood by adults and high school students. Some younger students will also enjoy them. You know your children best. I suggest you read these books first and then decide the best time for your children to read them.

**1984**, by George Orwell. When the year 1984 came and went, popular pundits looked around at modern society and smugly announced that Orwell was wrong, both in his predictions and in the date. They were completely mistaken on both counts. *1984* was meant not as a prediction, but as a warning, and the message is more pertinent today than it was when the book was written, or even in the year 1984. In the novel, the government's Ministry of Truth continually rewrites history, manipulating society's opinions and attitudes through Newspeak, a form of word-garbling that increasingly makes free and independent thinking impossible, and popularizes slogans such as "War is Peace" and "Freedom is Slavery." In our "real world" of today, literature and history books are being rewritten to reflect the desires of scores of minority pressure groups as well as current governmental policies, and the government bombards us daily with phrases such as "negative benefits" and "first strike defense," while telling us that "our" unbelievable military buildup — using more than fifty percent of the entire federal budget — is "to preserve world peace." The message of *1984* should be read and considered very seriously. The more we allow the meanings of words to become vague and cloudy, the more difficult true communication becomes, and the more easily our attitudes and beliefs will be manipulated by corporations, governments, or religious demagogues using repetitious slogans and doctrinal affirmations. No high school or college study of democracy and censorship is complete without a thoughtful reading of this book. We can't afford to look around complacently and say, "Well, it hasn't happened yet." If we don't move immediately to reverse the trend, it *will* happen — and its beginnings are already all around us. Ages 14 to adult. Code BT, $5.95.

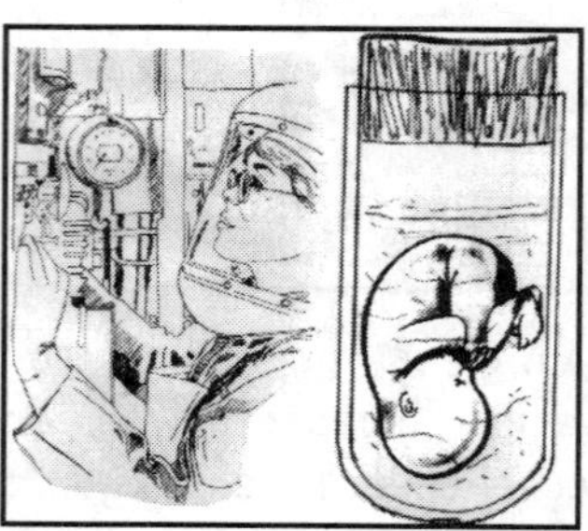

**BRAVE NEW WORLD**. One-hour old-radio program on cassette, with Richard Widmark. Based on the novel by Aldous Huxley about a society of genetic manipulation, in which the words "mother" and "father" are considered obscene and children raised without parents are the norm. Read the news, and say it won't happen. $9 plus $2 shipping. (May be combined with other old-radio tapes for a discount.)

**BRAVE NEW WORLD** is also available in paperback. Code HC, $11. If you'd like **BARRON'S STUDY NOTES**, add $3.95. If you order these together there is no charge for shipping the study notes.

**ANIMAL FARM**, by George Orwell. An amusing, biting satire on totalitarianism — and the dangers to democracy when it isn't carefully guarded. "We're all created equal, but some are more equal than others." A very funny, very serious, very disturbing book. Code BT, $9.95.

**FAHRENHEIT 451**, by Ray Bradbury. In a not-too-distant evolution of our society, in which most people spend the day conversing with their fictional television families, Montag is a fireman — not a firefighter, but a professional bookburner, working for an authoritarian state that endeavors to banish all printed material, and, by implication, all freedom of thought. When Montag accidentally reads some of the books he is supposed to burn, he begins to question — first his job, then the state. Unlike *1984* and *Brave New World*, this disturbing picture of total censorship ends with a hopeful note — which, however, shouldn't weaken its implicit warning. Older teens and adults. Code RH, $6.99.

**THE DAY THEY CAME TO ARREST THE BOOK**, by Nat Hentoff. Who would have believed *The Adventures of Huckleberry Finn* could cause the worst crisis in the history of George Mason High School? Certainly not Barney Roth, editor of the school paper. But when a small but vocal group of students and parents decide that the book is racist, sexist, and immoral — and should be removed from reading lists and the school library — Barney takes matters into his own hands. As the Huck Finn issue comes up for a hearing, Barney decides to write a story about previous censorship efforts at school. He's sure that investigative reporting and publicity can help the cause. But is he too late to turn the tide of censorship? This intelligent novel for teens and adults is entertaining and thought-provoking. *Publishers Weekly* called it "an outstanding work, given added value by the author's honest, comprehensive coverage of all sides of the argument over 'dangerous freedoms.'" Code RH, $5.50.

"It's mighty hard to figure, Jim. When Mark Twain first wrote about us, most everyone thought I should be in school. Nowadays, half the schools don't even want to let me in. Black folks don't like to read about us 'cause in the old days you was called a 'nigger,' an' thought nothin' of it, an' white folks don't want to read about us 'cause I'd rather go to Hell than send a man back into slavery, an' what neither of them wants for themselves, they don't want no one else to have neither. I tell you, Jim, I just can't figure it." **Thanks, Donn. No apologies to Mr. Twain.**

**LORD OF THE FLIES**, by William Golding. This is one of the books frequently targeted for removal from schools; I've forgotten why, but I think it's because of the few mild cuss words. I wouldn't worry about them. There are far more disturbing things in the book — ideas. According to Rousseau, Burroughs, and many others, a child will develop a healthy and mature perspective naturally, without being taught or trained. This novel explores the concept with a group of boys marooned in the wilderness, faced with the need to establish some sort of basic government for their mutual survival. Those of us who take democracy for granted consider its benefits obvious, but Golding's story is a reminder that democracy has taken thousands of years to develop, and may not be as "natural" as we would like to think. *Lord of the Flies* is also, in many ways, an "answer" to A.S. Neill (author of *Summerhill*) and others who advocate the enfranchising of children: Without a knowledge of history, without an understanding of the democratic process, without an acquired sense of fairness and justice, can we expect anyone — child or adult — to have an inherent desire for society's greatest good, and to leap over centuries of slow social evolution to an enlightened democracy? Golding's answer is not definitive; but it is certainly provocative. Older teens and adults. Code BT, $6.95. If you'd like the **CLIFFS NOTES STUDY GUIDE** the price is $4.95. No shipping charge for Cliffs Notes if you order them with *Lord of the Flies*.

Fiction allows the mind to wander freely and consider a wider variety of ideas than textbooks. Fiction can help us find constructive alternatives to today's problems within modern governments. I also concede that there is a need for some textbooks to learn the facts about government and how it does or should work.

> *Rebellion to tyrants is obedience to God.*
> — Motto on Thomas Jefferson's seal

## HOW THE U.S. GOVERNMENT IS DESIGNED TO WORK

The following three books and teaching guide are a "mice" way to introduce younger children to the U.S. government and its various functions. Cynical attitudes about government abound. If you have better ideas for running the country, then do what you can to make changes. In the meantime, for all its failures, I consider the U.S. government the best form available, barring the Hopi system of consensus. If we are to change the system, if we have hopes that our children will change the system, then we must first understand how it works. For too many youngsters, politics and government are thought to be dull and boring. These books are designed to help young children develop an understanding and interest in an institution that affects our lives on a daily basis. I think you and your kids will enjoy the illustrations; the architecture has been accurately represented. The last two pages of each book contain historical notes for parents and teachers. All books are in rhyming verse by Peter W. Barnes and Cheryl Shaw Barnes. Code VSP, $15.95 each.

The first book in the series is **WOODROW, THE WHITE HOUSE MOUSE**. Readers are introduced to the winner of the most recent mouse election, Woodrow Washingtail (yes, a mouse), and his family. Woodrow is sworn in just like human presidents. Kids are introduced to the various jobs the president does and the basic structure of the government. Ages 5 to 9.

**HOUSE MOUSE, SENATE MOUSE: Proudly Presenting the Squeaker of the House and the Senate Mouse-jority Leader**. This book explains very clearly how our laws are made, from researching a bill through the signing by the president. Well written and interesting for children to read. Ages 6 to 9.

**MARSHALL, THE COURTHOUSE MOUSE**. Explains the working of the Supreme Court. Marshall, the main mouse in this tale, is patterned after John Marshall. Again, the last two pages have historical notes of interest about the court and Marshall. Ages 8 to 10.

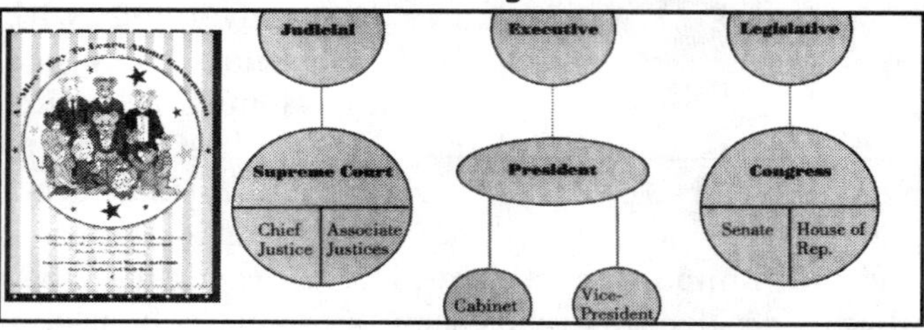


**A "MICE" WAY TO LEARN ABOUT GOVERNMENT**. A curriculum guide that covers all three books. Includes activities, research topics, role-playing exercises, a glossary, and an extensive reading list. Code VSP, $9.95.

> *The strength of the Constitution lies entirely in the determination of each citizen to defend it. Only if every single citizen feels duty bound to do his share in this defense are the constitutional rights secure.*
> — Albert Einstein

**CORNERSTONES OF FREEDOM**. These books explore several important aspects of U.S. history. Many full-color photos and black-and-white engravings, with clear text, almost give readers a sense of witnessing history in the making. Each book is 8x9½", 32 pages; reading level about 4th grade, interest level ages 8 to 12 or so. Code CP, $5.95 each; all four for $20. **The Bill of Rights, The Constitution, The Declaration of Independence, Thurgood Marshall and the Supreme Court.**

**THE VOICE OF THE PEOPLE: American Democracy in Action**, by Betsy Maestro and Giulio Maestro. A good introduction to civics. Includes development of the Constitution and covers the election process from local mayors to members of Congress, presidents, and appointment of Supreme Court justices. Explains what a member of Congress does and the division of powers in the three legislative branches, and demonstrates how voting makes a difference. Also included is basic information about the Constitution and the Bill of Rights. A very readable book, which amazes me, because there is also an impressive amount of information. 9x11", 48 pages, with good color illustrations. Ages 8 to 10. Code WM, $5.95.

**AMERICAN PRESIDENTS COLORING BOOK**. Portraits of all 42 presidents (Washington through Clinton) are drawn and ready to color. The background of each picture features significant events during each administration (e.g., James Madison standing before a burning White House during the War of 1812, Lincoln conferring with Union officers, Nixon debating Soviet Secretary Nikita Khrushchev in Moscow). Informative captions make this book a practical reference. Ages 8 to 12. Code DV, $3.50.

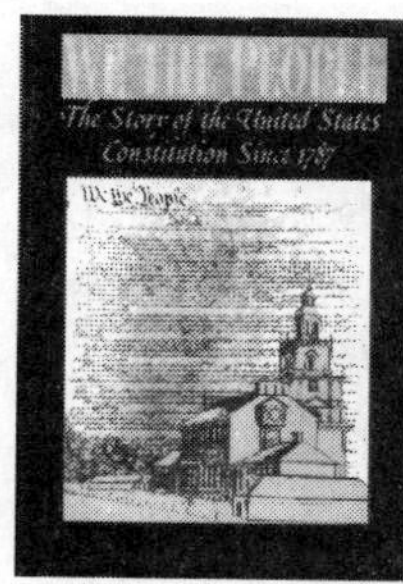


**WE THE PEOPLE: The Story of the United States Constitution Since 1787**, by Doris Faber and Harold Faber. At this time, most people consider democracy the highest form of government. This book traces the development of the Constitution from 1787, when 55 men met in Philadelphia to deliberate and write it, to the present. This is a well-researched and very readable book with many fascinating anecdotes about the famous and sometimes infamous people involved. It goes beyond the Constitution to cover the Bill of Rights, from 1791 to the 26th Amendment. The Fabers present lively commentary on the controversies within the country and the Supreme Court that have affected these amendments. The U.S. government as it stands now leaves much to be desired, yet in reading this book you'll come to appreciate the amazing vision of the men who wrote the Constitution and know that change for the better is possible. A great addition to all high school U.S. history studies. Includes the Constitution, the Bill of Rights, the amendments, and an extensive bibliography. Code SS, $15.95.

**THE PATRIOT'S HANDBOOK**, by George Grant, Ph.D. From a note at the back of the book: "G.K. Chesterton once quipped that America is the only nation ever founded on a creed. While other nations find their identity in geography, culture, ideology, or ethnic origin, America was founded on certain ideas about freedom, human dignity, and social responsibility." Educators in the early 19th century realized that if this experiment in liberty were to continue, the ideals held by the men who founded the country needed to be passed on to the young, and so they produced a handbook. *The Patriot's Handbook* is the modern equivalent, with introductions to the ideas, events, key documents, speeches, poems, songs, and personalities that have shaped the country. Brief biographies of presidents and influential people. A terrific resource for high school studies. Code HBSA, $14.99.

**THE U.S. CONSTITUTION: And Fascinating Facts About It**. A pocket-sized reference filled with facts and many really fascinating inserts about the Founding Fathers, signers of the Constitution, dates to remember, 20 briefs on landmark Supreme Court cases, and more. Ages 12 to adult. Code BT, $2.95.

**Right vs. Left —**

The *Washington Spectator* quotes some of "the true differences between Democrats and Republicans" from a newsletter called "Unconventional Wisdom":

"Democrats eat the fish they catch. Republicans mount them on the wall.

"Democrats buy most of the books that have been banned somewhere. Republicans form censorship committees and read them as a group.

"Republicans tend to keep the shades drawn, although there is seldom any reason why they should. Democrats ought to, but don't.

"Republican boys date Democrat girls. They plan to marry Republicans, but they feel entitled to a little fun first.

"Democrats have chapped hands and headaches. Republicans have tennis elbow and gout."

**Perils of Democracy**. Who should know better than an elected public servant what dangers there are in a democracy? In July 1989, the *Los Angeles Times* noted that California State Senator Bill Craven was worried about "the rise in citizens' initiatives, in which people sign petitions to enact changes in laws," and quoted Craven as saying, "[If we legislators] don't watch our respective tails, the *people* are going to be running the government."

---

*A politician thinks of the next election; a statesman, of the next generation.*

— James Freeman Clarke

---

**RespecTeen Speak for Yourself**. A free mini-curriculum for 7th and 8th grades, including seven lessons with worksheets (which you can reproduce if you need more than one set). Lessons include the legislative process, charting a bill from conception to law; reforms, with research on American reformers; investigating national issues; researching a national issue; learning about U.S. representatives and congressional districts; writing to Congress; and more. A lot to pack into seven lessons! If your child wants to carry this project further he can submit a letter to the RespecTeen contest — there are prizes. The contest has several levels; the winners from each state and a parent win a trip to Washington, D.C., to participate in a youth forum. Write to MS 855, Lutheran Brotherhood, 625 4th Ave. S., Minneapolis, MN 55415-9978. There is no religious content in these lessons.

---

Quoted in *Newsweek*: Robert Carroll, spokesman for Pratt and Whitney, explaining why his company charged the Air Force $999 for a single pair of pliers, said, "They're multipurpose; not only do they put the clips on but they take them off."

---

Free catalog of books by mail for thoughtful readers. Mostly adult books, but some for kids. Laissez Faire Books, 938 Howard Street, #202, San Francisco, CA 94103; laissezfaire.org.

**The Center for Living Democracy**, R.R. #1, Black Fox Rd, Brattleboro, VT 05301, offers an interesting publication with articles about the actions everyday people are taking in their own communities to improve their lives now and with future planning. Ask for a free sample and their book list.

**CANADIAN GOVERNMENT**

**CANADA VOTES: How We Elect Our Government**, by Linda Granfield. Does an admirable job of explaining the Canadian election system. Up-to-date. Ages 10 to 14. Code KC, $5.95

**O CANADA**, by Ted Harrison. Harrison illustrates his vision of the Canadian national anthem, "O Canada." Bilingual (French and English). Full-page full-color illustrations. All ages. Code KC, $5.95.

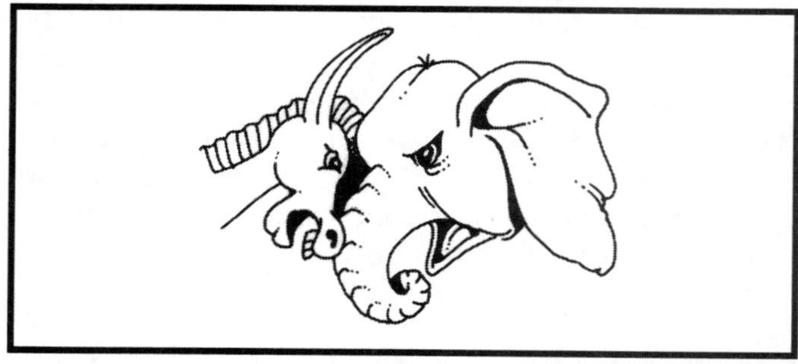

## CENSORSHIP AND CONSPIRACIES

Which came first, the right-wing censorship or the left-wing conspiracies? The extreme right complains that the schools are teaching secular humanism, and the extreme left complains that its First Amendment rights are being violated if children are told anything at all about religion. The right-wing arguments are based primarily on a strict, literal interpretation of the Bible; the left-wing arguments are based on a strict, literal interpretation of the U.S. Constitution. Education, caught in the middle and pulled by both groups in a tug-of-war, has stretched and snapped and gotten lost in the shuffle.

It's sadly true that public schools don't include much about religion, even in history courses. It's also sadly true that they don't include much about anything. Sometimes both sides seem to have some very valid, reasonable arguments and examples, and sometimes they both just bounce off the walls. The complaints and threats of both sides have scared textbook publishers, whose main desire (second to making money, of course) is to avoid offending anyone. Since someone, somewhere, either left or right, will be offended by anything at all, the publishers have thought it prudent to publish books that don't say anything, and find it very discouraging that some people are offended even by that. At present, despite a "liberal" administration and a growth spurt of fundamentalism, the left-wingers seem to be gaining ground in the schools and in the courts. Perhaps the irresponsible "rights" demanded by the far left will eventually result in an even greater reaction from the far right, which might result, for a while at least, in a more reasonable balance between the two. Probably neither side will be satisfied with a balance, but will continue to fight for increasing control, so the scales will continue to teeter-totter. Both extremes, the far-right fundamentalists and the far-left "secular humanists," are loud minorities. The "Moral Majority" was nothing more than a splinter of the right-wing minority, but there *is* a *real* moral majority — the great number of people who are not fundamentalists but disapprove of flag-burning and pornography; who don't believe the universe was created in six days, but do believe that homosexuality and hate-music are wrong. This real majority, out-shouted by the left-right extremists, is too intimidated by both groups to speak up in favor of a return to sound, "old-fashioned" moral values, academic competence, and common-sense education.

Let the far left return to being consenting adults in the privacy of their own homes, and let the far right teach Scientific Creationism in the privacy of their own homes and churches.

For far-left complaints, sometimes valid, about the far right, read publications of the American Civil Liberties Union; the War Resisters League (not to be lumped with other pacifist groups); Planned Parenthood; and anything you can handle by radical feminists, homosexuals (who, I understand, don't like to be called that), and Madalyn Murray O'Hair, who published *The American Atheist* magazine before she disappeared in 1995.

For far-right complaints, sometimes valid, about the far left, read **WHAT ARE THEY TEACHING OUR CHILDREN?** by Mel and Norma Gabler ($5.95 plus $1.50 shipping from Mel and Norma Gabler, Box 7518, Longview, TX 75607); **CHANGE AGENTS IN THE SCHOOLS**, by Barbara Morris ($9.95 plus $1.50 shipping from Barbara Morris, P.O. Box 2166, Carlsbad, CA 92008); **CHILD ABUSE IN THE CLASSROOM**, by Phyllis Schlafly ($5.95 plus $1.50 shipping from Crossway Books, 9825 W. Roosevelt Road, Westchester, IL 60153); **CENSORSHIP: Evidence of Bias in Our Children's Textbooks**, by Paul Vitz ($6.95 plus $1.50 shipping from Servant Books, P.O. Box 7455, Ann Arbor, MI 48107); and several passages in Mary Pride's **THE BIG BOOK OF HOME LEARNING** (listed elsewhere in this book).

Don't expect great intellectual feats from either side. Left-wingers take the Bible from school, claiming that exposure to a religious book is an infringement of their First Amendment rights. Right-wingers remove *Charlotte's Web* and *Peter Rabbit* from many schools because animals can't really talk, and *The Adventures of Huckleberry Finn* because Huck would rather go to Hell than betray an escaped slave. Joseph Scheidler, director of the ultra-right Pro-Life Action League, says "contraception is disgusting — people using each other for pleasure." Planned Parenthood, determined to match Scheidler's ignorance and stupidity, quotes his pious complaint to support its claim that making abortion illegal will "return women to a position of subservience." Both sides act as if their brains had been aborted.

I'm not a fundamentalist, as you've probably inferred by now, and I don't usually consider myself a right-winger in much of anything, but it seems to me that many of the arguments of the right wing are more valid than those of the left wing. I don't think "Bible science" should be taught in schools, but neither do I think that the recognition of Thanksgiving and Christmas as religious holidays will threaten anyone's liberty.

My brother says the older we get, the more conservative we get. I think I'm still as "liberal" as I've ever been, but the far left keeps moving so much further left that my liberalism seems increasingly conservative.

Kahlil Gibran tells of four frogs on a floating log, arguing about whether the log is moving, or the river is moving, or their movement is only in their thoughts. A fourth frog, who has stayed out of the argument, finally says, "All three of you are right. The river is moving, the log is moving, and we move in our thoughts." The first three frogs stare at the fourth for a moment; then all together, they rush at him and push him off the log.

Splash.

# PLEASE, *DON'T* COLOR MY WORLD

Fools rush in where angels fear to tread.
— Alexander Pope

**"BUT THE EMPEROR HAS NO CLOTHES!" the little boy cried.**
— Hans Christian Andersen

I've taken the liberty as editor of making a few changes I believe help to bring Donn's essay up to date. This has been a much misunderstood part of this book. Donn was colorblind. His intention here was not to hurt or make anyone feel defensive. His main point, which is still as relevant today as when he wrote it in 1991, is that *each of us has a unique cultural background*; that our own unique histories are important, but that we must keep our perspectives and priorities clear. While acknowledging our differences we must remember that we are one people and that our common goals are greater than our differences.

I find it interesting, but not alarming, that a Jewish home-school group and a Muslim home-school group are included in a published list of groups that excludes all "exclusivist" Christian groups — that is, those that accept as members only those who profess certain religious tenets. There are also Catholic and Mormon groups, presumably (although I don't know why) not so exclusivist as Protestants.

Interesting, because it seems inconsistent, but I'm frequently inconsistent, too, so I don't mind allowing others the same privilege. Not alarming, because the fundamentalist Christians have their own national network, and are in no danger of being unnoticed by anyone who is qualified to join. It seems to be true that birds of feather flock together, but I think it's a narrow way of thinking when the "feather" is a particular religious belief; however, I don't think these groups pose any threat to other home-schoolers — certainly not to me — so I don't find their existence any more alarming than their presence on a list that excludes other exclusivist groups.

I am very alarmed, however, by a different kind of exclusivist thinking that is growing, not only in general society, but also within the home-school movement: racism.

I would be among the very first to denounce any "all-white" home-school group or publication, and I don't see any difference between that and an "all non-white" group or publication.

Some newsletters are for "Homeschoolers of Color," and invite as subscribers "both Latina/o and Black home-schoolers ... and anyone else out there who identifies themselves as a person/family of color, regardless of nationality, percentage of color, language, religion, or any of the other factors that sometimes keep us apart." Unless you're white, that is, with "no percentage of color."

To the best of my knowledge, I have no "percentage of color" — but I have known blacks, some of whom were very close friends, and I have lived in the Hopi village of Hotevilla in Arizona, and I have taught blacks and Indians (along with whites, Asians, and Latinos) to read and write English, and Mexicans to read and write Spanish, and was once a librarian with an Indian assistant. I have known people of many races and ethnic backgrounds, in a variety of circumstances, and have gotten to know them all fairly well. We were not "colored" and "white" to each other, but just people. We all laughed and cried and bled in the same color, and I absolutely do not believe that their children "are not like everybody else's children."

Some of these special-interest homeschooling groups say their "children of color" have special needs as distinguished from children who are white. In other words, the needs and concerns of children "of color" are different from the needs and concerns of white children. Turn it around, and you have the bigoted argument with which white supremacists have justified their actions for centuries — that "colored" people don't have the same needs and concerns that white people have.

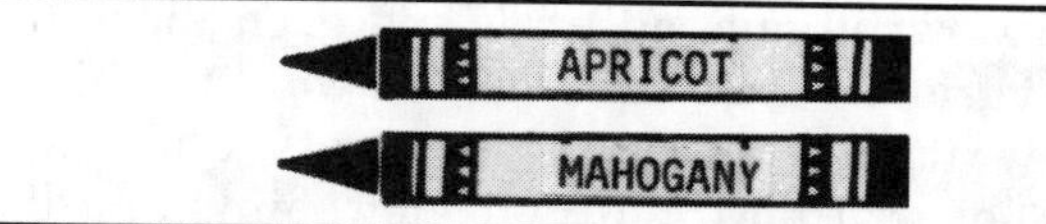


Have you seen Crayola's "multicultural" crayons, pencils, modeling clay, and washable paints and markers? Apricot, burnt sienna, mahogany, peach, sepia, tan, plus black and white for blending — "to help build skills and self-esteem," say the ads.

Of course, it's nicer to talk about "culture" than "race," but you won't convince me that those colors refer to culture. They refer to skin color, which is one of the factors often differentiating races. There is no such thing as a "black culture" or "red culture" — or "apricot" or "mahogany culture" — any more than there is a "white culture." All races have had as many differences among themselves as with each other. Some people of each race have built castles or pyramids while others of the same race were building mud huts.

I'm not against the skin-colored crayons. In fact, I think they're a good idea. I remember the frustration of trying to find a good skin-colored crayon — my skin, that is, or so-called "white" — when I was a kid. Light pink didn't work, and white was anemic. The larger crayon sets had "flesh," which was closest and worked the best.

Maybe the people "of color" want to think their needs are different because it was the white Europeans who enslaved or slaughtered their ancestors (and to some extent are still doing so, either literally or symbolically), but the Europeans were not alone in their guilt. Quite often they didn't even have to leave their ships to kidnap a cargo of Africans — because the people of some tribes were quite happy to sell the people of other tribes once they realized it was more profitable than killing them, enslaving them, or eating them. Africans had been enslaving each other long before the whites came along to buy slaves, just as earlier Europeans had enslaved each other, and just as many American Indians enslaved those of other tribes. The sins and crimes of white Europeans have been truly terrible, but they are not unique. With the possible exception of the Hopis and the Kalahari bushmen, there has probably been no society in human history that hasn't practiced its own full quota of atrocities on someone.

The Chinese invented gunpowder, but the Europeans discovered how effective it was in killing people — just other Europeans, at first, but eventually it proved to be just as effective when used on blacks, reds, browns, and other non-whites. I don't think history would have been much different if the power of gunpowder had been discovered first by people of some other race; only the names (and colors) would be changed.

While we're remembering unpleasant facts, let's not forget that some of the rich and powerful plantation owners in the antebellum Southern states were free blacks, who bought and sold other blacks at the same auctions attended by the whites. The bad guys haven't always been white.

White Europeans and their descendants have certainly wreaked havoc around the world, but they have also produced some of the world's greatest philosophies, scientific advances, and humanitarian impulses — including the American ideals of "life, liberty, and the pursuit of happiness" for all people, and the premise that "all men are created equal."

Because those ideals have been only partially realized is certainly no reason to discard them and revert to ethnic tribalism. We have made greater advances toward achieving them in the past three decades than in the previous three centuries. Some newsletters threaten to undermine all the advances begun by Rosa Parks and Martin Luther King Jr. just as surely as a "whites-only" policy would. They are not "celebrating diversity," as they claim, but merely emphasizing racial differences and turning their backs on the greater similarities of people, regardless of race.

This is not multiculturalism, but racial tribalism, which has been around since before people climbed out of trees to live in caves. It probably began when Og and his mate Ooga discovered that a single mastodon wasn't enough to feed their entire village and all the people from the next valley, too. Homo wasn't very sapiens then, so Og said, "I know, let's just feed the people who look like us." Ooga said, "That's logical," and they began throwing rocks at the people with different hair, eyes, clothing, and skin color.

Only recently, at least ten thousand years later, have we begun to find ways of living without throwing rocks at each other, and now some of those who have been stoned the most want to revive the attitudes that led to the rock-throwing in the first place.

We don't have to be identical to communicate with each other, nor do we need to have the same skin color to understand each other. Just because North American society doesn't revolve around the cultures of ancient Africa or China or pre-Columbian America doesn't mean that people whose ancestors lived there are being denied the right to identify with any ethnicity they choose. Not many have had the advantage of an Alex Haley to trace their roots for them, so it really is a choice, and the choices must often be fairly general and made at random. Africa is a very large continent, and the people who lived there before the whites arrived were just as diversified in their cultures — not to mention many aspects of stature and physiognomy — as European whites were. After so many centuries, so much intermingling of various tribes, so much interracial mixing, how does one decide which ancestors to claim?

I think M.B. Tolson had at least part of the best answer: "I, as a black poet, have absorbed the Great Ideas of the Great White World, and interpreted them in the melting-pot idiom of my people. My roots are in Africa, Europe, and America."

Having grown up in the United States, but living now in Canada, Jean and I still prefer to celebrate the American Thanksgiving in November rather than the Canadian Thanksgiving in mid-October. We still "feel" American, and continue to identify more with American history and heritage than Canadian. Our Canadian neighbors don't share our preferences, or several other family and cultural traditions we have, but that doesn't mean they are trying in any way to deny our ethnicity, nor do they think we are interfering with theirs. We accept each other and get along well. Occasionally, we compare some of the differences in our backgrounds, but our similarities — working for a living, raising a family, trying to stay sane and healthy in an increasingly complex world — are far more important than our differences.

Some special-interest groups seem to be saying, as are people "of color" throughout society, that if the prevalent histories and popular culture don't reflect their roots and viewpoints, then their ethnicity is being denied. To a large extent, this has certainly been true in the past, but modern society had begun rectifying the injustice even before the current fad of decrying the absence in history books (and in literature in general) of blacks, Indians, Native Americans, Hispanics, women, and other minority groups. (I've always assumed that women comprise about half of the world's population, give or take a few thousand, but lately many of them seem to feel they're in a minority, a large percentage of whom are black belts in karate, so who am I to argue? You open a door for one of them and get a thumb in the eye for your trouble.)

The victors usually write the histories, along with their own rationalizations and self-justifications, which certainly promotes a certain degree of inaccuracy, but I doubt that the history books would be any more objective or accurate if they were written by the vanquished.

Most North American history in the last four hundred years has involved descendants of Western Europeans more than people from other places around the world, so it seems natural, even if not "right," for history to have been written from their viewpoint.

The treatment by the whites of the blacks, browns, reds, and yellows has certainly been despicable, but it's still a fact, whether "right" or "wrong," that the whites have usually been pretty much in charge of things. Scores of minorities, religious and philosophical as well as racial and cultural (and even including many with various sexual differences), want the history books rewritten from their viewpoints, and insist that books not written from their viewpoints are discriminatory and racist. The societies of Canada and the United States have become much more diverse, racially and ethnically, but their legal and cultural backgrounds are mostly derived from Western Europe, so most of the histories will probably continue to be written from that viewpoint, although many recent publications have made a serious effort to include experiences and viewpoints of the minorities.

Some changes aren't being made fast enough to suit some minorities, however, so they're writing their own history books — but instead of writing new histories with a more balanced picture of life as it really was, with a sincere attempt at objectivity, they're writing specialized black, red, Hispanic, and women's histories, to be studied separately, or even exclusively. Black students may now choose to study black history only — which may help them know and appreciate their own ancestral heritage, but will hardly give them a realistic picture of their actual roles in world history.

Women study women; Indians study Indians; and so on. Each special-interest group thinks it is studying the hub of history, rather than an important but smaller spoke.

Our history books should include the many achievements — in the arts, politics, science, sports, music, education, etc. — of minority peoples who have been skipped in most history books of the past, but without emphasis, or even undue mention, of the color or race of the achiever unless it was a significant factor in the achievement. It's significant that Jackie Robinson was the first black player in major-league baseball, but the race or color of players since then has been much less significant. To concentrate exclusively on the achievements of any special-interest group — as in Black History Month — is even more false and deceptive than the abridged histories that have been in use. Studying any subject out of context greatly reduces its meaning. Such "studies" are often intended to increase the "self-esteem" of the minority peoples who have been too much ignored — but anyone whose self-esteem is dependent on being submerged in a larger entity, whether it's a race, a nation, a religion, or a place of birth, needs a different kind of therapy than fictional history will give.

I don't need to wear my hair as my ancestors did, or worship the same gods or dance around the same fires, to know that I have a place in the universe. It pleases me to know that I had two ancestors who fought in the Civil War and five ancestors on the Mayflower, but that knowledge isn't a matter of "pride" for me anymore than the hanging of another ancestor as a horse thief is a matter of shame. My ancestors

came from Europe, but I don't consider myself a "European-American"; I'm simply "American."

If the term "Afro-American" is used to identify blacks, what do we call a white person whose ancestors lived in Africa? Some American Indians — Native Americans — referred to blacks as "black white men," because they seemed so much alike except in skin color.

If students study only fragments of history, based on their own race, nationality, religion, or gender, society will become like scattered pieces of several jigsaw puzzles, growing steadily away from the American ideal of a cultural "melting pot" or the Canadian ideal of a cultural "mosaic." It will take more than all the king's horses and all the king's men to put the pieces together again.

Separating into groups based on race or religion won't put the pieces together again, either.

I fully realize that racial minorities have problems with poverty, education, and health that much of the white population doesn't have — but those problems will never be solved by a renewed emphasis on racial and cultural differences. It was exactly that kind of paranoia and exclusionary thinking — on the part of many races and cultures — that led to the problems in the first place.

If "people of color" really want to be included in the larger home-school community, they certainly won't achieve it by withdrawing into self-conscious shells, or by wearing placards proclaiming, "We're different" and "Nobody understands us." They'll achieve it, and be warmly welcomed, when they realize that we are all different in many ways, but the goals and values that we, as parents and as home-schoolers, have in common — happy, well-educated children — are far more important than superficial differences such as skin color or racial origins.

You may not agree with Donn; that's all right. We all come into adulthood with problems and differences; with possible disabilities related to color, religion, race, poverty, or even wealth; or physical, mental, or emotional challenges. To me, it's how we deal with them, the choices we make as we grow up and out of them, as we strive to make ourselves better people, that counts. The only people we can change are ourselves. If the goal is equality, we must live it.

## MULTICULTURAL LEARNING RESOURCES

*The conquest of the earth, which mostly means the taking it away from those who have a different complexion or slightly flatter noses than ourselves, is not a pretty thing when you look into it.*
— Joseph Conrad

**PEOPLES OF THE WORLD**, by Roma Trundle. Colorful introduction to the customs, traditions, languages, and beliefs of different cultures around the world. Topics include foods, crafts, folk dances, and celebrations. Detailed illustrations throughout, with many specific examples of customs, such as the Japanese bow of greeting, the body paint of the Nuba tribe, Indonesian batik, and how to wrap a sari. The major religions of the world are described in simple terms. Discover what makes our various cultures different and what we have in common. Ages 8 to 12. Code EDC, $6.95.

**LANDS, PEOPLES, AND CULTURES.** See "Geography."

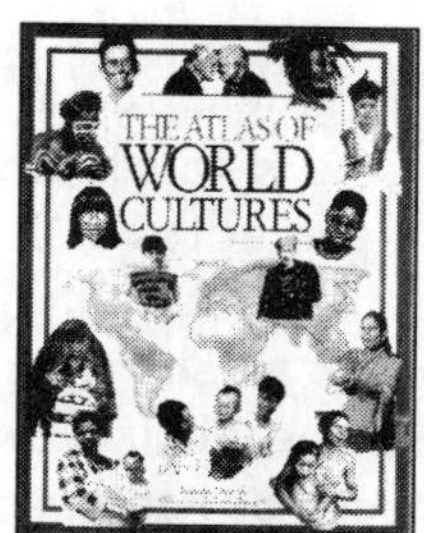


**THE ATLAS OF WORLD CULTURES**, by Brunetto Chiarelli, illustrated by Paola Ravaglia. Open this oversized 10x13" hardcover book and you'll find the flags of the world in bright color on the endpapers. The content of this atlas is much like any other atlas of cultures, with maps, charts, pictures, and information. What sets this one apart from the rest are the special-interest sections on language and writing, religions, food and costumes, art, dance and song, and cultures in conflict. This book is more than a reference book to be pulled off the shelf occasionally; there are so many maps and illustrations of people actively engaged in daily life that it's fun to just open it randomly and browse. I like the fact that the book was originally written in Italy. And guess what? There isn't a picture of a white North American male on the front cover! Ages 10 and up. Code PB, $19.95.

**MULTICULTURAL EDUCATION RESOURCE GUIDE**, by Cheryl Gorder. A wonderful compendium! Books, publishers, magazines, curricula and courses, textbooks, workbooks, toys and games, and so much more. Covers the spectrum of cultures. Code BBRD, $12.95.

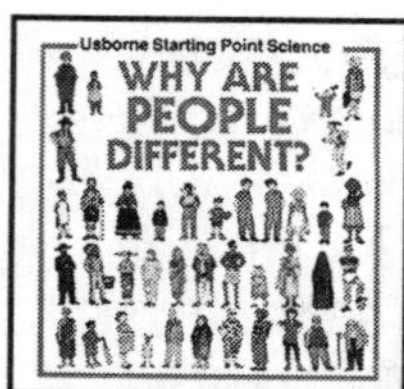


**WHY ARE PEOPLE DIFFERENT?** Now don't you go getting your politically correct back up in a huff until I'm done. This isn't *that* kind of book. Written for kids 4 to 8, this book is designed to give simple answers to common questions asked about why people are different. The text is simple and the detailed full-color illustrations complement the answers, allowing parents and children to discuss what they see and read. The book points out differences based on various circumstances — language, religion, geographic location, etc. — and makes its main point of showing how we are also the same. Numerous examples of being different, but the same. Code EDC, $4.95.

**CREATE A CULTURE: Complete Framework for Students to Use in Creating an Original Culture**, by Carol Nordgaarden. Using this book will help everyone understand just what "culture" means. By creating a fictional culture kids will increase their awareness of their own culture, allowing them to be aware of the similarities and differences with other cultures. You could hurry through this project, but I think you'll have much more fun if you take your time — maybe a whole year, because there's so much to do and think about. You'll have to make some decisions (e.g., name your culture; pick a time period, habitat, and modes of transportation; and so on). You'll be inventing and creating architecture, family structure, power structure, economy, currency, education, language, religion, rituals, folklore, clothing, toys, games, and much more. There are lots of ideas packed into this book to help you with all of these projects, and some suggestions for drawing your work to a successful conclusion. Fine for individual or group projects. Ages 9 to 15. Code LW, $9.95.

**ROUND THE WORLD COOKBOOK** has more than 40 international recipes. Like a night out at an exotic restaurant but better, because you don't have to go anywhere. Light a candle to mark this special occasion, dress up (or not), and put on appropriate music. Children and adults will find immense enjoyment from the food plus information about the food and eating traditions. Maps included. Ages 7 and up. Code EDC, $9.95.

**LET'S CELEBRATE! Canada's Special Days**, by Caroline Parry. Parry, a well-known folklorist, has packed 250 pages with information, cartoons, pictures, jokes, games, crafts, science experiments, poems, special activities, and the history of more than 250 special days of celebration. As diverse as Canada, with something for everyone to celebrate. This book is so culturally diverse that I really didn't want to put in the subtitle for fear only Canadians would be interested. You don't have to be Canadian to enjoy this book. It will be just as useful and fun in the U.S. or anywhere. Learn about Chinese birthdays, two season calendars, the winter solstice, Boxing Day, Black History Month, Lent, Turkish Children's Day, Coptic New Year, Oktoberfest, and more. For all ages. Code KC, $15.95. From the book: "Knock-knock! Who's there? Snow. Snow who? Snow idea, have you?"

### "OH, IT'S NOT SEGREGATION"

"Can an all-white student group at the University of Pennsylvania keep black students out? Oh, yes. A black woman was barred from a meeting of White Women Against Racism because the presence of a black woman would make whites uncomfortable as they examined their racist ways." *U.S. News & World Report*, February 12, 1996.

**FREEDOM CHALLENGE: African American Homeschoolers**, edited by Grace Llewellyn. If you're African American and having doubts that homeschooling will work for you because you're black, this is the book to help you see that it will — and very well. True stories written by those who have lived them. Code LH, $16.95.

### WHAT DO I CALL MYSELF?

A while ago I read a short article in *Reader's Digest* by Keith B. Richburg, author of *Out of America*. It was about his time as a journalist posted in Africa, a time when he confronted some truths about the birthplace of his ancestors — and about himself. He wrote, "I do not hate Africa or the Africans. What I hate is the senseless brutality, the way repressive systems strip decent people of their dignity.

"I am an American, a black American, and I feel no connection to this strange and violent place.

"You see? I just wrote 'black American.' I couldn't even bring myself to write 'African-American.' Is there anything really 'African' left in the descendants of slaves who made that torturous journey across the Atlantic? Are white Americans whose ancestors sailed across the same ocean 'English-Americans' or 'Dutch-Americans'? Haven't the centuries erased these ancient connections, so that we are now simply 'Americans'?"

**MARTIN LUTHER KING JR.** In a 1958 radio interview, "The Causes of Prejudice," Dr. King talks about the roots of prejudice and why it is so difficult to overcome them. He talks about the importance of using Gandhi's principles to find solutions. One cassette. Code AF, $12.95.

**CIVIL RIGHTS FOR KIDS**. See "History and Biography" for this very important book.

**SKIPPING STONES**. This is the best multicultural magazine for kids that I've ever seen. It is full of excellent and exciting prose and poetry by and about children from every imaginable background. There are book and video reviews; contributions from city and country kids telling of their hopes and dreams, their living conditions, and the problems they cope with on a daily basis; pen pals from around the world; bilingual pages; photos by and about kids; and more. Exciting! Low-income subscription allowance and multiple copy discount; write for information. Sample copy $5; subscription $25 (and worth it). Skipping Stones, P.O. Box 3939, Eugene, OR 97403-0939.

---

**A quote from a reader:** "I'm so glad you are a non-Christian group. I have nothing against Christianity, but I dislike exclusive special-interest groups. The special-interest groups would make more sense if they didn't filter their learning through a narrow point of view and those that were interested in learning about them could be included. I feel that home-schoolers have many more ideas and ideals in common to share than differences. The world is too small to wear blinders."

---

**Teaching Tolerance** is an organization devoted to the abolition of prejudice remaining in our society. They follow Gandhi's idea that "if we are to reach real peace in the world, we shall have to begin with children." For materials, write: Teaching Tolerance, P.O. Box 548, Montgomery, AL 36177-9621, and request, *as a teacher,* their Academy Award-winning video, **A TIME FOR JUSTICE**. You can also request **TEACHING TOLERANCE MAGAZINE**, free of charge; **STARTING SMALL** kits for elementary grades; and video and text education kits for secondary students.

**The Native American Homeschool Association** supports homeschooling as a way to preserve and incorporate native cultures into education. Write: Native American Homeschool Association, P.O. Box 979, Fries, VA 24330; expage.com/page/nahomeschool or expage.com/page/nahomeschool2.

**Syracuse Cultural Workers**, P.O. Box 6367, Syracuse, NY 13217, has a small, free catalog of interesting multicultural books for all ages.

**AKWESASNE NOTES**, Mohawk Nation, via Rooseveltown, NY 13683. This official publication of the Mohawk Nation at Kanawake has informative and intriguing news, articles, letters, and editorials by and about Native Americans of today. When writing for subscription information, ask also about Akwesasne Notes Posters and the Native American Calendar.

**Polychrome Publishing Corp.**, 4509 N. Francisco, Chicago, IL 60625, has a catalog of children's books concerning the Asian-Pacific-American community.

**Bison Books**, University of Nebraska, 312 North 14th St., Lincoln, NE 68588-0484, carries a large selection of books about Native American culture, plus some other very good titles. Request free catalog.

### EXCHANGE PROGRAMS

**AFS-USA**, American Field Service, 198 Madison Ave., 8th Floor, New York, NY 10016; 800-876-2377. Request Vol. 10, No. 4 issue, for exchange programs for kids 15 to 19.

**CIEE** (Council on International Educational Exchange), 419 Boyleston, 7th Floor, Boston, MA 02116.

**Rotary International**, 1 Rotary Center, 1560 Sherman Ave., Evanston, IL 60201.

**EF Foundation for Foreign Study**, 1 Memorial Dr., Cambridge, MA 02142; 617-252-6200.

**ASSE** (American Swedish Student Exchange), 800-733-2773.

**YFU** (Youth for Understanding International Exchange), 3501 Newark Street NW, Washington, DC 20016; 800-424-3691.

Please see *The Spirit That Moves Us* in "History and Biography" for literature-based resources for learning about prejudice and discrimination.

# GLOBAL AWARENESS

## HUMAN RIGHTS
## SOCIAL ACTION — VOLUNTEERING
## PEACE AND WAR
## MEDIA MONOPOLIES

"In the end, we will conserve only what we love,
we will love only what we understand,
we will understand only what we are taught."
From *The Diversity of Life*, by Edward O. Wilson

The world is shrinking.

Figuratively, because of the speed of modern transportation and communication, and literally, because some of the earth's substance is dissipating into space in the form of gas and some of the earth's substance is settling and becoming compacted.

Although codes of behavior vary from culture to culture, there are some standards that have always existed in nearly all of them. Among these is the law that it's wrong to hurt another member of one's own group, whether the group is a family, a tribe, or a nation. Murder or theft within one's own group is a punishable offense everywhere, even among those people whose highest awards and honor are for such actions if the victims are from another group.

As the world shrinks, the boundaries of our groups blend and overlap. We can no longer pretend, as we have for centuries, that humanity is not all one family, regardless of color or religion or place of birth.

"Am I my brother's keeper?" Cain asked God, but God knew Cain was being sarcastic, and didn't answer. The shrinking of our world is his answer now.

Most of the materials in this book relate, in one way or another, to global awareness — i.e., awareness that we occupy this planet with billions of other beings and life-forms, with whom we share the responsibility of preserving the health of the earth and its creatures. To do so, we need at least basic information about our fellow beings, and about both the good and the bad directions in which our species seems to be going. Entries in this section are those that most specifically address the subject.

---

*Our country is the world, our countrymen are all mankind.* — William Lloyd Garrison

---

**THE UNIVERSAL DECLARATION OF HUMAN RIGHTS: An Adaptation for Children**, by Ruth Rocha and Octavio Roth. Especially for ages 5 to 12, but interesting and informative for all ages. Based on the 1948 Universal Declaration of Human Rights, and beautifully illustrated, this book is an excellent introduction to the concept of human rights, and to the efforts being made by the United Nations to help countries around the world develop and protect human rights. $9.95 postpaid; checks should be made out to "U.N. Publications." Order #E.89-h from United Nations Publications, Sales Section, Room DC2-853, Dept. 202, New York, NY 10017.

Please consider *The Spirit That Moves Us*, in "History and Biography." It is an excellent literature-based program for the teaching of human rights.

**FACES**. Magazine of world culture from the publishers of *Cobblestone* history magazine and the American Museum of Natural History. Examines societies and individuals around the world: how they live, and their customs, prejudices, fears, and beliefs. Each issue centers on one theme — Asante World, Becoming Human, Coming of Age, Hands, Migration, etc. — with articles, puzzles, recipes, maps, and photo essays. Ages 10 and up. Cobblestone Publishing Company, 30 Grove St., Suite C, Peterborough, NH 03458-1454.

**TEACHABLE MOMENTS**. Two-page teaching guides mailed biweekly during the school year, exploring hunger, poverty, competition, gender roles, etc., around the world. Free. The Stanley Foundation, 420 E. Third St., Muscatine, IA 52761. The Stanley Foundation sponsors "Common Ground," a weekly program broadcast on public radio, featuring speakers involved with global issues. It is possible to get a listing of speakers and topics (and transcripts or cassettes). Write to them or look on the Web at www.commongroundradio.org.

**GAMES AROUND THE WORLD**. 40 ball games, string games, stick games, board games, brain teasers, running games, marble games, stone games, response games, and handicrafts from children of Nigeria, Thailand, Ghana, the Philippines, Egypt, Sri Lanka, Korea, and several other developing nations. The games require no expensive or elaborate materials, and can be played almost anywhere. They're best for young children (about 12 and under), but older children will find them interesting, too. Each 8½x11" game sheet has photos, instructions, and one or two little-known facts about the country from which the game comes. $3.50 plus $1 postage from the U.S. Committee for UNICEF, 331 E. 38th St., New York, NY 10016, or inquire about the price from UNICEF Canada, 443 Mt. Pleasant Rd., Toronto, ON M4S 2L8.

**TOWARDS FREEDOM**. A visionary magazine published by subscription. Their mission is "to publish an international news, analysis, and advocacy journal. TF seeks to strengthen and extend human justice and liberties in every sphere. Believing that freedom of the imagination is the basis for a just world, TF opposes all forms of domination that repress human potential to reason, work creatively, and dream." A few of the topics they have covered are reclaiming the earth, women's visions — ending the violence, global media, and rights and wrongs. An excellent resource if you want to convey this message to your children. 209 College St., Burlington, VT 05401-9953.

**Amnesty International**. A worldwide organization, independent of any government, political group, ideology, economic interest, or religious creed, that seeks the release of men and women detained in prison anywhere for their beliefs, color, sex, ethnic origin, language, or religion, provided they have neither used nor advocated violence. Amnesty International advocates fair and early trials for all political prisoners; it opposes the death penalty and torture or other cruel or degrading treatment of all prisoners. It acts on the basis of the United Nations Universal Declaration of Human Rights and other international instruments. Members are asked to contribute modestly to help support Amnesty International, and to participate in several supportive activities, including letter writing in support of prisoners of conscience, which has been found to be very effective in helping to gain the release of hundreds of prisoners around the world. Homeschooling families may find that participation in Amnesty International is a rewarding way to contribute to human rights around the world. We can't afford large donations to the various organizations we believe are helping to keep the world alive and somewhat sane, but writing three or four letters each month doesn't take much time or effort, and really does make a significant difference. Write for information to Amnesty International USA, 322 8th Ave., 10th Floor, New York, NY 10117-0398, or Amnesty International, 294 Albert St., Suite 204, Ottawa, ON K1P 6E6.

---

*In Germany they came first for the Communists, and I didn't speak up because I wasn't a Communist. Then they came for the Jews, and I didn't speak up because I wasn't a Jew. Then they came for the trade unionists, and I didn't speak up because I wasn't a trade unionist. Then they came for the Catholics, and I didn't speak up because I was a Protestant. Then they came for me, and by that time no one was left to speak up.*

— Pastor Martin Niemöller.

---

Asked what is the most important development of this century that will carry over and influence the 21st century, Howard Zinn (author of *A People's History of the United States*) replied, "Active, nonviolent action." — From a National Public Radio interview with Susan Stamberg

**PEACE AND WAR**

Forty thousand American soldiers died in Vietnam during ten years of war. In the poor countries of the world, 40,000 children under the age of 5 die of malnutrition, dehydration, or disease *every day*. Our family lives very simply, usually on the edge of poverty by North American standards, but we are healthy, educated, and well-fed, and live in a comfortable home. We are never so poor that we cannot send at least a small financial token to UNICEF, the United Nations Children's Fund, which is trying to combat

the economic, cultural, political, and natural enemies of these children. During UNICEF's annual Halloween campaign, we place collection boxes in local stores and the public library. We put UNICEF posters in store windows, and write letters about UNICEF to the local papers. We hang a collection box on our dining room wall and put odd pieces of change into it whenever we pass, and then add our own small donation to those we collect and mail a check to UNICEF, wishing we could do much more. The largest killer of children is simply dehydration caused by severe diarrhea, but a simple packet of oral rehydration salts can save the life of a child just hours from death. Two hundred children's lives can be saved by a donation of only $20. Enough measles vaccine to save 235 children's lives costs only $35. We can't think of a better use for our money — or a better way to go trick-or-treating at Halloween. For information on how your family can help in similar ways, at Halloween or anytime, write: United States Committee for UNICEF, 333 East 38th St., New York, NY 10016.

---

*The greatest evil today is indifference. To know and not to act is a way of consenting to these injustices. The planet has a become a very small place. What happens in other countries affects us.* — Elie Wiesel

---

**The Hunger Site** (www.thehungersite.com) is part of a U.N. program to feed people in need. The money comes from corporate sponsors (such as Sprint), and the amount of food donated daily is based on the number of people who visit the site that day. Please bookmark this site. It takes less than a minute to click on the button at the top of the home page and ensure that one more hungry person will receive something to eat. I do it daily when I first log on. One person *can* make a difference.

---

*Nobody made a greater mistake than he who did nothing because he could only do a little.* — Edmund Burke

---

**Organizations for Peace**. These are a few of the organizations that oppose war and actively work for non-violent alternatives, both on a personal level and on a global level. Most of these groups have religious motivation, but are non-denominational and non-doctrinal. Most of them publish newsletters or other periodicals and books, which will be valuable springboards for family discussions, even if you don't always agree with their views.

**American Friends Service Committee**, 1501 Cherry St., Philadelphia, PA 19102.

**Catholic Peace Fellowship**, 339 Lafayette St., New York, NY 10012.

**Central Committee for Conscientious Objectors** (CCCO), 630 20th St., #302, Oakland, CA 94612; 510-465-1617; cccowr@peacenet.org. On the East Coast: 1515 Cherry St., Philadelphia, PA 19102; 215-563-8787 or 888-236-CCCO. An agency for military and draft counseling. They also have two hotlines: Anti-Junior ROTC hotline, 800-NO-JROTC, and G.I. Rights hotline, 800-FYI-95GI.

**Fellowship of Reconciliation**, Box 271, Nyack, NY 10960.

**Mennonite Central Committee**, 21 S. 12th St., Akron, PA 17501.

**National Inter-Religious Service Board for Conscientious Objectors** (NISBCO), 1830 Connecticut Ave. NW, Washington, DC 20009; NISBCO@igc.apc.org. Counseling and advocacy services.

**Southern Christian Leadership Conference**, 334 Auburn Ave. NE, Atlanta, GA 30303.

**War Resisters League**, 339 Lafayette St., New York, NY 10012. Write for their book catalog. It's a good resource for kids and adults.

**Veterans for Peace, Inc.**, P.O. Box 3881, Portland, ME 04104. *The Washington Spectator* reported on April 15, 1990, that this is the fastest-growing veterans' organization in the U.S. Its president is retired Marine Corps Col. John Barr, who says, "There is a myth that military personnel are war lovers; in 30 years of service, I met no one who was genuinely fond of war." The aims of Veterans for Peace are to increase public knowledge of the human costs of war, restrain the government from military intervention abroad, end the arms race, and eliminate war as an instrument of foreign policy.

---

*The pioneers of a warless world are the young men who refuse military service.* — Albert Einstein

---

**AIN'T GONNA STUDY WAR NO MORE**, by Milton Meltzer. Well-documented stories of individuals and groups who have risked reputation, livelihood, and even life to protest war and violence. From the Colonial Wars and the American Revolution to the Vietnam War and the peace movement of the 1980s, the book tells the experiences and often severe consequences of following conscience rather than civil authority. Ages 9 and up. Code STM, $12.95.

**THE MINE ACTION WORKBOOK.** Produced under the aegis of Canada's Department of Foreign Affairs and International Trade, this downloadable workbook for is meant for ages 12 and up. You can find it on the Web at www.mines.gc.ca/english/education.

**The Institute for Non-Violent Education, Research, and Training** (INVERT). This very active group, affiliated with the War Resisters League, promotes non-violence training, draft and military counseling, war tax resistance, simple living resources, and the Maine Alternative Yellow Green Pages (listing Maine's green businesses). Although it is based in Maine I'm listing it here because it shows what a local or state organization can do. They will be glad to help anyone set up a similar organization. P.O. Box 776, Monroe, ME 04951.

---

*If a thousand men were not to pay their tax bills this year, that would not be a violent and bloody measure, as it would be to pay them, and enable the State to commit violence and shed innocent blood. This is, in fact, the definition of a peaceable revolution.*

— Henry David Thoreau

---

**Peace and War Books.** The War Resisters League sells many titles about disarmament and nuclear threat, draft resistance, conscientious objection, ecology and the environment, Gandhi, the Middle East, Latin America, militarism, pacifism and nonviolent action, prisons and capital punishment, socialism and philosophical anarchism, the Third World, and more. They have *Growing Up Absurd,* by Paul Goodman; *Human Scale*, by Kirkpatrick Sale; and many more, including some super-leftist and/or feminist and/or "gay" manifestos that I mostly ignore. Send for general information and a book catalog. You'll be invited to join and to donate money, but you don't need to be a member to order books. War Resisters League, 339 Lafayette St., New York, NY 10012. Here are a few of the books available from the WRL:

**WRITINGS ON CIVIL DISOBEDIENCE AND NONVIOLENCE**, by Leo Tolstoy. A collection of Tolstoy's major writings on conscience, with the main premise that peace begins only with the individual's refusal to participate in state-organized killing, and that we must seek ways to end our moral complicity and cooperation with the economic, social, and political processes which lead to war. Foreword by George Zbelka, the military chaplain who became a pacifist after blessing the pilots of the planes that dropped the atomic bombs on Hiroshima and Nagasaki.

**HUMAN SCALE**, by Kirkpatrick Sale. Schools, factories, businesses, and governments get out of hand when they are no longer *scaled to humans* — that is, when they become so big that humans become less important than the institutions which were intended to serve them. This is a thoroughly documented study of where and why things go wrong in nearly every facet of society, and what could be done about it. The chapter on education may be of particular interest to homeschoolers, although the entire book is fascinating, horrifying, and — if we're smart enough — hopeful.

**HANDBOOK FOR CONSCIENTIOUS OBJECTORS**. The definitive resource on draft regulations and support.

**YOU CAN'T BE NEUTRAL ON A MOVING TRAIN: A Personal History of Our Times,** by Howard Zinn.

**WHO'S CALLING THE SHOTS?** How to respond to children's fascination with war play and war toys.

**PEOPLE POWER,** by Susan Neiburg Terkel. Explores what is meant by "people power," how it works, and why it is important. This book is for young adults and adults and demonstrates how non-violence can be used for personal, national, and global self-defense.

**A MANUAL ON NONVIOLENCE AND CHILDREN,** edited by Stephanie Judson. More than 100 exercises, games, and agendas designed to help children gain an understanding of the value of cooperation and interdependence.

**NONVIOLENCE IN AMERICA: A Documentary History**. The best one-volume history available.

---

*I would no more teach children military training than teach them arson, robbery, or assassination.*

— Eugene Victor Debs

**Conflict Resolution Resources**. For excellent books specifically written for children about integrated and holistic approaches to conflict resolution, request a catalog from the Atrium Society, Education and Resources, P.O. Box 815, Middlebury, VT 05753.

## SOCIAL ACTION

**GLOBAL THOUGHTS, LOCAL ACTION**, by David McConkey. What can we, as individuals, do in our daily lives to improve conditions and relationships around the world? David McConkey is a home-schooler and is active in international development education. What we do — or don't do — can make a difference, and David gives scores of practical suggestions to show how we can contribute to a better world without leaving home. Although written primarily for adults, this book is suitable for high school students, and for discussion ideas in helping younger children gain global awareness. $4 postpaid from the Marquis Project, 707 Rosser Ave., Brandon, MB R7A 0K8.

**CHOICES: A Family Global Action Handbook**, by David McConkey. Thought-provoking articles, ideas, and practical suggestions to help families live and work in ways that promote global peace and understanding; also discusses peaceful parenting and nonviolent conflict resolution. Very good, very useful. $4 postpaid from the Marquis Project, listed above.

**INVEST YOURSELF**. A catalog of volunteer opportunities, including photos, articles, and listings of more than 40,000 opportunities for summer and full-time volunteers throughout North America and the world in a very broad range of programs: working with the aged; agriculture; arts, drama, and recreation; children and youth; community service; construction and trades; counseling; teaching; environment and natural science; health care; law; mentally or physically handicapped people; religious service; organizing; and more. Most programs provide room and board; some also give a small spending allowance. Some pay for transportation costs to and from the volunteer's home. A great way to travel, learn, and help others, for a few months, a few years, or a lifetime. $7.50 postpaid from the Commission on Voluntary Service and Action (CVSA), P.O. Box 117, New York, NY 10009.

**Institute for Peace and Justice**. A non-denominational group promoting family programs that include reading and activities for all ages, advocating parenting for peace and justice. This group is interested in "creating circles of peace to break the cycle of violence." For more information write the Institute for Peace and Justice, 4144 Lindell Blvd., #408, St. Louis, MO 63108.

**THE KID'S GUIDE TO SOCIAL ACTION: How to Solve the Social Problems You Choose — and Turn Creative Thinking Into Positive Action**, by Barbara A. Lewis. Here's everything kids need to take social action: step-by-step directions for letter-writing, interviewing, speech-making, fund-raising, media coverage, and more; petitions, proclamations, and news releases; addresses and phone numbers for government offices, other social action groups, and awards programs; and inspiring true stories about real kids accomplishing great things. This is the most comprehensive guide available for kids who want to make a difference in the world, written by a teacher whose own students' efforts have resulted in the cleanup of a hazardous waste site and the passage of two new laws. Ages 12 and up. 208 pages with photos and illustrations. Code FS, $18.95.

**THE KID'S GUIDE TO SERVICE PROJECTS**, by Barbara A. Lewis. This book has a slightly different emphasis than her book above. This book is focused on *service* projects that can be carried out within your community, county, or city that will make a difference in people's lives. Endorsed by Youth Service America. Ages 10 and up (and adults, too). Code FS, $12.95.

**WHATEVER HAPPENED TO JUSTICE?**, by Richard J. Maybury. A brief but clear and comprehensive examination of the ways in which the concept of "law" has changed from that of America's founders, who believed, says the author, that "all proposed legislation must be measured against the principles of Higher Law." Ages 12 and up, but adults, too, will find it very interesting and informative. From Bluestocking Press, P.O. Box 2030, Shingle Springs, CA 95682-2030.

---

*To see what is right and not to do it is want of courage.*
— Confucius

**DIRECTORY OF AMERICAN YOUTH ORGANIZATIONS**, by Judith B. Erickson, Ph.D. A guide to more than 500 clubs, groups, troops, teams, societies, lodges, and more organizations for young people. These are adult-sponsored, non-profit youth organizations. Homeschooled kids don't often get bored, but sometimes they need help finding the right direction for their energy and interests. These groups offer opportunities for young people to meet and share their particular interests. Here is a taste of the organizations listed: hobby; academic and honor groups; special-interest groups; career education and vocational student groups; science, math, and technology organizations; sports groups; sports groups for the disabled; civic, educational, and political groups; partisan and non-partisan groups; peace and global understanding groups; community development groups; religious organizations, both denominational and non-denominational; conservation and humane groups; service groups; self-help programs; and a lot more. Listings offer a good description of each group and complete contact information. Code FS, $21.95.

**Books for a Better Future**. New Society Publishers is a publisher of select titles about sustainable communities, eco-forestry, green business, peace, environmental studies and solutions, human rights, the third world, education, and much more excellent reading. Many books for all ages. Not left-wing rabble-rousers, but considered studies and proposals for working with present-day problems for a better tomorrow. We've reviewed a number of their books for you within these pages. Request a free catalog from New Society Publishers, P.O. Box 189, Gabriola Island, BC V0R 1X0.

Last year I watched a TV special on PBS about a program called Seeds of Peace, founded by John Wallach, in Androscoggin, Maine. This camp has many activities common to summer camps as we know them, but with a difference. The young people (teens) who come are from countries around the world where there is long-standing violent conflict: Bosnia and Herzegovina, Egypt, Israel, Palestine, Jordan, etc. By agreement, and with the endorsement of the heads of these troubled governments, these children come to look for ways to help themselves and their countries find and build peaceful solutions. The purpose of Seeds of Peace is to help these young people move past their prejudices, to see their "enemies" as people, to see that as people they have much in common,

including the dream of living in a peaceful society where death and destruction are not a daily fact of life. Seeds of Peace reaches for this goal through activities and discussions facilitated by highly trained personnel.

These young people come to Seeds of Peace with all the hatred and prejudice their societies have conditioned them to feel. They are armed with all the political, racial, or religious propaganda they have acquired since birth to support their point of view. I was going to say the propaganda inherent in their culture, but that is not true. It is not the cultures that hate. It is individuals, and it is conditioning fed by misinformation that breeds hatred and prejudice.

At first the participants begin with very strong feelings of cultural identity. They don't want to be separated from their countrymen. As "enemies" they don't know how to play together with those from other groups. They are suspicious. As the program progresses they begin to talk in small groups that are carefully monitored by the staff. The talk quickly becomes an argument. Everyone has a chance to voice his thoughts and opinions. You can see that at first it is very hard for these kids to sit and listen to someone else say why he and his country are right and the other wrong. The discussion gets heated, they yell at each other, some cry, and after a while they begin to really listen to each other. I was stunned by the emotion that finally drew these kids together in their first common bond. It wasn't love or caring about each other or a desire for peace or political solutions. It was the sharing of personal pain and fear. These are old young faces and they do not love each other at this point, but they all share the pain that comes with the loss of loved ones and the fear they have lived with all their lives. I am humbled. We are so innocent living here in North America.

Once the participants have established a common bond in spite of their differences, activities continue in a carefully planned progression. The campers begin to understand each other. They learn to play games together, they talk a lot, and they begin to make friends with those outside their own group.

The PBS program showed the last evening at Seeds of Peace. Along with a talent show and awards, the kids talked about what they had learned and what they wanted to achieve when they returned home. It was clear they had learned it is not the difference in cultures that creates and breeds violence and prejudice; it is the difference in the "facts" given by the media, it is the self-serving motives of the politicians, and it is never being allowed to see the "enemy" as an individual. Through the time spent at camp they found that as people, not cultures or countries, they had common dreams. These young people, maybe the leaders of the future, left with a determination to heal the differences wherever they could, to find ways to seek peace, with a place for all, because behind all the differences, they were finally able to see each other as human beings, each unique, each with something special to share. These young people found that after all was said and argued, they did have a common goal. They would all like to live in a peaceful place, without fear, and to create understanding, because fear and hatred cannot co-exist with understanding.

## THE MEDIA

**THE LORDS OF THE GLOBAL VILLAGE**, by Ben H. Bagdikian. This lead article in a special issue of *The Nation* assesses the alarming growth of the communications corporations; the shrinking of the media universe; and the consequent threat to freedom and diversity in global news, information, and culture. Meet a gallery of media barons such as Rupert Murdoch and Reinhard Mohn, who amass, homogenize, dominate, and devour media corporations around the world. "A handful of mammoth private organizations have begun to dominate the world's mass media," says the article. "Most of them confidently announce that ... they — five to ten corporate giants — will control most of the world's important newspapers, magazines, books, broadcast stations, movies, recordings, and videocassettes. Moreover, each of these planetary corporations plans to gather under its control every step in the information process, from creation of 'the product' to all the various means by which modern technology delivers media messages to the public — news, information, ideas, entertainment, and public culture." Very scary and thought-provoking. Essential reading if you're concerned about freedom of communication and ideas. Order by title. $4 prepaid ($5 in U.S. dollars for foreign addresses) from The Nation — Reprints, 33 Irving Place, New York, NY 10003.

Donn wrote that a while ago, and it is becoming more of a reality every day. The growth of the Internet has helped with the dissemination of information, but it is not nearly enough of a breakthrough to have much effect.

I've watched the book publishing industry over the last five years. You still see a wide variety of publishing houses listed, but if you look a bit further you quickly notice that they are not all independently owned. Many — way too many — are owned by very large national or international corporations. It is limiting what you will find in your local bookstore and the quality of the mass-market books available. The current trend in publishing seems to be to publish what the public will consume — and discard (e.g. romance novels and adventure thrillers) — rather than books of enduring value. I think many publishers choose new books to publish that are about on the level of the majority of TV programs — and most of those are not worth watching.

I urge you to support your small, local, independent bookseller. They will carry titles you will not find in Wal-Mart, Barnes & Noble, or Amazon.com, booksellers that base their businesses on mass-market sales rather on the quality of content.

# PHILOSOPHY AND RELIGION

## World Religions, Religious Thought, The Great Thoughts, Thinking

### EXPERIENCE

The battery-powered phonograph shuts itself off and I step out into the crunchy morning with the quiet joy of Mozart's thirty-fourth symphony still stirring through my veins. Wispy gray clouds fade away from the dawning sky, and sudden sunlight streaks through the frosty lace of the icy woods around me.

The moment is timeless. I lose myself in the simple magnificence of sparkling crystals, the shadows. Saplings and branches and towering trees are bent together under the weight of their jewels, curving together to form countless circles and arches, surrounding me in a cathedral of awe and wonder. Am I inside, looking out? Or outside, looking in?

A chickadee flies above me; a bashful rabbit pauses nearby; a phoebe calls; a hawk circles and soars away. Under the snow and ice over our little footbridge, the brook murmurs contentedly. They all have the answer.

Then I have it, too. There is no "inside" and "outside." Those are illusions I create when I separate myself from the reality around me.

### MANY PATHS

Whatever we believe or teach our children about God and our relationship to Him, it becomes increasingly important each day that we know, respect, and understand what others believe and teach. Whether we believe that ours is the one and only true religion or that there are many different paths to God and truth (or even if we don't believe in God at all), we need to understand at least the basic beliefs and teachings of others in the human family.

Some of the oldest legends and artifacts of human civilization indicate that people have always searched for truth and goodness; that they have always sought to understand the mystery of life, of being.

Religion did not begin two thousand years ago, nor four, nor five. Jesus was not the first to preach the return of good for evil, although others who have taught the same thing have been ignored and disobeyed just as much.

We teach our children that the universe and everything in it are basically good; that often what we call bad is only goodness distorted, or goodness frustrated, or goodness undeveloped. From a God's-eye view, even the most horrible criminals are never beyond redemption. They're just not ripe — but God has plenty of time. I don't believe that God gambles or experiments or makes mistakes. He won't punish parts of his creation for being slower to develop than others. A parent may say to a child, "I'm punishing you because I love you," but the Creator of billions of stars and flowers and grains of sand is never so foolish. Kindness, understanding, forgiveness, and patient guidance are facets of love; punishments are not.

What loving parent would sentence his child to eternal fear and suffering, no matter what the transgression? Yet there are still some who suggest that the Being whose love and goodness fill the void between the stars will do so for the crime of mistaken belief. Was Jesus lying when he told the parable of the prodigal son?

No doubt we are all prodigal — at times. We waste life, we waste time, still arguing — as did some medieval monks — about how many angels can dance on the head of a pin. "As if you can kill time," wrote Thoreau, "without injuring eternity."

We teach our children that people everywhere want to know God; that the followers of Buddha do not worship his statue, but that they believe in the Eightfold Path of Right Thought and Right Action as devoutly as Christians believe in the Ten Commandments.

In our home, we don't teach denominational dogma, but we often study about it. Our studies include ancient myths and legends as well as the various holy books that have grown from them. In comparing different religions of the world, our purpose is never to proclaim one better or more true than another, but to find what each has to offer for the betterment of humanity. We're curious about the various beliefs regarding creation and the afterlife, but we're more concerned with the moral and ethical teachings — as Jesus was. We're far more interested in the many similarities among various religions than in their differences.

All four of our children have attended various church services with their friends, and have made several interesting observations. The preachers all talk about Jesus quite a bit, but seldom say anything about Jesus's own teachings. The non-fundamentalist churches, of course, are not so concerned with damnation and redemption, but even these say little about applying Jesus's teachings to our own everyday lives. Far more is said about joy in eternity than about meaningful relationships here and now. In general, our kids have found that unbelievers are neither more nor less friendly and considerate than devout believers.

## CONVERSION

When Susan was in her early teens, she decided to attend Sunday school at the local Baptist church — initially just to be with her friends, so we saw no reason not to allow it. We had underestimated the church's techniques of persuasion. Susan was given homework — searching for specified Bible verses (almost always dealing with sin and redemption), competing for prizes in Bible-verse memorization contests, and writing short paragraphs about how her "life of lasciviousness and wickedness" could be changed by accepting Jesus as her savior. The church's literature, bought from a Midwestern publishing company, used adolescent psychology as a strong lever, insisting that Susan's awakening body and "confused thoughts" were under the control of Satan, and repeatedly telling her that she was sinful by nature and unworthy of God's love, which would be given to her only if she accepted God's sacrifice of his son. Recognizing the need of many adolescents to rebel and at the same time to belong to a group, the church distributed stories and articles about "Living With Un-Christian Parents" and "How to Convince Your Parents That They Are Wrong." Susan was encouraged to attend many extracurricular church activities. She stayed up late at night, studying the Bible, copying and memorizing passages — particularly from the Book of Revelations. In the morning, she was tired and antagonistic.

We told Susan we certainly had no objection to her being a Christian, if that was her choice, but that she should examine the church's teachings, investigate other churches, and learn more about Christianity before accepting the teachings of one particular church. Especially, we said, read the four Gospels. They are supposedly the basis of all Christianity; read them carefully, giving particular attention to the message of Jesus himself. She said there was no need to, because she had already found the truth. She accused us of being against the church only because she had chosen it, and then cried because God was going to throw us into a lake of fire and she would be the only one of our family to go to Heaven. She thought she would lose us. We thought we had lost her.

There are many, of course, who would feel that Susan was the only one of our family who had seen the Light. To us, any light that produces blindness is worse than darkness. After so many years of helping our children gain intellectual freedom, we were frightened by the ease with which others could inject intolerance and bigotry into one of them. We reminded ourselves that we should have known; we should have realized the emotional appeal, especially for a young teenager, of being one of God's Chosen.

Our other children were repulsed by the concept of a God who would throw people into a lake of fire, or simply snuff them out like candles.

One Sunday, Susan told us the church's preacher had told the congregation that Pete Seeger and Jane Fonda were communists, and he advised anyone who owned Jane Fonda's workout book to throw it away immediately, and to be careful not to listen to any of Pete Seeger's recordings. She was puzzled and apprehensive, having enjoyed our Pete Seeger records for years, and having looked through Jane Fonda's book in the public library. The principle of the issue wasn't new to our kids, but we were all a little surprised to see it pop up — ironically, in 1984 — in our small rural community in New Brunswick.

In the following week, our speculations about the preacher's concept of communism led into a lively discussion of Senator Joseph McCarthy's witch hunt of the '50s; the subsequent media blacklist of Pete Seeger, the Weavers, Paul Robeson, and many other entertainers because of their refusal to cooperate with the House Un-American Activities Committee (HUAC); and Jane Fonda's opposition to the Vietnam War.

We discussed the nature and dangers of stereotypes, prejudice, and false or incomplete information, and the humorous possibilities of political contamination from contact with an exercise book or a record of folk songs.

After Susan had been a militant born-again fundamentalist for about two years, her friends began drifting away from the church, and she slowly drifted with them.

We know now that Susan did learn from that experience — from the people she knew, from history, from the daily news, and from her own experiences — that there are many ways to find God.

As adults the children have all learned that those who have the most faith, hope, and charity are not always Christians or Jews or Buddhists, and that an atheist is not necessarily lacking in love and sympathy and generosity.

In this week's news magazine, how many reports are there of wars between religious factions — Arabs and Jews, Catholics and Protestants, Christians and atheists, even Christians against Christians?

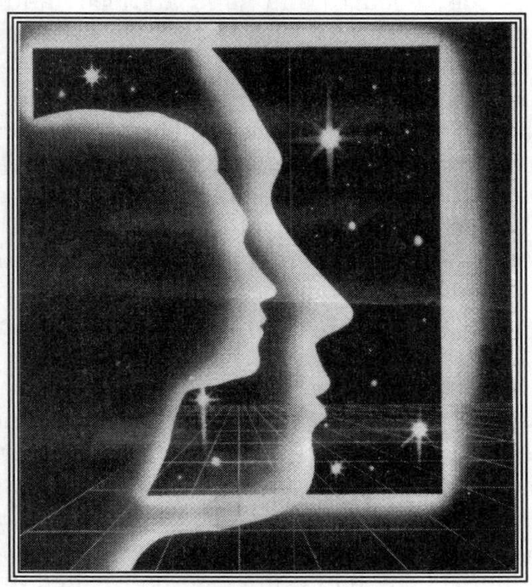

**CREDO**

I sometimes teach about God. Should I say "preach"? My text comes from dozens of holy books; from the many evenings I have lain in my sleeping bag, looking up at the stars; from the smell of new-mown grass; from the births of our children; from Strauss's *Also sprach Zarathustra*; from the sparkle of ice crystals on the tree branches; from the drowning sloth who puts her baby on her head to save its life from the flood rising around her shoulders; from the cut on my finger that knits and heals; from my eye, a small mass of fluid and membrane and blood and nerves, which transmits the image of a star or a flower or a sunset or a loved one to my inner self.

What I teach about God is too much for some, not enough for some, all wrong for some.

"Why, who makes much of miracles?" asked Walt Whitman. "To me every hour of the light and dark is a miracle, every cubic inch of space is a miracle."

When we hear or read of miracles, we look for something out of the ordinary, as if everything ordinary were not a miracle enough. There is no separation between the natural and the supernatural. God is not a remote being to whom we telegraph our requests, dabbling when he pleases in human lives, granting his favors as arbitrary rewards for obeisance or flattery. God is far more natural and more supernatural than that. God IS. All that is, is God. God is the I Am, the Word, the Way, Tao, the Great Spirit, the Over-Soul, the Force, all matter and non-matter, everything seen and unseen, all power and glory forever. Not a star or person or microbe is separate or distinct from God.

The early Greeks personified the earth as Gaia — Mother Earth — and saw all things earthly as being essentially one being, totally interrelated in a global ecology of earth and mind and body and spirit. British scientist James Havelock very seriously proposes the "Gaia Hypothesis" — that the entire earth functions as a single self-regulating organism. Lyall Watson, in *Supernature*, writes, "There is life on earth — one life, which embraces every animal and plant on the planet. Time has divided it up into several million parts, but each is an integral part of the whole. A rose is a rose, but it is also a robin and a rabbit. We are all of one flesh, drawn from the same crucible."

The God of which I teach is that same all-encompassing ecology — not only of the earth, but of the entire universe. Each of us is a droplet of water in the vast and unending Ocean of God. There is nothing that is not God. Our belief or unbelief, doctrine or doubt, searching or scoffing are also parts of what *is*, which is God. "No man is an island, entire of itself," wrote John Donne. "Every man is a piece of the continent, a part of the main; if a clod be washed away by the sea, Europe is the less, as well as if a promontory were, as well as if a manor of thy friends of thine own were. Any man's death diminishes me, because I am involved in mankind; and therefore never send to know for whom the bell tolls; it tolls for thee."

Those words, for me, are literally true, not only in a global sense, or only human, but referring to all things that exist, everywhere.

And how do we "pray"? The ancient psalmist told us: Be still —

"Be still, and know that I am God."

Not with words of supplication, or even of praise, but with surrender and quietness, with openness to let peace and love flow through us and become us.

**LESSON**

When Karen was twelve, she stayed overnight with a friend and went to church with her the next morning.

"The preacher asked how many were praying and their prayers weren't being answered," Karen told us. "A lot of people raised their hands. So the preacher told them their mistake was in saying, 'If it be Thy will.' Instead, he told them, they should praise God, tell him how much they love him, and then he'll give them what they want."

"Do you agree?" we asked her.

"That's just trying to butter God up," Karen said firmly, "and make him feel good, so he'll give us what we want. God is too smart for that."

**IN THE LIGHT**

Officer Archie O'Henry, on a routine patrol one evening, spotted a potted gentleman crawling on hands and knees under the streetlight.

"Can I help you, sir?" he called through his rolled-down window.

The man looked up and finally managed to focus on Officer O'Henry. "Lost my car keys," he explained.

The officer sighed, shut off his motor, and went to help. "Are you sure you lost them here?" he asked.

"Nope," said the man, "lost 'em over there, under that tree. Or maybe that one over there."

The officer scratched his chin. "I hope you won't think I'm being too critical, sir," he said, "but if you lost them over there, wouldn't it make more sense to look for them over there?"

The man hiccoughed and took a deep breath and said indignantly, "'Course not. There's no light over there."

**SERMON**

Calvin Coolidge, the Vermonter who became the thirtieth American president, was asked one day what the preacher had talked about in church that morning.

"Hell," Coolidge replied.

"Oh? What did he say about it?"

"He's agin it," Coolidge replied.

**LAST WORDS**

Preacher Jones, the traveling pastor, had decided to retire, and had finally found a buyer for his horse.

"Joe," he said, "I'm disappointed that you've never come around to be saved, but if you've got the money, the horse is yours."

Joe handed over the money, and Preacher handed Joe the reins.

"By the way, Joe, there are two things I should tell you about this horse. First, when you want him to go, you'll have to say, 'Praise the Lord.' Nothing else will make him move."

Joe frowned, but nodded his understanding.

"The second thing," Preacher said, "is when you want him to stop, you've got to say, 'Amen.' Nothing else will make him even slow down."

Joe frowned again, then nodded and swung into the saddle. He jabbed his heels into the horse's sides and said, "Giddap!"

The horse lazily turned its head to look at Joe, then stretched its neck down to nibble at some grass.

"Remember what I told you, Joe," Preacher said.

"Oh, all right," Joe said disgustedly. "Praise the Lord!"

The horse took off like a shot, neck stretched in front of him, tail flying behind. Joe grabbed the pommel and barely managed to stay in the saddle as the horse galloped away.

Just as Joe finally got himself settled comfortably in the saddle and was beginning to enjoy the ride, he noticed that the horse was going about forty miles an hour straight toward a cliff and his speed was increasing. Joe pulled back on the reins as hard as he could, shouting, "Whoa! Stop! Whoa!" but the horse galloped on.

Just yards from the cliff's edge, Joe remembered. "Amen!" he screamed frantically. "Amen!" The horse stiffened its legs, leaned back on its haunches, and slid to a stop, coming to rest two inches from the edge of the cliff, then stood trembling, anxiously waiting for Joe's command.

Joe looked down — three miles down — over the sheer cliff.

He sighed, wiped the sweat from his forehead with his sleeve, and said, "Praise the Lord."

**DIVINE COMEDY**

God, on a routine patrol one day, stalked me as I walked through the winter woods.

"Can I help you, sir?" he called through a curious chickadee.

I looked up. "I've lost the secret of the universe," I explained.

God sighed in a breeze, circled in a hawk, and came to help in a little flurry of snowflakes. "Are you sure you lost it here?" he asked.

"No," I said. "I think it was in one of those philosophies over there. Or maybe in one of those religions."

God chuckled in the brook. "I hope you won't think I'm being too critical, sir," he said, "but if you lost it in a thought, why are you searching for it in the woods?"

"The light is better here," I answered.

"Trying to butter me up?" God asked.

"No," I answered. "When Adam asked for creatures, you thought he said preachers, so you gave him a lot."

God chuckled in the brook. "Not bad," he said.

"Thank you," I said.

"Not *very* bad," God amended. "Have you heard the story about Calvin Coolidge?"

**PILGRIMAGE**

Our children must form their own relationships with the universe. Knowledge of God can't be taught; it must come from within. Trying to describe God with words is like dipping a bucket into the rushing brook beside our house: The water in the bucket, captured and held, is no longer the same as it was; it no longer bubbles and breathes and gurgles. We can hint and point a general direction, commensurate with our own understanding, but our children must find their own ways by themselves, when they're ready.

We agree with Thoreau: "They who know of no purer source of truth, who have traced up its stream no higher, stand, and wisely stand, by the Bible and the Constitution, and drink at it there with reverence and humility; but they who behold where it comes trickling into this lake or that pool, gird up their loins once more, and continue their pilgrimage toward its fountainhead."

We hope to give our children the strength and desire to continue that pilgrimage.

*God has no religion.* — Mahatma Gandhi

**ALL I SEE IS PART OF ME**, by Chara M. Curtis and expressively illustrated in full color by Cynthia Aldrich. A book of wonder and delight, suitable to use regardless of your religion (or non-religion). This is a child's journey of discovery, of learning that he is a part of, and connected in many ways to, the whole universe; a journey in which he understands that he has an inner life as well as a physical one. The exceptional author and artist combination makes this a treasure. Ages 2 and up, and if you think 8, or 18, or 88 is too old, you need it! This is one I will give my children for their children. Hardcover (because it will see lots of use). Code IA, $15.95.

**IN THE BEGINNING: Creation Stories From Around the World**, compiled and edited by Virginia Hamilton. Twenty-five intriguing stories from cultures around the world about the creation of the world and mankind. Illustrated with beautiful watercolors by Barry Moser. All ages. Code HBJ, $18.

**THE HERO WITH A THOUSAND FACES**, by Joseph Campbell. This audio-cassette adaptation of Joseph Campbell's best-selling book and popular PBS television show brings to life his insightful, poetic interpretation of mythology. Drawing on myths and legends from around the world, Campbell describes "the universal hero," asserting that myths are not merely enchanting fairy tales filled with demons, rituals, and romance, but are allegories that can help us make sense of the timeless mysteries of humankind's physical and spiritual worlds. Weaving traditional wisdom of the past with the modern struggle for identity and spiritual growth, Campbell demonstrates that folklore and mystic literature are potent sources of universal meaning that can serve as spiritual metaphors for modern man. Two cassettes, two hours. Code BT, $19.95. Also available in paperback: Code BT, $18.

**THE CELESTIAL RIVER: Creation Tales of the Milky Way**, by Andrea Stenn Stryer. Just as you and your children have looked at the stars and wondered where they and we came from, people over the centuries have done the same. The tales in this book span the centuries, with stories from Japan, Australia, Greece, Native American traditions, and many other sources, expressing people's fears, needs, and hopes. Ages 8 to adult. Code AH, $7.95.

**WISDOM TALES FROM AROUND THE WORLD**, by Heather Forest. A book filled with folktales, proverbs, and parables that impart lessons for living in a very readable, sometimes funny, and thought-provoking manner. Ages 8 to adult. Code AH, $17.95.

*Every religion is good that teaches man to be good.* — Thomas Paine

**THE OXFORD BOOK OF PRAYER**, edited by George Appleton. A selection of prayers combining traditional with modern, with material from the Bible and the Book of Common Prayer to a Ghanaian fisherman's prayer, including prayers from great non-Christian religions. The compilers looked first for spiritual quality; secondly for literary merit, whether of eloquence or simplicity; and, thirdly for "a living relevance," asking, "Does it ring true?" The prayers are arranged in subject groupings; there's a complete index. 416 pages. Code OX, $15.95.

**THE PROPHET**, by Kahlil Gibran. This beautiful and simple book of poetic prose tells us that work without love is worse than begging; that if there is a despot we would dethrone, we should see first that he is dethroned in our minds; and that children are the arrows of God, and we are His bows. "What is it to make laws but to trace around our own shadows on the ground? But what law binds him who walks facing the sun?" A book to read, reread, and browse in often. I would have chosen different subjects to emphasize and bring to your attention: love, marriage, giving, joy and sorrow, teaching. We consider this book a treasure in our house. Each of our children has a copy. I like to give it as a wedding present. Beautifully illustrated hardcover. Code RH, $15. Now available on cassette. Code RH, $12, but you'll miss the incredibly beautiful and sensitive artwork.

**DICTIONARY OF WORLD RELIGIONS**. A concise, authoritative compendium of information on the world's living religions, including Christianity, Judaism, Buddhism, Hinduism, and many others. More than 1,600 cross-referenced entries, with many key creeds, prayers, and mantras given in full. Hardcover, 848 pages, with 131 black-and-white photos and illustrations, eight pages of color maps, and more. Adults (reference). Code HC, $30.

**CONCISE DICTIONARY OF WORLD RELIGIONS**. A more affordable pocket edition: 700 pages, with 8,200 entries; topic index; and introductory essays about basics of each religion, movements, sects, cults, sacred texts, individuals, sacred sites, customs, ethics, and more. Cross-referenced and easy to use. Adults (reference). Code OX, $15.95.

**WORLD RELIGIONS**. This is a great way to examine the history, beliefs, and customs of the many peoples sharing our world. As travel, communication, and weapons of mass destruction all get faster, we have a much greater need to understand people who are different from us. Bigotry, hatred, and just plain misunderstandings can be avoided in many cases if we can understand and respect our differences as well as all we share as human beings. You'll find beautiful illustrations, photographs of religious works of art, festivals, and ordinary people involved in their religion. I don't care what your religion is — or even if you have none — this book should be part of your studies. Ages 10 and up. Code EDC, $9.95.

*My religion consists of a humble admiration of the illimitable superior spirit who reveals himself in the slight details we are able to perceive with our frail and feeble minds.*

— Albert Einstein as quoted in his *New York Times* obituary, April 19, 1955

**THE VARIETIES OF RELIGIOUS EXPERIENCE**, by William James. A comprehensive masterpiece that explores the personal, subjective, and mystical aspects of religion, considering religion not as a series of doctrines and beliefs, but as a direct experience of that force or essence of being we call "God." Modern Library edition. Adults. Code RH, $18.50.

*The sun, with all those planets revolving around it and dependent on it, can still ripen a bunch of grapes as if it had nothing else in the universe to do.*

—Galileo

**ATLAS OF BIBLE LANDS**, edited by Harry Thomas Frank. A collection of 43 terrain maps (28 in natural vegetation colors), 15 city plans (six of Jerusalem), and more than 80 illustrations in color and black and white of important Biblical sites, archaeological excavations, and artifacts. Hardcover. Code BT, $12.95.

**THOMAS JEFFERSON'S LIFE OF JESUS**. Also called *The Jefferson Bible*. While president, Jefferson compiled a version of the four Gospels that eliminated the virgin birth and resurrection and focused instead on the meaning of Jesus's life and how he lived. Like Thomas Paine and many others of his time, Jefferson was a firm believer in God, but did not accept the doctrines of sin, salvation, and vicarious atonement. He believed (as do many theologians today) that these doctrines were added to the teachings of Christ after he died, and had nothing to do with Christ's actual teachings. Not surprisingly, critics said that Jefferson was only rewriting the Gospels to suit himself, but he believed he was attempting to restore Jesus's real message. "It is in our lives and not our words that our religion must be read," he wrote. Whether or not one agrees with Jefferson, his *Life of Jesus* provides an excellent insight into the religious and moral beliefs of one of America's most important early leaders. It may also be useful in the way Jefferson intended it — as a look at Jesus's actual life and teachings without added doctrinal interpretations. Hardcover. Code BT, $16.

*The care of every man's soul belongs to himself. I cannot give up my guidance to the magistrate, because he knows no more of the way to heaven than I do.*

— Thomas Jefferson

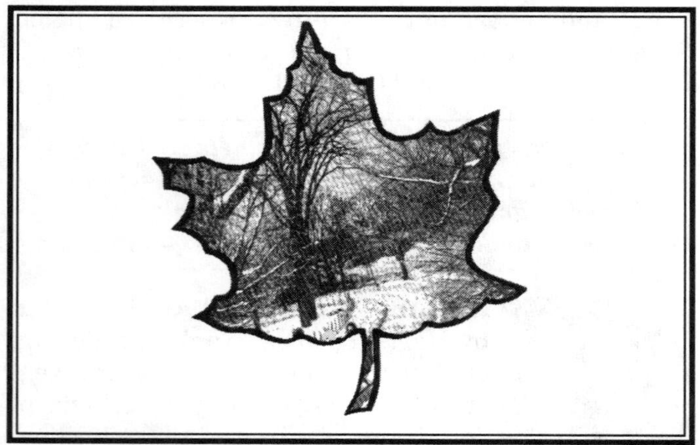

**Try This on Your Computer — Important Correction!!** In the first edition (1991), I said that in the mid-1800s Bishop James Ussher calculated that God finished the creation of everything on October 22, 4004 B.C., at exactly 6:30 a.m. I was wrong, on two counts, and I hope my faulty reporting didn't make you late for any appointments. Ussher (1581-1656), while Archbishop of Armagh, calculated that God finished the creation on October 22, 4004 B.C., not at 6:30 a.m., but at exactly 6:00 p.m. However, in 1859, more than 200 years later, Dr. John Lightfoot, vice chancellor of the University of Cambridge, said Ussher was wrong anyway. "Heaven and earth and man," he said, "was created by the Trinity on twenty-third October, 4004 B.C., at nine o'clock in the morning." (Now that that's settled, let's work on our grammar.)

**gy=c**. Look for this item in "Science" to learn why this might be God's signature.

**Biblical Coloring Books**. Ages 10 to adult. Code BB, $4.95 each.

**A COLORING BOOK OF THE OLD TESTAMENT.** Scenes from the Tickhill and other psalters, reproduced from manuscripts of the 13th and 14th centuries; interesting introduction to medieval art.

**A COLORING BOOK OF THE NEW TESTAMENT**. Ready-to-illuminate illustrations from the renowned St. Alban's Psalter and other Romanesque manuscripts.

**Dover Thrift Editions**. Code DV, $1 each. **Bhagavadgita, Tao Te Ching, Jewish Fairy Tales.**

**A BRIEF HISTORY OF TIME**, by Stephen Hawking. See my description and review of this book and six-hour cassette package in "Science." I mention it here because science and religion are both searching to understand the nature of the universe, and because Hawking's book might also be a brief history of God, although he only hints that this might be so.

**EINSTEIN AND THE BUDDHA**. See "Science."

**ZEN IN THE ART OF ARCHERY**, by Eugen Herrigel. This enduring classic in its field demonstrates several of the basic differences between "Eastern" and "Western" thought; more important, it shows how, through archery (or flower arrangement, or fencing, or almost anything) one can become aware of the absolute Oneness of everything. When the archer abandons his feelings of separateness for the target, when he realizes that he and the bow and the arrow and the target are essentially One, then he sees the futility of striving to hit the target — and the impossibility of missing it. Code RH, $10.

**Eastern Thought and Religion**. Books on karma, Universal Brotherhood, reincarnation, and more. The Theosophy Company, 245 West 33rd St., Los Angeles, CA 90007.

---

*Three things are necessary for the salvation of man: to know what he ought to believe, to know what he ought to desire, and to know what he ought to do.* — St. Thomas Aquinas

---

**NEW OXFORD REVIEW**. Ecumenical, intellectual "return to religion," praised equally by conservatives such as George Will and *Newsweek* and by liberals such as *Utne Reader*. Suggests that "the answers" are in the tradition of Moses, Jeremiah, Jesus, Augustine, Dante, Aquinas, Tolstoy, Kierkegaard, Buber, Niebuhr, Dorothy Day, and Mother Teresa. 1 year/$14; sample $3.50. Write: Room 576, 1069 Kains Ave., Berkeley, CA 94706.

The Bahá'í faith, while young in comparison to many of the world's religions, is worthy of investigation. It began in Persia (now Iran) in the middle of the 19th century, which certainly makes it a very young religion. Here are a few of its basic tenets: "There is only one God; all religions share a common foundation; mankind is one — the peoples of all races, nations, economic groups, and religious backgrounds are equal in the sight of God; each individual is responsible for investigating truth for himself; science and religion harmonize; men and women are equal, like the two wings of one bird." We recommend **THE BAHÁ'Í FAITH: The Emerging Global Religion**, by William S. Hatcher and J. Douglas Martin, and **THE BAHÁ'ÍS**, a compilation by the Bahá'í international community. Both books and general information are available from the Bahá'í Distribution Service, 5397 Wilbanks Dr., Chattanooga, TN 37343; www.bahai.org.

**NOAH'S ARK AND RAINBOW OF PROMISE.** Book and cassette. Written for young children beginning to read. Also easily understood if read to younger children. Cassette tells the story (with humor and songs) to reinforce the message. Ages 3 and up. Code EDC, $13.95.

**NOAH'S ARK.** Acid-free reusable sticker book, $9\frac{1}{4}$x$11\frac{1}{4}$". The book covers make a backdrop for the 30 or more full-color, reusable stickers in each book. Ages 7 and up. Code DV, $3.50.

**EASY-TO-MAKE NOAH'S ARK.** Cut and assemble an 11" model of Noah's Ark, complete with Noah, his family, and the animals, all two-by-two: polar bears, camels, ostriches, crocodiles, elephants, zebras, etc. Pieces are printed in full color on both sides of heavy stock. Full instructions. About ages 8 to 10. Code DV, $3.95.

**OLD TESTAMENT DAYS: An Activity Guide**, by Nancy I. Sanders. 168 pages filled with tidbits of information about the stories in the Old Testament, a timeline, and activities. Most materials you'll have around the house or can purchase inexpensively. Hours of fun and creative play. Ages 5 to 12. Code CRP, $14.95.

**Christian Book Distributors**, P.O. Box 7000, Peabody, MA 01961-7000, put out many free catalogs a year. Most items are Christian based. Some excellent movies as well as books, games, and more.

**THE CHRISTMAS STORY**, retold by Heather Amery and nicely illustrated. The illustrations make me smile. Written for beginning readers with some assistance from a friendly adult or older sibling. Can be read and understood by very young children. 98 pages. Ages 3 to 8. Code EDC, $4.50 paperback, $12.95 hardcover.

**BIBLE TALES SERIES**, by Heather Amery. These are Usborne books and you can trust them. They have taken some of the more popular and instructive stories and put them into a format designed for beginning readers. They're charmingly illustrated, and the pictures give clear clues to the words and their meaning. Ages 2 and up; beginning readers will do well with a little help. Paperback, 16 pages each. Code EDC, $4.50 each. **Daniel and the Lions, David and Goliath, Jonah and the Whale, Joseph and His Amazing Coat, Moses in the Bulrushes.**

**TAPESTRIES: Stories of Women in the Bible**, by Ruth Sanderson. Beautifully illustrated! This 9x$11\frac{1}{2}$" hardcover book is a collection of 23 stories of women in the Old and New Testaments. The stories are short and simple, yet well told. Young children will enjoy hearing the stories read aloud, and older children (8 and up) can read them on their own. Code LB, $15.95.

**DOROTHY DAY: Friend of the Forgotten**, by Deborah Kent. A moving testimonial biography to a woman of great Christian faith, a pacifist and protester, founder of the *Catholic Worker* newspaper and shelters. Recommended for ages 10 to 14, but I found extreme pleasure in reading it too — and so might you. Code ER, $8.

**Religion, Scriptures, and Spirituality**. Since the dawn of civilization, religions have expressed the concerns at the core of human existence: life's meaning and purpose, the significance of birth and death, moral commitments, and the proper conduct of life. Religion transcends *making a living* to guide us in *how we should live*. It involves us with what some theologians call "an other" — an inexpressible, non-rational part of existence that may be an emotional refuge or a source of spiritual nourishment and enlightenment. The history of the world is intertwined with religion, and can never be fully understood without a basic knowledge of the beliefs that have shaped it.

Each of these programs consists of two 90-minute cassette tapes, narrated by actor Ben Kingsley and featuring dozens of dramatizations and characterizations of great religious leaders, theologians, historians, and readers of the various scriptures. All code KP, $17.95 each, plus $2 shipping for the first set, 50 cents for each additional set. Ask about a discount for three or more sets. Order by number and title.

**Set 1: ORTHODOX AND ROMAN CATHOLIC CHRISTIANITY**. Both of these churches have their roots in first-century Christianity; their basic doctrines were summarized in the great Councils of the Churches, yet Orthodoxy and Catholicism have diverged through the centuries as each embraced different ideas about worship, ethics, and relations to politics and culture.

**Set 2: PROTESTANT CHRISTIANITY**. Since the 16th century, Christianity has flourished in a third form called Protestantism. In the Protestant Reformation, four distinct forms of religious expression emerged: Lutheran, Reformed, Anglican, and various radical extensions of those three initial movements. Succeeding developments extended this variety over the centuries, leading to the many sects and denominations of today.

**Set 3: JUDAISM.** Judaism is both a religion and a way of life. It has several major forms, or traditions (Orthodox, Conservative, Reform, and Reconstructionist); it is also the parent religion of both Christianity and Islam. Jewish sacred literature preserves the ancient oral tradition through the Hebrew Bible (Christianity's Old Testament) and other writings (in particular, the Talmud). Judaism exalts the divine gifts of the Torah, God's teaching or instruction.

**Set 4: ISLAM**. Islam began in the seventh century, and has evolved into various forms — Sunni, Shia, Sufi mysticism, and others — and is now a rapidly growing religion. This program also discusses the backgrounds and connections of related groups such as the Druse, Bahá'í, the Nation of Islam, and others.

**Set 5: HINDUISM**. Hinduism began in India about 1800 B.C.; several other religions and philosophies have sprung from it, including Buddhism and the Jain tradition (both sixth century B.C.) and the Sikh tradition (15th century A.D.). Vedanta, yoga, transcendental meditation, and other spiritual and meditative exercises are also related to Hinduism.

**Set 6: BUDDHISM**. Buddhism began with Siddhartha Gautama in the sixth century B.C. and has developed two chief forms: Theravada (or Hinayana) is found especially in Asian countries; Zen, a more recent form of Buddhism, is found throughout the world.

**Set 7: SHINTO AND JAPANESE NEW RELIGIONS**. Traditional Shinto was present in Japan from prehistoric times, and has greatly influenced Japanese culture. This program discusses various forms of Shinto, as well as new Japanese religions formed during the past 150 years.

**Set 8: CONFUCIANISM AND TAOISM.** Confucius, in the sixth century B.C., stressed family ethics and humanistic virtues and values. Taoism, beginning only a little later, is concerned with universal principles as well as social values.

**Set 9: NON-LITERATE RELIGIONS**. "Primitive" religious practices and understandings — those without a surviving sacred literature — are recognized by many to be in no way inferior to other religious beliefs. This program compares various non-literate religions, along with a discussion of their geographical concentrations and historical development.

**Set 10: CLASSICAL MEDITERRANEAN RELIGIONS AND MYTHS**. Mesopotamia, Egypt, Asia Minor, Canaan, Greece, and Rome have greatly and continuously influenced all of Western culture and civilization, and the literature and culture of the religions of these areas have also influenced Hebrew and Christian scriptures.

**Set 11: AFRICAN AND AFRICAN-AMERICAN RELIGION.** The religious ideas and practices of African peoples have much in common with each other, and with related religions in the Caribbean and the Americas.

**Set 12: NATIVE RELIGIONS OF THE AMERICAS.** This program discusses the religious heritage and cultures of North, Central, and South American Indians.

**Set 13: SKEPTICISM AND RELIGIOUS RELATIVISM**. Humanism, agnosticism, and atheism have always challenged traditional religious doctrines, yet reason alone — like religious faith alone — often raises more questions than answers. Can a religious commitment be reconciled with life in a rational, skeptical world?

**THE FAMILY TREASURY OF JEWISH HOLIDAYS**, by Malka Drucker and nicely illustrated by Nancy Patz. A true treasury that explains the most important Jewish celebrations and traditions. This book brings them all to life with music, stories, recipes, and projects. Code LB, $12.95.

**MAKE YOUR OWN JEWISH CALENDAR** This $8\frac{1}{2}$x11" book is designed to open and hang lengthwise on the wall. The top half of each two-page spread has lots of room to color your own picture. The lower section has space for you to write in birthdays and special occasions. Ages 6 to 10. Code DV, $2.95.

**RETURN OF THE INDIAN SPIRIT**, by Vinson Brown. A young Indian boy, raised in the city, visits the reservation and is inspired to attain the knowledge of his forefathers. Well told. Code TSP, $6.95.

**STORMY NIGHT**, written and illustrated by Michèle Lemieux. A book you and your child will explore many times and use as a springboard to probe and discuss many of life's puzzling questions. "Who am I?" "Is there only one me in the world?" "Imagine if we could switch bodies." "Is there anyone watching over me?" A book for parents and children of all religions and cultural backgrounds. Ages 8 and up. Code KC, $12.95.

**DREAMBIRDS**, by David Ogden. Opens with a quote from Chief Seattle: "And when your children's children shall think themselves alone in the fields, the store, the shops, upon the highway, or in the silence of the pathless woods, they will not be alone." The theme embraced here is the search for your true self and the recognition that "the source of all things is like a circle. It is where everything begins and everything ends." In some ways this is a very simple story of an Indian boy's search for his dreambird, yet there is a resounding depth that will appeal to all ages and all faiths. Large hardcover, with beautiful artwork on every page. Code IA, $16.95.

---

*Our humanity were a poor thing but for the divinity that stirs within us.* —Francis Bacon

**WALDEN, or Life in the Woods**
by Henry David Thoreau

I spent many of my childhood and teenage weekends and summers hiking and camping in the woods of southern Vermont, sometimes with one or two friends but more often by myself. One day, my sophomore English teacher, Walter Cohen, had written the title of this book on the chalkboard, and the subtitle made me wait eagerly for his explanation — which never came. At the end of the day, the note was erased. I realized much later that he had been sowing a random seed, and I may have been the most fertile ground in that particular class.

About that time, the early '50s, some of the world's best literature was being published in inexpensive paperbacks for the first time. Browsing in a bookstore one afternoon (a favorite pastime), I recognized that title and bought it — for 35 cents — and soon entered into one of the most important revolutions of my life. The first pages told me the book wasn't about camping at all, and not very much about life in the woods. It was about life in society, life in the world, life in the universe, life within oneself. How should I live my life? To whom or to what do I owe allegiance? How should I relate to other people, to society, to government, to my own existence?

"Why should we be in such desperate haste to succeed," Thoreau asked, "and in such desperate enterprises? If a man does not keep pace with his companions, perhaps it is because he hears a different drummer. Let him step to the music which he hears, however measured or far away" — not meaning, as many would have it today, that one should act capriciously or merely for self-gratification, but that one should listen for, and be guided by, the inner voice of conscience, of principle, of higher laws than those devised by governments. "I think that we should be men first, and subjects afterward. It is not desirable to cultivate a respect for the law, so much as for the right."

I devoured the book; it devoured me. What I felt was not so much agreement as recognition, as if many of Thoreau's thoughts were already in my mind and soul, hidden, waiting only to be called forth by an expression of them far greater than I would ever achieve.

Thoreau refused to pay his poll tax to Massachusetts, because that state supported the Fugitive Slave Act and the Mexican War, both of which he believed were wrong. For a while he was a schoolmaster, but was fired for taking his students on nature walks, and for refusing to whip them periodically to keep them in line.

Thoreau's essay "Civil Disobedience" has encouraged thousands, perhaps millions, to resist injustice, not through bloodshed and violence, but by personal withdrawal from the injustice. You can't stop the machinery of government, he said, but your deliberate opposition to its tyranny may throw a little sand in the gears. Gandhi, Tolstoy, and Martin Luther King Jr. credit their reading of "Civil Disobedience" as a turning point in their own educations and careers. No one, before or since, has so eloquently and accurately summed up the ideal relation of a person to society, to government, and to oneself.

Thoreau used words carefully and exactly, never settling for an approximation of what he meant, always choosing the word that precisely conveyed his meaning. He was a classical scholar, and likened the tending of his bean field to ancient battles — "Daily the beans saw me come to their rescue armed with a hoe, and thin the ranks of their enemies, filling up the trenches with weedy dead. Many a lusty crest-waving Hector, that towered a whole foot above his crowding comrades, fell before my weapon and rolled in the dust." He enjoyed puns — "If you are chosen town clerk, you cannot go to Tierra del Fuego this summer; but you may go to the land of infernal fire nevertheless."

*Walden* and "Civil Disobedience" shouldn't be required reading, because the person who isn't ready for them will get little from them, but every thinking person should have a copy, and browse in it occasionally, ready for the moment when Thoreau's words suddenly open the shutter and let the sunlight in.

I've read *Walden* many times, and reread bits of it — a sentence here, a paragraph there, often becoming absorbed and finishing the chapter — scores of times. I always discover something new in myself.

There are many editions of *Walden* and Thoreau's other works. I recommend the Modern Library edition, **WALDEN AND OTHER WRITINGS BY HENRY DAVID THOREAU**, which includes his two other books — *A Week on the Concord and Merrimack Rivers* and *Cape Cod* — and six of his most important essays — "The Allegash and East Branch," "Walking," "Civil Disobedience," "Slavery in Massachusetts, "A Plea for Captain John Brown," and "Life Without Principle." This is a durable, hardcover book, with clear text and a reasonable price. Code RH, $19.50.

**A MAN NAMED THOREAU**, by Robert Burleigh. An excellent introduction to Henry David Thoreau for all ages. Quotations from *Walden* have been woven with biographical facts and bits of Thoreau's philosophy to give an intriguing picture of an unusual man and his examination of conventional society. Many difficult concepts have been simplified without loss or distortion of meaning, making this a very good introduction to many questions of ethics and morality as well as a portrait of Thoreau.

I just learned that this book is out of print. If you've never read Thoreau this is a good introduction. If you've read Thoreau and found his style difficult, this little volume will unlock the secret of reading him with joy. Perhaps you can find it at your library.

> *Do not be too moral. You may cheat yourself out of much life so. Aim above morality. Be not simply good; be good for something.*
>
> — Henry David Thoreau

**WHAT DO YOU STAND FOR?**, by Barbara A. Lewis. Written for adults working with children in volunteer situations, this unique book is much more. It is a tool to help you and your kids explore your values and place in the community. It discusses courage, friendship, honesty, responsibility, empathy, forgiveness, loyalty, and more. It's thought-provoking and inspirational, with challenging activities to explore and develop individual values. Highly recommended. 224 pages. Ages 10 and up, Code FS, $19.95. Also see **BEING YOUR BEST**, written for children ages 7 to 12, in "Family Living."

**THE BOOK OF THINK, or How to Solve a Problem Twice Your Size**, by Marilyn Burns (a Brown Paper School Book). Did you ever have a traffic jam in your head? Did you ever feel as if on some days you just won't do anything right? Did you ever get yourself into a corner and know that whichever way you tried to get out was going to be the wrong way? If the answer to any of those questions is yes, then this book is for you. This book is about what to do when you are puzzled, or perplexed, or stumped, or can't get there from here. It's about using your noggin. It's about being smart even when you feel dumb. This book is about how to think even when you know you're fresh out of ideas. If you are a person who never has a problem, then don't read this book. Code LB, $13.95.

Exercise for people of all ages: Think about the things you want to do before you die. Make a list of at least 30 things. Look to see which are the most important and reorganize your list. Think about what you are doing to accomplish what you would like to do. Do this every year and keep your lists.

**WHAT DO YOU THINK? A Kid's Guide to Dealing with Daily Dilemmas**, by Linda Schwartz. You've talked about values — honesty, responsibility, forgiveness, and a lot more. Now it's a matter of learning ways to live those values and deal with the smaller everyday problems that can create dilemmas. This book presents daily situations that can cause problems. There aren't any answers in the book. The challenge here is to think about the problem presented and find practical, constructive solutions. Ages 10 to 14. Code LW, $9.95.

---

*Physical bravery is an animal instinct; moral bravery is a much higher and truer courage.*
— Wendell Phillips

---

**PSYCHOLOGY FOR KIDS #1 — Discover Yourself**, by Jonni Kincher. Are you an extrovert or an introvert, an optimist or a pessimist? Forty fun (and fascinating) quizzes, based on sound psychological concepts, will help you discover who you are and how you think about yourself. Ages 10 and up. Code FS, $16.95.

**PSYCHOLOGY FOR KIDS #2 — Learn About Others,** by Jonni Kincher. A companion to the book above. Lots to ponder and discuss. Are people more logical or emotional? Is there really a difference between the way males and females think? Do you think competition improves performance? Sharpen your observation skills. Learning about others helps us learn about ourselves. Ages 12 and up. Code FS, $17.95.

**THE FIRST HONEST BOOK ABOUT LIES,** by Jonni Kincher. This exceptional book is one of the most important you and your children will read and discuss — ideally, together. Serious and thought-provoking, yet also funny and full of experiments, examples, and games to help you explore truth; the nature of lies; and how they are used by you, on you, and around you. This book probes for the reasons for lying and promotes active questioning. Do lies serve a purpose, and if so, what purpose? This book won't tell you what to think, but it will help you establish good thinking habits about truth and lies. A good book to share and discuss — if you can get it away from your kids long enough to get a look at it. Ages 13 and up. Code FS, $14.95.

**GREAT IDEAS THAT HAVE SHAPED OUR WORLD**. Excellent cassette programs presenting the ideas of Paine, Jefferson, Thoreau, Garrison, Adam Smith, Mill, Burke, Hamilton, Hobbes, Locke, de Tocqueville, and others. See "History and Biography."

**GREAT CLASSICAL MYTHS**
**THE CITY OF GOD**, by St. Augustine
**THE WISDOM OF CONFUCIUS**
**THE WISDOM OF LAO TSE**
**THE WORKS OF PLATO**
See the Modern Library section of "Literature."

*There was never yet philosopher that could endure the toothache patiently.*
— William Shakespeare

**The Giants of Philosophy**. "Moderation in all things." "I think, therefore I am." "The unexamined life is not worth living." "And it is this that everyone understands to be God." These are the men whose thoughts have formed much of our Western civilization: Plato, Aristotle, St. Augustine, Immanuel Kant, and nine others. These are the men who have contributed greatly to the ideas we now have about happiness, love, art, God, morality, reason, justice, goodness, and evil.

The format of these presentations is the same as that of the Great Ideas That Have Shaped Our World (see "History and Biography"). The cassette tapes of the Giants of Philosophy are dramatized, with multiple voices portraying the author, contemporary observers, and critics, drawing on actual writings and quotations of the time and later history, with an overview narrated by actor Charlton Heston. Each tape is about 90 minutes long, divided into shorter segments — about 20 minutes each — for more convenient study. The social and historical background of each work is presented, as well as the effects, both immediate and long-term, that the work had on other thinkers and on society. There are numerous references to other works and historical events, demonstrating the continuing influence of the author's ideas.

Listening to these tapes is much better than simply reading the works that are discussed. The full background of the works and their influences on contemporary and future society are fully explored, giving a much deeper understanding than could be gained from the works by themselves. Code KP, $17.95 each, plus $2 shipping for the first set, 50 cents for each additional set. Ask about a discount for three or more sets. Specify "Giants of Philosophy," set number, and title. (e.g., Set #12, Dewey).

**Set 1: PLATO** (ca. 430-350 B.C.), Greece. Plato, the first great Western philosopher, thought that existing things are modeled on changeless, eternal forms. To Plato, human beings consist of an immortal soul and a mortal body; the soul has a love for the eternal, the good, the true, and the beautiful; these give life purpose, stability, and meaning.

**Set 2: ARISTOTLE** (384-322 B.C.), Greece. In revising Plato's ideas, Aristotle thought human beings are one with the rest of nature, yet set apart from it by their ability to reason. Aristotle codified the laws of thought, gave a complete account of nature and of God, and developed an attractive view of the Good Life and the Good Society. He was the first to describe physics, biology, psychology, and the standards of literature systematically.

**Set 3: ST. AUGUSTINE** (A.D. 354-430), Rome. St. Augustine, the first great systematic Christian philosopher, thought of Plato's eternal forms as ideas in the mind of God; he believed Christ provided the light of knowledge to the human mind. His detailed description of the City of God portrayed a divine ordering of human affairs.

**Set 4: ST. THOMAS AQUINAS** (1224-1274), Italy. The *Summa Theologiae* was St. Thomas Aquinas' monumental summation of the facts of Christian faith and knowledge. He offered proofs of the existence of God and set limits to the power of reason; he gave an account of the nature and constitution of the world, and outlined the soul's road to blessedness.

**Set 5: BARUCH SPINOZA** (1632-1677), the Netherlands. Spinoza took the unorthodox view that God, an eternal and infinite being, is identical with the world, and that we are therefore merely parts of the Deity. Human fulfillment is possible, he believed, only by rejecting our finite, flawed selves and identifying with the eternal within us.

**Set 6: DAVID HUME** (1711-1776), Scotland. Hume thought the entire world is constituted of the perceptions from our sense-experience. He had profound doubts about our ability to *know* anything with certainty; he was skeptical of science, and vigorously attacked others' proofs of the existence of God. He thought reason is a slave to our passions, yet was optimistic about human nature.

**Set 7: IMMANUEL KANT** (1724-1804), Germany. Kant believed that reason, the most fundamental human faculty, creates a world in which all events are causally connected; it enables us to act morally, to enjoy beauty, and to appreciate nature's magnificence. He forecast the possibility of a purely rational religion, and believed that the rule of reason might lead to permanent international peace. Kant believed that God's existence cannot be known, but he saw evidence of God in the moral order of the world.

**Set 8: GEORG WILHELM FRIEDRICH HEGEL** (1770-1831), Germany. Hegel aimed to make philosophy a comprehensive science and to restate the truth of Christianity in more precise language. For him, the state represents the divine on earth; our lives have meaning only as small parts of this larger entity. Hegel saw progress as the work of reason and of the "dialectic" — a historical process moving us through struggle and contradiction to a higher synthesis.

*What experience and history teach is this — that people and governments never have learned anything from history, or acted on principles deduced from it.* — Hegel

**Set 9: ARTHUR SCHOPENHAUER** (1788-1860), Germany. Schopenhauer was the most articulate and influential philosophical pessimist in the history of human thought. He believed that the space and time of ordinary life are illusions, and that we can flourish only at each other's expense. Life, therefore, is evil to the core, and pain and suffering are unavoidable; the price of escape is the total surrender of ambition, desire, and choice. (Compare this with the revelations that came to Siddhartha Gautama, bringing him to the realizations that made him the Buddha.)

*Every man takes the limits of his own field of vision for the limits of the world.*
— Schopenhauer

**Set 10: SOREN KIERKEGAARD** (1813-1855), Denmark. Kierkegaard believed that truth emerges only from our subjective, private lives, but neither the selfish search for pleasure nor a responsible social life can fully satisfy us. A deeply religious thinker, he believed that God's existence cannot be proven, but that only a religious leap of faith can make our own finitude bearable and endow life with meaning.

*Life can only be understood backwards; but it must be lived forwards.* — Kierkegaard

**Set 11: FRIEDRICH NIETZSCHE** (1844-1900), Germany. Nietzsche announced in 1883 that God is dead, reasoning that the world's injustices and suffering could not exist if God were still alive. He also believed that truth is relative, and proposed to replace the values of traditional morality with the idea that creative human beings can use their energy, strength, and intelligence to give purpose and meaning to their own lives.

*Man is a rope stretched between the animal and the Superman — a rope over the abyss.*
— Nietzsche

**Set 12: JOHN DEWEY** (1859-1952), the United States. Dewey believed that the scientific method, when applied to human affairs, can enhance personal happiness and community cooperation. Dewey believed that democracy is not so much a political organization as a way of life; it is best promoted by a rational and effective educational system. Dewey's educational theories, which grew out of his philosophy, have been greatly criticized, but are still very influential.

*The school is primarily a social institution; education, therefore, is a process of living and not a preparation for future living.* — Dewey

**Set 13: JEAN-PAUL SARTRE** (1905-1980), France. Sartre was a leading advocate of existentialism — the view that we must establish our own existence and individual dignity, despite a meaningless life and final death. Sartre asserted the ultimate reality of human freedom and the desperate need for personal responsibility.

*Man is not the sum of what he has but the totality of what he does not yet have, of what he might have.* — Sartre

*Every day one should at least ... read one good poem, see one fine painting and — if at all possible — speak a few sensible words.*
— Johann Wolfgang von Goethe

*I have gained this by philosophy: that I do without being commanded what others do only from fear of the law.* — Aristotle

*When angry, count ten before you speak; if very angry, a hundred.* — Thomas Jefferson

*When angry, count four; when very angry, swear.* — Mark Twain

*... ministers who spoke of God as if they enjoyed a monopoly of the subject.*
— Henry David Thoreau

*I hate people who are intolerant.*
— Laurence J. Peter

*Humanity is the Son of God.*
—Theodore Parker

*The test of a preacher is that his congregation goes away saying, not What a lovely sermon, but, I will do something!* — St. Francis de Sales

*Adam and Eve had many advantages, but the principal one was that they escaped teething.*
— Mark Twain

# ARTS AND ACTIVITIES

## CRAFTS, GAMES, HOBBIES, SPORTS PLUS ACTIVITIES AND GIFTS FOR THE HOLIDAYS

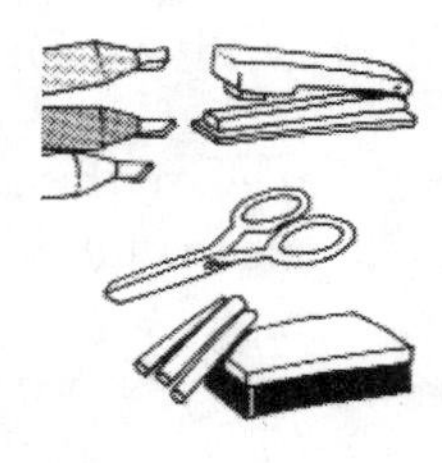

Arts and crafts aren't just time fillers or exercises in manual dexterity. These activities help fulfill a human need to create something unique and to express ourselves. Making good use of the materials in this section will help your children learn skills beyond what a strictly academic program provides. Enjoyment from these activities can build a foundation for future interests that will carry over into adulthood and become a lifelong pleasure — or perhaps a passion — or a way to make a living.

As you go through this section, keep in mind that many of these items would make wonderful gifts (as do many items in other chapters). We will be happy to gift-wrap items for you and include a card (you can supply your own if you like) and ship items to you or to a third party. Please keep in mind that we do not stock all of these items, and some take a while for us to receive. Please plan ahead to avoid disappointment.

**Necessary Items to Have on Hand** — Paper, pencils, crayons, watercolors, poster paints, finger-paints, scissors, ruler, glue, paste (glue sticks are neat), colored construction paper. Our kids never liked the oversized pencils and crayons supposedly meant for "little fingers." For older kids, ballpoint pens, colored pencils, and felt-tip markers.

### ART SUPPLY CATALOGS

**The Jerry's Catalog,** P.O. Box 58638, Raleigh, NC 27658; www.jerryscatalog.com.

**Dick Blick,** P.O. Box 1267, Galesburg, IL 61402-1267; www.dickblick.com.

### ART MAGAZINES

**The Artist**, P.O. Box 2120, Harlan, IA 51593.

**Watercolor Magic**, P.O. Box 5439, Harlan, IA 51593.

### ACTIVITIES AND PROJECTS

**THE MUDPIES ACTIVITY BOOK: Recipes for Invention**, by Nancy Blakey. Sound ominous? Imagine creating a hurricane in a bottle, a do-it-yourself radio show, edible art, and much more. Treat yourself and your kids to hours of fun. Ages 2 to 12. Code TSP, $9.95.

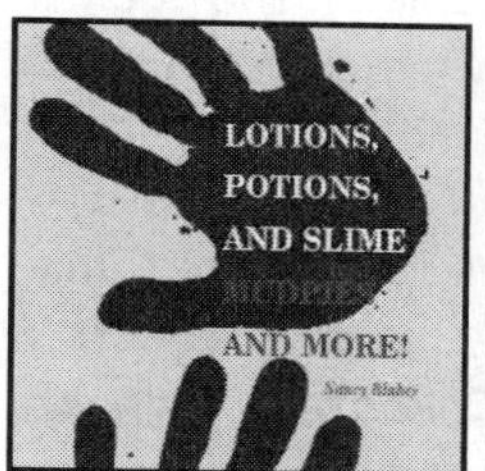


**LOTIONS, POTIONS, AND SLIME: Mudpies and More!**, by Nancy Blakey. 120 pages of fun, laughs, and goo for kids from 2 to 102. You'll find Crash Cookies and Feel-Good Paint, along with Electric Jell-O (absolutely safe). What more could you want on a rainy day when the kids are full of energy? Don't think, "I've already got enough mess!" Remind the participants that you're all equal. In other words, those who make the mess also clean up — or at least help with the cleanup. Code TSP, $9.95.

**What Shall I Do Today?** The full collection of these books won the Parents' Choice Award. None of these projects requires expensive or extensive supplies, just your child's imagination, and maybe a little help from you, depending on the age of the child. **WHAT SHALL I BE?** requires only a few old clothes for dressing up and some face paint if you have it, a little imagination if you don't. The directions are simple enough for young children to follow and full of ideas to capture the imagination. Older children will easily take these ideas much further. All paperbacks except

the collections. Ages 5 to 12. Code EDC, single titles $7.95 each. **What Shall I Be?** (see above); **What Shall I Cook?**; **What Shall I Draw?**; **What Shall I Grow?** (a green-haired creature, a giant sunflower, or alfalfa shapes to eat?); **What Shall I Make?**; **What Shall I Paint?**

Collection #1: **WHAT SHALL I DO TODAY?** Includes **Paint?, Draw?,** and **Make?** $18.95.

Collection #2: **WHAT SHALL I DO NOW?** Includes, **Grow?, Be?,** and **Cook?** $18.95.

**How to Have Fun!** Hours of fun are packed in these 32-page books. (That's about 25 cents a page.) Lots of information and interesting projects are packed into each page. Each book comes with clear, step-by-step, illustrated directions. Some of the projects may involve a bit of help from you, depending on the age of your kids. You may need to buy a few materials. There is a complete list of all required materials at the beginning of each project. Ages 8 to 12 *and up*, because you're never too old to learn to do something new. Code EDC, $7.95. **Batteries and Magnets; Beads, Bangles, and Bracelets; Collecting Things; Decorating T-Shirts; Face Painting; Hair Braiding; Masks; Paper Flowers** (making them); **Paper Superplanes** (making them); **Printing; Stencil Fun.**

**JUGGLING**. Completely unrelated to holding the baby, fixing dinner, answering the phone, letting the dog out, letting the cat in, finding the lost toy, and keeping track of the kids outside in the yard all at the same time.

**KITES.** How to make and fly them.

**MAKING MODELS**. Take the ideas from this book and combine them with a model castle, town, farm, or teepee village, and you have a super project.

**MAKING PRESENTS.** 64 pages, $9.95.

**ORIGAMI**. The creations in this book fascinate me. It's truly amazing what can be done with one piece of paper.

**PAPER ENGINEERING.** It's amazing what things you can make with paper! This book will amaze and intrigue young and old. Fun for the whole family.

**PAPIER-MÂCHÉ.** How to make it and many projects.

**SECRET CODES**. Lots of them for the household spy or those wishing to communicate in a secret language.

Many of the books listed above have related kits that are listed on page 379.

**BIG BOOK OF PAPERCRAFT**. A beginner's guide to making attractive things from paper, with clear, step-by-step directions. Wide range of projects includes paper planes, kites, puppets, greeting cards, and paper masks. Ages 7 and up. Code EDC, $13.95.

**RAINY DAY BOOK**. More than 100 ideas for games, gifts, and crafts, to cut out, sew, cook, draw, or build. Jokes are scattered throughout, just for the fun of it. Clear instructions and illustrations for a good range of skill levels and great results. Ages 7 and up. Code EDC, $14.95.

**DRAWING WITH CHILDREN: A Creative Teaching and Learning Method That Works for Adults, Too**, by Mona Brookes. Hundreds of very helpful tips on techniques and art materials, used with great success even with very young children. Code PTM, $15.95. This is a wonderful book!

***Revised* — DRAWING ON THE RIGHT SIDE OF THE BRAIN: A Course in Enhancing Creativity and Artistic Confidence,** by Betty Edwards. I seldom think about which side of my brain I'm using, but a few years ago when Karen was feeling frustrated by the elusiveness of a tricky subject she was trying to draw, we got out this book and tried its techniques. Hooray! Karen captured the subject she was after with little trouble, and went on to use the book's ideas to improve her artwork immensely. We both give it our wholehearted endorsement. Code BT, $16.95.

Children who like to draw and need some encouragement with writing will enjoy *Draw-Write-Now* in "English Language." The authors have made it very easy to learn how to draw a great variety of people, animals, and objects using very simple lines. Children are encouraged to write captions and stories with their drawings.

**PAPER AIRPLANES THAT FLY.** 8 fanciful full-color models to cut and assemble. Ages 12 and up. Code DV, $4.95.

**SPACE STUNT FLIERS.** Cut, fold, and fly 16 full-color fliers. Great fun. Ages 10 and up. Code DV, $3.50.

**CUT AND ASSEMBLE PAPER DRAGONS THAT FLY!** 8 full-color fierce-looking dragons that let your imagination fly too. Ages 10 and up. Code DV, $3.50.

Origami, paper folding, and paper craft books are available from Dover Publications (see "Free or Almost-Free Teaching and Learning Aids") at great prices. Some are listed below.

**MAKE YOUR OWN TIME CAPSULE,** by Steven Caney. Preserve the past; send a message to the future! The screw-top time capsule, made of shatterproof silver plastic, is roomy enough for dozens of artifacts — photographs, tickets, a diary, and many other keepsakes. The instruction and idea book tells how to prepare materials, and shows how to mark, map, and commemorate a time capsule. The book also includes a log, map grids, and forms to fill in; a sealing label with a serial number; envelopes; and identification tags. Ages 7 and up. Code WKM, $14.95.

**STEVEN CANEY'S TOY BOOK,** by Steven Caney. My dad used to make racing spools for me, and a little while ago I tried to remember how he did it. They're simple gadgets — a spool, a rubber band, a thumbtack, and a wooden match — but the secret kept eluding me. This book came to the rescue. Racing spools, clothespin wrestlers, a water lens, a pocket parachute, a tube telephone, a bull roarer, and much more. 50 very simple, inexpensive (or free, from household throwaways) games, pretending toys, building toys, action toys, discovery toys. Ages 2 to 12, and older kids will enjoy making these things for younger ones, or even for themselves on a rainy day. 176 large pages; many photos and line drawings. Code WKM, $8.95.

**STEVEN CANEY'S PLAY BOOK,** by Steven Caney. Another great book for kids of nearly any age, especially 3 to 12. How to turn cardboard, rocks, noodles, pencils, bottles, nails, and more into toy boomerangs, rings, salt gardens, sun clocks, bottle sandwiches, nail chimes, even a hammock made of 96 plastic six-pack carriers strung on clothesline. (Yucko. That's 576 cans of whatever. Better ask the neighbors if they'll help you guzzle.) 240 large pages, with many photos and line drawings. Code WKM, $9.95. (See also Caney's *Kids' America* in "History and Biography" and *Invention Book* in "Science.")

**Acid-Free Reusable Sticker Books.** The book cover makes a backdrop for the 30 or more full-color, reusable stickers. Books are $9\frac{1}{4}$x$11\frac{1}{4}$". Ages 7 and up. Code DV. Please mention that these are sticker books when you order to help us avoid confusing these with similar titles. Some have been listed in other chapters. **Horse and Stable**, $3.95; **Farm**, $4.50; **Zoo**, $3.50; **Building the Pyramids**, $3.95; **Egyptian Temple**, $3.50; **Medieval Castle**, $4.50; **Medieval Tournament**, $3.50; **Moon Exploration**, $3.95; **Pioneer Life**, $4.50; **Teepee Village**, $4.50; **Viking Village**, $4.50.

**Easy Punch-Out Stencils**. 8½x11" book, 16 pages. Code DV, $3.95 each. **Dinosaurs, Endangered Animals, Farm Animals, Funny Faces, Rain Forest Animals, Teddy Bear.**

**Punch-Out Masks**. All in full color on sturdy 9¼x12½" card stock. Punch out, wear, and play. Code DV. **Circus Clowns,** $3.95; **Dinosaurs**, $3.95; **Favorite Domestic Animals**, $3.95; **Indian,** $3.95; **Inuit**, $4.95; **North American Animals**, $3.95; **Prehistoric Animals**, $4.95; **Wild Animals**, $4.95.

Remember to check "Resources for the Early Years" for arts and activities for children under 6.

**Stained Glass Coloring Books**. 4¼x5¾" books. Translucent paper with designs to be colored. Hint: If you also color a little on the second side you'll get very interesting effects. Pages are removable so you can mount them on a window. These make inexpensive stocking stuffers. Code DV, $1 each. **Prehistoric Animals, Mythical Creatures, Unicorns, Fairies, Dragons, Flowers, Tropical Flowers, Wildflowers, Baseball, King Arthur, Fairy Tales, Legend of Sleepy Hollow, Egyptian Designs, Celtic, Valentines, Easter, Halloween, Thanksgiving, Christmas, Angels, Snowflakes, Jewish.**

**Clip Art**. Books filled with a great variety of illustrations, all copyright free. Illustrate your own storybooks. Impress the Department of Education with how "professional" your activity sheets are. Just clip the illustrations you want, glue them to your master copy along with your own typed or handwritten material, and take to your local photocopy shop for as many copies as you want. Useful for all grades and adults. Write: Dover Publications, 11 E. 2nd St., Mineola, NY 11501, and ask for their clip art catalog. Pick out what you want, but check their shipping charges. You can order all their books from us, and I think we charge less for shipping. A lot of their clip art is now available on CD-ROM for Macs and PCs.

**THE INDIAN HOW BOOK**, by Arthur C. Parker (Gawaso Wanneh). How Indians made canoes, teepees, traps, arrowheads, and pottery; Indian dances, songs, and rituals. Written by a man who spent much of his life with the Indians before their way of life was completely changed by "civilization." 335 pages, with 51 illustrations. Code DV, $7.95.

**Indian Items**. Tanned buckskin, jewelry findings, tomahawks, tools, soap, cane flute, and more. Request catalog. Crazy Crow Trading Post, P.O. Box 847, Pottsboro, TX 75076; 800-786-6210.

**INDIAN SCOUT CRAFT AND LORE**, by Charles Alexander Eastman. How to do numerous crafts. Loaded with projects and information. Code DV, $5.95.

**NATIVE CRAFTS**, by Maxine Trottier. 16 Native Canadian Indian crafts for kids 8-14. Includes seed and bead jewelry, clay pinch pots, totem poles, moccasins, and more. Code KC, $5.95.

*Indian Sign Language* and *Native American Sign Language* can be found in "History and Biography."

**GLOBAL ART: Activities, Projects, and Inventions From Around the World**, by MaryAnn F. Kohl and Jean Potter. A wonderful collection of activities and projects you won't find anywhere else. Great variety of things to do. Truly a global collection. There is a world map displaying the country of origin of each project plus bits of interesting information, too. Mostly household materials, but you may have to buy a few inexpensive items. Ages 8 to 15. Code GH, $14.95.

**PALMLOOM.** Interesting handicraft for all ages. Make scatter rugs, table pads, appliqué coasters, and more. The Palmloom Kit will fit into a pocket or purse, ready to use any time or place. It's fast and easy: Just wind strips of any type or weight of remnant materials—yarn, cord, or cloth; wool, cotton, or nylon—on the Palmloom, then bind it through the slots, and you have one finished unit. Join several units to make the finished product you want. Full directions included. $5.50 each or 2 for $10 postpaid from us.

**ON STAGE: Theater Games and Activities for Kids.** Author Lisa Bany-Winters knows how to share her knowledge of the theater, puppetry, pantomime, sound effects, costumes, makeup, and vocabulary to help you and your kids create something very special. Shakespeare said, "All the world's a stage." Remember — that includes your house! Ages 6 to 12. Code CRP, $14.95.

**ACTING AND THEATRE.** Thoroughly covers everything in the theatrical world, both creative and technical. Tells you how you can write your own script, using any story for a base. There isn't a better way to explore the inner workings of a story, and learn just what emotions and conflicts a character feels, than to stage a play. Ages 11 and up, but you can use your creative side and help the younger ones use the book. The sooner you start this kind of activity the better result you'll get. Younger children generally have fewer inhibitions about performing, and putting on a show is just plain fun. Code EDC, $9.95.

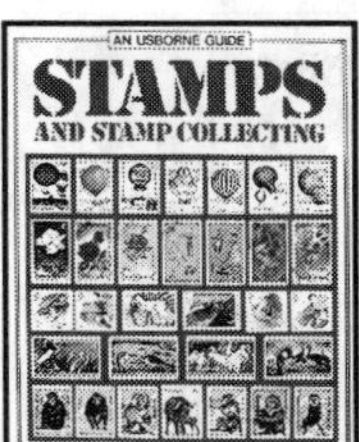


**STAMPS AND STAMP COLLECTING.** I am ignorant about stamp collecting. My working knowledge extends to paying for stamps and affixing them to envelopes. I know some stamps are beautiful to look at, and others I don't care for very much. Beyond their immediate usefulness they don't mean anything to me. I do know a lady who loves, values, and collects stamps as a serious hobby. On her recommendation I am writing this review. My friend says this Usborne book is the best she's seen — but best for adults, not kids. My friend has worked with various stamp collecting groups of adults and kids, and she tells me there's just too much detail in this book if you want your kids to be enthusiastic about collecting. If you do want the book, the price is $6.95. Code EDC. If you want your kids to enjoy collecting, write to the following organizations that have developed programs that work for kids.

**Kidstamp**, P.O. Box 948, Lenoir City, TN 37771. Send an SASE and tell them what you would like to do. They will provide free stamps, puzzles, games, and activities.

**International Society of Worldwide Stamp Collectors** (ISWSC), c/o Millie Feinberg, 3340 Dale Rd., Bensalem, PA 19020, or Carol Cervenika, 2502 Second St., Caddo Mills, TX 75136. They will send stamps, pages to mount them on, and mounting hinges. They will also help you find a mentor.

**YOU CAN START A STAMP CLUB.** Get a free copy of this brochure from the American Philatelic Society, P.O. Box 8000, State College, PA 16801. They also have a lot of great information and activities in the For Kids section of their website: www.stamps.org.

**Lots of Stamps**. Send $2 and receive a special collector's grab-bag of 200 U.S. stamps. My information says, "Limit 1 grab-bag per address. Adults only." So it's up to you, Mom or Dad, to write for these. Mystic Stamp Co., Dept. 5A290, Camden, NY 13316.

**How to Draw Series**. Each $8\frac{1}{4}$x11" book has 30 projects with line illustrations using simple shapes as a basis for creating figures that are fun and satisfying to draw. Code DV, $2.50 each. **Animals, Birds, Cars and Trucks, Cats, Dinosaurs, Dogs, Insects, Wild Animals.**

**Play With Boxes**. Kids love boxes, and Liz and Dick Wilmes have put together a super collection of things to make and do with large and small boxes. Create large and small projects, and your kids will have a ball decorating them. Create a boat, walk-along school bus, private book nook, play house, tent, games, and more. This could have gone in "Resources for Early Learning," but your 5-, 6-, and 7-year-olds might have missed out. Done with classrooms in mind but very easily adapted for use at home. More than 100 pages, including a good list of where to look for different-size boxes. Code GH, $12.95 each. Specify **PLAY WITH SMALL BOXES** or **PLAY WITH BIG BOXES**.

**BOXES**, by Lorianne Siomades. This one is designed for home use, with more than 90 pictured crafts and dozens of other ideas. You'll have fun just watching the kids! Ages 5 to 12. 48 pages. Code BMP, $5.95.

**PAPER BAGS**, by Judy Burke. An astounding variety of toys, gifts, and games you can make and have fun with — all out of simple paper bags. Ages 4 to 12. Code BMP, $5.95.

**FUN WITH STRING.** A well-illustrated book with projects to do with that ever-fascinating piece of string ... well, some people find it fascinating as well as useful. Code DV, $4.95.

**FUN WITH STRING FIGURES**. More projects for fingers. Code DV, $2.95.

**FUN WITH MODELING CLAY**, by Barbara Reid. Easy-to-follow directions for turning lumps of clay into fun, fantastic shapes and characters. Code KC, $4.95.

1956: Play-Doh was invented as a byproduct of the reformulation of a wallpaper cleaner.

**SCRIBBLE ART**, by MaryAnn Kohl. For the uninhibited, and even more for those who *are* inhibited about their drawing skills. 150 activities to stimulate imagination, creativity, and fun. Ages 3 to 12. Code CRP, $14.95.

**Curiosity Kits**. They're great! Send for their catalog. Lots of creative projects for kids as young as 4. They have projects I'd have fun doing. Some kits are scientific, some based on world cultures; there's body art, chalk paint, pocket friends, a tooth fairy pillow, and more. Reasonably priced. Curiosity Kits, 11111 Pepper Rd., P.O. Box 811, Hunt Valley, MD 21031-1203; www.curiositykits.com.

See *Play Lightly on the Earth* in "Ecology."

**EASY-TO-MAKE FELT BEAN BAG TOYS**, by Jane Ethe. Here's a collection of felt toys that youngsters will love and older children and adults can easily make. Full-size templates and clear directions. Useful information about using non-allergenic materials for stuffing. Ages 8 and up. Code DV, $3.95.

For cooks too young to read text, try *Pretend Soup* in "Resources for Early Learning." For teens and adults ready to learn more about delicious meals, seasonings, and cooking, **BLUE MOON SOUP**, by Chef Gary Goss

(owner of The Soup Kitchen in Northampton, Massachusetts, for ten years), will be a delight — and a treat for everyone lucky enough to be invited to the table. All recipes are suitable for vegetarians and meat-eaters alike. You'll find soup for all seasons, from ice cream soup to Ch-Ch-Chili. Good food, good kitchen safety rules, and nice extras such as a section on salads, garnishes, and breads provide hints for completing the meal. What makes a cookbook worth space in this book? We all have to eat, we all enjoy good basic foods served with a special zest that adds spice to the meal and life itself, and the illustrations by Jane Dyer are delightful. A hardcover book you won't outgrow. Ages 14 to adult. Code LB, $16.95.

**LOAVES OF FUN**, by Elizabeth M. Harbison, is just what it sounds like — and more. Even if you've never baked before, you'll enjoy baking these breads from around the world. Exploring these recipes will keep you well fed in body and soul, and teach you history and geography as you travel the globe. There's even a timeline history of bread! There is a good glossary that explains each ingredient and how it acts and interacts with the other ingredients. Nice illustrations and clear directions make this book suitable for children under six with adult help in the kitchen; ages 6 to 12 can use it on their own, or if you're older and like to bake bread, you can ignore the age recommendations just like I did. More than 50 recipes and activities, a multicultural journey with pita bread, pretzels, and plain and fancy breads for all seasons, all from ingredients you probably already have in your kitchen. Code CRP, $12.95.

**BAKE IT AND BUILD IT**, by Elizabeth MacLeod. MacLeod has combined a love of baking cookies, construction, and art into a book all cookie lovers will adore. Using five different cookie dough recipes your kids (or you) will learn to make and decorate gingerbread castles, holiday wreaths, jack-o'-lanterns, flowers, and much more. Instructions for baking, edible glue, and decorating. Ages 8 and up. Code KC, $5.95.

**LEONARDO DA VINCI FOR KIDS**, by Janis Herbert. A great blend of learning about art and science with lots of activities, a good glossary, a bibliography, a listing of museums and websites, and a timeline. Wonderful full-color illustrations. Ages 8 and up. Code CRP, $16.95.

**JUMP IN**, by Barbara Hall. 100 official double-Dutch rhymes and jump rope steps. Great exercise! Great fun! Rhymes, rules, and games to fill a summer afternoon or maybe even indoors if you have room. Instructions on how to turn the ropes, how to enter and leave, tricks, and more complex games with three and four rope turners — even a history of rope skipping going back to Egypt. Code CRP, $8.95.

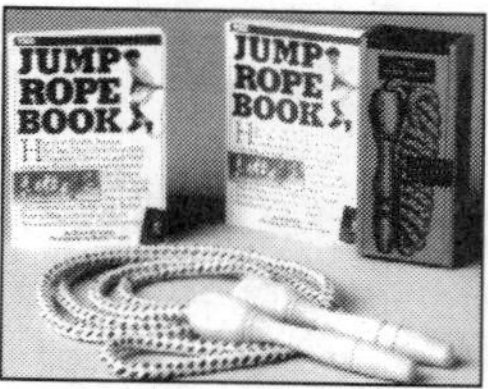


I wouldn't call jumping rope a sport, but it's good exercise and kids love to do it. The **JUMP ROPE BOOK** comes with a jump rope, offers info on how to do basic and fancy steps, explains rope jargon, suggests ways to decorate your rope, and details a variety of games. Code WKM, $9.95.

**Hotshots.** Pocket-size books for specialized interests. Well illustrated and packed with interesting facts that won't bore you. If you get bored, send it back! 32 pages. Ages 7 and up. Code EDC, $2.95 each. **Amazing Facts, Bikes, Brainbusters, Card Tricks, Chess, Computers, Drawing Cartoons, Drawing People, The Egyptians, Face Painting, Fancy Braiding (hair), Flags, Friendship Bracelets, Greek Myths, Hair Braiding, History of Britain, Joke Book, Kings and Queens, Lettering, Magic Tricks, Picture Puzzles, Rocks and Minerals, The Romans, Seashore, Secret Codes, Stars and Planets, Starting French, Swimming, Tennis, Travel Games, Trick Photography, Vampires, World History Dates, Your Body.**

**LOOK-ALIKES**, by Joan Steiner, is a book of more than 1,000 extraordinary and amazing visual puzzles the whole family will find fascinating. The more you look the more you see — and you'll be astounded at what you see! This oversize book is filled with full-color pictures of a circus, a house on a street, a harbor, a living room, and other interesting pictures. The great part is when you discover that the teddy bear in the pictures is made out of peanuts, a chair out of a pretzel and a Ritz cracker, and a dress out of a balloon and pistachio flowers. Nutcrackers form the towers on a suspension bridge, cinnamon sticks make a stack of firewood, and so much more. Every object you see is made out of everyday objects that are unrelated to the finished product. I was glad to find a key to all the pictures in the back of the book. You could spend a lot of your lifetime figuring it all out, yet there are so many common objects that 4- and 5- year-olds will have fun discovering the things they know. Code LB, $13.95, includes a CD-ROM, screensaver, and games. **LOOK-ALIKES, Jr.**, is available for kids ages 4 to 10. This book has more than 700 hidden everyday objects. Code LB, $13.95, includes a CD-ROM, screensaver, and games.

**Literature-Based Coloring Books**. Informative text and captions. All 8¼x11", 48 pages. Code DV, $2.95 each. **Aesop's Fables, Alice in Wonderland, Anne of Green Gables, Black Beauty, Child's Garden of Verses, Christmas Carol, Little Mermaid, Little Women, Mother Goose, Nutcracker, Pocahontas, Secret Garden, Shakespeare's Plays, Sleeping Beauty, Snow White, Tarzan, Treasure Island, Velveteen Rabbit, Wind in the Willows, Wonderful Wizard of Oz.**

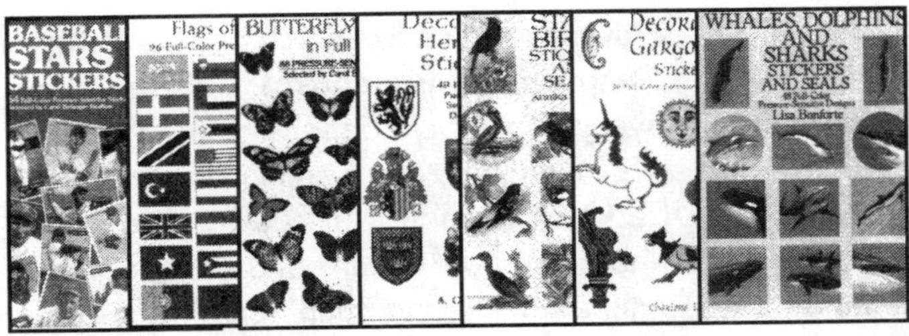


**Stickers and Seals.** All stickers and seals are in full color, and the book includes identification information. Fun anytime and good for small holiday gifts. Each book is 8¼x11", 8 pages. Code DV, $3.95 each, unless marked otherwise.

**AUDUBON BIRD STICKERS.** $4.95
**BASEBALL STARS STICKERS**
**BUTTERFLIES STICKERS.** $4.95
**DECORATIVE GARGOYLES STICKERS**
**DECORATIVE HERALDIC STICKERS**
**DINOSAUR STICKERS AND SEALS.** $3.50
**ENDANGERED ANIMALS STICKERS**
**FAVORITE BIRDS STICKERS**
**FAVORITE CATS STICKERS AND SEALS**
**FLAGS OF THE WORLD STICKERS.** $4.95
**GARDEN FLOWERS STICKERS AND SEALS**
**INSECTS STICKERS AND SEALS**
**POPULAR DOGS STICKERS AND SEALS.** $4.95
**RAIN FOREST ANIMAL STICKERS.** $4.95
**SEA LIFE STICKERS.** $4.95
**STATE BIRD STICKERS AND SEALS.** $4.95
**STATE FLOWERS STICKERS AND SEALS**
**TROPICAL FISH STICKERS**
**WHALES, DOLPHINS AND SHARKS**
**WILD ANIMALS STICKERS**

1902: Morris Mitchom named a stuffed bear to honor Teddy Roosevelt after reading that he refused to shoot a captured bear cub on a hunting trip.

**STARTING NEEDLECRAFT KIT**. Comes complete with everything you need to make a number of simple, satisfying projects, including a frog pincushion and a pocket mouse (Cute. I want one.) Illustrated text takes you from threading a needle and first stitches to appliqué and more. Comes with a tape measure, thread, buttons, needles, pins, and scissors. Ages 5 (with supervision) to 10. Code EDC, $13.95.

**DOLLS**, by Judy Ann Sadler. Clear, well-illustrated instructions for easy-to-make dolls. Most of the materials you'll have around the house or can purchase cheaply. Hours of fun making dolls using paper, peanuts, pencils, beads, buttons, yarn, and other common materials. Ages 5 to 10. Code KC, $5.95.

**MAKING RAG DOLLS** is an 80-page book with good directions for making a variety of dolls. It's written for older teens and adults, but you can use the ideas to create simpler projects for younger children. These dolls are so much nicer than many commercially made dolls that, for reasons I have never been able to fathom, don't have pleasant expressions on their faces. Code DV, $12.95.

There was a time I couldn't find a nice male doll for Derek, so I bought a set of toddler-sized clothes, added feet, hands, and a head and filled it with stuffing. The doll was almost as big as he was. He loved it!

**MAKE YOUR OWN OLD-FASHIONED CLOTH DOLL AND HER WARDROBE**, by Claire Bryant. Anyone who can sew can make any of these cute cloth dolls and clothing. Patterns are included, and more than 30 diagrams make it easy. Not for beginners, but you don't have to be an expert either. Code DV, $5.95.

**BEANBAG BUDDIES AND OTHER STUFFED TOYS,** by Judy Ann Sadler, has 12 different projects to make using old gloves, odd socks (yes! finally a good use for them), and scrap fabric. Easy-to-follow directions for hand sewing. Patterns are in the book. Your kids may start out making these to give away, but they may want to keep them when they're done. Ages 8 and up. Code KC, $5.95.

We never liked the Barbie fashion dolls or the male equivalents. We didn't want our children's play and fantasies to be centered around action figures such as G.I. Joe. Donn spent numerous enjoyable hours crafting dollhouses for each of our kids. Each house was unique, and each had a different doll family with a different lifestyle. He furnished each house, and I spent hours making doll clothes. We found that because we provided the kids with doll families their play centered around family life. The resulting play was gentle, with none of the violent people bashing that seems common with various popular hero-type dolls or spitefulness and false values generated by fashion dolls. Cathy had a large split-log house, and her people had a woodstove and a covered wagon for transportation. She wanted her family to homeschool, so Donn made miniature flash cards, books, pencils, and such from pictures in school catalogs, and he mounted them on cardboard. Karen's family had a homestead, gardened, and had a craft store. Her family included grandparents. Susan's family had a modern house, raised rabbits, and had a garden. She wanted, and Donn made, a circular fireplace in the middle of the sunken living room. Derek's family had a one-room cabin with a loft, and the man in his family was a forest ranger. Whatever you have for your children, keep in mind that the playthings they use will shape their play on many levels.

**MAKE THIS MODEL DOLL'S HOUSE** comes with baseboard, little paper people, and doll toys to make. You can make more people from magazine pictures or draw them yourself. All you need is glue and scissors or a craft knife. Finished size 24x18". Front panels swing open for access to the interior. Ages 9 and up. Code EDC, $9.95.

**KNITTING.** There are lots of beginners books available, but I particularly like this book because it has all the basic techniques *and* suggestions for developing your own ideas. Ages 11 (or whenever the desire and patience match) and up. Code EDC, $8.95.

**TOGETHER TIME**. A magazine that comes with craft kits, suitable for boys and girls ages 8 to 12 who like to make craft projects. The magazine is published monthly and arrives with three easy-to-do crafts, a monthly calendar to color, stickers, and more. All the materials are included, so it's easy on Mom. Bonus box with your first kit comes with crayons, craft glue, glue stick, scissors, and other nifty craft-making aids. $9.95 a month plus shipping. Creative Learning Institute, 7 Indian Hill Ave., P.O. Box 208, Portland, CT 06480-9986; 888-868-2263; www.togethertime.com.

**Creative Thinking.** Tin Man Press, Box 219, Stanwood, WA 98292, has a small, free catalog of unique creative thinking tools, activities, and books. Reasonable prices.

**Dot-to-Dot Books.** Pictures can be colored when they're finished. Good for learning number sequences. The number line at the bottom of each double-page spread is really nice, because young children can use it for reference if they need it. Ages 4 to 7. Code EDC, $3.95 each. Please specify dot-to-dot book when you order to avoid confusion with identical or similar titles. **Animals, At the Seaside, Dinosaurs, In Space, Machines, Nature, On the Farm.**

**BIG DOT-TO-DOT #1** includes *Animals, Machines,* and *On The Farm.* $9.95.

**BIG DOT TO DOT #2** includes *At the Seaside, Dinosaurs, In Space,* and *Nature.* $11.95.

**ZOOM FUN WITH FRIENDS.** More than 50 games, party ideas, jokes, etc. With a little help from this book, the kids will entertain themselves — and probably you too. Ages 10 to 15. Code LB, $7.95.

**ZOOM ZINGERS.** More than 50 body and brain teasers from the PBS TV show *Zoom.* Your kids don't have to have watched the show to have fun with these games, pun puzzles, and activities. An exceptional book that will liven up the house with laughter and put smiles on faces. This book can be used by one child alone or with friends. Ages 10 to 15. Code LB, $7.95.

**MY LITTLE HOUSE BIRTHDAY BOOK.** In the Little House books (see "History and Biography"), Laura described her birthdays and special parties. Using this book your child can create the same type of keepsake book that Laura used. There's plenty of room to write down thoughts about special party days and make notes about special ideas for a coming event, room for some photos, and a special pocket in the back for cards and special notes to be saved. Comes with a free colorful pencil. Big deal! Code HC, $7.95.

**NOW YOU SEE IT, NOW YOU DON'T.** Fascinating book about optical illusions and perspective drawings, with explanations of how they work — all with illustrations so you can test each one. Information about how we see, why our eyes can deceive us, optical illusions in art, and directions for making your own illusions. Fun for all ages. This book allows you to use your compass and protractor in the context of real mathematics, not just a geometry exercise. Code WM, $5.95.

**'M' IS FOR MIRROR**, by Duncan Birmingham. A delightful book with a page per letter of the alphabet, yet different from any other alphabet book I've ever seen. Eye- and mind-captivating pictures. To find the picture that matches the letter of the alphabet you slide the mirror (held at right angles to the page) across the page until the object appears. Like magic! Images suddenly appear and you just can't help but smile. Your kids will too. You're provided with a bookmark-size non-breakable mirror that needs only to be mounted on the heavy paper at the end of the book. For kids who like to be delighted, ages 5 to ?. (I had fun with it, and I'm a grandma.) Code PW, $7.50.

**GREAT DANCERS.** Coloring book covering the history of dance and dancers. Interesting and very detailed pictures to color. Ages 8 and up. Code BB, $4.95.

*Beauty in things exists in the mind which contemplates them.* — David Hume

**Coloring Books**. All $8\frac{1}{4}$x11", 48 pages. Ages 5 to 9. Code DV, $2.95. **The 3-D Alphabet, Ballet Class, Gargoyles and Medieval Monsters, Musical Instruments, Mythical Beasts, Peter Rabbit, Visual Illusions.**

**Easy-to-Make Models.** All you need are scissors and glue. Books are 9x12". Ages 6 and up. Code DV.
**PINWHEELS.** Colorful, fun, and easy. $3.95.
**PLAYTIME FARM.** Colorful rural homestead, with a barn, farmhouse, tool shed, well, chicken coop, animals, and more. $3.50.

1945: Slinkys came into being after a man and his wife watched a torsion spring tumble end over end.

**THE KIDS 'N' CLAY CERAMICS BOOK: Handbuilding and Wheel-Throwing Projects**, created by Kevin Nierman, written by Elaine Arima. For kids who love clay. How to set up a ceramics studio; make gifts; and learn various techniques, including wheel throwing, how to use a variety of tools, and hand techniques. Instructions for projects from start to finish. Ages 6 and up — interested teens will really benefit from this book. Code TSP, $16.95.

**MAKEUP**. This book may not be about your favorite teen activity, but if you have adventurous, curious teens, this book will give them good guidelines as to what works well. Step-by-step instructions explain the basics with good information about proper equipment. If they're going to experiment and learn, they may as well have good guides. Ages 14 and up. Code EDC, $6.95.

**HAIR BRAIDING KID KIT**. I'm sure you already know that most kids, girls in particular, love to play with hair — their own or anyone else's. With only a few simple accessories (no scissors) and some imagination, hair can become a natural entertainment center. This kit will provide materials for hours of giggles and fun. Perhaps it will be the coup de grâce at a slumber party. Ages 8 and up. Code EDC, $16.95.

**DRAGON MOBILES**, created by Anne Wild. Five fantastic full-color (on both sides) dragons, some 3-D, with clear instructions: cave dragon, sea dragon, fire dragon, Celtic dragon, and St. George and the dragon. Ages 12 and up. Code PW, $10.

**Explore the World of the Unknown** These books explore the frontiers between the known and the unknown. It's fascinating reading for the adventurous. Colorful diagrams and pictures. Ages 11 and up. Code EDC.
**UFOs**, $6.95.
**ESP?**, $5.95.

**DETECTIVE'S HANDBOOK**. Clues and suspects, catching crooks, fakes and forgeries, disguises, puzzles to solve, hidden loot to find, and more. Humorously presented and hours of fun. Ages 8 to 11. Code EDC, $12.95.

**PHOTOGRAPHY**. Step-by-step instructions for basic techniques, many helpful guidelines, and suggestions for producing good photos (without red eyes or missing heads). Combine photography with a journal or family album, or document a trip. Have fun! Ages 11 and up. Code EDC, $8.95.

**DO-IT-YOURSELF YEARBOOK**. Perfect for this year — or any year. Kids write about their friends, school, family, vacations, fads (!), favorite music, and more. What fun to look at in 5 or 10 or 20 years! Ages 8 to 12. Code LW, $10.95.

**Anti-Coloring Book Series**, created by Susan Striker. Throw out all your ordinary fill-in-the-spaces coloring books: All they require is a bit of manual dexterity. Either a child colors within the lines or he is judged (by himself or others) to be not very talented. Standard coloring books do nothing for a child's creativity, nor are they a means by which a child can express himself. Striker's books provide a creative platform for any child to develop imagination, express thoughts, and write short pieces if he is inclined to do so. Each page has more blank than designed space. Captions will stimulate thinking and original artwork that is a direct expression of your child's thoughts. Please order by number and title. Ages 9 to 13. Code HNH, $7.95 each.

1. **Draw Dreams, Nightmares, Wishes, and Feelings**
2. **Ideas and Imagining for the Past, Present, and Future**
3. **Discover and Design: Make Three Wishes on a Magic Lantern**
4. **Who, What, Where, and Why: Draw It the Way You Want**
5. **Transform Everyday Objects Into New and Amazing Images**
6. **Draw Secrets and Surprises, Hopes and Fears**
7. **Book of Exploring Space on Earth: Architecture and Interior Design Projects**
8. **Book of Masterpieces: Complete the World's Great Art** (includes color reproductions)
9. **Inventor's Anti-Coloring Book: Create Inventions, Devices, Contraptions, and Ecology**
10. **Mystery: Solve Mysteries of the Universe, Make Discoveries, Be Cops and Robbers.**
11. **Newspaper: Be a Cub Reporter, Movie Reviewer, or Create Comics.**

**Make Your Own Badges**. With a relatively small investment you and your kids can make your own 2¼" metal-backed safety-pin badges. We had a ball making them for ourselves and for gifts. We even made money selling some. Badge-A-Minute, P.O. Box 800, LaSalle, IL 61301; 800-223-4103; www.badgeaminit.com.

If you don't want to invest in the equipment you can send your artwork to us and we'll make a badge for you. **Home School Badges**. Your choice: THE WORLD IS MY SCHOOL (my personal favorite, and the one we sell the most of), I'M A HOME SCHOOLER, or THIS SCHOOL IS RUN ON KID POWER. $2 each or 4 for $6.50 postpaid. **School or Group Badges**. Send us a rough sketch or description of your design and the wording you want; we'll make it into a badge for you, like this one we made for the Manitoba Association for Schooling at Home. One custom-made badge $4. Each additional badge, same design and lettering, ordered at the same time, $1. For 10 or more badges of the same design, write for quantity discounts telling us how many badges you may want. **More Badges**. Send us your own artwork, magazine clipping, comic pictures, even a photograph, and we'll make it into a badge for you. You or your child can design and color your own picture, decorate it, and letter it. Good for unusual gifts, stocking stuffers, identification, group meetings, celebrations, I Love Grandma, or just plain fun. IMPORTANT: Your original artwork or clipping should be at least *two and three-quarters inches* in diameter; the part showing on the finished badge will be two and one-quarter inches. Badges from your finished artwork, $2 each. Five to ten badges at one time, $1.50 each.

**ARCHITECTURE EVERYWHERE: Exploring the Built Environment of Your Community**, by Joseph A. Weber. Architecture is all around us, and most of us don't know how to appreciate this art form. This book will connect you with the history and cultural development in your own community. The knowledge gained through reading and doing the numerous projects in this book will make a walk around your hometown or a tour of a new city much more exciting.

I found unexpected depth in this book. It goes far beyond learning the names of various building styles. This book explores everything from the first North American builders to ideas borrowed from other cultures; drive-ins: past, present, and future; and various building styles and how they evolved. The reader is frequently asked to be a detective, discovering things in the many photos or out in the community. You'll discover the evolution of private homes and commercial buildings as well as various building materials. There's a very good section on perspective drawing, and the reader is invited to draw and design his own creation. Ages 10 to adult. Code Z, $32.

**WHY DESIGN? Projects from the National Building Museum**, by Anna Slafer and Kevin Cahill. Great explanations and activities to help kids understand interesting and challenging design concepts. Lots of activities and well illustrated. Ages 12 and up. Code CRP, $19.95.

**THE ART OF CONSTRUCTION: Projects and Principles for Beginning Engineers and Architects**, by Mario Salvadori. Challenging thoughtful information and projects. Information about how we build and about the materials we use. Explores the physics inherent in construction and includes many creative hands-on projects. Ages 14 and up. Code CRP, $12.95.

1916: Frank Lloyd Wright's son John invented Lincoln Logs after thinking about an earthquake-proof hotel his father built in Tokyo.

**GREAT ARTISTS: 150 Art Projects for Kids to Use While They Explore the Styles of the Great Masters**, by MaryAnn Kohl and Kim Solga. The title is self-explanatory. 50 photos, 100 line drawings. Written specifically for ages 5 to 12, but if you're just learning to draw I don't think age matters. Code CRP, $14.95.

**THE STORY OF PAINTING** covers painting from the cave to modern art. Information is well presented, and all periods and styles are explained with text, illustrations, and reproductions. Very readable with some information about famous artists and their lives. Good introduction. Ages 10 and up. Code EDC, $7.95.

**DRAWING**. Overview of different media (pencil, charcoal, pencil crayons, etc.), techniques, and more. This will help a budding artist make the most of his talent and tools. Ages 10 and up. Code EDC, $6.95.

**For the Young Artist**. This series of books is designed to help create more professional results. Good, helpful suggestions for materials to use and clear step-by-step directions and illustrations to improve techniques. Ages 9 and up. Code EDC, $4.95 unless marked otherwise. **How to Draw Animals, How to Draw Buildings, How to Draw Cats, How to Draw Dinosaurs and Prehistoric Life, How to Draw Horses, How to Draw Lettering, How to Draw Machines, How to Draw Maps and Charts, How to Draw Monsters, How to Draw People, How to Draw Robots and Aliens, How to Draw Spacecraft, How to Draw Cartoons and Caricatures**, $5.95.

**HOW TO DRAW — DINOSAURS, GHOSTS, LETTERS, AND SPACECRAFT**. A combination of some of the books listed above. Code EDC, $12.95.

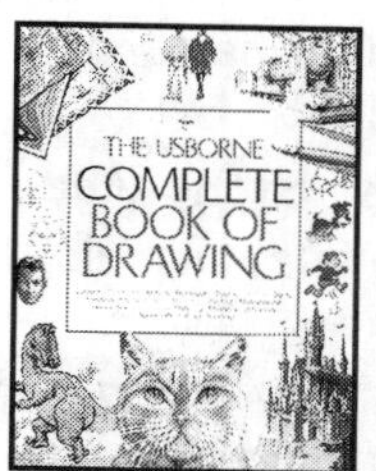

**COMPLETE BOOK OF DRAWING**. A comprehensive guide to drawing and painting, using some of the material from the How to Draw series listed above. More technical information to improve technique. Explains different styles from realistic to cartoon to collage. Includes a good reference section on materials and how to use them. Ages 10 and up. Code EDC, $17.95.

**Artists' Workshop Series**. Each of these books is especially designed for ages 7 to 13. These unusually creative projects, drawn from arts and crafts around the world, will enhance your children's creativity and give them the tools necessary to satisfy their creative desires. Well-illustrated, easy-to-follow instructions. All techniques are demonstrated using famous artists' creations. Techniques to duplicate special effects are demonstrated. These books are terrific. I wish we had had these when the kids were home! Code CT, $8.95 each, any 5 $40.

**MODELS**. Hopi kachina doll, teepee, African Nkonde figure, toy theater.

**PAPER**. Mexican papercut banner, Japanese marbled paper, Russian painted plates, Chinese monster headdress.

**FABRIC**. Peruvian appliqué, North American proggy rug, Central Asian hangings, block prints.

**FESTIVAL DECORATIONS**. Indian Diwali clay lamps, Russian Easter eggs, Shaker Christmas angel, Navajo prayer bundle.

**PORTRAITS**. History and techniques of various portrait artists, including van Gogh and Picasso. Activities include Egyptian effects, painting a self-portrait, and line design.

**LANDSCAPES**. Famous examples given and techniques explained. Uses plasticine, art tile, paper cut-out garden, Impressionist paintings.

**MYTHS AND LEGENDS**. Activities based on King Arthur, Alexander the Great, Sinbad the Sailor, dragon sculpture, waxy water scenes, Valentine cards, stained-glass secrets, voyages in art.

**ANIMALS**. Create pictures and models, Stone Age art, scaly reptiles, wax and tissue jungle animals, Aboriginal patterns.

**STORIES**. Each art example tells a story using a different technique. Each method is explained so it can be used in sponge painting and shadow play, water color, torn paper, and picture boxes.

**MEET THE GROUP OF SEVEN**, by David Wistow and Kelly McKinley, in collaboration with the Art Gallery of Ontario. Most Canadians know about this influential group of artists or have heard of them. This book describes how this group was formed, how and where they painted, why ten artists are considered to be part of this "group of seven," and much more. The interesting text is complemented by wonderful illustrations, photographs, and reproductions from several Canadian galleries. Full-color hardcover. Ages 8 to adult. Code KC, $12.95.

**Make Your Own Art Gallery** with these books. Each 9x12" book has 24 different full-color postcard-size cards, perforated for easy removal. Code DV, prices as marked. An inexpensive and easy way to integrate art and history studies. Shipping $2.50 any quantity. **<u>$3.95 each</u>: J.M.W. Turner, Twentieth-Century American Paintings, Twentieth-Century Sculpture. <u>$4.95 each</u>: Albright-Knox Gallery Masterpieces, Ancient Egyptian Art, Angels in Art, Audubon's Birds of America, Chagall, Currier and Ives, Dali, Degas Paintings, Great Paintings of the Old West, Hudson River School Paintings, Hummingbirds** (photos), **Impressionist Paintings, Japanese Prints, Jerusalem Windows** (stained glass), **Henri Matisse, Matisse** (cut-paper designs), **Matisse** (portraits), **Mexican Murals, Paintings of the American West, Picasso, Remington's Old West, Renaissance Armor, Renoir Paintings, Van Gogh Paintings, William Blake, Women Artists.**

**$1 Art Bargains**. Each $4\frac{1}{4}$x$5\frac{3}{4}$" book has six full-color pictures. Code DV, minimum order of 5, shipping $2.50 any quantity. **Ancient Mexican Postcards,**

**Book of Kells**, **Dali**, **Degas** (ballet dancers), **Edward Hopper**, **Gauguin**, **Indian Crafts**, **Kachina Dolls**, **Monet**, **Picasso**, **Renoir**, **Van Gogh**, **Western Paintings**, **Winslow Homer** (watercolors).

**UNDERSTANDING MODERN ART**. I much prefer looking at artwork I can understand without an interpreter. However, to give the devil his due, I read this book. I don't think I'll ever really understand a lot of modern art, but I know more about it and can appreciate more of it now. Well illustrated and well written, with explanations more easily understood than the art or the artists. Ages 11 and up. Code EDC, $9.95.

I really wish I could print this book in full color so you could appreciate the quality and beauty of the artwork in the books in this chapter.

**Art Prints**. Cheap! Create your own collection. 7,400 prints of paintings and other art objects and architecture throughout history and updated continually. Prints are 5½x8". Black-and-white prints 8¢ each, full-color 18¢ each. Choose any quantity you want. Fully indexed by title, period, school, artist, or date. 246-page catalog, $3 plus $1 postage. The University Prints Catalog, Box 485, Winchester, MA 01890; www.universityprints.net.

Take a tour of the Louvre from the comfort of your own home at www.louvre.fr/louvrea.htm.

**Full-color reproductions** of the world's art masterpieces are available from Art Extension Press, P.O. Box 389, Westport, CT 06881; www.home-school.com/Mall/Artext. One hundred 3x4" prints $22.50, accompanying text $15, plus $4 shipping. Free brochure.

*I shut my eyes in order to see. — Paul Gauguin*

Since your parents are trying to teach you at home, Karen, you're lucky to have a grandmother who has a Ph. D. in Art History. Now, this is Hunt's "Lady of Shalott." I don't remember the story, but... ah... uh...

It's in the time of King Arthur, Grandma. The girl is afraid of a curse, so she stays in her tower. One day she saw Lancelot in her mirror. She looked at him, and the curse struck her; in the autumn, she died. Tennyson wrote a poem about it.

## GAMES

### Cooperative! Challenging!

### *NO REFEREE NECESSARY!!*

Yes, it is possible to play games without a referee. Playing games is — or should be — a friendly social act. How strange that in most games players work to eliminate others, to outsmart them, to take advantage of another's oversight, age, or weakness. The games below call for cooperation, not competition. Some are mostly a matter of luck; others call for thinking skills. Some are mostly for one age group, and others will allow players of different ages to work together. A few games can be played by oneself if no one else wants to play. A number of these games come with suggestions for variations so you actually get more than one game in a package. I'm limited in space so I'm going to list just a few for each age group. If you're interested in a full-color catalog send $1 and ask for the Cooperative Games Catalog. All these games are code FP. Shipping is $4 for the first game. Add $2 for each additional game.

### FOR THE VERY YOUNG

**HARVEST TIME**. The object is to plant and harvest your garden before winter. It's possible if you work with everyone else. Bilingual rules (English/French). 2 to 4 players (more if you play with partners), ages 3 to 7. $14.

**BEAUTIFUL PLACE**. An ecology game for children! Environmental concepts are presented in a simple way. The object is to restore the planet before the pollution clouds take over. You can do it if you work together. 2 to 4 players (more if you play with partners), ages 4 to 7. $14.

**FUNNY FACE** will have everyone in giggles. Lots of funny pantomime. This is an active game that plays very quickly. It's a favorite because it's never the same twice. 3 to 18 players (great for the family or a party), ages 3 to 8. $14.

**THE SECRET DOOR**. One of the most popular with young children. Definitely a cooperative mystery game. Besides needing a bit of luck, you'll need your memory and thinking skills. 1 to 8 players, ages 5 to 8. $14.

**HUGS AND TICKLES** will make everyone feel good. Just watch out for the Blues! Part of the game is to pass on a hug, tell a joke, dance, or sing a song. Fun for the family or a party. 2 to 12 players, ages 5 and up. $14.

### 7 TO ADULT

**INVESTIGATORS.** Be part of a private investigating team. Solve cases of smuggling, theft, and blackmail. Move around the city avoiding guard dogs and tough guys, and try not to get tied up. Use a disguise or a special tool kit. This game moves quickly. Tricky but fun. 2 to 8 players. $18.

**SKY TRAVELERS**. You are a peaceful people who crash on an island. You must search the shore, sea, forests, and mountains for repair materials for your ship. You meet UTOC's (ugly things out of control). You use your powers to deal with them, but you must not harm anyone. Dire consequences if you do! 2 to 4 players. $18.

### 10 TO ADULT

**OUR TOWN** requires a higher level of strategies. Develop your city's economy and avoid going bankrupt. You must decide what will work best as a private enterprise and what will be best cooperatively owned and operated. Rules for easy play and for a more advanced game. 2 to 6 players. $22.

**NEW AMERICA**. Be part of a research and development team to redesign the socioeconomic system before it's too late. The focus is on energy and resources, but many other fields are explored. Very suitable for thinking friends. Designed to provoke discussion. 2 to 4 players. $22.

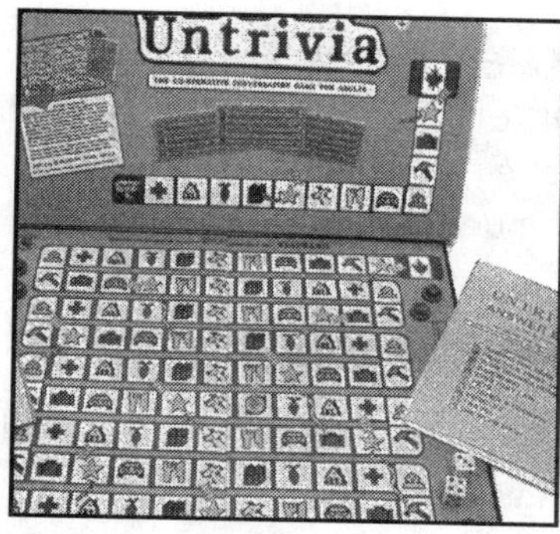


**UNTRIVIA**. Finally! A game that asks practical questions about child-rearing, gardening, everyday law, travel, health, and more. It's fine if you think you have the answer and maybe better if you discuss it before deciding. This is more the way our family always approached Trivial Pursuit. This game has "goof" tokens! A relaxing conversational game for older teens and adults. Highly recommended. 2 to 12 players. $24.

## STRATEGY GAMES

**MAZE**. A cooperative form of chess. An intricate strategy game that is different every time you play. Wizards can make a veritable study of this game. Beginners can play an easier game. Basically a two-person game, but can be played alone. Ages 12 and up. $25.

**ZEN BLOCKS** is a cube game for thinking and intuitive players. Easy games for the young and tough games for teens and adults. Many solutions to this puzzle. A good logic game. Play alone or with as many as 13. Ages 6 to adult. $16.

## BOOKS YOU SHOULD POSITIVELY, ABSOLUTELY HAVE, NO MATTER WHAT

******GAMES MANUAL****** Many times when we didn't have a birthday to celebrate and the kids wanted a party, we would have an "unbirthday party" and invite everyone's friends. Each person brought a small gift costing less than $5 that would do for a girl or a boy. We played games and had ice cream and cake — complete with lots and lots of candles. Everyone helped to blow out the candles (picture it!). I wish we'd had this collection of games to use. This book has 170 co-op games and activities for ages 3 to 12. Little or no equipment needed; good for small or large groups. Most games can be played indoors or out. You'll never do better than this for price or value. Code FP, $4.

**SPORTS MANUAL**. Features 60 co-op sports games for ages 10 to adult. Detailed manual for athletics, gymnastics, team sports, stick and ball events, co-op billiards, and horseshoes, plus suggestions for running a co-op field day. 36 pages. Illustrated. Code FP, $4.

**PARLOR GAMES**. A collection of 50 unique parlor games that are played cooperatively. Amusing and challenging games for small and large groups. Little or no equipment needed, for a quiet evening or lively party. Ages 12 to adult. Code FP, $3.75.

**MARBLE GAMES**. I always had marbles that I loved, but I never knew what to do with them. Now I do. This is a collection of 50 marble games. Line drawings illustrate the text. Ages 6 to 12. Code FP, $3.75.

**EVERYBODY WINS!** by Jody Blosser. This books lists 45 *non-competitive* party games and activities for children. You don't need to have a party to have fun with these games and activities — just several children, or you and your child can do these together. Almost every activity in this book comes with a bonus — it teaches skills such as counting and coordination. I particularly like the introduction, in which Blosser gives you a very clear idea of the difference between activities that produce real self-esteem and ones that just make your child feel good at the moment. Materials needed are around the house or not expensive. Each activity listed comes with information about preparation time, a list of materials, age level, what procedures to follow, and some helpful hints for success. Code ST, $16.95.

**Other Games to Play! And Where to Find Reviews.** The games listed below are made by Aristoplay. Like us, they believe that learning can be fun. They also agree that learning is something that parents and children can and should do together — that's why many of these games can be played on different levels at the same time.

**DON'T BUG ME**. See "Mathematics."

**INVENTORS, EXPLORERS, and SCIENTISTS**. See "Science."

**MONEYWISE KIDS**. See "Mathematics."

**SOME BODY**. See "Science."

**TIC TAC TWICE CLASSIC**. See "Mathematics."

**TRUE SCIENCE**. See "Science."

**WHO'S AT HOME?**. See "Science."

**ARTDECK.** A game to introduce you to the masters, Impressionism to Surrealism. Learn about art while enjoying an afternoon or evening card game. Artdeck contains a miniature collection of modern art by 13 of the world's greatest artists, from Monet to Miró. There are 52 cards depicting four major works of art by each artist represented; 13 artist cards feature information about the artists and their work. The 52 paintings depicted are from 16 of the world's great museums, including the Louvre, London's National Gallery, the Metropolitan Museum of Art, Boston's Museum of Fine Arts, and the National Gallery of Art in Washington, D.C. 2 to 4 players, ages 12 to adult. Code A, $15 plus $4 shipping.

**STARTING CHESS** is an ideal book for beginning players. Animated illustrations show basic moves and some tricks. Basic rules clearly explained. Ages 8 and up. Code EDC, $4.95.

*All new and revised* — **THE KIDS' BOOK OF CHESS AND CHESS SET**, by Harvey Kidder. The origins of chess, patterned after medieval battlefields, help explain the movements of the chess pieces. Pawns, the common infantry, advance step by step. The knight's leaping L-shaped move is the warrior on his charging horse. Powerful bishops line up beside the queens and kings, as in the Middle Ages' alliance of church and state. Readers are led through the fundamentals of beginning, middle, and end games, and shown winning strategies for offense and defense — how to castle, how to protect pieces, how to control the center of the board, how to identify the opponent's key square and bear down with an attack until checkmate is reached. The book is accompanied by great illustrations, and you get a full-size 32-piece chess set, with a folding board. Code WKM, $14.95.

**Usborne Guides to Playing Chess.** Profusely illustrated introduction, with clear step-by-step instruction in more advanced techniques. Suitable for all ages. Code EDC, $7.95 each. Specify **Advanced Chess** or **Chess Puzzles.**

**BOARD AND TABLE GAMES FROM MANY CIVILIZATIONS**, by R.C. Bell. Encyclopedic work on 182 different games: mah-jongg, hazard, wei-ch'i (go), backgammon, pachisi, and more. Code DV, $9.95.

**Mudpuppy Press**. Catalog of great puzzles for little ones. Great puzzles (starting with 5 to 8 pieces on up to 36), books, and more. Galison Books, attn: mail order, 28 W. 44th St., New York, NY 10036.

**WILDLIFE JIGSAW PUZZLE.** 360 pieces, beautifully colored. Features animals from around the world. 25 inches in diameter. Ages 9 and up. Code EDC, $12.95.

**CHRONOLOGY JUNIOR**. A game that asks questions such as "Which was invented first, the Tootsie Roll or the Hula-Hoop?" "Was the paper clip invented before or after Christopher Columbus discovered America?" Players build a timeline. Covers history, science, geography, and politics. Ask about the standard Chronology game, too. For ordering information and catalog, call Mind Ware, 800-999-0398; www.mindwareonline.com.

**TIC TAC TWICE** is a game of logic, strategy, and patterns — all math skills, but without the "math"! Like tic-tac-toe, to win you must place four markers in a row, but with this game you are playing on two boards at the same time. Magnetic boards (good for traveling); your choice of Animals or Insects edition. 2 players, ages 7 and up. Code A, $10 plus $3 shipping. For the classic version of this game, see "Mathematics."

**FACE PAINTING KIT.** Full of ideas. You get five water-based, *washable*, nontoxic, colored paints, and an applicator. Lots of color illustrations so even beginners will get good results. The artistically inclined will find their own way. The book says it's for ages 5 to 8, but I think they're wrong. I think this is best for ages 10 and up or teens and adults to use on themselves or younger kids. Faces: clown, robot, Dalmatian, lion, cat, and more. Ages 10 and up. Code EDC, $15.95. **FACE PAINTING** book only, $7.95.

**CALLIGRAPHY KIT**. This 48-page book makes it easy to create beautiful handwriting, which I consider an art form in itself. Includes three calligraphy markers in red, black, and blue, with broad, medium, and scroll points for the pens. Ages 11 and up. Code EDC, $14.95.

**BEADS, BANGLES AND BRACELETS KIT**. This 32-page book explains and illustrates how to use beads, clay, and many other materials included to make your own jewelry. Lots of quick and easy projects that will provide satisfying results. Includes four colors of clay, assorted colored beads, salt crystals, gold wire, paint, embroidery floss, and bracelet tubing. Ages 8 to 12. Code EDC, $20.95. **BEADS, BANGLES AND BRACELETS** book only, $6.95.

**PAPER FLOWERS KID KIT**. Enjoy flowers in your house all year round or give them away. Hours of creative fun. Poppies, daffodils, roses, crocuses, and more. Comes with colored paper, florist wire, and a 32-page book, well illustrated with clear directions. Supplies for 25 flowers. Ages 8 and up. Code EDC, $16.95.

**ORIGAMI KID KIT**. Comes with 55 multicolored sheets of paper in different sizes, plus clear instructions in a 32-page book. Make butterflies, jumping frogs, snapping dragons, and more. Ages 8 and up. Code EDC, $15.95.

**DECORATING T-SHIRTS KID KIT**. The catalog review of this book says, "You and your kids will ... create beautiful and ingenious designs." I won't guarantee anything but the fun. You get four fabric paints, an outlining pen, a paint brush, a craft sponge, and more than 40 designs to choose from, just in case your kids happen to run out of their own ideas. Helpful step-by-step directions for cartoons, dinosaurs, and more. Ages 8 and up. Code EDC, $19.95. **DECORATING T-SHIRTS** book only, $7.95.

**STENCIL FUN KIT**. Create your own gift cards and matching envelopes, stencil one side of a breadboard to make a gift, get creative with T-shirts, and have fun. Comes with acrylic paints, sponge applicator, stencils, glitter, and a couple of $5\frac{1}{2}$x$4\frac{1}{2}$" cards with envelopes. Clear, well-illustrated instructions. Ages 8 and up. Code EDC, $15.95. **STENCIL FUN** book only, $7.95.

**PAPIER-MÂCHÉ KID KIT**. This kit contains all you'll need. The paints, glues, markers, pencils, and crayons are nontoxic. Easy directions will help ensure a successful creation, and the skills learned will carry over into other art projects. For creative kids ages 8 to 12 (and adults). Code EDC, $15.95. **PAPIER-MÂCHÉ** book only, $7.95.

**FRIENDSHIP BRACELETS KIT**. All your child needs to create the latest in kid fashion. Clear, full-color illustrations. Everything included to make braided, woven, or beaded bracelets, with directions for 12 styles. All your child needs to add is imagination. Ages 8 to 12. Code EDC, $9.95.

**BOOK OF MAGIC KIT**. Who doesn't enjoy a little magic? What kid can resist? Magic wand, props, deck of cards, silk scarf, and dice all come along with a well-illustrated book about the secrets of performing illusions. Let your kids entertain you. Ages 10 and up. Code EDC, $16.95.

Need more origami paper? **Variety Pack**, $3.95; **Animal Prints**, $4.50; **Patterned Paper**, $4.95; **Rainbow Patterned**, $4.95. All code DV.

## SPORTS AND RECREATION

**IN PURSUIT OF EXCELLENCE: How to Win in Sport and Life Through Mental Training**, by Terry Orlick, Ph.D. A must for parents and children involved in competitive sports. I also think this is an important book for all of us who seek excellence within ourselves. I bought this book because Derek competes on a very high level with horses, and I thought he would enjoy and learn from it. I got surprised! I read and learned a lot in terms of my own life before wrapping it up as a gift. Orlick has competed extensively and has coached hundreds of Olympic athletes. He speaks from his own experiences. A man very aware that "winning" is not everything, that getting there has to be important and rewarding in itself, and that there have to be balances with life outside the arena. He is a man who understands just what it is inside a person that makes him a winner, in sport and in life. Ages 14 to adult. Code BT, $15.95.

**THE COOPERATIVE SPORTS & GAMES BOOK**, by Terry Orlick. Terry has had years of experience working as an Olympic contender, as a professional coach, and with children. He believes in personal excellence *and* cooperation. He believes that through cooperation each child can feel free to do his best without feeling inadequate or intimidated. Hours of fun for small and large groups. You'll find considerable advice concerning how to help each child or group have the most fun. More than 200 games for all ages and abilities, indoors and out, with little equipment needed. The emphasis is on fun and imagination. You'll have no "losers" with these games. Orlick includes pointers for teaching and playing. Perfect for the family, parties, and support groups that have activities for children during a meeting or outing. Code RH, $18.

**RUNNING SKILLS**. If you or your kids are runners, or want to be, this book will help you improve your stamina and technique and get more enjoyment from your efforts without unnecessary injury. Well written with good illustrations. Ages 11 to 15. Code EDC, $5.95.

**THE WINNING ATTITUDE!**, By Michelle Kwan. A very good book for teens working to excel in any sport or endeavor, whether it's good grades, great music, or excellent writing; it's not just about ice skating. Kwan discusses the most desirable attributes for winners and their counterparts — the demons that can be problems. Code LB, $9.99.

**MAGIC ON ICE**, by former junior Canadian figure skating champion Patty Cranston. A look behind the scenes, with full-color photos and profiles of favorite skaters past and present. Also warm-up exercises, practice drills, and how-to tips. Interviews with top coaches and judges give kids an insight into the life of competitive skating. Ages 8 to 16. Code KC, $5.95.

**YOGA KIT FOR KIDS**. Nicely put together by Leah Kalish and Diane Spahn. Comes with an excellent beginner's instruction book. Yoga can be much more than a gentle form of exercise, but this beginner's kit is just an introduction and nothing more. A cassette tape of classical music is included (nice touch), and there are games you can play using the yoga you learn aided by a bit of imagination. Suggestions are included. This could be an excellent way to take a break from concentrated study. It's a combination of exercises building strength, flexibility, and balance, followed by quiet relaxation. You can count it as PE if your state requires physical education in your program. It's gentle and non-competitive. Ages 4 and up. Code IM, $19.95 plus $3 shipping.

**CREATIVE MOVEMENT FOR CHILDREN**, by Joan Koralewski, M.A., is about exposing your children to the joy and experience of creative movement. This is more about movement than dance, but for young children it can be almost the same thing. Many good ideas for experimenting and exploring. No special equipment except for common household objects. $12 plus $5 shipping. **CREATIVE MOVEMENT II** presents 25 intermediate and advanced ideas for dancers ages 12 to adult who have had previous dance experience, $11 plus $3 shipping. Write: Joan Koralewski, 12 N. Paradise Dr., Orem, UT 84057.

**STARTING BALLET** is written for beginners and shows all the basic moves with delightful illustrations. Lots of ideas, yet leaves lots of room for creativity. Ages 5 to 8. Code EDC, $4.95.

**Yo-Yo Tricks**. Send a #10 SASE for a free Yo-Yo Trick pamphlet. Write: Duncan Toys Co., P.O. Box 5, Middlefield, OH 44062.

**USBORNE SOCCER SCHOOL.** Developed with professional coaches and players, this book covers ball control, passing and shooting, dead ball skills (whatever that is), and defending. Tips for games and exercises. Great photos! Ages 8 and up. Code EDC, $14.95. There are more books in this series. For information send a #10 SASE.

**STARTING SOCCER** is for the very beginner. Rules and play are clearly explained and illustrated. Lots of practice ideas. You don't need a whole team to play and have fun playing soccer any more than you need a whole team to play baseball — improvise! Ages 8 and up. Code EDC, $4.95.

**HORSES AND RIDING**

These books from Usborne are for serious riding and horse enthusiasts. They are full of detailed information with illustrations and photos that make the text very clear. You'll learn about daily care of your horse or pony, grooming and stable management, and how best to show yourself and your horse. Ages 8 and up. Code EDC, $5.95 each. **First Pony, Grooming and Stable Management, Jumping, Showing.**
**Riding School** (a one-volume collection of all these books), $14.95.

Derek and I did a lot of riding and competing together over a period of years. We enjoyed the people, the horses, and the challenges. We were discouraged and disgusted with some of the (unwritten) requirements at some amateur shows and competitions. We found that even on beginning levels many judges deducted points or were influenced by "improper clothing," e.g., wearing jeans rather than breeches in an English class, or using tack that was not "regulation," meaning not having a second cinch in a Western class. We'd assumed that judging would be based on how well the horse and rider performed. Silly us! At the time we really couldn't afford designer clothes for us or the horses. It took some of the fun out of what we were doing. If your child is going to compete, find out what will be expected so you can meet those expectations or prepare your child to deal with this prejudice.

**HOLIDAYS**

**HOW TO MAKE HOLIDAY POP-UP CARDS**. You'll never have to buy them again. I hope no one feels this book is only for kids, because everyone can have fun making these holiday cards. Directions to make cards for more than 30 holidays, plus notes about each, so you will learn something new while you devise your own creation. Ages 8 and up. Code KC, $10.95. Use the book and you'll save a lot more than that!

**Punch-Out Window Decorations**. Each book has a variety of full-color decorations that 6-year-olds and up will enjoy punching out and putting up. Can be used again and again. Code DV. **Chanukah**, $3.95; **Christmas**, $3.95; **Easter**, $2.95, **Easter Bunny Village.** Houses and *lots* of bunnies, $4.95.

**Early Learning Coloring and Activity Books**. For preschool through 1st grade. Good fun. All books 8¼x11", 32 pages. Code DV, $1 each. **Christmas Fun, Christmas Puzzles, Easter Fun, Halloween Fun, Night Before Christmas, Thanksgiving Fun.**

**Halloween Fun!** All you need is glue and scissors or a craft knife. These fantasy models have moving parts, "see-inside" sections, and baseboards. Donn did the wizard's castle, and we really got a kick out some of the comic details. Ages 9 and up. Code EDC, $9.95 each. **Haunted House, Wizard's Castle.**

**PRESS-OUT MODEL NATIVITY**. This is a three-dimensional model that the kids will have fun putting together. All pieces are die-cut to push out and slot together. Easy to do. Would make a lasting holiday decoration. 11x17" base. Ages 7 and up. Code EDC, $12.95.

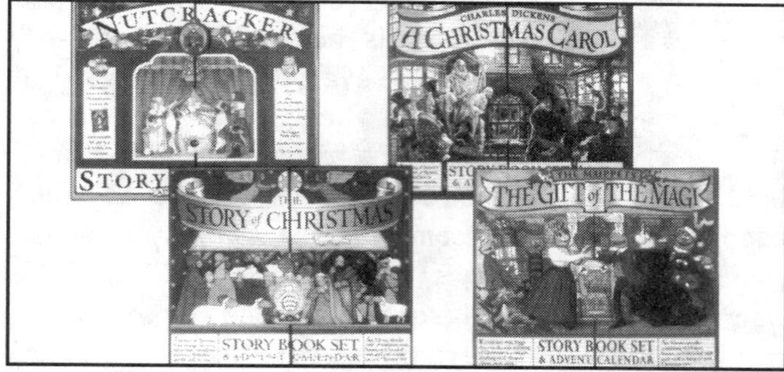


**Advent Calendars**. Storybook and calendar. Code WKM, $16.95 each. **The Christmas Story, The Nutcracker, A Christmas Carol, The Gift of the Magi.**

**Wall Calendars** make nice gifts. All full color unless otherwise stated. Code BT, $10.95 each. **Audubon Calendar, Gnomes and Friends** (beautiful, enchanting illustrations by Rein Poortvliet), **Greenpeace, Little House Calendar** (pictures from the book series), **Monet, National Geographic: America's National Parks, Native American** (black-and-white photographs from the American Museum of Natural History), **Norman Rockwell, Sierra Club, Timelines of African-American History** (interesting dates, people, beginnings, and turning points), **Working Mothers** (animal mothers and their young), **Wolves.**

**MAKE YOUR OWN CALENDAR**. This is a perennial item. There's a new one every year. It comes with basic full-color illustrations by Sue Dennen, yet with plenty of room for your child to personalize each page. Entertaining and interactive. Invites young artists to paint, draw, or paste in their own unique pictures and color the borders. Comes with 198 full-color stickers. Ages 6 to 10. Code LB, $7.95.

**THE MAGICAL MOBILE, INCREDIBLE CUT-OUT BUTTERFLY CALENDAR** Wow! 12 big full-color butterflies to cut out, to hang as decorations or make into a mobile. Calendar comes with puzzles, stickers, information, trivia, crosswords, and more. A kid's delight. 17"x11" before opening. Code WKM, $12.95.

**Page-a-Day Calendars**. Code WKM, $9.95 each.
**BOOK LOVER'S**. Quotes from and about books.
**LITTLE ZEN**. Philosophical thought for each day.

**CHRISTMAS ORNAMENTS**. 12 full-color decorations to punch out, fold, and glue. The nice thing about this book is that you can use the patterns to create your own variations. Easy to do. Age 5 and up. Code DV, $4.95.

**SANTA'S WORKSHOP AND VILLAGE**. Full-color pieces punch out to form a nice scene. Just punch out, fold, and glue together. The kids will have fun making this, rearranging all the pieces, and making up stories to go with it all. Code DV, $4.95.

**CHRISTMAS VILLAGE**. Book opens out to make an 18½x12" backdrop for the 75 reusable stickers. Hours of fun. Great characters. Code DV, $3.95.

**PUNCH-OUT CHRISTMAS STENCILS.** 8½x11" book with a variety of designs. Code DV, $3.95.

**DECORATIVE PAPER SNOWFLAKES.** Challenging and rewarding work for those with manual dexterity. Code DV, $4.95.

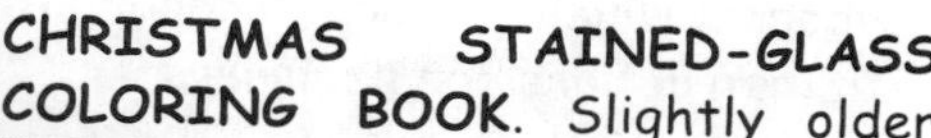

**CHRISTMAS STAINED-GLASS COLORING BOOK**. Slightly older children will enjoy coloring this. Code DV, $4.95. **TWELVE DAYS OF CHRISTMAS**, $3.95.

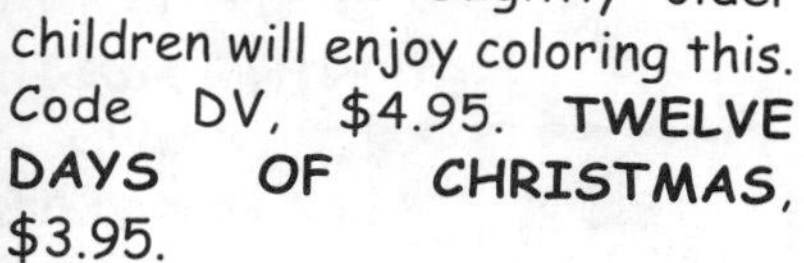

**A CHRISTMAS CAROL** (abridged) on cassette with book, plus the book **CHILDREN'S CHRISTMAS STORIES AND OTHER POEMS**. Code DV, $5.95.

**CHRISTMAS STORIES AND SONGS**. Boxed set of five books, including stories by Charles Dickens, O. Henry, and E.T.A. Hoffmann. Code DV, $5.

**THE NIGHT BEFORE CHRISTMAS,** a special edition by Jan Brett. Playfully illustrated, this is a book you'll be glad to have in hardcover. Reading this with your children will become part of your Christmas traditions — and when there are grandchildren you'll feel a special pleasure in sharing this unique edition of a classic story. Code PTN, $16.99.

**BELIEVE**, by Mary Engelbreit. A beautifully illustrated hardcover treasury of classic Christmas stories. Mary has collected her favorite quotes, poetry, prose, and songs and illustrated each with pictures the whole family will enjoy. Among the classics are "The Gift of the Magi," and "A Visit from St. Nicholas." She also includes interesting facts about holiday customs around the world. Embossed cover, ribbon marker. A book to last a lifetime. Code BT, $29.95.

# MUSIC AND DANCE

*If it sounds good, it is good.*
— Duke Ellington

*Without music life would be a mistake.*
— Friedrich Nietzsche

Music is a common chord in all of us, and we respond to it in conscious and subconscious ways. Music is a poetic expression of our innermost feelings painted in sound. It can express our anger, love, frustrations, dreams, loss, and joy, and reflect our soul. It is a gift to be enjoyed in every way possible. Some of us can create it, some play it, and some of us can barely hum a tune, but we can all enjoy it.

I was lucky to enjoy music in many forms while I was growing up. I studied dance for years; sang in several choruses; played piano moderately well, but without great talent; played clarinet, not as well; played the violin with promise (I was told); and found playing the drums absolutely boring. It wasn't until I reached my mid-teens that I found the right instrument for me (the guitar), one I felt could help me express what I couldn't put into words, one that vibrated with my inner being and gave it expression. I think every child should have the opportunity to learn at least one instrument. Speaking from my experience I would not, as a parent, be discouraged if a child started and stopped music lessons or changed instruments over a period of years. Many people try various instruments before they find the one that's right for them, and many adults who had music lessons as a child and stopped playing start again later in life.

Children love music. They feel it and move to it; they love lullabies and story songs. (They even respond to music in utero.) There's lots of great children's music available to listen to, and there are thousands of good songs to sing and learn. Don't let the language of music — the notes, the musical alphabet — discourage you. It's very simple in its basic form, much simpler than learning English or French. It is a gift you can give your children that will last long after the lessons are forgotten.

If you've never played an instrument, I suggest you start with a recorder. It's inexpensive and not complicated to play. A piano is also a good beginning instrument because the keyboard is very logical and it is easy to relate to the written notes. If a piano is beyond your means, don't give up! Get an electronic keyboard, which is much cheaper. They usually come with instructions for beginners.

## BEGINNING MUSIC STUDIES

**SOUND CHOICES: Guiding Your Child's Musical Experiences**, by Wilma Machover and Marienne Uszler. I love it! It's for everyone who would like to provide some musical experience for his children. If you just want to give your children a casual acquaintance with music, this book has a lot more than you will need, yet it offers the best ideas for even the most basic experiences. The scope of this book goes far beyond choosing an instrument and providing lessons. There are extensive sections of other music resources that address the needs of various age groups, with suggestions for parents. You'll find chapters on practical issues: singing lessons, electronic instruments, very detailed suggestions for choosing a teacher, practicing, different learning systems (Suzuki, Orff, etc.), and much more. There's well-researched information about recognizing the musically gifted. Even more important is the chapter devoted to children with special needs, covering music as therapy; help for the physically limited, the learning disabled, and those with varying degrees of hearing or sight loss; and information about adapting instruments and other ways of making it possible for these children to make music. Each section of the book is followed by a listing of resources: books, CDs, videos, camps, and organizations. Sprinkled in with all this information about music is a lot of commonsense psychology about listening to your children and how and when to encourage them. Code OX, $19.95.

**PRACTICING FOR YOUNG MUSICIANS: *You Are Your Own Teacher*,** by Harvey Snitkin, Ph.D. This is the best book I've ever seen concerning the motivation for practicing and effective practice strategies. It will give you and your child strategies that take the nightmare out of practice time. This book puts the student in charge. After all, learning to play mostly takes place *between* lessons during practice time, not during the lessons themselves. Fun to read. Highly recommended for all adults, teens, and parents of younger musicians — ***and all music teachers***. Code HMS, $14.95.

**FIRST BOOK OF MUSIC** really is for beginners. It answers such questions as "What is music?" Nice introduction to different types of instruments and how they work. Includes suggestions on how to make simple instruments with materials you'll have on hand. Discusses high and low pitches, using your voice, musical ideas, drawing and painting music, recording music, moving to music, music around the world, listening to music, and things to consider when choosing an instrument. Ages 6 to 10. Code EDC, $9.95.

**THE STORY OF MUSIC** covers the development of instruments and musical styles around the world, from the first instruments to electronic music. Good commentary about major composers from historic periods and good illustrations. Not a how-to-play book. Ages 10 and up. Code EDC, $7.95.

**LEARNING TO READ MUSIC**. A home-study course with an 80-minute cassette program and a booklet containing 90 diagrams that teach time signatures, sharps and flats, repeats, rests, clefs, and more. Excellent explanations for beginners ages 10 and up or an adult refresher course. Code AF, $14.95.

**Musical Coloring Books.** Historically researched and accurate. Ages 13 and up. Code BB.

**A MUSICAL ALPHABET.** Very interesting portraits and caricatures of many well-known composers. $4.95.

**WOLFGANG AMADEUS MOZART.** Portraits of Mozart and his family, suitable for framing after coloring; with interesting, informative text. $3.50.

**LUDWIG VAN BEETHOVEN**. Beethoven's life story in pictures. $4.95.

**WOMAN COMPOSERS.** From the Middle Ages to the present; famous and lesser known composers. $3.95.

**PETER AND THE WOLF BALLET.** Drawn from Nicholas Benois' famous ballet of 1947 at La Scala. Great pictures of Prokofiev's story, along with amusing, informative text about musical instruments. $4.95.

**NUTCRACKER BALLET.** The story of the ballet and of its different productions, with illustrations by Alexandre Benois. $4.95.

**GREAT DANCERS.** A history of dance and dancers, with a portrait of each great dancer's greatest role. $4.95.

**SLEEPING BEAUTY BALLET.** The famous, elegant costumes by Leon Bakst for Diaghilev's production of this ballet. $4.95.

**KEY TO THE KEYS**, by Gale Pederson. This is a basic home-study course that provides easy, enjoyable piano lessons for ages 10 to adult. Code AF.

**VOLUME 1**: the basics of fingering and chords, and the playing of simple melodies. One cassette and illustrated booklet. $15.95.

**VOLUME 2**: increasingly advanced piano-playing skills. Two cassettes and booklet. $21.95.

**SAVE** — both for $35.

MUSIC TO SING AND SONGBOOKS

**THE I CAN'T SING BOOK: For Grownups Who Can't Carry a Tune in a Paper Bag ... But Want to Do Music With Young Children**, by Jackie Silberg. What a title! What a book! And not just for those who feel they can't sing. Great ideas for musical enjoyment without any technical terms. Silberg makes it all so easy that anyone can make music by putting together high and low sounds, simple rhythms, cheek popping, and body sounds. Also included: games, activities, simple homemade instruments, answers to frequently asked questions, and more. I've always had music as a part of my life and shared it with the family, and I still wish we'd had this when the kids were home. For adults with children birth through 10, but you're never too old to learn. Code GH, $12.95.

These books have familiar tunes specially arranged to suit children's voices. Easy-to-play piano, keyboard, and guitar accompaniments. Ages 3 and up. Code EDC.
**NURSERY RHYME SONGBOOK.** $9.95.
**NURSERY RHYME STICKER BOOK**. $6.95.
**ROUND THE WORLD SONGBOOK**. $9.95.
**FRENCH SONGBOOK FOR BEGINNERS.** $6.95.
**CHRISTMAS CAROLS**. 25 well-loved songs. Melody line is also suitable for playing on the recorder, flute, or violin. $10.95.
**CHILDREN'S SONGBOOK**. Music for piano, recorder, and guitar. $10.95.
**MUSIC PACK: NURSERY RHYME *TAPE*** (about 40 minutes), **NURSERY RHYME SONGBOOK,** and **STICKER BOOK.** Code EDC, $19.95.

**BORN TO SING**, a terrific program put together by Julliard-trained Elizabeth Howard and Howard Austin. Step-by-step instruction on all the basic and advanced vocal techniques. You'll get immediate results in vocal control, power, and range. Covers most vocal styles including Broadway, classical, jazz, country, blues, rock, and pop. So what more do you want? Private lessons? You won't come much closer than this without going out and paying someone a lot more. Do this first and you'll be ready for much more when you do seek a teacher. Four cassettes and booklet. Ages about 12 to adult. (Use this and you won't have to confine yourself to singing in the shower.) Code AF, $39.95.

**STORIES AND SONGS FOR LITTLE CHILDREN**, told and sung by Pete Seeger with many of his best songs for kids (and playful adults), including "Abiyoyo," "Froggie Went a-Courting," and more. Code AH, cassette $9.98, CD $15.98. One of my favorites.

**WHERE HAVE ALL THE FLOWERS GONE: A Musical Autobiography**, by Pete Seeger. An exceptional autobiography written by a man still full of life and good humor. You'll find many of Seeger's famous songs and many others (all with words and music), photos, and line drawings by Seeger and others. This book traces not only his life, but the history of politics, labor, segregation, the peace movement, his efforts to clean up the Hudson River, and much more. Pete Seeger has worked for world peace and understanding through music and song all his life. The music has the melody line and guitar chords; some pieces have tablature. High school age and up if you're reading and playing, but the music can be shared with all ages. I fell in love with this book the moment I opened it. A very special sharing by a very special man. 285 pages, large paperback. Code SO, $17.95.

**THE AMERICAN SONGBAG**, edited by Carl Sandburg. A collection of 280 songs, ballads, and ditties sung by people in the making of America. Piano accompaniments. 495 pages. Code HBJ, $22.

For early childhood music and related learning activities, see "Resources for the Early Years."

**BOUND FOR GLORY**. Woody Guthrie's legacy includes this remarkable autobiography. His son, Arlo, gives an inspired performance as he reads parts of his father's biography and sings Woody's songs. Two cassettes, 3 hours. Code BT, $16.95.

**THIS LAND IS YOUR LAND**, words and music by Woody Guthrie with a tribute by Pete Seeger, paintings by Kathy Jakobsen. Nearly everyone knows the song "This Land Is Your Land," even if they don't know who wrote it. Woody wrote this while hitching rides from California to New York in 1940. This book is a pictorial journey through the land and its people. It's also a songbook with *all* the original verses Woody wrote. Along with Pete Seeger's tribute to Woody there is a brief biography. If you like to sing, if you want to give your kids the pleasure of a pictorial trip through the land with bits of history thrown in, this book is for you. Hardcover. Code LB, $15.95.

**I WAS BORN ABOUT 10,000 YEARS AGO**, a *very* tall tale retold and illustrated by Steven Kellogg. The lively young storyteller takes us on a fanciful trip through biblical and historical settings, with humorous and improbable results. A treat for the imagination. Includes guitar chords and a simple piano arrangement to go with these words or variations from other recordings, or some you just make up on your own. Illustrated with humor and creativity. For young readers and musicians with a funny bone. Code WM, $5.95.

**THE CAT CAME BACK**. A classic folk song about a cat that just wouldn't go away, no matter what poor Mr. Johnson did. Fun to sing, and the musical notation is included along with the great illustrations. Code KC, $4.95.

**Folk Songs of the United States and Nova Scotia.** John and Alan Lomax's classic book, *Folk Songs of North America*, is no longer available, but these two volumes have all those great songs, spirituals, hollers, game songs, lullabies, courting songs, chain-gang work songs, and more, with notes about the origins. Code DV.

**AMERICAN BALLADS AND FOLK SONGS** (Vol. 1). 672 pages. $13.95.

**OUR SINGING COUNTRY** (Vol. 2). 464 pages. $14.95.

**SONGS AND BALLADS FROM NOVA SCOTIA**. 361 pages. $9.95.

## LEARNING TO PLAY AND FIRST MUSIC BOOKS

The recorder is an ideal first instrument. It's physically easy to use, and the one-line melodies make learning to read music easy. If you don't read music, you'll quickly learn and be able to help your child.

**First Music Series.** These books are good introductions for children and adults. Designed for beginners, they introduce all the basic skills and theory and include graded practice tunes, with lots of tips for getting the best sound. The books include pop, folk, and classical pieces to play, plus games, puzzles, and fascinating facts about the recorder or piano. The publisher says ages 6 and up. I'd say age 6 with parental involvement or ages 8 and up on their own. Code EDC, $10.95 each. **First Book of the Recorder, First Book of the Keyboard, First Book of the Piano.**

**Recorder Kid Kit.** Book and recorder. $22.95.

***Warning*:** Your dog may howl. Gus has definite musical preferences. He groans and mutters when I play in the key of D minor on the guitar, but only with some pieces. It puzzles me. He is completely intolerant (as in howling mad) of the recorder and the flute when I play them, but he is not at all bothered by a recording of these instruments. I try not to take this personally. If you love classical music and/or the recorder, listen to *Souvenir*, an RCA CD recording of Michala Petri on recorder with Lars Hannibal on lute and guitar.

---

*Of all noises I think music is the least disagreeable.* — Samuel Johnson

---

**LEARN TO PLAY KEYBOARDS.** For older beginners. Much like the *First Book of the Keyboard*, but progresses faster, with more detail and information given. Ages 12 and up. Code EDC, $9.95.

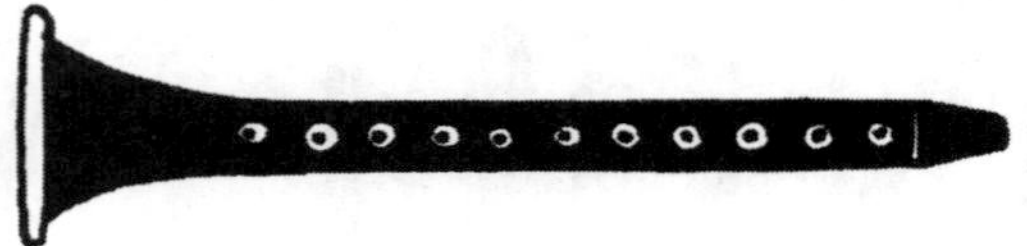

**USBORNE PIANO COURSE.** Two books to get you started. Clear, easy text and straightforward exercises allow your child to progress at a steady pace. Musical terms are explained clearly. Familiar tunes and original compositions are included for practice. These books have just about the same content as the *First Book of the Piano*, but the lessons are broken down into smaller increments so they are better for younger kids. Ages 5 and up. Code EDC, $7.95 each. Specify **Book One** or **Book Two**.

---

*Music is your own experience, your thoughts, your wisdom. If you don't live it, it won't come out your horn.* — Charlie Parker

---

**LEARN TO PLAY THE GUITAR.** This book provides solid technical background on acoustic, electric, and bass guitar, with step-by-step instructions and tunes for practice. Ages 11 and up. Code EDC, $10.95.

I used Frederick Noad's books *Solo Guitar Playing*, books one and two, when I started to learn classical guitar. These books are excellent, but I recommend working with a teacher because there are specific techniques that should be acquired when you begin this type of playing. I started out on my own, and it wasn't until I met another classical guitarist that I learned I was playing all the right notes — but I wasn't using the correct techniques to bring out the melody properly. I didn't have to start over from scratch, but I paid a price for my ignorance and independence.

### MUSIC TO SING AND PLAY

**MY FIRST BOOK OF AMERICAN FOLK SONGS.** 25 classic songs with very easy piano arrangements. I like this one. Code DV, $3.95.

**MY FIRST BOOK OF COWBOY SONGS.** Standard favorites that will be fun to sing and not too difficult to play. Code DV, $3.50.

**MY FIRST BOOK OF HYMNS AND SPIRITUALS.** 26 favorites with easy piano arrangements. Wide selection, including "Simple Gifts," "Amazing Grace," "Go Down Moses," and more. Code DV, $3.95.

**MY FIRST BOOK OF CHRISTMAS SONGS.** Easy arrangements that will please everyone. A good start. Code DV, $3.95.

**MY FIRST BOOK OF CLASSICAL MUSIC.** 20 themes by Beethoven, Mozart, Chopin, and others in easy piano arrangements. Very satisfying pieces to play, including Beethoven's "Pathétique" sonata and Brahms' Lullaby. Code DV, $3.95.

Don't let the term "classical music" fool you into thinking it's inaccessible. This kind of music expresses every possible human emotion. Just listen, feel, and enjoy. If you want to learn the difference between a sonata and a concerto, a symphony orchestra and a chamber group, see the Usborne books (code EDC).

**EASY TUNES SERIES.** Each book has a collection of more than 100 tunes, including jazz, folk, classical, and modern. Most have music for just one instrument, but a few pieces in each book include duets with another instrument. Helpful hints about techniques and reading music; playful illustrations. Sprinkled with facts and background information. Books begin with easy tunes and increase in difficulty. Ages 8 and up. Code EDC, $10.95 each, unless otherwise stated. **Easy Guitar Tunes, Easy Piano Tunes, More Easy Piano Tunes, More Easy Recorder Tunes, Easy Violin Tunes,** $9.95.

**THE GIFT OF MUSIC,** by Jane Stuart Smith and Betty Carlson. If you'd like to enrich your listening pleasure by learning about classical music composers, I recommend this very accessible book with interesting biographical information about composers and music from the age of the psalms to modern times. Each chapter has further reading and listening suggestions. Good glossary and a chart showing the progression of music and a few of the other arts through the ages. Mainly about the composers' lives rather than about music of specific periods. Ages 14 and up. Code CW, $15.99.

---

*Music is the universal language of mankind — poetry their universal pastime and delight.*
— Henry Wadsworth Longfellow

---

**Learn to Play the Classics.** These two books require basic piano skills. They have a nice selection of pieces that progress from relatively easy to more difficult. Nice notes about the composer's life and work. Most pieces are arranged to be played solo, but a few have a music line for flute, recorder, etc., to be played as duets. Music shared more than doubles the pleasure of the participants. Code EDC, $10.95 each. **Learn to Play Beethoven, Learn to Play Mozart.**

---

*Music heard so deeply that it is not heard at all, but you are the music while the music lasts.*
— T.S. Eliot

---

**USBORNE BOOK OF PIANO CLASSICS.** This book has much more than just 80 pieces of great music. The contents are arranged by period and type — baroque, classical, romantic, theater, dance, religious, etc. — with information explaining why each is unique, plus very brief biographies of the composers. There's an excellent glossary and a section with notes about playing specific pieces. It makes me wish I had time to take up the piano again. Lovely selection of pieces for hours and a lifetime of enjoyment. Code EDC, $17.95.

---

*Don't play what's there, play what's not there.*
— Miles Davis

---

## MUSIC THEORY

**MUSIC THEORY FOR BEGINNERS.** The vast majority of young children need to play and enjoy music before theory will be of interest. This book is for beginning adults and teens (and younger, if they are very involved and interested in studying about music). I learned a lot more from this book than I thought I would and thoroughly enjoyed it. Excellent information about basic music theory and exploring intervals, transposing, phrasing, chord structure, ornaments, glossary of terms, symbol chart, and more. Covers some music history and the development of written music. Lots of interesting and fascinating side notes, diagrams, and charts. Code EDC, $8.95.

**UNDERSTANDING MUSIC** (an Usborne Introduction). This complete introduction to music covers every style from classical to punk (yuck!). It highlights the main features of each style and the life and times of those who wrote and first performed it, explains the theory and science of music, and puts it all in historical context. A full description of instruments and instrumental groupings is given, as well as suggestions for music to listen to. Ages 9 and up. Code EDC, $9.95.

The air in music the wing forsakes. All things move in music and write it. The mouse, lizard, and grasshopper sing together on the Turlock Sands, sing with the morning stars. — From John Muir's letter to Jeanne C. Carr, from Yosemite, 1874.

**DANCE AND BALLET**

**BALLET** is a complete guide to the world of ballet with beautiful color photographs. The text is written for about age 10, but the desire to dance usually comes much earlier. It you have a budding ballet dancer, the photos alone make the book worthwhile. 64 pages. Code EDC, $9.95.

There is a program about movement to music for young children in "Arts and Activities."

**ONE VERY SPECIAL PROGRAM AND OTHER RESOURCES**

**MAKING MUSIC WITH CHILDREN**, by John Langstaff. The easiest way I know of to make music a part of your day is to use John's teaching videos and books, even if you don't know a thing about music. If you love music, you'll really love the charm with which John introduces songs and activities to go with them. Each video explains ways to teach singing on pitch (the right sound), experiments with rhythm (I think all children love this), movement activities, tone and dynamics, and part singing (yes, beginners can do this too!). There are step-by-step instructions for teaching songs, how to build an orchestra out of "found" objects, and how to use sound to express feelings and ideas. The music is as diverse as you could wish for,

from many different cultures: folk songs, singing games, street chants, story songs, sea chanteys, canons and rounds, and much more. You'll find that your children will ask to watch and take part in the video action on their own time because they will really enjoy it. This is a great program for individual families or groups. These are really worth the investment, as you'll use them over an extended period of time — and you and your children will carry the enjoyment for years to come. Code LP.

For individual families:

**Program 1: Ages 3-7**. Video, instructions, words to songs. $24.95.

**Program 2: Ages 7-11**. Video, instructions, words to songs. $24.95.

**DISCOUNTED SET of Programs 1 and 2 bought together**. $44.95.

For a group working together:

**Program 3: Ages 3-7. Making Music in the Classroom** (adapted from Program 1 above). $29.95.

**Program 4: Ages 7-11 Making Music in the Classroom** (adapted from Program 2 above). $29.95.

**DISCOUNTED SET of Programs 3 and 4 bought together**. $54.95.

*** **Extra word books** available at $4.95 each.

*New* — Expanded complements to the above programs with *more* sing-along versions of all the songs. **LET'S SING!** Ages 3 to 7. **LET'S KEEP SINGING!** Ages 7 to 11. $19.95 each, or both for $35.95. For extra sets of word books, music, and instructions, add $8.95.

**Classical Kids**. This series (which deserves all the awards it's gotten) is a wonderful and gentle introduction to classical music, the most famous composers, and their work. Each selection comprises a dramatic story, a bit of history, and the featured composer's music — all blended for imaginative listening. Like other recorded works, these will be listened to many times. Someone on National Public Radio said the other day that listening to radio (or recorded)

music and stories is "the finest visual medium." I agree and would add that it's all in your head. Ages 5 to 12 (except for *Daydreams and Lullabies*). Code BT, CD $18.98 each, cassette $10.98 each, unless otherwise marked. Specify CD or cassette.

**MOZART'S MAGNIFICENT VOYAGE**. The Dream Children are about to be written out of Mozart's most famous opera. Hoping to change their fate, they enlist the help of the composer's young son, Karl.

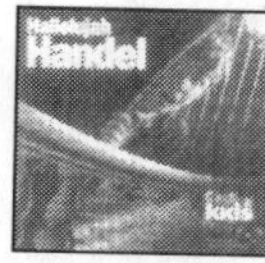


**HALLELUJAH HANDEL**. Katarina and Maestro Handel discover a young orphan boy with a mysterious past: He sings like an angel, but refuses to speak.

**TCHAIKOVSKY DISCOVERS AMERICA**. Tchaikovsky arrives in New York in 1891 for a grand opening at Carnegie Hall and takes a surprise adventure by train to Niagara Falls.

**VIVALDI'S RING OF MYSTERY**. A young violinist meets the great composer Antonio Vivaldi and travels the canals of Venice in search of her past. (Available in French with English translation. CD $21.98, cassette $14.98.)

**MOZART'S MAGIC FANTASY**. A young girl finds herself in the fairy-tale world of Mozart's *Magic Flute*. With a talking dragon as her guide, Sarah helps the prince find his princess.

**BEETHOVEN LIVES UPSTAIRS**. Young Christoph exchanges letters with his uncle about the chaotic arrival of an eccentric new boarder, Mr. Beethoven. In the end, he is won over by the great composer's music. (Available in French with English translation. CD $21.98, cassette $14.98.)

**DAYDREAMS AND LULLABIES**. Follow a young family from playtime to bedtime. A magical mix of classical music and classic poetry and poems written and performed by children. Features music from Bach, Beethoven, Mozart, and Vivaldi, with many classical lullabies. Ages newborn to 6.

**MR. BACH COMES TO CALL**. Mr. Bach visits a little girl at the piano and brings along his magic orchestra and choir.

Sets: **Music Box #1** — Beethoven, Vivaldi, and Handel or **Music Box #2** — Tchaikovsky, Bach, and Mozart. CD $52.98 each, cassettes $29.98 each.

**CLASSICAL KIDS TEACHING NOTES**. These notes provide additional background information, discussion topics, and activities divided by age group, with suggestions for exploring the music across the curriculum. Specify the individual title from above. $9.95 each.

## FINDING INSTRUMENTS AND MORE MUSIC

**Music for Little People**, P.O. Box 1460, Redway, CA 95560. Great free catalog! Music on cassette or CD. Nice variety of recordings with young people in mind. Musical instruments and other related items.

**Rhythm Band Instruments, Inc.**, P.O. Box 126, Ft. Worth, TX 76101.

Ask your local public school music teacher, or anyone who gives music lessons, for information about getting instruments (and reconditioned instruments) and instruction. Although the public schools, with one exception, would not allow our children to participate in their music programs, we found that the music teachers, when approached outside of school, were most helpful.

**Lark in the Morning**, P.O. Box 1176, Mendocino, CA 95460; larkinam@larkinam.com; www.larkinam.com. Write for a catalog of musical instruments. Great variety for all ages, from all cultures.

**Harps of Lorien** (P.O. Box 77, Questa, NM 87556-0077) makes a variety of beautiful handmade harps and is a good source for harp music. They offer a Kinder Lyre especially designed for youngsters. The seven pentatonic strings suit a child's voice range, have a soft sound, and are used extensively in Waldorf schools. Please mention you heard about them from us.

**Courtly Music Unlimited**, The Pillars, 84 Main St., Warrensburgh, NY 12885; 800-2-RICHIE. Play the recorder! Make your own music. Beginners and experienced players can get personal attention from Richie and Elaine (Julliard graduates). Instruments, instruction, and music tailored to your needs.

---

*Music has charms to soothe a savage breast,*
*To soften rocks, or bend a knotted oak.*
— William Congreve, *The Mourning Bride*

**Daedalus Music** (P.O. Box 6000, Columbia, MD 21045-6000) has an interesting catalog of music at discount prices.

**The Leonard Bernstein Society** (P.O. Box 3930, Milford, CT 06460-2088; 800-328-6622) offers a catalog with marvelous videos of Bernstein's Young People's Concerts with the New York Philharmonic. They're expensive. The catalog also lists videos on art, artists, and singers, and CDs of various musicals.

**HOW TO PLAY THE HOHNER HARMONICA.** Hohner Harmonicas will send you a free copy of this step-by-step guide. Write: M. Hohner, Inc., P.O. Box 15035, Richmond, VA 23227.

**Sing Out** is a non-profit organization formed to preserve the cultural diversity and heritage of traditional folk music from all countries and cultures, and to encourage the practice of folk music as a living phenomenon. For more information about membership and receiving their quarterly magazine, write to Sing Out Corporation, P.O. Box 5253, Bethlehem, PA 18015-0253.

**American Orff-Schulwerk Association**, P.O. Box 391089, Cleveland, OH 44139-8089. Movement, speech, song, and instrument playing are integrated to teach the elements of music; improvisation is encouraged to develop creative thinking. Free information.

**Suzuki Musical Instruments**, Customer Service, P.O. Box 261030, San Diego, CA 92196-1030. Write for a free catalog of musical instruments and related items.

If you would like a good, structured, Christian classical music program, write to Debra Flewelling, Tree of Life Book Service, 443 Weston Rd., Weston, NB, Canada E7K 1B1. Book and two CDs. Non-Christians can ignore the religious content.

**The Boston Ballet Order Center**, P.O. Box 9200, Waltham, MA 02154. Small free catalog of books, videos, and cassettes.

*Bach*
*gave us God's Word*

*Mozart*
*gave us God's laughter*

*Beethoven*
*gave us God's fire*

*God*
*gave us music that we*
*might pray without words*

# FOREIGN LANGUAGES



## LEARN TO TALK YOUR WAY AROUND THE WORLD
## OR
## TO YOUR NEIGHBOR

The best way to learn a language is to grow up with it. The next-best way, we're often told, is to live in the country in which the desired language is spoken. I think the next-best way is to live in the country and use some good books, tapes, or other study guides. I became fairly fluent in Spanish while living in Mexico, but if I hadn't studied the grammar and vocabulary at the same time, my Spanish would have been limited to that of the uneducated poor people with whom I spent most of my time. The same is usually true even in learning one's native language: If one's family and everyday associates speak ungrammatically, one's own speech will be the same unless an effort is made to improve it through study and practice. If you want to learn a language but don't expect to be living where it's spoken, or you want to learn some of it before you go, there are many different ways of learning: tapes, phrase books, classroom studies, and so on. Finding someone in your community to act as a mentor is an excellent way to learn a language and make new friends. We've investigated and tried several methods, and we believe the selections we've made are among the best language-learning aids available.

I've considered some of the new computer software programs for learning languages and found that although you can hear native-born speakers, the sound isn't as clear as on an audiocassette. Although some of the software came highly recommended, I found myself getting numb after the novelty wore off, and my eyes didn't like staring at the monitor. I wouldn't want my children using software for learning a language, even though the multimedia effects were quite good.

Cathy traveled and lived in Mexico for several months after high school. She started studying Spanish at home with the book *Madrigal's Magic Key to Spanish* and used an advanced cassette course. She didn't finish either the book or the cassette course before she left, but these resources gave her a good basic working vocabulary and an idea of the grammatical construction of the language. She learned enough to have a great time and make some very good friends.

Donn, on his first trip to Mexico, assumed that there would be English-speaking people on the bus between Texas and Mexico City to ease his language transition — but there weren't. There are many words in Spanish that are similar to English, requiring just a change in accent. He found that the little bus-stop stores offered drinks for sale — Coca-Cola, various beers, and coffee — all easy to say and all easy to drink. It was a bumpy road, and it wasn't very long before he realized that his phrase book lacked something very important. You can pantomime many things, but have you ever had to pantomime, in public, "Where is the bathroom?" There is no substitute for a good bilingual dictionary. Don't leave home without it!

If you are beginning language study with young children you will find that all the beginning programs are incomplete. Your kids will want words that are not on the tapes or in the books. You'll want a good bilingual dictionary: one that goes from English to your target language *and* from the target language to

English. You will also be better prepared to help your kids if you study along with them or use a more advanced course at the same time. It will give you a better understanding of the pronunciation and grammatical construction. I think everyone will benefit from using more than one program for young learners. The variety will increase vocabulary and decrease the chance of boredom through listening to the same thing repeatedly. The more exposure you get to the sound of the language the better your ears will hear it, and your pronunciation will improve.

## LANGUAGE TOOLS

**Beginner's Picture Dictionaries.** Words are grouped thematically so they appear in context. Each page has a large, detailed, and entertaining picture (a park, a house, a store, etc.) with all the details labeled in the target language. Words are listed in alphabetical order in the back, in English, with the target language and a pronunciation guide. The back of the book has a guide to grammar and conjugated verbs. Ages 9 and up. Code EDC, $12.95 each. Specify French, German, Italian, or Spanish.

**Essential Dictionaries.** 3,000 words listed in English and the target language. Easy to use. Ages 12 and up. Code EDC, $7.95 each. Specify "Dictionary," French, German, or Spanish.

**Dictionaries for High School and College.** These are excellent dictionaries, with all entries listed in the target language to English and English to the target language. More than 80,000 (70,000 for German) entries of words and phrases, more than 100,000 translations, help with sentence structure, practical appendices, and more. Code OX. Specify French (800 pages), $16.95; German (800 pages), $14.95; or Spanish (992 pages), $14.95. Other languages available upon request. Send us an SASE.

**Essential Guide Books.** Useful for teens traveling on their own. These books have up-to-date, useful phrases and expressions for almost any situation. Words and phrases only — not safety or currency exchange information, etc. Code EDC, $7.95 each. Specify "Essential Guide," French, German, or Spanish.

From *Reader's Digest*: "My brother-in-law helps teach English as a second language. He thought one student was making lots of progress with the nuances of English until the man proudly told the class that after he had moved, he called the power company all by himself and explained in English: 'I've changed my dress and want to be turned on.'" Contributed by Joy Johnson.

**Flash Cards.** Sets of 50 sturdy cards with a picture on one side and the word with a picture on the other. Use your imagination and create some games to go with these. Code EDC, $8.95 each. Specify French or Spanish.

**54 FAMILY CARD GAMES with cassette tape.** Outstanding! A Parent's Choice Award winner. Play games like gin rummy, solitaire, concentration, and go fish by forming sentences (5,000 possible in all). The vocabulary is centered around the family and everyday phrases and includes numbers and days of the week. The 45-minute audiocassette uses native speakers and ensures that you will learn the proper pronunciation. Side one covers the vocabulary. Side 2 introduces Deck Master, an interactive language-building game. Each card has a color code (red, blue, and white), a French or Spanish word or phrase with a phonetic guide, a picture representing the words or phrases and the English equivalent of the phrase, and a numeral accompanied by its foreign language name and the English equivalent. The instruction booklet explains how the cards are used and describes several of the possible games. Having the cassette for learning proper pronunciation is an asset. At first the only flaw I found with all of this was that the rules for more games could easily have been included, but then I realized you can use your imagination or adapt other games that you know. Code PTN, $12.95. Specify French or Spanish.

**PHRASE-A-DAY.** You and your children will enjoy the variety of everyday phrases and expressions and learn them without much effort at all. Organized by season; all voices are native speakers. You'll get two cassettes and an activity/coloring book. A good supplement to any language program. Ages 5 to 11. Code AF, $24.95 each. Specify French or Spanish.

**CULTURE CAPSULES.** Recorded in English, these tapes will familiarize first-time travelers — or the curious — with basic customs and traditions, manners and language usage, forms of greeting, traveling within the country, cuisine and ordering food, festivals, and more. 60-minute cassette. Ages 12 to adult. Code AF, $14.95 each. Specify China, France, Germany, Italy, Japan, Portugal, or Spain.

**FOREIGN LANGUAGES AND YOUR CAREER,** a handbook by Edward Bourgoin, explains how to put your language skills to work in many occupations and professions. Includes addresses for information sources. Code AF, $9.95.

A mama cat was playing with her kittens in the back yard. A dog came along and started to bark, scaring the kittens. The mama cat barked right back and the dog ran away. The kittens were surprised to hear their mama barking. The mama cat said, "I always told you it was important to learn a second language."

— From my Uncle Al, who travels a lot!

**PAGE-A-DAY CALENDARS.** 365 interesting phrases, tidbits, and trivia for those just learning the language and those well-versed. Ages 12 to adult. Code RH, $9.95 each. Specify French or Spanish.

**Received in the mail, for $3.99:**

> **NEW TRANSLATOR WANTED**
>
> ELECTRONIC MOSQUITO REPELLER
> "Use special frequency and waveform
> to repell the mostquito away
> "No harm to human beings and pets
> "Simple and, safe operation
> :Only one UM-3 battery
> "Effective distance: about 4 meters
>
> Experiments Report
> Mosquitos frequently infect you place in Summer, especially at night, They are extremely irritating as they disturbed our sleep and the most annoying of all is the difficulty in getting rid of the itch & soreness. After, ordinary mosquito increase or "Electrified Mosquito Killer" are used. However, the odour is unbearable and the abuse of some of them may become dangerous. In order to do away with the above nuisance, "Electronic Mosquito Repeller" has now been produced. According to the research of insect ecology, most of biting mosquitos are female ones in spawning period. A spawning female mosquito is very disgusted at the approaching of male mosquito. Therefore, the frequency of Repel-It' is made to imitate the sound signal of male mosquitos to repell female mosquitos away.
>
> MADE IN HONG KONG

**WORDACE.** Software for your computer, PC or Mac. Its massive bilingual dictionary and thesaurus will give you the right word or verb and conjugation. Many languages. For information call Transparent Language Inc., 800-332-8851; www.transparent.com.

From the *Seattle Times,* October 24, 1999, the Tech News column, "Free, instant translation":
**Free Language Translation Software.** Babylon (www.babylon.com) is downloadable software that works as an instant language translator and dictionary. The program works by loading a large dictionary onto your hard drive. Add-ons make the translation/dictionary program work in nine languages, including Hebrew and Japanese. Currently, Babylon is available only for Windows 95 and 98.

## FIRST BOOKS

**First Picture Word Books** have intriguing illustrations of kids and adults doing everyday things (some of them silly) and having fun. The appropriate descriptive word is printed in the target language with English underneath. Picture word books are perfect for creating a discussion using the new words. Each book has a pronunciation guide and dictionary (foreign language to English). The Cheshire Cat and I agree that it would be more useful if it went both ways (e.g., English to French and French to English). Each double-page spread has a picture of a cute little  duck to find. The publishers recommend these books for ages 2 and up, but use your own judgment. Code EDC.

**FIRST HUNDRED WORDS.** Your choice of French, German, or Spanish, $8.95 each. Matching sticker books are available for French and Spanish, $7.95 each. Videos are available for French and Spanish, $19.95 each. Special savings for a package with *First Hundred Words*, matching sticker book, and video, $29.95 (not available for German).

**FIRST THOUSAND WORDS.** Available for French, German, Hebrew, Italian, Japanese, Russian, and Spanish. Ages 3 to 12. Hardcover. $12.95. Cassette tape and book for Spanish only, $21.95.

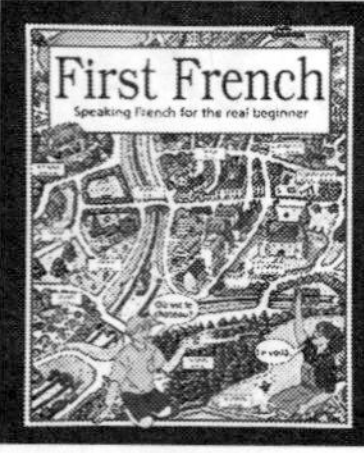

**First Language Books.** Use your beginning language skills and expand your vocabulary by following the exploits of an eccentric family at home, at school, or on holiday. Available in French and German. Your choice: **AT HOME, AT SCHOOL**, or **ON HOLIDAY**. Ages 7 and up. Code EDC, $6.95 each. All three of these books (in French) in one volume, called **FIRST FRENCH**, $12.95.

**Fun and Adventure.** Use that language! Two exciting *bilingual* stories with entertaining picture puzzles to do. The pictures have so many details to spot (and enjoy) that these books will be read again and again. Comprehensive word list and simple pronunciation guide for words and phrases in the back. Ages 7 and up. Code EDC, $5.95 each.

**L'ÎLE FANTASTIQUE** (Fantastic Island; French)
**CHÂTEAU MYSTÈRE** (Mystery Castle; French)
**LA ISLA FANTÁSTICA** (Fantastic Island; Spanish)
**EL CASTILLO MISTERIOSO** (Mystery Castle; Spanish)

**Language Picture Word Books.** 8½x11" books, 15 pages. Black-and-white scenes with people, animals, places, and things all labeled in the target language. No pronunciation guide, but a bilingual dictionary is included. For all ages. Code DV, $2.95 each. Specify German, Hebrew, or Italian. Spanish and French versions are listed separately below.

**BEGINNING LANGUAGE COURSES FOR CHILDREN**

**SPRINGBOARD LANGUAGE.** Introduces young children to foreign languages in an active, play-oriented way. Ideal for ages 4 to 8. Adult guidance is usually needed, but familiarity with the foreign language is not necessary; everything is on the cassettes. It's like playing Simon Says in another language. Activities include singing, coloring, playing games, and cutting out shapes. Two cassettes and a 40-page book. Code AO, $16.95 each. Specify French, German, or Spanish.

**SPANISH FLASH CARDS.** Designed to help children recognize words, these cards introduce Winko Bear/ Winko Osito, who demonstrates words and actions through pictures on the cards so that even children who can't read can understand the word needed and can say it. The target word is on the front. On the back is the part of speech (just nouns and verbs), the target word again, and an example of its use in a sentence in English and in the target language. Young children can then do the action shown: run to the door, turn on a light, walk to the table, etc. I think Winko is cute! Code AF, $12.95 each. Specify French, German, or Spanish.

**STORYBRIDGES FOR CHILDREN**. For slightly older children. Children learn French, German, or Spanish by joining Sadie and Sydney, the storyteller's young helpers, in repeating key foreign-language words and phrases spoken in the context of familiar stories: "Goldilocks and the Three Bears," "Little Red Riding Hood," "The Turtle's Music," "The Nightingale," "The Shoemaker and the Elves," and "Peter and the Wolf." By learning new words and phrases, your children will actually help tell the story. Each program consists of three cassettes. Code AF, $29.95 each. Specify French, German, or Spanish. Available for Spanish only is a 48-page activity workbook. Code AF, $8.95.

**LEARN FRENCH TOGETHER ACTIVITY KIT.** This is a program designed especially for children ages 4 to 8 and their parents so you can learn French together. It comes with a 48-page workbook and 40 play and learn stickers. You and your child will acquire proper pronunciation from the 60-minute cassette. Your child will enjoy this basic beginning language program for itself and because it is something special he can do with you. Specify French, Italian, or Spanish. Code RH, $14.95.

**TEACH ME TAPES.** A good beginning for ages 3 to 12. Lots of music to sing and pictures to color. They've made a good selection for beginning vocabulary and include musical action songs such as "Head, Shoulders, Knees, and Toes." Most songs will be familiar, and you'll learn new ones, too. Very upbeat, clear sound for easy learning. All tapes have native speakers, and each comes with an activity book. Code TM, cassettes $13.95 each, CDs $15.95 each. Specify Chinese, French, German, Hebrew, Italian, Japanese, Russian, or Spanish. Songbooks are available in French and Spanish only, $7.95 each. Not essential, but nice if you really enjoy the tapes in this program.

**TEACH ME MORE!** These tapes will take you and your child further in your skills and language adventure. Each comes with an activity book. Code TM, cassettes $13.95 each, CDs $15.95 each. Specify Chinese, French, German, Italian, Japanese, Russian, or Spanish.

**TEACH ME EVEN MORE!** And that's what this lively program will do. Only French and Spanish are available so far, but I'm sure the rest of the series will be available soon, because they are so well done. Each comes with an activity book. Code TM. Cassettes $13.95 each, CDs $15.95 each. Specify French or Spanish.

**TEACH ME TEACHING GUIDES.** Available for all three Teach Me levels, these are a good idea. You'll get addresses for pen pals and a lot more. Specify language and level. Code TM, $6.95 each.

A note from one of our readers had this story:

A linguistics professor was lecturing his class one day. "In English," he said, "a double negative forms a positive. In some languages, though, such as Russian, a double negative is still a negative. However, there is no language wherein a double positive can form a negative."

A voice from the back of the room piped up: "Yeah, right."

**LEARN FRENCH, GERMAN,** or **SPANISH.** For ages 12 and up. Good introductory books. The humorous illustrations will help maintain interest, and the tapes provide proper pronunciation. Since these books use a conceptual approach — things in the kitchen, at the store, on the phone — you will learn more than simply isolated words and phrases. Well done for this age group. Book and tape sets for French and Spanish. Sorry, no cassette available for German. Code EDC, $21.95 each. (Books only, without the tape, $10.95 each.) Specify French, German, or Spanish.

**Complete Language Courses for High School and Adult Learners.** These extensive language training programs include basic, intermediate, and advanced lessons, all produced by native speakers. They emphasize communication skills, provide repeated practice, and allow frequent review, and come with hours of audiocassettes, textbooks, and transcripts. If you want foreign language skills for college entrance, travel, or enjoyment (none of these being mutually exclusive), these programs are the best. You won't need anything else. You can succeed with these courses in as little as 25 minutes a day. (The secret is to *do it every day.*). These courses were designed for use by the Foreign Service Institute for personnel going overseas. We regularly carry French, German, Hebrew, Italian, Russian, and Spanish. If the language you want to learn is not listed, send an SASE for more information. We have access to more than 50 languages in this format. *All prices have been reduced 15%.* All code AF.

**FRENCH**

Basic Part A: 12 cassettes (15 hours), 194-page textbook. $158.

Basic Part B: 18 cassettes (25 hours), 290-page textbook. $185.

Basic Advanced Part A: 18 cassettes (27 hours), 332-page textbook. $208.

Basic Advanced Part B: 18 cassettes (22 hours), 235-page textbook. $208.

**GERMAN**

Basic German Vol. 1: 10 cassettes (9½ hours), 171-page textbook. $158.

Basic German Vol. 2: 8 cassettes (8 hours), 179-page textbook. $132.

Basic German Vol. 3: 18 cassettes (17½ hours), 375-page textbook. $208.

**HEBREW**

Basic Hebrew: 24 cassettes (24 hours), 552-page textbook. $218.

**ITALIAN**

Modern Spoken Italian Part A: 8 cassettes (8 hours), 124-page textbook. $158.

Modern Spoken Italian Part B: 8 cassettes (8 hours), 136-page textbook. $158.

**RUSSIAN**

Modern Russian Part 1: 24 cassettes (28½ hours), 480-page textbook. $220. Workbook, $11.95.

Modern Russian Part 2: 24 cassettes (28½ hours), 479-page textbook. $220. Workbook, $11.95.

**SPANISH**

Programmatic Spanish Vol. 1: 12 cassettes (17 hours) 464-page textbook and manual. $158. Workbook, $7.95.

Programmatic Spanish Vol. 2: 8 cassettes (12 hours), 614-page textbook and manual. $140.

Basic Spanish Advanced Level Part A: 12 cassettes (13 hours), 614-page textbook. $158.

Basic Spanish Advanced Level Part B: 12 cassettes (12½ hours), 471-page textbook. $158.

If English is your second language and you would like to improve it, we have a number of different resources available. Send a #10 SASE for information, and tell us your native language.

**LANGUAGE 30.** Brief language courses based on the U.S. military "speed-up" methods designed for military and embassy personnel. Includes two 45-minute cassettes with all phrases spoken in both English and the target language by native speakers and a convenient phrase book. Stressing conversational and useful words and phrases, the course offers 1½ hours of guided, repeated practice. Two short sections by Charles Berlitz, one introducing the course with helpful tips on its use, and another on the social customs and etiquette of the country. Good refreshers, or can be used as a crash course if you need basic language skills in a hurry. More than 35 languages available. High school and up. Code AF, $17.95. Specify Afrikaans, Arabic, Chinese (Mandarin), Czech, Danish, Dutch, Finnish, French, German, Greek, Hebrew, Hindi, Hungarian, Indonesian, Irish, Italian, Japanese, Korean, Latin, Northern Sotho, Norwegian, Persian, Polish, Portuguese, Romanian, Russian, Serbo-Croatian, Southern Sotho, Spanish, Swahili, Swedish, Tagalog (Filipino), Thai, Tswana, Turkish, Vietnamese, Xhosa, Yiddish, Zulu.

## LATIN

**ARTES LATINAE.** Designed for independent study, this classical Latin course combines modern teaching techniques, a sequential text, and extensive use of audiocassettes. This is not a Christian-based program. Best for high school students and adults. Code AF.
**Part 1,** 444-page text and 8 cassettes ($4\frac{1}{2}$ hours), $160.
**Part 2,** 440-page text and 8 cassettes ($4\frac{1}{2}$ hours), $160.
**Parts 1 and 2** bought at the same time, $295.
**Part 3,** 404-page text and 6 cassettes (3 hours), $145.
**Part 4,** 203-page text and 6 cassettes (3 hours), $145.
**Parts 3 and 4** bought at the same time, $260.

"I love the Latin program. Both my sons and I are really learning it. It's hard to believe that you can actually learn a language on your own, but this method works." — Happy customer

**Greek and Latin.** All levels, beginner to very advanced. Textbooks, literature, easy readers, filmstrips, cassettes, and more. Classical literature in the original text or in translation. Write for a catalog: Bolchazy-Carducci Publishers, Inc., 1000 Brown St., Wauconda, IL 60084.

**Native American Languages.** For information on audiocassette courses, send us a #10 SASE. Specify Cherokee, Chickasaw, Choctaw, Kiowa, Lakota, Lenape, Mohawk, Navajo, or Passamaquoddy. Also legends on tape, one side in the native language and the other side in English, and Native American music on tape.

**Asian Languages.** Asian books (for all ages), games, language courses, and more. Write for a free catalog: Cheng and Tsui Company, 25 West Street, Boston, MA 02111-1268.

**Japanese.** Books on Japan, Japanese culture, and language material for all ages. Write for a free catalog: Kodansha America, 114 Fifth Ave., New York, NY 10011.

## FRENCH

**STARTING FRENCH.** Pocket-size reference book. Best small reference book I've seen. Ages 7 and up. 32 pages, 7x$4\frac{1}{2}$". Code EDC, $2.95.

**HARVEST TIME** is a bilingual English/French game for ages 3 to 7. See "Arts and Activities."

**FRENCH ALPHABET.** $8\frac{1}{2}$x11" coloring book. Code DV, $2.50.

**FRENCH PICTURE WORD BOOK.** Black-and-white scenes of people, animals, places, and things, all labeled in French. No pronunciation guide, but a bilingual dictionary is included. For all learners. 15 pages, $8\frac{1}{2}$x11". Code DV, $2.95.

**MY FIRST FRENCH ABC PICTURE COLORING BOOK.** Each double-page spread of this $8\frac{1}{4}$x11" book is devoted to a letter of the alphabet. You'll find many illustrations of commonly used words to color, with the French word printed clearly beneath each. Good for all beginning French students. Code DV, $2.50.

**Tales for Young Children.** 32-page books, unabridged with full-color illustrations. Code DV.
**L'histoire de Jémima Cane-de-Flaque/ Jemima Puddle-duck,** $1.50.
**L'histoire de Pierre Lapin/Peter Rabbit,** $1.

**SING, DANCE, LAUGH, AND EAT QUICHE!** A collection of original and traditional French songs, this is a delightful introduction to French vocabulary. Explanations between songs are in English so everyone can follow along. Includes a one-hour cassette and an illustrated book with lyrics (and interactive actions) and an easy recipe for quiche. An excellent addition, once you've started with the basics. Code AF, $21.95.

**BONJOUR LES AMIS.** The three 50-minute videos in this series feature Moustache the cat, a playful feline, who introduces 4- to 6-year-olds to French language and customs. The series covers simple words

and phrases used in family celebrations, food, colors, etc. Code AF, $24.95 each, or all three for $69.95. Specify #1, #2, or #3.

**L'Ecole Chez Soi** has a resource catalog for homeschoolers. Contact Janice and Robert Beaudoin, St-Bruno, Quebec, at 514-461-1922.

**CORRESPONDENCE COURSES IN FRENCH.** Complete elementary school courses, covering all subjects, in French for Francophones or advanced students of French. I've checked on recent prices and they're under $90 per year, per course, in U.S. dollars (between $100 and $130 in Canadian dollars). They also offer advanced studies. Write for a catalog: Ministère de l'Éducation Nationale, Centre National d'Enseignement à Distance, 31051 Toulouse Cedex 1, France.

**FRANCE.** A magazine devoted to the country and culture. Not sold on newsstands; write and ask for a sample copy. P.O. Box 318, Landisburg, PA 17040.

---

*Never doubt the courage of the French. They were the ones who discovered that snails are edible.*
— Doug Larson,
United Features Syndicate

---

**FRANCE TODAY.** A magazine about France. Good information and travel guide. P.O. Box 1522, Martinez, CA 94553-9902.

**LES BONS MOTS: How to Amaze *Tout le Monde* With Everyday French**, by Eugene Ehrlich. Buying this book may be like "un chat en poche" (literally, a cat in a bag; in English, buying a pig in a poke). You'll be surprised at how delightfully Ehrlich gives an example of a French idiom and its pronunciation, and then explains it in both languages. You'll learn many important, amusing, and useful expressions that you would never find in a textbook, and how to use them. For example, "hurler à la lune" (ür-LAY ah-lah lün) means "go fight city hall." It translates literally as "howl at the moon," which Ehrlich explains is an expressive way of saying, "raise a futile voice against a person in high position." Did you know that "avoir un besoin," which translates literally to "to have a need," is what you want to say when you need to find a toilet? If you say in French, "Qui se sent morveux, qu'il se mouche," it means "If the shoe fits, wear it." Literally, this means, "If one's nose is running, let him blow it." This book was written for adults but is quite suitable for an interested intermediate or advanced student. (I originally purchased this book for a 13-year-old French immersion student. His mother says that when she hears him chuckling in his room, he's usually reading this book.) Code HH, $23.

## HEBREW

**FIRST THOUSAND WORDS IN HEBREW.** Great variety of amusing pictures to help you learn. See the description of First Picture Word Books above. Ages 2 to 12. Hardcover. Code EDC, $12.95.

**HEBREW ALPHABET COLORING BOOK.** Ages 5 to 12, more or less. Code DV, $2.50.

**HEBREW ALPHABET STICKER BOOK.** For fun. Code DV, $1.

**HEBREW PICTURE WORD BOOK.** Good for all beginners. Code DV, $2.95.

## SPANISH

**BUENO.** I highly recommend this quarterly magazine for kids and adults who want extra fun learning Spanish. Information, games, books, bilingual stories, and more Spanish resources. $10 a year U.S./$20 foreign. Send a #10 SASE for a free sample to: Bueno Books, 1700 Wagon Gap Drive, Round Rock, TX 78681. A sample of things you can order from Bueno:

**MOMS AND DADS/MAMIS Y PAPIS.** Bilingual coloring book with complete sentences in English and Spanish. Grades 2 to 6, $1.95.

**NOW YOU'RE LEARNING ESPAÑOL.** A gentle introduction to Spanish for the young (and young at heart). Fun verse to help you learn more than 60 useful words. 32 pages, $5.95.

**BILINGUAL COOKING/LA COCINA BILINGUE.** More than 100 recipes in two languages. Learn Spanish (or English) while you explore new foods. 224 pages, $9.95.

**20,000 WORDS IN SPANISH IN 20 MINUTES.** Using what you know to learn what you don't know. Easy! Many English words are the same in Spanish with just a change of accent or pronunciation. 188 pages, $15.

**FIRST THOUSAND WORDS IN SPANISH**. This kit contains the same book listed earlier in the chapter, but adds a workbook for ages 12 to adult. There is also a tape, which is pretty standard: They say it, you say it. Pronunciation is clear. My biggest complaint is that they tell you where (in the book) to find the duck. That's criminal! It spoiled half my fun. I've complained, and maybe they'll change it. Ages 6 and up (younger, if you want to play the tapes so your kids get used to the sound of the language, which isn't a bad idea). Code EDC, $21.95.

**ARROZ CON LECHE (Rice Pudding): Spanish Game Songs for Children**. Music with bilingual lyrics accompanies 12 popular traditional games children play in Spain and Latin America. Six circle songs and games, one similar to our Red Rover, and three that can be played in a variety of ways. One cassette and booklet with cultural notes (and a recipe for rice pudding). Ages 4 to 9. Code AF, $17.95.

***Revised*** **— MADRIGAL'S MAGIC KEY TO SPANISH**, by Maria Madrigal. *This is THE BOOK* with which to study Spanish, along with a good cassette course (such as Language 30, above) to help you learn the proper accent and pronunciation. "At this moment you know several thousand Spanish words even if you have never seen or heard a Spanish word," says the author in her preface. Many of those words are identical in spelling and meaning to the English, such as *popular, capital, animal, hotel, radio,* and *actor*. Many others are different only by one or two letters, such as *Atlantico, Pacifico, dramatico, restaurante*, and *importante*. Spanish is a very phonetic language, with very few exceptions to spelling and grammatical rules. This book will teach you how to recognize words that are identical in both languages, how to make Spanish words from the English words you already know, and how to form easy sentences right away. Before our kids were born, Jean and I took this book with us to Mexico, and received many compliments on our quick grasp of Spanish. Perfect for high school students and essential for parents working with younger children. 496 pages. Code DD, $12.95.

(This book's a lifesaver! Madrigal will have you speaking Spanish immediately. I couldn't have survived in Mexico without it. Our book is falling apart from use. One of the reasons I love Spanish, apart from the fact that I just enjoy the sound of the language, is that English spelling has always vexed me, and unlike French with all its silent letters, Spanish is almost completely phonetic.)

By the time you get about halfway through Madrigal's book, you can add Tom Blodget's **MUSICAPAEDIA!** Level 1, with its lively, upbeat set of lessons learned through music. This is a multisensory learning experience. The lyrics teach grammar in a natural way so you won't even have to think about it, and each song has an interesting story line. It's easier to accept repetition when it's done to music, so this learning form will liven up your day and will work for you on a subconscious level. The tunes are catchy, and I find myself tapping my feet, wanting to dance, and humming along with little or no effort. (For a more balanced assessment, I asked a family with children to test this program. They didn't find it particularly exciting and didn't care for the music. Beats me!) I think you'll learn the songs so quickly that the sequential lessons, puzzles, and worksheets will just add to the fun. The well-thought-out lessons are easy to use. Older kids can work with this on their own. The 68-page book includes a glossary and a CD with songs followed by the karaoke music at the end (allowing your own singing). For grades 8 to 12, late 1st- or 2nd-year students. You can preview it on the web at www.musicapaedia.com. $29.95, plus $3 shipping; money-back guarantee. Tom is working out discounts for groups so that you can buy a varied number of books and CDs and purchase according to the needs of your group. Write us for more detailed information. If you enjoy the Spanish language you'll probably enjoy *Gracias a la Vida*, by Joan Baez, an all-Spanish album. I have the record. Amazon.com sells the CD.

**MY FIRST SPANISH ABC PICTURE BOOK COLORING BOOK**. Each double-page spread of this $8\frac{1}{4}$x11" book is devoted to a letter of the alphabet. You'll find many illustrations of commonly used words to color, with the Spanish word printed clearly beneath each. Good for all beginning Spanish students. Code DV, $2.50.

**SPANISH PICTURE WORD BOOK.** Black-and-white scenes of people, animals, places, and things, all labeled in Spanish. No pronunciation guide, but a bilingual dictionary is included. For all learners. 15 pages, 8½x11". Code DV, $2.95.

**Spanish Stories.** Stories to read with pictures to color. You may want a bilingual dictionary for use with these books. All books 8½x11". Code DV, $2.95 each.
**LA SIRENITA** (*The Little Mermaid*)
**LA BELLA DURMIENTE** (*Sleeping Beauty*)
**BLANCANIEVES** (*Snow White*)
**EL CUENTO DE PEDRO, EL CONEJO** (*The Tale of Peter Rabbit*)

**Spanish Stories**. Smaller format than the stories above. 32 pages, unabridged, with full-color illustrations. Code DV.
**EL CUENTO DE PEDRO, EL CONEJO/PETER RABBIT**, $1.50

**EL CUENTO DEL GATITO TOMASIN/ TOM KITTEN**, $1

**SING, DANCE, AND EAT TACOS!** Original and traditional Spanish songs introduce Spanish vocabulary and traditions. Explanations between songs are in English. A nice addition to your Spanish program after you've gotten started with the basics. One-hour cassette and illustrated book with lyrics. Code AF, $21.95. Oh, yes — also a recipe for tacos!

There are many excellent Usborne stories available in Spanish for ages 4 and up. Send an SASE for a list of titles.

**Books in Spanish.** Write for a free catalog: Astran, Inc., 591 S.W. 8th St., Miami, FL 33130.

**EVERYBODY HAS FEELINGS: The Moods of Children/TODOS TENEMOS SENTIMIENTOS**,

photographed by Charles E. Avery. A bilingual book with simple text and outstanding pictures of the multicultural world of children. Unless taught otherwise, children naturally see different skin colors, yet see beyond them. This small book with English and Spanish text will give you the opportunity to talk about feelings common to all of us and increase your Spanish vocabulary in a meaningful way. Ages 5 to 8. Code GHS, $8.95.

If you haven't found what you're looking for here, you want more extensive language materials or literature in a foreign language, or you just want more choices in language materials, I recommend you write to Calliope Books, Route 3, Box 3395, Saylorsburg, PA 18353 for a catalog. They specialize in excellent language materials for all ages and have an extensive catalog with learning materials and foreign language books at all learning levels.

# COMPUTERS

## *DONN AND I ACTUALLY HAVE SOME DISAGREEMENT!*

Our option message has changed. Please listen carefully.
For quality service your call may be monitored.
Please press 1 for service in English.
Press 2 for routine services.
Press 3 for non-routine services.
Press 4 if you know your party's extension.
Press 5 if you would like to access a directory.
Press 6 if you detest this menu and would like to speak to a person.
Please hold and enjoy this junk music while your call is connected.

"If you think computers will make you smart, then you'll believe having a library card will make you well-read." This was a smart remark — and you may take that any way you'd like to — that I overheard on National Public Radio. I apologize for not remembering the name of the speaker.

Donn wrote his part of this chapter in 1991. After I took computer classes we had some interesting discussions and ongoing disagreement about computers. At that time computers were just moving into our lives, mostly through big business. They were expensive and more difficult to use than the ones available now. Today they are a part of nearly everyone's daily lives, either directly or indirectly, whether we like it or not. This book comes to you compliments of a computer. Times have changed, and I know his perspective would be different now, but I believe many of his objections, observations, and reservations are still important to consider. I know it is highly unjust to take advantage of his inability to respond, but I now have the last word, and I intend to make the most of the situation!

"Computers are man's most beautiful creation," said U.S. Navy Captain Grace M. Hopper, who set the standards of computer language for the Pentagon (in 1991). "All children older than four should have their own computers. We may even get a generation that can spell."

That's like saying anyone who owns a gun will know how to make bullets.

Or using a calculator means you can do basic math or make change.

Or owning a TV and VCR implies you can program your remote control.

Or owning a car means you can fix it.

Or reading this nonsense means you can't add on at least ten more examples.

Captain Hopper must mean that all previous generations, those unlucky enough to have grown up computerless, can't spell. She may be right. A little while ago, I was looking through the diary my grandmother kept during her first year as a schoolteacher. That was more than ninety years ago, and my grandmother was sixteen. Not once in the diary did she spell "computer" correctly. In fact, she avoided the word completely.

Although excessive love of gadgets and gimmicks is the root of much evil in the world, it's good to be familiar with the basic usage of some of those gadgets. Books are tools of communication and learning; cars and planes take us to interesting places; telephones help us to reach out and touch someone. We try to help our children become book-literate, telephone-literate, and even airplane-literate.

(See what happens when a word is suddenly uprooted and transplanted into foreign soil? "Literacy" used to be related only to the ability to read and write. Then computer folk tacked it on to the word "computer," with the guilt-trip implication that if you're not able to operate one of the new-fangled gadgets, it's tantamount to the other kind of illiteracy. In other words, "literacy" came to mean "competency," which gave it an added dimension, but also robbed its original meaning of much of its potency. E.D. Hirsch Jr. compounded the felony by tacking the word to "cultural," with the implied parallel suggestion that a lack of cultural knowledge and awareness is as serious as the inability to read and write. Okay, then, why can't I say "telephone-literate" and "airplane-literate"?)

I have little interest in computer literacy. Computers are undoubtedly very useful tools, but I am unconvinced that they're essential to a happy life or a creative career. An apple a day may keep the doctor away, but an Apple a day may increase society's need for psychiatrists.

Donn, I don't disagree with your conviction that a happy life or fulfilling career can be had without ever using a computer, but there is much to be said in favor of being able to use one.

I am now one of the "computer-literate." (Pardon the terminology.) No, I don't know *how* they work, but I can use one with ease. No, it hasn't taught me to spell; however, I am freer to use my reading vocabulary because I know the spelling will be corrected (if I remember to use the spell-checker). I am no longer chained to the dictionary, a time-consuming activity when I have no idea how a word is spelled. I readily admit that Microsoft Word doesn't know how to spell pteranodon; the spell-check function can't tell a typo from a typewriter, and the dictionary and thesaurus in this software program are not as extensive as our old-fashioned bound volumes, but I am less inhibited and freer to concentrate on my writing because I no longer have to disrupt my work to look up many words.

The computer is faster and more accurate with the math I need to use in the business. I can even keep the checkbook up-to-date and make it balance. I like the ease with which the computer can generate reports that instantly tell me into which hole all the money has disappeared.

The computer keeps my work more organized. It insists I file each piece of work when I finish it. Even better, if I can't remember where I filed it, the computer knows and can retrieve it for me. I certainly can't say the same for myself and the unfiled paperwork lying in piles around the office.

To address your comment about computers improving the standard of living for psychiatrists: If computer use leads to the need for psychiatric help, then a rapidly increasing segment of the world is already in deep trouble. Computer use is multiplying even faster than bitey-bugs on a camping trip or in the garden. When my first computer crashed, I needed a box of tissues and a regular backup program, not a psychiatrist. I felt I'd lost half my memory. I wondered if my experience was similar to knowing that your Alzheimer's disease is progressing. I knew I'd lost things, but I couldn't remember just what. Looking back on that event, maybe I should have had my head examined for not having a regular backup program.

I do agree with you on the most important point. The computer is a useful tool, but like all tools, it does not make for a happier life. Shane (in the book by the same name) said, "A gun is a tool. It is only as good or as bad as the man using it." Satisfactory living comes only from within yourself and your relationship to the people and the world around you. If you think you need a computer to be happy, you do need a psychiatrist.

On a larger scale, computerized society becomes increasingly impersonal, and the value of life becomes reduced each day by a few more decimal points. On a smaller scale, people who use computers a great deal tend to think in computer-like patterns, in which life becomes a series of problems to be dealt with in a systematic, orderly manner, with a logical solution to each problem at the end of each operation. Life is seldom that orderly and logical. Solutions are reached by feelings, hunches, and intuitive empathy as often as by orderly examination.

Yes and no, Donn. I think you would have changed some of your thinking by now if you had a computer to use. Yes, computerized society is becoming more and more impersonal in many ways. I detest some of the more common computerized services. The "phone menu" here in New Brunswick is enough to frustrate a saint. Mabel at the local exchange would be faster and friendlier. When a computer makes a mistake, it takes forever to straighten the problem out, and you definitely need a *person* to help you and to correct the computer. Computers do have their limitations. However, I love the ATM at the bank. It's always much faster than the tellers (and sometimes friendlier), and the waiting line is never as long. Being able to do research on the Internet at any hour of the day on any subject is a boon. Taken altogether, I think today's computers are as good or as bad as the people programming them and the manner in which they are used.

Donn, if you could watch me use the computer, I'm sure you would quickly realize that it hasn't improved my logic, or made my work habits much more systematic. It's better at filing and spelling, and many other logical and consistent tasks, than I am, but it doesn't offer "solutions" to my problems.

*Computers are useless. They can only give you answers.* — Pablo Picasso

Answer e-mail
Let Gus out
Write kids
Balance checkbook
Answer the phone
File papers and catalogs
Fill orders
Eat?
Let Gus in

I agree that real-life solutions are often reached through feelings, hunches, and intuitive empathy. A computer can extrapolate, but only within the limitations of data supplied by a person. The day computers make imaginative, intuitive leaps to reach conclusions, we had better hope the science fiction buffs have figured out what to do about it. There is already quite enough trouble with computer use when we can more or less control what they do.

To give the devil his due (to use one of those strange phrases that seem to make sense until you examine them), Mario Pagnoni almost convinces me, in *The Complete Home Educator* (now sadly out of print), that computers are not the bad guys I think they are. His explanation of the uses and values of a computer, especially as a learning tool, is the clearest and most convincing I've found. I'm just as suspicious of computers, and as concerned about their detrimental influences on human ways of thinking, but Mario's book has shown me that computers can be controlled and can have a proper place in the home or homeschool. Maybe.

I think there is definitely a place for computers in education. One thing you've never seen, Donn, is the growth of the Internet. Access to an overwhelming amount of knowledge is easy. The Internet provides information on any subject you might care to investigate, and you don't have to go further than your computer to find it — and you can check out many (maybe too many) sources around the world. Computers make it possible for students to participate in high school and college classes that are actually taking place miles away. Donn, you would love being able to sit here in our quiet woodsy home, in the comfort of your own chair, with a cup of coffee in hand, and follow a NASA mission, or look over the shoulder of a scientist working on an archaeological site halfway around the world. I think you would concede, without quibbling, that it can be a valuable learning tool.

Computers have also changed our means of communication forever. I correspond freely with our kids, now scattered across the continent, and I hear from them far more often than I would without my computer e-mail. Communication is so fast and easy we frequently carry on conversations through the course of a day or an evening. I've even continued your exchange of junk mail with your brother, but I can do it faster and it's delivered right to his desktop! I can just as easily and quickly correspond with people on the other side of the world.

I know you would be concerned that computers tend to separate people from "living." I don't think computers isolate people from one another. People isolate themselves, with or without a computer. It is a matter of use and misuse. I believe our mental, spiritual, and emotional growth can come only from interacting with other people.

The greatest advances in art, music, literature, philosophy, and science have been made by men and women who were open to inspiration, hunches, and wild guesses. Computers often do away with the need for creative thinking: Just feed the problem into the keyboard and wait for the computer to find the solution. This approach may produce rapid and astonishing advances in the already existing arts and sciences, but it is incapable of producing new arts and sciences. The computer's "reasoning" can be based only on information and procedures that are fed or built into it; a human being — genius, mystic, or you or I — unfettered by controls and programs, with circuits and synapses of flesh and spirit infinitely greater than anything of silicon and magnetic impulses will ever be, can leap light-years while the computer is still singing "Daisy, Daisy."

The possibilities of extrapolation open to a computer may be nearly infinite, but that extrapolation must still be based upon existing data. Any situation or problem of life processed from a computer's view is reduced to a paint-by-number picture. No matter how the combinations or choices of colors are varied, the end result is still no more, and usually less, than the original.

Again, yes and no, Donn. Computers will probably never be capable of the truly creative thought process. Yes, Donn, I'm hedging my bets with the word "probably," because computers and programming are changing rapidly. We have computer-generated music, but to me it will never equal the genius of Beethoven or Mozart, and synthetic music will never equal a live performance. A computer can make a picture, but it will never rival Monet. But computers have changed, and software programming is changing so rapidly most of us can't keep up with it. I think that as servants of creative and inquisitive people, computers can work out complex problems faster, eliminating hours of computation with a pencil and paper.

I do agree with you that computers can give us knowledge but not "living." I think it's possible to lead a very satisfactory life without ever learning how to use a computer. The benefits from this new technology are many, yet I know in my heart that in many ways the joy of discovery will never be as great when gained through a computer as it is through active hands-on experience or through interaction with people. A joyful life is created through interacting with your family, friends, the people in your community, and your surroundings. A computer picture of a desert sunset or a recording of wolves howling will not instill peace in your soul or raise the hair on the back of your neck. The audiovisual experience translated through a machine doesn't engage the spirit. A picture may be worth a thousand words; a hug and a laugh with someone you love is beyond price.

Our job as parents must include finding a sane balance between use and misuse of computers. Computers, like televisions, can be overused "baby-sitters." Flashy software programs are relatively cheap and will distract a child (and some adults) for a long time. There are Internet sites that are not suitable for children (or most adults). As with the television, remember that there is an "off" button.

As more educational computer opportunities become available, we need to evaluate not only the programs, but our children's needs. There are complete home education courses available in computer format. The information in some is excellent, but I don't think it's a healthy way to learn. In most cases I think it's still better to use books, activities, and hands-on learning. Calvert School has put out a King Arthur CD-ROM. It's packed with information: a marvelous collection of classic artwork in vivid color, a variety of myths to compare with actual history, an audio guide to pronunciation, and an interactive game. With the exception of the game (which I think would be much better if played as a board game) and the pronunciation guide, the rest would be better in book form.

Before you consider using computer resources, consider your child as well as the educational possibilities. A computer user spends most of his time sitting, using the keyboard, and staring at the monitor. Anyone sitting for hours at a computer risks injury to his eyesight, carpal tunnel syndrome, back problems, circulatory problems, and more. Our human bodies, young and old, are not designed to sit still for long periods of time. How long do you want your child to sit in one position, staring at one spot? Consider how much you want your child to learn by himself at the computer and how much you want to be an active part of his learning and his life. I consider moderation and vigilance the key to making constructive use of this relatively new tool. I can hardly wait to finish this book and put more activity back into my life. I know it hasn't been good for me.

We don't want paint-by-number lives, for ourselves or for our children. We're willing to accept the benefits and beneficial possibilities of computers, but I am not convinced that they will make any significant contributions to the world in any terms of real human progress. The art of living, if reduced to lines and numbers, would no longer be art and hardly living.

**BEGINNING COMPUTERS**

These first four books are friendly introductions in easy-to-understand English. Jargon is clearly defined. Recommended for ages 10 and up. Don't be shy about using them if you're older — the simple directions and explanations are good for all beginners.

**STARTING COMPUTERS**. An ideal first guide for young beginners with Windows 95 or 98. Learn how to draw pictures, work with text, and combine your written creativity with your artwork. Jargon-free language and clear illustrations make this easy to use. Ages 10 and up. Code EDC, $9.95.

**WINDOWS 98 FOR BEGINNERS.** A clear and concise Usborne guide. Jargon-free language with step-by-step instructions to help you and your kids develop your word processing skills, make better use of your computer, explore the Internet, and much more. Ages 10 to adult. Code EDC, $10.95.

**BUILD YOUR OWN WEBSITE.** A good book to use to learn the basics. Ages 10 and up. Code EDC, $9.95.

**THE USBORNE COMPUTER DICTIONARY FOR BEGINNERS.** Takes the mystery out of the jargon and specialized vocabulary. The kids will enjoy learning from this book, and you'll want to use it so you can understand your kids! Ages 10 and up. Code EDC, $10.95.

**Encyclopedias**. There are a lot of them for computers. Look at the ones in the library and decide which you like best.

There are many magazines for computer users: *PC Magazine*, *Windows*, and many others. When I got a computer I was assaulted with offers for computer magazines. I didn't know enough to know what I needed, and therefore spent money for magazines that I couldn't use. Most were too technical. For myself, and certainly if I had kids at home, I would subscribe to **FAMILY PC**. It's well-rounded in the topics it covers and will answer some reader questions that are sent in. *Family PC* reviews the latest equipment, upgrades, websites, software for family use (including educational software and ratings done by families), and more, and it does it all in understandable language, not jargon. More content and less advertising than others. $14.95 in the U.S. Family PC, P.O. Box 55414, Boulder, CO 80322-5414; www.familypc.com.

### DO IT YOURSELF
### LEARN TOUCH-TYPING

***Revised* — MASTER YOUR KEYBOARD**. Designed for use with your computer, word processor, or typewriter. The notes with this say it is an introductory program that will teach touch-typing in only four hours, whether you're a complete beginner or use a hunt-and-peck method. I won't guarantee you will learn this in four hours, but it is one of the easiest and most enjoyable typing courses we've seen, and certainly the fastest. For high school students and adults. Three cassettes and exercise book, Code AF, $34.50. **SPEED AND ACCURACY AT YOUR KEYBOARD** is the second volume of this series, and provides 20 30-minute exercises to give you advanced typing skills with a minimum of time and practice. Code AF, $34.50. **Both courses** $64.

**Mavis Beacon** has an excellent typing program for older kids and adults. About $40 from Mindscape, 800-231-3088 or 617-761-3000; www.mindscape.com.

**LEARNKEY'S QUICKTIPS VIDEO**. Free from LearnKey, Inc., 1845 W. Sunset Blvd., St. George, UT 84770. Helpful training tips for using WordPerfect, Excel, Access, Microsoft Word, and other PC applications. Runs about 20 minutes. Write on your school letterhead.

**VDT FACTS**. A one-page sheet that explains potential risks to the fetus when a pregnant woman spends too much time in front of the computer. Be sure to include the number (09-410-00) when requesting this free information sheet. March of Dimes, Julietta Ackerman, 1275 Mamaroneck Ave., White Plains, NY 10605. Available in the U.S. and Canada.

**VDT USER'S GUIDE TO BETTER VISION**. A guide to help you protect your vision when using the computer. American Optometric Association, Communications Center, Dept. DP1, 243 N. Lindbergh Blvd., St. Louis, MO 63141-7881.

Got problems? Your printer won't print? Modem won't dial? Need help with Windows-based software, hardware, networks, printers, etc.? Call The Home Computer Help Line: 900-884-2001. They charge $1.99 a minute, and the average length of call is about seven minutes. Probably faster and cheaper than calls to your dealer if you didn't buy locally. They can answer most questions, and if they have to do research they will call you back at no charge.

**For Your Ambitious and Serious Future Computer Programmer**. If you have a child with excellent computer skills who plans to work in programming and is interested in Microsoft certification, write to Transcender Corporation, 315 10th Ave. N., Suite 113, Nashville, TN 37203-3498, for information.

**COMPUTERS**. A Peterson's guide to the industry. Top-level professionals inspire readers and share their insights about working in the industry and what it takes to build a career. Interesting text and graphics. Covers training, responsibilities, pluses and minuses of different jobs, salary, career growth expectations, perks, travel potential, and where and how to get jobs. Code PTR, $9.95.

### THE INTERNET

**INTERNET FOR BEGINNERS**. This is what you need if you're feeling lost in cyberspace and don't know the difference between a web and the Web. This book tells you exactly how to get connected, describes the hardware and software you will need, and helps you select a service provider. It goes even further and shows you how to connect with NASA (and how your children can send their names to Mars!), send e-mail, download files, and explore the World Wide Web. There are some safety tips, but not enough. If you want your kids to use the Internet/Web safely, you should investigate some of the programs that will limit where they can and cannot go. Ages 10 and up. Code EDC, $9.95.

**WORLD WIDE WEB FOR BEGINNERS.** Reviews the basic information in the book above, plus it has more advanced information about using the Web for research, downloading programs, buying and selling online, creating your own Web page, advanced page design, vocabulary section, useful addresses (kid-safe), and a section about possible future developments. Ages 10 and up. Code EDC, $9.95.

**INTERNET FOR KIDS**, by Dr. Barbara Kurshan and Dr. Sara Armstrong. A great book full of fun and educational Internet resources for all. How to find penpals, explore other countries, see NASA images, communicate with experts, and so much more. Available for free ONLY IF you mention your source, which is my source: **The Guide to Free Computer Materials.**

You must request this on your school letterhead and state your position (instructor, grade 4, or whatever). Write: Sybex, Inc., Julie E. Simmons, 2021 Challenger Dr., Alameda, CA 94501. Only one per school instructor. Available in the U.S. only.

**THE ONLINE CLASSROOM: Teaching with the Internet**, 3rd edition, by Eileen Giuffré. This book will save you hours of online time. It begins with the basics and includes K-12 lesson plans (which you can use or not). Topics include e-mail, the Web (and using search engines), page design, chat, videoconferencing, and Java. Learn how you can explore Canada, Mexico, and whales; communicate with people around the globe; and much more. Code FS, $26.95.

**Educating.net Website Resources** is an education search engine with information on homeschooling, distance learning, scholarship assistance, K-12 information, and much more. You'll find it at www.educating.net.

**UNCLE SAM'S K-12 WEB**, by Laurie Androit. I've listed some of the government websites below, but there just isn't room for all the good ones. This book provides an excellent guide to the many available sites for parents, students, and educators. A real help for busy parents — you'll use this book for years. Covers the natural world, the environment, health and safety, the U.S. and the world, community and people, words, reading and the arts, work, money and the mail, transportation, energy and technology, math, science and space, education, and more. Code CRP, $24.95.

## ONLINE SAFETY

Depending on the age and nature of your child, safety may or may not be a very real concern. As reported in the *Christian Science Monitor* by Mark Clayton, "Douglas Rehman, a special agent in the Florida Department of Law Enforcement, estimates 250 to 300 nationwide charges of child sexual exploitation using the Internet have been brought in the last two years." Many online service providers now have adult hosts to monitor children's sites, but not all. If you feel the need to have some control over your children's investigation of the Internet, I suggest you use a censoring software program that can be personalized to your taste.

Here are some guidelines for parents and kids, taken from *Cruising Online: Larry Magid's Guide to the New Digital Highway*, written for the National Center for Missing and Exploited Children (800-843-5678) and the Interactive Services Association.

1. Never give out identifying information — address, school name, telephone number — in a public message (chat room or bulletin board).
2. Know what your child uses online.
3. Never allow a child to arrange face-to-face meetings without permission, and you should accompany him to a meeting in a public place.
4. Never respond to messages or bulletin board items that are suggestive, obscene, belligerent, or threatening, or make you feel uncomfortable. (This sounds too obvious to mention, but the temptation to just say a few words will give the other person your e-mail address!)
5. Report child pornography by calling the number listed above.
6. Remember that people online may not be who they seem.
7. Remember that not everything you read online is necessarily true.
8. Set reasonable guidelines and discuss them with your children so they understand the reasons behind them.

I've never found any objectionable material on the Web, but then I haven't the time or the interest to look for any. I have had unsolicited suggestive e-mail delivered to my desktop by spammers. I have heard many people complain about material found on the Web, and I agree that the material they said they found was not suitable for children. Using a computer for study or just for fun is great, but I think the bottom line is whether or not you trust your kids to stay with constructive material. If you're not sure, or want to be sure, use one of the filtering programs below.

Software programs to help you guide your child's web use:
**CYBER PATROL** from Microsystems Software, 800-489-2001; www.microsys.com
**NET NANNY** from Trove Investment Corp., 800-340-7177; www.netnanny.com/home.html

These sites will keep you informed about Net safety:
**SAFESURF**, www.safesurf.com
**RECREATIONAL SOFTWARE ADVISORY COUNCIL**, www.rsac.org
**THE INTERNET ADVOCATE**,
www.monroe.lib.in.us/~lchampel/netadv.html

**COALITION FOR QUALITY CHILDREN'S MEDIA**. This is a non-profit coalition of the media industry, educators, and child advocacy organizations. Their aim is to evaluate and rate children's videos, CD-ROMs, and television programs. Their standards: no gratuitous violence or sexuality; no physical or verbal abuse; no racial, gender, cultural, or religious bias; and no condescension toward children. Products are judged by educators, parents, and children. To find out more about their Kids First program or to become a member, write: Coalition for Quality Children's Media, 112 W. San Francisco St., Suite 305A, Santa Fe, NM 87501.

## ONLINE CLASSES AND DISTANCE LEARNING

**NovaNET**, University Communications, 3895 N. Business Center Dr., Suite 120, Tucson, AZ 85705, offers 12,000 courses, grades 4 through high school, and some vocational training. Students download their courses and have access to a personal tutor. Write for prices and more information.

For use by children, high school students, and adults: The **HOME SCHOOL VILLAGE** is an interactive website with chat rooms, college information, career advice, helpful links, downloadable files, and more. www.home-school-village.com.

For distance learning, contact **GLOBAL VILLAGE LEARNING**. High school and more than 20,000 college and trade school classes available, fully accredited, including high school diplomas and dual credits. A wealth of information and resources if you want computer-based learning at home. Global Village Learning is located at 145 Main St., Brunswick, Maine. If you can go in person, it's a great place to find resources. *For homeschoolers on a budget, they even offer refurbished educational workstations and software to run on them. This includes laptops.* For more information, contact Frank Heller, global@GWI.net; www.netschoolofmaine.com.

**EDUCATION AND CAREER ADVANCEMENT NEWS**. This resource and information kit directs students to a website they can use to practice for the SAT, ACT, GMAT, and other tests. Write: Kim Connolly, Media Relations Coordinator, test.com Inc., 1300 East 9th St., Cleveland, OH 44114; www.test.com. You can also go directly to the website. There is a fee for taking the sample tests.

For enrollment and other information about quality distance learning for credit-granting courses in English/ESL, math, science, social studies, and languages, check out www.cyberschool.k12.or.us.

**Educational Courses on the Internet**. If you research some of these, you'll find a wide variety of topics and usually open enrollment.
California Virtual University: www.california.edu
UCLA Online: www.onlinelearning.net
University of Phoenix Online: www.phoenix.edu/index_open.html
Boise State University: www.boisestate.edu/conted/schedule/internet.html
Cyberseminars: www.cyber-seminars.com

Seattle Pacific University, Division of Continuing Studies, 3307 3rd Ave. West, Seattle, WA 98119-1997; 800-482-3848; www.spu.edu/depts/soe/conted.html. Offers distance learning K-12.

If that isn't enough, check out more learning opportunities from About.com's Distance Learning site: www.distancelearn.about.com.

**PETERSON'S DISTANCE LEARNING GUIDE 2000**. If you and your family are planning to use distance-learning resources, this is the most complete guide available and will be well worth the investment. Code PTR, $26.95.

## ONLINE RESOURCES

Online shoppers can now look for the **BBB-Online Care seal**. The Better Business Bureau will now give this seal to any company that has been online for more than a year and complies with their business standards. You can click on the seal and pull up a full BBB report on the company, including its address, ownership, and service record, or you can go directly to the BBB site (www.bbbonline.org) for a searchable data-base. If you are unhappy with one of the companies you have done business with, you may lodge a complaint and the BBB will mediate the dispute.

**Primary Sources**. The Library of Congress offers an extensive collection of material on the Internet: www.loc.gov.

www.appleprof.com is a growing site created to assist the increasing number of non-traditional learners who are preparing for or in college. The site will eventually have 200 information modules covering study skills, life skills, and first aid. The latter will include physical and mental health issues and concerns. The most relevant to independent learners will be the study tips, memory tricks, time-saving suggestions, active note taking, and ways to read faster and retain more. There's more on this site worth investigating. I think some of the strategies suggested for writing papers and test taking have more emphasis on pleasing the professor and getting a good grade than on learning something because you care about it. The two aims are not mutually exclusive, but ... The site also covers information about dating, humor, renting apartments, managing money, community service, rape, abuse, conflict resolution, leadership skills, and a lot more.

**Visit the Smithsonian!** An amazing collection of Americana. Terrific graphics! Primary sources for your history research. Well-researched and -written articles. Best for curious junior high students; great for high school research and curious adults. www.si.edu. And for younger children there's the excellent www.kidscastle.si.edu. The Smithsonian also publishes a wonderful magazine; if you don't want to subscribe, you can still have access to it at www.smithsonianmag.si.edu.

At www.juniornet.com you'll find safe, commercial-free games, stories, activities, and more, chosen from good children's magazines: *Highlights for Children*, *Ranger Rick*, *Sports Illustrated for Kids*, *Weekly Reader*, and *Zillions*.

4-H information: www.fourhcouncil.edu.

www.tourbus.com lists and reviews a lot of interesting and some very educational sites. Worth investigating.

www.billnye.com is the site for the PBS show *Bill Nye the Science Guy* .

Visit the National Geographic Society at www.nationalgeographic.com.

Robert Krampf offers weekly science experiments by e-mail. Safe, cheap, fun, sometimes very dramatic. To get on the list e-mail krampf@aol.com.

World Wildlife Fund: www.worldwildlife.org

The Global SchoolNet Foundation aims to connect kids of all ages around the globe: www.gsn.org.

www.homeschoolheadlines.com offers information, support, and practical advice. Get the news about the news.

Hundreds of free detailed lesson plans relating to PBS (Public Broadcasting Service) programming: www.pbs.org/teachersource.

If you're shopping for a computer, call the following numbers for free catalogs so you can compare values. These companies have been in business for a long time and have excellent reputations: PC Connection, 800-800-1111; MAC Connection, 800-800-0002; CD-ROM Warehouse, 800-237-6623; Tiger Direct, 800-888-4437; Educorp, 800-843-9497; Inmac, 800-547-5444.

If you own a Mac or are thinking of buying one you can get help or information from 800-SOS-APPL or 800-538-9696; 800-662-9238 in California.

www.biography.com is very good for history and research. You'll find a lot from popular culture, but the classroom section is rewarding.

### Canadian Web Resources

www.ucalgary.ca/~dkbrown/authors.html has links to many well-known kids' authors.

www.cbc4kids.ca focuses on kids 8 to 13 with news, sports, drama, science, and more from CBC radio.

I could give you a longer list of websites to

visit and places to look for software, but that's not my area of expertise. Rebecca Rupp, in *The Complete Home Learning Source Book* (see "Homeschooling and Education"), has a multitude of resources and good ideas about how to make the best use of them.

### SOFTWARE RESOURCE CATALOGS

**Educational Resources**, 1550 Executive Dr., P.O. Box 1900, Elgin, IL 60121-1900. Hardware, software, educational programs. Excellent programs for kids.

**Scholastic Software** (sold by, but not created by Scholastic) can be excellent or terrible. Caveat emptor. Free catalog: 800-724-2424.

**Edmark Software Catalog.** Edmark has been in the business of educational products for a long time. Very consistently good software for kids ages 5 to 14. Money-back guarantee. They also have a very good Internet filter program. Edmark, P.O. Box 97021, Redmond, WA 98073-9721; 800-320-8379; edmark-team@edmark.com; www.edmark.com.

**Electronic Courseware Systems,** 1210 Lancaster Dr., Suite D, Champaign, IL 61821-7028. Software for all ages.

**MECC**, 6160 Summit Drive North, Minneapolis, MN 55430. Some very exciting software.

**Optimum Resource, Inc.**, 5 Hitech Lane, Hilton Head, SC 29926. Preschool to 12 years.

**School Zone Publishing,** P.O. Box 777, Grand Haven, MI 49417. Lots of early learning materials.

I think I would use the following resources *very* sparingly, if at all. I really don't think kids this young need to learn much, if anything, on the computer — or from one, but kids this age are almost always curious about everything older siblings or their parents do. Remember, there will be plenty of time for them to use a computer when they are older.

**KIDware** from the Mobius Corporation offers learning software programs for kids pre-K to grade 2. KIDWARE, 405 North Henry St., Alexandria, VA 22314.

**READ, WRITE, AND TYPE.** An integrated program to teach all three skills at the same time. It works. Mac or PC. Ages 6 to 8. About $20 from The Learning Company, 800-716-8506; www.learningco.com.

**"efficient instruction elsewhere,"** by Donn Reed. As you must realize by now, Jean and I take education very seriously, but laughter is high on our curriculum agenda. I've wondered at the lack of humor in most homeschool publications. Mary Pride is witty sometimes, but not funny. Others are "funny," but not humorous. Homeschooling is usually treated as if it's too sacred to speak of lightly. Despite the slings and arrows of my outrageous family, I published this book of cartoons about confrontations with suspicious school authorities, disapproving relatives, curious neighbors, and the continuing challenge of providing "efficient instruction elsewhere." Several publications asked to borrow a few of the cartoons. On the other hand, John Holt wasn't impressed. Most of the cartoons are now in this book, which saves me the bother of printing and binding a separate book, and saves you the bother of writing out another check (in case you'd be tempted to).

**HOLT ASSOCIATES, INC.**

Dear Donn,

On this matter of EFFICIENT INSTRUCTION ELSEWHERE, I have been stalling around for a while, but guess I can't stall around any longer. I just don't think it's funny. ... Your book is full of sayings which are certainly true enough, but, for whatever reason, they just don't strike me as particularly funny. I don't even get a smile out of them, much less a guffaw. The other thing that might redeem the book would be if the cartoons were unusually well-drawn, but I am not telling you anything you don't already know if I say they are barely beyond the stick-figure stage.

Hope this won't offend you, or lessen in any way my admiration for the many kinds of good work you are doing.

Best, John Holt

# TELEVISION

I disagree with the fairly common belief that many kids of today can't read because they watch too much television. I think they watch too much television because they can't read, which is not the same thing. (I think it's safe to lump video and computer games in with TV in this instance.)

The great public furor over "why Johnny can't read" began before TV became a common household appliance. Public school teachers, not realizing that the teaching methods they had learned were different from those of the previous generation, and feeling perplexed and frustrated by their students' reading failures, thought they had finally discovered the reason for those failures.

Like many other things, television can be a useful tool of learning (as well as a source of good entertainment), or it can be an escape from life. There are times when I resent its intrusion into our lives, even with good programs, and I can understand and sympathize with those who choose not to have a television. On the other hand, I'm just as impatient with those who preach against it as I am with those who watch it for ten or twelve hours a day. If your kids' minds are being turned into soggy oatmeal by too much television, there's no need to throw away the television, as many critics suggest; just cut down on the viewing time. If you can't control your kids' television use, how will you control anything else in their lives?

The number of hours we spend, as a family, in watching television varies from year to year, depending somewhat on our other activities and somewhat on the programs available. Our choices are limited to the programs available in our area, through one Canadian network, one American network, and the American Public Broadcasting Service. We check the TV guide in the local newspaper for National Geographic specials, wildlife and science shows, vintage movies, and occasional music or movie specials. Jean and I choose about a fourth of the programs, although the kids might have chosen the same ones. Our average, over the years, has been about ten or twelve hours a week, although not everyone watched all the shows. A "special," such as *The Ten Commandments*, would add to our time.

Some of the kids wanted to watch some of the soap operas, but we discussed them all democratically and then Jean and I democratically ruled them out.

Some people say that kids will eventually tire of too much television, and shut it off without adult direction. We experimented with that approach a few times, but neither Jean nor I had the stamina to follow through. Many of our kids' friends were hooked on soap operas, and talked of the characters as if they were real acquaintances. If there was a saturation point for them, they hadn't reached it.

Our kids have always spent at least three hours reading for every hour spent watching television. They read before TV, after TV, and even during commercials. They also knit, crochet, and draw during both the programs and the commercials.

One evening, after an episode of *Hill Street Blues* in which a character mentioned casually that a certain situation was "like something out of Kafka," Cathy said she had recently read one of Kafka's stories that didn't seem to fit the allusion. Our discussion of the subject added new dimensions to her studies as well as to the television program.

Sometimes we have discussed the shows, especially if we thought the kids might need help in putting them into useful or healthy perspectives. Some of the situations and people in many of the big-city settings would have been confusing or even incomprehensible to kids whose only contact with cities had been brief visits to relatives in New York, Chicago, and Boston.

*Sesame Street* was a favorite when the kids were younger. We assumed, like millions of other parents, that it was Good For Them, but after a while we no longer thought so, and we were glad when the kids finally tired of it. John Holt has criticized the show's flashy bombardment of letters and numbers, and we agree with him, but we became more concerned with the relationships of the characters. Most of them are selfish, sarcastic, and inconsiderate. They criticize each other constantly, usually in a bossy nagging way, or whine about their own misfortunes. Our kids always needed at least an hour of active physical play to counteract each hour of *Sesame Street*.

The only children's show that never disappointed us was *Mister Rogers' Neighborhood*. Mister Rogers' cheerfulness is never artificial, and he really believes that you — *you*, to whom he is speaking — are a very special person, just as you are. We were sorry when the kids eventually outgrew it and wished there might be a similar show for older kids.

Even on the programs we enjoy and think are "worthwhile," we are often jolted by the subjects of drugs, violence (both physical and psychological), sexual promiscuity, homosexuality, prostitution, and rape, but we never reject shows just because of them (although we used more "parental discretion" when the kids were younger). Such subjects, unfortunately, are part of everyday conversation throughout society, and our kids need to know how to deal with them. Playing ostrich won't help. So we judge each show by its treatment of such subjects: Is it realistic and accurate? What is the attitude of the show's main protagonist? We accepted the early *Dallas* shows because the "good" characters tried to lead moral lives. We reject *Three's Company* because promiscuity and homosexuality are treated lightly, with double-meaning jokes and naughty winks. Our children's friends who attend public school and watch television for forty hours a week won't keep their "knowledge" secret, so we have the choice of helping our kids understand the subjects or moving to a remote island.

We never tried to develop a formal philosophy about television, but we soon reached several informal rules.

Television, like most other tools, is neither good nor bad in itself. For us, the weekly average of ten to twelve hours has never seemed harmful, and at least half that time has been either directly or indirectly informative and educational, as well as entertaining. We always try not to be arbitrary in our decisions about which shows will be allowed. We're always willing to try a new show if the kids want it, and then we discuss it, although Jean and I retain final veto authority. In limiting viewing time or choosing programs, we always discuss it with the kids; they may disagree with us, but they understand our viewpoint, and usually accept our decisions graciously. We don't grant viewing as a reward, or withhold it as a punishment. We don't use television as a baby-sitter.

There are many good shows on television — art, nature, science, history, sociology, music, theater — and throwing away the TV in spite of them would be like throwing away all our books because there are so many bad books being published.

We live in a small rural community, fairly isolated both geographically and culturally, which makes television especially valuable for us; but in any situation, the judicious use of television can be very broadening, showing us other countries and ways of life, the deep-sea adventures of Jacques Cousteau, and the exploration of outer space.

Television is certainly not a substitute for books, but neither are books a substitute for television.

One evening, through the combined miracles of intrauterine filming and television, we watched the hazardous journey of a sperm, its union with an ovum, and the magical growth of the resulting single cell into a human being — transparent, without eyes or ears, rapidly developing features and losing its atavistic tail, floating weightlessly inside every mother who has ever lived.

We've watched births and deaths, and thousands of lives, both animal and human. We've attended concerts, not sitting somewhere back in the balcony, but wandering freely through the orchestra, savoring each instrument's voice, then standing with the conductor to hear the blended sounds. Sometimes we spend a few minutes with Grand Prix racing or a prize fight or Billy Graham — not because they have particular meaning in our own lives, but because seeing them increases our knowledge and understanding of those who consider them to be of great importance. We've seen presidents, dictators, winos, junkies, and saints.

Through that little black window, we travel in time and space, and our little home in the woods is everywhere in the world and the universe.

## RESOURCES

**History and Literature on Video**. Also science, art, travel guides, ballet, and opera. These are among the best sources of videotapes, including several movies of classic literature, history, and historical fiction (along with standard, popular movies and a lot of junk).

**Pacific Arts**, 11858 La Grange Ave., Los Angeles, CA 90025. Videos from PBS; prices begin at $19.95.

**Critics' Choice**, P.O. Box 749, Itasca, IL 60143. Thousands of video titles; most prices as low as $19.95.

**Columbia House Video Club**, 1400 N. Fruitridge Ave, Terre Haute, IN 47812. Large quarterly catalog and smaller monthly catalogs offering thousands of titles, often with special offers.

**The Video Catalog**, P.O. Box 64267, St. Paul, MN 55164-0267. Many great classics and historical fiction, travel, documentaries, performing arts, and more.

**Time Warner Viewer's Edge**, P.O. Box 3925, Milford, CT 06460. Some very good titles and reasonable prices.

**Barnes and Noble**, 1 Pond Rd., Rockleigh, NJ 07647. Scores of classic films, including the original *Tale of Two Cities*, which is far better than the modern remake.

---

The average American child watches at least 20,000 murders before graduating from high school.

---

## SUPPLIERS OF INSTRUCTIONAL VIDEO PROGRAMS

**Agency for Instructional Technology**, 1111 W. 17th St., Bloomington, IN 47402.

**Direct Cinema Ltd.,** P.O. Box 10003, Santa Monica, CA 90069.

**Intermedia**, 1600 Dexter Ave. N., Seattle, WA 98109.

**Lucerne Media**, 37 Ground Pine Rd., Morris Plains, NJ 07950.

**Pyramid Film and Video**, P.O. Box 1038, Santa Monica, CA 90406.
**Social Issues Resources Series, Inc.,** P.O. Box 2348, Boca Raton, FL 33427.
**World Book, Inc.,** Customer Service, Station 58, Merchandise Mart Plaza, Chicago, IL 60654.

**Program Guides.** Educational-TV program guides, giving advance notice of coming shows, synopses, individual projects, discussion questions, and recommended resources. $15/year from Prime Time School Television, 120 S. LaSalle, Chicago, IL 60603.

**Discount Videos**. More than 1,000 how-to, travel, and other educational videos; also VCRs, TVs, blank tapes, etc. No membership fee, no minimum purchase, no obligation. Catalog $1. Teachers Video Club, 3230 Nebraska Ave., Santa Monica, CA 90404.

**The Video Schoolhouse**, P.O. Box 5101, Carmel, CA 93921. Rent or buy more than 5,000 "how-to" videotapes, on gardening, cooking, arts and crafts, hobbies, hunting, fishing, self-improvement, business, and much more. Catalog $3.

**The Coalition for Quality Children's Media — Kids First**. An organization that rates videos and software. Their standards are high, and you can trust their ratings. Write: Coalition for Quality Children's Media, 535 Cordova Rd., Suite 456, Santa Fe, NM 87501, for more information. There is a membership fee, but it's not much if you buy or rent a lot of videos or are looking for good software programs for your kids.

**Encyclopedias**. There are a lot of them for computers. Look at the ones in the library and decide which you like best.

**Public Broadcasting Programs**. Catalog: WGBH Boston, P.O. Box 2284, S. Burlington, VT 05407-2284; 800-255-9424. (Yes, they are in Vermont, but I don't know why.)

**Gateway Films/Vision Video**, P.O. Box 540, Worcester, PA 19490-0540. Free catalog.

---

*If you read a lot of books, you're considered well-read. But if you watch a lot of TV, you're not considered well-viewed.* Lily Tomlin

---

Posted on www.educationnews.org on September 16, 2000, from the *New York Post*: "George W. Bush, who has decried the 'pervasiveness of violence' in Hollywood, served on the board of a movie company that financed more than two dozen R-rated films, including a gory 1986 slasher flick."

# HIGH SCHOOL



## TRANSITION TIME FOR PARENTS AND KIDS
## DEVELOPING STUDIES, STUDY OPTIONS
## GRADUATION AND DIPLOMAS
## PLANNING AHEAD FOR YOURSELF AND YOUR KIDS
## AVOIDING YOUR FEAR OF AN EMPTY NEST

Experimentation throughout the grade school years enabled us to discover the various ways each of our children learned best. Our philosophy about learning didn't change when our children reached the high school years, but we did find ourselves doubting and questioning ourselves again, challenged by different types of problems, and investigating new learning options. It was a time of trials and errors. Here are some of our observations and the lessons we learned.

**We learned that our children continued trying on various roles throughout the time they were at home.**

From the time they could move about freely, the kids played at many roles — father, mother, dog, lion, cowboy, nurse, clown, superhero — testing each one, experimenting with their own possible roles in society. Throughout, they have felt secure in their knowledge of belonging to the family. Actually leaving the family someday was not a reality. Academically we found that basic skills and a general knowledge of the world — reading, writing, arithmetic, history, geography, government, science, and beginning literature — fit well into the ages from six or seven to thirteen or fourteen, roughly equivalent to the ages spent in the first eight grades of public school.

At puberty, as the body begins rapid changes and emotions become stronger, the mind also grows suddenly and rapidly. Our children began to realize that they really would leave home someday, and the world was still a huge, intimidating mass of uncertainties. They looked forward to being on their own as adults, but at the same time were apprehensive about it. They wanted more time, more preparation, and more practice.

Once again they tried on different roles, this time outside the home, testing themselves in community functions, clubs, and traveling alone — fitting into groups larger than the family and separate from it. Some of them experimented with popular teen fashions — dress, makeup, slang, music, and opinions. We noted that because there were rarely other homeschoolers in our area, our kids related to their friends and tended to think in terms of grade levels, with a definite division between elementary school and high school, based on their ages more than on their actual studies and achievements. We observed that our children's own desire and capacity for a deeper and broader educational base — which we may call "high school" — was roughly concurrent with adolescence.

**Adolescent Problems and Transitions**

Adolescence is a time of rapid changes and can cause a variety of difficulties. Homeschoolers are not necessarily exempt. One minute adolescent kids think and feel they know it all, and the next they doubt and challenge themselves and everything around them. Sometimes they feel they know themselves well, other times not at all. We sometimes felt we knew our kids well, other times not at all. Cathy and I suddenly seemed to be having frequent arguments. We were surprised, hurt, and confused by this. As soon as Donn realized that these disputes were basically a power struggle between Cathy and me we were able to deal with the problem. I realized that my knee-jerk reaction was a part of my built-in conditioning — from my past relationship with my mother — coming back to haunt me. Cathy and I started discussing issues as they came up and found ways to resolve our problems. Sometimes I'd have to take a "time out" to think before answering so I could really consider my answers.

Adolescence can be a roller-coaster ride for parents as well as kids. All of a sudden the time spent with diapers, runny noses, and "he hit me first" can look easy in retrospect. This is the time when all the years of homeschooling and working together can provide a secure base for everyone.

Everyone has problems. No child is perfect. No parent is perfect. Each of us does the best we can at the time. Sometimes our best is not what's needed, or is not good enough. We've had our share of problems over the years. Sometimes Donn and I could see we'd made a mistake in handling problems with the kids. We spent time thinking and talking to find a resolution to the problem. In retrospect, there are things we could have done differently. We had power struggles with the kids, were too strict, were too lenient, said yes when we shouldn't have, said no when we shouldn't have. At times Donn had serious doubts and fears and wondered if he had the right to create a homeschooling book when we, or the kids, had problems. We have dealt with lying, stealing, drugs, alcohol, and personality conflicts. Homeschooling didn't exempt our family from dealing with problems that occur with children in public schools. Homeschooling did create strong family bonds that gave us a better understanding of each other and the strength to deal with these problems and resolve them creatively and constructively. It's a case of on-the-job training and learning. Kids don't come with a training manual.

### Other Challenges That Come With Adolescence

Beyond the psychological and emotional challenges that come with adolescence there is the tendency by parents to prematurely encourage the kids into early career choices. We felt it was important not to do this.

Some public schools encourage children as young as eleven or twelve to choose their academic and vocational futures. Twice that age would be a much better time for such choices, if they must be made. We encouraged our kids not to make choices and decisions, but to watch and explore their own feelings and desires — to watch their general inclinations, and follow them, but without committing themselves beyond their present interests.

Our kids saw many of their friends move steadily, or so it seemed, toward definite goals, but they rarely envied them, whether the goals were college, careers, the military, or working in the local frozen food plant. They knew that many of their friends had been programmed by parents, teachers, aptitude tests, guidance counselors, or even economic necessity to make early decisions, often based on narrow or incomplete data, and that many would probably be frustrated and unhappy adults.

With high school, as with earlier learning, the children's own interests and preferences were the best indications of the direction their studies should take. Working with them, we could help them discover and develop fields of study that would give them broad and solid foundations for nearly any career or lifestyle, as well as the knowledge, skills, and self-confidence to develop other foundations if their interests changed.

We tried to show our children the broadest fields of possibilities, always emphasizing that there's no need to make an immediate choice — that following one's own interests and instincts, not as a goal but as an exciting journey, would lead naturally to a happy, creative life. If a child of ten or fifteen (or any age) has a particular talent or interest, and is determined to follow it, that's good — provided that determination doesn't become a dutiful consistency without a continuing interest. How many adults would like to change careers or lifestyles when they're thirty or forty or fifty, but don't dare to, or don't feel capable of doing so? Any early choices made should allow for the possibility of a more desirable alternative suddenly popping up at any time, and the freedom of thought and circumstance to accept that alternative.

**We learned that we needed to reexamine our goals, to continue to focus on the kids' interests, as we worked to impart lifelong learning skills.**

Much of our education was introspective; that is, we frequently examined what we were doing as we did it, continually looking for ways to improve our learning, abandoning methods or materials that weren't working well and searching for others that were better. We had read and discussed John Holt's *How Children Learn*, applying it to ourselves, testing it against our own experience. Despite the title, many of John's observations can be applied to how *anyone* learns, at any age.

Our approach to many of the subjects, as you have seen, was often different, sometimes oblique — as with Derek's study of sharks. We often introduced new subjects, or new facets, and we led, guided, instructed, and questioned, but we let the kids' own interests determine the scope and direction of our leadership. Sooner or later, their interests usually led them not only to all the fields and subjects prescribed by law or convention, but to many others as well, and often beyond the levels expected in public schools. We tried to lead the kids in the directions where their interest was low, feeling some general knowledge was necessary for a liberal arts education. We made an effort to not force higher math or higher levels of some skills on the kids who seemed to have little inclination for the subject. Our aim was to see they had the skills to learn whatever might be useful to them in the future.

(Derek and I did have an interesting conversation about his studies. When I asked him if he felt he had learned what he needed to know before leaving home, he said no. He went on to explain that he wished he had had more math, so I asked him if he felt we should have pushed him to do more. He chuckled and said, "No. I resisted. You and Dad did all you could do for me. It's my fault I didn't learn more." I asked if he'd had any trouble learning the math he needed after he left home, and he assured me that he hadn't. I've heard similar stories from other parents. In comparing stories we all felt reassured.)

This has proved itself to be a reasonable approach for our kids. To the best of my knowledge none of the kids has felt handicapped because of the education he did or did not get at home. Since leaving home, all of them have learned higher math or other skills when they have had use for them. Along with whatever knowledge they had when they left home, they have taken the all-important skill of knowing how to learn with them.

### Trials and Errors

We learned the pros and cons of correspondence schools. We concluded that they covered only the basics, and we and our children wanted more depth in our learning experiences.

Many of the conventional high school subjects are part of a good beginning. Cathy enrolled in the American School of Chicago, possibly the best known of the many correspondence high schools. At that time, the entire four-year course cost about five hundred dollars, which we were allowed to pay in small monthly installments. Each of this school's courses consisted of a basic textbook and examination booklet, sometimes including a brief study guide. Cathy read a chapter, wrote out a test and mailed it in; the test was graded by the school and returned, usually with brief comments. Cathy had three or four courses at one time; when one was completed, she began another. The textbooks were average; i.e., not outstanding, but adequate. Her algebra text was based on "new math," which none of us liked, and her general science book seemed to be poorly written and confusing.

After we had seen half a dozen of Cathy's courses, Jean and I realized we could provide a much better education ourselves, choosing our own textbooks, and, not so incidentally, save at least two hundred dollars. We sent for, and studied, the catalogs from several correspondence high schools and found most of them to be like the American School. They offered little more than fifteen or sixteen textbooks, a few brief study guides, a series of short tests (most of which could be completed quite easily by reading the questions and then searching the text for the answers), and a diploma. A conscientious student can learn a great deal from them; a lazy student could receive high marks and a diploma almost as easily. Most of the schools offered some individual attention if the student had problems or specific questions.

Extension courses offered by universities and state departments of education usually have a much wider range of subjects, sometimes with laboratory materials (when appropriate), and more personalized tutoring, by mail or telephone. A supervisor approved by a local school official often is required for courses taken for credit. Non-credit courses require no supervision, and usually cost much less.

At least half the correspondence high schools whose catalogs we received were not accredited, which means that they have not yet been "certified" by an independent examining board. The majority of these schools had curricula identical, or at least very similar, to those that were accredited. Diplomas from these non-accredited schools are genuine and represent at least as much study and learning as most accredited correspondence schools or public schools.

None of the high school programs we examined seemed to meet our needs. We felt that the education itself was far more important than the diploma, and all the correspondence courses lacked many of the subjects we felt were most desirable or necessary. As thousands of functional illiterates receive fully accredited diplomas from public schools, more and more colleges and employers realize that the decorated parchment may mean nothing at all except that the student has met minimal attendance requirements.

### How We Developed Our High School Studies

We decided that our own curriculum was superior to that of almost any public or correspondence school. We broadened our literature base considerably by adding books from many different genres and many cultures. We read much of the literature together and discussed it. We talked about the ideas and characters, the authors and the time in which they lived, how they were influenced by the people and events around them, and how they in turn influenced their times and the world. We found biographies to supplement and deepen our understanding of history and literature and incorporated geography. We spent more time talking about the development of philosophy and religion throughout history and in our own time. We read about nature and ecology. We used several scientific magazines as well as textbooks and discussed developments and possibilities for the future. We talked about world news, world conflicts, and conflict resolution. We used public television, *Smithsonian* magazine, *Newsweek,* and many audio and videocassettes as well as numerous books to investigate and learn about the arts. We read and discussed psychology and personal ideals. We studied languages (French and Spanish as well as English). We talked about the meaning of life, in both the totally abstract and the intensely personal. Jean and the girls all played musical instruments — guitars, recorders, flute, clarinet, keyboard — and sang together. All the kids stuck mostly with basic practical math and geometry except for Karen, who studied more advanced math because she wanted to do it.

Other activities, many of which are discussed elsewhere in this book, were just as much a part of the education we provided: youth groups, 4-H, ball games, skiing, skating, sliding, carrying firewood, churning butter, building our barn, building our house, square dancing, gardening, cooking, washing dishes, caring for our farm animals, gathering maple sap, traveling, and on and on. The kids had jobs at times — working in a grocery store, the library, a secondhand bookstore; cleaning a stable; picking potatoes; picking rocks; baby-sitting. They learned how to save money and how to spend it, how to study catalogs and decide what to buy, and how to evaluate their purchases afterwards.

We always sought ways to expand the children's knowledge and experience far beyond that of our rural home. Cathy and Karen participated in national 4-H exchange programs, Cathy traveling to Alberta and Karen to Manitoba. Cathy worked once a week as a volunteer helper in a public library, and the following summer was hired as a full-time assistant. The next year she was a counselor in a girls' camp in Vermont. Karen visited relatives in Vermont and New York, went to Virginia and New Hampshire for two-week visits with families we had "met" by correspondence, and worked for a few hours in John Holt's office in Boston. Susan won a trip into the past at New Brunswick's Kings Landing Historical Settlement (see "Reading, Writing, and Spelling"), and went on month-long Outward Bound trips in Maine and Texas. She, too, worked at a summer camp. If you can't afford to send your kids as a camper, help them get jobs as counselors or assistant counselors! Derek worked in a sporting goods store and later cleaned horse stalls to pay for riding lessons and the opportunity to be near horses. He later worked at a riding camp in Virginia as a counselor-in-training. It wasn't long before he was training horses and riders at stables near home.

Cathy continued her American School studies until she had finished the few courses that were left on hand, but augmented them substantially with our own materials, then shifted to our own curriculum. We had learned an important lesson. We sat down with Karen and worked out her high school courses, and then sent away for books and other materials. The skeleton of her academic work was *High School Subjects Self-Taught*, edited by Lewis Copeland, a comprehensive distillation of 28 subjects (This book is out of print. Amazon.com is currently selling the fourth edition, dated 1989, in one volume for $79.95 and four volumes for $89.95. Barnes & Noble online is selling the 1989 one-volume edition for $89.95. I can usually find one given some advance notice for $30. If you would like to sell this back to us when you are done we will buy it back so we can make it available to others.) A few subjects, such as history and science, needed supplementation, for which we used several of the "Made Simple" series and various other books especially pertinent to Karen's interests. Karen finished all 28 courses in *High School Subjects Self-Taught* in two very intense years of study (her idea) and went on to expand her studies in literature, psychology, art, and miscellaneous reading. With a few books from the public library, Karen had a complete high school education for less than three hundred dollars (not including all the books and other materials we already had on hand).

Susan used our own high school program for two years and then wanted to enroll in the local high school for the remaining two years. We rejected this idea because we didn't like the curriculum or the presence of drugs and alcohol in the school. We compromised on The Meeting School, a small private school in New Hampshire (discussed elsewhere), from which she graduated.

Derek also followed our high school curriculum for a couple of years. When he was 16 he began working part time, saving his money for a car, and began supporting himself. He still read voraciously, but drifted away from academic studies to pursue his longtime ambition to work with horses by obtaining a job teaching riding and training horses in a stable. This was a good choice for him. He now rides and trains horses for a living.

**GRADUATION TIME**

As the children gained knowledge and the necessary skills for living independent lives, Donn and I pondered the meaning of a graduation ceremony. We recognized its importance, not for the diploma — a mere piece of paper — but as a rite of passage into the world at large.

We felt that a diploma from Brook Farm School would have at least as much moral validity as any public or correspondence school diploma. We wrote a rough draft and had the local print shop set it in type and print it on a standard diploma form. It cost about twenty dollars, and to us was much more valuable than others that might have cost us several hundred dollars, but would have represented much less work and learning.

This is how the local newspaper reported Cathy's graduation ceremony:

**Unique Graduation Ceremony**
THE OBSERVER, Hartland, New Brunswick,
Wednesday, June 20, 1984

Brook Farm School celebrated its first high school graduate, Catherine Barbara Reed, 17, at a unique graduation ceremony held at the Women's Institute Hall in Knowlesville, Saturday, June 16. A family enterprise, Brook Farm School is operated by Donn and Jean Reed.

Donn Reed opened the Commencement and Awards Ceremony, and welcomed the 35 guests present. He then presented certificates to Catherine and Karen for maintaining exceptional standards of study, workmanship, perseverance and independent endeavor, and to Susan and Derek for outstanding work and progress in specific areas of investigation, study, and accomplishment. Notes of appreciation were given by the four children to their parents.

Rev. Maynard Rector offered the Baccalaureate, after which Mr. Reed presented Catherine with her diploma. In his address, Mr. Reed said, in part, "Basic academic skills ... are all parts of the education in our school. Several other subjects are just as much a part of our education — the study of other countries, and their people, other ways of thinking, other beliefs about humanity and God and the universe. Activities such as daily chores, ball games, participation in 4-H and youth groups, jobs away from home, are invaluable parts of education."

Presenting the Class History, Mr. Reed said, "Through the modern miracles of airplanes, buses, satellite, television, and first-class mail, Brook Farm School has drawn freely upon resources and instructors from around the world."

In the Valedictory Address, Catherine said, "I think my education has given me imagination, a sense of truth, and a feeling of responsibility, which I hope to share with people wherever I go."

Following the reading of the Class History, the Last Will and Testament, and the Class Prophecy, the ceremony ended, and guests sat down to a potluck supper. A copy of Catherine's yearbook was presented to each guest.

Catherine is leaving shortly to work as a camp counselor at a private girls' camp in the States, after which she plans to continue her education.

**Just how important is an "official" diploma?**

I've checked with all four of our kids, and none has ever been asked to physically present a high school diploma. When applying to a college or for a job, the question is usually "Did you finish high school?" or "What is the highest level of education completed?"

**So, what *do* I do with this piece of paper?**

## GRADUATION
## A TIME OF DREAD OR CELEBRATION?
### Parental Transitions
Do You Fear an Empty Nest?

Homeschooling is a way of life. I hear from many parents that they dread the time when their children will be gone and this lifestyle will disappear, too. Some parents fear they will no longer be needed, that there will never again be anything as meaningful in their lives. For some parents these thoughts create anxiety, for others panic, and some see this time as a doorway to the future offering new adventures in living and learning for themselves. I know how easy it is to get caught up in the daily routines and activities of homeschooling. As homeschooling parents we work very hard to help our children look ahead to their future. It is vitally important to remember that we too have a future. Through exploring what lies ahead for yourself, you become a model for your children of how to take control of a new part of your own life.

If you're afraid you will no longer be needed, that the meaning of your life will diminish, you are mistaken. You will always be a parent, and your children will need you at all stages of their lives. However, your role will change over time. Children are born to become increasingly independent. Remember how easy it was to adjust to the myriad changes that occurred over the first few years of your children's lives. It was a natural progression from having a totally dependent baby to having a toddler. At some point you will stop being the chauffeur and hand over the car keys. You can teach, guide, and lead by example, and then at some point you must trust your children and trust the life process itself. As your kids become adults they will look to you more as a longtime trusted friend. Although it is rarely said, when your children leave home — for short periods of time or forever — they do so trusting that you will be there for them if they need you. The love and shared memories remain, but your job description changes and your own developmental challenges change.

When you think about your life after the children are on their own, imagine all the things you haven't had time for while you were involved in the complex daily routine centered around your children. Just as you have worked to make your children aware of the many possibilities for their lives, you too should envision a future filled with possibilities, whether it be continuing your education, creating or finding a job, developing your artistic talents, finding satisfaction in volunteer work, gardening, reading, or working with other children. There is a future for you to dream about, to work toward, to bring into reality. This is a time to renew yourself and a time to celebrate a job well done.

For Donn and me, the end of our homeschooling journey had much in common with the beginning stages of our adventure — it was a time of questioning and doubt, a time for reflection and anticipation and new joys. Our children are now scattered across the country, and we've found that the bonds of love, companionship, and understanding formed over the years of living, working, growing, playing, laughing, and crying together overcome the distances between us. As our children became increasingly independent, we found a new maturity, a deepening of respect, and a new feeling of equality developing between us. These intangible rewards of the homeschooling years are lifetime treasures, a living legacy binding our family together through the years.

I used to wonder what an empty nest would be like: Would I find it traumatic when the last child left home? When the time came, Donn and I were surprised at how naturally our lives filled with a variety of interesting and challenging options. Unlike children, these interests didn't require us to be on call 24 hours a day. I went back to college part time, studying computers, sign language, and emergency medicine, and began a serious and engrossing study of classical guitar. Donn worked more intensely on his writing. Both of us enjoyed the time we had to refresh our relationship, to work and play together, just the two of us. We treasured the times when the kids came home, filling the house with their love and laughter. When they left again, we felt immense satisfaction that they were happy establishing their own lives.

(Warning! You may still get those late-night calls. So far we've had: 1) Guess what? We're getting married! 2) We just had a baby! 3) One that started with "Everything's all right, but ... I'm calling from the ambulance." Once a parent, always a parent!)

### OPTIONS FOR CONTINUING EDUCATION

Today, you have more options to explore than we did. One recent development is the increased number of community and private colleges, as well as some universities, allowing homeschooled students to take higher-level courses for credit while still in high school. Community college courses are relatively inexpensive. If you have been a resident of the area for at least six months, there are usually scholarships or reduced rates available.

Another option is to use a computer to participate in the rapidly expanding possibilities offered by high school and college distance-learning courses on the Internet. I get excited when I think that a student can take a class which may originate across the country (and be able to interact with the class as it takes place), monitor an archaeological dig in Egypt, or follow a space mission — all from a home computer. Distance-learning classes can provide stimulating and challenging opportunities for your children — and you. It's possible to get full credit for your distance learning that can help with college admissions. If you don't have a computer your child may be able to use one at the library or a community resource center. If the course taken is a non-credit course, be sure to document the work done and create a portfolio.

Please see the listings in "To College or Not" for some exciting possibilities you can use while your kids are still in high school.

### CAVEAT EMPTOR!

With all the wonderful opportunities available for learning at home through distance courses, there are still pitfalls you should know about. *Home Study Opportunities*, by Laurie M. Carlson, is fully reviewed in "To College or Not." This is the only book I've found that discusses a variety of problems that can occur. If you plan to use correspondence courses or other distance-learning programs you should read this.

### RESOURCES FOR THE HIGH SCHOOL YEARS

**THE ALMANAC OF EDUCATION CHOICES**, Jerry Mintz, editor in chief. More than 300 pages of listings and information on more than 6,000 alternative schools and programs in the U.S. and Canada. You'll find private, community, alternative, home-based, and correspondence listings, with basic information about each and contact information, along with other resources. Code SS, $20.

### CORRESPONDENCE COURSES

**American School**, 850 E. 58th St., Chicago, IL 60637. Offers general high school course and college prep course. Payment plans available.

**Citizens' High School**, 5575 Peachtree Rd., Atlanta, GA 30341. Offers high school diploma program. Offers more than 50 subjects. Payment plan available.

**Clonlara Home-Based Education Program**, 1289 Jewett St., Ann Arbor, MI 48104. Write for the most current information.

**Home-Centered Learning**, P.O. Box 92, Escondido, CA 92025.

**Home Study International**, 6940 Carroll Ave., Takoma Park, MD 20912. Offers preschool through high school diploma program.

**Newport/Pacific High School** (branch of ICS, International Correspondence Schools), 925 Oak St., Scranton, PA 18515.

**North Atlantic Regional High School**, 25 Adams Ave., Lewiston, ME 04210; www.NARSdiploma.com. Not limited to Maine families. Grades 7 to 12. Parent-selected, parent-directed studies.

**Phoenix Special Programs**, 3231 W. Clarendon, Phoenix, AZ 85017. Nationally accredited non-traditional courses. Free brochure.

**Puget Sound Community School**, www.pscs.org. Offers online classes.

**Quantum Educational Systems and Technology**, 8792 Stonehouse Dr., Ellicott City, MD 21043. Middle school, high school, and advanced-placement science courses.

**Seattle Pacific University**, a division of Continuing Studies, 3307 3rd Ave. West, Seattle, WA 98119-1997; 800-482-3848; www.spu.edu/dcs. Offers K-12 distance learning.

**Seton Home Study School**, 1 Kidd Ln., Front Royal, VA 22630.

**The Sycamore Tree**, 2179 Meyer Place, Costa Mesa, CA 92627.

**University of Nebraska at Lincoln**, 33rd and Holdredge sts., Lincoln, NE 68583.

**Canadian Branch of ICS** (International Correspondence Schools), 9001 Avon Road, Montreal West, PQ H4X 2H2.

Canadians, see **Alberta Distance Learning Centre** in "Support Groups, Organizations, and Correspondence Schools."

For independent study, see *Peterson's Independent Study Catalog* listed in "To College or Not." There are numerous listings for courses available to high school students.

For a list of accredited high school and college distance-learning programs, see "Computers." You can also write to the Distance Education and Training Council, 1601 18th St. NW, Washington, DC 20009-2529, and request their Directory of Accredited Institutions. It's free.

**International Study**. Free information from the Council on International Education Exchange, 205 E. 42nd St., New York, NY 10017-5706.

**THE EDUCATIONAL REGISTER**. Descriptive listings of hundreds of private schools, boarding schools, summer study programs (academic, remedial, music, computer, etc.), and summer camps and trips, listed by geographic area (e.g., Northern New England, Mid-Atlantic, Canada, Abroad). Descriptions include curriculum; programs; extracurricular activities; number, age, and gender of students; and cost. Many listings seem to be for upper-middle incomes, but scholarships are often available, and sometimes, depending on the age of your child, he can become part of the staff and take part for the cost of transportation — and maybe be paid. When Derek was 15, we looked for a summer riding camp we could afford — meaning one with almost no fee. Nonexistent, of course. The description in *The Educational Register* of Hazelwild Farm Camp, in Fredericksburg, Virginia, seemed just right, except the $400 per week fee. Derek wrote to the camp's director, telling of his experiences in riding, training horses, winning trophies, and teaching other riders. He was accepted as a counselor-in-training and spent eight weeks riding, coaching, training, and making friends, and he paid $200 (which he had earned the previous winter) for the entire summer. *The Educational Register* is FREE to parents and educators. Request a copy from Vincent/Curtis, 224 Clarendon St., Boston, MA 02116; www.vincentcurtis.com.

**Institute of Lifetime Learning**, American Association of Retired Persons, 1909 K St. NW, Washington, DC 20049, offers free booklets on many subjects, including art, anthropology, history, literature, philosophy, and physics, with suggestions for further study and self-tests. Write for free information and a full list of subjects.

**Accelerated Learning Programs**. Several video and audiocassette programs that promote enhanced skills and achievements in reading, memory, note taking, test preparation, math and algebra, communications, confidence, and motivation. The materials have been used and tested by thousands of high school students, whose scores jumped very dramatically. For more information and a catalog, write Learning Forum, 225 Stevens Ave., Suite 103, Solana Beach, CA 92075.

## OTHER RESOURCES

**THE TEENAGER'S GUIDE TO SCHOOL OUTSIDE THE BOX**, by Rebecca Greene. The book to use to put real spice into the high school years. It's full of real accounts by teens about their experiences with internships, mentorships, volunteering, study abroad, community service, apprenticeships, and numerous other exciting learning experiences. Many of these opportunities can be done from home and others involve travel. Details in the book explain how to scout out opportunities and evaluate them so you know if they will be right for you, how to prepare, what to expect, how to make the most of your experience, and how to overcome obstacles such as cost and distance. Greene has good listings of where to go to find out more about hundreds of programs. Good for teens and other young adults. Code FS, $15.95.

**WORTH THE RISK: True Stories About Risk Takers,** by Arlene Erlbach, is not about being a hero or doing foolish stunts. This book will help you learn how to plan a new venture like starting a new business or overcoming a fear or disability. It is about learning, planning, persistence, and personal growth. It's about learning from your experience, whether it succeeds or fails. Full of suggestions and probing questions so you can assess yourself and your project. Ages 10 to adult. Code FS, $12.95.

**TRADITIONAL LOGIC: An Introduction to Formal Logic**, by Martin Cothran. Designed for high school students and parents who wish to tackle this challenging subject. No prior training necessary. This is not to be confused with creative thinking, or critical thinking. Traditional logic is a discipline established by Aristotle in the fourth century. Lesson plans are included, with clear instructions, and each book includes an answer key. Specify book one or book two. $24.90 each from Memoria Press, 4103 Bishop Ln., Louisville, KY 40218.

**CREATING PORTFOLIOS, For Success, School, and Life**, by Martin Kimeldore. Although this was not written for homeschoolers preparing college portfolios, it is an excellent fund of useful and imaginative suggestions for creating four different portfolios: personal, student, project, and professional. This is certainly a useful skill for college entrance and job applications, but more than that, it is a creative way to compile your work and celebrate your life. Suggestions for collecting, selecting, organizing, and presenting essays, computer printouts, photographs, maps, and more. Ages 12 and up. Code FS, $14.95. There is also a teacher's guide with suggested ways to implement and evaluate portfolios and to adapt them to students with special needs. Code FS, $14.95. More about creating portfolios in "To College or Not."

---

*Learning is the very essence of humility, learning from everything and from everybody. There is no hierarchy in learning. Authority denies learning and a follower will never learn.*

— Jiddu Krishnamurti

# TO COLLEGE OR NOT



## Internships and Mentors and Other Alternatives

Parents and young adults begin to have renewed doubts about homeschooling and feel more pressure during the high school years, for several reasons. For parents the obvious discomfort is caused by thoughts about whether or not they have prepared their child adequately for the future — including college, if that is the goal. Many students wonder what they would like to do after graduating and feel they must face the traditional choice between college and work. Many homeschoolers are challenging that choice, and I feel this is healthy.

If you are having doubts about getting into college, relax! Getting into college is no longer the "BIG QUESTION" it used to be. I know of no college or university that has turned down a homeschooled student's application *because* he was homeschooled. Increasingly, colleges and universities are coming to appreciate homeschooled students because they are more self-motivated, because they know what they want to get from their continuing educational experience, and because they know how to direct their own studies far better than many of their traditionally educated peers. Colleges actively seek out students with these abilities. Pat Farenga of *Growing Without Schooling* says some colleges are now sending recruiters to homeschooling conferences!

These are the important questions to consider when thinking about college: Is college attendance necessary or desirable to reach the long-term goals of the student? Is it necessary or desirable to attend college in the traditional manner? Would an internship or working with a mentor be more productive? If more formal education is the right way to reach the end goals, what is the best manner to prepare for it?

The answer to the first question should be answered by your young adult. If you feel your child should attend college just because it feels like the best option to you, but your child is opposed to the idea, you should read Herbert Kohl's book (listed below). It will help you sort out this problem. If you have been homeschooling, I hope you are aware that there is no point in anyone pursuing a college education without inner motivation.

If you're still reading, you probably need to seriously consider the second question: Is it necessary or desirable to attend college in the traditional manner? There are many pursuits in life that will necessitate attendance, on campus, at a college. If this is the course your young person has decided to pursue, you will need to search for the appropriate institution. Your local library should have books listing colleges and universities along with notes about their specialties, if any. The Peterson's guides listed below will help, too.

For those wishing to pursue more education in a non-traditional manner, there are many opportunities available, and it is no longer as difficult to find them as it used to be. Although there are jobs and careers that require college attendance, there are many that require only the necessary knowledge, in which case an apprenticeship or learning through work experience may be more satisfactory.

Fortunately, one of the blessings that come with non-traditional education at all levels is the ability to pick and choose the best possible resource or resources for each individual circumstance. Community colleges are lower in cost and available to everyone. Your young adult can attend as many or as few classes as he wishes, making it possible to work part time and take classes. An option to consider for your college-bound high school student is taking one or more college courses while still doing most of high school at home. This can be done through local colleges or community colleges, through correspondence, or over the Internet. One of the benefits of the increasing number of high-school-age homeschoolers is that more and more traditional learning institutions are becoming responsive to requests for part-time attendance and participation in their programs.

Unfortunately not all institutions welcome homeschoolers on any level.

**COLLEGE OR NOT?**
**BOOKS TO HELP YOU MAKE THE DECISION**

***Warning!*** If you want and expect your kids to go to college, do *not* let them read this book, unless you are willing to consider other options. If you'd like to help your child find a way to live a fulfilling life doing work he loves whether it involves college or not, then all of you will benefit from the following book:

**THE QUESTION IS COLLEGE: On Finding and Doing Work You Love**, by Herbert Kohl. Yes, if you've read through "Homeschooling and Education" earlier in this book, you've seen this listed before. It brings us full circle, back to evaluating the true needs of educational goals. I hope you've reread this book. If not, this is the time to do it again — and for your young adult to read it, too. In spite of the warning, which may make you feel this book is anti-college, you should know it is not against college. Kohl questions the need for college, and that need will vary according to your long-term goals.

In the first section of the book Kohl challenges you to think deeply about lifetime goals — what constitutes satisfactory living — and you may find yourself evaluating your needs as well as those of your children. Kohl will help you see how important it is to support your child in whatever decision he makes about college, and help you consider whether or not taking time off before or during college would be advantageous. The second and third sections have specific tools to help your young adult determine what will be the best course of action after high school — and how to achieve it. There are charts to set up a career profile and a thorough explanation of how to use this information. The appendices have useful information about further resources you or your young adult can use to find other opportunities for the future. Code HMN, $15.95.

**THE CLOSING OF THE AMERICAN MIND: How Higher Education Has Failed Democracy and Impoverished the Souls of Today's Students**, by Allen Bloom. The fact that the "Education Summit" came to pass is a sign that the government is still behind the times, but it is interesting that they have finally noticed what many of us have been aware of for a long time: that the schools are failing a frighteningly large number of students. In this now-famous book, the author probes the state of American education and assesses the intellectual and moral confusions of modern students. Although Bloom has been accused by critics of elitism, in that he seems to be writing primarily of Ivy League collegiate education, I think many of his conclusions are valid, and can easily be applied to other segments of society and education, whether or not that is his intention. As homeschoolers, we certainly agree with Bloom that modern education is sadly lacking in some of the most fundamental essentials. The question is, do we agree on what is lacking, and on the possible remedies? Even if we aren't directly concerned with public education on the elementary and secondary levels, most of us would agree that many of those wishing a college education will probably go to college, which makes Bloom's indictment more relevant to us. Having withdrawn our children from an inadequate elementary school system, do we want them entering an inadequate college system? Bloom's comments and numerous historical anecdotes, tracing the educational system back to the time of Plato, are certainly worth reading, and should make us examine our own philosophies very carefully, even if we end by disagreeing completely with everything he says — which is not likely if we are serious about education. Code SS, $13.

"From Home to Harvard" is the headline on a recent article in *Time* magazine. It's a catchy title, but the only thing related to Harvard was a quote from Marlyn McGrath Lewis, director of admissions: "Often we're impressed by what someone has done under unusual circumstances ... and homeschooling fits the bill." There were a couple of other interesting statistics in the article. Stanford University admitted 26 percent of the 35 homeschooled applicants in 1999, "nearly double its overall acceptance rate." The article also stated that many colleges look at standardized test scores when considering homeschooled applicants and that the scores in 1999 "averaged 1100 on the SAT — a full 81 points above the national average — and 22.8 on the ACT, compared with the national average of 21."

**AND WHAT ABOUT COLLEGE?**, by Cafi Cohen. This book has just been updated to give you the best information about helping your young adult prepare for and be accepted into college. Cohen explains how to use your homeschooling to your best advantage. You'll find detailed information about admissions policies (what to include on your application), test requirements, scholarships, study tips, and related resources and websites. Learn how to find the college that will suit your needs and just what to include with your application. Includes sample transcripts, résumés, application essays, sample eclectic curricula, a listing of colleges that have accepted homeschoolers, and a planning checklist, plus good information about college through distance learning. $18.95 from Holt Associates (see "Homeschooling and Education" for the address) or from us. Code BT.

**FROM HOMESCHOOL TO COLLEGE AND WORK: Turning Your Home-schooled Experiences Into College and Job Portfolios**, by Alison McKee. This clearly written book is an excellent guide for all parents and students learning at home, no matter what your particular "brand" of learning. It will help you learn how to take advantage of your unique experiences to apply for college or work. McKee outlines when and how to begin your documentation, how to compile your data, and how to put it together in a final form — all with examples. There is also a good list of resources if you feel you need more information. Highly recommended. There may be flashier books, but this one has all the basics you'll need. Code BH, $10.

### STUDY SMARTER, NOT HARDER

**"How to Study" Program**, by Ron Fry. Unlike most books with similar subjects and titles, which I wouldn't give shelf (or review) space, this series is really useful for all high school students, and especially for home-schooled students who plan to go to college. The author's style is informal, encouraging, and often funny, and his advice and suggestions are practical and easy to employ. Code CP.

**"ACE" ANY TEST,** 96 pages, $6.99.
**GET ORGANIZED**, 96 pages, $6.99.
**HOW TO STUDY**, 224 pages, $9.99.
**IMPROVE YOUR MEMORY**, 96 pages, $6.99.
**IMPROVE YOUR READING**, 96 pages, $6.99.
**IMPROVE YOUR WRITING**, 96 pages, $6.99.
**MANAGE YOUR TIME**, 96 pages, $6.99.

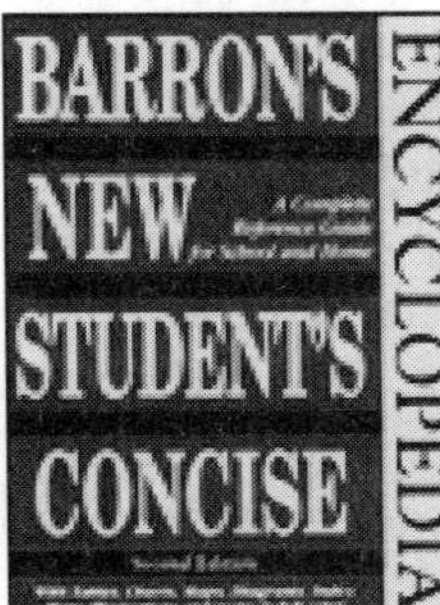


**BARRON'S NEW STUDENT'S CONCISE ENCYCLOPEDIA: A Complete Reference Guide for Home and School**. This is a single-volume encyclopedia of "essential information" for high school and college students. A review of all major subjects (24 in total) is presented in the form of A-to-Z entries or by topic within these general academic sections:

LIBERAL ARTS: Music, Art, Language and Literature, Philosophy, and Religion.

SOCIAL STUDIES: American and World History, Government, Geography, Economics, and Business.

MATHEMATICS AND COMPUTER SCIENCE

SCIENCE: Astronomy, Biology, Chemistry, Earth Sciences, Technology, Physics, and Psychology.

In general, the information presented is reliable and comprehensive. One disadvantage is that most information (except mathematics and a few other subjects) is arranged *alphabetically*, as in an encyclopedia, rather than chronologically or around a central theme, which makes study somewhat difficult — in history, for instance, in which the chronological sequence of cause and effect is of major importance. However, these sections still serve very well as mini-reviews, refresher courses, and — the best use of this book — basic reference points and starting guides for more intensive study using other materials (library books, encyclopedia, etc.).

The mathematics section is very complete, from simple arithmetic to calculus and trigonometry, but is also very brief. For more detailed study, which you'll probably want, we recommend *Essential Math* or *Arithmetic Made Simple* (see "Mathematics") for high school math.

The U.S. history is fairly complete, but brief; world history is skimpy.

Another section, "Study and Learning Workshops," provides advice and guidelines to help students make efficient use of study time and achieve their highest possible marks when taking tests. Detailed instructions are given for writing term papers and making full use of library research facilities.

A section on "life outside the classroom" contains information — some of it very useful — about basic health and nutrition, exercise programs, and first aid, and offers practical tips for managing personal finances. The book also contains many excellent maps, including historical maps and many charts and tables, including weights and measures, metric conversions, holidays, and time zones. More than 1,000 pages. Code BE, $29.95.

### TEST PREPARATION

I recently heard Dr. Ruth Simmons, president of Smith College, on National Public Radio, speaking to the Commonwealth Club of California. From poverty to becoming the first black woman to achieve the title of college president, she has filled her life with rich accomplishments. When she spoke of college admissions tests, her opinion was that the students who sometimes do the poorest will actually have the greatest potential. She did not mean you shouldn't study and work hard if college is your goal. She meant that many students of great potential will not have great test scores, which is why Smith College (like many others) asks for an essay. This is the place to show off your homeschooling work; your original thinking; and your ideas, ideals, and goals. By the way, Smith also invites parents to write something for them.

Not all colleges and universities require SAT or College Board testing. Plan ahead. If you're faced with official testing, read about it. Your child can achieve higher scores if he understands more about the testing procedure, and there are ways to increase scores without "knowing more."

We used a number of "test preparation" guides over the years, not with any intention of preparing anyone for a test, but as comprehensive curriculum guides and basic reference works. The guides for the SAT, the SSAT, and the GED, especially, include full review and instruction in the basic subjects that are generally considered part of a good high school education. We usually ignored the tests, unless the kids wanted to do them to discover "weak" points, but we gained much useful information from the instructional sections.

---

*Training is everything. The peach was once a bitter almond; cauliflower is nothing but a cabbage with a college education.* — Mark Twain

**HOW TO PREPARE FOR THE COLLEGE-LEVEL EXAMINATION PROGRAM (CLEP) GENERAL EXAM**. The most comprehensive practice and review book for the CLEP, with thousands of typical questions, plus 15 practice exams with explained answers. More than 650 pages. Code BE, $14.95.

**PASSING THE GED: A Complete Preparation Program for the High School Equivalency Examination**. Provides instruction, study tips, and review in writing skills, social studies, sciences, reading skills, and math, in 30 lessons. Contains a diagnostic test and three model GED exams with explained answers and vocabulary drill and requirements in each state. Code BE, $14.95.

**14 DAYS TO HIGHER SAT I SCORES**. Includes the book *Basic Tips* and two 90-minute cassettes to help develop test-taking skills. The tapes review math and verbal skills; the book contains two prep tests and a model SAT with answers. Code BE, $16.95.

**HOW TO PREPARE FOR THE SAT I**. Complete preparation for a major college entrance test, with seven full-length exams modeled after the SAT I. All answers explained. Extensive math and verbal reviews, and a review of the Test of Standard Written English. More than 600 pages. Code BE, $14.95, $29.95 with CD-ROM. There isn't anything extra or different on the CD-ROM. It just allows you to use your computer along with the book and a pencil.

The FairTest website has the following FAQ:
**What Does SAT Stand For?** Nothing. Initially titled the Scholastic Aptitude Test and then the Scholastic Assessment Test, it is now officially named just SAT I because of uneasiness at ETS and the College Board about defining just what the test measures. "SAT is

not an initialism; it does not stand for anything," say the testmakers.

Good news! The National Center for Fair and Open Testing (FairTest) now lists more than 280 four-year colleges and universities that do not use ACT or SAT scores for admissions decisions. That is an increase of more than four dozen institutions in the last couple of years. FairTest also found that there are hundreds of other undergraduate institutions that are not using only the standardized tests for admissions purposes. You can get a free updated list by sending a #10 SASE to "Tests Optional," Fair Test, 342 Broadway, Cambridge, MA 02139; fairtest.org/optional.htm.

**HOW TO PREPARE FOR THE *CANADIAN* GED.** This has all the features of the U.S. book listed above. Complete sections cover all the necessary information. You could use this as a guide for your high school curriculum and expand it in areas of special interest. Code BE, $18.95 Cdn.

### IDEAS

Here are a few hints for using the Web as a resource for finding and applying to college. Use the College Board at www.collegeboard.org, Kaplan at www.kaplan.com, or the Princeton Review at www.review.com to help you plan when to take various exams, file applications, and a lot more. One of the features you'll find on some online sites that may be particularly useful is a series of multiple-choice questions along with SAT scores to help you match your young person's interests to a suitable college. Many college applications can be filled out online, but I think particularly for homeschoolers, because our kids offer so much more than the typical public school students, it's best to send in a regular application and take advantage of the opportunity to write about special abilities and experiences.

learninfreedom.org/colleges_4_hmsc.html is an excellent site to find out about colleges that have accepted homeschoolers. If you don't have a computer, it's worth a trip to a community access center or the library to use their computer.

**Berea College**, located in Berea, Kentucky, is one of the best tuition-free colleges available to students and families unable to pay for other college options. Students sometimes pay room and board if possible. All students work 10 to 15 hours per week. Berea has excellent courses and a work program for students. Based on Christian values, it draws 80% of its students from Appalachia. If you live outside this area you may still apply. Berea College, Berea, KY 40404; 606-986-9341, ext. 5083; www.berea.edu.

**Peterson's Guides**, P.O. Box 2123, Princeton, NJ 08543. Free catalog of annually updated guides to secondary schools, colleges, universities, camps, private schools, and career education courses, such as *Guide to Two-Year Colleges*, *SAT Success*, *Summer Opportunities for Kids and Teenagers*, and many more. You can order any or all of these books either from them or from us. Compare shipping prices. Ours may be lower. You may also find these in your local library.

### CAVEAT EMPTOR!

**HOME STUDY OPPORTUNITIES: The Complete Guide to Going to School by Mail**, by Laurie M. Carlson. Unfortunately this book is now out of print. Try to find it at your library, because the greatest value in this book lies not in the listings (although I saw many that were new to me) but in the warnings given about programs that look good, and may be good or even excellent, but will not give you credits you can transfer to other schools or universities. Carlson gives very specific directions for finding out about the school you are investigating, telling you where to go for help finding the information you need. Her warnings are just a very small part of the book, but imperative reading if you are considering an alternative program that is not part of a well-known institution.

### OFF-CAMPUS EDUCATION

**College by Correspondence**. For those who prefer to continue their studies at home or while working, there are hundreds of institutions that offer college credits and even grant fully accredited degrees, mostly or entirely by correspondence. The cost is far below that of an on-campus education. Usually, the correspondence program can be completed in a shorter time than an on-campus program would take, if you're in a hurry. Another advantage is being able to work at the same time if you find it necessary or desirable. The credits and degrees thus earned are completely legal and are recognized throughout the world as being just as good as if they were obtained on campus. One can earn a bachelor of arts, a bachelor of science, a master's in several fields, even a law degree and several doctorates — all without ever attending a school except through a post office. It is often possible to earn a full degree without taking any courses, by having one's work, hobbies, previous training and study, military service, and travel experiences evaluated.

Some of the best college-by-correspondence programs are offered by:

**Chadwick University**, 2112 11th Ave. South, Suite 504, Birmingham, AL 35205; 800-767-2423. Offers accredited B.S. and M.S. through distance learning. Write or call for a free catalog.

**Home Study International**, 6940 Carroll Ave., Takoma Park, MD 20912. Doesn't grant degrees, but courses are fully accredited. Make arrangements with a local college or university to earn its degree using some or all courses from HSI.

**State University of New York**, Albany, NY 12230; SLN.suny.edu/SLN.

**University of Nebraska at Lincoln**, College Counselor, Division of Continuing Studies, 511 Nebraska Hall, Lincoln, NE 68588. The College Independent Study program offers the opportunity for high school juniors or seniors to earn college credits while still in high school; for students who are attending on-campus college classes to make up academic deficiencies; and for students who are off campus (at home or elsewhere) to expand their academic background without attending classes. More than 100 courses are offered. Non-credit college-level courses are also offered in specific professional and personal interest areas. Counseling for students is available.

**University of Phoenix**, P.O. Box 52031, Phoenix, AZ 85072-9352; 877-879-4723; online.uophx.edu/onlinebiz. B.S. and M.A. degrees through distance learning.

**University of Wisconsin Extension Service** believes in making high school and college courses available to those who want them. Very supportive. Call 800-442-6460 to talk with an adviser or request a catalog.

## IN CANADA

**ATHABASCA UNIVERSITY**, 1 University Dr., Athabasca, AB T9S 3A3; www.athabascau.ca. Very comprehensive and inexpensive. Full degree programs entirely by mail. For residents of Canada only (unfortunately). A four-year graduate program (B.A. or B.S.) costs less than $1,000 per year. Write for current catalog.

**UNIVERSITY OF GUELPH**, Independent Study, Guelph, ON N1G 2W1. Offers a variety of courses.

**PETERSON'S GUIDE TO DISTANCE LEARNING PROGRAMS 2000.** Incredible guide to two- and four-year degree programs — or just exciting study. Created in cooperation with the University Continuing Education Association, this is the only comprehensive guide providing details on thousands of degree and certificate distance-learning opportunities in almost 800 accredited institutions in the U.S. AND CANADA. Wow! If you want to study at home, this is for you. 636 pages. Code PTR, $26.95.

**PETERSON'S INDEPENDENT STUDY CATALOG.** Lists hundreds of onsite as well as reputable correspondence and distance-learning opportunities (for high school, college, and lifelong learners) and what each offers. Helpful information answering common questions (e.g., who should consider independent study, why consider it, what it offers, questions you should ask before registering with a college, how it really works, and how to finance your studies). **U.S. and Canadian listings.** Code PTR, $21.95.

**BEARS' GUIDE TO EARNING COLLEGE DEGREES NONTRADITIONALLY**, by John Bear, Ph.D. This book has been revised to such an extent they've changed the title! It's now called **BEARS' GUIDE TO EARNING DEGREES BY DISTANCE LEARNING**. It's still the best resource for earning a bachelor's, master's, doctorate, law, or medical degree through a wide range of unconventional methods. Discusses more than 2,500 schools and programs. 400 brand-new listings. 480 pages. Code TSP, $29.95.

**COLLEGE DEGREES BY MAIL & INTERNET**, by John Bear, Ph.D. The best guide to the 100 best accredited non-traditional institutions that grant degrees at undergraduate or graduate levels without requiring attendance on campus. Code TSP, $12.95.

**College Without College**. Fully accredited college degrees may be granted for non-college work, general life experience (travel, military service, knowledge gained through work experience, and teaching your kids at home), or proficiency in specific areas of knowledge (such as writing, math, or a foreign language). One of the best of several institutions offering such degrees is the University of the State of New York, 7

Columbia Circle, Albany, NY 12230-5159. Write for free information about the College Proficiency Examinations and the Regents External Degrees Program. This isn't a program for which a recent high school graduate would qualify, but it is a practical possibility for anyone to consider for the future, if one foresees a need for a degree but prefers to spend a few years in work or travel. If this is something you will possibly want to do, be sure to keep a journal of your work or travel experiences.

**A Degree From an Expensive College Without Paying the Full Price**. Most colleges and universities will accept up to three years' worth of credits from other colleges and universities, including accredited correspondence courses. If you have enough money for one year at an expensive school, make it your last. Build credits in cheaper schools or by correspondence, or both, then transfer to the more expensive school for your degree.

**College Credit "Banking."** The Regents Credit Bank of the State University of New York, Albany, NY 12230, will, for a very reasonable fee, keep records of all college credits you earn through any accredited institution, including correspondence courses, and will send a complete transcript to any institution or agency at your request. In this way, credits earned through several different institutions or life situations can be combined into a single transcript. Write for more information.

---

*By working faithfully eight hours a day you may eventually get to be boss and work twelve hours a day.*
— Robert Frost

---

### IS A CAREER DESIRABLE?

Common opinion these days — or "conventional wisdom," as it's sometimes called, although it's seldom very wise — is that it's important to decide upon a career as early in life as possible, and to work diligently to achieve that career and to advance in it. In the United States and Canada, the question "What do you do?" usually means "What do you do *for a living*?" In most other parts of the world, although the earning of money is considered a necessary part of one's life, "What do you do?" refers to one's hobbies, avocations, or personal interests — "What do you do for enjoyment?" Not everyone is fortunate enough to have his strongest interests coincide with means of earning money; many people resign themselves to working for money at jobs they don't care for, but are able to fill their other hours with more interesting activities, and don't feel their lives are wasted. Many people are content to have a variety of jobs during their lifetimes, although much of society sees this as being unsettled and indecisive, if not downright shiftless. "Jack of all trades, master of none" used to be the common pejorative applied to someone who didn't stay settled in one line of work.

I have never had a desire for any one career. Since I left high school, I've worked at many things — road construction worker, newspaper editor, psychiatric aide, migrant farm worker, freelance columnist, sawmill edgerman, etc. Usually, I stayed with the jobs for as long as I enjoyed them; when my enjoyment began to wane, I moved on to something else. Many times I have had the opportunity of staying with a job and advancing in it — "making a career" of it — but I knew I'd soon become bored and wish I were doing something else. "A foolish consistency," said Emerson, "is the hobgoblin of little minds." Not *consistency*, but a "*foolish* consistency" — being consistent just for the sake of being consistent.

Even now, although most of my monetary income is derived from my books and our mail-order book service, not all of our *living* comes from them. We have a cow and chickens and pigs and a garden, and a great deal of our living comes from a sort of part-time farming, although it doesn't bring us any money. The monetary value of the food we produce through our own efforts could be expressed as the amount of money we would have to spend to buy it, but that doesn't say anything about our enjoyment and satisfaction in raising it. We'd rather put the time and labor into milking the cow and collecting eggs than half the time into earning money with which to buy milk and eggs produced by someone else.

There is nothing dishonorable in having a variety of work, either concurrently or consecutively; a peripatetic career can be as remunerative and often more satisfying than the single-minded pursuit of only one kind of work.

Choosing a career should be done only if one wants a career.

## FINANCING THAT COLLEGE DEGREE

Keep in mind that public universities may not be the cheapest schools. Public institutions rely on government money. It is only a limited amount, and they are not at liberty or likely to give complete scholarships. A private university may have an endowment fund and be able to afford anything from a partial to a complete scholarship.

Fill out the Free Application for Federal Student Aid. This will determine how much your family is expected to contribute to your child's tuition. Make sure you check with the admissions officer about *all* the scholarship possibilities. (At the University of Rochester in New York, any student with a combined SAT score of 1350 or above is guaranteed a $5,000 to $10,000 annual scholarship.) The advice from Peterson's (the people who put out the great college and career guides) is that the less-selective schools tend to be the most generous with scholarship money. Look for schools where your student will be in the top 25 percent of all applicants. Look for schools with good regional reputations but little national visibility, such as Lewis and Clark College in Portland, Oregon. Their names may not be well known, but they are academically sound and you are more likely to find smaller classes. With high grades from a smaller college it is always possible to move to a bigger institution with more scholarship money.

The library is a good place to start looking for scholarship money. Check out the College Board's *College Cost Explorer Fund Finder*, which will help you match interests and talents with available scholarships. Look for private grants. Many civic groups, private foundations, professional organizations, and corporations award grants. Westinghouse gives out from $1,000 to $40,000 in science awards. Coca-Cola also gives out awards.

➡ *Haggle!* There is more competition for students these days, and sometimes you can play one school against another. It may sound petty, but it is an ancient tradition and I doubt you'll surprise anyone if you do it.

Before filling out an application for college or financial aid, look in the library for the following books. They will help you make the most of your financial situation, whether you are in dire need of financial help or have enough income so you don't think you qualify for help. Look in the Princeton Review's *Student Access Guide to Paying for College*, by Kalman Chany, and the College Board's *College Costs and Financial Aid Handbook*.

## FINDING SCHOLARSHIP $$$$$$

For scholarship searches on the Internet, use FastWeb.com (www.fastweb.com), which is a FREE web service. It will match your student with appropriate scholarships. There is a fairly lengthy registration process, but you can't expect good results without completing all the possibly pertinent information. FastWeb has a database of 180,000 scholarships and will deposit the results *and* future updates to your personal mailbox. With help like this, there is every reason to believe you will find some financial help.

The federal Department of Education has a "student gateway to the U.S. government," www.students.gov, where you can find information about planning and preparing for two- and four-year programs; applying for student aid, including federal, state, and private sources of grants, scholarships, and loans; how to repay those loans; and testing.

**WINNING MONEY FOR COLLEGE**, by Alan Deutschman, a Princeton University graduate who graduated debt-free! Dissatisfied with Peterson's guides? Deutschman writes about where to find alternative, additional sources of money based on talent and achievements. Many privately sponsored sources are listed. 205 pages. Code PTR, $12.95.

## ODDBALL SCHOLARSHIPS

Check these out and then do some research of your own. Anything is possible! List from the *Christian Science Monitor*, July 10, 1996.

➡ Gertrude J. Deppen Scholarship at Bucknell University, awarded to a teetotaling, non-smoking resident of Mt. Carmel, Pennsylvania, who doesn't like sports.

➡ Beckley Scholarship Foundation: $700 to left-handers at Juniata College.

➡ Evans Scholarship Program: full tuition and housing for seniors in the top 25% of their class who have caddied for two years at a golf club.

➡ Antique Weapons Research Fellowship: $5,000 to students willing to write a scholarly report on antique weapons to be published in the American Society of Arms Collectors bulletin.

➡ Two/Ten International Footwear Foundation: $2,000 awarded to children of footwear industry workers.

➡ The Billy Barty Foundation: $2,000 to "students of short stature."

➡ United Daughters of the Confederacy Scholarship: $400 to $1,500 awarded to descendants of Confederate soldiers.

**SCHOLARSHIPS, GRANTS AND PRIZES**, a Peterson's guide. Lists more than 2,200 programs offering more than 800,000 awards, and some of these are in the wacky list above. The list may seem funny, but it might get you where you want to go, and you'll have the last laugh. Who says you have to take money seriously? 540 pages. Code PTR, $26.95.

**COLLEGE MONEY HANDBOOK**, a Peterson's guide. One of the best, and this one tells you about the things you don't know that might hurt you. 717 pages. Includes the *Access Advisor* CD-ROM disk to help you estimate costs. Code PTR, $26.95.

You can find out about student loans for college by writing: U.S. Department of Education, 400 Maryland Ave. SW, Room 2097, Washington, DC 20202.

Free financial aid information from the U.S. Department of Education: grants, loans, and work-study programs, and much more. Worth writing to the Consumer Information Center, Dept 506 X, Pueblo, CO 81009. Request the booklet "Financial Aid From the U.S. Department of Education: Grants, Loans, and Work Study."

Free information about whether you're eligible for student aid. Request "Meeting College Costs" from College Board Publications, Bibliography of Financial Aid, 45 Columbus Ave., New York, NY 10023.

**FINDING MONEY FOR COLLEGE**, by John Bear, Ph.D., and Mariah Bear, M.A. Includes much standard stuff and a lot of ideas no one else has mentioned. 168 pages. Code TSP, $8.95.

## INTERNSHIP AND MENTORING PROGRAMS

**THE NATIONAL DIRECTORY OF INTERNSHIPS** offers opportunities for undergraduates, graduates, high school students, and others. More than 600 pages; more than 85 fields of interest. National Society for Experiential Education, 3509 Haworth Dr., Suite 207, Raleigh, NC 26709.

## OTHER ALTERNATIVES

**VOCATIONAL AND TECHNICAL SCHOOLS**, a Peterson's guide for those who are following dreams and have chosen not to go to college. Peterson quotes a study that shows vocational and technical graduates earn more money than two-year college graduates. Within these 640 pages you'll find a guide to 5,000 skills-training programs. Details include tuition, financial aid, apprenticeship programs, and more. Code PTR, $34.95. Specify east or west of the Mississippi River.

***Revised* — THE COMPLETE GUIDE TO ENVIRONMENTAL CAREERS IN THE 21ST CENTURY**, by the Environmental Careers Organization. Very comprehensive overview of the entire range of environmental career fields: parks, outdoor recreation, air and water quality management, education and communication, land and water conservation, fisheries and wildlife management, forestry, and more. This is probably the most complete and reliable source of information today for students, recent college graduates, volunteers, career counselors, and anyone interested in working to protect the environment. 464 pages, with photos and a good index. Code IP, $17.95.

**Travel and Get Paid for It**. Eight-week training course for many aspects of hospitality and travel industries — hotels, motels, airlines, steamships, etc. Classes taught by training staff from Hilton, Sheraton, TWA, Princess Cruises, etc. The school claims 92% job placement after graduation. I wouldn't recommend this work for a lifetime career for creative people, but there are often temporary work positions in these fields that might enable young people to receive substantial discounts or even be paid for traveling. Write for information: Echols International and Travel School, 303 E. Ohio St., Chicago, IL 60611.

**CAREERS IN CAMPING**. Pamphlet describing several professional camp jobs (administrator, trip leader, program director, etc.), with advice on the necessary training and how to get it, where to find the jobs, etc. Free from the American Camping Association, Bradford Woods, 5000 State Road 67 N., Martinsville, IN 46151.

**NANNIE NETWORK, INC.,** 6700 Cabot Drive, #L-11, Nashville, TN; 877-626-6963. Teenage and young adult women are placed in homes around the country to work five or five-and-a-half days a week, about ten hours per day, caring for children and doing light housekeeping (preparation of children's meals, laundry, and "generally helping to maintain the household"; no heavy housework.) A one-year commitment is usually required, but shorter terms are sometimes available. Live as a member of the family, and receive a minimum weekly salary, paid vacation (usually one or two weeks), room and board, free time during evenings and weekends, and sometimes use of a car. The Nannie Network matches applicants with host families; no placement fees are charged. Write or phone for more information, application, and reference forms.

**AUDUBON EXPEDITION INSTITUTE** (affiliated with Lesley College) offers great opportunities to travel, work, and study. Mission statement: "To inspire, educate, and transform students into informed, skilled, creative, and compassionate leaders who effect, through their initiative and global vision, the conservation of all life." For the adventurous and committed student. Write for a catalog: Audubon Expedition Institute, P.O. Box 365, Belfast, ME 04915; 207-338-5859; www.getonthebus.org. Ask about their informational video.

**WORK YOUR WAY AROUND THE WORLD**. A Peterson's guide to finding the right jobs, either prearranged or on the spot. Detailed listings. 528 pages. Code PTR, $17.95.

**TEACHING ENGLISH ABROAD**. Another Peterson's guide; offers a country-by-country look at employers, job requirements, working conditions, and details on 200 training courses. 478 pages. Code PTR, $16.95.

**ADVENTURE CAREERS: Your Guide to Exciting Jobs, Uncommon Occupations, and Extraordinary Experiences**, by Alexander Hiam and Susan Angle. How to get a grant to teach public health in Nepal, apply to the Peace Corps, work on a kibbutz, support yourself during a year of travel through Europe or Africa, and much more. Lots of practical how-to information, lists of contacts and phone numbers, and firsthand accounts of experiences of a number of teen and young adult adventurers who didn't want just a "secure" and comfortable career niche. Teens and adults. Code CP, $11.99.

# BIRTHING AND BABIES

## Pregnancy, Nursing, Early Parenting

## Pro/Anti-Choice

This chapter contains resources for birthing and parenting. Our ideas about parenting have frequently differed from the norm. Our ideas about childbirth are our own. The piece below, **OUR WAY**, is our story. It is intended as something to consider and think about. Our approach was right for us in the late '60s and early '70s, and we would probably take this approach again now. Today, you have many more birthing options available to you than we had more than thirty years ago. Currently, midwives are reputable and available, doctors and medical attitudes about birth have changed, and the special birthing facilities at the hospital no longer seem to be holdovers from the Middle Ages. The most important decision you'll make about how you want to give birth should be based upon what will make you feel the most comfortable.

### OUR WAY

When Jean and I were expecting our first baby, in 1966, there was very little literature about natural birth. We had read enough to know that we wanted an undrugged birth, but we took for granted the "necessity" of birth in a hospital.

From the beginning, we felt that both the pregnancy and the birth were *ours*, together. All we asked was permission for me to be present during the labor and delivery.

"Oh, no," the doctor said. "We have enough problems without having fainting husbands all over the floor."

So Jean and I decided, tentatively, to have the baby at home. We began studying all the books we could find on childbirth, gynecology, and relaxation techniques (mainly yoga). We left the question of "where" open to the last minute. We bought and familiarized ourselves with the few supplies necessary for a home birth, but kept our suitcases packed, ready to throw into the car. If either of us felt even a little insecure or worried about having the baby at home, we'd go to the hospital.

The time came and we felt fine. We tingled with anticipation and quiet excitement. The labor was a typical 18-hour, first-baby labor: tiring, but completely without pain. Throughout the labor, I stayed with Jean, rubbing her back, moistening her lips, and being a brace for her legs — except for the few times when I tried to find food for myself. Each time I put on a pot of coffee or a pan of beans, another contraction began and I ran back to help.

Cathy was born in a little log cabin in northern Vermont, forty miles from the nearest hospital. She began nursing right away, while I massaged Jean's uterus to reduce the possibility of excessive bleeding. The only thing that went wrong with Cathy's birth was that I burned three pans of beans and boiled away six pots of coffee.

Karen was born in 1968 in our home in Vermont, with six feet of snow drifted outside the windows. This birth was not only painless, but very actively pleasurable. We had never read about this aspect of birth, and it took us both by surprise. What a long way from the pain and agony of conventional myth! (Years later, a sympathetic doctor said, "Yes, I've seen it a few times. It may even be that many women have orgasms during birth, but interpret them as pain, because the sensations are more intense than anything they've experienced previously, and because they have been conditioned to expect pain.")

Susan was born in 1970 and Derek in 1972, both in a log cabin in the mountainous Central Interior of British Columbia, also forty miles from the nearest hospital. Both births were work, but relatively easy, completely painless, and physically pleasurable.

I was lucky. With each of our four children, I had a period of about a month with Braxton-Hicks contractions coming about every other day and lasting about an hour or two — gentle practice, warm-up exercises for the labor to come. The only problem with these contractions was deciding if I was truly in labor or not. Did we dare go to town or go visiting, or should we stay at home, just in case?

Cathy came easily. I worked hard, but the labor was so gradually progressive I stayed completely relaxed, totally focused inward and aware of all the new and different sensations and of all the muscles working in harmony, performing the job they were designed to do, without interruption or interference.

We put the camera out with the birth supplies and forgot about it! My only regret over the years is that I didn't take a picture of Donn holding Cathy right after she was born. Like a variation of the Madonna and child, Donn glowed. He was totally enraptured. He was so caught up in the wonder of the experience that when I asked him if we had a girl or a boy, he just stared at me, his face suddenly, totally, blank. To him, at that moment, it was completely irrelevant. He hadn't looked!

Cathy came gently and gradually into this world; Karen, I swear, came into this world pushing with her feet! I had the usual warm-up contractions on and off for a month. The day she was born, I had contractions just before lunch, and knowing we were close to the birthing time, I didn't eat but fixed lunch for Donn, Cathy, and Mother (Donn's). We expected this second labor to be shorter, but didn't feel we could give Cathy, two and a half years old, all the attention she might need without interrupting my concentration. Mother was good enough to come and stay with us.

I decided that labor was "for real" while cleaning up after lunch. Mother took Cathy to the neighbor's and planned to come back in an hour or two. Shortly after they left, I began to feel the urge to push. I told Donn and he laughed at me! He said he'd start getting things ready soon. I told him I didn't think we should wait. He looked at me and decided this wasn't the time for a debate; he would just "humor me" — and I knew he was humoring me. As we started fixing the bed together, I told him that with the next contraction I was going to lie down and he could just humor me a bit more and take a look to see what, if anything, was happening. With the next contraction, I did, and he did, and I will admit that both of us were surprised to find that the baby's head was beginning to crown. We did get the bed set, just barely in time. Now the contractions were really strong. I love the urge to push. I don't think there is anything else in the world that is so totally compelling and feels so completely right. I had two pushing contractions on the bed and Karen came into the world — and with the most incredible orgasm. This took Donn and me by surprise. Just like our lovemaking, it was a feeling of Life celebrating Life. It seemed so very unfair that Donn couldn't be a part of that, too.

We tried telling people about our experience. Many thought us liars. A few women patted me condescendingly on the shoulder and told me I didn't have to make up stories. To those who were truly interested and asked what made the experience so extraordinary for me, I've always answered: my ability to feel completely relaxed and at one with myself, my sexuality, the natural process of birth, my husband, and the order and wonder of the universe.

Here's Derek before he's even a minute old.

Some people have wondered how we could let our young children witness birth. Brought up to see birth as a natural process, and having witnessed animal birthings, with only minimal explanation they understood what they might hear and see. As children will do, they adopted our attitude and found there was nothing to fear — there was only the wonder and magic of seeing a baby come forth. See how the girls have their hands out?

**AS YOU EAT, SO YOUR BABY GROWS**, by Nikki Goldbeck. A 16-page guide to nutrition during pregnancy, endorsed by La Leche League and others. Order from Ceres Press, P.O. Box 87, Woodstock, NY 12498. Request a list of their books and ordering information.

***Revised 4th edition* — HUSBAND-COACHED CHILDBIRTH**, by Robert A. Bradley, M.D.; foreword by Ashley Montagu. In 1966, when our first daughter was born, a husband's participation in childbirth was considered very radical; today, in many areas at least, it has become common. This book is one of the very best in discussing the father's role and the ways in which his presence and participation contribute during both pregnancy and childbirth. We recommend this book very highly to all couples expecting a baby.

This was the book I relied on the most. I read and reread it before the birth of each of our children. Bradley has great common sense and a natural, relaxed approach to birthing; he conveys confidence in the naturalness of pregnancy and birth, and the rightful place of the father during this time. The new edition has added sections about different birthing methods, natural prevention and healing for common problems associated with pregnancy, and a chapter called "Daddy Helped Born Me." Code DD, $12.95. To find out more about the Bradley Method of birthing, write: Husband-Coached Childbirth, Box 5224, Sherman Oaks, CA 91413; 800-4ABIRTH; www.bradleymethod.com.

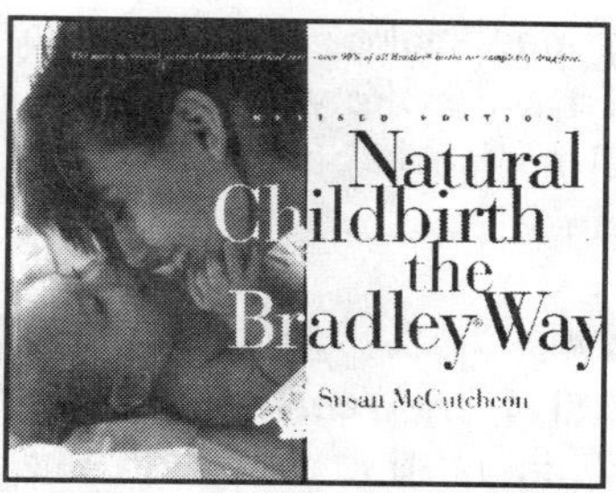


**NATURAL CHILDBIRTH THE BRADLEY WAY**. Cathy assures me that this book is much like *Husband-Coached Childbirth*, containing the same basic information, but that it appeals to women more than men. I trust Cathy's judgment. I know she's had good reason to research this very carefully. Code BT, $17.95. P.S. She just gave birth to a baby boy last March using the Bradley Method. It was a wonderful experience for her and her husband.

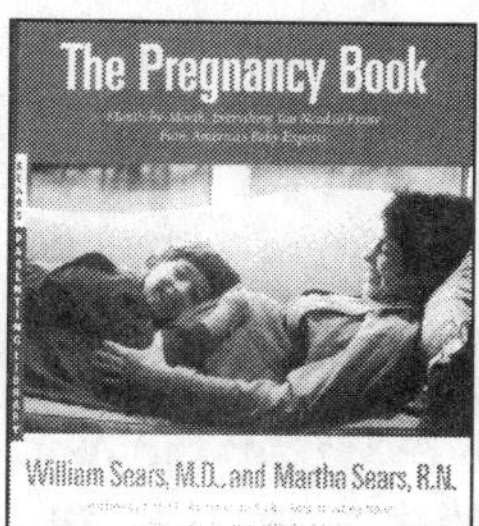


**THE PREGNANCY BOOK**, by William Sears, M.D., and Martha Sears, R.N. A very thorough nutritional and physical guide to use when you're pregnant. Many insightful comments about how to enjoy this special time as well as how to cope with various physical problems that may occur. There is some general discussion about different methods of childbirth, along with a note emphasizing that each woman is different and that it is essential to do your homework about various methods, basing your decision on what will be right for you. Code BT, $21.95.

**THE BIRTH BOOK: Everything You Need to Know to Have a Safe and Satisfying Birth**, by William Sears, M.D., and Martha Sears, R.N., authors of *The Baby Book* (listed below). A wonderful, very complete guide to birthing. Many approaches are examined, including VBAC (vaginal birth after cesarean). A history of birthing; choices in childbirth; getting your body ready; tests, technology, and other interventions that happen on the way to birth; cesarean births; easing pain in labor; why birth hurts and why it doesn't have to; relaxing for birth; how the doctor can help; best birth positions; labor and delivery; composing your birth plan; and real birth stories. Up-to-date and thorough. I'd use it if I were ever going to have another baby. Code BT, $13.95.

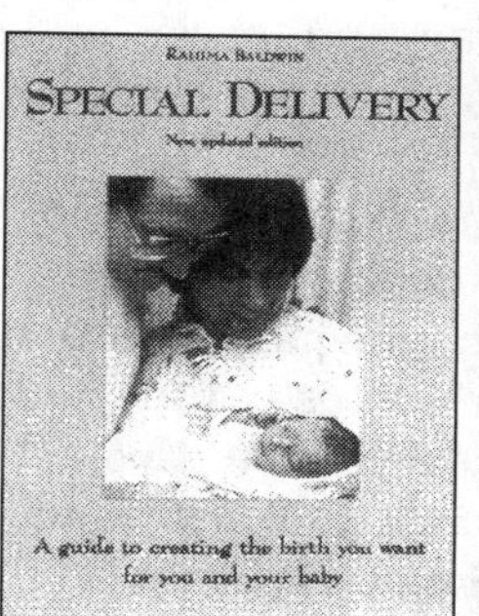


**SPECIAL DELIVERY: The Complete Guide to Informed Birth**, by Rahima Baldwin Dancy. For couples who want to take greater responsibility for the birth of their baby, whether at home, at a birth center, or in the hospital. Times have changed, and fortunately many doctors and hospitals are finally changing. Pregnancy and birth are seen as a natural process. The focus of this book is on people rather than technology or methodology. A great book to help you figure out what will be best for you. 8½x11", with photographs, a bibliography, an index, and drawings. Code TSP, $18.95.

**GENTLE BIRTH CHOICES**, by Barbara Harper, R.N. Boxed set. The book is a guide to making informed decisions about birthing centers, birth attendants, water birth, home birth, and hospital birth. It provides good information about a model of maternity care that reduces the need for high-tech crisis intervention and focuses instead on preparation and good health for mother and child. The book has illustrations and birth photos. The video includes six actual natural births demonstrating different positions and techniques. Code IT, $39.95. Book only $16.95.

**40 WEEKS TO MOTHERHOOD** — a great poster. See "Science".

"One of the problems in our culture is that we do not like the act of birth. We avoid talking about the process. Too many women fear it — endure it. The secret to a satisfying birth is to embrace it, not escape from it. If we prepare for birth spiritually, mentally, and physically, and then welcome birth as a natural, beautiful event, childbirth becomes a whole new opportunity for joy." Page 20 of **UNASSISTED HOMEBIRTH: An Act of Love**, by Lynn Griesemer, available from Terra Publishing, P.O. Box 80514, Charleston, SC 29416-0514. The word "unassisted" means giving birth out of the hospital and frequently without a trained attendant. Even if you plan a hospital birth, this book will help you explore your own conditioning and attitudes. It can inspire you to have a better birthing experience anywhere.

**A CHILD IS BORN: The Drama of Life Before Birth**. Photographs by Lennart Nilsson; text by Jirjam Furuhjelm, Axel Ingelman-Sundberg, and Claes Wirsen. This is an awesomely beautiful photographic record of life developing inside the womb, from conception to birth, and of birth itself. Children and adults will feel as if they're gazing into a magical world with all the full-color photos in this new hardcover edition. Imagine: This is what you looked like inside your mother when you were five weeks old. Code DD, $29.95 hardcover, $19.95 paperback.

I just read Laura Shanley's book **UNASSISTED CHILDBIRTH**. It's been so long since we had our last birthing that I'd forgotten a lot of the reasons we had chosen to birth at home, besides the fact that we wanted to be together. It was an eye-opener all over again. Well-researched facts about how women give birth, and why the experience can be so degrading and depressing as well as physically, mentally, and emotionally exhausting for some, with unnecessary complications caused by the very people who are supposedly helping. Many excellent examples of how birth should be and could be better. The publisher says it's out of print, but you can get a copy directly from Laura for $18, if you don't wait too long. She has only a limited number. Laura Shanley, 760 36th St., Boulder, CO 80303. For more information about unassisted childbirth, see Laura Shanley's website: www.unassistedchildbirth.com.

**NEW NATURAL PREGNANCY: Practical Wellbeing From Conception to Birth**, by Janet Balaskas. A reassuring and empowering book that pays tribute to the psychological and emotional changes and growth that occur during this time — a nice contrast to the books that focus on the physical aspects of pregnancy and birth — with numerous constructive ideas for coping with these changes. It offers a good yoga routine, massage techniques, nutrition advice, natural therapies for preventing and healing common problems, and holistic healing ideas. Beautiful photos and good drawings. I like it. Code BT, $15.

Much important and interesting information about birth and parenting is available from Informed Birth, P.O. Box 3675, Ann Arbor, MI 48106. Write for information.

You will be able to find great online resources for pregnancy, birth, nursing, and much more at www.monarch-design.com/baby/index.html.

**YOGA FOR PREGNANCY** by Wendy Teasdill. Gentle, risk-free exercises to help prepare you for birthing and a speedy recovery. Color illustrations and clear explanations make this easy to use. Staying fit will make your pregnancy easier, and you will feel so much better before, during, and after birth. Code KT, $15.95.

**PRENATAL YOGA AND NATURAL BIRTH**, by Jeannine Parvati Baker. This is the story of one woman's growth and experiences through four birthings (one a set of twins) in the hospital and at home. If you are already doing yoga this book will help you make the most of your physical and spiritual journey through pregnancy and birth. I feel you should already be familiar with and practicing yoga to get the most out of this very unusual and spiritual book. Jeannine says of her last birth, "I had prepared somewhat for this being painful as my last delivery had been. Yet this time the pulse of birth feels wonderful! I am building up to the birth climax after nine months of pleasurable foreplay. With one push the baby is in the canal. The next push brings him down, down into that space just before orgasm when we women know how God must have felt creating this planet." A book for the open-minded. Code FP, $10.

**THE BABY CHRONICLES**. Make your own permanent record, beginning with your third trimester and continuing through your baby's first year. Lots of questions are asked with blank spaces for you to fill in, so your calendar becomes a very personal record. There are places for pictures (Mom — before, during, and after pregnancy), helpful hints on each page, comical illustrations, and lots of stickers to mark special events (last toe sighting, baby's first bath, first smile, etc.). Code LB, $10.95.

**MOTHERING MAGAZINE**. One of the leading international magazines devoted to natural childbirth, breastfeeding, child-rearing, and midwifery. Covers family issues; pros and cons of vaccination, dental care, discipline, childhood illnesses, and baby supplies. Bimonthly. $18.95 per year, add $5 for foreign addresses. P.O. Box 1690, Santa Fe, NM 98504-9774; 800-984-8166.

**WELCOME HOME**. Not a homeschooling publication but supportive of women making the transition from the work force to being home all the time with their children. Published monthly. Sample copy $2; call for a free info packet. 8310A Old Courthouse Rd., Vienna, VA 22182; 800-783-4666; wh@mah.org.

**La Leche League International**, P.O. Box 4079, Schaumburg, IL 60168, is an international organization with branches in 60 countries. They offer a wonderful array of books and information about breastfeeding, birthing, and parenting, with some special books for fathers, whole foods, and other related subjects. Their free catalog is exciting. Among many other excellent books, they have the classic **THE WOMANLY ART OF BREASTFEEDING**, which I highly recommend. If you live in Canada, ask about their main Canadian office and resources in your province.

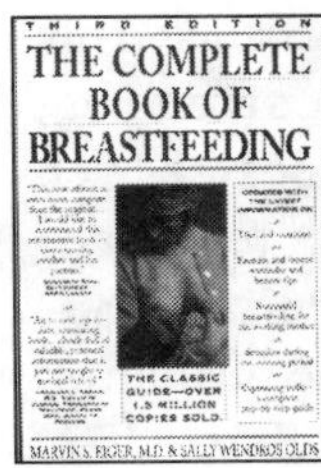


*Revised* — **THE COMPLETE BOOK OF BREASTFEEDING**, by Marvin S. Eiger, M.D., and Sally Wendkos Olds; completely revised. This book is now a recognized classic even by the American Academy of Pediatrics, which now recommends exclusive breastfeeding for the first six months and thereafter as long as mother and child desire. Advice and information on every aspect of breastfeeding, including how immunity of the mother transfers to the baby, cognitive development, sexuality, special needs of single and working mothers, the role of the father, drugs, exercise, nutrition, nursing premature babies, and an expanded resource section. If you're considering breastfeeding you need this book. Even though we were convinced breastfeeding was the natural way to feed a baby, this book gave us a multitude of scientific reasons to do so and offered solutions to various common problems. Code WKM, $10.95.

**THE BREASTFEEDING BOOK: Everything You Need to Know About Nursing Your Child From Birth Through Weaning**, by Martha Sears, R.N., and William Sears, M.D. The Searses' book is a combination of medical knowledge and experience — they've raised eight children. This book contains the same information as the one listed above, but with the addition of the attachment parenting perspective. Rather than talk about the "role of the father," the Searses assume Dad will be an intricate part of pregnancy, birthing, and child-rearing. Mom, if you're a single parent or if you feel like you're doing the child-rearing mostly by yourself, get the book above. If raising your children will be a joint project, then this is the book you want. Code BT, $14.95.

**GAMES TO PLAY WITH BABIES**, by Jackie Silberg. Here are some stimulating ideas for things to do with your little ones from birth to one year. Chapters include games for growing and learning, games for bonding, kitchen games, laughing and fun games, arts and singing games, finger and toe games, bath and dressing games, and going to sleep games. Code GH, $14.95.

***New Edition*** — **YOU ARE YOUR CHILD'S FIRST TEACHER**, by Rahima Baldwin Dancy. In a time when most parents are bombarded with scores of approaches to "raising" their children, this book introduces a way of insight and understanding that will be very welcome to many. Chapters include "Caring for the Newborn," "Helping Your Toddler's Development," "The Development of Fantasy and Creative Play," "Nourishing Your Child's Imagination," "Rhythm," and "Discipline in Home Life." Black-and-white photos, 396 pages. Code TSP, $14.95. This is among the books we have given (or will give at the appropriate time) to our children.

**WHOLE CHILD/WHOLE PARENT**, by Polly Berrien Berrends. "Once I had a dream," the author says in her introduction. "In the dream I was to receive a diploma as a spiritual teacher or guide of some sort. ... But before me there stood an enormous mountain of laundry. To receive my diploma I would first have to climb over this huge heap of laundry."

Many books tell you how to clothe, feed, amuse, and educate your children; many others tell you of ways to indoctrinate your children with particular beliefs, or to "modify" their behavior according to your wishes. This book will lead you on an exciting path of discovery of the wholeness, the one-ness, of you and your children and of all aspects of your lives together. The usual subjects — clothing, diaper rash, toys, books, playtime, discipline — of most child-care books are here, but with an entirely different perspective. They are thoughtfully and lovingly considered from a viewpoint of truth — not the dogmatic "truth" of a particular creed that must be taught, but the inner essence of being that is discovered and experienced. *Whole Child / Whole Parent* is a book to browse in frequently, to keep next to the window for rainy-day reading and on the nightstand for the last thoughts before sleeping. A classic book we will give each of our children at the appropriate time. Code HC, $17.

**THE BABY BOOK: Everything You Need to Know About Your Baby From Birth to Age Two**, by William Sears, M.D., and Martha Sears, R.N. Forget Dr. Spock! This book is the best one available to help you and your baby begin your lives together. This book favors attachment parenting, "and if Dad doesn't realize how important he is in the first few years of life, this book will get him involved — and he'll love it." The Searses say, "There is really no such thing as one best way to parent a baby, just as there are no perfect babies and, would you believe, no perfect parents. ... Being a parent requires on-the-job training. Too much advice from 'experts' can ... interfere with the beginning parents' intuition. ... We are going to show you how to become your own experts." The book begins with a definition of attachment parenting and then moves on through birthing, preparing for baby, getting the right start, postpartum family adjustments, and common concerns during the first few weeks. The next section deals with feeding your baby. Although the Searses favor breastfeeding, they also recognize that for various reasons some women can't or don't want to breastfeed. This section has excellent information about feeding your baby with safety and love if you are not nursing. Then comes a large section of the book devoted to parenting: carrying your baby, nighttime parenting, fussy or colicky babies and how to help them, and a lot more. Good suggestions for working parents, the adopted baby, twins, special-needs babies, and mixing babies and pets. (This last topic gave me a chuckle; this section is divided between "Have Pet — Add Baby" and "Have Baby — Add Pet.") Part IV is about infant development and behavior through the toddler years and toilet training. Part V focuses on health and safety. 686 pages with a good index. Code BT, $21.95.

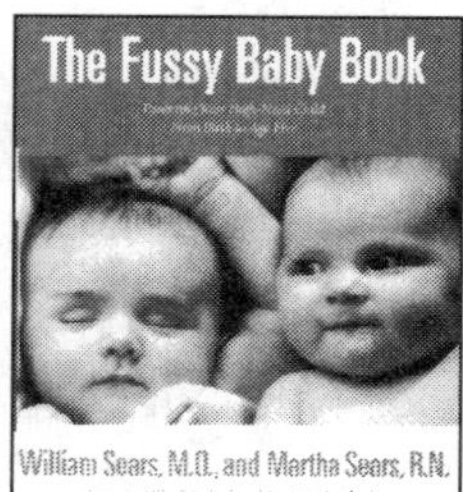


**THE FUSSY BABY BOOK: Parenting Your High-Need Child From Birth to Age Five**, by William Sears, M.D., and Martha Sears, R.N. This is not about children with disabilities. This book is about healthy children with more needs than the average baby. The "fussy" baby is more intense than most babies, is hyperactive, feeds frequently, awakens frequently, is unpredictable, doesn't like to be put down, and more. A fussy baby is demanding, unsatisfied, and very difficult for parents. After having three "normal" babies, the Searses' fourth baby was "fussy," and at first they felt responsible; then they paid more attention to what this child needed and realized the difference was in the child. Filled with wonderful and loving suggestions for dealing with your "high-need" child and for taking care of your own needs at the same time. Code BT, $12.95.

**NURTURING**. An international journal to encourage attachment parenting. A must for parents seeking information and support. If you really want to be close to your children and understand their needs and how to fulfill your needs too, you will treasure this magazine. You'll find articles on birth, breastfeeding, emotional issues, and health. Of all the magazines for parents I've seen, this one comes closest to representing our feelings and philosophy about raising children. Ads for baby- and parent-friendly products. Write for sample issue: 3213 W. Main, Suite 153, Rapid City, SD 57702; TNParent@aol.com; www.nurturing.ca

**NATURAL CHILDHOOD**, by John Thomson. An analytic and holistic look at parenting and childhood. I think this book begins with too much discussion of conventional psychoanalytic theories demonstrating the development of current understanding of childhood development over the past century. However, if you're not familiar with these theories, it's good background. I started getting excited when Thomson moved on to presenting an overview of thoughts about childhood by Eric Fromm, Erik Erikson, A.S. Neill, Jean Piaget, Joseph Chilton Pearce, and others. Thomson states in his introduction that this book was written "in defense of childhood." Certainly in this day and age childhood needs defending. In spite of a plethora of parenting books, prenatal and postnatal services, toys, playgrounds, Head Start programs, special baby foods, etc., the real lives of children are too frequently ignored in favor of what will serve our materialistic society. Childhood is all too often not valued for itself. Reading Thomson will stimulate your thinking about the prenatal development of a baby, effective postnatal communication on a child's terms, creative play, health and healing, education, and schooling. Thompson introduces you to this century's innovators in education, including John Holt, Rudolf Steiner, Maria Montessori, and others. He presents an overview of some alternative schools (including human-scale education) and homeschooling. There is an extensive list of books for further reading about parenting and education; addresses for craft supplies, toys and games, musical instruments, and natural-fiber clothing; special-needs resources; and much more. I enjoyed my journey through this book and found many well-expressed ideas, some that were new to me. I also disagreed with some things, but agree or disagree, I found the book thought-provoking and stimulating. An exceptional resource for those about to be parents and those with young children, as well as those of us interested in exploring childhood in greater depth. Code SS, $20.

**NATURAL PARENTING: A Practical Guide for Fathers and Mothers: Conception to Age 3**, by Peter and Fiona Walker. I wish we'd had this when our children were young. Sound advice about developing the best attitudes toward pregnancy, birth, and developing family bonds. Breathtaking photos of developing babies in the uterus. Excellent massage and yoga exercises for pre- and postnatal well-being for mother, father, and baby. Very important proactive things a father can do for his wife during pregnancy and birth. Also a section on teaching your baby to be at home in the water and learning to swim. Code BT, $12.95.

**PRO/ANTI-CHOICE**

As I've said elsewhere, I sometimes send contributions to the World Wildlife Fund, Amnesty International, UNICEF, and similar organizations.

My small contributions of money or effort should indicate that I'm opposed to nuclear war; pollution of the earth; the torture and unlawful imprisonment of peaceful civilians; and the slaughter of whales, elephants, and dolphins.

As mailing lists get traded around, other organizations solicit my support, having inferred, through some sort of logic I can't follow, that my opposition to wanton slaughter of animals and to irresponsible use of the earth means I also favor the killing of babies.

The few churches that still believe in the sanctity of life — human life, at least — oppose abortion, so pro-abortionists claim it's a religious issue only, and therefore protected by the First Amendment.

Does the study of law include a study of logic? The writers of the First Amendment, reacting in part to the theocratic monarchies of Europe, stipulated that the federal government may not establish a religion, so today's students of law and justice infer that "separation of church and state" means the government should have no jurisdiction over the subject of abortion — because, they say, it's a religious matter.

Most religions also oppose suicide, stealing, and murder. Does that mean governmental legislation on these issues constitutes interference in religious matters? If the killing of unborn babies is a "personal" or "religious" matter, and therefore protected by the First Amendment, how long will it be before the killing of an unwanted five-year-old is also a "personal" or "religious" matter?

Those who say abortion should be made legal because women will get abortions anyway (and shouldn't be "forced" to risk their lives with illegal methods), might as well use the same argument for speeding on the highway, robbing banks, and forcing children into prostitution. The logical extension of their argument is that some people will do those things anyway, so let's make them legal.

In most cases, once conception has taken place, a choice has been made, whether carelessly or deliberately. From that moment on, there are many choices and decisions to be made, but murder should not be one of them. Killing a baby isn't made into something less by hiding it under a bushel of evasive impersonal euphemisms such as "fetus" and "product of conception."

Now you know why I just drop some of my mail into the wastebasket. And I'll even risk being put on a right-wing mailing list by suggesting that if you think killing unborn people is wrong, write to the National Right to Life Committee, 419 7th Street NW, Suite 500, Washington, D.C. 20004, to learn more about what's being done about it and what can be done.

# FAMILY LIVING — SIMPLE LIVING

## CONFLICT RESOLUTION
## HOMESTEADING AND GARDENING
## SUMMER AND TRAVEL OPPORTUNITIES

**JOURNAL OF FAMILY LIFE** is a quarterly magazine with a minimum of advertising and a broad range of interesting articles about family life and community, published by the Free School in Albany, New York. Articles feature interviews or written work by provocative thinkers with ideas that directly concern family issues. There's also some poetry and written work submitted by readers. The issue I've just read contains an interview with Grace Llewellyn, a thoughtful story of one family's coming-of-age ceremony for their son, an interview with Joseph Chilton Pearce, and a book review about the dangers inherent in using Ritalin for ADD, among the many other articles I enjoyed. They have a health column, book reviews, a wisdom tale, and other regular features. Single issue $6 plus $2 postage. Subscriptions $22 per year. (Add $8 for overseas delivery.) More information: *Journal of Family Life*, 22 Elm St., Albany, NY 12202; jflmag@aol.com; www.empireone.net/~freeschool.

**THE SIMPLE LIVING GUIDE**, by Janet Luhrs, begins with a quote from Thoreau about simple living, and I thought I would simplify my life, reduce my heating bill, and burn the book. I wasn't impressed with her application of Thoreau's thoughts, but since it arrived as a gift from Cathy, I gave it a second chance. First, Luhrs explains that simple living does not necessarily mean poverty and deprivation. She then goes into depth about how to become more aware of your priorities and how to achieve them. Good financial advice, with lots of resources listed. Enjoyable reading. I'm still not in agreement with her use of Thoreau, but the rest of the book makes sense. Code BT, $20.

**VOLUNTARY SIMPLICITY**, by Duane Elgin, is not about living in poverty. It is a book about living within the context of balance with our daily needs (as opposed to wants), global awareness, personal growth, and seeking the richness within our lives. Elgin is very aware that lasting changes in our society will come from individuals making changes in their own lives and not from government, although these changes will eventually be reflected there. Code BT, $10.

**MEMORY SKILLS** will give your kids an advantage when they study. It's a boon for parents and teachers, too. Tips and techniques to improve your memory, then some tests you can give yourself to gauge how well you've done. This will help you get names and faces together correctly, and help with studies and Trivial Pursuit. I won't guarantee that the kids will remember to pick up after themselves, but they should at least remember that you told them to do so. Ages 11 and up. Code EDC, $5.95.

**SURVIVAL SKILLS**. This book provides basic knowledge for survival in a variety of circumstances. (For people like me it should begin with the directive to read *Memory Skills* first, so I'll remember to take my bee-sting kit when I pick berries.) Excellent ideas for putting together your own first-aid kit and knowing what you can do in emergencies. Ages 11 and up. Code EDC, $5.95.

If you really care about survival at home, in town, or in the wilds, enroll everyone in your family, 14 and older, in a CPR course. It doesn't cost much, and that small investment in time can save a life — yours or someone else's. *Survival Skills* won't teach you CPR, but it will be a good beginning.

**KIDS TO THE RESCUE! First Aid Techniques for Kids**, by Maribeth and Darwin Boelts. This book is designed to be used by parents and prereaders together or older children learning the basics of first aid. This is not a complicated book. Very practical, down-to-earth information every child should know so he will not be too frightened to help. They recommend, and I agree, that each section be read, discussed, and then acted out. This book will help your child help others and himself. After assimilating the information, your child will know what to do in certain situations as well as when and how to get help from an adult. Topics covered: bleeding, broken bones, chemical burns in the eye, choking, clothing on fire, dog bite, electric shock, burn, insect sting, nose bleed, poisoning, snake bite, something in the eye, and unconsciousness. This is not an alarming book, and it does not go into gory consequences. Code PP. $7.95.

**THE MERCK MANUAL — HOME EDITION**. How many times have you taken one of your children, or yourself, in to see a doctor and after his exam he has excused himself for a few minutes? Did you know what he was doing? There's a good chance he did not know what the problem was or was unsure of the treatment. It's likely he was consulting the Merck Manual for physicians. It's been the main reference guide for doctors across the country for almost a century. We've used it for years and have been very glad to have it for reference, although we sometimes found the medical terminology difficult to understand. Now it's available written in layman's English all of us can understand. This comprehensive work covers all known diseases and disorders and has in-depth information about symptoms, diagnosis, treatment options, prescriptions, over-the-counter medications, and more. You won't find holistic information here, but it's still very useful. Easy-to-use, illustrated format. Code BT, $29.95 hardcover (1,509 pages), $7.99 paperback (1,620 pages).

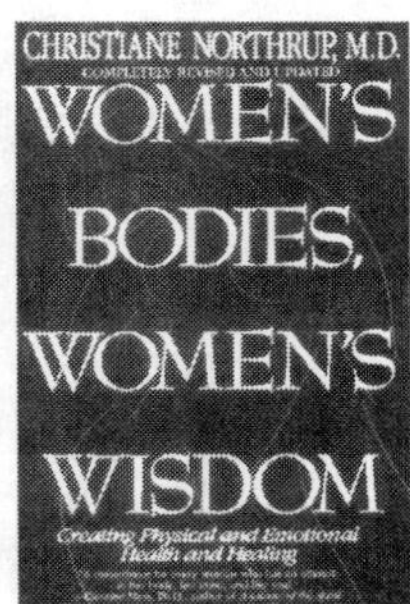


**WOMEN'S BODIES, WOMEN'S WISDOM: Creating Physical and Emotional Health and Healing**, by Christiane Northrup, M.D. A complete reference on women's health, written with wisdom and knowledge, and drawing information about healing from almost all forms of the healing arts. A holistic reference work for holistic women written in terms every woman can understand. It's the first place I turn when I want information about my health. 906 pages, including a good index. Code BT, $17.95. Christiane Northrup supports Public Broadcasting by presenting a variety of workshops during their fund-raising periods. She's a lively speaker. If you can't stand the pledge drives then tape the show so you can fast-forward through the pledge breaks.

**Five Kids and a Monkey**. A three-book series by Nina Riccio for ages 7 to 11. Code CA, $7.95 each. Each book has a unit study guide full of activities, puzzles, and games for $5; no shipping charged for the study guide if ordered with the book, and you can order as many unit study guides as you need.

**SOLVE THE GREAT CUPCAKE CAPER**. Cartoon characters solve a mystery and learn interesting and very useful knowledge about foods, food groups, reading product labels, and how to eat well.

**INVESTIGATE A VICIOUS VIRUS** explains what a virus is, how it works, germs, and the immune system. Made lively with the same set of cartoon kids.

**BANISH THE STINKIES** will make you and your kids smile as you go through this adventure about keeping clean to stay healthy.

**THE FAMILY NUTRITION BOOK: Everything You Need to Know About Feeding Your Children From Birth Through Adolescence**, by William Sears, M.D., and Martha Sears, R.N. Sound advice and good information. There are a few things I disagreed with, but on the whole this is a very sensible book about good food. It's not fanatical. For example, it won't tell you your kids' teeth will rot and fall out if they eat white sugar, but you'll learn about different sugars and their effects on the body. It won't make you feel guilty if you or your kids eat junk food, but it will tell you why some foods are called "junk food." Code BT, $19.

**I AM NOT A SHORT ADULT**, by Marilyn Burns. A Brown Paper School Book about how to make the best of being a kid. Often much of growing up is spent getting ready for what comes next (kindergarten is preparation for first grade and so on). This is a lighthearted book about the serious business of being a kid *right now*, about relationships within the family, money, work, TV, and legal rights. A book for creative thinking about what you can and can't control and how to make the best choices for yourself. Ages 10 to 16. Code LB, $13.95.

**WHAT IS A COMMUNITY? FROM A-Z**. A very good question for all of us to think about. I live in a small rural community where there are a number of community activities. Most of us have more than a nodding acquaintanceship, and when someone needs help the community, as a group, pitches in to help out with whatever is needed. I have lived in the city, where I frequently didn't know who lived next door. I also know that people in some cities have formed "communities" around shared ideas. This book discusses the qualities that make up a community — the people, culture, government, economy, buildings, and services — and how communities are interdependent. It draws the conclusion that our planet Earth is our most important community. Ages 7 to 10. Code CT, $7.95.

I'm not sure if you'll get the following books for yourself, your children, or your parents. Whomever you get them for I'm sure you will all benefit by building a stronger family and deepening the ties and understanding across the generations. When we have lived in small rural communities we have marveled at the cross-generational ties and interaction. Now, with our kids grown and living far away, and with the addition of three young grandchildren, I have a new appreciation of the ties that bind us together. Not so long ago, when the world was less mobile, it was common for several generations to live within easy visiting distance of each other. It is far less common now, but it's just as important, if not more so, that we maintain the continuity of family ties.

**MY GRANDFATHER AND ME** or **MY GRANDMOTHER AND ME**, both written by Jane Drake and Ann Love, are special scrapbooks for kids and grandparents to use together. There are ideas for sharing, collecting, and recording memories. There are spaces for filling in the family tree; for noting likes and dislikes, talents, and special family stories; and lots of room for photos and drawings. There's even a pocket to contain letters and souvenirs, plus a punch-out space on the front cover for a photo of the authors. Ages 5 to 105. Code KC, $4.95.

**KIDS AND GRANDPARENTS: An Activity Book**, by Ann Love and Jane Drake. You can use this book even if the grandparents in your family live across the country — or on the other side of the world. Packed with ideas for things to do and share across the generations by creating together or swapping crafts, recipes, cassette tapes, and more. Ages 6 to 106. Code KC, $10.95.

**SOMETHING TO REMEMBER ME BY**, by Susan Bosak with Laurie McGaw, is a very special book. I debated whether it belonged here or in "Resources for Living With Chronic or Terminal Illness." It's here because although it deals with death, this book is for the living — to keep alive in memory the special people who have touched our lives. The most important thing in all our lives is the love we give and receive, and it is the one and only true lasting legacy. From the book jacket: "It's the little things, the simple things. It's the big, warm smiles and warm snuggly hugs. It's the moments that make memories ... it's a gift that both young and old can give each other. It's the most important gift we can all give. *Something to Remember Me By* is a celebration of the gift of love, and of memories and legacies across generations." Throughout this universal story of a grandmother and her granddaughter over the years, you will find delight for your eyes through the illustrations, it will touch your heart, and it will leave you with a smile and tears. The message is simple: Share the moment. Take the time, now; for what you do today will be your legacy.

Although the story is about a grandmother and granddaughter, you can expand on the ideas presented to include any important family relationship. Each hardcover book comes with a 24-page Reader's Companion with ideas of things to do *together*; of greater importance are the opportunities to discuss relationships, intergenerational bonds, and, if appropriate, death. The last few pages of the guide have a wonderful list of books with intergenerational themes for children and resources for adults. Code CP, $15.95.

**MY FAMILY TREE WORKBOOK**, by Rosemary A. Chorzempa. This book has all the information you or a child 10 or older will need to get started with your genealogy. I like this book because it provides places to write about your personal history: where you were born, schools attended, where you lived, favorite things, family stories, reunions, ethnic heritage, and special notes about ancestors. There's a glossary and a list of places to go for help in your research. A book to keep through the years. Too bad it's a paperback and not hardcover. Code DV, $2.95.

Host an international exchange student through the American Intercultural Student Exchange. Find out more at www.aise.com.

**COMING OF AGE IN AMERICA**. Dr. Margaret Mead contrasts the "shoulds" and "oughts" of traditional childhood and adult development with the realities of our present culture. Particularly of interest to people interested in the cultural background of changing and alternative lifestyles. Although some statements are dated (e.g., prior to the 18-year-old vote), the emphasis on the *quality* of life versus *quantity* is still just as valid. This talk gives a good basic background for understanding many current social issues. A few humorous moments too. 80 minutes; recorded in 1965. Order by title and #35010. Code AF, $12.95.

**HOW PEOPLE CHANGE**. Dr. Margaret Mead describes how our attitude toward change is crucial to our attitude toward the world as a whole, and what is required to effect changes in people and cultures. 25-minute audiocassette. Order by title and #35002. Code AF, $13.95.

**COPING SKILLS FOR PARENTS AND KIDS,**
**or**
**Don't Throw the Baby Out With the Bathwater and Other Very Tempting Solutions**

**WITHOUT SPANKING OR SPOILING: A Practical Approach to Toddler and Preschool Guidance**, by Elizabeth Crary. This book begins with the statement "One of the basic principles of human relationships is that you can change only yourself; however, when you change yourself, you change the relationship." An excellent place to start. This will not be an easy book to work through, but it is a provocative one that can help you create a philosophy of discipline that will be a positive experience for you and your children. Crary presents information from several schools of thought: Parent Effectiveness Training, behavior modification, transactional analysis, and the Adlerian-Dreikurs approach. She recognizes that each person is unique, and she offers ways to deal with a wide variety of situations. Mostly she will help you develop a philosophy of discipline that will be effective without hitting (why use a euphemism for hitting?) your kids. Chapters include "Before You Begin," "Steps in Problem Solving," "Avoiding Problems," "Increasing Appropriate Behavior," "Teaching New Behaviors," "Decreasing Inappropriate Behavior," and "Putting It All Together." Code PP, $12.95.

**THE DISCIPLINE BOOK**, by William Sears, M.D., and Martha Sears, R.N. Based on the theory of attachment parenting. I like this book. The philosophy is one of observation and appropriate response without physical or psychological violence. The Searses do not believe there is ever a need to spank (I really want to say "hit") a child; however, they recognize that some very loving and committed parents do spank/hit their children, and they have included some very good advice and thought-provoking ideas for those who do feel the need to spank/hit their children. They also offer alternatives to spanking/hitting. This book covers important issues from birth through age ten. You'll learn how to say no in a positive manner; deal with temper tantrums; provide structure as well as freedom; deal with biting, hitting (how can we condemn children for hitting if we hit them?), whining, sibling rivalry, morals, and manners; and use discipline for special times and special children (the hyperactive child, the special-needs child, the shy child, etc.). Very thorough, very compassionate. Code BT, $13.95.

**MISS MANNERS' GUIDE FOR THE TURN-OF-THE-MILLENNIUM**, by Judith Martin. Manners? Who needs this? I'd say everyone. This 742-page book will guide you through all social occasions. More important, it can show you ways to defuse difficult situations within and outside the family. Yes, this is especially important in family relationships. We often forget that in the course of our daily lives. If we as adults use good manners and consideration with our children we set a good example and are much more likely to be treated with courtesy. Code BT, $15.95.

**GOOD MANNERS**. A whimsical coloring book following the progression of proper behavior through the ages. Ages 8 to adult. Code BB, $4.95.

**HOW RUDE!**, by Alex J. Packer, Ph.D. Written for teens, this guide is sometimes funny and sometimes serious. I am disappointed that Packer felt he had to use pop teen language. I find it condescending, and I think most kids will too. This book contains some information I'm confident no homeschooler will ever need, because, with very few exceptions, our kids relate well to people of all ages. The social guidelines are sound. There's a discussion of the history of manners that includes the issue of whether manners are sexist; having manners vs. being fake; formal dinners (different courses, silverware settings, etc.); family etiquette; and suggestions for behavior during interviews, at the theater or symphony, at funerals, and at bar and bat mitzvahs; and a lot more. *Miss Manners* is written for adults; this is for teenage needs. 463 pages including index. Code FS, $19.95.

We found that conflict resolution works much better if "blame" is not the issue discussed. We felt that blame was counterproductive, because what is past is past; it can't be changed. The current need is a solution. We discussed individual points of view so that all parties involved could see the other perspectives. This does not necessarily mean agreement, just understanding. We put our emphasis on finding solutions and compromises, and finding ways to avoid similar problems in the future. Children of all ages look to their parents for guidance not only for finding an immediate answer, but to learn "how" we go about finding solutions. It can require a great deal of time and patience, but these lessons are ones that last a lifetime and are worthy of our time and effort. The immediate issue will disappear, but the ways in which we help our children learn to deal with conflict in a peaceable manner will last. It is an example we can set. It is a gift we can give.

**KIDS CAN COOPERATE: A Practical Guide to Teaching Problem Solving**, by Elizabeth Crary. An innovative, inspiring, and very practical approach to learning how to help children listen, consider, and cooperate. Crary writes clearly about why kids quarrel and offers concrete ways to help kids learn to settle problems. There is a section for working with preschoolers and a separate one for school-age children, recognizing that issues change and older children can use more complex problem-solving skills. There is also an excellent section about child-parent conflicts. I think this book has many excellent ideas for coping and resolving family conflicts. I highly recommend this book to all imperfect parents with imperfect children. I didn't agree with everything, but that shouldn't surprise anyone. Code PP, $12.95.

The following book would be fun to use in a group, although it will be just as useful for individual use.

**BEING YOUR BEST: Character Building for Kids 7-12**, by Barbara Lewis. All of us strive to do our best. That includes kids too, even when they squabble with each other, refuse to cooperate, or get mad at us. When kids act inappropriately they are learning what works and what doesn't work in a given situation. In writing this book Lewis has given us valuable tools for helping our kids sort out important ideas and clarify their thinking about many important issues that will affect them throughout their lives. As homeschooling parents our goals should go beyond teaching the 3 R's and include models for good living — for being good people, good neighbors, and good citizens of the world. Lewis's book is a practical approach to developing these skills with quizzes, cartoons, and practical writing exercises. If your kids don't want to write, you can discuss the topics, which is a good idea anyway. Subjects covered in this book are caring, citizenship, cooperation, fairness, forgiveness, honesty, relationships with family and friends, respect, responsibility, and safety. Included are positive examples of real kids making a difference. This book will help your kids see that what they do can make a real difference. This book is a younger sibling to **WHAT DO YOU STAND FOR?** in "Philosophy and Religion." Code FS, $14.95.

**A LEADER'S GUIDE TO BEING YOUR BEST**, by Barbara Lewis. I generally consider most books that need a "guide" to have been incompletely written in the first place. No so with this. This guide has reproducible pages with good questions to be answered, and there are many useful and constructive ideas for discussions and activities. This book can be used easily with individual children or with groups. Code FS, $18.95.

**GROUNDED FOR LIFE?!**, by Louise Felton Tracy, M.S., doesn't sound like a book homeschoolers should need, but if you have adolescents in the house and are finding communication difficult or having other problems, this book can help. It will call for introspection on your part and some changes in your approach to problems. This isn't a book about "tough love"; it's about identifying problems, developing listening skills, and exploring natural consequences, and it's filled with constructive suggestions that will help you create the kind of relationships you want most. Code PP, $12.95.

**GETTING THRU TO KIDS: Innovative Approaches for Pre-Schoolers to Teens**, by Phillip Mountrose. Similar to the book above but for helping you deal with younger children. Mountrose recognizes that the only person you can change is yourself, and in doing so you change the way others relate to you. Being a parent is challenging. Being a parent and homeschooling calls for more intricate skills. This book can help. I fully agree with Gene Lehman's assessment in *LUNO*, (5/28/97; see "Homeschooling and Education"): "Although problem solving was a major concern for Mountrose ... his basic five-step plan for problem solving has universal applications, not just for children under age 6 but even for resolving adult problems." Chapters include "Helping Yourself, Helping Kids," "Finding the Balance," "Building Trust," "Learning to Listen," "Exploring Feelings," "Handling Anger," "Setting Good Boundaries," "Learning From Our Mistakes," "Dealing With Complaining," "Getting Results," and a lot more. Interesting books in his bibliography. Code BT, $12.95.

**WHAT TEENS NEED TO SUCCEED**, by Peter L. Benson, Ph.D., Judy Galbraith, M.A., and Pamela Espeland. If you are just beginning to homeschool a teenager or taking your teenager out of school for the first time, he may feel lost and need more resources to help him learn to structure his time, energy, and new life. This book may be what you're looking for. Designed for teens in school, its value to your teen will be in the ideas for becoming more involved with family and community. Good ideas to help with self-assessment and forming goals. Many other resources listed. Code FS, $14.95.

## RECREATION AND SUMMER IDEAS

**The American Hiking Society** has a catalog of volunteer positions available in national and state parks and other public lands. Positions include fire lookouts, campground hosts, and trail workers. For a catalog send $5 to AHS/Helping Out, 1015 31st St. NW, Washington, DC 20007.

**SuperCamp**. A 10-day program from Learning Forum. SuperCamp offers intensive, motivational, and lifelong accelerative "learning how to learn" skills in a camp atmosphere. Activities will stretch teens intellectually, emotionally, and physically. The focus is on effective reading methods, writing strategies, innovative note taking, creative problem solving, memory techniques, and more. Sports and other activities are offered. Learning Forum believes every person is capable of learning, that people learn in different ways, that belief in oneself is vital to success, and that respect and caring for each individual are essential. Campuses across the U.S. and abroad. For more information write: SuperCamp, 1725 South Coast Highway, Oceanside, CA 92054-5319.

**PETERSON'S SUMMER OPPORTUNITIES: For Kids and Teenagers**. Wondering what will make the summer memorable for your kids? This book has almost 2,000 reviewed listings of opportunities. Travel the U.S., Canada, or Europe; be a camper, a counselor, or a guide; learn new skills, develop talents, improve your sports or academics; get ready for college; and make new friends. Something for everyone, including the gifted and specially challenged. Details given on day and residential programs, courses, special activities, costs, financial aid, accreditations, and more. There's a new edition every year, but if you get one it will probably be good for several years. More than 1,300 pages, including a great index. Code PTR, $26.95.

**Summer Activities for Teens and Up**. Are you looking for constructive projects that will challenge your older children and give them a unique opportunity to work with others their own age, under supervision? For projects near home or overseas write the Quaker Information Center, 1501 Cherry St., Philadelphia, PA 19102, or phone 215-241-7024. Request information about short- and long-term youth programs and additional learning opportunities with the American Friends Service Committee and other organizations. Programs last a weekend or months. Some programs pay and others don't. Most programs have no religious orientation.

**Canyonlands Field Institute**. A remarkable place to enjoy and study the Southwest. Take part in their programs as an individual, group, or family. They offer special programs for teens and even courses for university credit. Canyonlands Field Institute, P.O. Box 68, Moab, UT 84532; 800-860-5262.

**Wild Quest**. An Outward Bound-type program with more emphasis on environmentally ethical travel through the wilderness and a natural science/history focus. Learn wilderness skills for safe, comfortable, environmentally ethical travel through areas of the U.S., Canada, and Mexico. Staff is primarily made up of educators. Cost is about half what the other outfits charge. Free catalog and information. 888-217-8226; applications@wildquest.org; www.wildquest.org. The Outward Bound wilderness program offers a special scholarship rate for first-time participants if they need assistance. Maybe Wild Quest does too.

**Interested in working abroad?** Write for free information from Work Abroad, CIEE, 305 E. 42 St., New York, NY 10017; 212-661-1414, ext. 1126.

**KIDS CAMP! Activities for the Backyard or Wilderness**, by Laurie Carlson and Judith Dammel. Lots of activities to help young campers build an awareness of the environment, learn about insect and animal behavior, and enjoy the outdoors, whether near or far from the back door. Ages 5 to 12. Code CRP, $12.95.

**Au Grand Bois** is a family camp offering a variety of outdoor activities as well as crafts, etc. for the entire family. Au Grand Bois, Ladysmith, Quebec J0X 2Q0, Canada; 819-647-3522; bm567@freenet.carleton.ca; mha-net.org/users/agb. Comment from a reader who has been there for a women's retreat: "Great food! Great place!"

**THE KIDS CAMPFIRE BOOK**, by Jane Drake and Ann Love, is full of great ideas for fun around the campfire. Lots of related activities. Ages 12 to adult. Code KC, $14.95.

**CAMPING AND WALKING**. A very practical guide to having a good time with fewer blistered heels and fewer burned meals. This book will tell you how to read a map and use a compass so you may not need the *Survival Skills* book (listed above). Lots of information here for the beginner and some things even an expert would like to know. Ages 8 and up. Code EDC, $12.95.

**Looking for a camp?** The American Camping Association has a website (www.acacamps.org) where you can search their database by location, special needs, specific activities, or other characteristics.

**2 STORY OUTHOUSE**

## HOMESTEADING AND GARDENING

**THE ENCYCLOPEDIA OF COUNTRY LIVING**, by Carla Emery, has 858 pages packed with just about all the information needed to live in the country. A truly encyclopedic work, with everything from soup to soap, farm machinery (including horses), buying land, and wood cookstoves. Information about gardening from scratch and how to preserve all it produces; purchasing a cow or goat, caring for it, milking it, and using the milk, including making butter; raising poultry for meat and eggs; growing and using herbs; starting home industries; and a lot more. Code BT, $27.95.

**WHOLE EARTH MAGAZINE** (formerly called *Co-evolution Magazine*). A quarterly publication with alternative living resources, excellent reviews, and informative articles — a prime publication for those who want to improve their lives and preserve the planet. Subscriptions: $24 in the U.S., $32 in Canada, $39 all others. U.S. funds only. 1408 Mission Ave., San Rafael, CA 94901; 888-732-6739.

**BACKHOME MAGAZINE** is dedicated to sharing knowledge about self-reliant living with a direct hands-on approach. It covers organic gardening, solar and renewable energy, alternative homebuilding, home business, alternative education, crafts, and all topics related to living in harmony with the land. Subscriptions, $18.97. Sample issue $4. Write BackHome, P.O. Box 70, Hendersonville, NC 28793; www.backhomemagazine.com.

**FIVE ACRES AND INDEPENDENCE**, by Maurice Kains. A classic. Detailed information about planning buildings, gardens, etc., to create an integrated working homestead. Code DV, $7.95.

**Radical Weeds!** Christie Sarles and Jillian VanNostrand have started a series of garden books for people — primarily women, but not exclusively so — who prefer natural, safe, holistic living and healing. Each of the following books is chock-full of the information you need to create a weed/herb garden to help you live better. This can even be done in containers in the middle of the city. Each herb or weed is illustrated with a meticulous drawing, historical background and uses are explained, and cultivation and harvest information and preparation are described. Uses are spelled out. It gets better: Each book comes with a ready-to-mail postcard that entitles you to a *free packet of seeds* for each herb in the book. You mail the postcard just before your growing season begins, so the seeds are always fresh. I usually ignore endorsements on books and products until after I reach my own conclusions, but I was pleased to see these books recommended by Christiane Northrup, M.D. (author of *Women's Bodies, Women's Wisdom*, listed above). Code RW, $11 each.

**WILD WOMAN'S GARDEN: 7 Radical Weeds for Women Over 40**. You probably aren't ready for this book yet, but you'll get there. Learn to cope with menopause and midlife changes the natural way.

**SERENITY GARDEN: 7 Radical Weeds for Natural Stress Relief**

**EN GARDEN! 7 Radical Weeds for Life Support and Repair**

**ROOTS, SHOOTS, BUCKETS, & BOOTS: Gardening Together With Children**, by Sharon Lovejoy. A wonder book of theme gardens, bean tunnels, a moon garden, a sunflower house, a flowery maze, a snacking and sipping garden, and much more. There's a how-to section that will assist the beginning gardener, myths and stories related to growing things that will intrigue young and old, and snippets of information about wildlife that will be attracted to your garden creation. It's winter, but this book makes me want to grab the nearest kid and start planning summer fun. This book goes well beyond just growing flowers and vegetables. It's about having fun in the garden. Code WKM, $13.95.

**STARTING GARDENING** is written for children (and parents if you're new to growing things). Lots of ideas, and directions for successful gardening. You don't need acres of land. Small pots in an apartment can be just as much fun and just as rewarding. Ages 5 to 8. Code EDC, $4.95.

**GREEN THUMBS!**, by Laurie Carlson, is the perfect way to begin gardening with children ages 5 to 12. Lots of good advice and information is slipped into many projects that you can do with your children or they can do on their own. Easily understood text and lively illustrations. Code CRP, $12.95.

**GOOD BUGS FOR YOUR GARDEN**, by Allison Mia Starcher, tells you how to identify and encourage the "good guys" in your garden. Good reference and fun to read. Hardcover; well illustrated by the author. Code WKM, $10.95.

**GENTLE SPIRIT**. A magazine about families, homesteading, homeschooling, natural living, and a lot more. Well written, with a variety of content. For subscription information write: Gentle Spirit Magazine, P.O. Box 246, Wauna, WA 98395; www.gentlespirit.com.

If you can find it, get *How to Have a Green Thumb Without an Aching Back*, by Ruth Stout (now out of print). It's full of incredible information about organic gardening using mulch. I've used this book to the point that mine is falling apart and I need a replacement. Using mulch has saved me hours of weeding — and my garden looks clean and neat without any fuss. I've heard you can find copies of this book at www.abe.com, an alliance of used bookstores.

**Gardening help online** for those without green thumbs: www.gardenguides.com.

**Homesteading Books**. Just about everything you need to know about gardening, cooking, preserving, building and maintaining a homestead, raising and caring for animals, home crafts, and alternative energy. Scores of books by some of the most respected authors in the field. Request a catalog of books for country living from Storey Communications, Inc., 105 Schoolhouse Rd., Pownal, VT 05261; www.storeybooks.com. Note: If you find it difficult to order from them, send the title and ISBN (book number) to us along with a check (don't forget our shipping charge; $2.50 for the 1st book and 25 cents for each title after that) and we'll get them for you. You may find our shipping charges lower in any case, but check to be sure.

If you're interested in rugged wilderness homesteading, try to find books by Bradford Angiers. He talks about everything from building a log cabin to putting up Saskatoon jam for the winter.

Reading *Crusoe of Lonesome Lake*, by Leland Stowe, won't teach you how to build a log cabin or survive in the wilderness, but it is the true story of Ralph Edwards and his family's life as they carved out a homestead in the wilds of British Columbia. It's an inspiring story. Good reading even if you're not interested in tackling grizzly bears while you work in the garden. Ralph's daughter Trudy has been instrumental in saving the trumpeter swans.

**VETERINARY MERCK MANUAL**. A definitive reference book for all animals. Used by all veterinarians. It's technical and written for vets, but in our homesteading experience we found it to be well worth the investment. Covers symptoms, diagnosis, prognosis, medications, and treatments. Hardcover, 2,305 pages. Code BT, $32.

Our dogs and cats have always been considered family members, and we always treated their medical problems in the same way we would treat a human member of the family. **LOVE, MIRACLES, AND ANIMAL HEALING**, by Allen M. Schoen, D.V.M., and Pam Proctor, is the best veterinary guide I've found. There are wonderful stories of healing, but the best and most useful part is reading about Schoen's approach to combining alternative and conventional treatments and the importance of the loving connection that exists between our pets and ourselves. The book includes animal massage and a chart of the most important acupuncture points. My local physical therapist used the acupuncture points illustrated in this book for my cat Ruff. It turned out that he had a broken bone, which acupuncture couldn't heal, but it did relieve the pain. A real relief for Ruff and me. An excellent book to inspire those who are considering veterinary medicine. Code SS, $12.

**Real Goods**, 555 Leslie St., Ukiah, CA 95482, 800-762-7325; service@realgoods.com; www.realgoods.com. This catalog carries many excellent books for independent living, alternative power, organic gardening, etc. Expensive. Look for the original suppliers.

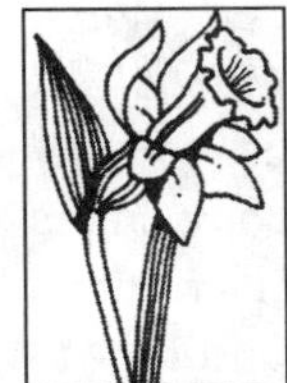

**GARDENING HOW-TO**. A magazine with great information about growing flowers and vegetables, with regional articles, books, help on what to do when the animal kingdom shows up, and a lot more. Official magazine of the National Home Gardening Club (worth joining). For information: 800-324-8454; visitors.gardeningclub.com.

**THE HERB NETWORK** is a seasonal publication packed with information about growing, drying, and using herbs for your family or a business; a Q & A column; historical information; and much more. By joining the Herb Network you get a free sample of each herb currently discussed, and can become part of a co-op buying program. For more information write: The Herb Network, P.O. Box 152, Oshkosh, NE 69154-0152; herbnetwork.com.

**ORGANIC GARDENING** magazine is a good source of information. It's readily available wherever magazines are sold.

**NATURAL LIFE**. Canada's alternative life newsmagazine. Write for information and price: 272 Hwy. 5, R.R. 1, St. George, ON N0E 1N0.

For those of you who are interested in living or learning more about sustainable living and building, renewable power, and organic gardening, I suggest you write to Chelsea Green Publishing, P.O. Box 428, White River Junction, VT 05001, and ask for their book catalog. Check their shipping charges. Ours may be less.

**THE NATURAL HOUSE**, by Daniel Chiras, is outstanding because he clearly explains the options for building natural homes (straw bale, rammed earth, adobe, papercrete, and more — 13 in all), the costs, and the pros and cons, and provides a resource guide at the end of each chapter. Includes advice in combining conventional and alternative building materials. Chiras also understands the need to build with style and substance. Code BT, $35.

**GENETIC ENGINEERING, FOOD, AND OUR ENVIRONMENT**, by Luke Anderson. This is becoming a big issue that will affect all of us. Here is a book that explains what genetic engineering is; why it's being done and who controls it; and what the implications are for health, farming, and the environment. Read this, then decide how you feel about the issue. If you're not in favor of it there are suggestions for what you can do about it. Code CG, $7.95.

**THE SOLAR LIVING SOURCEBOOK**, by John Schaeffer and Doug Pratt. This is the 10th edition of this classic. Filled with how-to information on designing renewable energy systems using sun, wind, and water, with listings of where to find materials. Included are articles about sustainable living, homesteading, etc. We started with this and learned a lot. Our book is dog-eared from use. Code BT, $30.

**INVERT**, P.O. Box 776, Monroe, ME 04951. For information pertaining to sustainability, peace, social justice, and more, request their resource list. An SASE would be appreciated. A recycled SASE would be even better.

**GOING SOMEWHERE?**

**AUTO REPAIR FOR DUMMIES**, by Deanna Sclar. Auto repair is conventionally in the male domain, and I'm a total ignoramus once the hood is up, and here's a book by a woman that makes it almost clear to me. Boy, am I embarrassed. This book is the answer for those of us (male or female) not born with wrenches in our hands. Concise, direct, simple explanations help the reader understand the major systems of an automobile and take the fear out of dealing with maintenance and repair. If you don't like greasy hands, at least you'll be able to talk to a mechanic as if you know what you're talking about, but probably, with this book, you won't need a mechanic. More than 300 illustrations. 480 pages, comb-bound so it will lie flat while you refer to it as you work, so you won't get grease all over it. Code BT, $19.95.

Almost as essential as the spare tire and rest stops are books to keep the troops happy and relatively quiet. (Well, maybe just quieter.) And you can play too — if you're not the driver or the pilot.

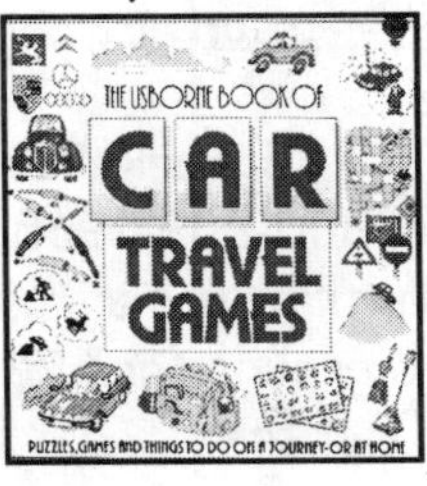


**CAR TRAVEL GAMES**. There are lots of games and activities here to challenge a wide age range. Read the book before leaving home. As a parent you'll be glad to know it begins with suggestions about how your kids can help get the car ready for the trip. It calls for a few materials you might not have on hand. Some games require thinking skills, some just luck. There are short notes throughout with interesting facts. On page 15, try changing the name of the game to "Grandfather's Big Fat Toe!" **AIR TRAVEL GAMES** is just as good. Maybe better because you won't be driving and can join the fun. Ages 7 and up. Code EDC, $4.95 each, both in one volume $8.95.

**Over 21?** Travel as a courier. You must be over 21 and be willing to travel when and where your job takes you. Overseas travel is usually seven days or less, but who cares if you can get there?! For more information contact the International Association of Air Travel Couriers (IAATC), Box 1349, Lake Worth, Florida 33460.

**TRAVEL WISE WITH CHILDREN: 101 Educational Travel Tips for Families**, by Mary Rodgers Bundren. It's just what it says. There are many activities and hands-on projects to do. Some projects are to be done even before you leave, and they will make your trip much easier. You'll build far more than memories using the ideas in this book. Code BT, $12.95.

**Free maps and travel information** about any state. Call directory assistance for toll-free numbers (800-555-1212) and ask for the state tourism office. Easy!

For information about interesting things to see and do in your state, check your library or bookstore (in desperation, write to us) for Moon Publications travel handbooks. These are also available for parts of Canada.

To find recreation or historic sites, outdoor fun, national parks, and more activities in your area or in an area you'd like to visit or study, try www.recreation.gov.

**AMERICAN STUDENT TRAVEL**, 16225 Park Ten Place, Suite 450, Houston, TX 77084, 800-688-1965; www.astravel.com. Fun and educational trips in various parts of the U.S. with well-supervised groups for kids ages 10 to 18. Be a chaperone and travel free!

**FUN ON THE ROAD**, by Ted Wade (author of *The Home School Manual*). A small collection of good games to play while traveling. You can easily copy pages for repeated playing. Mostly for children who can read, but there are good bingo-type games that can be played by non-readers. Ages 6 and up. $2, plus $1.30 for shipping, from Gazelle Publications, 11580 Red Bud Trail, Berrien Springs, MI 49103.

**WELCOME TO ROAD SCHOOL: The Real Classroom**, by the Marousis family. "Many people dream, but few people pursue those dreams." This is their story, told through selected journal entries of a year traveling, camping, exploring, and learning. A fascinating story in itself. If this is something you've dreamed about, you'll also find much useful information about planning for the road and financing your trip. I enjoyed their trip. Code BBRD, $14.95.

**The Room Exchange**, 800-846-7000 or 212-760-1000 in New York, is a wholesale agency that brokers leftover rooms in thousands of hotels in the U.S., Canada, and the Caribbean. You can get last-minute discounts and bigger savings by calling in advance. If you find a good deal, you can reserve on the phone and pay with a credit card.

**TRAVEL TIPS**

Colleges frequently have empty rooms during the summer. Call the university housing office. Rooms can be as little as $15 a night.

Drive cross-country for free (and maybe get paid) as an auto transporter. Check the yellow pages for Automobile Transporters. Good driving record required, and frequently a $200 refundable deposit. You pay only for food, fuel, and lodging.

Intervac U.S. (415-435-3497). For a $35 annual fee, they'll provide three directories — with more than 7,000 contacts in all 50 states and 25 countries — of people who want to trade homes for a vacation.

At www.homeexchange.com you can search for home exchange listings and contact owners directly at no cost.

## VOLUNTEERING AND SERVICE

**CHILDREN AS VOLUNTEERS: Preparing for Community Service**, by Susan J. Ellis, Anne Weisbord, and Katherine H. Noyes. Outstanding for group leaders; useful for adults volunteering. Offers techniques to recruit, train, and design projects for children under the age of 14. 68 pages, 8½x11". Catalog #2-102-2. For price and ordering information write: Energize, 5450 Wissahickon Ave., Philadelphia, PA 19144.

**INVEST YOURSELF**. A catalog of worldwide volunteer opportunities published by the Commission on Voluntary Service and Action. This book gives you basic information about each program, the name of a contact person, and the address to write to for complete information. Most programs provide room and board and a small allowance. *Invest Yourself* is $8 plus $3 postage ($5 outside the U.S.) from CVSA, P.O. Box 117, New York, NY 10009. Also ask about their quarterly newsletter.

**VOLUNTEER VACATIONS: Short-Term Adventures That Will Benefit You and Others**, by Bill McMillon. For teens. Information and ideas for fun and constructive vacations. Short essays by others who have done this. 412 pages. Code CRP, $16.95.

More books about opportunities for volunteering are listed in "Global Awareness."

# MISSION IMPOSSIBLE: REFLECTIONS

## THE SPIRIT IS WILLING, BUT...

See the blank box above? It's there in memory of a nice idea. I'd planned several pages, at this point in the book, for the kids to write and share their thoughts and feelings about their experiences with homeschooling and moving out into the world. For the most part they are very willing to share their thoughts, but getting something in writing from them was impossible. They have their own lives, and this is, after all, my book, not theirs. Here's an update.

As the kids left home, one by one, at first for very short periods, then for increasingly longer periods, they continued to find that the entire world was their school, and no matter where they were, life was learning. It's been exciting and challenging, and sometimes has been very different from what they or we have expected.

Cathy had tentatively planned to work in Third World countries after high school, but after spending several months living and traveling in Mexico she settled in Brattleboro, Vermont. She was familiar with the town after visiting her grandmother and spending several summers as a camp counselor in a nearby town. She obtained a job as a full-time librarian, based on her experience at our local library. When she wanted to see another part of the country she went to Virginia, where she joined a company that raised money for volunteer fire departments and emergency services. Still wanting to travel around the country, she moved to Northern California, staying with some of our old friends, and worked in a school library, drove the school bus, and fell in love. She and her husband, Michael, married in Scotland and now live in Sacramento. Over the years she has taken courses in business and health and nutrition at a community college, and obtained specialized financial training to learn about debt management so she could help others. She has held a number of office management jobs and is very active with the American Cancer Society. Up until the birth of her first child she was employed by an association of hospitals and health systems. She now works part-time so she can stay home and take care of her baby.

Karen finished her high school academic studies in two years (her idea, not ours) and went to New York City to study art. Although we felt she wasn't ready to cope with full independence, especially in a large city, we couldn't hold her back. We felt her months in New York were a learning experience, some of it very good and some not so good. After a short time back at home she moved to Florida, lived with my mother, and entered college, where she received high marks and was on the dean's list. Since then she has worked in the advertising department of a newspaper, in a high-tech optical company, and as an office manager and accountant. She has gone back to college for advanced computer training and taught software design at Clark University, near Boston. She is currently a very successful independent software consultant in New Hampshire, where she lives with her husband and two beautiful and wonderful daughters.

Susan spent her last two years of high school at the Meeting School in New Hampshire. Donn's impressions of the school when he visited with Susan before enrolling her were good. In the end we were not satisfied with the education she got there, but she came away with much of value, including some lifelong friends, and she feels the Meeting School was a good experience for her. She spent the next year working, saving money, and traveling around the country with friends in a car, which almost made it back home. She decided to pursue a career in outdoor education, working in programs such as Outward Bound. She was accepted at Prescott College in Arizona, which she attended for two years. She enjoyed her first year but left after the second because of extreme frustration at not being able to get the courses she really wanted. In the years she remained in the Prescott area she studied Intrinsic Breathwork and became a trained leader, enabling her to lead workshops and give individual counseling. Using these skills, she has worked as a behavioral health technician with abused and delinquent teens at Mingus Mountain, a residential treatment center for delinquent girls. After seven years in Arizona she moved to

New York State and attended Mercy College as a part-time student while working full time at Green Chimneys, another residential treatment center for abused youth. She has just moved back to Arizona and completed a year at Yavapai College, earning a place on the honor roll. She is now pursuing a B.Sc. in psychology in the adult degree program at Prescott College while she works, again, at Mingus Mountain and continues her private Intrinsic Breathwork counseling work.

Derek has always wanted to work with horses. He began working in various stables while still in junior high school. To put foundations under his dreams, he cleaned numerous stalls (at the rate of $2 an hour) in exchange for lessons, and eventually was asked to begin giving lessons. At times stable owners left him in charge of a barn, with thousands of dollars worth of horses, while they went on vacation. He learned to manage veterinary problems, lessons, complex feeding routines, stable management, and clients. He has worked as a barn manager, trainer, and riding instructor, and has competed in horse shows in Vermont, Quebec, North Carolina, Florida, Kentucky, and Colorado. Lest your kids read this and think it's all very glamorous, they should keep in mind it involves an incredible amount of physical work. Derek frequently spends his days in the barn from 6:30 a.m. to 9:30 p.m. He doesn't mind. He loves his work, and he and his fiancée now live and work in Colorado.

I have deliberately left out information about whether or not our grown children will homeschool their children. Donn and I made the decision to homeschool our children, and it was right for us. I will be extremely pleased if our kids homeschool their children, but not disappointed if they choose differently. I expect some of them will homeschool and some of them won't. It's not my decision to make. Our children, with their life partners, will make their own decisions based on what is right for them. I have complete faith that they will choose to do what is best for their families.

## REFLECTIONS

Donn (1994)

After all the years of raising children and teaching them at home, Jean and I stand back (as we have done frequently through the years) and ask ourselves if we have achieved what we had hoped to achieve. Have we prepared our children adequately for life on their own? Has the education they have received with us really been a better preparation for them than public education would have been? We made many mistakes, although we watched for them and tried to correct them. Sometimes we set our goals too high for our children and for ourselves; other times, our goals may not have been high enough. We listened to our children constantly, and watched them, trying to anticipate and meet all their needs — academic, intellectual, social, physical, and spiritual, both immediate and eventual. Most of the time, I think, we succeeded, although we always wished we could have done better. We aimed for perfection, for ourselves and for our children, knowing it would never be reached, but also knowing that the higher our aim, the higher our achievements would be.

Despite setbacks, problems, and occasional disappointments, we have enjoyed these twenty-four years, and have no regrets about having chosen to teach our children at home. Not to have done so would have left us with much less meaning and happiness in our lives, then and now. We and our children continue to be very close. That alone is great success and wealth. With the wisdom of hindsight, we know there are many changes we'd make, but the decision to home-school would stand.

"By their fruits ye shall know them," says the Bible, which I guess means the final judgment rests not with us, but with our children, and with the people who will know them through their lives. The real measure of our children's education at home will be the degree to which they achieve success and happiness in their own lives, and in the influence they have on the world around them. Jean and I are confident that they will continue to make us proud of them, and we'll feel honored to be judged according to the people our children are and are still becoming.

I think that's the best any parents can hope for.

Jean (2000)

Our goal as parents (and teachers) was to raise healthy, happy, loving children into caring and independent adults, capable of caring for themselves and others and able to make positive contributions to the world around them.

As I sit here in our woodsy home, surrounded by memories of smiling faces and shared laughter and tears and embraced by the house we built, I feel an immense amount of satisfaction. I, too, feel there is much we could have done differently, better, but I know we did the best we could at the time. I feel intensely grateful for the years we all spent together. Would we do it again? Absolutely.

No one knows what the future will bring to any of us, but with ten years for retrospection since the last fledgling left home, I feel the time and experiences we had in living and growing together are beyond price and more valuable than any tangible reward. Our children are good people and doing well with their own lives. I am immensely proud of all of them for what they have made, and are making, of their lives. Of greater importance than anything else, our children are my friends. When Donn died, I don't think I could have survived without their love and support. Each in his own way has given and continues to give me strength and love and encouragement. Donn and I gave them life and brought them into this world. They, in turn, have made it possible for me to continue without him. I could ask for no more.

## DONN REED TWO or DONN REED, TOO

Daring to be, with fierce integrity, friend.
Open to truth universal. Ready to go
Nebula hopping and shopping for stars and stopping for fun
Anywhere people are silly or batting their cilia.
Long, lanky, loony, loving, learned and loyal.
Dawn dawns on Don; Don dons Donn; I'll be doggoned!

Buck-naked boys bound through woods, each with stone club,
Ready to kill the nearest wolf or deer or bear,
Unless, of course, a small horse or cow would do in lieu.
Cowed and cold we quit, redressed, empty-handed, non-bucolic.
Ecstasies of starlight and laughter surrounded our campfire.

Recalling that we mingled blood one distant yesteryear
Evokes in me an atavistic urge,
Empowers me with mystic-fingered grace,
Delivers me again to archetypal brotherhood, friend.

Leonard J. Nadeau,
Lifelong friend
December 20, 1995

# I MET HER ON THE BUS

She was going two hundred miles, back to college from a weekend visit with her grandmother. I was going ten miles, home from the store. Her guitar case was on the luggage rack and she had long blond hair and I sat beside her. Three months later, on Groundhog Day, 1963, we were married.

When we built our first home, we worked together, hauling and lifting logs, fitting, chinking, and nailing on the roofing. We've built other homes since then, and we've worked together to make them strong and warm.

With an affluent, suburban childhood, she had no home-making skills. She taught herself to sew and mend, to make shirts and darn socks; to cook on a woodstove; to bake pies, cookies, cakes, and bread; to churn butter and make cottage cheese.

When we decided to start a family, we wanted to share the experience of childbirth, but every doctor we consulted refused my presence in the delivery room: "We can't have fainting husbands all over the floor."

We went to the bookstore and the library, and we studied obstetrics, gynecology, and yoga breathing. We delivered our first child, Cathy, in a small log cabin, miles from the nearest neighbor. In following years, we delivered Karen, Susan, and Derek, all at home, all four without complication or pain.

She nursed each of the children at least a year, and we carried them everywhere, and they always knew they were loved and wanted.

We've worked together in the garden, the hayfield, the barn. She can milk a cow, nurse a sick calf, pitch hay, shovel manure, catch runaway pigs, and be midwife for a pig.

Her pie crusts are light and flaky, a slice of her bread makes a meal complete, and her doughnuts are my special reward.

She has stood spellbound by the Northern Lights, entranced by the call of wild geese flying north, and breathlessly excited by the musical howl of northwestern timber wolves.

Her fingers fly on her guitar and her singing is magic, whether playing classical or folk, Bach or Dylan, loving or growling.

She's five-foot-five, still slim and shapely, and becoming more beautiful every day. Her golden hair is silvery now, but still falls free and long, like spring rain and the morning mist. Her eyes sparkle, she smiles, she laughs, she works and plays, she hugs our children, and she's the best there is. She's a natural woman, whose love flows like a river, warm as summer, strong as a mountain.

With her, my fields are always green, my skies are blue; she nourishes me, feeds my soul. We are two shafts of grain, blown by the wind, north or south or east or west, leaning together, in sunrise and sunset, under clouds and rain and storms, under clear skies and stars, sunlight, moonlight, darkness, whispering together in the breezes, our roots intertwined in the earth, our stalks together in the air, our heads together in the sky.

Sometimes I think I will burst with the awesome mountain of love I have for her; and when I feel her love, I am grateful: Thank you, Jean.

And humble: Bless me, wife.

And glad: Let's dance! Dance! Dance!

And proud: Look, world, look at this woman of mine. There's no better woman anywhere; she's the one I'll take to the stars with me—

Oh yes oh yes oh yes.

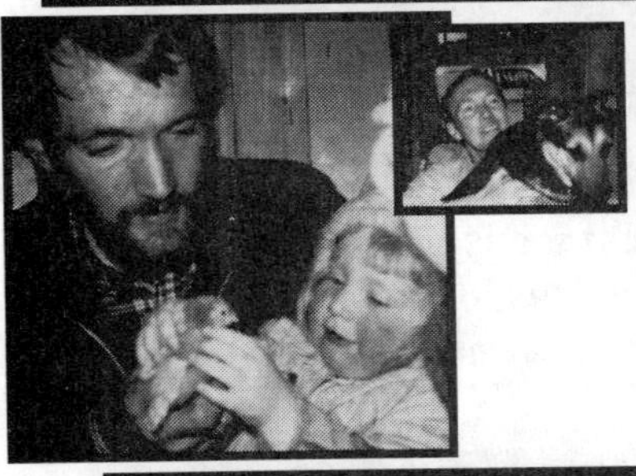

# THAT BUS RIDE

That bus ride changed my life, making unexpected tours and stops for thirty-seven years. I'm still on the bus. Donn was taken off five years ago, but my life is far more than I imagined it would be because he sat next to me.

Tall and thin, he had hair that came down over the collar of a leather jacket with a large peace symbol on the back. He was soft-spoken and poetic, analytic, philosophical, and mysterious, with a mind-blowing wit and sense of humor and fun.

With a gentle hand and loving heart he led me out of the wilderness of my adolescent rebellion. I felt cherished and safe. I fell into unconditional love with the man and with our challenging and adventurous life.

He was blessed with an irrepressible love and reverence for all life. The days were not long enough, the nights too short. There was never enough time to turn all the dreams into reality. But, oh! He taught me to slow down, to cherish the dreams and savor the moment.

We were blessed with four healthy children, and I was blessed with a man who taught me what a parent should be. The babies were ours, together — all things shared except the nursing, and he often complained that he wished he could do that too!

Thank you, Donn, for your love. For the joy of living that you shared and inspired in me. For making me laugh at myself. For showing me, when discouraged, that the glass was half-full, not half-empty. For leaving me a living legacy of love in our children, by creating a work of love that allows me to continue working with you.

Thank you, Donn, for giving me so much in life that I cry with joy for what we had — and still have.

Thank you, life, for giving me a man to fill my days and nights with wonder and love.

I am waiting for the stars, Donn, and you.

## OUR GUARANTEE

We want you to be happy and satisfied with your purchases from Brook Farm Books. We understand that it can be difficult to buy through the mail. If you are not satisfied with anything you purchase from us, you may return it ***in salable condition within 30 days*** for a full refund of your purchase (but not your postage) or credit toward other merchandise (your choice of cash or credit). If your order arrives damaged or we made a mistake in your order, return it, and we'll reimburse you for postage and correct our mistake or replace your order. Please be sure to package items for return with care, as the postal service doesn't really care what's inside a box and packages are not treated with great care or respect.

## POSTAGE

Listings that don't include postage or specify "postpaid" have a letter code just before or after the price. Believe it or not, the letter codes are set up to save you money.

For the **first item** in **each** letter code, add $2.50 for postage. For **each additional item *with the same code,*** add 25¢. The more you order within any one letter code, the less the postage is per item.

**IMPORTANT!** If your order totals $100 or more ***before*** adding postage fees, deduct five percent from the total **AFTER** adding the postage fees. If you feel confused by this, look at the sample order on page 461.

## HOW TO ORDER

Use our sample as a guide in ordering from us. All information is essential for accurately filling your order. Please type or print your name and address very neatly. Lack of handwriting skills is not necessarily a sign of low I.Q. (look at your doctor's handwriting), but it makes speedy delivery of your order impossible. If we have trouble reading your name or address we are willing to guess, but the post office may return it, and then we're all in trouble. We have an unusable check and the books that belong to you, plus a disappointed and possibly very mad customer (also you). Please add your telephone number and e-mail address in case there is a question about your order. We will respect your privacy. We do not sell, share, or rent our customer list or information with anyone for any reason.

## SPECIAL ORDERS

We can get almost any book that is in print. If there is a book you would like us to get for you, send the title, author, and (if you have the information) the name of the publisher and the ISBN (International Standard Book Number, a ten-digit number unique to each book). Shipping charges will be based on our normal shipping rates.

## PAYMENT

We will be happy to help you with your orders during regular business hours, Monday through Friday 8 a.m. to 5 p.m. EST. We will stay open Friday evenings until 10:30 p.m. EST. We accept Visa/MasterCard and American Express orders by phone or mail as well as checks and money orders.

Most of our suppliers and most of our customers are in the United States, so all prices are listed in U.S. dollars. All payments should be in U.S. dollars. Please make checks out to Brook Farm Books.

TO ORDER BY CREDIT CARD: Call toll-free: 1-877-375-4680.

If you'd just like to talk or consult with us, please call 506-375-4680 or e-mail jean@brookfarmbooks.com.

**U.S. orders** should be sent to:

Brook Farm Books<br>
P.O. Box 246<br>
Bridgewater, ME 04735

*****Maine residents,** please add 5% tax to all orders.

**Canadian Orders.** We apologize for the inconvenience of paying in U.S. dollars, but it is a necessity due to Canadian banking regulations at the Bank of Nova Scotia. Please remember to add the or GST. All Canadian orders should be sent to: Brook Farm Books, Box 101,Glassville, NB E7L 4T4.

## PRICES

Our suppliers all note that their prices are subject to change without notice, which means we have to tell you the same thing. Most prices are relatively stable, but of course they do increase sooner or later. If the increase is $5 or more we will contact you before shipping.

## BOOK CLUBS, READING GROUPS, AND RESOURCE CENTERS

We want to support your efforts. We are happy to offer you a 20% discount. Write and tell us what you need.

## SHIPPING

Items in stock are usually shipped within three days of our receipt of your order. Please allow two to four weeks for 4th-class mail, sometimes longer, depending on the season and how the postal workers feel. ("Christmas rush" doesn't mean things move faster.) If you are in a hurry add $5 for priority shipping.

## GIFTS AND GIFT WRAPPING
## GIFT CERTIFICATES

We will be glad to gift-wrap an item for you at no charge. You may include your own card with your order. If you would like us to add a card for you, please let us know the occasion for the gift (e.g., Christmas or birthday). **Please** print the name and address of the recipient **clearly**. You may also send a check and we will send you a gift certificate to give, or we can send it directly to the recipient.

## THREE KINDS OF "OUT OF STOCK"

The first two aren't bad.

First kind: We have a very small business and can't keep all items in stock all the time. When an item is out of stock with us, we just order it from a publisher or supplier and usually have it within a week or two. If an item is out of stock but already on order and we expect to ship within 30 days, we probably won't notify you about the delay. If we expect shipment to be later than 30 days, we'll send you a note saying so. Expected shipping dates are only approximate, because we're dependent on the whims of the publishers and their shippers. Most publishers and other suppliers are very prompt and thoughtful, but a few are consistent in sending late and/or incomplete shipments, often with no explanation.

Second kind: Our regular supplier is out of stock and follows the same procedure — ordering from the publisher and sending the item on to us, still within a week or two.

Third kind: The publisher is out of stock, which really means the current printing is sold out and the book is being reprinted, and anyone who knows when the book will again be available has been sworn to secrecy. This doesn't happen often, but when it does, it could be a long wait. Usually we'll refund your money and suggest you try something else. Or we'll tell you and you can let us know if you want to wait.

## OUT OF PRINT

Publishers' minds often seem on a par with those of public educators. They undoubtedly have very good reasons for discontinuing publication of some very good books, but their logic eludes me. I wish the publishers could share some of the embarrassment I feel when I have to tell you that a book you've ordered (on our recommendation) is now out of print. Luckily for all of us, it doesn't happen often. When it does, I'll try to suggest a substitution, but I won't substitute without your permission unless the substitution is really comparable, in both content and price. If you don't like the substitution just return it for a full refund, including postage.

If we write to you that many (perhaps even *all*) of the items you've ordered are out of stock, please bear with us. All the items will already be on order and will be sent to you as soon as possible. We have a very small company (and Gus is really very little help, although he sometimes has a lot to say), and we just can't keep all the items we sell in stock all the time. We try to keep the most popular items in stock, but even those sometimes sell out unexpectedly, and we scramble to rebuild our stock. Rather than hold up your entire order to ship all at once (if you've ordered several items), we'll probably ship items to you as we receive them, so you may receive your order in installments. We're a lot friendlier than computers, even if we aren't as efficient.

## CUSTOMER SURVEY

**We'd like to hear from you.**

Please fill this out and mail it back to us. It would be nice if you added your name and address (not all of you buy this book directly from us), but it's not necessary. We feel that having the following information will help us to help you.

What type of information or materials do you need most?

What would you like to see more of (essays, commentaries, books, cartoons)? What subjects?

What would you like to have less of?

How can we improve our service to you?

Do you buy many of the items we list from other sources? (It's all right to say yes. We'd just like to know how you use this book.)

Comments?

Questions?

Would you be interested in having Jean come to give a workshop for your conference? What topics would you like to hear her speak about?

ORDER FORM



TO

BROOK FARM BOOKS
P.O. BOX 246
BRIDGEWATER, ME 04735

OR

BROOK FARM BOOKS
BOX 101
GLASSVILLE, NB E7L 4T4

Please make all checks payable to Brook Farm Books

DATE: March 1, 2001

Please send me the following items:

| Page# | Qty. | Item/Title | Price | Code | Postage |
|---|---|---|---|---|---|
| 123 | 1 | What Your 1st Grader Needs to Know | 11.95 | BDD | 2.50 |
| 123 | 1 | Aesop's Fables | 1.00 | DV | 2.50 |
| 123 | 1 | Story of King Arthur and His Knights | 8.95 | DV | .25 |
| 123 | 1 | Robin Hood | 8.95 | DV | .25 |
| 123 | 1 | Listen & Read Child's Garden of Verses — book and cassette | 5.95 | DV | .25 |
| 123 | 1 | Atlantis Globe | 49.99 | RPL | 4.00 |
| 123 | 1 | Drawing With Children | 15.95 | PTM | 2.50 |
| 123 | 1 | Book of Where | 13.95 | LB | 2.50 |
| 123 | 1 | Book of Think | 13.95 | LB | .25 |
| | | | | | |
| | | Subtotals | 130.64 | | 15.00 |
| | | + | 15.00 | | |
| | | Subtotal | 145.64 | | |
| | | Minus special 5% discount for orders $100 or more | 7.28 | | |
| | | Subtotal | 138.36 | | |
| | | Add Maine state tax or GST if applicable | | | |
| | | TOTAL ENCLOSED | 138.36 | | |

**FOR COMPUTER USERS**

You can now place orders by e-mail when you use your credit card. To ensure the safety of your information, we suggest sending your order and half of your credit card number in the first e-mail. Then send a second e-mail with the rest of the card number and the expiration date.

E-mail: jean@brookfarmbooks.com

Name:

Address:

E-mail:

Circle one: Visa MasterCard American Express

Card #:

Exp. date:

Signature:

Phone:

WE DO NOT RENT, SELL, OR TRADE YOUR INFORMATION.

**Attention Canadians:** Canadian titles not listed under Canada or Canadian are marked *

# A

# B

## C

# D

# E

# F

# I

## J



## K



## L

## M

# N



# O

# P



# Q

# R



# S

## U



## V



## W

# X, Y, Z



## *ATTENTION!*

At some time in the future we will be publishing an updated list of materials that have had price changes or gone out of print. We will also include new materials that have come to our attention that we want to share with you before the next edition.

If you would like information about this interim publication, please send us an SASE.

# WISH LIST